This edition first published by Verso 2002
© Verso 2002
Translation © Krzysztof Fijalkowski and Michael Richardson 2002
First published as Georges Bataille, à la mort à l'oeuvre
© Editions Gallimard 1992
All rights reserved

This paperback edition first published by Verso 2010

The moral rights of the author and the translators have been asserted

2 4 6 8 10 9 7 5 3

Verso
UK: 6 Meard Street, London W1F 0EG
US: 20 Jay Street, Suite 1010, Brooklyn, NY 11201
www.versobooks.com

Verso is the imprint of New Left Books

ISBN-13: 978-1-85984-153-2

British Library Cataloguing in Publication Data
A catalogue record for this book is available from the British Library

Library of Congress Cataloguing-in-Publication Data
A record for this book is available from the Library of Congress

Typeset by SetSystems Ltd., Saffron Walden, Essex
Printed and bound by CPI Group (UK) Ltd, Croydon, CR0 4YY

Georges Bataille

Georges Bataille

An Intellectual Biography

MICHEL SURYA

Translated by Krzysztof Fijalkowski
and Michael Richardson

VERSO

London • New York

This edition first published by Verso 2002
© Verso 2002
Translation © Krzysztof Fijalkowski and Michael Richardson 2002
First published as *Georges Bataille, la mort à l'œuvre*
© Editions Gallimard 1992

2 4 6 8 10 9 7 5 3 1

Verso
UK: 6 Meard Street, London W1F 0EG
USA: 180 Varick Street, New York, NY 10014–4606
www.versobooks.com

Verso is the imprint of New Left Books

ISBN 1–85984–822–2

British Library Cataloguing in Publication Data
A catalogue record for this book is available from the British Library

Library of Congress Cataloging-in-Publication Data
A catalog record for this book is available from the Library of Congress

Typeset in 10.2 on 13.6 Sabon by
SetSystems Ltd, Saffron Walden, Essex
Printed by Biddles Ltd, Guildford and King's Lynn

Contents

III

IV

Contents

V

Contents

Death is the most terrible thing and to maintain the work of death demands the greatest strength.

F. G. W. Hegel

Foreword

On 8 July 1962, a man died. He was buried in a small cemetery at the summit of Vézelay hill. The austere and inconspicuous tombstone is inscribed:

GEORGES BATAILLE
1897–1962

A name on a tombstone, two dates and some books: the remains of a dead writer. Frequently he effaced himself beneath his books. Sometimes they, too, vanished. While he lived, no one could completely efface Georges Bataille, yet he was scarcely better known than his books. Today they are among the most significant. They are also among the most scandalous.

While he lived, Bataille scandalised because he discussed eroticism as a dark truth, a truth laid bare, because he also discussed what as a rule is – through fear or platitude – suppressed about death: it fascinated him. Dead, Georges Bataille still fascinates.

In considering someone over whom silence has fallen, a biography seeks the secret of the fascination his work exerts. This will undoubtedly elude us. The truth of a biography is that, no matter how close it may at times get, in the end this secret eludes it, it should be condemned to the silence that descends along with the tombstone. This is a truth that is both delicate and heart-rending.

I think as a girl takes off her dress. At the extremity of its movement, thought is indecency, even obscenity.

G. Bataille

Writing is powerless: it lacks the face and nudity of a prostitute to speak quite abjectly about the human life it has made of itself a façade and that debauchery renders it to truth.

G. Bataille

We are not in the habit of taking account of it, if we reflect or speak, but death will interrupt us. I will not always have to pursue the servile search for truth. Every question will finally remain unanswered, and I will conceal myself in such a way that I will impose silence. If others take up the task, they will not achieve more and death will cut them short, as it did to me.

G. Bataille

I

In the beginning was death

'Considering my "conception" – the loss from which *I exist* (*I exist*, which does not simply mean that my being exists, but that it is clearly distinct), I notice the *precariousness* of the being within me. Not that classical precariousness founded in the necessity of dying, but a new and more profound one, founded on the small possibility I had of existing (that there was only my originating being and not some other).'[1]

A man is not merely mortal (if he were, his ontology would be less 'black', less comical), he is also unlikely. The 'good fortune' to exist – in other words his infinitesimal possibility of being what he is rather than someone else – is measured through all the slippages which might have made him another being, or (why not?) left him without a future at all. The *self* that he was (or was promised to be) had so much more 'likelihood' – incomparably more – of not existing. The erotic conjunction of the progenitors (as Bataille himself later noted) establishes a singular combination of being among 225 trillion other possibilities.[2] A throw of the dice! The pure void (is this not what Bataille would say?) is a measureless probability more oppressive than any conception: it was *infinitely* probable he would not be born.[3] The void from which he randomly emerged is infinite. (Bataille said so clearly: his being is the only one there is. His alone was extracted from the void. *All* others are the void in so far as they are not him. They are distinguished from him by everything it is possible to imagine could be, a probability that is clearly infinite.) And the precariousness of this being in which he will preserve himself as a refusal of that void will be measureless.

In 1961 – a year before he died – in an interview in the weekly *L'Express*, Georges Bataille moved (or started to move) towards his own name for the first time. For the first time he endorsed (or almost endorsed) the circumstances that caused him, when younger, to write under pseudonyms. From that moment there would be nothing further to separate him from the author of *The Story of the Eye* (Lord Auch) and *Le Petit* (Louis Trente). In these two books, as we shall see, he tried to speak the truth about his memories. But, in unmasking himself, he also unmasked his relations; in unreservedly reassuming his name, he unmasked his father. Nevertheless it is premature to claim that Bataille, in this interview, finally unmasked himself. He did not say he was the author of either *The Story of the Eye* or *Le Petit* (which were then known only confidentially). Had he done so, no doubt the masks would finally have been lowered. At most, Madeleine Chapsal, who conducted the interview and wrote the article, spoke for him: 'Certainly Bataille, who has not ceased to seek places and moments at which "the heart skips a beat", is still alive. Moreover, he is prepared to give some not unimportant information about his background: his tabetic father had general paralysis and became mad, as did his mother.'

A highly indignant reaction soon followed. Georges Bataille's brother, Martial, denied his assertions.[4] Certainly there is nothing to prove that their father, Joseph-Aristide Bataille, was mad. It was Lord Auch and Louis Trente – Bataille's pseudonyms – who made the claim. With the interview, Georges Bataille confirmed it. Martial denied it. Who to believe? Was one pusillanimous and did the other get carried away? Fifty years after the events took place, forty-five years after the death of the subject who suffered them so terribly, the two brothers were equally sincere. For both, the facts were distressing.

The horror – which can be measured still more strongly by repeating that a half century had passed – seems deep-rooted. The evidence suggests it was something suppressed. Was Bataille's offence that he did not keep silent? At least this is the accusation Martial made against him. When he said, as though he was sadly glorying in it: 'I saw . . . what no one saw . . . This will all be obliterated with me', Georges replied: 'I have found no other means of rousing myself from it than in expressing myself anonymously . . . in spite of everything, this is the best means I could find.' In both cases, the horror had been such that it was necessary either to suppress it completely or to speak of it, although from behind a mask, at the risk of terrifying. In both cases, the cost was not negligible and spared neither.

The odd thing remains that, whatever their differences, whatever they revealed or suppressed, they nonetheless agreed to bear witness to a horror outstripping anything an adult, even an elderly one, can lay to rest in childhood. However they confronted it, they were suddenly so agreed to make a confession of it, a confession so long deferred that (and this is not the least paradox), by their brief and lively exchange of letters, they appear to dispute the impossible privilege of having, as children, had the more violent vision of this shattering horror. Martial protested in vain that their father was not mad, that their mother did not become so in her turn, but conceded something which was no less oppressive: 'I was close to our parents, spending day after day in grief and despair. It was unimaginable because I saw what you did not see, what no one saw. Events that are not known and of whose existence no one suspects. I alone was led to witness them and I have always wanted to be the only one. This will all be obliterated with me.'

Nothing but what was unseemly or humiliating could have measured the horror. And the two men (both tired and sick) certainly did not wish to. What one of them pledged to the void, the other was perhaps ready to reveal as one does a wound: we see that Georges Bataille ceaselessly exhibited everything publicly. Evidently this cuts to the quick where the work begins (I will say how) and perhaps is where it returns without being aware of the fact.

Martial Bataille's silence lasted to the end.[5] What remains is to judge what Georges Bataille said. And what he spoke about was terror (did he ever speak of anything else?): 'Besides, I can tell you that, concerning what is at stake, I came out of it in a turmoil that lasted for life. What happened fifty years ago still causes me to tremble.'[6]

There is no shortage of memories. However, they have a singular quality: they are amazingly alike. So closely, so profoundly, so obsessionally alike that one is tempted to ask whether, faced with the sight of his father, the child did not himself become mad. (In fact, was he the only one who went mad? And was this madness wrongly attributed to his father? Or did the father's madness cause the child to have a breakdown? Georges Bataille's vision was hallucinating, no doubt about it, but he was never insane.)

Joseph-Aristide Bataille is not the most important 'father' in literature, nor is he the least strange, however. In any event, we know few clear things about him, so few that one is inclined to believe that this silence was partly intentional. He was born at Gajan, in the Ariège, where he does not seem to have lived for long. While he was still young, he probably moved to his mother's home region: to Garandie, to be precise, an austere village which Bataille would later discover in his turn and which he described with a restrained horror: 'Constructed on a crater slope without trees or church, a simple mass of houses in a demonic landscape.'[7]

He was thirty-five – no longer a young man – when he met and married Marie-Antoinette Tournadre (and his brother married her elder sister twenty-two months later; there seems no doubt that this marriage was a direct result of the first). What did he do before that? He seems to have undertaken medical studies (there had previously been no doctors in his family; he would have been the first) without finishing them. Instead, he entered government and became a civil servant: he was successively a college bursar,[8] an employee of Melun prison (should we see this as the origin of the violent aversion Bataille maintained all his life for prisons?[9]), then a postmaster. This was the job he had when his sickness came to light.

Joseph-Aristide Bataille was thus forty-four when his second son, Georges, was born, and he was already weak. Syphilis (which had no doubt become manifest between the birth of the two children, that is between 1890 and 1897[10]), before overtaking him entirely, had already taken away his sight (or, more accurately, his look). Georges Bataille was born of a man who was for the first time closed off from the world outside, of a blind man ('absolutely blind'). Worse: he was fathered by this man.[11] Was the sickness not such as to dissuade him from giving life to a child? Apparently not: Georges Bataille was born on 10 September 1897.

Three years later, the sickness had not abated. Joseph-Aristide Bataille lost the use of his limbs: 'When I was born, my father was suffering from general paralysis, and he was already blind when he fathered me; not long after my birth, his sinister disease confined him to an armchair.'[12] He had fifteen more years to live, fifteen years which not only he but also his family had to endure: a wife whom Georges and Martial acknowledge, each in his own way, to have lived a martyrdom; fifteen years in which they both grew up.

Bataille was not unaware that a Christian could see election in such a fate: 'My father, the blind man and the paralytic in one man'. He was so aware of it that no doubt he momentarily believed it. Yet he preferred to see it as destiny (is not destiny a sort of objectless choice?): 'So much horror predestines you!'

Such a destiny is only imaginable: the wide open eyes of the child on a man whose own are closed. A man? It is not certain that Georges ever thought his father really was a man (but any child, in his place, would have doubted in the same way).

More distinctly than a man – and *a fortiori* of a father – he would remember an ascetic, an 'involuntary ascetic' or 'a repugnant ascetic'. As he spoke of him, he essentially recalled (difficult as it must have been to make such a disclosure) his father as being closer to an animal than a man: sickness, cries . . . and bodily functions. Why the latter? Was it because nothing better exposes his dead eyes (eyes that will never be so exposed as when dead)? 'the weirdest thing was certainly the way he looked while pissing. Since he could not see anything, his pupils very frequently pointed up into space, shifting under the lids, and this happened particularly when he pissed.'[13] Dead though they were, they were still eyes and what they did not see drew the gaze more shiftily than living eyes, being marked by a hole (a cleft?) in the centre of the face that acquired a sort of strange strength which is a more exposed truth than the organ of urination. 'He had huge, ever-gaping eyes that flanked an eagle nose, and those huge eyes went almost entirely blank when he pissed, with a completely stupefying expression of abandon and aberration.'[14] These eyes, open to the void or the abyss, this truth of eyes that were more real than those of the living, were eyes of a 'madman', or of a saint (a 'madman' to the extent that one chooses one's 'fate'; a 'saint' to the extent that one chooses 'election'): how could a child fail to be fascinated?

Georges Bataille recalled less – at least he said less – about the urination ('in a small receptacle while sitting in an armchair'), the sound it made (by going into a receptacle), the smell or even the organ of emission, than about the whiteness of the eyes seeking in the night what, within reach of the jet, he pissed over: the gaping eyes appeared to seize the obscenity of the living organ between dead legs. No doubt to the eyes of the child this eye was absolutely obscene (which is anything but complacent; we will see that, in speaking obsessionally about eroticism, Bataille will act no differently: the truth of eroticism is less that of bodies than that of the void in which they embrace).

The father's blindness could at times be contagious. What the father did not see, and as if obeying the order of things ruled over by not seeing it, the child in his turn would not see: 'My father remained in the gloom since to put a light on had no meaning for him. If no one else was there, no one would put the light on and I would stay there, I remember, in a state of very deep prostration, even disgust.'[15]

But it must also be a demand to see (it could not be otherwise): to see for himself what his blindness had concealed from him, and to see it himself, in prey to what it hid from him. We need to consider this: in 1900 (when Georges was three years old) this man was no longer even able to take a step into the night into which his eyes had taken him.[16]

There is no doubt that the symptoms Bataille describes are precisely those the sickness produces: stabbing pains ('Stabbing pains tore animal cries from him'), visceral crises, motor, sensory and digestive problems also affecting the sensorial reflexes, the genitals and the sphincter ('for example he sometimes shat his pants'[17]). Everything Bataille says gives credibility to the tabetic symptomatology.

Nevertheless, isn't the disclosure exaggerated? Or could the excessiveness simply be the child's fatigue? A fatigue in proportion to the generally unbearable way his father was forgetting himself. It would be careless to think that Bataille's insistence upon recounting these 'scabrous' details resulted from provocation and nothing more. It is far more serious than that. Joseph-Aristide Bataille was no less *under* him, *under* the child's eyes . . . and in calling for his help: 'He would get out of his blind paralytic's bed . . . it was very hard . . . (I would help him).'[18] The child had to place him on the bedpan on which, getting out of bed 'with difficulty' and most often wearing 'a cotton nightcap (he had a pointed grey beard, ill-kempt, a large eagle's nose and immense hollow eyes staring into space)',[19] the convenience the bedpan was intended to offer, the discretion into which the invalid had to try to maintain his needs (with the aid of a cover that, not being able to see, he could not usually place very well), the needs that in fact, without embarrassment, he satisfied under the eyes of everyone (of his son, but what eyes would he assume for a child conceived in blindness other than eyes likely to see *everything*), the spectacle of 'brutalising abandon' he gave, with eyes rolled back, leaving *excreta* in the bedpan.[20] Georges Bataille recalled all this as the spectacle of a man who no longer had anything to offer the child emerging from the night, anything but the vision of a 'beast' on whom space twice closed like a trap.

Georges Bataille loved this man. He said so simply without thinking he should add that this love owed nothing to pity. If pity was involved, it would no doubt have been for his mother. On the contrary, 'the very contrary to the majority of male babies, who are in love with their mothers, I was in love with my father'.[21] This love lasted until he was fourteen. Fourteen years of a life that were – no doubt – not always as black as this (there is every reason to imagine that things got worse). A life, however, that was at the very least dark and austere when, by fits and starts, it did not become exemplarily tragic. (Did not Martial also say that his childhood was only 'sorrow and despair'?). At fourteen – why, we do not know – hatred took the place of this love, a 'deep and unconscious'[22] hatred. We do not know (and Bataille tells us nothing) about what took place. We do not know what happened, however horrible it might have been, to cause what the child had considered 'lovable' suddenly to become hateful for the adolescent. But he evoked this dark and cruel hatred: 'I began vaguely enjoying his constant shrieks at the lightning pains caused by the tabes,[23] which are considered among the worst pains known to man. Furthermore, the filthy, smelly state to which his total disablement often reduced him . . . was not nearly so disagreeable as I thought. Then again, in all things, I adopted the attitudes and opinions most radically opposed to those of that supremely nauseating creature.'[24] He was fourteen: puberty distanced him from his father. The 'chosen one' ('in one figure, the blind man and the paralytic') became the 'reprobate'. In a disgusting way, he was God (he will, once again, be God; as we shall see: abandoned, betrayed); henceforth he is 'that supremely nauseating creature'. No doubt nothing had essentially changed, and yet everything predictably became worse. It was from 1911 (when he was fourteen) that Georges Bataille dated the first signs of madness, which for Martial seems never to have existed. (It is known that tabes, in the tertiary phase of its development, produces madness; it should be mentioned that in 1911 Martial Bataille left the family home to do military service, from which he would return only when the war was over; he could therefore not have known much about his father's last years, except for brief stays on leave.) It is less likely to have been a durable and constant madness than several attacks: 'One night, we were awakened, my mother and I,[25] by vehement words that the syphilitic was literally howling in his room: he had suddenly gone mad.'[26] If there is nothing to indicate that such scenes had not occurred before, this one would be distinguished by the fact that for the child it would destroy 'the demoralising effects of a strict upbringing'.[27] It would be distinguished by reason of being openly and for the first time sexual. 'The insane blind man' cried to the doctor who had come without delay and was for a moment alone with the sick man's spouse, 'Doctor, let me know when you're done fucking my wife!'[28] The violently sexual character of this scene is remarkable for several reasons: Bataille revealed the need, on all occasions, to find its equivalent. *Story of the Eye*, he said, bears witness to it; as would – one imagines – later narratives in their turn.

It was a madness that seems almost to have been contagious: Marie-Antoinette Bataille, he says, also lost her mind. This was no doubt less 'madness' than a temporary loss of sanity,[29] but it was significant: significant for the fact that Marie-Antoinette, the mother of Georges Bataille, appears in the two accounts of his childhood[30] only at these times of the collapse of her sanity. It is significant, too, that Bataille systematically only spoke about this in the worst light. At no time did he seem inclined to turn away from it. (Provocation, or the complacency with which he has been reproached? Is it not rather that, for him, only the worst was true? His accounts of childhood conform to the same laws as his fiction: the worst alone spoke truly.)

Joseph-Aristide Bataille occupies an essential place in the two accounts just mentioned. But until now, not a word about his wife! In fact, she appears only when Georges Bataille admits no longer having anything but hatred for his father. No sooner does she appear than she suddenly goes 'mad' (Bataille remembers her – at least that is all he describes – only as being sick and crazy in her turn). After this, the apparition of the 'crazy' mother brings with it, as an unmasked doubling of the promise of death made to the father, an anguish linked to the mother's suicide. (Did not this form of blackmail in anticipation of her own death add to the living corpse-like state of the father?)

Madness and suicide carry the interest of these two accounts ('Coincidences' and 'W.–C.') to a completely different, maternal, pole. The overabundant presence of the father was not suddenly less, but to this is added a third presence which dramatically responds to it only in pushing things to what they could only be: the worst. But what could this 'madness' involve? Marie-Antoinette Bataille seems to have been melancholic for several months, a melancholy haunted by 'absurd ideas of damnation and catastrophe'.[31] (Bataille makes it clear that she suddenly lost her sanity after her own mother had made a revolting scene in her presence.[32]) It was a sometimes violent melancholy that caused him to fear, if we are to believe him, that she would attack him. Losing his patience with her, it came to blows and he struck her.

This melancholy (manic-depressive, he specifies) seems to have been strong enough for her to twice try to commit suicide. The first attempt failed: '[we] finally found her *hanged* in the attic.'[33] The second time as well, when it seemed to be her own decision:

> A short time later, she disappeared again, this time at night; I myself went looking for her, endlessly, along a creek, wherever she might have tried to drown herself. Running without stopping, through the darkness, across the swamps, I at last found myself face to face with her: *she was drenched up to her belt, the skirt was pissing the creek water*, but she had come out on her own, and the icy, wintery water was not very deep anyway.[34]

The authenticity of what Bataille says about his childhood is certainly open to question (more than that of any other). There can be no doubt that all these accounts are organised in such a way that we could unreservedly say they are fictional. It is no more frequent than acceptable for someone to speak of their own parents in such a way.

For a long time doubt about them has thrived: we have no assurance that Bataille was telling the truth. When it comes to it, no other assurance than Bataille's own: 'A few people, reading 'Coincidences', wondered whether it did not have the fictional character of the tale itself. But, like this 'Preface', 'Coincidences' has a literal exactness: many people in the village of R. could confirm the material . . .'[35] Perhaps he took pleasure, as his brother complained, in darkening, in tarnishing what did not at all warrant such indignity. Perhaps he reported hallucinations that belonged to himself alone, to his own disturbance, and which were otherwise unjustified (this is what Martial tried to say). Nevertheless, there can be little doubt that, a couple of details apart, Bataille told the truth. A couple of details, possibly of importance. For example, it is not impossible that this father, in spite of his state and his pain, could also be affectionate. But is not the affection of an invalid and a madman (holding out his hands, *blindly*, to grab a young child) also terrifying? Joseph-Aristide was certainly syphilitic. He certainly reached the final stage of this disease (almost twenty years passed between its onset and its end), and suffered from the most violent symptoms connected with it. He (virtually) certainly, at least momentarily, lost his sanity (the diagnosis of dementia is too often associated with this disease for there not to be every possibility that Georges Bataille was telling the truth). His mother certainly lived in dread for almost twenty years, more often kind, patient, resigned than intemperate, and, in the end, she herself became demented and crazy (to say more than this could only be a hypothesis). Bataille probably told the truth, however amazing it may appear, a truth that perhaps did not say *everything*. To close friends he may have admitted, without saying more about it, what was still worse. Worse, a sick and mad father; worse, a mother entirely linked to him in a way that she experienced her own martyrdom (is it so incredible that finally she also lost her reason?); worse, especially these two children as powerless witnesses of a drama which, in any event, went beyond them, though they saw its essential elements, two children too different in age and temperament to help one another endure it. Their two testimonies are not unreliable. We knew that of Georges Bataille: he was too dark and aggressive not to take pleasure in being able to leave things open to doubt. Now there is also, brief and contradictory as it may be, the testimony constituted by his brother's two letters: that of a man who his whole life had observed the most scrupulous silence, who never accepted that Georges Bataille should make something shameful or scandalous of the situation; whatever his reservations, his testimony leaves no room for doubt. It came late, fifty years after the events in question. We have seen how overwhelming was what the two men – both old and worn out – admitted. What was most overwhelming was perhaps that, to admit it, they had both waited until they were close to death.

One letter, written forty years earlier (in 1922), said nothing different and had a similar tone. The same vague exasperation seeps through it, the same difficulty of resigning himself to speaking of it, accompanied by the same apparent pleasure in making the admission while at the same time withholding it (Bataille did not say everything. We notice that he even made a rather knowing and theatrical evaluation of what could and could not be spoken), a brutal as well as temperate testimony. This letter was written to a young girl (we shall have occasion to meet her again), who had clumsily provoked him (but this annoyance seems feigned and seems to be simply a necessary pretext for the admission) by imputing his 'extravagances' to madness:

> I get furious when my exuberance or extravagances are attributed (or
> I think they are attributed) to madness. And you will easily understand

that on this point I am easily offended . . . I have a personal experience of real madness which I admit is painful since I saw *my father and mother successively become mad*. And, goodness, this might unfortunately incline you to understand me in a more hurtful way than ever. But a simple inclination, I believe, for it was the morphine given to him that destroyed my father's sanity and I would ask you not to force me to recount the extremely tragic circumstances in which my mother became sick. I will add only that such a lamentable succession of misfortunes would cause most people to founder.[36]

If this admission authenticates the double and successive madness of his father and then of his mother, it falsifies (morphine) and denies (syphilis) the reasons and hides the circumstances of what he himself calls such a lamentable succession of misfortunes.

'Turn the world upside down, turn the world, quite ineluctably, upside down'

It is not exactly known when Joseph-Aristide and Marie-Antoinette Bataille moved to Rheims (to 65c, rue du Faubourg-Cérès; this was their only home in Rheims). It is unlikely to have been later than 1899 or 1900. The reason for the move is also unknown. They had no family ties with the city. It may well have been due to an administrative transfer: Joseph-Aristide Bataille was apparently a postmaster.[1] Whatever the reason, Georges Bataille spent all his childhood and school days at Rheims.

We know little about his childhood: his memories of it are rare, except when they closely concerned his parents (at any rate those offered are rare). No memories of games or friends. Nothing which would in any way associate his childhood with innocence or the marvellous. Even the city was terrifying, terrifying in its industrial architecture, with the chimney stacks of factories 'between the sinisterly dirty sky and the stinking, filthy ground of spinning mills and dyeing works'. Not one recollection which does not relate to his father's affliction (and the terror and disgust it provoked). This was no doubt the case when, bored as a boarder at secondary school, he claims to have been devoted to the joys of self-mutilation: 'I had grasped my pen and, holding it in my clenched right hand like a knife, I repeatedly buried the steel nib in the back of my left hand and forearm. Just to see . . . and also: *I wanted to inure myself to pain.*'[2]

All the same there was something more serious, 'sicker' ('sick' in proportion to the obsession with terrors associated with the sufferings of the family). Bataille certainly never set it down so bluntly, but for a long time he had been convinced that his father had made obscene advances towards him (incestuous and pederastic advances; later he would even speak of 'rape'). This was alleged to have taken place in the cellar of the Rheims house, a real cellar reached down a long and narrow stairway resembling 'those in Piranesi',[3] also associated with lasting and recurrent terrors – of rats and spiders for instance – he never lost. The most he was to say, in a text prudently entitled *Rêve*, was that he saw his father again 'beckoning his obscene hands [towards him] with a venomous and blind smile'. 'This memory seemed to me the most terrible of all.'[4] For a long time, until late in his life, he remained convinced that his father had made 'untoward' gestures towards the child he then was ('It had the effect of reminding me that had he been young, my father would have liked to abandon himself with pleasure to something atrocious towards me'). This idea was only dispelled years later when he realised that, rationally, it would have been impossible for his father, sick as he was, to have assaulted him or even to have gone down into the cellar of the Rheims house. If Bataille went down to the cellar, it must have been alone and accompanied only by his own terrors. Nevertheless there is no doubt that any affectionate gesture his father made towards him could have seemed 'untoward' and 'obscene'. One cannot expect a child already placed in such an 'unhinged' situation to establish a good filial relationship.

He had little to say about his school life. He was a poor pupil, a fact he actually emphasises: he was lazy, and seemed almost proud of it, being 'the most indolent in the class, indeed in the whole school'.[5] Lazy and arrogant: he was 'convinced that one day, since such a lucky insolence was sustaining me, it was I who was bound to turn the world upside down – turn the world, quite ineluctably, upside down.'[6] His studies from the most junior years to the lower sixth were at Rheims lycée,[7] as a boarder it seems, although certainly not at the beginning.[8] It is worth noting that Bataille was a boarder, because that was what he wanted. This was no doubt, as he later claimed, to avoid too close a relationship with his parents. The precise reasons are not known, but in January 1913 (when he was sixteen), during the school year, he decided not to go back to school. Was this his decision or was he, as he said, 'practically' expelled? He made both claims. From January 1913 to the summer was a long period of idleness, during which he explored the countryside around Rheims on his bicycle.

Upon returning to school in September 1913, he was, at his own request, registered as a boarder at Épernay College, seven miles or so from Rheims. He undertook his first baccalaureate there, which he passed in June 1914.

'The thunderbolt pilots all things'[1]

Of all dates possible, 1914 is perhaps the most clearly symbolic of those that might be used to make a history of Bataille's life. Certainly this is the time when what had hitherto been only a drama became a tragedy; both his father's fate and his own were to be dramatic with outcomes that were tragic.

In 1914 three events took place (though we shall see that a fourth gives them a quite different appearance) which Bataille himself indicated as among the most determining factors of his youth. The first was his discovery that 'his interest in this world was to write, in particular to develop a paradoxical philosophy'. Was it that simple? It would seem not. It is not merely that we really do not know how he arrived at this conviction (there is nothing that helps us to understand it); we can also not be certain that he did not backdate this discovery. In fact it is doubtful whether Bataille was already contemplating writing philosophy, and, if he was, even more doubtful whether it would have so soon taken the form of a paradoxical philosophy; doubtful since this was the very year (Bataille himself supplies this double and simultaneous dating) he became a convert to Catholicism.

That his father should suffer without any relief had an exemplary effect on him, as did the fact that he could not believe that the horror of his situation made any sense; and that there was no God to bring him reprieve. Bataille, at the age of seventeen, would give meaning to this horror. The relief his father refused (his father being irreligious and his mother indifferent) was invoked by Bataille, weary of this affliction. It is not known by what route he arrived at this, nor whether anyone helped him. In 1914 he discovered God, and became a convert. (This is why it is doubtful whether he simultaneously imagined himself undertaking to write philosophy, what is more one that was paradoxical. *A priori*, revelation dispenses with philosophy; *a fortiori* with a heterodox one.) As to the conversion there can be no doubt: Bataille attended Cardinal Luçon's morning services at Rheims cathedral during the summer of 1914, until the latter left for Rome for the Conclave (as Bataille noted in his first book, *Notre-Dame de Rheims*). And in the summer of 1914, probably at the cathedral, he received the sacrament of baptism.[2] But one should immediately make clear the circumstances in which Cardinal Luçon's services were held, to whom they were principally addressed (the armies stationed at Rheims), and hence the context in which this sudden conversion took place (without necessarily having to imagine that this context altered or justified it). On 3 August 1914, Germany declared war on France. On the eve of the declaration, Belgium (despite its neutrality) had been forced to allow passage to German troops. By 7 August Charleroi and by 23 August Namur had fallen to their forces. It was from these two towns that the offensive was organised which, passing through the Meuse valley, Charleville and Rethel, soon reached the gates of Rheims. On 5 September, with the occupier's artillery in position at Mesneaux, four miles from the Marne's main town, Rheims was promptly declared an open city. It would seem this did not satisfy the assailants. The latter (the Twelfth Saxon Corps) opened fire without warning. The first day of shelling alone left sixty dead and 140 wounded. From 5 to 12 September, in a short but endless week, Champagne's capital was bombarded and ransacked; it was almost completely destroyed.[3]

But by 4 or 5 September, Bataille was no longer in Rheims; like the majority of the civilian population, he had been evacuated. This evacuation would be of little interest if it had not been accompanied by circumstances that were not only dramatic (the drama at this point engulfed all the citizens of Rheims and the surrounding populations who had taken refuge in Rheims since the beginning of August), but singularly tragic as well. Bataille and his mother were no doubt following the order to evacuate at the end of August (at this time Martial was at the front), but at the cost of leaving behind his father, her husband, whose disability chained him to this city pledged to fire and destruction. The circumstances of this separation remain unclear. In all likelihood Joseph-Aristide Bataille resigned himself to it. It is even probable that, as a father concerned for the fate of his family, he enjoined them to leave; they left for Riom-ès-Montagnes.

Nevertheless there is no doubt that Georges Bataille experienced this departure as an abandonment (which effectively it was, whatever its reasons and however impossible it would have been to avert it).

Doubly caught in the dreadful trap of his disabilities, a third disaster now closed in around Joseph-Aristide Bataille: total solitude in the most desolate of cities which everything suggested was fated to devastation. The fate which had crippled him and made him insane now moved to a new level of absolute tragedy. Abandoned to his fate by his own family, a man who was doubly excluded from the outside world, his feet bound and his eyes staring into space, with no one to help him but a housekeeper, was left *alone* to confront the terror of his own end in a city that, as if in sympathy, was mutilated in its turn (by the end of hostilities on 5 August 1918, Rheims was to have gone through 857 days of concerted bombardment).

Neither his wife nor his son would see him alive again. Fifteen months later, in November 1915, having heard he was dying, they found only 'a fastened coffin in the bedroom'.[4] Of all Bataille's childhood experiences, this was no doubt the key: 'On 6 November 1915 . . . two or three miles from German lines, my father died abandoned'.[5] It was not enough that a sort of destiny, predating anything the adolescent Bataille could have done, combined to doom his father, his mother and himself, but it also placed him in a position that caused a sense of guilt that would never leave him. Guilty of having failed in what little he could have done: *to see, to see* to the very end. Guilty *a fortiori* because he was a sinner: it must be remembered that the 'abandonment' (as we shall describe the departure from Rheims and the separation, since this is the word Bataille himself used) came at exactly the same moment (to within a month, even a few days) as his conversion to Catholicism, and original debt. By being baptised, Georges at once redeemed and *acknowledged* the 'fault' in which he had been born. He fell into a realm which, as an unbeliever, he had not previously understood.

We should try to understand this as he could have himself understood it. This death was no longer that of a saint (one of the elect) or of a madman (one of the 'doomed'), but of a god. His abandonment alone was of these proportions: 'No one on earth, or in the heavens, was concerned with the anguish of my dying father', he wrote.[6] God, abandoned and betrayed, mocked and stripped beyond anything Bataille could have imagined: 'I abandoned my father, alone, blind, paralytic, mad, screaming and twitching with pain, transfixed in a worn-out armchair'.[7] And since Bataille had just recently converted to Christianity, why not express this in Christian terms (he could not have failed to admit this himself): as Peter thrice denied his master, so he thrice disavowed his father. Firstly, whatever the reasons for flight (and certainly they were not surmountable), by leaving him alone in Rheims. Secondly, knowing how close his death was, in not returning to him (giving way to his mother's 'madness'; there can be no doubting that Marie-Antoinette Bataille's lapses of reason and suicide attempts were contemporaneous with the fifteen months her husband spent alone in Rheims. A self-punishing delirium, no doubt? But also a violent hostility and more violent dread of the idea that she and her son would join him). The third disavowal is more symbolic: being converted to a God of succour, to the consoling God of Christianity. Bataille says so forcefully: his father lived without religion and died without religion. It is more than a little noteworthy, even if it was chance that made it so, that what is called Bataille's conversion (and as we shall see, it was lasting) corresponded exactly with his father's abandonment in Rheims. What the sick, 'mad' man was bent on living through quite unaided (and what strength he must have needed to succeed in doing so!), the adolescent, confiding it to a priest ('I rarely went a whole week without confessing my sins' he said of himself at this time), lived through at the feet of a substitute god. Of course, only the magnanimous, merciful God of the Christians could justifiably claim to overcome the stubborn fatality of this tragic god. Only he was powerful enough for such a fate not to be completely without enlightenment. It is not an overstatement to see this as Bataille's third abandonment of his father, since he himself would say: 'My piety was only an attempted evasion: I was desperate to elude my fate and I abandoned my father'.[8] As for his father, he would not elude it. Blind, sick, 'mad', he unreservedly said *Yes*, no matter the terrible price to pay. Not to abandon him, to keep watch over him (was this not what the blind father enjoined him to do?), that alone would have been to say *Yes*, when to kneel before a priest and a redeeming god was profoundly to say *No*. The first, blind, sees what no one sees and which God conceals. The second – does religion not say 'to have one's eyes opened'? – intentionally blinded himself. It took a long time (longer, as we shall see, than he himself said) for Georges Bataille to rid himself of this cunning God, a long time before he admitted the truth to which this benign but tragic god of a father obliged him to open his eyes: the truth of death is the truth of night, something which the blind man *already* knows.

This must be understood: if Bataille was never definitively an atheist (at least never in the sense in which atheism was not a question for him), this is not because there is no God, or because God is dead, but because there is something stronger than God – stronger because blind ('God in his disability is blind when to see is my disability'), blind and mad. In his way, Joseph-Aristide Bataille was the 'madness' of God. Alone, he faced it: the supplicating confrontation of the blind man with the abyss, what is more that of a paralysed blind man, unable even to throw himself into that abyss. Twice at least (we will see there were many other times) Bataille later indicated how completely he was won over to this god, and how inevitable that fate was for him: 'Sometimes I imagine that I shall die abandoned, or even that I shall remain alone, living and with no strength. Why would I avoid my father's fate?'[9] And 'Today, I know myself "blind", measureless, a man "abandoned" on the earth like my father'.[10]

The impossible[11] is not a truth of Silenus (Silenus condemned to an untenable *No*, Bataille to an impossible *Yes*);[12] it is a Dionysiac truth, a 'bacchante's truth': a truth of scorched eyes.

'It is natural for a man, in encountering the destiny that belongs to him, to have an initial moment of recoil.'[13] What Joseph-Aristide Bataille laid bare with his empty eyes was death. It was natural for Bataille, an adolescent, to recoil, and just as inevitable that one day he should return. By an extraordinary reversal – from abandonment to the most profound agreement, from refusal to the greatest acquiescence – it was paradoxically not seeing that allowed Joseph-Aristide to *know* (his son said: 'I have seen . . . what dead eyes discern'[14]), that Georges in his turn, in order to know (determined 'to be lucid . . . to the point of dying blind'), would beg no longer to see: 'God, who watches over my efforts, give me the night of your blind man's eyes'.[15] He also said: 'It is necessary, in the end, to see everything with lifeless eyes, to become God, otherwise we would not know what it is to sink, to no longer know anything.'[16] There can be no doubt that Joseph-Aristide Bataille was what in an imaginary way, after the God of Christianity, he prayed to and entreated. Praying to him, entreating him, kept Bataille at his father's side, obedient, long before he knew it, to this Hegelian injunction: 'The spirit is this power only in knowing how to look the negative in the eyes and knowing how to stay close to it'.[17]

Ave Caesar

Joseph-Aristide Bataille died on 6 November 1915, at eight in the morning, at 69c rue du Faubourg-Cérès in Rheims.[1] Since September 1914, Georges Bataille had been living in Riom-ès-Montagnes with his mother in the house of his maternal grandparents, who also lived there. His grandmother Anne Tournadre died shortly afterwards on 15 April 1916, and his grandfather Antoine Tournadre much later, on 16 January 1923.

At Riom-ès-Montagnes Bataille lived a pious life. All the time that his father remained alone in Rheims (and much longer), and that his mother lived in prey to the disorder of her mind (apparently recovering after the deaths of her husband and mother, in November 1915 and April 1916), Bataille spent studying, taking trips and pursuing pastimes. The studies were his preparation by correspondence for his second baccalaureate (in philosophy), which he passed in June 1915. The trips were cycle rides to Châteauneuf, north-west of Riom; to the ruins of the Apchon château in the south-east; to the Monts de Cantal, the remains of a former volcano in the south, and to Salers where he seems to have often visited medieval remains.[2] The pastimes were hunting and fishing. (We must be wary of imagining Bataille as a young man steeped in nothing but devotion, spending his days in prayer and meditation. In the same way we must be wary of seeing him as a puny, malingering young man, only turning from the pleasures of adolescence through an inability to respond to them. The rare accounts we have of him at this time show him, on the contrary, capable of rivalling, if not excelling, the best of his friends – the Angrémys, the Delteils. We know he liked hunting; he also fished, in the most sporting way – getting trout from the river bare-handed. He also played tennis.)

The most important part of his time was nevertheless spent piously.

This at least is what the testimony of Georges Delteil, his closest childhood and teenage friend,[3] leads us to believe:

> Aged twenty, in our Auvergne mountains,[4] he lived a saintly life, imposing on himself a discipline of work and meditation. . . . This was in a fine austere house, that of his grandfather, situated in the centre of the village, a stone's throw from the old romanesque church where one evening he got himself locked in; deep in his prayers or reflections, he hadn't heard the sacristan close the heavy doors.[5]

His kneeling before a Rheims priest in August 1914 continued to dominate his life, and was to do so for a long time. There is no doubt that Bataille believed in the absoluteness of this kneeling, and of the absolution it marked. For him, this activity alone seemed able to respond to the merciless absoluteness that the two 'madnesses' of his father and mother forced him to live out. It is as an exemplary young man – his morals and deference were exemplary – that we should portray him between the ages of seventeen and twenty-three (we will see that he remained so noticeably longer). His faith led him to write his first book in 1918, a book as pious as he was: *Notre-Dame de Rheims*. Above all, it led him to contemplate becoming a priest, after apparently having wanted to be a doctor; his cousin Victor Bataille, who was ten years older, seems to have dissuaded him from this by making him see that as a widow his mother would not have had the means to allow him to pursue such studies. This, moreover, is also how Bataille justifies not having undertaken philosophical study.[6] So this left holy orders: monasticism or priesthood. In one form or another (his preference was to become a monk), there is no doubt that for several years Bataille cherished the ambition of devoting himself to God. This is confirmed by a year spent at a seminary, beginning in the autumn of 1917 and ending in summer 1918.[7] With the war over, he did not remain there (we do not know why), but enrolled at the École des Chartes in Paris.

Before going to the seminary, he had been conscripted, a conscription of fairly short duration which did not take him to the front. Unlike several of his close friends, he had only a brief and almost abstract experience of the war: 'circumstances were such that I never needed to fight'.[8] He was a sick soldier, imagining each day, amid the wounded and sick who were older than I, the hell to which I remained destined. . . . My life, like that of the soldiers among whom I lived, seemed enclosed in a sort of apocalypse, distant and yet present between the hospital beds.[9]

He did not go to the front, though it seems the possibility was there. He would have responded to the call, he later said, not because he had a taste for the hostilities but as one responds to anguish when it becomes excessive.[10]

Mobilised in January 1916, he returned to Riom-ès-Montagnes in January 1917, discharged for health reasons ('fell seriously ill and was discharged in January 1917', he said of himself; the First World War is linked to his first attack of pulmonary illness). In October 1918 he was in Paris, having abandoned the seminary, but with *Notre-Dame de Rheims* written and published. By ministerial decree dated 8 November 1918, he was admitted to the first year of the École des Chartes.

'Laid out like a corpse'

Should *Notre-Dame de Rheims* be counted among Bataille's books? Perhaps not. It has only an anecdotal interest, no literary value (we must admit it: Bataille displayed no trace of precocious genius). It is anecdotal and, essentially, biographical: the most precise and sure of possible testimonies about Georges Bataille's youth,[1] and the strength – be it sometimes foolish (and without doubt this is how he would himself judge it, having all his life observed the most complete silence about it) – of his Christian convictions.[2]

Innocent? Devout? Foolish? The book is no less strangely significant: less for its faith than for the way he tried to suppress it. We could read it in the way the young (twenty-year-old) Bataille could have claimed to have written it, as an apologetic address to the young people of Haute-Auvergne. At a time of fire and ashes, he wanted to retain hope and reveal the light. *Notre-Dame de Rheims* (there was the war and the hopes that affected everyone, but also his own history: was this not where he was converted?), attacked and destroyed by 'barbarians', spoke loud and plain about the symbolic world that irreligion seemed to want to end; still standing, it spoke also, or especially, about how nothing, neither irreligion nor force, could touch the depths of the soul, which was entirely impregnated with Faith, with the Church and with France. The light that is Notre-Dame de Rheims is as immemorial as it is incorruptible.

Yet one could also read this book the opposite way, against its nature (which offers the advantage of conferring a paradoxical, as well as hypothetical, interest to it), less for what it says than for what it doesn't, for what, of its impossible 'truth', seeps out in line after line: we know how difficult it was for Bataille to have left his father, alone and in all likelihood dying, in a Rheims that fire promised to consume. The book, entirely devoted to Rheims and to its grandest and proudest building, obstinately says nothing about this. Not a word. Of this beloved man, stripped of his dignity, of this ravaged 'god', of this 'madman', who, moreover, remained alone, nothing. His father is completely erased: completely erased at the impossible price of a silence cast over his 'sacrifice' (a silence so much more remarkable, so much more incomprehensible in that, having left Rheims before the destruction of the cathedral had begun, Bataille only saw it ripped apart and reduced to rubble because of his short visit to the city precisely in order to attend his father's funeral). Impossible because whatever care Bataille took to eliminate it, it rose up as evidence of his deep delusion. Paradoxically he hid his innocence there. In this way, Rheims cathedral, delivered up to fire, could be a glorious substitute for this unexhibitable god.[3] Is this line of thought imprudent? How can it be avoided when, in this text filled with aggrandising qualifications, this admission appears: 'among us there is too much pain and gloom and all things rise up in a shadow of death'? Or this, otherwise explicit and confusing: 'I see [the cathedral] as the highest and most marvellous consolation left with us by God, and I think that, whether it lasts or is in ruins, it would remain *a mother* [my emphasis] for whom to die.'

This says at once almost nothing and everything: abandonment: 'It was in a sudden fever, flight for some, for others invasion with the German army'; the madness of mothers (of his own): 'women became mad because, in their flight, they were separated from their children' (did his mother not nearly lose him when he wanted to go back to his father? Was not this the time she became 'mad'?); the choice he made to stay with his mother: 'it remains for us a mother for whom to die'; but especially blindness: 'the luminous equilibrium of life is broken, because no one remains whose eyes have not been burned by the reflection of fervid flames'. There can be no question that the city, the victim of flames and destined for destruction, should turn the man caught in its trap into one condemned man among others; fire condemned the city (against its nature) and its inhabitants to the fate of blindness. And if one still doubted that the address might not return us, in an unconscious homage, to what it intended to suppress, it would be enough to add these two citations in which the cathedral, glorious, immemorial and lasting as it was, had suddenly become – in an immeasurable way – human: 'It had ceased to give life'; 'it was laid out like a corpse'.

The school of the flesh

Pious and fervent as he then was, it is not surprising that Bataille should be reading pious and fervent literature. Above all this affected his intellectual training – we have seen how heterodox this was: he was not a formally trained philosopher – which first and foremost comprised edifying books. Nothing could alter (and nothing would erase) the fact that, whatever he was about to read – as we shall see, Proust, Dostoevsky, Nietzsche – would be read after (one is tempted to say *in the same way as*) he had 'read' God with piety and fervour.

This is why the information supplied by his friend and fellow student, André Masson, is so valuable: in 1918–19, Bataille's assiduous bedside reading was *Le Latin mystique* by Rémy de Gourmont. *Le Latin mystique* is made up of pungent, wild, violent and often splendid texts dating from the fifth to the eighteenth centuries, attributable to some of the most eminent figures of the devout Middle Ages. They serve not least as an apologetics; this is even their essential intention. But this is not what makes them interesting here. Their aim (it is curiously, obsessively, always the same) is to encourage impious souls to renounce the flesh ('rejection of the flesh is without doubt essentially Christian', Rémy de Gourmont writes), less because the flesh is odious (if it were, not knowing it would suffice) than because it is terrifying. As such, it gives rise to a veritable demonology. The flesh as presented by saints and preachers is nothing but sickness, nothing but pain; and even if it might avoid these, it would remain (and this is enough to prove how completely and intrinsically hostile it is to God) condemned to rot. Christian flesh is no doubt a tarnished flesh; it is certainly a mortal flesh, either mortal or commanded to be so, since it is never dead enough. The flesh is never so cruelly dead that God forgives it for being born from the sin which, in the beginning, was committed against him: 'Let us kill this flesh . . . kill it in the same way that, with the death caused by sin, it has killed us', says the saint Jean Climaque. No denunciation is ever enough. By a violent, punitive, rhetorical effect, the flesh is all the more permitted to condemn itself; it is not enough for it to be mortal (that is but its fate), it is not enough for it to consent to this condemnation: it must wish it upon itself.

The religious writers (evangelists, rather than mystics) collected by Rémy de Gourmont are among the most ardently contemptuous of the flesh. The most ferocious of them is Odo de Cluny (one might even say the most mad – his ferocity is that of one possessed): 'sad and great', as Rémy de Gourmont says of him, 'whose boldness of expression turns one pale to the point of fainting'.[1] But one cannot ignore how much famines, catastrophes, natural disasters and atrocities of all kinds can give rise to this deprecation of the flesh:

> The body's beauty lies entirely in the skin. In fact, if people could see what lay beneath the skin, blessed like the lynx of Bœotia with eyes that can see within, the very sight of women would be sickening to them: this feminine grace is nothing but suburra, blood, humours and gall. Consider what is hidden within the nostrils, the throat, the belly: filth everywhere. And we who find it repulsive to touch vomit or manure even with a fingertip, how could we wish to hold in our arms a mere bag of excrement![2]

We are justified in finding the touch of flesh repulsive since, however beautiful it is, it is so intrinsically condemned to disintegration that, even embraced and loved, it is no less already rotten. This is what Saint Bernard tells us: 'Reflect that you shall die, in long sighs and harsh choking, in every pain and in every terror . . . your body will be turned, in pallor and in horror, putrid and fetid, into worms and food for worms.'

Not only is the flesh mortal; worse still, it is sexualised: by an entirely Christian syllogism, apologetics wasted no time in saying that it is mortal because it is sexualised. It is not a question of whether or not Bataille shared this syllogism (the evidence is that his work is largely made up of similarities in nature of this order). The point is that this syllogism arose at this time to horrifying and edifying ends, and that a claim was made for the moral judgement of the flesh, become evil to the point that it could be nothing more than *death*: evil and the devil. The preachers agree on a demonological vision of the flesh: the flesh is not only mortal, it is mortifying, and God alone can save us from it. But the trade of the flesh affronts its atonement, which this God attempted to effect through crucifixion. And it is this sexualisation – in other words, in the Church's teaching, woman – which stands in the way of man's salvation. It is she who makes him ungodly, she who makes him deny grace. These deranged evangelists cannot find words harsh enough to explain how treacherous and deceitful the flesh of woman is, and how mortal is man's desire for it. Because she is death, she is also, insidiously, the devil: all the more repugnant for being desirable, all the more devilish for being beautiful. In a fury, Anselm of Canterbury says: 'Woman will stop at nothing, believing everything to be allowed her. She dares do everything the impetuosity of her lust craves; fear and modesty, all gives way to her whim. She despises the most sacred laws, every vow: whether it is shameful or ferocious, at the moment of pleasure she is happy.'[3]

If Bataille only retained one thing from the long years of his belief (we will see that he retained several), it would have been this: he never loved the flesh, at least never in the sense that he could imagine it without repugnance; in any case never in such a way that he could not see the kind of death to which it, and whoever was wedded to it, was consigned. As freely, as indulgently as (in his debauchery) he gave himself over to his desires, it was in the knowledge that the terror it inspires is at least as great as its beauty. And if the flesh is neither as dirty or as tarnished as God's touts would make it seem in seeking to turn this to their advantage, it remains so in so far as it is, above all, desirable: the dirtier and more tarnished it is, the more tragically it tells us that no God lies behind it to promise another beauty, an ideal one that will not decay – that God is dead. And God is all the more dead the more dirty the flesh is, and the more sullied it is, the more it is beautiful.

But this was not the only thing that could impress Bataille, and which could be more lasting than his reasons to be a believer. What he might have found 'edifying' in 1919 (stories of the martyrs) was to reappear several years later (1925), resurfacing in such a way that its significance could appear to him independently of any apologetics: the pure and simple fascination of horror. Don Ruinart, quoted at length by Rémy de Gourmont, indulgently (perhaps even with delectation) describes in minute detail what the atrocities endured by the Christian martyrs might have been like (the appalling cruelties inflicted on their bodies spoke, in exemplary fashion, of how little they valued them; the body was so insignificant that any part of it could be gloriously sacrificed to God); what the *ungulae*, the iron nails, tongs whose pincers were made of teeth imprinted on the flesh when clamped together were like; and the *unci*, a sort of hook pinched out at the end of a long stick with which 'the entrails were torn out . . . through the large openings in the sides made by whips'; and the *pectines*, iron combs used, Don Ruinart eloquently says, to comb 'like a bloody fleece the dismembered belly of Thea of Gaza'.

For whatever different reasons, Bataille, who, we will see, was fascinated for over forty years by one of the bloodiest of tortures (the Chinese torture of a Hundred Pieces), must also already have been affected by the accounts of Christian tortures. It is possible and even likely that he saw in them the opposite of what he would later see: in 1919, the boundless magnanimity of a God whose love could be a grace to the torture victims, such that they sacrificed themselves with rapture; in 1925, the absence of God, an absence as absolute as the horror endured was absolute, an absence nowhere so evident as in the place where horror would call out to it (but we shall see that such a horror, one that nothing can justify, is no less 'enrapturing').

Such a reading, a fascinated reading (remember that André Masson specifically tells us that *Le Latin mystique* was Bataille's 'bedside reading') is not so common for a young Christian that we should not remark on its dark and 'disordered' character. Bataille's Christianity is not only one of salvation. If he had been looking for escape, he would have been drawn to edifying reading of course, but the kind (which is plentiful) in which the character of consolation prevailed. On the contrary, he whose childhood we now know to have been made up of terrors, a powerless and overwhelmed witness of a flesh that each year was more pitifully in decay, chose for meditation texts that consign the flesh to the most violent and savage of fates. His Christianity was thus not entirely an escape (an evasion) as it might have been five years earlier, and as he himself explained it.

'Hard brow and clear eyes'

However pious and puritanical he was in his first year in Paris, it remains doubtful that Bataille disparaged the flesh to the extent (as Odo de Cluny enjoined him) of still being chaste. We know from several letters sent to his cousin and confidante Marie-Louise that at this time he was smitten by one of his childhood friends, Marie Delteil. If we can guess that this love was not his first, for Bataille it was certainly the first that counted.

There would be nothing exceptional about this – after all he was twenty-two – if he did not deny it. For it is in the way in which he denied it that his first stirrings of passion were brought to the attention of his cousin, as denial and repentance: 'This year's experiences have very much detached me from all doubts. Emerging from the cowardice I have shown over the past few months and from having pursued indulgence under unpleasant passionate pretexts to the extent of refusing what was most real within me in order not to offend, *I want and I know how to make my life.*'[1] While Bataille does not say the flesh is sinful, his complaint shows concern that what he has witnessed of it has distanced it from himself and what he felt he should be: 'I am tired of the idiotic forgetfulness in which I have subsisted for six months. You will still find me [he warns his cousin] with my old ideas and projects.'[2] Everything he did had to be judged. Clearly, he denounced some of his proclivities. And these are ones of which he disapproves so aggressively: 'As I told you, I continue to skirt around misanthropy. It is as though I have developed in a hothouse and you won't recognise me. I warn you I'll be peevish and harsh.'

But he does not decry love and the flesh entirely. If he felt that the love he experienced in Paris (though maybe there were several[3]) kept him away from what he ought to be, there was another in Riom, with a childhood friend, who brought him closer to it; this is the very least he affirms. We do not know when and how they declared their love. There is no doubt that Georges Bataille had known Marie Delteil for a long time (she was the sister of his oldest friend, Georges Delteil, and the daughter of his mother's doctor): is it for all that what is usually called a childhood romance? Or was it declared considerably later? It is only in 1919 that he firmly decided to marry her and it is with firmness – almost with arrogance – that he announces it to his cousin:

> And first, God willing, I'll marry Marie Delteil. Conceding this as an act of my will, it is not a matter of a vain seduction and you know how I have been seduced. It is only a matter of my will and if this act, in full possession of myself, displeases you, it is because you do not love me as I want to be loved. . . .

> I think that to will oneself according to one's strength cannot leave someone who loves one indifferent, and I would like you to recognise in it all the light that has guided me on the path of a life that friendship truly has us share and that one must love sufficiently to will oneself great.

God willing? He was not. And it was presumably not God who was unwilling as much as the young woman's parents. To understand why it is crucial to consider what Bataille was at twenty-two. Those determined to see the autobiographical figure of Bataille in the narrator of *Story of the Eye*, dissolute to the point of scandal, are a long way off course, as far away as possible, in fact, from what he was at that time: straightforward ('I love her in complete constancy') and respectful to the scruples of customs: 'It remains that I have in some way not a single hope in this respect for she is really too much a good girl and, besides, I will not accept her without her parents' consent.'[4]

Georges Bataille asked her parents for the young woman's hand and they, as was after all foreseeable, refused. Not that they had any doubts about the young man (Georges Delteil recalls the reputation Georges Bataille had then in Riom-ès-Montagnes: a model young man with the best possible future[5]), but the two families knew each other too well for a 'spectre' not to be superimposed on the possibility of the union: that of Joseph-Aristide Bataille, syphilitic, blind, sick and . . . mad? They soon made Marie realise that she had to consider the marriage 'as absolutely impossible', something about which Georges Bataille seems not to have been excessively surprised: 'after all, I was under no illusion, I knew that my marriage could have drawbacks, that I had more than an average chance of having an unhealthy child, and I find it quite understandable that they reject me but they should have done so a little earlier.'[6]

This event calls for some comment. The first, and it is not the least symbolic, is that Joseph-Aristide Bataille, even dead, continued to have an effect upon his son's life in a way the latter tried to escape. The marriage would have reconciled him with himself (at least this is what he claimed) and would have protected him from the tendencies he recognised and denounced within himself. His father, dead for four years, made this impossible, and he could no longer really define and distinguish good from evil or discern what meaning desire had in relation to them: 'I no longer know what to say in so far as my life seems uncertain and dark.'

So uncertain and dark that Bataille (and certainly for one of the few times in his life; perhaps it was also the only time he felt really humiliated) thought of killing himself: 'I would willingly do away with myself.' Suicide is rather doubtful: in the same letter he says two or three things which, in contrast to the rest, indicate the sort of man he is starting to become, just as he himself foresaw how things would be without from then on being able to avoid them: 'Why be worried about me. As much as I had a hard brow and clear eyes with which to look[7] it does not matter to me if the sky is a marvellous blue or a sinister grey, because the only thing that is real is the quite powerful face I have. . . . I no longer know what will go through my head because for a long time now my poor head has borne so many things predicting all kinds of adventure.'[8]

At the beginning of November, Bataille returned to Paris for his second year at the École des Chartes. However 'upright' his love had been, it does not appear to have been his only one (but probably the only one which seemed to him to be of the kind to link him with his 'old ideas' and 'old projects'): 'Nevertheless, I have not ceased to love another in spite of myself while there is perhaps no further obstacle between herself and me than ten days of holiday to complete.'[9]

Tumult and withdrawal

After finishing top of the class at the end of his first year at the École
des Chartes, he spent a second year there which presents no special
interest except for something he himself never appears to have mentioned: with the new academic year, in October, his mother moved to
Paris and set up a home, which her two sons Georges and Martial
shared, at 85 rue de Rennes. Was this second year less studious than
the first (he ended the year third in his class rather than top, as he says
he regularly was)? This is not significant, although the fact that he
hesitated ever more visibly between a civil and a religious life does
appear to be. His studies might seem to justify this hesitation: did they
not prepare him for a civil career? But there is no doubt he was still
planning to become a priest (there is no room to doubt he was telling
the truth in saying that 'until 1920 hardly a week went by in which I
did not confess my sins'). As far as we can guess today, the hesitation
appears even more diametrically drawn. One pole of attraction
involved the most total withdrawal: it was more monasticism than
priesthood that attracted him. The other, the liveliest dispersal, a life
made up of far-flung journeys, preferably to the Orient. Of these two
inclinations, we shall see that the second was eventually to prevail,
although in fact the future lying in store for him was a sedentary life,
as far from cloisters as from minarets. But for at least two years, from
the summer of 1920 to that of 1922 (more likely still until 1924–5),
Bataille was to be consumed with the idea of leaving Paris and
answering the rather Rimbaud-like call to 'see as much as possible of
new lands'. A letter to his cousin Marie-Louise[1] leaves no doubt about
this: 'I need only recall that in particular on 23 August 1920 I was as
preoccupied as could be with going to the Orient; at the time the taste
for travel was so pronounced in me that a month later I applied for a
teaching post in America' (thus at the end of September 1920). He did

not obtain this post; but it is rather strange that in the same month, after a study trip to London (at the British Museum, as I shall discuss later), he took the opportunity to stay, even if very briefly (Bataille says two or three days), at the Quarr Abbey monastery on the north-east coast of the Isle of Wight. This stay cannot have been simply fortuitous; neither could it have been linked to his research at the British Museum. So he must have organised it and, if so, it was because, however strong his desire to roam as far as possible, he did not discount the possibility of bringing it to an end in an almost contemplative way. In the only account he gave of this stay, peace and meditation prevail, as though it was imperative for him to protect himself from the 'adventures' his imagination promised him: 'a house surrounded with pines, beneath a moonlit softness, at the seashore; the moonlight linked to the medieval beauty of the service . . . in this place I only experienced the exclusion of the rest of the world, I imagined myself within the walls of the cloister, removed from the tumult, for an instant imagining myself a monk and saved from an interrupted, discursive life . . .'[2]

He was pulled in two directions: one involved an interruption from the world's tumult; the other was towards that tumult itself – more accurately, towards complete immersion in it. Two years later, in Madrid, nothing seemed to have changed; he even expressed himself in astonishingly similar terms: 'The only really serious thing in our insignificant existence is agitation; I will personally be happy when I have taken this restlessness a little further' (he was now thinking about Tibet). Would tumult have won out over withdrawal? Probably. But would he not, as would be logical to deduce, have lost his faith? This is what he himself often said, dating this abandonment from 1920. We shall see that this was not at all the case. By 1920 he could at most have become detached from the idea of a contemplative withdrawal.

At most, the former of the two attractions (travelling or being a recluse) would have prevailed. But there is nothing to make this certain: more likely, contemporaneously with his studies, he would have continued to hesitate between these two extreme possibilities had not, as I have suggested, life chosen a compromise solution for him that would see him dispersed rather than ascetic, but not to the point of undertaking any of the long journeys of which he had been dreaming for several years.

The depths of worlds

Between these two possibilities there arose a discovery that was to have a decisive effect upon the choices that Bataille was hesitating over; it would be equally decisive, too, in its long-term effect, to the extent that it would remain so integral to his work from start to finish that it might be said to be inseparable from it and could without distortion be seen as one of its revelatory keys. This key is *laughter*.

While staying in London to undertake research at the British Museum (London will appear several times in his work) he was able to meet Henri Bergson, the first philosopher he had met and apparently the first to have caused him to question the problem and nature of philosophy. Bataille did not conceal the fact that in 1920 he had read none of Bergson's works (it appears that he had not read anything of any philosopher). In anticipation of the meeting, he read – no doubt in haste, but the book is short – *Laughter*. It disappointed him: '*Laughter*, like the philosopher himself, was a disappointment.' (He added: 'At the time I had a tendency to go to extremes', a phrase which leaves things open to question and is at the very least premature.) It was a disappointment to the extent that what Bataille found simultaneously in laughter was essential (and might we say that he found it because of Bergson or in spite of him?). The subject merited a different treatment than the one given by Bergson. Though he was disappointed in both the man and the book, they provided Bataille with a revelation: laughter is the foundation; it reveals what is at the depths of worlds. Immediately he felt it was the key, that one could be possessed by laughter, and that by resolving this enigma, he would have resolved everything. Where the prudent and 'philosophical' Bergson believed he had perceived 'useful and reasonable knowledge', 'methodological in its madness', which he claimed could only emerge from 'a very calm, well-integrated surface of the soul', where, as he supposed, 'pure intelligence' required 'a momentary anaesthesia of the heart',[1] on every point Bataille perceived the opposite: an irrational engulfing both of the heart and the soul in the knowledge of the depths of worlds. For him, laughter was definitively distinguished from the comical (the comical never interested Bataille except derisively) as being equivalent to God. It was thus a trepidation, of the gravest kind!

Laughter is no more a morality than God; like Christianity, it is a revelation. And this, as far as he was concerned, was Bergson's error (he acts like those who make Christianity a morality): 'Let's say, henceforth, that this is especially the sense in which laughter "chastises morality". It makes us immediately try to make clear what we should be, what finally no doubt we will one day truly be.'[2] Even then,[3] for Bataille, it was the opposite: laughter was unrestrained. But – he was still a Catholic – it is through God that laughter is devoid of restraint (later he would be able to say that it is the absence of God that marks laughter; right at the end of his life Bataille even said that laughter is the 'laughter of death'). For, vivid as this revelation had been, it would be false to believe that laughter immediately replaces the revelation he had in 1914 in which he knelt down before a crucifix. For the moment they could coexist: the Bataillean *laugh* in 1920 is still Catholic, as he made clear:

> at the beginning of this experience, I was animated by a very specific religious faith that conformed to a dogma and this was very important to me, even to the point that, as far as I could, I reconciled my actions with my thoughts. But it is certain that from the moment at which I recognised the possibility of delving as deeply as possible into the realm of laughter, its first effect upon me was the disintegration of all that dogma had brought me in a kind of diffluent tide. I then felt it was quite possible for me, from that moment, to maintain all my beliefs and the actions which linked me to them but that the tide of laughter I had endured had turned these beliefs into a game. . . . From that moment I could no longer cling to them except as something laughter had surpassed.[4]

A transitory period began in which Bataille was able to maintain his beliefs (all of them: he insisted on recalling how orthodox these were and how careful he was to observe their prescriptions) within the vertigo produced by the discovery of laughter. It even seems that, during this period, his beliefs were rekindled and enriched. It was only later (as we shall see, around 1922–3) that Bataille would see laughter in a completely different way, as an affirmation rather than a denial of death. A sense of descent rather than elevation. And such laughter dissolves: it even dissolves God.

La emoción

Nowhere does humanity lean over the empty depths of
life with greater obstinacy than in Spain.

Having returned to Paris, Bataille began his third year at the École des
Chartes, and between 30 January and 1 February defended his final
thesis, '*L'Ordre de la Chevalerie*: A thirteenth-century tale in verse
with an introduction and notes'. By decree dated 10 February he was
awarded the title of palaeographic archivist, coming second in his
year,[1] and as a result was sent to the School of Advanced Spanish
Studies (later the Casa Velázquez) in Madrid: by tradition the best
student went to Rome and the second best to Madrid.

We have two sources on the stay in Madrid, distinct enough in
nature and written at sufficient interval to shed light on one another,
so that we have no reason to suspect Bataille of having retrospectively
imposed on his recollections a kind of narration typical of maturity
rather than youth. The Spain he later described does not accord with
the one he discovered in 1922; evidently what he claimed to have
found was not quite what he really experienced. The first source is
contemporaneous with his visit, consisting of long, detailed and confiding letters to his cousin Marie-Louise; in all likelihood we can trust
their content, however much he might have respected the obligations
of the kinship ties linking him to their recipient. The second comes
twenty-four years later, in the form of an article published in a journal
edited by him in 1946 on the subject of Spain.[2] If the same visit and
the same events are thus described twice, we shall see two differences.

One thing Bataille says in 1946 is nevertheless correct: 'After a few
months I realised I was in a different moral world.' This is accurate
but also ambiguous, since Bataille spent no more than a few months
there, tending to support the idea that, if he discovered Spain during

his first visit in 1922, it could not have been until the very end of his stay.

Before finding Spain serious and tragic, before he perceived the Spanish people as more anguished than any other, he spent a long time in an indifferent and resigned solitude:

> I'm in Madrid, not as you might think in a state of either exhaustion or desolation, but in that mixed state characterised by the fact that it is made up of neither exhaustion nor desolation. What is more, this state is totally unpleasant, obviously. It comes from the fact that at no time in the day do I feel the slightest pleasure in seeing anyone's face. There's no need to bemoan this, just that in the end this absence tires you out. One never weeps for want of laughing, but one still suffers . . .[3]

Far from being keen or impatient to go out and meet Spaniards, far from immediately feeling, as he would later say, that they unconsciously inherit an 'authentic, apparently spontaneous culture of anguish',[4] he seems to have lived a withdrawn existence, devoting himself to solitary experiences of meditation which were important and intense enough to appear regularly in his letters. For in Madrid he was *dreaming*, methodically; he complained to his cousin that 'most poor people dream in a way that lacks scientific character or method. Strictly speaking, it's a universal misfortune.' If, as he says, there are ways to breathe in tobacco and opium smoke, why would there not be ways similarly to impregnate oneself with dreaming: 'This is why I'm patiently inventing a method of making myself dream in the humblest of circumstances. . . . To imagine burning kisses or fragrant dusks while looking at statuettes that are no more expressive than a German beer glass or a tuppenny neck tie.' A subsequent letter gives an insight into this method in the form of a pithy formula:

1. Take an average-sized cigarette of quite pale tobacco.
2. Take on a totally expressionless face like that of people sleeping.
3. Become elated.

The dream begins like a stream flowing on a moonlit night.

This formula calls for two comments. Firstly, that at the same time in Paris the surrealists, who were initiating themselves (at René Crevel's instigation) in the practice of provoked dreaming, were not acting very differently. Secondly, the instruction to become elated is strangely reminiscent of Nietzsche; Bataille, alone in Madrid and still a Christian, knowing nothing about Nietzsche, was himself experimenting with techniques and thinking which relate in different ways both to surrealism and to Nietzsche.

In Madrid he was *dreaming* and above all thinking about going away. We have seen that since the summer of 1920 he had cherished the plan of making long journeys:

> I am only obliged to recall that in particular on 23 August 1920 [what does such a precise date, given two years later, mean; what event does it allude to?] I was completely taken up with going to the Orient. . . . Of course, I have never since come across anything which would contradict in general terms this stalled wish (not so much to live abroad as to see as much as possible of new lands). . . . Of course, what I'm saying to you here is so true that it is becoming pointless and above all impossible ever to talk about it again.

In Madrid (though surely he already was abroad) his aims were exactly the same: 'I have very little to tell you about my current life, whose principal pleasure [neither enthusiastic nor desolate, as we have seen] consists in working out projects and saving up to accomplish them.' And these projects can be named: he told himself that in 1922, once his stay in Madrid was over, he would go to Morocco – perhaps to Fez, and definitely to Rabat.[5] And later he would go to Tibet, which seemed to him the fitting end of all journeys, because, as he said, 'of the difficulty, the cold and the altitude' (apparently considering the 'journey' as ascetic rather than initiatory) and, perhaps jokingly, he adds, because of the polyandry: 'found out that the lovely Tibetan women have several husbands at the same time. How glorious it would be for the traveller who, going to live in this pleasant land, would bring back such courteous customs.'

When he was not indifferent, he was unhappy: 'These last days have been the worst I have yet had in Spain', and impatient to leave. This seems to have been what Bataille was like in Madrid, at least for some weeks.[6]

What Bataille would not say later either was that the Spain he was to discover (since he managed to emerge from his reverie and go out to meet it: 'I'm starting to sense a Spain full of violence and sumptuousness') would be essentially Catholic. It was the Spain of 'highly spiced' lavenders, some of which had 'the distinct character of an Inquisition torture'; the Spain of a sun 'as resplendent as a baroque monstrance';[7] the Spain of mountainous peaks 'truly torn to bits and lifted high into the sky'; finally the Spain of Isabella the Catholic when she drove Boadbdil from the Alhambra.

The letters written from Madrid leave little doubt: in 1922 Georges Bataille was a Catholic, so clearly, so manifestly a Catholic it would be hard to see what distinguished him from the Catholic he had been four years earlier in Riom-ès-Montagnes when he wrote *Notre-Dame de Rheims*. Even the solemn, inflated style of this first book appears again here and, remarkably, on the subject of sacred architecture: 'Towards the mountain one can consider, in chaotic surroundings that nevertheless have an infinite horizon, the mass of the Escurial where the bells, whose violence truly makes one feel giddy and where, with a pungent unease, bizarrely exalted, there gives out from this sizeable tomb, in panting and broken voices, a simple and clerical grandeur.'[8]

Evidently the tumult had still not entirely rid him of his faith. God resists laughter and the world. London only provided a temporary upset, not enough to take with it the resistances built up around the most scrupulously Christian dogma. And if Bataille uttered a vow at the end of this long letter, it was certainly not because anything might get the better of God, quite the reverse: 'I dream of spending my life in such infinitely renewed constrictions . . . it is right that the good Lord should sleep tonight with an easy conscience on our account.'

What we have just read, reflected faithfully and confidently by the letters, would later be edited out by Bataille to the benefit of something else which appears in them only by allusion. The evidence shows that the effects of a late 'reconversion' would cancel out what he knew had to be due to sheer piety. 'For several days, and every evening, I went to see a dancer every time she danced . . .' This is what he wrote in 1946, adding splendidly: 'The dance, essentially miming anguished pleasure, frustrates a challenge that catches the breath. It communicates an ecstasy, a sort of suffocated revelation of death and the feeling of touching the impossible.' This same dancer, no doubt, is evoked in the letters in less 'ecstatic' if no less erotic terms (it is doubtless the first written erotic suggestion we know from him): 'I saw a native dancer who looked like a panther with a lithe little body, nervous and violent. A little animal of this breed seems to me one that could set a bed on fire in a more devastating way than any other creature.'

But of the two other apparently defining events the letters say nothing (no doubt they only took on this aspect in retrospect): one is the *cante hondo* tournament[9] he attended in Granada[10] and the appearance of a flamenco singer, Bermudez ('He sang – rather, he threw out his voice in a sort of excessive, rending, prolonged cry which, when you thought it was exhausted, reached, in the prolongation of a death moan, the unimaginable').[11] If the letters make no mention of this competition, Alfred Métraux's account seems to confirm the 'tense' character it had for Bataille: 'His enthusiasm was so lively, the images he evoked so beautiful, that forty years later I can convince myself that I myself took part in this festival.'[12]

Nevertheless it was another event which most visibly brought out the violent, tense nature of Spanish festivals: on 17 May 1922, Bataille was present at the death of the young bullfighter Manolo Granero (barely twenty years old) in the Madrid bullring; spectacularly wounded, 'Granero was thrown back by the bull and wedged against the balustrade; the horns struck the balustrade three times at full speed; at the third blow, one horn plunged into the right eye and through the head.'[13] This mutilation gripped and fascinated him. The hold and fascination were to last, no doubt less as completely immediate sensations here than as retrospective ones as well (they would only take full effect when they found their place in the fantastical mechanism of *Story of the Eye*). In fact, Bataille was only in a rather poor position to witness the horrific event personally and immediately: 'I was on the opposite side of the ring, and only learned the details of the whole drama from the published accounts – or photographs. . . . I didn't know at what moment, in the arena where the vast crowd got to their feet, a stunned silence fell; in sunlight, this theatrical entrance of death, at the festival's height, had an evident, expected and intolerable quality.'[14]

But from this overwhelmed festival, whose horror highlighted rather than diminished its meaning, from this evident, expected and intolerable beauty of a death bursting out in the sun, a sun scarcely heavier than the resigned, stunned silence of the crowd, was born – and no doubt this was *profoundly* true, whether or not it happened at once – the sense of the most disturbed pleasure, a pleasure that was aggravated (like a tooth), worked up: 'From that day on I never went to a bullfight without a sense of anguish straining my nerves intensely. This anguish did not in the least diminish my desire to go to the bullring. On the contrary, it exacerbated it, taking shape with a feverish impatience. I *then began to understand* that unease is often the secret of the greatest pleasures.'[15]

Which Bataille should we choose? The pious one or the one beginning to be disturbed by the most fierce and equivocal pleasures; the one who sees a dancer as a 'panther' to 'set a bed on fire' or the one who mentions the love he bears a French girl (Miss C., whom we shall meet later) 'of such a deep and delicately feminine sensibility', a veritable 'Beatrice, since she is a little hieraticised and has a true theological rigour'?[16] The truth about this visit, and about the young man Bataille still was, is apparently to be found at *both* these two opposing extremes (and not at all *between* them), the same ones we saw emerge from his stay in London in 1920 (the dating of these appearances is of course symbolic; at best they mark out a long, slow evolution, and there are no grounds for considering them as sudden and imperative as the conversion of 1914 seems to have been). Bataille was still a fervent Christian, of this there is no doubt (even if in more than one way he later dissembled the fact), a fervour that could be just as naïve as that which spurred the writing of *Notre-Dame de Rheims*. A Christian, certainly, and he does not appear to have had any desire to be otherwise – on the contrary. But as for the 'infinitely repeated paroxysms' he prayed his belief would supply, as it happened it would be from quite different events in Spain that twice or three times they would be produced. Interposed between the Andalusian sun, which in 1922 he saw as 'a baroque monstrance' and the 'torrent of the guts' with which he replaced it in 1927,[17] was the memory (first real and then reconstructed) of the heavy mortal sun of the Madrid bullring.[18]

Letters to an unknown woman

One of the paradoxes of this body of work is that, while it is among the most self-exposed, it leaves us in suspense about more than one essential point. Admittedly, this is not such that Bataille should be accused of negligence, for his work – we need to remind ourselves – is only incidentally, or additionally, autobiographical. It may illuminate three or four aspects while, at the same time, disregarding so much else, consigning it to shadows, while not allowing us to infer that he considered the former more important than the latter. Without any doubt a more subtle, and less coherent, play is at work here (it is only possible to read and speak about Bataille in an incoherent way). Even the very depictions presented as autobiographical (or presumed to be) are not so exact they can be unreservedly accepted. For instance: 'I've said that at the age of twenty a tide of laughter swept me away . . . I felt I was dancing in light. At the same time I surrendered to the joys of free sensuality. Seldom does the world so satisfyingly laugh at someone who returns the laughter.'[1]

We can be sure that Bataille was not swept away by such a wave of laughter when he was twenty. It cannot be so because, on several occasions, he dated his discovery of *laughter* (in the sense we have seen that he understood it) to 1920, when he was twenty-three. It cannot be accurate for another, more definitive, reason: he was twenty in 1917, the year he was demobilised and entered the Saint-Flour seminary (he was about to write the highly devout *Notre-Dame de Rheims*), and at that time he was pious, contemplative, puritanical and, we know, wished to devote himself to God.[2] Light and sensuality had by no means made his world sensual and filled with laughter like no other. Is this a simple error or a simplification (which is what being twenty means)? It is more than likely that we should see it as representing Bataille's ever present concern to distance the time he shed his burden of Catholicism. Was he ashamed of it? Though uncertain, this is not impossible. At any rate, one day he dates this renunciation at the latest at the age of twenty, on another at twenty-three, while several of his close friends have said he was twenty-four. . . . The letters he sent from Madrid leave little doubt that he had lost his faith completely only when he was twenty-five, if not twenty-six. Subsequent, then, to his return to Paris in 1922.

But what was he like in Paris? Still pious or quite free of all religious proclivities? One thing is likely: the stay in Madrid was not so long that what we know about it can hide a violent change. There is in all probability still something remaining of the pious young man who could be perceived in the letters to his cousin. And such it was that he returned to Paris, doubtless no longer convinced of his vocation (we have seen that it was in 1920 that he seems to have abandoned this idea), but still close enough to it to recall it at the end of his letters. If Spain was not immediately decisive, there is little doubt it became so in the long term. Bataille afterwards wanted people to believe that determining factors were the *cante hondo* tournament in Granada or the bullfights, especially the one that caused the death of Manolo Granero. The letters he wrote, however, make no allusion to either. What predominated in them was, on the one hand, the sacred architecture of the Alhambra and the Escurial and, on the other, the sense of boredom and wish for distant travel, to go to the Orient or at least leave Spain. To our knowledge, this desire appeared in 1920 and remained with him when he returned to Paris. It is probably necessary to see a confirmation of it in the fact that he enrolled at the School for Oriental Languages. He acquainted himself with Chinese, with Tibetan (as we saw, he wanted to go to Tibet because it seemed a fitting culmination of all possible journeys) and with Russian (as we shall soon see, if he did not manage to visit the Soviet Union, this apprenticeship would still be useful for him[3]).

Indecisive and anguished, swinging between self-deprecation and sarcasm towards others, between provocations and regrets, fearing boredom and threatening suicide, determined on the best (an upright life) and giving way to the worst (or what he believed to be the worst), modest to the point of excess and yet arrogant, and so on. This is how Bataille seems throughout a long correspondence, less amicable than no doubt insidiously amorous (but the relationship it evokes does not seem to have been anything more than friendly), with a young girl I will refer to here as Miss C.[4]

These letters hold considerable interest in that Bataille reveals himself with sufficient plausibility and sincerity to give us the means of recognising the sort of person he was between 1922 (and the end of the stay in Madrid) and 1924 (when he would meet those who would later support this account), and how he *tottered*.

'Totter' is probably not the right word. It suggests the harshness of a fleeting movement. Among other things, these letters have an importance in also deferring the moment of *transition*. Certainly it happened at that time. And yet, it happened only in part. Reading them makes it finally possible to date not so much Bataille's 'reconversion' and loss of faith (we have seen that it could only have been a gradual process) as their first manifest effects: effects which in their turn would amplify this reconversion and loss. Bataille would abandon God by surrendering to temptation. This he did in one movement. He did not give religion up after doing what it proscribes. It was by succumbing that he moved away from religion. So much so that he would finally abandon God.

Bataille was unable to explain clearly what temptation meant for him or what it meant to succumb to it. Obviously, and even though these two words are absent from the correspondence (their absence is itself revealing, considering the direction already indicated), it is under the auspices at least of error, at most of sin, that he experienced temptation and consented to it (the word 'sin' is no doubt neither immoderate nor displaced). It is in every case the word he used, much later, when far from concealing that he could have been a young Catholic, he insinuated that his Catholicism might almost have been heretical: 'I do not believe that, to the extent that I had a Catholic faith, I was in the least bit on the road to saintliness; I was also perhaps on the road to sin. It was a combination . . . and saintliness certainly did not predominate.'[5]

For Bataille consented to what he succumbed to, however great the fear that repeatedly seized him, and with however much bad faith he found absolution. He both consented and fled (refused): 'I have not the slightest desire to surrender to unbearable feelings'; 'I don't at all want furious pleasures.' The nature of the fear taking hold of him left no doubt: he needed *either* to be chaste ('What is my ultimate reason to be chaste?') *or* to consent to excess ('It is a matter of a pleasure which, I believe, goes a very long way beyond my faculties of assimilation'). No half-measures were possible. If he still drew upon Christianity in the effort he made to repel the temptations to which he was prey, it was certainly no longer in the usual sense in which any consent to the flesh would betray it, but in that in which the flesh could not be offered to temptation except under the sign – so much rarer and already dramatised – of *excess*.

He explained this excess to his reader (with a doubtless displaced insistence; he knew he was defiling the trust she placed in him and, obviously, whatever his protestations of shame, he was *taking pleasure* in them):

> I also know it is difficult for me to spare you an explanation. . . . It is absolutely essential that I no longer see a certain woman. That's easy enough in the sense that I have only seen her once. This is why: she is absolutely monstrous and yet I have no sort of disgust because after all there is something rather magnificent about monstrosity and especially because, for me, this woman is absolutely beautiful.[6] Perhaps you will surmise that my life is awful? I hope not: you would be wrong. In fact my only difficulty at present is that, so long as I do not see the woman again, I will live the purest life possible.

Confessing himself so indecently had a sly meaning: from beginning to end these letters show him seeking from this idealised young girl the will that alone he was incapable of maintaining not to see the woman again. Binding himself to her opinion as his intimate friend and knowing beforehand that her judgement would humiliate him, he made a promise.[7] He promised not to see this woman who was so beautiful as to be monstrous and from whom he had taken pleasures which attracted him all the more strongly because they went beyond what he found tolerable (all the more so because they scared him). He promised not to return to the place where he would risk meeting her.[8]

Although this promise, he said, was irreversible in nature, irreversible because shame was added to it,[9] he did not for long hide from his reader that it was wholly impossible to restrain himself: 'I think', he wrote in the same letter, 'that in general it is necessary to avoid definitive resolutions. I also think that there are no *bad* pleasures, etc. I cannot really hide from you that my thoughts are also a mass of very immoral things.'[10] The lure was more powerful than all the promises which, moreover, no one was urging him to make. More powerful was the temptation of slipping (for what he enigmatically calls 'certain reasons of intimate sincerity') into 'brutality and bestiality'.

Obviously, this was not the only time Bataille vacillated. If we can see him slipping towards the sort of disordered sexuality that even his friends would later reproach him for or which would at least amaze them, we cannot be sure that it was the first time he had done so. We may perhaps deduce this from a passage in which regret suggests boredom: 'The suffering of an overly parsimonious life is really too great when one had already known an exuberant prodigality'.[11] An 'upright life', if 'innocent, open-hearted' friendship, may still, in his view, have been cherishable and worth the effort, but not to the extent that he would hide either what he thought ('a mass of very immoral things'), or even what he wanted and indeed valued. Suddenly accusatory, perhaps for the only time in these letters – Bataille protests against his reader's suspicions:

> I get furious when people attribute (or I imagine they attribute) my exuberance to madness. . . . I see a sort of disrespect in it concerning the only things for which for my part I can address any respect. By this I mean feverish passion, restlessness of the spirit and *desire*. It therefore shocks me to see the degree to which these virtues can be explained away as a distasteful degradation, a little as if I were a Catholic to whom someone would speak with vulgarity about a very holy sacrament.[12]

The portrait of Bataille these letters convey is undoubtedly varied. If he was no longer a believer, he retained more than one aspect (purity, chastity) of religious morality, and if he was slipping towards pleasures that would lose him this aspect, it was not without fear or remorse. If he provoked his reader, it was in order to invite the risk of her reproach which would humiliate him, and if he called upon and repeated the humiliation into which without further warning she placed him, it was still through imploring her to love him better and to love him more. If he called so willingly and strongly for a friendship which would dictate such letters to him (and these would oblige their reader in return), it was more desperately to deplore his solitude, and if she only broke this solitude at long intervals, it was because such letters seemed excessive and frightened her. If he was affirming himself strongly ('I still have sound judgement'), it was in order, a few lines later, not to hide the fact that he was also really a coward. If he begged and implored, it was not without 'the set purpose, at once hateful and diverting, of scorn [for you]'. If he praised existence and pleasures which, in the end, he would be unable to renounce, it was no longer without several times threatening death ('it needs to end on a bridge'[13]), and if he was friendly, even obsequious, it was not without himself recognising that it was egoistically . . .[14]

One could certainly picture this as a primitive psychoanalysis where the addressee, under cover of friendship, was the confidante in spite of herself (he insists on it: it is friendship which links him to her, but not to the point that she must eliminate the idea that what makes him write to her so often and over such a long period could be other than friendship). In fact, none of the elements constitutive of an analysis and, as far as one can imagine, of the analysis Bataille embarked on in 1925 at the instigation of his anxious friends, are lacking here, at least in outline. The annoying character in Dostoevsky's *Notes from Underground*, with whom this self-portrait, in some ways in spite of himself, seems to have more than one point in common, may also come to mind.[15] Finally this can be imagined (imagined in a literary way): with Miss C., to whom he admiringly attributed, in a letter to his cousin, a 'real theological inflexibility', he would not give up what he retained of 'theology', a little as Valmont, with the Presidente de Tourval, would not give up what he retained of love. The provocation these letters are could thus have this meaning: in them he put an end to himself as a *believer*, resolutely and furiously shattering his belief into pieces. Thus, after nine or perhaps ten years, he put a definitive end to the period inaugurated with his conversion in August 1914.

'When you have to embark on the seas, you emigrants'[1]

He does not seem to have made any of the journeys for which his study of languages at the School of Oriental Languages prepared him. The only one we can be certain about took him to Italy, although we do not know when: at a guess, 1923. If it is worth mentioning here, it is because it evidently came just after his loss of faith: 'I laughed at my pleasure in living and my Italianate sensuality – the softest, most graceful I know of. And I laughed to discover the extent to which life had played with Christianity in this sun-blessed spot, changing the anaemic monk to the princess of *A Thousand and One Nights*.'[2] However literally we wish to take this, Bataille also seems to be speaking about himself – yesterday an 'anaemic monk'; today, by the grace of existence, laughing at the Christianity which would wish to prevent him from being what sensuality invited him towards: a princess from the *Thousand and One Nights*. In Italy he went to Sienna. Once again sacred architecture drew his attention, but this time quite differently from Notre-Dame cathedral in Rheims or the Escurial. What seized him in the Duomo in Sienna was not trembling (trembling on his knees) but laughter. For the first time, a religious edifice presented itself for what it was, *empty*: 'Of questionable taste, multicoloured and gilded.' Nothing in him bows down or lies prostrate now. To the solemnity of the edifice, to those who kneel, Bataille opposes the free and upright sensuality of streets, light and women.

I have suggested the date of 1923 for this journey. It would thus mark the definitive end of his religious 'commitment'. But the fact remains that we do not know exactly what happened. However invaluable the letters to Miss C., they hardly do more than suggest *by default* that their author was becoming progressively, rather than suddenly, distant from his belief. There is effectively only a short two-year period separating the return from Spain and his getting to know his first friends, among them Michel Leiris. At the start of 1922, Bataille was still devout or at least humble before God. By the end of 1924 he was leading 'the most dissolute lifestyle'.³ How should we understand this? How, in such a short time, did Bataille go from being a young man mindful of the prescriptions of religion,⁴ religious himself – even a mystic, as his fellow student at the École des Chartes, André Masson, described him – to being a dissolute man, 'frequenting dives and prostitutes', drinking and gambling in select circles?⁵ Not only does the loss of faith appear to have been definitive, it was also violent. Bataille emerged from one state only to adopt its radical opposite: devout in 1922, debauched in 1924. The worst is not that we do not know exactly when this turnabout occurred, but that we do not know how it came to be so definitive and spectacular. For Bataille's debauchery from 1924 had to be spectacular for Leiris to note it and recently confirm that this was indeed his first memory of their meeting. Libertinage was not so rare at the time as to be worthy of comment: on the contrary, in intellectual circles, after the butchery of 1914–18, it could be indulged in without anyone taking offence. This does not seem to have been the case for Bataille. His faith was complete and lasting; its loss appears brutal (if not sudden). We know that in Madrid Bataille began a novel in the style of Proust; so he had already, no doubt at length, read him. Proust could have been the first to lead him away from the world of religion. Then in 1922 came Gide (*Les Nourritures terrestres* [*The Fruits of the Earth*] and *Paludes* [*Marshlands*])⁶ and above all Nietzsche (*Untimely Meditations* and *Beyond Good and Evil*⁷); no doubt they led him even further away. Bataille said on several occasions that his reading of Nietzsche was decisive (though not until 1923). What Proust had begun to wear away, Nietzsche undermined, in a way so violent (too much so, no doubt) that Bataille recoiled: 'I was overcome and I resisted.'⁸ At first he recalled all the things that could help him reduce the effects of this devastating reading: 'It is natural for a man encountering the destiny which belongs to him to experience an initial moment of recoil'⁹ (we can clearly see how Bataille might have stepped back: for example, by reading Claudel's *Cinq grand odes*, which parallel the concerns of *Notre-Dame de Rheims*, and could act as a spur to continue the 'work' begun in 1918).

Bataille would only 'resign himself' to Nietzsche, as though to the destiny laid out for him, in 1923. But in doing so, he experienced what Nietzsche had undertaken: 'On my own, I'll have to face the same difficulties as Nietzsche – putting God and the good behind him, though all ablaze with the ardour possessed by those who lay down their lives for God or the good.'[10] Bataille was ardent, inflamed, no less than he had been as a Christian. But what Nietzsche beckoned him towards, what everything (like the laughter he discovered in London) had been beckoning him towards in the years before Nietzsche had any part in it, was abandonment of God and goodness: everything, indeed, that had until then sustained him. Not a lesser conversion than the one that caused him to kneel before a crucifix, this was a conversion in reverse. A conversion whose implications he doubtless did not immediately grasp, but which he nevertheless must have recognised for what it was: radical. All the more radical in that, in so far as he was immediately able to judge, Nietzsche is not merely the philosopher of the will to power, but also, he said, of evil.[11] In place of the good justified by God, Nietzsche points to evil, at the behest of a morality turned inside-out like a glove. There remains a God who is *dead* (or not so much dead as absent) who is not replaced with anything: whose place is vacant. With God denounced, the 'do this or that' of the preachers is reduced to nothing. The only preaching he permits himself to hear is that of Zarathustra who is, even more than God, 'a seducer, laughing at the tasks he undertakes'.[12] Bataille now realised, this time thanks to Nietzsche, that the laughter he had discovered in London in 1920 (and then in Sienna), in all its cataclysmic depth, in no way had to be justified to God, but to himself, himself alone:

> Certainly, the moment I started to conceive of the possibility of descending as far as possible into the realm of laughter, the first impact was a feeling that everything dogma offered had become decomposed after having been swept away in a sort of diffluent tide. At that moment I felt it was after all quite possible to maintain my faith and related behaviour, but that the tide of laughter sweeping over me had turned my faith into a game, a game in which I could continue to believe, but which had been transcended by the dynamics of the game given to me by laughter.[13]

Henceforth no project, no salvation would be connected to him. The immoderation of Nietzschean intoxication was no doubt felt by Bataille in Sienna. Denying God (Bataille denies God, but only someone who was once entirely devoted to him can truly, violently deny him), Bataille chooses a flesh stripped bare: nothing justifies it more than the desire that inflames it and the laughter that shakes it. It alone is what God was: an abyss. This in a way was the lesson taught by his father, but this time with nothing sick, deathly or damning about it: 'Here I am, a *self*: awakening, emerging, from a long period of human infancy, in which people relied on each other for everything.'[14]

One has to come back to this: 'My piety was merely an attempt at evasion: I wanted to escape my destiny at any price, I was abandoning my father.'[15] In reply to the *No* his conversion of August 1914 made him exclaim, his 'reconversion' of 1923 bade him express a completely unqualified *Yes*, a *Yes* as profound as the lightness, the playfulness, the one who speaks it finds in the world. This needs emphasising because it is not through a sudden lack of religion (in the usual sense of the word) that Bataille forsook Christianity, but because, for the absoluteness he ascribed to it, he substituted an even more intense one, because, however absolute the Christian *No* might be, the Nietzschean *Yes* is so much more so.

Much later Bataille would say, in terms worth repeating here so as to anticipate any misinterpretation which might arise from the close and apparently paradoxical proximity in which he maintained Christianity and 'Nietzscheanism' throughout his life: 'Nietzsche's atheism is of a singular nature, an atheism of a man who *knew* God, who had the same experience of God as the saints. . . . Everything moreover commits us to believe that Nietzsche's teaching requires an initial assimilation to Christianity in order to be followed.'[16]

> Our ancestors were Christians who in their Christianity were uncompromisingly upright: for their faith they willingly sacrificed possessions and position, blood and fatherland. We do the same. For what? For our unbelief? For every kind of unbelief? No, you know better than that, friends! The hidden Yes in you is stronger than all Noes and Maybes that afflict you and your age like a disease; and when you have to embark on the seas, you emigrants, you, too, are compelled to this by – a *faith*.[17]

The paradox is that Bataille should be presented as a nihilist (as was Nietzsche), he who better than anyone made the above injunction his own: 'not the least contradiction is that his work, devoted to the anguished search for an expression at the limits of the impossible, often takes on the appearance of a relentless negation, when at the same time he never stopped saying *Yes* to the world, without limit or reservation'.[18]

The joyful cynic

From September 1922 to the end of 1924, we have reason to believe that Georges Bataille was a young man who was most often on his own. He formed his most constant friendships only in 1924. Until then the only friends he could count upon appeared to be André Masson, his fellow student from 1918, and Alfred Métraux, who entered the École des Chartes just as he was leaving it. Bataille met Alfred Métraux a few days before leaving for Madrid. From the start, they had in common a 'dark sense of physically resembling one another', a resemblance ('the same height, the same very black hair, the regularity of features, and probably even a kinship of expression, with a mingled air of gentleness, passion and resolution') so striking that, according to Fernande Schulmann,[1] they were frequently mistaken for brothers. The two young men called one another 'vous' but their ties were deep. They spent three or four hours walking together along the rue de Rennes (where Bataille lived), or along the Champs-Élysées in the mornings. Bataille would speak of Gide and Nietzsche; Métraux of Marcel Mauss, whose course he was following[2] and into whose teaching he gradually initiated his friend.

Torments and enthusiasms were common to them both. To Métraux's reserve (the reserve of someone recently arrived from the provinces, from Vaud), Bataille, for whom everything was permitted, seems to have striven to oppose his morality of cynicism (we must remember that this was already 1923 at least, if not 1924): 'Dare to be the cynic you are', he urged. According to Métraux,[3] the 'joyful cynic' is, if not the title, at least the theme of a draft novel on which Bataille was working at that time, about a cynic who, after many adventures, ends up killing a tramp.

Bataille only made a belated and distracted mention of this abandoned novel during an article about Samuel Beckett (on *Molloy*, as if the animality of the title character had the power to resuscitate that of the tramp). Waiting for a train at an interchange station, the adolescent Bataille (he said he was between fifteen and twenty, without being more precise) had a very long conversation (lasting for part of the night) with an old 'vagabond' who was happy with the life fate had brought him and happy that his fate made an impression on the adolescent: 'Encountering him had such an impact on me that a little later I began writing a novel in which a man who had met him in the country killed him in the hope of gaining access to his animal immediacy.'[4]

Georges Bataille and Alfred Métraux shared everything ('we became inseparable'[5]), including women in 'black silk pyjamas, with long gold cigarette-holders and boyish haircuts, moving around in poorly defined and rather ambiguous surroundings . . .'[6] Alfred Métraux's testimony is the first we have that leaves no doubt about Bataille's 'reconversion' and, far from evoking any piety, introduces its opposite into his life. For the first time it is clear how much his readings of Gide, Nietzsche and Dostoevsky seem to have influenced him.

'Tristi est anima mea usque ad mortem'

Bataille made no secret of the fact that he was not educated as a philosopher (he even, almost provocatively, insisted on it). His education – it was wartime – gave him only a rough grasp of it, the bare essentials. All in all, in this field he had only a philosophy baccalaureate and the knowledge he gained from the course textbook ('bound in green cloth', he recalled). Partly on purpose ('I deliberately had no wish to be a specialist philosopher'), partly for want of the means to do so, once he had sat his baccalaureate he did not take up the study of philosophy. At least that is what he said. We may recall that he seemed to be heading more towards the study of medicine than philosophy; also that, for want of taking up either, it was theology he chose by enrolling at the Saint-Flour seminary, which was much more congenial to the person he then was. Everything suggests that in 1922 (when he was twenty-five and home from Madrid), with one or two exceptions, Bergson for example, he had not read any philosophy.

If he read in Paris (and he was still not reading very much), it was unmethodically, letting chance decide his encounters. To reading, Bataille preferred reflection, in a disconnected way, moreover, subject to complete disorder. Such free and disorganised reflection (but of a kind preliminary to any conceptualisation) was not enough to constitute thought; reflection only supported now and again by a few randomly procured reference points is liable to impotence. Bataille did not underestimate this: 'I was limited to reflecting, yet I was very aware of the abyss separating my embryonic reflections from the aimed for result.'[1]

Once his jubilation had passed, the dizzying effect of Nietzsche would certainly not have been enough to take him beyond this impotence. The help of an intermediary was required; this privileged intermediary was undoubtedly, from 1922 (or 1923) to 1925, Léon Chestov.

It is no surprise that Bataille later emphasised his differences from Chestov rather than their similarities. Yet on closer inspection, their similarities are considerable. It was not only the fact that Chestov's philosophy 'began with Nietzsche and Dostoevsky', as Bataille put it, that attracted him. Actually, at the time Bataille knew little of Nietzsche, and apparently nothing of Dostoevsky. The Nietzsche he knew, however much he was shaken by what he read, arose from out of nowhere. Chestov would seem to have put him back into his history; whatever reservations Bataille had in admitting this, this history was *also* that of philosophy. Nietzsche's genealogy – it was Chestov's as well – appeared to him for what it had to be: made up of Pascal, Plotinus, Tertullian, etc.,[2] writers, Bataille would have us believe, of whom he had read little if anything. For Chestov, Nietzsche's thought was a reconquest, overcoming even those he claimed to disprove: it no longer emerged *ex nihilo* from a chaos without links or reference points. It would no doubt be pretty close to the truth to suggest that Chestov was responsible for Bataille leaving behind a 'poetic' (idealised) reading of Nietzsche.

Chestov not only guided Bataille in his reading of Nietzsche, he initiated him into Dostoevsky. Everything suggests that this discovery was decisive. The young Bataille might be seen as 'Dostoevskian': not only because of the explicit reference he made to the great Russian novelist in the sole remaining fragment of his first book *W.C.*; it may also be inferred from accounts by Métraux, according to whom Bataille wanted to follow the maxim 'everything is permitted' (echoing Dostoevsky's famous axiom 'nothing is true'), and Leiris. He first persuaded Leiris to read *Notes from Underground*; in addition, Leiris depicts him at this time as 'frequenting dives and the company of prostitutes like so many heroes of Russian literature'.[3] Leiris also suggests that the hero of *Notes from Underground* influenced Bataille 'by his obstinacy in being what in popular terms one calls an "impossible" man, ridiculous and odious beyond limit'.[4] Finally, Leiris portrayed the Bataille of 1924–5 as: 'impossible' certainly, debauched beyond a doubt, and a gambler like many of the heroes of Russian literature in general and Dostoevsky's in particular. Bataille gambled – often with money, and sometimes with his life at Russian roulette.

But the affinities between Bataille and Chestov were deeper and more lasting still. What fascinated Léon Chestov most about Nietzsche and Dostoevsky was their conversion; in other words, how their respective thoughts one day let go of their moorings, exposing them suddenly to the risk of a nudity that nothing was still able to justify. Chestov says this in a general and in the end not very interesting way: 'The history of the transformation of convictions! Is any history in the whole field of literature more exciting?' But he also says this of Dostoevsky in more precise terms: he 'not only set fire to what he adored; he also heaped mud on it. It was not enough for him to hate his former faith, he had to despise it'.[5] And he speaks in identical terms of the Nietzsche of *Human, All Too Human*. How can one avoid thinking of Bataille, at this same time, as acting no differently (did he tell him this, or did his shyness prevent him?). How even can one avoid imagining that Chestov had an influence – of whatever kind – on the loss of faith Bataille experienced?

The similarities certainly do not end there. Bataille found in Chestov a master in anti-idealism, an anti-idealism that was to be as complete as it was definitive (and which he would never renounce). Chestov had in fact written: 'It is possible that we must add to the list of scourges that assail poor mortals yet another – idealism.'[6] Bataille, with only a few nuances of tone (his would be notably less pitying), was to write the same thing around 1929–30. Even the architectural metaphors, in a kind of indirect response to the very young Bataille of *Notre-Dame de Rheims* as well as the only slightly older one of the letter from Madrid where he talked about the Escurial, find a resolute fighter in Chestov:

> In one respect idealism is like the despot states of the Orient: from the outside everything looks splendid, built to last for ever; but inside it is awful. This explains the at first sight incomprehensible phenomenon where an apparently innocent doctrine becomes the object of a terrible hatred on the part of people whom one would not suspect of evil tendencies. One can say with certainty that the bitterest enemies of idealism were, like Nietzsche and Dostoevsky, extreme idealists and that the 'psychology' that has blossomed so magnificently in these last few years was the work of apostates of idealism.[7]

The Bataille who had given himself entirely to God, who had considered becoming his representative, was an idealist. He would soon be the most violent of its apostates and the most careful of its denouncers: there was to be nothing that resembled this shameful idealism in any way he would not punish. Nevertheless Chestov pushes the disenchantment further. He never calls for apostasy. He is even darker than Nietzsche: if he is close to Nietzsche's conversion to anti-idealism, he is even closer to an (imaginary) Nietzsche that Pascal might have caught in the snare of his spite, a Nietzsche who would have asked himself just one question: 'Lord, why hast thou forsaken me?'[8] He has none of the evangelistic zeal of the Nietzsche of *Zarathustra*. He would gladly advise us to turn away from the solitude and horror his choices point towards, even if we lack the power to do so: 'He who wishes may turn back towards Kant. You are not certain to find what you need there, a "beauty" of whatever kind. There may perhaps be nothing but monstrosity and ugliness.'[9]

Idealism is the object of such hostility (for all that a calm, resigned hostility; his thought has nothing furious about it) for Chestov that he is not afraid to claim that the most beautiful and attractive forms that wish to establish their reign in our soul are a response to nothing but 'our basest impulses'. We shall see that Bataille would soon say exactly the same thing; what he was to say, in appealing to Sade, Chestov would already have said about Dostoevsky: 'He was the only one in the whole universe to envy the moral grandeur of the criminal.'[10] For, by a brutal reversal of the most commonly held conventions, it is moral conscience that evil can claim to be most proud of. Before Dostoevsky (and no doubt Bataille learned it from Chestov) no one had said of 'the ghost of former happiness', which we are endlessly assured is the one thing that might turn us from the most bitter pessimism, that it is from this and this alone that all evil comes.

The Nietzschean injunction, at least as deduced by Chestov, is 'Know or die!' One way or the other there lies the abyss.[11] Chestov often uses this word to indicate what depths a finally derationalised conscience reveals; it is a word Bataille would use just as often. God or no God, nothing is as intellectually unacceptable as that which Aristotle raised to the level of an indifferent truth: the theory of the excluded middle. Chestov (and Bataille as well, as we shall see) was interested only in those questions to which reason declares itself powerless to respond. Only the abyss they open up beneath your feet interests him. The abyss of a world without morality; morality belongs – Chestov says this directly, in a way analogous to how Bataille would in his turn describe it – 'in the cowshed'. We can imagine that, if Chestov had stopped there, this would already be enough for Bataille to have drawn on him in the most useful way. But he went further still, far enough for Bataille's most profound thought, no doubt unbeknownst to him, to find the means to develop. 'One should not be ashamed when reason says "it is shameful"; truth appears when reason affirms something is senseless; and where it indicates a perfect impossibility, there and there alone is total certainty to be found.' Admittedly, this is not Chestov but Tertullian; it is doubtful whether Bataille ever read Tertullian before Chestov quoted him.

The philosophy of Léon Chestov in this period was fed by tragic writers (this would not entirely be the case right to the end). And he describes the philosophy of tragedy: it is one 'of despair, of madness, even of death'.[12] But this might be a paradox (and if so, Bataille himself would never resolve it): the greater the aversion to Christianity, the stronger the latter becomes. Curiously, it feeds on whatever harms it. Chestov says this superbly: 'God demands the impossible, he demands only the impossible.'[13] So impossible is what he demands, it is as though he did not exist, except as desperate, mad or dead. What drives one from Christianity (and does so violently) is also what draws one to it. Chestov also has this characteristic, which would have no small influence on Bataille: he relates Nietzsche to Christianity. And in thus making him the third peak of a triangle, formed with Pascal and Kierkegaard, he makes him the savage, unruly inheritor of the Old Testament mysticism – that of Abraham, for example, but an Abraham who is more desperate than Job.[14] This Nietzsche (all things considered, a not very accurate one), this Christian Nietzsche, the Pascalian one (but, for Chestov, Pascal is in turn 'Nietzschified'), would also be Bataille's.[15] There is no doubt that this phrase, written nearly thirty years after Bataille left Chestov behind, is profoundly Chestovian:

> The God of Abraham compels humanity to the commandments, but does not *submit* the divinity to them. Nietzsche's way of seeing is also closer to the activity of grace opposed to works (to moral merit), but these doctrines themselves have always been eliminated, according to appearances, by reason of the tearing that they impose on the simplicity of good people. We can also see in Nietzsche's immoralism, so generally unrecognised, what he saw in it: a hyper-Christianity.[16]

Léon Chestov (under his real name Lev Izaakovic Schwartzmann)[17] arrived in France in 1920, fleeing the Russian Revolution which he had supported – of which he had deeply approved – before turning against it. Bataille often visited him at his home in the rue Sarasate in the

evening; thus the two men exchanged few letters. However, the degree
of interest Bataille had developed in Chestov's work is clearly indicated
in one such letter,[18] in which he says he is preparing a study (it is not
known if this was an article or a book) on it.[19] How far did this work
get? We do not know, but nothing remains of it today, and what is
more Bataille never referred to this project (not even to Michel Leiris,
even though he knew Bataille was part of the set formed around the
Russian philosopher). It nevertheless indicates beyond a doubt that he
had a deep enough knowledge of this work to aspire to undertake a
study of it. It also clearly indicates that in 1923 he was perceptibly
more attracted to philosophy than he later claimed.[20] Last and not
least, it testifies the importance of an influence which curiously he
never entirely admitted as such, paying Chestov indirect and contradictory homages, acknowledging that he had the merit of introducing him
to things he did not know, but saying that these never became essential
to him ('He guided me with great sensitivity in the reading of Plato. . . .
What he could tell me of Plato was what I needed to hear, and I cannot
see who would have been able to tell me this if I had not met him'),
while reproaching him, paradoxically, for what in the end he really
owed him: an apprenticeship in thinking through violence.[21] It was to
him that he owed learning (as he admits) that 'the violence of human
thought is nothing if it is not its fulfilment'.[22] And yet, he claims, it was
because Chestov was leading him away from this violence that he had
to take his distance from him.

The words with which Bataille evoked Chestov's memory thirty-five
years later indicate at the same time a tender, filial ('I admire the
patience he took with me as at the time I could express myself only by
a sort of sad delirium'[23]) and doubtless distorted debt. In all likelihood
the truth is different: Chestov invited him to the abyss of a desperate
thought. All the more desperate since at this time Bataille was not
ready to accept it. Among the first émigrés from socialism, Chestov no
longer believed that a 'good society' existed; worse, if there was one, it
would not respond in the least to the tragic sense of the impossible
demanded by God. His political thought (although he may not have
yet have had one) leaned freely towards the Dostoevsky of *Notes from
Underground*: 'Let ideas triumph! Let us liberate the peasants! Let us
establish just and merciful courts! Let us put an end to the old system
of military conscription! – His soul would not feel any lighter or
happier. He would be forced to confess that if, instead of all these

fortunate events, catastrophe were to strike Russia, he would perhaps feel even better.'[24] The Bataille who, in 1924, was to meet his first surrealist friends (Leiris, Fraenkel and Masson) could only protest profoundly against a thought that not only consented to the state of the world, but worse still called out for catastrophe to engulf it, like the desire for the abyss. The violence of Chestov's resignation is in no doubt, no less than Bataille's not to be resigned.[25] It is perhaps that of a man of a different generation. It is no doubt that of an exile. We shall see that, strangely, it would in turn later be that of Bataille: a resignation to the state of the world after he had called for catastrophe on it, for which he was violently reproached. In 1925, Bataille stopped seeing Léon Chestov; and he says this in a phrase that seems to explain it: 'like all my generation I had to turn towards Marxism.'

The planned study of Chestov's work was never carried out. Instead, Bataille collaborated with Teresa Beresovski-Chestov on the translation of his book *L'Idée de Bien chez Tolstoï et Nietzsche (philosophie et prédication)*,[26] published by Éditions du Siècle in 1925. Pierre Klossowski was the only person to note how lasting Chestov's influence was to be on Bataille, noting at the time of *Acéphale*, just before the war, that he 'himself [was] haunted by his reading of the Russians, of Chestov in particular. The whole atheology of *Acéphale* rests on the idea that the death of God does not terminate in an atheism; it is the remains of Golgotha: it is not definitive, it continues.'[27]

II

Torpid Maurras and decrepit Moscow

It would doubtless be imprudent to claim that there was a discernible moment when Bataille's life came to be linked with that of his contemporaries. But one thing we can ascertain is that the encounter took place in 1924. Just as certainly, it was progressive. Until then there is nothing to show that Bataille had any interest in politics. What changed in 1924? Nothing immediately. However, in 1924 he met Michel Leiris and André Masson, who were both soon to become surrealists, and Théodore Fraenkel, an ex-dadaist. These encounters did not influence Bataille so greatly as immediately to give him a pronounced interest in politics, but they were instrumental in gradually inclining him to be aware of the domains surrealism had entered: aesthetics and politics. These were seen as a central concern of everyone in his generation, whether Bataille admitted it or not (and he probably did).

In October 1924 (I will use this date as an arbitrary landmark), Anatole France died.[1] France, who was the great conscience of the left in the period after the war – the founder of the increasingly marxist review *Clarté*, a collaborator on *L'Humanité* – was mourned by everyone: Aragon brought attention to this in order to deplore it, in one of those impatient and harsh turns of phrase whose secret he then held: by everyone from 'torpid Maurras' to 'decrepit Moscow'.[2] Mourned by everyone? Not quite! The unanimous litany roused the surrealists' indignation. At the instigation of Pierre Drieu La Rochelle (close to the surrealists, if not himself a surrealist) and Aragon, they hastily put together a pamphlet with the title *A Corpse*, so much more abusive for being directed against the *great dead man*.[3] They were soon followed by others. The review *Clarté*, which France himself had created in 1919 with Barbusse and Vaillant-Couturier[4] (or a least a fraction within the review comprising Jean Bernier, Marcel Fourrier, Magdeleine Marx and Paul Vaillant-Couturier), published as its issue of November 1924 a pamphlet against Anatole France, sparing neither the French Communist Party nor Moscow. But in contrast to the surrealist critique, *Clarté* took the viewpoint of orthodox marxism: the posthumous rallying of the French workers' party to the bandwagon surrounding the reformist France was brought into question by *Clarté* from a strictly revolutionary point of view. An extreme fraction thus seemed to be emerging to the left of the Communist Party.

If it is not without importance that momentarily people from different outlooks and interests (some militants, the others intellectuals) came together, something which moved Victor Crastre (of *Clarté*) to say allowed a glimpse of the 'possibility of an accord between poetry and revolution', and which a not insignificant fraction of *Clarté* (Crastre, Fourrier, but especially Bernier) would work assiduously towards, it should be mentioned that this could not have occurred had several events not preceded it and made it possible. In 1924, on 21 January, Lenin died. We know the internal struggles that took place over his succession. We also know that Trotsky emerged from them in a weak position. Less well known is that a French intellectual, Boris Souvarine, a member of the central committee of the PCF since 1920 (the date of its creation) and a member in Moscow of the three leading institutions of the Comintern (its presidium, its secretariat and its executive committee) from 1920 to 1924, publicly took the side of Trotsky, through fidelity to the ideals of the revolution more than by any allegiance to Trotskyism, as also did the dissident fraction of *Clarté* in France (essentially Jean Bernier) and the surrealists. They did not all support Trotskyism. Souvarine was often resistant towards it. Nevertheless, the fact is that in France he was Trotsky's most active and useful supporter. Bernier was a Trotskyist, in a provisional and perhaps confused way, as for a long time were the surrealists. But what was important was not whether or not they were Trotskyists, but that several groups found themselves to the left of the workers' party due to an initial dissidence, to which other names and people soon rallied as other disagreements arose.

It is clear that three men played a considerable role in these ideological trends. They were André Breton, endowed with all the prestige of nascent surrealism (most young artists were keen to be part of it); Boris Souvarine, the most respected French communist intellectual, the director of the only official theoretical organ of the party, *Le Bulletin communiste*, from 1920 to his exclusion (I will say a lot more about him later); and Jean Bernier, an active figure of the extreme left since just after the war.

Bataille would get to know these men well. At different times, they respected or hated him. They joined him for common actions and broke with him, saying why loudly and clearly. It is also highly significant that fate would often cause their public and private lives to cross (hardly surprising for someone like Bataille; rather more so for a character like Souvarine) and their public accusations against one another often contained elements that were highly secret, if not less admirable. It is a constant feature of this period that friendship – and love – played a role that could unite them in their undertakings together one day, only to tear them apart the next. This has been noted – perhaps too often – about surrealism. We shall see how Bataille, Souvarine and Bernier were also linked or separated by things other than just ideas.

In 1924, Bernier had a role he would never again hold as a mediator between surrealism and communism, between poetry and revolution (Francis Marmande calls this role that of a 'ferryman'). He has been described as tall, built like an athlete and handsome. Above all it was said, not always kindly, that he was a jack of all trades. In any case, he made a show of being a militant, a writer, and a political, music and sports columnist. This was too much for one person, especially in the view of Breton, who did not like journalists, especially when they were also dilettantes . . . If he valued Bernier, from the start he also mistrusted him. For Bernier, the 1914–18 war was the beginning. Like others of his generation, he returned from it disgusted not only with the charnel-house it became, but because it was also a senseless one. Those who returned from the horrifying 'stupidity' which had led to this war did so as confirmed pacifists. Departing for it as a bourgeois, Bernier returned a rebel 'with the confused idea that I had an enormous score to settle with the leadership and its brainwashing'.[5] He was ready, along with others in France (Raymond Lefebvre, Barbusse, Vaillant-Couturier, etc.) who were sympathetic to revolutionary positions, to rally to Lenin's indictment of the 'imperialist war' and 'social-patriotism'. With them he founded the ARAC (Republican Association of War Veterans) in 1917. Much as Breton may have scorned his dilettantism, he and the surrealists were no less impressed by the man himself. Of course being the same age meant they shared the experience of the war, and they had a lot else in common: they were intellectuals (Bernier wrote novels, which was unusual among revolutionaries); they were well read in the essential texts of marxism-leninism (though Bernier doubtless knew them incomparably better); they were all fascinated by Freud (very few revolutionaries had read Freud attentively); they were friends with Drieu La Rochelle (Bernier, at least as much as Aragon, was his intimate companion). This was doubtless why Bernier undertook patient work from 1921 to 1924 that involved trying to bring together the positions of the surrealists with those of the communists, at least those of the *Clarté* group (since it would never entirely be part of the PCF). In 1924, when Anatole France died, he was an organiser, along with Édouard Berth, Marcel Fourrier and Georges Michael, of the dissident fraction of *Clarté* which in 1921, at the Third International in Moscow, chose revolutionary action and, at the party's Eighth Congress in 1924, supported Trotsky (a position that, as we have seen, Souvarine, at the time one of the leading figures in the Comintern, also adopted). The choice Bernier made in 1916 of revolution against poetry (or perhaps it would be more accurate to say of revolution *before* poetry), in 1924 tended to connect with the diametrically different poetry of the surrealists. Jean Bernier really was a ferryman. He opened up links by which a lot of young intellectuals could commit themselves. He enabled the hypothetical compatibility of the figures of the poet and the revolutionary, a compatibility clearly distinct from what France, Barbusse or Rolland before him typified.

Different as Souvarine and Bernier were, both enjoyed the esteem of the surrealists – an esteem so enthusiastic that Simone Kahn, Breton's first wife, even suggested that they were the most important political influences on Breton in the early days of surrealism. The year 1924 saw the appearance of the first issue of *La Révolution surréaliste* (in December). It had been preceded, on 15 October 1924, by the *First Manifesto of Surrealism*. Boiffard, Vitrac, de Chirico, Noll, Desnos, Péret, Morise, Aragon, Reverdy, Soupault, Delteil, Man Ray, Ernst, Masson and Picasso were grouped around Breton. Surrealism was *also* (one is tempted to say *especially*) what was at stake. Whether or not he agreed, Bataille would participate in it first hand or from a distance. Linking himself with several of those who had made it their own, he would – albeit from outside – know its promises and its futility. One thing is certain: he was never so distant from surrealism that the reconciliation of aesthetic, intellectual and political imperatives was not equally important for him.

Magnetic field

Georges Bataille came to know Michel Leiris at the end of 1924 through the intermediary of Jacques Lavaud who, like Bataille, was a librarian at the Bibliothèque Nationale. Leiris sketched an early portrait of Bataille where we find that same cynicism Alfred Métraux had noticed shortly before:

> His non-conformist mind [was] marked by what it was not yet customary to call black humour. . . . Somewhat thin, with a style both romantic and of his time, [he] possessed (in more youthful form of course, and less discreetly) the elegance he would never lose. . . . His close-set, darkened eyes, brimming with all *the blue of noon*, went with his teeth that oddly suggested a forest animal, often uncovered by a laugh that (perhaps wrongly) I judged to be sarcastic.[1]

Neither 'flamboyantly attired' nor 'extravagant', elegant but conservatively dressed ('I always knew Bataille dressed in a very bourgeois way':[2] 'there was nothing Bohemian about him'[3]). There was nothing Bohemian about Bataille but, as photographs of the time show, he displayed an elegance that was close to dandyism, a cynical dandyism.

Michel Leiris met him shortly before he joined the surrealists. Rather than joining, it might be better to say he converted (there is little doubt Leiris would reject this word but it is closer to what Bataille felt): 'At first I sensed the change in Leiris's attitude only dimly, but very soon I had a clear sense of what it involved: a moral terror emanating from the ruthlessness and craftiness of a rabble-rouser.'[4] A sort of silence fell between them, a silence maintained by Leiris, which brings to mind that of lovers about their fortune and the converted about their happiness. No sooner linked (although Bataille felt, wrongly according to Leiris, that the latter did not at first attach as much importance to their new friendship as he did) than a distinction in nature came into force. From this time, Leiris had the advantage over Bataille of 'knowledge': 'Leiris was, of the two of us, the initiated one.'[5]

From the ideas which they threw around together when they met, they had an admittedly fleeting intention, one night when their path took them to a little brothel on the street next to the Porte Saint-Denis, that the three of them (with Jacques Lavaud) might found a movement called *Oui*, 'implying a perpetual acquiescence to everything and which would have the advantage over the *Non* movement that had been Dada of escaping what was childish about a systematically provocational negation'.[6] But nothing remains of this idea – which was already entirely typical of Bataille who, in denouncing Dada (in his words 'not stupid enough'), also denounced in advance what surrealism was to try to be.[7] Entering surrealism as one does a religion, Leiris thus returned Bataille to his solitude (I repeat: it matters little whether this was exactly true, but Bataille felt this). A disordered solitude; as he himself said, nothing interested him at the time but 'the disconnected and the inconsequential', except for the desire for 'a dazzling life'; 'Personally I was nothing but the locus of empty agitation. I wanted nothing and could do nothing. There was nothing within me which even gave me the right to speak in a muted voice.'[8]

It was thus through the intermediary of Leiris that Bataille came to know surrealism; a paradoxical knowledge of someone who was *a priori* excluded. What the surrealist Leiris was – what, on his insistence, he eventually agreed to tell him – convinced Bataille in advance that he could expect to gain nothing for himself by joining the movement. Was this a hasty, irritable or jealous judgement? The fact remains that, perhaps alone of his generation ('nobody among the active youth at that moment misunderstood the dominating role of Breton. All the same Bataille remained an isolated figure'[9]), he expressed reservations about surrealism that were clear enough to outweigh any solicitation. The words he used to judge what Leiris let him guess and understand were definitely those of a man who glimpsed the worst: 'I feared a boisterous fraud'; 'I immediately thought that the dense world of surrealism would paralyse and suffocate me.'[10] The contagion of surrealism was such that, far from finding allies, he found himself on the contrary reduced to solitude and silence: 'I was suddenly faced with people who assumed an authoritative tone'.[11] It was the tone of those who know the appropriate cure for the tumult. Bataille differed from them only in not believing in the appropriateness of the cure; and in leaving unanswered the question of knowing if there was any cure for his tumult (no doubt in the end he asked himself if it would not be better not to attempt the cure).

A few months later, Bataille joined up with the third of his oldest friends (after Alfred Métraux and Michel Leiris), Théodore Fraenkel. Less of a novice than Bataille – he had been Breton's friend since 1906 and had participated energetically in Dada – Fraenkel was at this time distancing himself from any tumult, surrealism included. He never hid his disdain for writing; we only know an apocryphal Cocteau sonnet by him, published by Pierre-Albert Birot (in the journal *Sic*), and a poem in *Littérature* made up of sentences from a phrase book put back to back.[12] Bataille's recollection of his friend in 1924 was of a 'very quiet night bird'. This silence was very soon something they had in common; let us not forget that, until the age of thirty, Bataille was silent and shy rather than loquacious and free (which did not stop him from giving this self-portrait in the same period: 'I had both an unstable character and one that was clinging and impulsive, inconsequential, unconstrained and anguished'[13] which, he added, he always had been). A silence that was one of sadness rather than hostility against anything, 'with a sort of nocturnal sadness, but ridiculous deep down'.[14] To their two silences a third was added, graver and more astray, a surrealist who was one of the most sincere, as different as could be from the arrogant assurance of someone like Aragon: that of Antonin Artaud.

Bataille and Artaud met for the first time in a brasserie on rue Pigalle. Their silence was only broken by asides from Artaud and Fraenkel. Was Fraenkel, who was less cowardly than his surrealist friends, ready to take medical care (he was already a doctor) of the 'madman' Artaud – the 'scoundrel' whom Breton would soon denounce – as he was ready, with Bataille, to support his choice intellectually? Artaud, at the opposite pole to Breton, raised the spectre of surrealism's 'madness'. To the prudish and prudent Breton (whose delirium never went beyond what his reason was able to master), Artaud showed what the stakes of surrealism should have been had everyone practised what they preached. He was in some ways the black, disintegrating side of Breton, as the latter, in his own way, admitted much later: 'Perhaps he was at even greater odds with life than the rest of us were. . . . He was possessed by a kind of fury that spared no human institution . . . Be that as it may, his fury, by its astonishing power of contagion, profoundly affected the surrealist procedure.'[15] Contrary to Breton, Bataille saw Artaud as calm and overwhelmed rather than savage: 'He did not laugh, was never puerile, and although he didn't say very much, there was something emotionally eloquent in his rather grave silence and terrible edginess.'[16] Artaud and Bataille did not have the opportunity to get to know each other better. The somewhat mechanical linking of their two names since the early 1970s should not mislead us: it indicates little more than the posthumous importance assumed by their works, which are among the century's most significant, but during their lifetimes there existed between them or their work nothing more than distant relationships or affinities. To the 'boisterous fraud' knowingly orchestrated by Breton, Artaud opposed a shadow which early in his work Bataille could believe was also his own. Just now and again it still was; at the time of Artaud's incarceration he wrote 'I had the feeling that someone was walking over my grave.'[17]

The first issues of *La Révolution surréaliste* gathered together individuals of differing backgrounds and outlook around André Breton (the Breton of the first *Manifesto*). This was true of Gérard Rosenthal (known as Francis Gérard), Mathias Lübeck and Jacques-André Boiffard, who came from the magazine *L'Œuf dur*. It was also true of Georges Limbour, Jacques Baron and Max Morise, who came from the magazine *Aventure*. None of them had been a surrealist before 1924.

Another group, this time still an amorphous one, with no leader or journal, without a doctrine or an ideology – rather than a group, a spontaneous crystallisation of aesthetic and human affinities – soon joined *La Révolution surréaliste*: the one generally labelled the rue Blomet group. At its heart was a man – a painter – André Masson.[18] Since 1922, Masson had had a studio at 45 rue Blomet that was 'very Dostoevskian in its dilapidation', as Michel Leiris was later to write,[19] where his friends met. The first of these was Roland Tual, the second Max Jacob. The latter offered first Antonin Artaud and then Joan Miró, who in turn took a neighbouring studio, the benefit of André Masson's hospitality. It was through the intermediary of Max Jacob that Jean Dubuffet and Georges Limbour soon arrived, and through Roland Tual that Michel Leiris came and found what he described as having been 'his formative environment'. Finally, Armand Salacrou became a regular visitor, and Gertrude Stein and Ernest Hemingway occasional passers-by.

As we can see, despite its informality, a group formed itself that, once Breton and Masson had met (and got on with each other; their understanding was complete and immediate), partly joined *La Révolution surréaliste*. Tual, Artaud, Miró, Limbour and Leiris were among the latter; they were choice recruits for the newly-born Surrealist Group but (and one wonders if Breton sensed this) they already formed a faction. Effectively they had enjoyed an independence of spirit and a moral freedom around André Masson at rue Blomet that some of them, when the fascination waned, were not to find again for a long time. André Masson made no secret of it: rue Blomet lay heavily on rue Fontaine with the weight of its natural heterodoxy. It is certainly not a matter of casting doubt on Breton's ability to fascinate; nor on his ability to suggest to everyone's approval (and participation) aims that without him they doubtless would have been unable to express. No one at that time knew better than he how to reconcile fury and passion. The problem was rather that of the price he obliged them to pay for this reconciliation. As determined as the goal he proposed, to everyone's enthusiastic assent, so too were the means to attain it, which he made a condition for all concerned. Much later, Masson had no hesitation in seeing in this determination a religious if not a demiurgic whim. But did he and his friends sense this at the time? And even if they had, it would have taken more than one point in common with their group for (almost) all of them to rally together as one. The harsh severity with which Masson and his allies judged Breton and his goals and the means to attain them may well have been retrospective. All the evidence suggests that in 1924, those joining did so with nothing but enthusiasm. If Masson saw in himself and his friends 'schismatics taking power', and in rue Blomet 'the home of dissidence', it was for two reasons that only gradually became clear. The first is that at rue Blomet one was freer than Breton would ever tolerate: sexually free (Masson was already known as an erotic painter), free to drink and to smoke opium, all things Breton fiercely forbade. Far from him, and whatever declarations of fidelity they made him, at rue Blomet they carried on living as before. The second reason is more intellectual: Masson and Breton's opinions basically differed on Nietzsche and Dostoevsky. They fascinated Masson, while Breton hated them.[20]

(Nietzsche and Dostoevsky were, moreover, not the only authors read at rue Blomet who were not read at rue Fontaine; there were also the German romantics, the Russians – doubtless Tolstoy, perhaps Léon Chestov – and the Elizabethans.)

But there was something else more serious and, as we shall see, more decisive. There was agreement on the goals, but not so much on the means; more specifically on the vital one (so vital that it is itself close to being one of surrealism's goals): morality. As Masson emphasised, the moral question was never raised at rue Blomet. Never did he or any of those close to him judge one another, or any artist at all, for anything other than his work. If the work was admirable, so of necessity was its author. This was never the opinion of Breton, who required an author to be as morally beyond reproach as his work before bestowing his admiration on him (thus Breton attempted to discredit Rimbaud to Masson because of his morality). Did those at rue Blomet sense what trials such an intransigence might contain?

It would seem not: the alliance took place in the spring of 1924. It was at roughly the same time that the rue Blomet group joined that of rue du Château. Here again, rather than speaking of a 'formalised' group, it would be better to talk about a 'place'. What is commonly called the rue du Château was, all in all, a 'paltry' turn-of-the-century outhouse that Marcel Duhamel's grant could pay for. But Jacques Prévert and Yves Tanguy moved into the outhouse they refurbished with him. Sent over by Breton, Péret favoured integrating this new group into the movement. A 'chapel' as rue Blomet had been ('There were several poles of attraction. Rue Fontaine was the Vatican, then there were smaller chapels like rue Blomet, not ordained chapels but meeting points for friends. This must all be spoken of in religious terms. It is evident that the papacy was André Breton, and Breton absorbed all the smaller chapels, including rue Blomet, which was a big chapel but a chapel all the same'[21]), as a chapel rue du Château pledged its allegiance in turn to its new papacy. Certainly, the atmosphere there was right: they very quickly became surrealists, and with fewer scruples and a greater curiosity. As André Thirion (who lived there for a long time) clearly states, whole sections of culture ignored at rue Fontaine were taken up at rue du Château, valued just as highly as more noble ones: 'Jazz and American films, horror movies, newspaper features and crimes, the stupidities of everyday life, insubordination, the melancholy poetry of penny machines, and the deadly boredom of the industrial suburbs'.[22] No doubt they were more surrealist there than at rue Blomet, and faithful in different ways; if they were less solemn and grave than Breton, they made no claim to differ essentially from him: it is a mistake to see, as some have readily done, a contradiction in nature and an imminent rebellion between the headquarters (the Holy See) and its annexe. Rue Fontaine and rue du Château (unlike rue Blomet) shared a hatred of Bohemia and its excesses (drugs, homosexuality), the denunciation of libertinism, making a rule of monogamous love, and having a general rigour at all times on morality.

Whatever their differences, rue du Château and rue Blomet (perhaps due to their relative proximity: one is in the 14th arrondissement and the other in the 15th) joined together closely enough for it soon to be possible to meet friends of one place in the other. No doubt one would fail properly to grasp the history of surrealism without acknowledging that within it friendships were at work over which Breton, the ideologue, had little control. It was not uncommon to meet at rue du Château (which Breton rarely visited) Roland Tual, André Masson, Michel Leiris, Raymond Queneau, Max Morise, Jacques Baron, Robert Desnos . . . All individuals who, when disenchantment set in, were to find themselves together in the same mutiny.

These two surrealist annexes had considerable influence on the movement; not in modifying it essentially, but because from them came a number of new ideas[23] (not all of which found expression within surrealism) before they also gave rise to the rebellion of the dissident surrealists. No doubt they also had an equally significant importance in Bataille's life. Introduced by Michel Leiris, he quickly became a regular at rue Blomet (and the friend of André Masson with whom he had more than one taste in common: for Nietzsche and Dostoevsky, for Greek myth, and for eroticism), before becoming one at rue du Château. This requires the comment that it was not enough for Bataille to judge Breton unfavourably in 1925, that not only was he one of the few, if not the only one, not to agree to ally himself with him, that not only did he gradually develop a line of thought that was totally opposed to Breton's; but that Bataille also had to befriend some of those most enthusiastic for the cause he was denouncing, and patiently to try and dissuade them from it. We know he made this his challenge. It is hard to gauge how great his influence really was: undoubtedly considerable at rue Blomet (helped by friendship); uncertain at rue du Château. On this we only have the testimony of André Thirion, a staunch surrealist, henchman of Breton, and one of the least liable to leniency: 'Nor was rue du Château haunted by the metaphysical and political concerns of rue Fontaine. Yet we were very open to the influence of a person of great stature, a true loner, whose work was shaped by a coherent philosophy: Georges Bataille.'[24] The anachronism – in 1927 or 1928 Bataille had no coherent body of work – matters little. The fact remains that rue du Château was very open (so he was not yet the enemy accused by Breton) and that he could exercise his influence there. Thus if Bataille was only acquainted with the close fringes of surrealism (its holiday retreats away from the Vatican), if he was not above making frequent visits to those living at rue du Château, after developing lasting friendships with some of those at rue Blomet, it would seem that at some point he was in a position to exert a budding influence on them. This influence is partly explained by the curiosity and greater doctrinal flexibility of those of rue du Château (as we have seen, they were certainly moral in the sense that Breton understood the term, but without excess or ostentation; certainly they agreed to the dogma pronounced from rue Fontaine, but without this ever becoming exorbitant, for example to the point of going against friendship). It was an influence that, when difficulties and boredom set in among the surrealists, was capable of being perceived as a rallying point instead of and replacing that of Breton.

In 1925 Georges Bataille was far from hoping ever to have such an influence. He still knew little about surrealism; of Breton, he only knew the *First Manifesto* which he could only find 'unreadable', and *Soluble Fish* about which, through shyness and distrust of his own judgement, he agreed with that of Leiris: as favourable as possible. And in his eyes automatic writing found little more than a bored favour: 'I was as fond of disorienting games as the next man but, in my humble condescension and provocative timidity, only in an idle way.'[25]

It was only right that the sceptic Bataille should try to distance Leiris from surrealism, and that the enthusiast Leiris should try to bring Bataille closer to it. And it was through his intervention that for the first and only time Bataille collaborated on *La Révolution surréaliste*. The pretext was not an article or a text (which would have over-extended the welcome to a newcomer), but a translation. More specifically, it was a transcription from Old French of the *Fatrasies*, thirteenth-century poems unique in their complete lack of meaning. They were requested, in Breton's name, in writing by Michel Leiris on 16 July 1925. This transcription was to have been published in the October 1925 issue of *La Révolution surréaliste*, and eventually appeared in the March 1926 issue. But it was published anonymously: neither Bataille's name nor his initials appeared anywhere in the journal. Bataille's sole contribution to *La Révolution surréaliste* might just as well not have happened.[26]

But it did happen, and it invites the comment that it is certainly untrue that Bataille was hostile to the surrealists from the beginning. It is also untrue that he made them his enemies *in advance* (as he freely and frequently implied), or that he never wished to join them. One need only hear what he himself said of his first meeting with André Breton to prove this. The meeting seems to have been organised by Michel Leiris, so that Bataille could hand over his transcription of the *Fatrasies*. The precise date is unknown, but the setting was the Cyrano, the surrealists' regular café on the place Blanche. He was not only charmed by those he spoke to that day (Breton, Aragon, Éluard and Gala), in fact they impressed him, in particular by the feeling that they gave out 'that the silence of the world lay within them'.[27] He was also impressed by their almost hypnotised languor, their 'manner of being so insidiously out of line', the appearance they gave of living a 'majestic life', even though it might be based on nothing but a whim.[28] They impressed him: 'I loved (or admired) them'. Was Bataille on the point of being won over by the languor their silent attention gave off? Did he at that moment consider giving in to the fascination Breton had over people and submit to his authority that, shortly before, he was calling brutal and despotic? There seems to be no doubt that at that moment he could have considered becoming a surrealist. His closest friends already were; in fact, there was not one of them who did not wish to be. Breton's prestige was great, and Aragon was truly seductive. Who was he to criticise them? One must remember that in 1925 Bataille had still not written anything, with the exception of *Notre-Dame de Rheims* which (unsurprisingly) he did not boast about. No doubt he was already suspicious – his first conversations with Leiris more than suggest this – but what did he have in reply that he could use and defend to his advantage, what means did he possess to show himself to Breton and his friends as he alone knew himself *to be*? Had he not admitted to being profoundly sick of 'my empty life, with no reputation or means; so envious of the authentic life these recognised writers embodied. At the same time I was so tired of being envious, so angry at the idea of the most furtive concession'?[29] But the fear of making concessions held him back: if we are to believe him, his weariness of not being known by anyone for anything he had done was less than the extreme confidence he had in himself. His shyness and embarrassment were only matched by 'an excess of certainty'.[30] But in fact it would seem that this certainty should be understood negatively: he knew precisely what he did not want to be (however much he was sometimes weak enough to desire it): 'I knew I lacked the strength to face them as I was. They threatened . . . to reduce me to a powerlessness that would literally suffocate me.'[31] For Bataille to enter surrealism, if indeed this is what Breton wanted, would have been a major concession. But neither Bataille nor Breton seriously considered this. Bataille only really liked the silence Breton maintained around him, taking advantage of it to speak carelessly and without 'cruelty towards the self', 'without the subtlety which doubts and protests, and without the terrible panics in which everything becomes undone'.[32] As for Breton (who quickly judged those with whom he spoke – in the case of this newcomer, unfavourably), he seems, according to Leiris, to have dismissed him less with a condemnation than with a curse: Bataille was nothing but an 'obsessive'.

Bataille claimed not to have taken much notice of this malicious opinion; it was not so serious that he considered it to be more of a threat than Breton's friendship, judging from those of his surrealist friends who submitted to it. According to him the problem was not whether Breton liked him or not, but whether he liked others as they liked him. The problem was the existence of a world (an 'unbreathable' world) where only what moved him could be moving, where only that which he considered to have meaning and value had any, a world only accepted by 'the least submissive minds'. In fact, Breton's opinions and judgements marked out a line whose crossing signified whether or not one was counted among the elect; there was a far side – belonging – and a near side – rejection (or exclusion). Whether or not he wished to cross this line, Bataille would have to remain on this side of it. From that moment he made his decision to discourage his friends: 'I felt the need to protect those whom I liked, or who mattered to me, from this influence.'[33]

*

Bataille met Aragon again, once more thanks to Michel Leiris, late one night at Zelli's, and thereafter by chance. At the time, Bataille had read Aragon's *Anicet ou le panorama* and *Feu de joie*,[34] as well as *Le Paysan de Paris*, which he liked. Aragon was admired by those around him: his kindness and willingness often made people prefer him to Breton. Above all, he was seductive (something that, in Bataille's eyes, Breton was not: he was fascinating, not seductive). There is no doubt that if he had been forced to choose between the most influential members of early surrealism, he would have chosen Aragon (for his violence and flair for insults). But Aragon soon disappointed him: 'He was not a fool, but he was not intelligent either.'[35] On the rare occasions they met, Aragon's need to behave as an admired individual should before a 'mediocrity' (it was not without irony that Bataille thus described himself) hurt him less than it amused him. Aragon, one of the most prestigious and feared of the surrealists, made him realise that surrealism was what he had predicted it would be: a fraud.

> What we shared was a common feeling of misfortune at living in a world that we felt had become empty – of having, for want of profound virtues, a need for ourselves, or for a small number of friends, to assume the appearance of being what we did not have the means of being. The Russian revolutionaries wondered whether they were true revolutionaries: they were. The surrealists knew they could not be authentic Rimbauds, but within themselves they knew they were as far from the Revolution as from Rimbaud.[36]

Thus they were powerless to combine together revolution and poetry in any way, being neither one nor the other. It would seem he already had the dubious pleasure of turning the duplicity and good fortune within which Aragon was entangled against him: hesitating between vanity and anguish, tempted by his brilliance (to act as if the ills of a time that was becoming hollow did not exist, or as if he had found the answers that would help him escape them) and, late at night, unmasked, to reveal what an innocent *he really was* underneath. Of the two men, the most adept was perhaps not the more false: Bataille only feigned ignorance and foolishness – he listened to him for a long time – the better to denounce what infamy and boasting surrealism seemed to him to be: 'Once again I know nothing . . . about all the things you have talked about so eloquently, but don't you have the feeling that you are pulling rabbits out of a hat?'[37]

The mortuary chasm of debauchery

Lasciate ogni speranza voi qu'entrate

In 1920, Georges Bataille was a pious young man destined for a brilliant career. The rare testimonies we have, like those of Georges Delteil, his friend from Riom-ès-Montagnes, and of André Masson, his young fellow student at the École des Chartes, agree in describing him as then being reflective and romantic, torn between a taste for chivalry and religion, but in either way inclined towards noble ambitions and feelings. However much light the letters he sent to Miss C. throw on the years from 1922 to 1924, we finally have only a meagre understanding of what caused a young man who was clearly still devoted to God at the end of his stay in Madrid (even if he no longer seems to have wanted to devote himself to his service) to become the one Michel Leiris met in 1924: 'When I met Georges Bataille, he already lived the most dissolute life. He was debauched, a drinker and a gambler. He played in select circles and was often cleaned out, appallingly so.'[1] As a debauchee, he began to visit brothels. When? What was it that caused him to start? Neither he nor his friends have ever given an explanation. The fact is that brothels, from 1923, or at the latest the beginning of 1924, would be an essential part of his life, and he would never cease to visit them assiduously, spending 'fortunes' in them.[2] At the time this was not so rare as to single him out (Breton may have proscribed brothels, but Aragon and Drieu went frequently). To have been so soon reproached for it, he must have done so in a different way, making it indefensible, to the extent that it was shocking . . . Perhaps only as an 'obsessive' could: 'I understood Breton's horror of me. Had I not encouraged it? Was it not true that I was an obsessive?'[3]

In brothels he found pleasure, pleasure that was 'dirty' and indefensible, which no one achieves without being lowered in advance to the shadiness, ugliness and obscenity that characterised these places and their regular customers. The chasm Bataille sought some years earlier in churches was illusory. It was illusory because God answers it (it is a chasm only in appearance). 'My true church is a whorehouse – the only one that gives me true satisfaction.'[4]

> I differ from my friends in not caring a damn for any convention, taking my pleasure in the most base things. I feel no shame living like a sneaky adolescent, like an old man. Ending up, drunk and red-faced, in a dive full of naked women: to look at me there, sullen, with an anxious curl of the lips, no one would imagine that I am coming. I feel utterly *vulgar* and when I cannot attain any object I at least sink into a real poverty.[5]

The brothel was freedom, a freedom of naked bodies at whose feet genuflection was more real than before a crucifixion, and of bodies delivered up to an ignominious trade. The freedom of brothels costs more than the price of pushing open their doors. It is still necessary to measure the dread they reveal, and this dread is divine. It is divine because it is shameful and because it is indefensible. The procuress is God who ordains the faked climax of touched and possessed women, forever available to desire as if they knew no limit. The whore is God, who opens up like a suffering night, deeper than any woman because under her flesh there is emptiness, a sky lower than a body lying down – emptiness and not God.

> I undressed so many women at the brothel. I drank, I was intoxicated and was happy only if I was indefensible.
> The freedom one has only at the brothel . . .
> At the brothel I could take off my trousers, sit on the assistant madam's knees and cry. That was of no consequence either, was only a lie, exhausting the miserable possibilities nonetheless.[6]

But the brothel is also death, it is so much more death in being fascinating: 'This is not at all a woman, but a corpse with no fear of causing a scandal and which rises up in the drowned temple with the blinding clarity of filthy love.'[7] Filthy as churches ought to be, and entering them should be a trepidation. 'But I did not come into this frightful church with an insolent tranquillity and, on the contrary, am chilled and paralysed. I entered the stifling realm of corpses only in torment, in an almost corpse-like state.'[8] To enter a brothel stripped, more naked than any saint ever was. Naked to the point of shame, to the point of humiliation, to the point of abasement and tears. The brothel provoked tears, rather than consoling him. It is the chasm and holds nothing back. It alone has the nature of a condition: that of the Godless body, of the body promised to death, of the decaying body:

> As it was really necessary for me to be at the height of this circumstance I secretly imagine, in a flash of heat, and so as to laugh [only laughter would rise to the level of this terror], that I am not a young, trembling, inexperienced and troubled student but an old bullfighting horse which lost her filthy entrails days ago on the sand of the ring! It would be possible for me to lay my nostrils on the marble at the tip of her patent-leather shoes, her large stupid and ridiculous head, her glazed eyes, perhaps even encircled with flies.[9]

The cadaverisation of the naked and prostrate body is the free truth of the brothel, a truth of a fly in the light – a truth of God. The girls are God's 'saints', whom he loves: they are the ignominious testimony of his love. Naked and erect, a man vertiginously falls from grace for he knows the beast within him is this God without clothes: the truth of a body like a bitch.

In the Bataillean topography (we will see that there is one which is precise and limited), the brothel is substituted for the church, or at least it conciliates church and arena, shadow and light, stone and sand, bread and blood: their double and hostile sacrifice: 'In a few moments, I will bite into her accursed body with my whole mouth and in the course of our angelic excitement for certain now, all the famous legends of God and the saints arrive like packs of hounds barking out our two souls and at the same time our two bodies cast to the beasts.'[10]

The philosopher and the rake

In 1926 Georges Bataille was twenty-nine. He had parted company with Léon Chestov, though not before the latter had given him 'the basis of philosophical knowledge which, without having the character of what we usually expect under this name, in the long run no less became real'.[1] In the meantime he had joined up with several of the most important surrealists, without, however, subscribing to what had linked them together. He could now take stock of the challenge of his times, something in which, like it or not, he too was implicated, and of how the answers others (essentially the surrealists) suggested to him obliged him to find his own. And he wrote his first book, *W.-C.* It was not the first to be published (*Notre-Dame de Rheims* had been, but *W.-C.* would not be) but the first he was willing to speak about (unlike *Notre-Dame de Rheims*, which he was never to discuss), the first he would in some way recognise as his own, and the one with which we could justifiably say that his work began, even if he destroyed it.[2]

Bataille mentioned this destroyed book for the first time in 1943, in *Le Petit*: 'A year before *Story of the Eye* [in 1926, therefore], I had written a book entitled *W.-C.*: a small book, a rather crazy piece of writing. . . . it was a shriek of horror (horror at myself, not for my debauchery, but for the philosopher's head in which since then . . . how sad it is!'[3] The philosopher and the rake: and between them, the horror. We know what kind of philosopher Chestov tried to make Bataille; we also know how, being the extremist he said he was, the rake in him protected him from it. Perhaps *W.-C.* was just this: the philosopher and the rake sliding into the same disorder under the pseudonym of Henri Troppmann.

As this book no longer exists, we can try to reconstitute it in broad terms, using the few suggestions we do have – those Bataille himself supplied, few as they are. The most he put forward was a drawing illustrating it: an eye, the eye of the scaffold, opened in the lens of the guillotine. This drawing bore a title from Nietzsche: 'The Eternal Return'. There is little doubt that the guillotine evoked the infamous assassin Troppmann, beheaded on 19 January 1870 for having murdered the eight members of the Kink family in September 1869.[4] So this is the individual Bataille made the principal protagonist of this story (although from what we know, the story bore no relation to this news item) and its pseudonymous author (the name with which Bataille meant to sign it). But Troppmann would reappear in his work: his name would be that of the narrator and principal character of *Blue of Noon*. Neither is there any doubt that the eye opened in the lens of the guillotine is, with only slight changes, the one we find again in *Story of the Eye*, perhaps a more 'gloomy' one (as Bataille himself calls it), but hardly any less undignified: W.-C. was, he said, 'violently opposed to all dignity'. It would appear that the gloomy indignity of W.-C. demanded the 'thunderous' indignity of *Story of the Eye*.

Michel Leiris, who read this book – and who remembered it – is more forthcoming. Thanks to him, we know that, before he gave his name to the pseudonymous author of W.-C., Troppmann was the character under whose auspices Bataille took the stage. It is also thanks to him that we also know that the first chapter survived the destruction (whether in its entirety or revised) and is now known to us as the introduction to *Blue of Noon*. Finally it is also thanks to Leiris that we roughly know the story: that of a beautiful, rich young Englishwoman called Dirty who, after an orgy scene in a room at the luxury Savoy Hotel in London (this is in fact the opening scene of *Blue of Noon*), gives herself over 'in the company of the narrator, to an orgy with the costerwomen from a fish market, in the market itself'. And he adds this detail which better helps us picture what Bataille was like in 1926–7; 'a certain Lord Arsouille type (who vanished later when Bataille stripped himself of all surface romanticism, though he still burned under his sage exterior) appeared in the two successive chapters, in which everything takes place between the two extremes of an aristocratic luxury and literally a fishwife's vulgarity.'[5]

Nothing but this outline remains of W.-C.; but these two main characters, Troppmann and Dirty, reappeared in *Blue of Noon*, written in 1935 and published in 1957, after having appeared under the title *Dirty*.

Finally there is also the fact that, like a faint echo of this aborted title (*W.-C.*), Bataille chose to sign *Story of the Eye* with the pseudonym Lord Auch, a provocative contraction of 'Dieu aux chiottes' ['God in the shithouse'].[6]

'I write in order to erase my name'

An introduction is essential: it is not enough for us to understand what Bataille's work was, it should also be made clear how, more than once, it obscured his life. I will explain: there was not one man born in 1897 called Georges Bataille who wrote some of the most beautiful and most terrible books of twentieth-century French literature. Or not only one. There is not *one* Georges Bataille but *several*, variously called Lord Auch, Louis Trente, Pierre Angélique. Georges Bataille used pseudonyms (he is not alone in this but we shall see that he used them differently) and in such a way that before we begin to gain an understanding of his work, we need to see under what signs he placed it, with which names (and perhaps why) he signed it when he did not sign with his own name.

A name bears a kind of flagrant and sad evidence. Today we still know only imprecisely what it is; imprecisely in what we recognise of ourselves in it; more imprecisely still if it is right for our works to be attributed to it.

This much is true: the name is the name of the father. But what we have said about the relations between Joseph-Aristide and Georges Bataille allows us to suppose that a testimony can rarely be more violent than in their case.

The author of *Story of the Eye* (but of *Madame Edwarda* and *Le Petit* as well) is as much Georges Bataille as Lord Auch (and Pierre Angélique and Louis Trente). To distinguish them would have only an uncertain meaning. Rather than highlighting the greater freedom that Lord Auch had to write the book than Georges Bataille, what is important is to show that, as much for the book as for its title, the adopted pseudonym determines a 'real fiction' (the tale is fictional, but the book is real) in which, at best, the father would be absent, to which, at worst, he would be sacrificed.

It is certainly not possible to neglect the social and professional reasons that may have caused Georges Bataille to have recourse to a pseudonym. As an employee of the Bibliothèque Nationale he was a civil servant and would have had no choice but to avoid the allegation that he was responsible for a book that was published and sold clandestinely. Without any doubt, these reasons were significant, but they do not preclude deeper and more determining ones.

What does a pseudonym do? It hides. But it *also* breaks with the formality of a name that has been handed down. It does not simply abstract a writer momentarily from the civil, social and perhaps affective grip of his forefathers, it symbolically puts them to death by depriving them of the posterity through which they could claim to survive themselves. To don a pseudonym, even momentarily, would then be a sovereign action, breaking with the heritage and the debt (with God, that is!), an act of pure expenditure, bearing witness to a prodigality in which ostentation, paradoxically, is more important than dissimulation.

But with Bataille things are not so simple. It has been stated probably too often – he said so himself once – that he wrote to erase his name and, with it, the memory of his father. This is possible, and quite likely. We have seen how, in *Notre-Dame de Rheims*, Joseph-Aristide Bataille was so obviously absent only in order to re-emerge as its fundamental reason, that which, even silenced, even denied, justified the fact that the book was written. In its way, this effacement consti-tuted an impossible and paradoxical homage. The same thing is true of *Story of the Eye*, which Lord Auch signed on Georges Bataille's behalf. The final pages of this book ('Coincidences') are there in order to attest (in the most explicit way possible) that the pseudonym chosen (Lord: God in the English of the Scriptures; Auch: vulgar abbreviation for 'in the shithouse') raises the value of the name of the father – in dramatis-ing it, to be sure – rather than effacing it. 'God relieving himself'.[1] Bataille gives the exact explanation of it in 'Coincidences'. In so doing, he not only reappropriates the authenticity of the tale (its authenticity, not its truth), he illuminates its psychic substratum. Anyone seeing this man relieving himself with eyes rolled upwards, on his chair, in the sight and knowledge of all (and of the child who was Bataille), would call up an amplified, dramatised, horrific, double, the one designated by the pseudonym: the omnipotent God, impotent in his turn, and shitting under him. So, rather than taking us away from the real (civil, social and affective) the pseudonym leads us there with so much more violence that it permits it a lesser, or a 'displaced' empire. *Story of the Eye* and *Le Petit* (by Lord Auch and Louis Trente) overexposed the spectral, monstrous, mad, paternal presence neither more nor less than that of God.

We can readily agree that the pseudonym is a mask, a mask which a writer places over his face and his name and, in the same gesture, places over his father's face and name. Under a mask, the only part of the face that is visible are the eyes. But what remains visible of a blind man's face under a mask? Nothing but two dead eyes appearing absurdly in the clefts arranged for their use. The pseudonym, a mask borne by Bataille over his name and his father's face: only what was dead remains visible. The mask in this case had the paradoxical effect of hiding what was living and leaving bare what was dead; of showing only what is horrible and inhuman of two dead eyes in a face: 'When what is human is masked, there is no longer anything present but animality and death'[2] (the mask could be considered as the fundamental phantasm of *The Story of the Eye*: the cleft, the dead eye . . .).

Each time Bataille used a pseudonym, he did not merely barter with the living (one name for another; a real filiation for another, which is imaginary). More terribly, he bartered with the living against the dead. His pseudonyms are not a variation of his name; what they fix is the name shown bare and dead.

Other, clearly philosophical, reasons can be conceived for this evasion, this abstraction to the confession of the *name*. Jean-Noël Vuarnet (speaking, it is true, of Kierkegaard) suggests this: if, having recourse to the rhetorical artifice of the pseudonym, the philosopher differentiates himself, outlines, de-localises himself, it is, ultimately, to escape all judgement (in fact, Kierkegaard is the only philosopher who does not 'expose himself' once, or who exposes himself only by hiding himself better: for which the pseudonymic dissimulation was the means to expose himself): 'Participating at once of fiction and theory, pseudonymical fantasising constitutes a fragmentary and unfinished corpus very analogical to the dionysiac corpus of book-fragments and fragments of a book that Nietzsche signs by a single name . . . This fantasising has meaning only in relation to the subjectivity of a "private thinker" who, at odds with all social order, reveals himself as essentially suspect: *guilty, not guilty?*'[3]

This is not just an abstract idea. Georges Bataille died when he was sixty-five without having lowered the masks and without having collected together the various names he took under his own.[4] Born from him, Lord Auch, Louis Trente, Pierre Angélique died with him ('the mask is chaos become flesh'[5]) after he had obstinately maintained them in silence, after he had lived in their company as if they each represented for him a concealed door (admittedly, they were not secret for anyone close to him. They all knew he was the author of *Madame Edwarda*, *Story of the Eye* and *Le Petit* . . . But what interests us is that Bataille *never* agreed to any of these books being published in his name). What is most amazing is that, no matter how hostile, no one ever 'betrayed' him. Neither Breton, in respect of *Story of the Eye*, nor Sartre, in respect of *Madame Edwarda*, nor any of his friends.[6] The clandestinity in which one part of Bataille lived under assumed names (maintaining the delusion of an ardent but presentable work, and concealing the fact that, underneath, a more ardent one still urged him to expose himself) was never betrayed by anyone, anywhere, in any way.

The *Œuvres complètes* of Georges Bataille homogenise everything he wrote, under whatever name he wrote it. But when he was alive, he was never concerned with such simplicity (or, if he had, there must have been reasons to dissuade him from it). Except for Kierkegaard, no important philosophers have taken several pseudonyms (no doubt philosophy is not so shameful). And there are few important writers who have died without laying claim to their works, to *all* their works (*a fortiori* if, as is the case here, they count among the greatest). The play Bataille maintained with his names, real and borrowed, is quite different and positively complex. Why did *Story of the Eye*, *Le Petit* and *Madame Edwarda* require the use of a pseudonym? And why did not *The Impossible*, *Alleluia*, *L'Abbé C.*, and *Blue of Noon* – even though they are no less 'scandalous'? What criteria did Bataille apply? They escape us. Throughout this book, it is important to keep this in mind: Bataille's tales (for it is they and they alone that involve the use of pseudonyms) would know three types of different treatment that nothing can explain in a completely satisfactory way. The first was what appeared while Bataille was alive under his own name; the second appeared under pseudonyms without ever raising the veil; the third (*The Dead Man*, *My Mother* . . .) was published after his death.

For Bataille died in 1962 with part of his work hidden under him (in this way he differs from others who also used pseudonyms) as an unavowable folly, a folly of the name (of the father, of God). Dionysus with his body in pieces would at the same time become a Dionysus with his name in pieces: a world where God is no longer is a world open to all possibilities of pseudonymity.

The torture of a Hundred Pieces

The victim at the stake, the hanged man in the garden of torture, the crucified man, the terror inspired by this appalling representation in churches, the terror of kneeling and trembling: Bataille retained all these images from his days as a believer as memories and perhaps even more as a predilection. In doing its worst – the undignified and nauseating death of a God – Christianity no doubt rightly perceived the key that opens up its mystery, ambiguous and obscure as well as hallucinatory. Like Nietzsche, Bataille retained his love for this pitiful, naked God.

But in 1925 he responded to the hallucination of a different torture. In Madrid in 1922 he experimented with methods of waking dreams. In 1938 he would devote himself to disordered and spasmodic meditations. In 1925, he immersed himself in black and immediate delights. The empire of the cross is that of evil: for Bataille, as for Pascal, Nietzsche and Chestov, the news of the resurrection falls on deaf ears. In Christianity, only the abandonment on the cross at the sixth hour interested him, only the Christ of the most outrageous dereliction. The cross bears the empire of a limitless evil (only very late on would he try to think Evil through), but it is an evil that seizes hold, that hallucinates, that *ravishes*. In 1925, Adrien Borel[1] sent him a photograph of a torture practised in China, the torture of a Hundred Pieces. This substituted for the representation of a deicide, idealised by its very nature, one that was the trivial execution of a guilty man, devoid of all salvation. The torture victim was Fu Chou Li, guilty of murdering Prince Ao Han Ouan. The emperor's leniency (!) granted that he should not be burned as decreed, but cut to pieces, into a hundred pieces: cut up alive. Georges Dumas may have been and Adrien Borel certainly was present at this execution on 10 April 1905, and brought back photographs of it.[2] Adrien Borel brought one of these to Bataille's attention. One thing is clear: 'This photograph had a decisive role in my life.' This was a role equal, one can assume, to that of the discovery of laughter, and to that of Nietzsche as well: a role that shook his world to its core. The hallucinatory appearance of these photographs (we do not know which of those reproduced here was sent to Bataille in 1925; they were all eventually to belong to him) is due – perhaps because of the injection of doses of opium[3] – to the fact that the victim looks 'ravished' and ecstatic. Whatever the horrors of the torturer's meticulous work, whatever the pain he had to endure, with his hair on end and eyes rolled back, what one can see on his face is an indefinable expression. Is it a pain so great we are unable to recognise anything we have ever seen in a human face before? Or is it a joy, a demented, ecstatic joy? Dumas rashly claimed the latter (rashly because his book is that of a scientist).[4] Bataille had no doubt he was right, and no doubt that one must read the photograph in this way for it to gain all of its intolerable beauty.

These photographs obsessed him. He often spoke of them, and always kept them. One day, the torturer would become the object of his terrified attention: 'The Chinese executioner of my photo haunts me: there he is busily cutting off his victim's leg at the knee. . . .';[5] on another, it would be the victim: 'The young and seductive Chinese man . . . left to the work of the executioner, I loved him.'[6] One day sadism informed the scene, providing its key: 'My purpose is to illustrate a fundamental connection between religious ecstasy and eroticism – and in particular sadism'[7] (one cannot help but think of the erotic sadism of saints kneeling at the foot of the cross). On another, sadism was quite absent: 'I loved him with a love in which the sadistic instinct played no part: he communicated his pain to me or perhaps the excessive nature of his pain, and it was precisely that which I was seeking, not so as to take pleasure in it, but in order to ruin in me that which is opposed to ruin.'[8]

The ecstasy Dumas rashly ascribed to the victim would much later, by a kind of masochistic contagion ('When I die I want it to be under torture . . . I'd like to laugh when I go to my death'[9]), be known by Bataille in his turn. In 1938, when a friend introduced him to yoga,[10] he would use this photograph to judge the 'infinite capacity for reversal':[11] 'I was so stunned that I reached the point of ecstasy.'[12]

Anguish is the key; an anguish with no remaining limits, an anguish tied to disaster. Crucifixion was little more than a 'happy' torture: God and redemption gave it its two meanings. But this was two too many: horror is only horror when it is laid bare. So it alone is sacred: the greater it is, the more divine ecstasy is: 'What I suddenly saw . . . was the identity of these perfect contraries, divine ecstasy and its opposite, extreme horror.'[13]

The reversal was in fact infinite. The photographs Bataille discovered in 1925 and published a year before his death, in 1961,[14] that is thirty-seven years later, welled up in his work like one of its essential springs: the prodigality of Aztec torture, anguished eroticism, senseless waste, are all possible images of this Chinese Dionysus: cut to pieces, 'hideous, crazed, lined with blood, as beautiful as a wasp'.[15]

The priest of Torcy[1]

Were Bataille's judgements at that time those of a 'sick' man? He said the Sienna cathedral was laughable, even though common sense is generally agreed that its beauty is without equal; whereas the flaying in the Hundred Pieces torture, a picture which should legitimately disgust us, was beautiful, as beautiful as a wasp. At best, such judgements would be those of an obsessive (as Breton said); at worst of a sick man. For he not only visited brothels (for Breton, he might be nothing but a libertine, but that was enough to justify his reproval), he did so as one might descend to the underworld. And this would no longer be as a libertine but as a madman (except for the 'girls', have brothels ever been like hell?). He was not simply devoted to the flesh; it disgusted as much as dazzled him and fascinated as much as oppressed him. In all things, he tried the worst and trembled like a man who enjoyed the horror it brought him. Doctor Dauss, who was alarmed by the 'virulence and generally by the obsessions of his writing' (what was he referring to? W.-C.? Others that Leiris had read?) advised him to undergo analysis. Bataille did not take kindly to his friends' concern. From those who, having left behind the childish impulsiveness of surrealism, he expected to join him, making their own what overwhelmed him, he received only kindly attention and solicitude: 'I suffer – just barely – from the pusillanimity that made them say I was sick.'[2]

Yet Bataille yielded to their advice, probably not because he feared the worst but because he did not envisage it. (There is no doubt about this: he was no longer, nor would he ever again be, really suicidal. The *Yes* was stronger for him than all the *Noes*.[3]) But by his own testimony, he was suffering. He suffered the 'series of inauspicious mishaps and failures which he resisted' – his words, speaking of himself in the third person. What were these failures and mishaps? We do not know. There can be little doubt that one should count among them the solitude into which his refusal of all concessions placed him, as well as his literary failures. He would soon be thirty and had not yet 'written' anything, having been unable to finish either *Le Joyeux Cynique* (let us call it this in the absence of knowing the title he intended to give it), or *W.-C.*, or of course his study of Léon Chestov. How could he therefore not be envious (and unhappily envious) of the celebrity of the surrealists? Except for some articles published in the review *Aréthuse*, the first to which he had contributed (an article on Charles Florange in July 1926, another in two parts on the 'Money of the Great Mongols' in October 1926 and January 1927[4]), occasional articles for a palaeographer-archivist attached to the Office of Medals of the Bibliothèque Nationale, he had finished nothing he had embarked on and had only been read by a small core of true friends.

Did he follow a proper analysis? He acknowledges he did not. There are several reasons for this. The personality of the analyst, Adrien Borel, is one.[5] A founder member of the Psychoanalytical Society of Paris, a specialist in drug addiction and consultant at Saint-Anne hospital, he was also a friend of the surrealists, who valued him. He was especially a heterodox Freudian: he relished dogma as little as Bataille, even that of the founder. Élisabeth Roudinesco cast some supplementary light on the practice of Adrien Borel which gives some idea of how he could have been compatible with Bataille's intractable spirit. With him, treatment was above all else 'therapeutic, adaptive and founded with attention to suffering'. It was, in short, 'not very rigorous' and not 'ritualised', *a fortiori* with creative people (Borel had several in analysis, mainly surrealists[6]) who, she says, he allowed to struggle with the violence of their unconscious.[7]

The second reason is that it seems highly unlikely that Bataille would have had the necessary patience to submit to a real analysis. In truth, as a real analysis this one lasted for hardly more than a year, one that is besides difficult to situate with certainty. It was in 1925 that Borel entrusted Bataille with the photos of the Hundred Pieces.[8] But it was in 1927 that he wrote *Story of the Eye*, which we know Borel read, chapter by chapter. At best we can assume the treatment took place – this is only a hypothesis – between the incompletion of *W.-C.* and the end of *Story of the Eye*. On the other hand, there is little doubt, as Élisabeth Roudinesco suggests, that Borel left his patient battling with obsessions re-emerging from his childhood in addition to those connected to his life of debauchery. *Story of the Eye* bears witness to this in a quite exemplary way. The analysis could therefore roughly have been this: on Borel's side, an encouragement to write; on Bataille's, a writing producing a series of images in response, which in turn oiled the keys of the analysis; keys which probably threw a new light on the book, enabling him to carry it to a conclusion. To some extent it was, if the word could be used, an 'applied' analysis, as is said of research. Borel assumed an attentive and kindly position. He encouraged and commented: he steadied and supported the heavy obsessional material of the narrative (which could well have alarmed him) when necessary. Everything did not immediately fall into place. He sometimes contributed to the findings. For instance, the testicles of the bull in *Story of the Eye*: never having seen any, Bataille imagined them as bright red like 'the animal's erect penis'. Without Borel's involvement, they would no doubt have remained in that state in the final text. In correcting it, he not only satisfied the laws of anatomy, but also allowed the fantastic flow appropriate to the book to be restored in its entirety. The testicles of a bull have an ovoid form and the appearance of an ocular globe . . . So much so that they assumed a meaning half way between the dead eye of the father (Joseph-Aristide Bataille) and the dead eye of the priest, by way of the enucleated bullfighter (an enucleation, we recall, which Bataille witnessed in Madrid in May 1922, but here there is both enucleation *and* castration). Adrien Borel, reacting to the writing, encouraged admission and, when necessary, worked on all the possible meanings with Bataille.

A short epilogue entitled 'Coincidences' provided the ending of *Story of the Eye*. It places the narrative at a distance at the same time as admitting its autobiographical fantasy basis. Without possible doubt, the man speaking here is no longer the narrator of the tale, is no longer the person brought to his downfall by the extreme sexual stimulation of the tale. It was Bataille himself, evidently finally capable of analytical autobiography. Having completed *Story of the Eye*, he knew, with the aid of analysis, how much the imaginary is involved in it, and how, by paths previously unknown to him, he had drawn material from displaced and deferred admissions: the author of this account is not so distant from the narrator as he would have believed without Adrien Borel. And this is the key, as much of *Story of the Eye* as of any possible narrative: these were now to develop in the nearest realms of existence. They give the secret password of this existence while operating a deliberate work of decentring and metamorphosis.

Short as this analysis was, no one, especially those involved in it, doubted that it was effective. This was about the time he lost his timidity, his inhibition and his silence. He said himself: 'it changed me from being as absolutely obsessive as I was into someone relatively viable.'[9] The word he used at the time was 'deliverance'. The analysis managed what the work alone could not have done (deliver him from this morbid state): 'the first book I wrote [*Story of the Eye*] . . . I was able to write it only when psychoanalysed, yes, as I came out of it. And I believe I am able to say that it is only by being liberated in this way that I was able to write.'[10]

Bataille remained Borel's friend and in attributing to him a sort of paternity for the possibility of writing, Bataille found a dedicatory ritual to symbolise it which he respected for the rest of his life: he sent him the first numbered copy of each of his published books.[11]

Triunfo de la muerte

'I grew up very much alone and as far back as I can recall I was frightened of anything sexual.'[1] As chance would have it, this first sentence of *Story of the Eye* would also be the first of the *Œuvres complètes*[2] (chance, since it was apparently written in 1927, ten years after Bataille's first text). It opens both; it is their ideal *incipit*.

Nevertheless, this sentence calls for an introductory remark: certainly it uses the pronoun *I*, and certainly it is Bataille, or more precisely Lord Auch, his pseudonym, who utters this *I*, the same I (yet different every time) we shall find throughout the fictional works. But is it entirely real? Is it not rather entirely imaginary? Would it not simply be unwise to take it as autobiographical? And simply thoughtlessness – perhaps also a form of contempt – to take it as merely imaginary? Is it not more often alternately one, then the other, a knowing play on them, as they are thrown on the table like dice, obeying a logic that eludes us even as it forces us to pose the question?

This remark is also a question – one to which we may never know the answer: every one of Bataille's narratives was written in the first person. But *Story of the Eye* does not essentially narrate this *I*. In two senses, and in two reasonably distinct sections, it has three protagonists. Three, but two of them are the same throughout: the narrator (an adolescent boy, one imagines) and a girl, Simone, 'the simplest and most angelic creature ever to walk the earth',[3] a girl who 'so bluntly craved any upheaval that the faintest call from the senses gave her a look directly suggestive of all things linked to deep sexuality, such as blood, suffocation, sudden terror, crime; things indefinitely destroying human bliss and honesty'.[4] There is no doubt that this is above all her story; that of her impossible and divine caprice. The others, including the narrator (under whose auspices Lord Auch-Bataille is portrayed), make this caprice, no matter how devastating, their quest: she is the source of the contagion.

The two teenagers, first alone and then to the detriment of a third character, Marcelle, who is pious and docile rather than spineless, become initiated into ever more extremely disturbed behaviour, until the powerless victim of their games, subjected to a limitless terror, hangs herself. It is wrong to think there is anything sadistic in the ferocity of the trials she has to endure. They are *innocence* itself. Her fatal condition is that she was their designated victim. All three obey this fate without restraint, carried along by what is illuminating about such a destiny given to desire.

Alongside Marcelle's corpse, Simone loses her virginity to her young lover, and commits the final outrage on it, one worthy of this risible and devastating martyr. She pisses on her face, the eyes of which remain open: 'those eyes, extraordinarily, did not close.'[5]

If it is extraordinary that, given the defilements hitherto committed by the adolescents, it is only in the presence of this corpse that they embrace and enter each other, if it is extraordinary that the two very young lovers are finally joined together only when *seized* by this dead body, it is because it alone could give their act the extreme gravity, the character of a penetration of a devastated world, it would otherwise have lacked. It alone, as befitted their tastes, defiled the desire they had to love each other beyond all pleasure. Simone's body, like a night, only suddenly becomes penetrable because its double, that of Marcelle, pure beyond compare, *innocent* (yet without being able to resist the fate of her end), hangs itself. Death opens up bodies, allowing them to be penetrated by those who, because horrified, make this horror the measure of the love incarnated by the night's body. Simone's body becomes a hell; this hell is so powerful that she and her lover will from that moment love each other with sadness and ferocity (though no ferocity could match the one that turns them into lovers beyond measure); for Marcelle's death is a laceration. Simone's cruelties, and the narrator's too, are certainly extreme, as is her pain. Simone defiles herself as Marcelle has made herself innocent. This does not make Simone in any way less pious; but she does so with desperation. Her trance is that of a 'fowl with its cut throat', of someone in convulsions. The chaos into which she hurls herself, since it flays her and tears her apart (and it is only desirable because it flays and tears her), because from the games to the dramas (from the eggs she plunges into the toilet bowl to the eye plucked from the priest which she swallows with her cunt), inaccessibly innocent as it was, the world has become violently, ostensibly *guilty* to the core. Guilty to the point that it will be put right only by giving in to its chaos.

This chaos is that of a 'saint' (the saint Marcelle could not be), the first of the Bataillean hagiography, the youngest and, perhaps for that reason, the most determined.[6] Because she has no restraint she is evil, she is beyond doubt God. A God equal to what is devastating about the desire that throws bodies onto one another; devastating on the same scale as what separates them, now that he is dead. Whatever limits one is ready to transgress (but one must be ready to transgress them *all*), death prevents one from ever becoming conjoined. From his first book, Bataille made this a kind of law for his work. Marcelle's death reveals precisely the violence to which all eroticism that knows of which nothingness it is the impossible (the unappeasable) desire to escape is pledged. *Story of the Eye* can legitimately be considered Bataille's first book: it is a novel of initiation into death for the same reasons that it is an erotic novel.

'I am as happy as ever with the fulminating joy of *The Eye*: nothing can wipe it away. Such joy, bordering on naïve folly will forever remain beyond terror, for terror reveals its meaning.'[7] This is not the place to detail the extravagant, naïve episodes of *Story of the Eye*. But in fact, *beyond* anguish, they take a black, out-of-control, 'fulminant' joy (all the stronger for the intensity of the anguish) in sullying, devastating, mutilating and killing – an *ardent* joy in which Bataille consumed what a short while before he had cherished, denied what he once believed, laughed at what he had been. Of all the books he wrote it is certainly the one in which laughter is the most perceptible and, as far as we can imagine it, the closest to that in which in London in 1920 he discovered the power for reversal . . . The obscene laugh of an apostate.

Here it would be worth stopping to consider *Story of the Eye*'s final scene. It takes place in the church of the Santa Caridad hospital in Seville, beneath two paintings by Valdès-Leal, 'pictures of decomposing corpses' (their titles, *Triunfo de la muerte* and *Finis gloria mundis*, could easily be sub-headings for *Story of the Eye*). He who in 1920 was thinking of becoming a priest and in 1922 was still commending himself to God at the end of his letters from Madrid, who was so sincerely pious that he then became impious, delivers an unfortunate young Sevillian priest, 'blond, very young and handsome', into the bedazzled charge of Simone. If he is a priest, Bataille ferociously strings him a rosary of insults: he is a 'church rat', a 'sordid being', a 'frightful ghost', a 'larva'; worse still, a 'sacerdotal corpse'.[8] It is upon him, upon his 'corpse' that are heaped the combined excesses of the two adolescents, accompanied by a tragic master of ceremonies, an Englishman of cold sensual delights, Sir Edmund (who is the third character of the second part; the one who in a way takes the place vacated by the dead Marcelle). The story closes upon this priest ('sexual delirium, blasphematory unleashing and murderous rage'[9]), a martyr in his turn, but this time a foolish one, idiotic, a caricature of the martyrdom endured by Marcelle (whose martyrdom was innocence), as he expires while coming, 'tragically gorging himself on pleasure', his 'body erect, and yelling like a pig being slaughtered'. As a martyr, he too would witness the posthumous outrages of Simone: for the dead Marcelle it was extraordinary that her eyes 'did not close' (remember how important the eye gouged from the bullfighter Granero was for the story, as the ersatz eye of the cooked testicle of the dead bull is to those of Simone). The priest will have to keep his open, better than open; at Simone's request, Sir Edmund will extract one eye with which, innocent at last, pacified, she will *play*. Inserted into her most intimate place, then pissed upon, it finally appears to the narrator as what he expected it to be: the pure, pale blue eye of Marcelle, *crying*: a vision of 'disastrous sadness'.

It is doubtful that one could find anything that compares to this book. Bataille published it anonymously and clandestinely;[10] it is hard to imagine how he could have done otherwise. However, the year 1928 saw the publication of several books that might make one think it was more liberal than previous years: *Hécate* by Pierre-Jean Jouve, *Irène*, since attributed to Aragon,[11] *Belle de jour* by Joseph Kessel and *Le Dieu des corps* by Jules Romains . . . *Refaire l'amour* by Rachilde and *Aphrodite* by Pierre Louÿs also appeared, as did a profusion of 'soft core' books that were sometimes quite lightweight beneath their provocative externals (*Femmes suppliciées* by Jean de La Beucque, for example). Evidently this was a time for a literature of pleasure, in fact this was so clear that it spurred leagues of decency into making the Church remind its faithful of their duties: 1928 was the year that Abbé

Bethléem updated the 1905 edition of the compendium *Novels to Read and to Forbid (since 1500)*,[12] and Pope Pius XI distributed his famous encyclical *Casta Connubi* on Christian marriage. The leagues did not stop there: the one that made its goal the 'reinstatement of public morality' organised several congresses against pornography; it succeeded in raising the number of convictions for the sale of books deemed obscene or likely to contravene moral standards. A large number of declarations were made by those who despised this moral laxity, and they tell us fairly clearly which monsters were perceived to be threatening the times: 'We are under the reign of the most cynical and revolting amorality. Private and public life, theatre, literature, politics, the stock exchange, the press, the business world, nobility or middle classes, everything spreads corruption, the desire for bestial pleasures, and orgies, lies and impostures.'[13]

It seems unlikely that Bataille felt concerned with any of this. He stands totally apart from all of the above (including Jouve, Kessel, Romains, etc.). Certainly, none of the books listed above can even come close to matching either the violence or the frenzy of *Story of the Eye*. Just as certainly, and no doubt this is a key point, unlike his contemporaries Bataille does not turn pleasure into anything worth fighting to liberate further. Bataille very quickly sensed the importance of interdiction and taboo. He never wanted these to be reversed or abolished, or even their realm to be reduced. To understand his position precisely, we must imagine that he could have been prepared to defend them, even if only so that he alone would not lose the possibility of transgressing them. (He would never waver on this subject. If it ever happened that limits were absent, then the possibility – the sovereign possibility – offered to just one individual, with a few others, to experience them would vanish.) A second reason justifies his position: he is a debauched man, and not at all a libertine:

> But as of then, no doubt existed for me: I did not care for what is known as 'pleasures of the flesh' because they really are insipid; I cared only for what is classified as 'dirty'. On the other hand, I was not even satisfied with the usual debauchery, because the only thing it dirties is debauchery itself, while, in some way or other, anything sublime and perfectly pure is left intact by it. My kind of debauchery soils not only my body and my thoughts, but also anything I may conceive in its course, that is to say, the vast starry universe, which merely serves as a backdrop.[14]

These lines from *Story of the Eye* state unequivocally both what Bataille's 'erotic' thought was in 1928, and what kind of key this story is; only death is filthy enough, it alone uses debauched bodies to tell the truth of their desire: it is desperate.

Could he have expected the surrealists to be less distant from him, and to say a few things about eroticism that he might find less idiotic? It would seem that he awaited with interest, if not impatience, the publication of issue 11 of *La Révolution surréaliste* in which the enquiry 'Recherches sur la sexualité' was due to appear. Whether they could be less distant from him is debatable. The stated position of André Breton on surrealist eroticism in the enquiry (in fact positions vary perceptibly from speaker to speaker; not all were as strict as him, for example on the issue of homosexuality; nevertheless one is justified in feeling that the sexual morality of surrealism, which André Thirion and his friends professed to follow more or less scrupulously, is that of Breton alone) is a long way from Bataille, a long way from his writings. For Breton, love alone justifies eroticism, a love which, it goes without saying, is monogamous and elective.[15] For Bataille, debauchery is enough, at most love enlivens excess. For Breton there is no question that 'unknown bodies' might be 'employed' as 'erotic elements'; he even rejects the idea indignantly. We now know what recurrent and obsessive use Bataille makes of them in *Story of the Eye* (as the title indicates, this book is the story of an object). For Breton, love is so singular and exclusive that it is inconceivable that a third party might take part in its embraces.[16] *Story of the Eye* twice adds a determining third party (Marcelle, then Sir Edmund) to the turmoil of the two young lovers (when it is not simply the crowd; that of the bullring, for instance). For Breton, there can be 'no question of having consciousness of external danger in physical love'. Bataille on the other hand has a taste for this fear and plays with it; only danger gives the anguish which reveals its meaning. Breton 'dreams' of closing down brothels, as he dreams of closing down asylums and prisons. Bataille regards them as a church, for him they are 'the only really voracious ones'. Breton asserts that he is 'neither sadistic, nor masochistic'. Bataille insolently makes no secret of being alternately both. Neither Breton nor any of those around him evokes death (amazingly; in this the surrealists hardly seem Freudians) nor scatology (except for Péret; but his is a blasphemous scatology, not at all justified merely by a taste for the 'soiled'). Bataille denies neither being a necrophile (a little later he would emphasise this tendency) nor being a scatophile, saying that eroticism was both, since they alone reveal its true nature.

The publication of *Story of the Eye* in 1928 clarified (or at least rendered irrevocable) why Bataille three years earlier had believed himself 'unsurrealisable'. There is little doubt that the affinities he might have felt he shared with Breton (if he ever thought he did) were slight compared to what separated them. *Story of the Eye* astounded some surrealists; those of rue Blomet no doubt, who were his oldest friends, and perhaps those of rue du Château. We do not know what Breton thought. The judgement he made to Leiris in 1925 (that Bataille was an 'obsessive') was most likely only reinforced. This was not so according to Jean Piel, who related this contradictory anecdote: 'A new guy had just been introduced to Breton who was so quiet and shy you couldn't get much out of him, but who had in his pocket a manuscript so extraordinary that the man was probably a genius.' This is factually untrue (Bataille cannot have been introduced to Breton in 1928, since he had been already in 1925, at the time of the publication of the *Fatrasies* in *La Révolution surréaliste*), but what does seem convincing in this account is the ambivalent relationship of fascination and repulsion Bataille maintained with the surrealists.[17]

Story of the Eye was published (thanks to René Bonnel) in 1928 in an edition of 134 copies, with no publisher's name, to Pascal Pia's design, accompanied by eight original unsigned lithographs (in fact by André Masson). It was only reissued in 1944 by K. Éditeur, in an edition of 199 copies, with original aquatint engravings by Hans Bellmer. The re-edition is, in fact, a revised edition (the so-called Seville 1940 edition). The third and last edition during Bataille's lifetime appeared in 1952–3 (the date is uncertain), published by Jean-Jacques Pauvert; this is the so-called Burgos 1941 edition. These three editions together make less than 850 copies. All three were signed with the pseudonym Lord Auch. The first edition to be attributed to Georges Bataille only appeared in 1967, in other words forty years after the book had been written, and five years after the death of its author.

The eye at work

It is surrounded by a halo of death that an overly pale
creature initially arises which, under a sick sun, is nothing
but the celestial eye it lacks.

It is true that we do not know the exact nature of the analysis Bataille
followed under Adrien Borel. *Story of the Eye* gives a glimpse of it.
Other texts written between 1927 and 1930 do so perhaps better, at
the very least in a more naked, and raw, way. The first of these,
L'Anus solaire, is earlier than *Story of the Eye*: we know he wrote it in
January and February 1927. Other texts, though written over several
years,[1] form a totality that can be read without serious error as one
and the same – albeit unfinished – book (in the *Œuvres complètes* they
have been gathered together under the title of *Dossier de l'œil pinéal*
('The Pineal Eye')[2].

Admittedly none of these texts are fiction, yet it is still not certain
that they clearly differ from *Story of the Eye*. They certainly amplify it:
at the very least they 'dramatise' it. *The Solar Anus* is the first of them,
written, as I have said, before *Story of the Eye*. But it not only predates
the novel; it was a preparation for it. Is it not closer to the sinister
nature W.-C. presumably had, and as explosive, in its way, as *The
Story of the Eye*? In it we find eggs like those Simone immersed beneath
her in toilet bowls . . . They are also rotten. Eyes already appear,
punctured as well, but they are the eyes of judges, not yet of priests.
'The gross and loathsome bundle of entrails' that the horned mares
expelled with a soft and repugnant noise on the sand in the arena is
again expelled, but onto the surface of the world from the volcano, its
anus. *Story of the Eye* laughs where *The Solar Anus* trembles in prey
to 'night and terror everywhere'. Such terror 'that the eyes can no
longer bear the sun, nor coitus, nor corpses, nor obscenity': all the

things the eyes of Lord Auch, the author of *Story of the Eye*, could bear.

But essentially it is the sun that the eyes cannot bear. Eyes are crippled in proportion to how loathsome the sun is. Loathsome because, seen by Bataille in 1927, the sun is 'nauseating and pink like a glans, open and urinating like an orifice'; it is 'filthy'.[3] The sun is filthy and what it erects is filthy. The erection of the plant is filthy and so is that of the tree, both of which promise to fall, either withered or struck down. That of people is also filthy: a sort of brief rising of a ghost over a coffin, immediately weakened. The earth and the sea obey lavish vibratory movements, to which plants, trees and men oppose their absurd erectility: plants and trees towards the sun; men – powerlessly and impotently – towards woman.

Whether it be filthy or obscene, the sun *blinds*. This word is to be understood in two ways: 'the blinded sun or the blinding sun, it doesn't matter which'.[4] The image is not simply banal. Bataille was no longer unaware, since Chestov initiated him to Plato, of what an ideal triad constituted: there is the eye, there is the father, and there is the sun.[5] But to whatever ideality Plato dreamed, Bataille was not unaware how much more, however solar this triad appears, it could reel in horror. The lack of the first of its elements could be enough to cause this. The sun is solar, obviously, and fathers are dead: this is what the eye they have given us allows us to know about the erection which *we are* between the earth where they are and the sky where the sun is. But what eye does a blind father bequeath? A staring eye, a dead eye. And the triad is reversed: the eye is dead, the black sun and the parents living. Putrid was the sun stared at by the dead eyes of this blind father. Blind is the sun stared at by the living eyes of the child of a putrid father. What was on high is cast down. What is elevated wears itself out, collapses: 'The sun is at the bottom of the sky as a corpse is at the bottom of a well.'[6]

The texts of 'The Pineal Eye' are hardly more placid and do not say anything different, although they do so in a different way: we wonder how, doubtless in a rather 'mad' way, they speak in terms borrowed from rationality. Bataille went back to zero, even though the eye might see (in fact, his own saw), has the weakness of not having evolved in conformity with the movement of the erection of man on earth (for in fact, it is self-constituted). He has retained the archaic constitution of the crawling (and the squatting) state of the earliest men: what he sees is servilely linked to the earth. He responded with absurd obstinacy to the erection of the body towards the sun, hiding from sight. Except by twisting the nape of the neck, he *saw* nothing of the sun but the light, and even then only by refraction on what it illuminated.

'The horizontal axis of vision, to which the human structure has remained strictly subjected in the course of man's wrenching rejection of animal nature, is the expression of a poverty all the more oppressive in apparently being confused with serenity.'[7] If the eye is doubtless not blind (was this not already an initial result of analysis? Does *Story of the Eye* envisage it other than as blind?), it is at the very least crippled. However absurd it may seem, Bataille will find a remedy in this infirmity. All, scientists included, agree in placing an atrophied gland in front of the cerebellum (not the least interesting thing about this is that – like the eye, like eggs, and like the testicles – it should be oval), where in a rudimentary way Descartes placed the seat of the soul, which, in Bataille's time, was agreed to have the characteristics of an eye remaining in an embryonic state. Of this pineal gland, since this is what it is called, Bataille did not want to make a less illuminating, less definitive use than Descartes: it is and will be the embryo of an eye destined to provide man with a vertical vision that will no longer be terrestrial but solar.

From this eye, as it plunges into the sky, 'as beautiful as death, as pale and implausible as death',[8] the most terrible and violent flashes may be expected. Because it is situated at the top of the skull, it bears witness to the fact that mankind was destined to be able to look the sun in the face, hideous as it is; it was destined *to see* in the most burning, most incandescent way. Sick? Bataille said without naïvety: 'During this period, I did not hesitate to think seriously of the possibility that this extraordinary eye would really come to light through the bony roof of the head, because I believed it necessary that, after a long period of servility, human beings would have an eye just for the sun . . .'[9]

But in the end would this eye be solar? Far from it: of the putrid, corpse-like sun it is able to see, it assumes a black nature that is putrid and corpse-like. For another vision, invidious, dazzling, is superimposed on that of this eye risen from the cranial box, one Bataille had at London Zoo in July 1927: that of the nudity of a monkey's anal rump. What in human beings has, since they have stood erect, withdrawn deep into the flesh and hidden from sight, in the monkey juts out, 'a beautiful boil of red flesh', in an obscene and illuminating way. If the pineal eye resembles anything, it is something as raw and violent: it will have its obscenity and wildness. And Bataille pictures the look of this new eye in the resemblance of what could rise up from such a rump like 'discharges of energy at the top of the head – discharges as violent and as indecent as those that make the anal protuberances of some apes so horrible to see'.[10] Those he saw at London Zoo threw him into a 'sort of ecstatic brutishness'. The brutishness and ecstasy would be no less than to allow this protuberance, so prominent as to be like a 'great pink (disgusting) penis, drunk with sun' '(*drunk and penetrating it, a corpse at the bottom of the well*) which would have vibrated, forcing me to emit atrocious screams, the screams of a magnificent but stinking ejaculation'.[11]

The eye at work in analysis. I could equally well have said: the father at work in analysis. It had taken fifteen years, and this analysis (however brief it had been), for the effacement of *Notre-Dame de Rheims* in its turn to be effaced. *Story of the Eye* is in some way the precipitate (miraculous in its way) of this analysis. The 'Coincidences' with which the narrative closes speak for the first time about what – deferred and decentred – was responsible for its black joy. *The Solar Anus* does not bare other elements, although it does deal with them in a more convulsive and delirious way. 'The Pineal Eye' brings it to an end, an end that is less a reconciliation than a consent, according to the evidence. Of the images (doubtless one could say visions) which Georges Bataille's father forced him to face up to, all or almost all – deferred, metamorphosed – re-emerge in the texts written in this period: with the erection of the body on the surface of the earth (this paralysed man); with the pineal eye and its violent bedazzlement (his dead eyes); with the obscene and miraculous beauty of the anal protuberances of monkeys (the sick man on his seat with his trousers down); with the sockets and their parcel of loose entrails (this man shitting himself while he watched); with the incandescence of the putrid sun (perhaps the city in flames as he lay dying) . . . Other examples could be cited. The least eloquent is admittedly not that of the volcanoes which for a long time Bataille associated with his father and generally with death.[12] Volcanoes, at least as much as the eye, cut into these texts like slopes made of flesh (or orifices of the earth) from which would rise up, at different times, excrement, entrails, orgasms, fires and dead people . . .

'I was not insane but I undoubtedly made too much of the necessity of leaving, in one way or another, the limits of human experience, and I adapted myself in a fairly disordered way so that the most improbable thing in the world (the most overwhelming as well, something like foam on the lips) would at the same time appear to me necessary.'[13]

Don't waste my time with idealism!

Paris 1929. More than just another tremor was visible on the surrealist horizon; it was a fracture, the first in its history, and, in retrospect, certainly its most significant. A lack of direction was becoming apparent and the movement was running out of steam. Breton had to suggest new goals around which everyone could rally, as in 1924; but finding anything that would not betray what united the surrealists was not so simple. Breton's sway over those faithful to him had not diminished, but several of them had evolved. New horizons had opened up that appeared not to contradict their commitment to surrealism. Only Breton could call them to order:

> At the end of 1928, the surrealist world was aswirl with currents, attracted by outside lures, invitations and vicissitudes [one would think we were reading about an order of recluses], perturbed by André Breton's severity and his demanding personality. He was as severe in morals as in the criticism of ideas and works. It wasn't always easy to grasp his frames of reference and applications because he made a strict point of frequently redealing the cards and changing the rules in order to avoid any codification.[1]

Was Breton afraid the movement would congeal? That once suddenly assured of its strength and necessity, it would freeze (and so effectively die)? Far from congealing or freezing, on the contrary the movement demonstrated its vitality, but also an entropy. It was not paralysis that seemed to threaten certain of its members but their dispersion that threatened the movement. Strict in nature, even austere in its ways (austere like a religious movement: one cannot state too firmly the *religious* character of surrealism as described by André Masson; with the enthusiasm of its first few years dissipated, surrealism no longer answered the totality of the desires of those who formed it. Others sprang up that Breton, powerless to control, pronounced heretical. Henceforth he knowingly, skilfully (he gave off a science of power unusual in a poet), maintained tensions, outbursts and break-ups. At best, he controlled them; at worst, he provoked them. He alone was their master, and mastered their worrying succession. In his eyes a group with fewer members was better than one ridden with dissension. More than any other sovereign, Breton discriminated and pronounced the movement's reference points of right and wrong; and accepted or rejected followers according to these prescriptions. What the movement had been founded upon had within a few years become its rules. It now fell to the man who, to universal consent, initially pronounced the rules to which surrealism should devote itself, the rules it *represented*, to defend them alone, intransigently. This Breton did.

We know what the rules and aims were. It is not entirely clear that Breton deliberately set himself to redealing the cards and changing the rules of the surrealist game, as Thirion felt he did. On the contrary, it would even appear that for a long time the cards and the rules remained as they were: as they had first been dealt, and Breton held the only hand.

He was in no doubt that they had to be kept working; that this was the only way for surrealism to resist what threatened it on all sides. But this took no account of the free availability of those, even the most faithful, who joined surrealism so as to conquer a surfeit of freedom, perhaps the only one possible, not to give it away entirely. In fact they had evolved: what they had initially agreed to, unreservedly, even enthusiastically, and which had caused them to accede to the fascination exercised by André Breton, no longer had the same hold over them. What was more, even the movement itself had evolved, imperceptibly but in its entirety. In the interval a political direction had begun to prevail, an orientation towards social revolution of which not everyone approved.[2] It was also true that certain names were beginning to stand out: Breton, of course, who had just published *Nadja*, but also Éluard (*Capitale de la douleur*) and Aragon (*Traité du style*). All three attained their first, relative, notoriety, which was not just limited to a surrealist readership. The others might have felt themselves reduced to the role of ideological firebrands, the best (or the quickest to take advantage) among them dividing up the privilege of a distinction that was ultimately very literary (and thus not particularly surrealist).

The tensions provoked within the movement by Breton, who was an adept ideologist, tore it apart. Artaud had abuse heaped on him during a lecture he gave at the Sorbonne in 1928; it is not certain that everyone agreed. Some may have felt that the pointlessly (perhaps ignominiously) insulting pamphlet *Au grand jour* ('we have vomited this bastard out today') went too far. Vitrac and Soupault were not spared either: they too were excluded. Artaud was guilty of being an actor, Vitrac of writing plays, and Soupault novels . . . More than just failings, these were betrayals.

Before them, Max Ernst and Joan Miró, two of the leading painters of early surrealism, were denounced in equally violent terms: accused of handing over 'weapons to the worst partisans of moral ambiguity'.[3] Consciously or not, in subjecting the criteria of aesthetic judgement to criteria of moral judgement (which is what André Masson along with the rue Blomet group had deplored from the start), Breton was tending to adopt an attitude that was inherently idealist.

In breaking with some of his closest collaborators (and friends), Breton knew the ructions to which he would be exposing the movement unless it became possible in one way or another to close ranks around a cause or an action whose necessity no one would question. Luckily enough, 1928 provided one.

In 1928 René Daumal and Roger Gilbert Lecomte appeared on the Parisian scene. Could the Grand Jeu group be an alternative to surrealism? Could it really claim to rally the disenchanted and dissident? It does not seem ever to have been capable of doing so.

They seduced Breton; or perhaps he was seduced by the idea that new groups might appear on the fringes of surrealism over which he could exercise influence short of control. The idea was that the defections chalked up would be compensated by newcomers; that surrealism would find new frontiers and grow in size with new members whom Breton would allow not to be, strictly speaking, surrealists as long as they brought it new ideas and values. One had to think big, think beyond the limits of the movement alone. He and Aragon had the idea of a summit to which all would be invited.[4] A letter was composed on 12 February 1929 and sent by Raymond Queneau to nearly eighty recipients,[5] inviting them to choose between individual and collective activity (even though the latter was not defined in advance), 'and requesting the explicit names of those with whom one would agree to participate in any necessary joint activity. The accent was on the importance of individuals, and recipients were asked to judge whether they would refuse to take part in certain public *or private* acts.'[6] In this way Breton's concerns for expansion could be met; so could those for clarification. Some could judge this to be a dubious procedure: that of an inquisition, if not a trial. Breton saw in it the possibility of counting up the membership, of galvanising them around a new project, and of making an overture to others without making any concessions on the grounds for moral compatibility. The manoeuvre did not succeed; the blunder by one of the Grand Jeu's members, Roger Vailland, who had just written an article praising the highly suspect Chief of Police, Chiappe (whose sympathy for the Leagues was universally known), short-circuited Breton.[7]

Bataille, one of the few not to belong to any group, was also called to this meeting. So in 1929 he was once more offered the opportunity to move closer to the surrealists and to Breton, and to forge allegiance; he declined with a phrase Breton would be unable to forgive for many years: 'Don't waste my time with idealism!'

The donkey's kick

When the word *materialism* is used, it is time to designate
the direct interpretation, *excluding all idealism*.

Idealism was the enemy, the enemy that in 1929 Bataille would step by
step undertake to overcome. What is surprising is not that he would
create a review which in its entirety would make this its rationale (it is
unlikely he would have found the means), but that this would come to
be grafted onto a project of which he was far from being the only
person involved or the principal instigator and whose *a priori* perspective revealed few affinities with his intentions.

Jean Babelon and Pierre d'Espézel, former editors of the very serious
art and archaeology journal *Aréthuse* (to which, as we have already
seen, Bataille had contributed on several occasions), suggested to
Georges Wildenstein the idea of a journal to replace *Aréthuse*, with the
title *Documents*. A dealer in old masters and publisher of *La Gazette
des Beaux-Arts*, Wildenstein agreed, accepting the idea that the field of
investigation should extend to ethnography. Georges-Henri Rivière,
assistant director of the Trocadero Museum, was also involved in the
origins of the project, constituting a laudable guarantee of seriousness.

In 1929, Georges Bataille was a mongrel. One part of him belonged
to the community of 'scholars': his first articles were published in
Aréthuse, where only his competence as a palaeographic archivist
(probably one of the most gifted of his generation) was called upon.
No more was required of him: more precisely, it is hard to see how he
could have been allowed a greater role. The other part was devoted to
offending taste and reason: *Story of the Eye* and *The Solar Anus* could
hardly be further from what a serious review would publish in its
columns (his collaborators were probably unaware that he was their
author). Entrusting him with the general secretariat of *Documents*, a

sort of disguised editorship,[1] was an acknowledgement of his capacity as a young 'scholar' (as a doctor, he would later say ironically), not as a writer, even less as a scandalous writer. The restless nature of the project is clear: the presence of members of the Institute, museum curators, librarians and historians of art on the editorial committee indicates without possible doubt its pretensions and aim. *Documents* was to be a scientific review, and he was expected to respond seriously to what a scientific review should be.

But what happened was, to say the least, unusual. Attracted by Bataille, without whom *a priori* they would not have had anything to do with it, the first surrealist dissidents joined the editorial board: Georges Limbour, who filled the function of editorial assistant when he felt like it (Pierre d'Espézel did not approve of this casual attitude, and he reproached Bataille for the fact that his assistant had no sense of order or method; Michel Leiris and then Marcel Griaule would succeed him), Jacques-André Boiffard, Roger Vitrac and Robert Desnos.[2] From then on, a strange tussle took place between the most suspect and least predictable of the young writers on the editorial committee and those who could be called conservatives; it is unlikely that the latter understood its rationale, and the publishers of the journal more than once had reason to complain about this. Georges-Henri Rivière was unsparing in the support he gave to Georges Bataille, and Pierre d'Espézel recalled the idea they started with: 'We need to return to the spirit which inspired the first draft of the journal, when you and I spoke about it to Mr Wildenstein.'[3]

The beginnings were nevertheless cautious: Bataille at first hardly went beyond what he had written in *Aréthuse*. A judicious reserve restrained him from pushing ahead with provocation. This did not last. What, in the text advertising the launch, could pass for a concern for the enlargement of the field of investigation ('The most provoking, as yet unclassified, works of art and certain unusual productions, neglected until now, will be the object of studies as rigorous and scientific as those of archaeologists') very quickly – in fact from issue 4 – assumed considerable importance. What is contrary to the 'rules of decency', and what is commonly suppressed by a platitude, were no longer used as an adjunct, a curiosity, a 'plus' that this journal took pride in, in contrast to its rivals: they became its essential character. 'The provoking and the unusual, if not the disturbing'[4] were the mark of the publication itself, side by side with austere and characteristic studies by the personalities who would continue to publish in it.

'Yet we had to wait until issue 4 to see Bataille – a stubborn peasant, who gives the impression of acting in all innocence while never for a moment letting go of his intention – decide to put his cards on the table.'[5] On the title page of issue 4, 'Miscellanea and Illustrated Magazine' was added to 'Doctrines, Archaeology, Fine-Arts and Ethnography'. How could anyone fail to notice? Its true colours were revealed. Bataille's articles could finally take the direction for which he had patiently become involved in this unusual gathering. His anti-idealism was unleashed, aided by those who joined him at the beginning: Alberto Giacometti and Gaston-Louis Roux, who at the time no one yet knew, Salvador Dalí, who was not yet a surrealist, Pablo Picasso and Joan Miró. It was suddenly interested – miscellanea permitting – in Afro-American music hall, jazz, Hollywood cinema and its stars, in cabaret songs and popular imagery (Croquignol, Ribouldingue and Filochard, cartoons[6]): the conflict with the austere initial project is measured by what it was tending to become.

The uneasiness of Pierre d'Espézel, which he expressed to Bataille from April 1929, was justified: 'After what I have seen up to now, the title that you have chosen for this journal is hardly justified except in the sense that it gives us Documents about your state of mind. It is too much and yet not quite enough.'[7] He merged his reservations with a single, harsh threat: the suppression of the journal. Perhaps we should be amazed it did not happen sooner. He waited until January 1931 and the fifteenth issue to carry out the threat.

A stubborn peasant, as Michel Leiris amiably said, Georges Bataille did not act recklessly. He knew how lucky he was to control a journal, whatever constraints he must at first accept and whatever resistance he would encounter. There is no doubt that, patiently and stubbornly, he conceived *Documents* as a war machine against surrealism; as an advanced position over its territories to which its dissidents would rally one by one.

His patience and circumspection were all the more remarkable in that in 1928, in another journal, *Les Cahiers de la République des Lettres, des Sciences et des Arts*, he published an article which left no doubt about the nature of the themes he would develop and his way of developing them. In this intoxicating article ('Vanished America', published to mark the first great exhibition of pre-Colombian art), in a way that would quickly become what, for lack of a more appropriate word, one might call a method, Bataille integrated a capital reserve of scientific knowledge with his own preoccupations, indeed his most dubious fascinations. Light, the sun, jokes, blood, sacrifice, death were the things around which he constituted *The Solar Anus* and 'The Pineal Eye'. The Aztec people gave him the opportunity to consider them in another way, from another angle, legitimised by the ethnographic pretext. Speaking of this people in a way that science would be unable to find fault with, Bataille was still speaking, in an exemplary way, of himself: 'doubtless a more blood-spattered eccentricity has never been conceived by human folly.'

The Mexican gods in particular overwhelmed him: 'ferocious and strangely malicious'. This people – in their way more religious than any other, religious to the point of horror, to the point of loving death – preferred the bitter aloe of their cruel and malicious gods to the sugary sweetness of the Christian God. They were gods so strong they deserved the way this people honoured them: sacrifices by the thousands, cutting up the bodies, opening up their bodies and taking out their beating hearts, cooking everything and eating it. All that amid the greatest merriment with which they were, in return, blessed. Mexico bore witness to 'the most streaming human abattoirs', and for its people – 'astonishingly happy with these horrors' – death was nothing or, better than nothing, something for which they had an enticing avidity: 'There seems to have been an excessive taste for death among this people of extraordinary courage.' A religion of death, a religion which looked to love death, not through resignation, but by excessive force, had an immeasurable advantage over Christianity, which bowed, judged, wept and terrified. To the point that Cortès, the conquering Christian, did not, as history incorrectly claims, win out over these 'savages': to the death he brought with his God, the Aztecs replied by *theirs* in a sort of hypnotic delirium, 'a veritable enchantment'. Having arrived at the summit of their happy vertigo, they wanted in their turn to vanish into the abyss. Only this vanishing had the free and irrepressible character of their juvenile cruelty. It was the only possible result: that of an 'insect one crushes'.[8]

It would be wrong to regard this impenitent meditation on death (impenitent and happy), in which the Aztecs' enchantment occupies something of what we have seen in Fu Chou Li's 'enraptured' torture, only as Bataille's interpretative delirium. Anthropology does not contradict the main lines he opened. More than this, according to the anthropologist Alfred Métraux, it has real insight. Insight, for Métraux, was required to see the Aztec gods as 'tricksters, mischievously fond of practical jokes, often as whimsical as they were cruel'.[9] And Bataille was ahead of his time: 'By a sort of curious intuition, he also proved to be the precursor of a whole school of anthropologists who sought to define *ethnos*, in other words the hierarchy of social values which gives each civilisation its own value.'[10]

Georges Bataille's way ('way' is perhaps more accurate than 'method'), at work from this first important article, would soon become this: a knowledge hastily acquired through a few reference texts, conversations, and something extra, at the very least – something intuitive rather than deductive and insightful rather than logical in character – assuredly personal in nature (born of play with experiments on himself), something extra that most of the time was singularly *carried away* and yet illuminating. Bataille would act no differently when it came to politics, economics and sociology (as we shall see: even his closest friends were often tempted to take exception to such an unorthodox 'way', before partly or completely rallying to his opinion and following it).

The articles in the first three issues of *Documents* were more prudent. 'The Academic Horse', published in the first issue (April 1929) hardly did more than stick some banderillas into 'the idealists' platitudes and arrogance',[11] favouring 'decaying forests' and 'stagnant swamps' over what is 'harmonious *and* ruled'.[12] 'The Apocalypse of Saint-Sever' (issue 2, May 1929) showed the same prudent reserve; at most, in passing, Bataille put in a plea for 'the salutary value of dirty or blood-stained events'[13] without making a further comment. 'The Language of Flowers', with sly didacticism, plunged the sword a little more deeply into surrealism. Admittedly, flowers are beautiful, it is commonly agreed, but not in themselves; only because they conform to what must be: *to the human ideal*. Defoliation proves this, baring the flower's sexual organs when they are pubescent and therefore ugly. What is a defoliated rose if not a 'sordid-looking tuft'? But there is worse: between the sky, without reaching it, and earth, through its roots, 'nauseating and bare like vermin', the flower derives its fragile beauty 'from the stench of dung'. This stench is like its sign; that of its inevitable withering: wilted, it stops being the beautiful thing everyone agrees on, to become the 'tatters of air-borne dung'.[14] The flower as the symbol of love has the definitive 'smell of death'. Desire and love have only a little to do with ideal beauty, except in withering and tarnishing it. Their liberty represents: '. . . a disturbing mockery of all that still is, thanks to miserable evasion, elevated, noble and sacred . . .'.[15] The end of another article by Bataille published in the same issue sketches, without naming them, those people *Documents* would soon denounce: 'When the word *materialism* is used, it is time to designate the direct interpretation, *excluding all idealism*, of raw phenomena, and not a system founded on the fragmentary elements of an ideological analysis, elaborated under the sign of religious relations.'[16]

If the first three issues of *Documents* more or less warily set the fuse, the fourth lit it. Georges Bataille signed no less than three notes or articles which were extremely fiery. The appearance of the Blackbirds, a negro revue, at the Moulin-Rouge was the occasion for some lines that no longer held back: '. . . we decay with neurasthenia under our roofs, the cemetery and mass grave of so much pathetic crap.'[17] But the most fiery of these three articles undoubtedly is the one entitled 'Human Face', a title beneath which we guess that another is more crudely discernible, 'Human nature'. That is, there are humans but not human nature. A photo offering an interesting assortment of people is enough to show this: a wedding, for example, a 'repulsive' assortment of 'vain ghosts'. No young person would fail to acknowledge having the most charming of their fancies changed by this 'senile soiling' by those from whom they were born. This ascendancy is not merely shameful; it denies the existence of *human nature*. The most eminent qualities generally ascribed to this belief, the very ordinary monstrousness, a 'monstrousness without madness', of this wedding reduces them to nothing. Bataille could not make a more violent attack. He was attacking the most insipid deference: the one accorded to his generation . . . The tone is set. *Documents* would be the abscess burst each month from surrealism: what the latter had not dared be, what its violence would have been if it had not been prevented, *in extremis*, by Breton's fierce desire, to match it with the best, that is the most worthy, reasons. Surrealist violence is dictated by superior considerations. If everything is grist to its mill, it was neither blindly nor desperately. It is justified against the grain by the order it denies, that of the 'slave-traders', 'businessmen' and partisans of 'moral equivocation'. The formidable surrealist revolt finds its rationale and authority in the world it condemns and yet relies upon. Bataille's absolutely solitary revolt is justified by nothing but itself: the good no longer has a God to guarantee it, nor does evil have a God to blaspheme. Its only authority is its bad temper and its rage. If it denounces, it does so with no claim to change anything. If it decides to destroy, it is with no hope of replacing anything. If it exists, it is without an outcome . . . In short, it has no other authority but itself, the one that horror makes its rule.

It is only moralists who claim that horror must be fought. Bataille did worse: he recounted it in great detail and obligingly allowed himself to be fascinated by it; a lucidity of eyes open to the sun. It is moreover remarkable that in the fifteen issues of *Documents* he did not once cite the name of André Breton. To the commiseration which Breton showed him in 1925, Bataille replied with a commiseration that was at least as great. What annoyed him was idealism; whether Breton and his friends recognised themselves in these proceedings is secondary: they are not designated by name. A suddenly clear-sighted tactician, Bataille was confident enough to let Breton be the first to commit himself by insulting him. He then had a good enough hand to match him, turning the power relations to his advantage when Breton, given his status, should legitimately have held the upper hand.

'The Big Toe' (an article published in issue 6 of *Documents*) appeared in this context as the unrestrained parody of poetic idealism. The object chosen is no longer a flower but what everyone thinks of as being the lowest and most unworthy thing. In fact, Bataille only emphasises this unworthiness. The fate which consigns it to mud and dejection, the fate which consigns it to dung and also 'corns, callosities and bunions', this fate is that of people erroneously considered noble.[18] If such people take pride in their erection towards the sun, their feet give them the necessary foundation in mud and faeces. Their feet indicate that life is made of an 'oscillating movement from filth to the ideal and from the ideal to filth'.[19] Such a life is consigned to rage; a rage 'it is easy to call down upon an organ as low as a foot'. The foot is so low that, like the fall (the failure of the foot to maintain equilibrium), it is death. And because it is death it is the most human and most desirable thing possible.

> The meaning of this article lies in its insistence on a direct and explicit questioning of *seductiveness*, without taking into account poetic concoctions that are, ultimately, nothing but a diversion (most

human beings are naturally feeble and can only abandon themselves to their instincts when in a poetic haze). A return to reality does not imply any new acceptances, but means that one is seduced in a base manner, without transpositions and to the point of *screaming, opening his eyes wide*: opening them wide, then, before a big toe.[20]

Poetry is the second of the names of idealism. To the 'halfheartedness', the 'loopholes' and the 'deliria' disclosed by poetic impotence, Bataille intends 'to oppose a black rage and even an incontestable bestiality'.[21] The journal *Documents* was supposed to be had in six months become an anti-surrealist war machine. For the first time Bataille 'found himself in a position of ringleader'. This was a position he used to his advantage in order, if not to denounce, at the very least to reduce, with the help of some dissidents, the undivided power André Breton exercised over intellectual youth.[22] Obviously *Documents* never attained the notoriety of *La Révolution surréaliste* and, after it, *Le Surréalisme au service de la Révolution*; equally obviously, no matter what splits surrealism might have undergone, no matter what losses it had to resign itself to, *La Révolution surréaliste* retained the privilege of being the most widely read and most representative of the avant-garde journals, and that it was relative to it that all others defined themselves, *Documents* included. *Documents* lasted just two years where *La Révolution surréaliste* lasted for five, but in two years, through its grouping and through the margins, *Documents* made clear what surrealism was not; what, under the aegis of Breton, it could not be. *Documents* was a doubtful taste in surrealism's mouth; Bataille was a bad tooth in Breton's (an expression we shall come across several times). And its 'madman', since none could emerge within surrealism itself. If Artaud drove *words* mad, Bataille drove ideas mad. Worse, he turned them rancid. He was the 'mad', uncontrolled philosopher within the very reasoned enterprise of surrealist unreason. In a way that eluded all control, eluding surrealism above all, undoubtedly outside the rules, Bataille 'philosophised' the surrealism of which Breton was only (and this was his weakness) the theoretician, sometimes the ideologue, but never the philosopher. More than fleeing the authority of their mentor, the dissident surrealists joined what the logic of the thought in which Breton had schooled them called for, so that this thought was finally restored to itself: to its impossibility. The surrealist marvellous only painfully concealed the butchery the war had been. Bataille's 'bestiality' was more attentive to the despair and disgust into which the war had cast a whole generation. Hateful as the war had been, Bataille did not hold out the hope that a world in which it would be absent would ever exist. More *bestial* still, since it was not in any way possible to recall people to their true nature, he said that what was fascinating was that they might not have one. Bataille's bestiality was to have eyes wide open on the beasts they were, and to open those of a few others. If he was a surrealist in a certain way, it was to the point that he alone thought its unthought (the impossible).

André Breton made surrealism the instrument of the *marvellous*; he wanted retribution for the hatred in which it was held and the ridicule which, he claimed, everyone cast on it: 'Let's speak plainly: the marvellous is always beautiful, anything marvellous is beautiful, it is even only the marvellous that is beautiful', he wrote in the *First Manifesto*. At the other extreme, Georges Bataille made *Documents* the instrument of the *monstrous*.[23] Monstrous is the 'play of mankind and its own decay', and it is cowardly that this game 'continues in the most dejected condition without one having the courage to confront the other'.[24] It is in what is lowest, most vile, most dirty, that Bataille, with all that had gone before for people nauseated by such a cowardly flight, sought the uninterpretable truth of existence: 'What is really loved is loved especially in shame'.[25] Love of the marvellous says, profoundly, *No*, to existence: it bears witness against it. True to himself and to the project he discussed with Leiris and Lavaud in 1924 to form a *Yes* movement, involving a permanent acquiescence to everything, Bataille consented to the world to the point of it turning one's stomach and making one 'froth at the mouth'. He consented to so much, so profoundly, that this nausea and this slime are the love that one could have of this world, a love bearing witness to the point of shame. Shame is the truth of this love as the sun is the truth of eyes wide open on decay. A shame which necessarily manages to reach bedazzlement and vertigo . . . A truth of a bedazzled, vacillating, man who bites through his finger while looking at the sun . . . A truth of a woman smashing her face and tearing out her eyes . . . The truth of Vincent Van Gogh who took his severed ear 'to the place which most disgusted him': to a brothel.[26] 'Sacrificial Mutilation and the Severed Ear of Vincent Van Gogh', one of Bataille's last articles in *Documents*, is one of the most beautiful and unsettling, with the *marvellous* and depressing character of sunflowers, those flowers restlessly painted by Van Gogh that all day long *stare at* the sun, ordering their rotation on its course. For the first time in painting, Van Gogh painted them wilted, burned, disheartening. The sun, through contagion, infects the one who made it his ideal.

Later, another journal created by Georges Bataille entitled *Acéphale* took as its emblem (drawn by André Masson) a man whose head is amputated from its body. *Documents* could legitimately have taken for its emblem a donkey or, better, a donkey's head, 'whose comic and desperate braying would be the signal for a shameless revolt against ruling idealism'.[27] *Documents*, the donkey's kick against surrealism.

'Excrement philosopher'[1]

'It is worthwhile to know just what kind of moral virtues surrealism lays claim to . . .'[2] It should not be overlooked that surrealism (Breton) demands respect for 'moral virtues'. More essentially, as soon as it was threatened, it even appeared as nothing but that: a morality. This was never so manifestly true as in 1929 when, with some people starting to take liberties, Breton had to call the movement back to the principles that gave it birth and that continued to form its goal.

It was now already two years at least since Breton had begun to doubt if he would ever reach the goal he could glimpse. On meeting the Yugoslavian surrealist Marco Ristic, in December 1926, weary and discouraged, he admitted that 'attaining the marvellous is something awful, impossible'. The listener deduced from this that 'Breton had lost many of his illusions, and a part of his faith in what surrealism would achieve'.[3] It is true that it cost him dear when he felt himself obliged to exclude Robert Desnos, the price of friendship and admiration. Others left of their own accord or put themselves in a position to be thrown out. The movement was feeling the undertow for the first time.

However important the people excluded were (the time for exclusions had arrived), they indicated the movement's fragility and how much room there was for doubt that it would ever achieve its goals. Unattainable or not, these presumed goals justified Breton in employing the most repressive means, given that in the end these were preferable to the break-up of the movement. There was thus no other choice than to rally the faithful back to what had initially brought them together (back to their 'vows') and to point out for disapproval those who had contravened it. This is a common practice to galvanise the members of a movement (or a sect, religion or party) in a common vendetta directed against those who, through their actions, are alleged to have threatened its declared interests. It was in this climate of weariness and bitterness

that Breton set to writing the *Second Manifesto of Surrealism*, a kind
of poetic-political programme that was put into action, here excom-
municating, there rehabilitating, here reaffirming the movement's
origins, there pointing out new ends. This *Second Manifesto* does not
have the enthusiastic tone of the first; if it expands it, it is in proportion
to what threatens it (it closes off more than it opens up).

Not without reason, it is remembered for its extreme violence. But
it is also moving. Breton recognised the monsters threatening him and,
worse, that these monsters did not *all* come from outside; some sprang
from surrealism itself. He was no longer in the position of a man who
can be proud of *all* the enemies he can name. Justifiably or not, he had
made some among the very first of his closest collaborators, and these
would not be the least violent. Desnos was one of them; Breton, not
without 'sadness', recalled how 'essential, unforgettable' his role had
been.[4] As for the others – to each his due – they were the object of just
as much disenchantment: 'Each day brings us new indications of
disappointments which we must have the courage to admit, if for no
other reason than as a measure of mental hygiene, and inscribe in the
horribly debit side of the ledger of life.'[5]

Breton was weary, and in proportion to this weariness, he was
exasperated. This exasperation, this fit of anger that made him write
that the simplest surrealist act consisted of going down to the street,
revolver in hand, and firing at random into the crowd (too simple an
act to be truly surrealist; Breton would long regret this rash phrase),
were the same ones which, with a sort of sad violence in drawing up
surrealism's horribly indebted balance sheet, made him pronounce the
exclusions, one by one: Antonin Artaud, accused of 'lucre' and of
'notoriety', was the first to be named; but the worst had already been
said: 'For a long time we have wanted to unmask him, convinced that
a veritable bestiality was driving him.'[6] Next, heaped up pell-mell in
the surrealist ossuary, came Carrive ('Gascon terrorist'), Delteil ('disgusting'), Gérard (for 'congenital imbecility'), Limbour (for 'scepticism,
literary coquetry'), Masson (for 'megalomania' and 'absenteeism'),
Soupault (for 'a new low of dishonour' and for being 'a rat running in
circles around his rat cage [with his] items which appear in scandal
sheets'), Vitrac ('a veritable slut of ideas'), Naville, taken to task at
length ('whose insatiable penchant for notoriety we are patiently waiting
to devour him'), Baron (for 'crass ignorance'), Duchamp (like Limbour,
for 'scepticism'), Ribemont-Dessaignes (for having meanwhile become

the author of 'odious little detective stories'), Picabia (for having collaborated in 'the remarkable garbage pail known as *Bifur*'); each one, according to his faults, 'fools, frauds, or artful schemers but who, in any case, have only the worst intentions as far as the revolutionary movement is concerned'.[7]

Finding himself forced to turn these defections into major excommunications (even if only to continue giving his power a positive thrust), Breton additionally needed to single out, for the hatred of the faithful, the external enemy, close at hand it went without saying, the only one he deemed likely to encroach upon his territory. The first of two outside groups to benefit (!) from a denunciation of principles was the Philosophies group of Morhange, Politzer and Lefebvre[8] who, three years earlier, had been branded with 'bad faith, arrivism, and counter-revolutionary ends', and whose major fault seems to have been to have enjoyed the confidence of the Communist Party leaders. The second group was *Documents*, or more precisely 'Mr Bataille'. Compared to the preceding names, those of *Documents* and Bataille presented the advantage of supplying a new, fresh foe. When the *Second Manifesto* was published (in issue 12 of *La Révolution surréaliste* on 15 December 1929), *Documents* had only been in existence for nine months, with seven issues to date. This was not much, but it seemed enough in Breton's eyes to justify devoting the longest and most sustained of his attacks to Bataille: a whole page and a half of the magazine (six pages in book form) when the aforementioned excommunicants, all in all, were given only a few lines if not just a few words.

If there *is* idealism in surrealism (Breton, of course, denies this: 'There was, for us too, the necessity to put an end to idealism *properly speaking*, the creation of the word "surrealism" alone would testify to it'), it is for its defence and explanation that Breton proceeds prior to any argument with Bataille. No doubt it is this 'properly speaking' (it is my emphasis in the quotation) that was responsible for the profound misinterpretation on the part of the two men. In any case, what Breton does not consider idealist, was so for Bataille, and idealist of not the least detestable kind. Breton, by suddenly placing surrealism under the dubious auspices of Nicolas Flamel, hoped that the analogies the latter proposed with alchemical research would liberate the human imagination 'after centuries of the mind's domestication', to take 'a stunning revenge on all things'.[9] But the soul must also adopt an attitude that is propitiatory in every way: divorce itself from vulgar things, cleanse itself of all sickness or weakness of spirit, hold itself in a 'pure, bright place, wherein white wall hangings are everywhere apparent'. All wise men have clung to the brilliant cleanliness of their clothes as to that of their souls, and it must be exemplary that the surrealists, as alchemists of the mind, should be at least as demanding,

We can see that this is far removed from Bataille. Breton, before any polemics, reminds the reader what surrealism is: this search, in a profound way. Did 'Mr Bataille' have grounds to take offence at this? Breton pretends to be shocked; he pretends to be shocked that, when he pronounces the conditions for the apparition of the marvellous, Bataille protests against 'sordid quests for every integrity'. Breton's ingenuousness is fairly blatantly simulated; the surrealist soul is only suddenly so 'angelic' the better to say what satanic shades Bataille's soul is made of when he only considers 'in the world that which is vilest, most discouraging, and most corrupted';[10] and that, far from holding up this world, 'befouled, senile, rancid, sordid, lewd, doddering', for reprobation or denunciation, he delights in it. If it does not occur to Breton that, with his surrealism exasperating him, he is close to making a fool if not an obscurantist of himself, it does clearly appear to him that Bataille's delight is that of a sick man (he does not beat about the bush in this diagnosis), a victim of 'a state of conscious deficiency, in a form tending to become generalized', of 'psychasthenia'. It is simple: the desire for the marvellous is that of a healthy man; the taste for the morbid that of a sick man. Breton does not waste time on nuances, and is even less concerned about justifying his 'clinical' categories with notions borrowed from a psychology that is rigidly normative (also as little Freudian as possible) when it is not, as it sometimes turns out to be, repressive. Ending on a lyrical note, Breton pleads for clean robes and gold, and denounces, as appropriate, Bataille's abject inclination for flies ('Mr Bataille loves flies. Not we') as an object of universal disgust.

The triviality of Bataille's tastes would be of little consequence (probably they would never even have bothered Breton) were it not that he had been in a position to gather around him the principal refugees from surrealism, the very ones distanced from it for a 'defect'. Henceforth it is his double, predictably his negative double, that Breton has in mind: 'Perhaps Mr Bataille is sufficiently forceful to bring them together, and if he succeeds in this effort the results, in my opinion, will be extremely interesting.' But – and this is not often noted

– whatever ill temper Breton displays, whatever insults he throws at Bataille, discreetly and almost respectfully he acknowledges in him at least one virtue, one he acknowledged very rarely and which he considered so discriminating that he denied it to almost all the former surrealists: rigour. To surrealism's 'harsh discipline of the mind', Bataille opposes 'a discipline which does not even manage to seem more woolly, for it tends to be that of the non-mind . . .' And no less explicitly, 'I am amused, moreover, to think that one cannot leave surrealism without running into Mr Bataille, so great is the truism that the dislike of discipline can only result in one's submitting oneself anew to discipline.'[11]

Breton had found someone – and something – on surrealism's fringes to fight against. Quite involuntarily, *Documents* tightened the movement's ranks. And this movement found its defections partly compensated in autumn 1929 by the arrival of new members: René Char, René Magritte, André Thirion, Luis Buñuel and, by a swing back of the pendulum, Salvador Dalí, who for a while had been close to *Documents* before drawing to surrealism. In 1930 others would come, not least Alberto Giacometti. Against Bataille proclaiming 'the sordid quests for every integrity', Breton seemed to have been right to reaffirm that surrealism was less than ever disposed to 'dispense with this integrity'. These unexpected reinforcements justified in retrospect the intransigence of his purges.

The castrated lion

'The Second Manifesto of Surrealism is not a revelation, but it is a success. The genre of the hypocrite, traitor, drill sergeant, sacristan, in short of the cop and the priest, could not be bettered.'[1]

Did André Breton expect his old friends to reply to him? The majority, having participated in surrealism for a long time, had retained its taste for polemic, invective and insult. With the *Second Manifesto*, Breton did not accomplish much more than a police report: the *ad hominem* attack, under the pretext that it was justified by considerations of morality, amply established an ideological polemic (which could encourage the view that, in surrealism, personal issues prevailed). The response was in a no less personal or insulting style, and in all probability a lot more violent than he could have expected.

The reply borrowed the form and the – ironical – title of a pamphlet the surrealists had written in 1924 on the death of Anatole France: *A Corpse*. This claimed to bring to an end the paralysing funeral homage which 'from torpid Maurras to decrepit Moscow' the illustrious deceased had received. Breton had thus laid himself open to the possibility that one day this corpse might be returned to the bed of surrealism.

The extreme violence of the response is still striking. Robert Desnos, the one whose loss was most sincerely regretted by Breton, set the tone. With insults: 'And the final vanity of this ghost will be to stink eternally among the stench of the paradise promised by Breton the crook's imminent and certain conversion.' Not content with this, he continues, speaking on behalf of his old friend as 'the slug's soul': 'I am satiated with the meat of corpses: Vaché, Rigaut, Nadja, whom I said I loved. Crevel, whose death I was really counting on, has buried me with his own hands, depositing the droppings, with justice and tranquillity, on my carcass and my memory.' In comparison, the others were almost magnanimous. All the same, Prévert branded him a 'Fregoli adjusting his Christ's beard in secret', this 'Déroulède of dream' and 'pope' spitting 'everywhere, on the ground, on his friends, on his friend's wives'. Vitrac called him a fraud ('cowardly, envious, greedy, gullible and pitiable') who was taken seriously only by 'a few aged schoolboys and women giving birth to monsters'. Baron regarded him as a venal hypocrite (for example, he derided Diaghilev one evening, only to welcome him with open arms the next day at the Galerie surréaliste) and as a 'larva more decayed than the utmost petit-bourgeois'; Leiris called him necrophagous (for having lived off the corpses of Vaché, Rigaut and Nadja); Limbour brought attention to how artificial his philosophical knowledge was ('Hegel was hard to read but hadn't Croce done an excellent study of him?'), Boiffard was ironical about 'the imbecility' of certain of his expressions ('To a degree of expression or nearly: action, we are outlaws'). He would be pardoned nothing, either by Baron for having 'never brought anything but the darkest confusion', or by Ribemont-Dessaignes for giving way to denunciations which 'have the character of everyday extortion exerted by newspapers sold to the police'.

Bataille was not to be outdone; in fact, his rage excelled. He had the advantage over the co-signatories of *A Corpse* of never having 'served' Breton, and also the advantage of having allowed Breton to make the first attack. He deliberately played on this double advantage as though, of the two, he was the one who had the authority to be disdainful: 'I have nothing much to say about the personality of André Breton since I hardly know him. His police reports don't interest me.' With the first banderilla posted, it was immediately followed by a second, more wounding still: in addition to being a 'cop', Breton was also a 'priest'. He was an 'old religious windbag', a 'soft strumpot'[2], 'fine for little castratos, little poets and little mystic-mongrels'. Even more, he was so much a cop, so much a priest, that he was no longer even a man, but a beast, and one of an 'unspeakable species, the animal with a great mop of hair and sputtering head': a 'lion', a 'castrated' one it went without saying . . . or better than a lion, even castrated: an 'ox'. Breton was a beast, an ox, and dead (along with surrealism). Which earns him this ignominious epitaph: 'Here lies Breton the ox, the old aesthete and false revolutionary with the head of Christ.'[3] In 1930, the most stinking odours (the least respectable ones) rose up from the sewers of angelic surrealism. The 'soiled, senile, rancid, sordid, improper, shabby' world

Breton reproached Bataille with delighting in, provided Bataille and several former surrealists with equally degrading epithets to describe the person who claimed to make surrealism an example of probity and morality.

Today we may not realise how shocking this was. In fact, by putting to one side the element of open and unrestrained violence (dictating to its authors the most insulting of epithets to heap upon someone they had, a little earlier, regarded as at least a master, if not a friend), one can see what these texts share: an accusation Bataille for a long time alone had made and which no one then would have accepted without being laughed at – the accusation of idealism. For a long time, no one, whether they knew surrealism intimately or from a distance, whether they liked it or not, could see the justification for such an accusation, because it was not suspected that surrealism could be anything but what it claimed to be. But Bataille was quick to formulate it, doing so from a clearly materialist point of view: surrealism could only be erroneously considered as materialist since it only laid claim to what was *low* the more effectively to abstract it, in his view, from the dignity of baseness.

Breton doubtless did not expect such a retort. It affected him so much that people who had not signed the pamphlet (people whose views were important to him) had to declare their solidarity with him: 'For a while he thought everyone would desert him.'[4]

Thirion's hypothesis is that only Bataille could conceive of such an outrage. He believes that the overall insulting tone was down to Bataille, who was also responsible for the insulting language and the filthy terms used. Thirion suspected him of having ideologically infiltrated the rue du Château surrealists who were incautiously open to the influence of this 'person of great stature, a true loner, whose work was shaped by a coherent philosophy', although he accused him of having 'harshly criticised the superficiality of philosophical discussions at Breton's home and the focus on magic, Freud, and Marx'. This would be why his criticism gave the signatories of *A Corpse* 'what is known in far-left jargon as an ideological foundation'.[5]

This is too many virtues at once for one defendant. The hypothesis certainly serves to attenuate the errors of Breton's old friends. But apart from being implicitly insulting to them (insinuating that, even freed from Breton's influence, they would immediately fall under an influence of a similar nature), it is to all appearances inexact. Breton's character and the fact that several of his friends were fed up with accompanying him in chasing chimeras which, once defined, became jealously erected into dogmas, could be enough to justify both the tone and method of the pamphlet. Without Bataille, would not Desnos have thought, said and perhaps written as he had? Did Bataille do anything more than bring the others together? Did he have the ideological influence Thirion assumes? Michel Leiris doubted it. One thing is certain: it was Robert Desnos (and not Bataille, as has sometimes been said) who came up with the idea. He was the one who suggested both it and the title to Bataille. On Bataille's admission, he only gradually became involved. Admittedly the idea attracted him (who could doubt it . . . it constituted the possibility of a dazzling revenge on Breton's scorn?) and he passed it on to Georges-Henri Rivière who also agreed with it and raised the necessary funds. In the meantime, Desnos had second thoughts, less out of magnanimity than because he feared the pamphlet would have the opposite effect to that intended, in other words it would increase Breton's renown. Bataille appeared to share this view, but it was too late: things had been put in place. He persuaded Desnos to write the text he had conceived (and, in fact, among the twelve contributions, his was doubtless the most violent, proving that it was not due to sudden magnanimity that he doubted the enterprise). Ribemont-Dessaignes, Roger Vitrac, Jacques Prévert, Michel Leiris, Jacques-André Boiffard, Max Morise, Jacques Baron, Georges Limbour, Raymond Queneau and Alejo Carpentier wrote theirs.[6] Jacques-André Boiffard devised the photomontage of André Breton with eyes closed and head wreathed with a crown of thorns (Breton was *thirty-three* years old). The pamphlet was published on 15 January 1930 in 500 copies of which we can presume that barely half were distributed.[7]

'Surrealism's secret affectations'

> Having hastened to address myself to a coward as to a
> coward, I here invite anyone who still feels that *above all*,
> he has a spurt of blood in the throat, to spit with me in
> the face of André Breton, at the clown with closed eyes
> adapting Sade to surrealism's secret affectations.

Did this polemic end with the publication of *A Corpse*? It seems not,
even though it is not clear what new developments in it the two parties
made. According to Bataille, Breton forbade anyone from shaking his
hand; Breton claimed Bataille and his friends were guilty of assaults on
his private life.[1] It is hard to know today what really happened, but
the wounds were such that it is not impossible that, in one form or
another, each party sought to aggravate them still further.

We know Bataille wanted to take things further. But it is not certain
he felt he had emerged from the confrontation over *A Corpse* to his
advantage. It is even less certain he was happy with it. Chance had it
that in order to reply to Breton's opening attack he had to associate
himself with people with whom he shared neither motives nor goals.
Of the twelve signatories, he was one of the few never at any point to
have been a surrealist. He therefore had no need to mourn a truth and
a commitment that had once been theirs. And the brief text he added
to it reveals more frustration than the pride he could legitimately take
in never having been duped. Was this why he undertook in a way to
write it again in the form of open letters to his comrades? Was it so
that his motives would be clear to everyone at last, and so that, as
distinct from those with whom he had rallied for a moment, they were
not ascribed to personal issues? The fact is that, this time on his own,
in a solitude he judged to be his own responsibility, he doggedly
worked to redraft one by one the objections he had from the start
formulated about surrealism.[2]

A single name could amplify all these oppositions to their most extreme intensity: that of Sade. Sade enjoyed an unrivalled prestige among Breton and his friends, one such that he (and he alone) had the privilege of exemption from the strict moral categories followed by the surrealists. Nothing in him, no matter how *odious* he may have been (and the surrealists might have been more logical in considering him in this way), was not sublimated by his intemperate violence in overcoming *all* servitude. In Breton's eyes, no doubt, the overwhelming nature of this servitude justified him in behaving in whatever way he saw fit, given that this was seen *a priori* as subversive. By a highly strange casuist's twist of the argument – since in the end nothing proves Sade *wanted* to subvert and was not just seeking his own liberty – the ends arbitrarily ascribed to Sade justified his use of means that elsewhere surrealism denounced without exception.

Bataille viewed all this as a fraud: the surrealists, he said, were in no way authorised to appropriate the Marquis's mortal remains. In fact they should be the last to lay claim to them. Indeed, how could they be claimed by a man as carefully prudish as Breton, who said he hated libertinage, who found brothels (like prisons and asylums) repulsive, who daily extolled singular, 'mad' love, and fidelity, and who defended the most 'domestic', least perverse and deranged, eroticism against all attacks (as witnessed by the *Recherches sur la sexualité*)? Which Sade could he be claiming if not one who was filleted and quite dead (one can imagine what Sade might have said about Breton)?

All the same, Sade was quoted at length, religiously even, at the rue Fontaine. He was revered, lauded, but without letting anyone be 'Sadean'. But worse than forbidding anyone from being surrealist *and* Sadean, even to claim it was to forfeit surrealism. For Bataille, this was more than hypocrisy (which would still only be a moral judgement), it was a fraud: 'It has seemed fitting today to place these writings (and with them the figure of their author) above everything (or almost everything) that can be opposed to them, but it is out of the question to allow them the least place in private or public life, in theory or in practice.'[3]

Is it appropriate to make of Sade what Breton made of him: an (oneiric) idea; more dubiously, an idol; entirely tragically, a primitive god, praised and hated, adored and execrated (Bataille adds maliciously: and excreted: 'he is only an object of transports of exaltation to the extent that these transports facilitate his excretion')?[4]

Either way, Bataille considered Breton and the surrealists to be either hypocrites or swindlers. Bataille would long maintain this rage,[5] but it would never have such a violent outburst as in these 'open letters'. A choice had to be made: either Breton and his friends are Sade in their turn (to the extent that reading him committed them to this), at the very least allowing that they should try to be, or else they should remain silent. But it is not at all tolerable (or logical) that what demands admiration in Sade should be held against Bataille. Not that he claims to be Sade (one must be clear on this: Bataille is not Sade nor does he claim to be), but he requires that the surrealists, if they lay claim to him, must accept in theory and practice the consequences stemming from the overflow of the 'excremental forces' he put into play; and at the very least he demands to be granted the right to experience it for himself to the utmost possible limit without Breton, like some old bestower of blessings, immediately accusing him of obsessions.[6] In doing this, he does no more than give a reminder of Sade's due: what is due the man, and his work. It is of very little importance that in reading Sade, *in his own way* practising him, he adds something now and again which is not there. It is right to say that Bataille is not exactly Sade (right and ultimately pointless: certainly he is so only very slightly, even if he is in many ways the closest to him among his contemporaries; just as he would never exactly be Nietzsche, far from it, even if, of twentieth-century French philosophers, he is, if not the one who gets closest to him, then the one who most usefully continues him); thus Bataille is not exactly Sade, but the discovery of him he had made fairly recently[7] assured him forcibly of the reasons he had for living out the experience of his own derangement. It is right to say, in fact one should stress (unless I am completely mistaken), that Bataille, unlike Sade, is not a libertine, but debauched, which distinguishes them profoundly. The eroticism Bataille puts in play soils, spoils and wrecks. By projection, it shares common cause with an obsessional representation of death. It wrecks memory, self-indulgence, vows, the possibility of beauty or salvation, fidelity, education, morality, women, God . . . it's all the same. The libertine adds while the debauched man takes away. The first lives in an economy of accumulation: of pleasure, of possession . . . the second in a spending economy, one of loss, waste and ruin.[8] What Bataille would say about his meditation on the torture of the Hundred Pieces ('this was rightly what I sought, not to enjoy it but to destroy within me what is opposed to that destruction') could also be said about his eroticism. There is nothing in this that could in any way be attributed to Sade. And yet, however far Bataille might be from him, through his debauchery, through his taste for the 'dirty', he is a thousand times closer to him than the hypocrites and cheats who solicit the 'marvellous' and 'poetry' as others solicit God. What Bataille said of Sade is half Bataillean and half Sadean: 'the excessive violation of modesty, positive algolagnia,[9] the violent excretion of the sexual object coinciding with a powerful or tortured ejaculation, the libidinal interest in cadavers, vomiting, defecation . . .'[10] Is this inventory more Sadean or more Bataillean? What matters here is that in no way is it surrealist, that it is made up of words Breton never used nor would have dared to (if he even read them). And so that things are absolutely clear (except that they doubtless never will be, as people have since obligingly insisted on comparing the two men), Bataille, *in thinking through* Sade, no doubt the first in France really to do so, created a concept, a negative and aleatory one like all of the sporadic concepts he ever created: that of *heterology*. This means simply the science of what is *completely other*, so repulsively *other* that one could also call it *scatology* on condition that at the same time we add to what is made dirty (filth) what is saintly: in this case the most precise term would be *agiology*. This concept is not simply a provocation aimed at Breton. We shall see that, in its appearance from *The Solar Anus* and 'The Pineal Eye', the concept would soon be used by Bataille in a political sense (thus demonstrating that reading Sade has private *and* public consequences, something the surrealists carefully avoided admitting). Everything we have so far seen to have fascinated Bataille is found in the concept of agiology: sexual activity (diverted of course from its useful functions), defecation, micturition; death and the worship of corpses; *taboos*, ritual cannibalism, sacrifices, laughter and sobbing; ecstasy and, in a single sacred combination, the attitude before death, shit and the gods; brilliant and lecherous women, ruinous spending . . . All this, which came as much from Bataille himself (from his childhood, as we have seen) as from the bloody eccentricity of the Aztecs, from the young Chinese torture victim as much as from Sade, from the bullfight as much as from the potlatches analysed by Marcel Mauss,[11] from the brothels as much as from the prominent 'shit-stained behinds' of monkeys, here finds a meaning as concerted as it is definitive. Several of the great texts of political sociology to come would have their starting point in this concept which serves to describe the processes of excretion against processes of appropriation throughout the works.[12] Bataille did more than stigmatise Breton. He forged against him the rudiments of a political philosophy to which, in the most paradoxical way, Breton would eventually rally, as we shall see. Once again and in two different ways Bataille was proved right by this tenacity and rage: firstly through the brief political alliance of Breton, and then by the belated and unexpected homage the latter paid him one day in conversation with André Masson, on the eve of war: 'Georges Bataille (he told me in a wonderful gesture of sincerity) is the closest of all of us to Sade.'[13]

The angel and the beast, part 1

Did Bataille ever end his hostility to surrealism? It has to be doubted. For at least ten years (from 1925 to 1935), it was at the heart of most of his statements and was sustained by polemics that were constantly renewed, each time more violently. Their interest is not inconsiderable. After having been an object of study (doubtless as long as it seemed subversive), surrealism is tending to become an object of legend and of the academy. Nevertheless the history of surrealism today is no longer quite the same (perhaps it is more academic; but certainly far less legendary) as the one we can see from from the position that Bataille and Bataille alone occupied, a position which catalogued almost all its poetic, aesthetic, sexual, metaphysical . . . and political aspects.

Surrealism's fault, as he saw it, its 'cowardice', his accusation of its 'senile cunning', was due to the fact that, powerless to admit that the spirit of subversion is justified by nothing but itself, it immediately sought to make use of a *superior* authority, seeking then to create new values. Whether in the mind, in poetry, in the absolute, in the surreal, there is no shortage of abstract authorities, pure of all contingency, able to buttress the revolutionary in his ideal of having done with the world as it is. To its baseness, he responds in the name of what no one can deny is (morally) superior. But Bataille asked: what can be born of this 'redemptive light' suspended above the world in the expectation that its purest representatives will derive from it the spirit of their sovereign subversion? He replies with: 'infantile ethical tendency', 'utopian blindness' and 'Lamartinian bliss'.[1]

With an unequalled lucidity (Bataille was *also* a political thinker, no doubt one of the most difficult because he escaped all common categories, one of the most astonishingly modern because he was disenchanted before so many others), long before everyone rallied to the view that otherworldliness is one of the best means to bestiality,[2]

Bataille denounced the surrealists' stupid belief (which they shared with all idealist revolutionaries) in the radiant and Icarian idea of a *super-eagle*. If revolutions fail, if they come to be the opposite of what they claim to be, simply replacing the authority they oppose with an even more rigid one, it is because this idea is the consequence of a disturbing theoretical breach of trust which admittedly satisfies the ideal but not at all the real. It is a breach of trust that gambles on a humanity that theory is powerless to admit is filth as much, if not more, as it is ideal, and that persists in a cowardly way to refuse to give way entirely to 'radical evil'.[3] He alone knew the evil, the abjection and the filth that no politics could hope to bring to an end. Because he knew what a corpse he had (to be destined to become one is no different: he wrote at this time, 'my own corpse still obsesses me like a dirty trick, obscene and consequently horribly desirable'[4]), because he insisted on the stinking odour he already was, because he knew the irrepressible laughs and sobs by which this corpse and this odour suffocate, he was tormented by no justificatory light and by no God. Did one have to begin with such baseness, 'to speak' from such baseness, in order to articulate sooner than anyone what the destiny of the revolutionary century would be: 'A castrated Icarian revolution' (as they all, sooner or later, are) travestied in 'a shameless imperialism exploiting the revolutionary urge'? Bataille, shamelessly, prophesied it (Bataille as a prophet of misfortune?) and by the same token accused incorrigible simpletons and optimists in advance of having disguised the claims of the most base parts as the claims of the highest parts. In reality, he was saying nothing other than what he had said about the surrealists' use of Sade for indirect ends: they dignified him wrongly. They dignify even the invidious – even Sade, even slaves – without realising that this disguised dignity is daily exposed to the denial of base and servile facts, to the violent resurgence of the unassimilable (the heterogeneous) world, 'befouled, senile, rancid, sordid, lewd, doddering . . .'.[5]

Bataille even includes Nietzsche, and this is a surprise, among the ranks of impenitent Icarians. Nietzsche's impulse to break, he said, did not come from below, but from on high. Admittedly, he did not forget what his meaning of the ground was, any more than he forgot that for him sexual foundations governed superior psychic reactions, or what his laughter was, but still, borne by who knows what deplorable inclinations to elevate everything with a flick of the rudder, these claims again become noble, elevated, even romantic. Like the surrealists,

Nietzsche is for this reason a reactionary thinker and his values, like those of surrealism, are 'rigorously impractical and scandalous'.[6] They all – in this they are not distinct – hoist everything on a poetic high: as evidenced by the significant use they made of the lamentably idealist prefix *Sur* in 'Surhomme' and 'Surréalisme'.

To this idealist representation of the solar and sovereign eagle (imperialism in politics, the idea in metaphysics), to the representation of the supereagle (utopia turned into fascism: a castrated Icarian revolution), Bataille opposed for the first time an image strangely drawn from Marx, less from the revered Marx than from a lesser-known one who wrote: 'In history as in nature, decay is the laboratory of life' – the image of the mole. To the eagle, to the supereagle, Bataille opposes this 'old mole', the very one that made its sky in the swarming, disgusting and decomposed earth of societies, repellant to the delicate nose of utopians who, in the entrails of the earth and of the proletariat, associate 'base' and 'repulsive' images with swarming, decaying, blinding, nights, tombs, caves, and the anus . . . It is in this hole, in this collapse, that human liberty must be safeguarded from all the calls to 'Attention!' compelled by its 'idiotic elevation':

> The earth is base, *the world is world*, human agitation is only vulgar and perhaps not acknowledgeable: this is the shame of Icarian despair. But to the *loss of the head*[7] there is no other reply: a crass sneer, vile grimaces. For it is human agitation, with *all* the vulgarity of needs small and great, with its flagrant disgust for the police who repress it, it is the agitation of *all* men (except for this police and the friends of the police), that alone determines revolutionary mental forms, in opposition to bourgeois mental forms.[8]

'A man is what he lacks'

It is difficult today to know what sort of man Bataille was in 1930; we know roughly what he did, but little about who he was. Certainly it has to be accepted that we lack documentary evidence. Neither Bataille nor any of those close to him have left any decisive testimony on this period. But it is *also* impossible not to take into account what might be intentional about this silence. Bataille eludes us less than is generally assumed, but he eludes us all the same. And there is every reason to believe that what this silence hides corresponds fairly precisely with what those involved did not wish to be said. The image of an *intellectual* Bataille (and only *intellectual*, even if he could be scandalous on occasion), the readily given image of a man tempered by age, as the photographs of him depict him – mature (in most of them), sleek and handsome – seems to verify what those who were then close to him have consented to allow us to know. If he had just been a libertine we would gladly agree to say that he had 'lived his life' as a young man. But his debauchery is a problem, and no doubt is even frightening. Libertinage has a socially admissible sense, but not debauchery (as I have said, libertinage is acquisitive and capitalist; debauchery is ruinous and nihilistic). The Bataille of the post-war years, an *apparently* mellowed man (it is undeniable that he took pains to give this impression), is the man one would like to think he always was: nothing conflictual, nothing abhorrent. This silence could perhaps throw us off the scent had it not been broken (just) by one or two words from a few individuals. Unquestionably, as we have seen, Breton was afraid to allow him any justification; later on, Sartre, too, described him as 'mad'; meanwhile Souvarine and Simone Weil also considered him, respectively, a sexual deviant and a sick man. It is thanks to those who wished to denounce him, and not to those who loved him (though perhaps they pitied rather than loved him, and feared rather than encouraged him), that we can roughly guess at who he was. But it is also thanks to his books, in not inconsiderable measure: autobiographical or not, we can take them *symptomatically* at their word: it has too often been said and accepted that Bataille was a wise librarian, devoted to his work and fantastically productive. With due respect to those reassured by this image, it does not seem to have been true at all, and was even less so before the war.

The question arises here of a character trait that, if it was prevalent above all after 1950, was also no doubt present (to what degree we do not know) before 1940. Bataille very quickly learned to gauge those freedoms he could claim and those he could not. In other words, what freedom was *socially* possible for him. Bataille was not the kind of man ever to wish to make an example of himself. Not that he feigned his nature; but, if he was scandalous (and clearly he was), it was discreetly so. One part of him (the chartist, in particular the former Christian, but most of all his childhood part) knew how to respond skilfully to the social and professional duties imposed on everyone. They never got the better of him; and they never had such hold over him as to catch him unawares or unable to respond. He was no doubt even better able to deal with them than anyone; his unfailing courtesy (which he quickly made into a 'religion';[1] no one was more courteous), his affability which was never merely casual, the extreme attention paid to one and all, his patience and equanimity, not to speak of his seductiveness, the extraordinary innocence of his lovely blue eyes, all of these he learned quickly and ever better to offer to whomsoever expected them of him. Did this make him ambiguous or hypocritical, and a Jesuit, as was sometimes later said? What matters here is not whether or not he was (and I shall return to this), but that it was behind this appearance, on the reverse of this coin, that he arranged a freedom that was all the less constrained because hardly anyone suspected it. Bataille never really concerned himself with what people thought of him, for good or ill: good helped him; ill threatened his advance; rarely is so little romanticism found about someone's façade. If he was tactful, it was in proportion to his tactlessness; if courteous, in proportion to his savagery; if conformist, in proportion to his freedom (it should be made clear that he was *also* tactful, courteous and conformist). And if he was so highly concerned about his respectability[2] – as people have taken pains to point out, whether or not they understood it – it was because ultimately he valued above all else what he knew no one would openly grant him: the experience of a life which would repudiate its morality more in its essence than in its outward forms. He is too often remembered as a delightful and 'tidy' man (his care for sober elegance is described by Leiris, as if this were the only thing that ought to be said about him) for it not to have to be stressed that he was only ostensibly both of these things (and I would admit that in this he was hardly Sadean or Nietzschean, and also that it absolutely cannot be called hypocritical) because he was – perhaps underneath or perhaps elsewhere – barbaric and 'dirty', as he himself liked to say. He acted as a man who knew what horror and bestiality sex involved, as a man who very early on – even in advance – knew that any social behaviour is likely to be irreconcilable with it, in so far as one knows what is due to both, to sex and to society, and how incompatible everyone's demands are; he knew this so well that he stated it explicitly:

> Your sex is the darkest and most bloody part of yourself. Lurking in the washing and in the undergrowth, it is itself a sort of half being or animal, alien to your surface habits. An extreme conflict exists between it and what you show of yourself. Whatever your real violence, you present a civilised and polished aspect to others. Every day you seek to communicate with them, avoiding clashes and reducing each thing to its poor common measure so that everything can harmonise and be ordered.[3]

So much was at stake – a limitless freedom – that Bataille knew it was better to appear to obey the limits observed by all than, sanctioned by those limits, to risk losing it. Admittedly we cannot be sure that this was already so in 1928; but in all likelihood it was beginning to be the case. One must, moreover, gauge how scandalous *Story of the Eye* could have been. What would he have gained by laying claim to it loud and clear, or from being proscribed as Sade was (certainly less seriously, but there is no doubt that the freedom claimed by Sade convinced Bataille of the reasons he might have not to run this risk)? What would others have gained that he himself would not lose? This much at least must be understood: Bataille was never a militant for any erotic liberation.[4] And he never believed that one should overturn any of the limits agreed upon by a society and observed by all (we shall even see that, however paradoxical it may seem, he would have occasion to defend them). So scandalous was *Story of the Eye* in 1928 that he kept it secret. As we have seen, he signed it with the pseudonym Lord Auch (itself a provocation as few others were). No doubt few at the time knew that he was its author. Certainly his friends did, but did his colleagues at the Bibliothèque Nationale; his associates at the highly serious art and archaeology journal *Aréthuse* to which he had been submitting articles since 1927; or his in-laws who gave him a girl in marriage who was not yet of age? (Bataille was married in 1928; no extreme desire for conformity should be read into this: between the wars marriage was almost universally respected, even by the least subservient and most anarchist.)

But to know what his life was during these years one no doubt needs to look at it again in detail, however few the documents and accounts giving us access to it. Georges Bataille joined the Bibliothèque Nationale in 1922, being appointed a trainee librarian on 22 June. Two years later, on 3 July 1924, he was appointed librarian of the Medal Department: a choice promotion for someone so young. He remained there until 18 January 1930, when he was transferred to the Printed Books Department. His professional life does not therefore appear to have been touched by the disorder of his private life; and, unlike many (among them the surrealists, who did not lose the opportunity to use this fact to denounce the peaceful insobriety of a man sequestered in a library rather than the Bastille),[5] he received a salary, a salary which, if we believe Jean Piel (but all testimonies concur), he frittered away in brothels (in which 'he spent a fortune'),[6] when he did not lose it gambling. The transfer from the Medal Department to that of Printed Books nevertheless calls for comment. If his professional life does not seem to have been perceptibly touched by the disorders of his private life, it would nevertheless appear that the administration did not have particular cause to be pleased with him, at least not in the way it would have hoped. If, as I said, *Story of the Eye* does not seem to have caused him any problems (presumably no one knew he was its author), this was not the case with *Documents*. The journal, it is said, created a great fuss right at the heart of the quiet establishment, especially over Bataille's article 'The Big Toe'; such a fuss that Leiris speaks of a veritable 'scandal'. Too many people have suggested today that the decision to move Bataille from the Medals to the Printed Books Department amounted to a reproof for it not to be in all likelihood true, but it does not seem that this was the only reason for it. The quiet librarian, all too complaisantly portrayed here, was also the target of a readers' petition occasioned by his over-frequent late arrivals or absences.[7] It is no secret that Bataille, except right at the beginning, did not possess an irreproachable devotion to his profession.

Of his emotional life between 1922 and 1927, nothing certain is known. But it is not possible to imagine his life as simply debauched and without emotional involvement; Bataille always liked to combine them (no doubt they helped to give each other meaning and intensity). Except for Miss C., the only woman who leaves any trace is the one photographed with him in Nice, at the Baie des Anges. It seems she may have constituted a more lasting relationship than others.[8] Michel Leiris did not remember any of these in particular, but several fleeting ones. The first we really know about was also his future wife. Their meeting would seem to have dated from 1927 (it is unlikely to have been earlier). The young woman was Sylvia Maklès, and she was notably younger than he was: in 1927 she was nineteen and he was thirty. According to Élisabeth Roudinesco, Sylvia Maklès and Georges Bataille met in Raymond Queneau's studio flat in the Square Desnouettes, near the Porte de Versailles, where several writers were meeting along with Adrien Borel (this seems perfectly possible: we recall that at that time Bataille was undergoing analysis with Borel). Laurence Bataille gives a very slightly different version of this first meeting. According to her, they were introduced to each other through the intermediary of Sylvia's older sister Bianca, a former medical student (coincidentally along with Aragon and Breton) and the wife of Théodore Fraenkel; ultimately the two accounts do not really contradict each other.

Sylvia was of Romanian-Jewish descent, and born in France. Apart from Bianca, she had two other sisters: Simone, who would marry Jean Piel, and Rose, who would marry André Masson (two of Bataille's closest and most faithful friends). The marriage of Sylvia and Georges Bataille took place on 20 March 1928 at Courbevoie (as Sylvia was not yet of age, her family's consent was required). The couple had as witnesses Simone Maklès for Sylvia and Michel Leiris for Bataille. So Bataille left 85 rue de Rennes, where he had been living with his mother and brother since 1919, and moved in with his young wife, first at avenue de Ségur in the studio of a painter friend, and then at 74 rue Vauvenargues in the 18th arrondissement. They lived in this flat until the end of 1928. At the start of 1929 they moved to 24 avenue de la Reine in Boulogne-sur-Seine, and they kept this home until the end of 1930, when they went to live in Issy-les-Moulineaux, at 3 rue Claude-Matrat.

The more we know of the life of Bataille the writer in these years, the more his private life eludes us. And it is not the least paradoxical thing about this body of work, which strips things bare like no other, that it has only the minimum, and generally nothing but bad things, to say about his private life. It is a fact that, looking back, there is a complete silence about happy moments, leaving this strange impression – unacceptable to a biographer – of a black and completely accursed life. It would in fact be a mistake to see Bataille only in this light. Leiris insists, and rightly, that Bataille loved life, and loved it so much that he could say *Yes* to it without the slightest reservation, whatever the dramas he was living through (the movement he wanted to found in 1924 is without a doubt closest to what Bataille believed all his life: the only one which fits the morality he never rejected). But it is true that not a single line in his writing, *not one*, alludes to the *meeting* with Sylvia, to his love for this woman, or to whether he was happy or not; not one line lets us picture whether or not this love was touched by the disorder in which Bataille lived. Yet everything leads us to think that Bataille did not really change his life, that he did not stop frequenting nightclubs and brothels, and that he participated in (and perhaps organised) orgies. Did they include her? He made all – or nearly all – of the women he loved his accomplices. It is unlikely that this was not also true of the first of them we know about – all the more unlikely since this was a period in which he most openly lived out his dissolution, sufficiently so (though still not much, as we have seen) for it not to be a secret to those at all close to him.[9] This absence of private life in his work calls for at least two comments. The first is that it would not always be the case: we shall see that at other times whole pages would have a notably autobiographical character, even if it remains impossible to verify how and to what extent. The second is that in this too Bataille can be distinguished from the surrealists (it really does seem that we cannot fail to see them as opposites on every point). Not that he was less ardent than any of them (the debauched Bataille was also emotional; moreover, he would not be the only person to be seduced by the considerable charm of Sylvia Bataille) but, unlike the others, he did not write the slightest poem or text that was anything like an ode to love from which, in some way or another, a scent of the marvellous might emanate; with Bataille no love poetry is possible. The sole explicit allusion he made came considerably later, more than thirty years on: it consisted of saying that *Blue of Noon* bore witness to the crisis experienced at the time of his separation from Sylvia, but without being an account of it (according to Laurence Bataille, there is no doubt that the character of Edith in *Blue of Noon* is in fact Bataille's wife, as that of the 'mother-in-law' is Sylvia's mother[10]). The only literary evocation of this marriage is thus not only retrospective, but also irredeemably negative, nothing but bad, as in general were all those of his private life, those of his parents, his childhood, and also that of his mother in 1930.

In fact on 15 January Marie-Antoinette Bataille died, at her Parisian home. The final allusions Bataille made to his mother – dark if not insulting in tone – go back to the period of the war (1915 to be precise), and to the violent disagreement which kept them apart: should they or should they not return to Rheims to be with the dying man who was husband to one and father to the other? Bataille bluntly says that this idea drove her mad and that they even had to fight to prevent this madness threatening him (if it evokes 1915, this text was written in 1927 or 1928, at the end of *Story of the Eye*, a book it is hardly likely she would know before her death). Of the life they lived in Riom-ès-Montagnes between 1915 and 1919, and the one they lived together in Paris from 1919 to 1928 (it is not without interest that Bataille lived with his mother until he was thirty-one, two years before her death), once more not a word. Yet there is no doubt that he held this woman dear, as plenty of accounts confirm. But the fact remains – and this more than anything is Bataillean – that he only ever spoke ill of her and that, after the long, long silence about her from 1915 to 1930 and after the insult paid to her in 1915, there promptly came (as though nothing worse could be said than this) an outrage, a rending and posthumous outrage that is so present in the work that it can only be capital in its way, even if it is important to relate it here with the strongest reservations. The reservations to note are of at least two kinds: firstly, such an outrage (though certainly this is a clumsy word unless it is taken in the same way I used for *Story of the Eye*, in the sense of a *homage*) was analogous to one Bataille read in Krafft-Ebing's *Psychopathia Sexualis*. Did he take this over in its entirety, in which case it would be a question of a fiction which, as such, would shed light on his œuvre without telling us anything biographical? Or was this reading superimposed in a parasitic or identificatory way onto what Bataille already instinctively knew to be pathological? To tell the truth, we do not know (by its very nature such a moment has no witnesses).

Nevertheless Bataille twice presented this outrage as being real,[11] and on two other occasions he incorporated it into a story, *Blue of Noon*, which there can be no doubt, unlike *Story of the Eye*, is in large part indebted to autobiographical elements (even if, as we shall see, these can only with difficulty be disentangled from fictional events). Moreover, Bataille's necrophilia is constant in this period – as in fact it always remained – so constant that it lends credibility to the claim without, of course, proving it. Such an event, true or not, in fact belongs to the world in which Bataille lived, a world in which desire only bursts forth forcibly, violently – without which it is nothing but a weakness of the flesh – when provoked by the extreme horror of death, the extreme and repugnant 'filthiness' of corpses. Debauchery is a 'mortuary abyss', and the brothel the church in which they are laid bare. The brothel is a church: a morgue. Bataille was not faced by death so frequently for us not reasonably to suppose that he wanted to experience (in a certain way, to see proven) its sexually convulsive nature. The horror he demanded whores should make him feel through his desire would in return be communicated to him by death in the form of the most violent and transgressive desire.

The dead woman – his mother – is on her bed, stretched out between the two candles for her vigil, alone, arms at her sides, and so with her hands not clasped. The narrator (but is it really so unwise to see him as being Bataille? Doubtless not so much unwise as, for the faint-hearted, shocking) is asleep in the room next door (in so far as the scene is real, it took place at 85 rue de Rennes): 'I cried and cried, shouting all the time.' So far this is only natural from a devoted son, as we know Bataille was . . . But, from the bedroom where he was to the one where *she* is (she, meaning his mother, her mortal remains), he advances, barefoot: 'In front of the corpse I kept quivering – I was frightened and aroused. Aroused to the limit.' He takes off his pyjamas, and 'then I – you understand . . .'[12]

Elsewhere, outside any novelistic context, describing the same scene, Louis Trente (pseudonymous author of *Le Petit*) says more baldly: 'I masturbated naked, in the night, before my mother's corpse'.[13] This (if it is real) calls for comment, less to diminish its obscenity than to accompany it with its most extreme reasons: what springs up from transgression is located beyond the scandalous, at the same time as it belongs to it entirely. One may kneel and pray before a corpse, what is more that of a loved one ... The religious world answers with the attitudes conforming with the significance it gives death, however intolerable the latter may be. And thus death takes on the sense of these attitudes. But one can do more than this: more, and worse. The worst would consist purely and simply of reversing the dilemma we find ourselves in (was he speaking of himself or creating a fiction?) and claiming that the fiction is that which presupposes that a God exists who understands the justice which tears are beseeching and the consolation being sought by the kneeling. Of course, the horror of death is real, and so are tears. But what about kneeling, prayers or supplication? In so far as the events recounted four times by Bataille, in noticeably the same way, are accurately described (and according to those close to him, it is quite possible to imagine Bataille doing that at this time), their character does not differ substantially from the sacred character of any other more credible action. Does masturbating in front of the mortal remains of a loved one tear someone apart any less? It is certainly no less of a homage. The homage of a godless man who knows the abyss to which the shrouded body is bound.

Had Bataille wanted us to understand this better by pushing things to the very limit, he would still not have told it differently. Describing the scene, he adds:

> I slept badly and recalled that two years earlier during my mother's absence I abandoned myself to a drawn-out orgy in this room and in this bed which was serving as the support for the corpse. This orgy in the maternal bed took place by chance on the night of my birthday: the obscene postures of my accomplices and my ecstatic movements in the midst of them were interposed between the birth which had given life to me and the dead woman for whom I experienced a desperate love which was expressed on several occasions by terrible absurd sobs. The extreme sensual pleasure of my memories led me into the orgiastic bedroom to masturbate passionately as I looked at the corpse.[14]

This time, there is scarcely a trace of fiction. To the woman who gave him life (in circumstances we have already seen), he now pays the homage of a man who knows what his life is, the most desperate and the most desirable, destined to die in his turn, spilling out life where another who once gave birth to him shed hers.

Marie-Antoinette Bataille, born Tournadre, was sixty-two years old. 'Absolutely withered away', he said, but doubtless he was not forgetting that she had been beautiful. What he does not say is that, sleeping in the room he had just left to join the corpse, his wife was in her turn expecting a child. Laurence Bataille, daughter of Georges and Sylvia Bataille, was born on 10 June 1930, five months after the death of her grandmother, the one person who really knew what Bataille's childhood had been like.[15]

'An obscene and horribly desirable trick'

It seems we must picture Georges Bataille, after *Documents* ceased publication, in a state of the most extreme solitude, and probably also greatly disheartened. Neither the pamphlet *A Corpse* nor *Documents* could delude anyone. Breton was wrong to fear that Bataille would lastingly gather the outcasts of surrealism around him; he was wrong to fear the formation of an alternative or contrary Surrealist Group. Obviously there was not, or not yet, a group around Bataille, and at this time it was probably not his intention to form one. Gathering together the twelve signatories of the libel against Breton was completely circumstantial: they were 'never united by anything other than hostility'.[1] Even *Documents*, which came to an end in January 1931, did not create a lasting ideological group. It was born of contradictory wishes and directed with obstinacy by Bataille in a quite different direction to that envisaged; and he said quite legitimately that these people of wholly different viewpoints came together as a result of circumstances. The solitary figure André Thirion described in 1927–8 was no less so when *Documents* ceased publication – no less so, but differently. He had written a book (*Story of the Eye*) which was fascinating (or disgusting) but in a confidential way. He had edited an important journal (although it never enjoyed the notoriety of *La Révolution surréaliste*). Therefore, as Michel Leiris said, he had, for nearly two years and for the first time, been a 'ringleader'. His singularity, the outlook he had (which at the time he was alone in having), could legitimately have made him a *mentor* able to bring together the maximalists of the philosophical, aesthetic and political ultra-left. If this did not happen, it was because Bataille himself – whenever others might have come together in agreement with him – raised the stakes, pushing provocation further. Even if he complained about being condemned to the 'most dismal isolation', there is little reason to doubt that he was himself responsible for it. Virulent as his articles in *Documents* had been, they were far from equal to the violence and provocation put into play in the 'Open Letters to Friends'.[2] Violence, provocation, rage: 'the dog's rage against so many calm faces who have forgotten what the most wretched contractions of hatred were'.[3] Rage against his own body (amazingly, even when his existence gave the impression of being calm, this rage would never leave him; one year before his death, he would still describe himself as an 'enragé'). It seems that it was at this time that the most violent evocations of death to which he knew he was *also* promised appeared. Bataille continually pondered his death. He lived in a way people rarely live: *with* death. The fascinations born earlier (no doubt in adolescence), and heightened by the bloody sacrifices of the Aztecs and the Chinese torture of the Hundred Pieces, were amplified to the dimensions of a representation brought down on himself and trimmed – or skinned – of all useless metaphysics: 'My own death obsesses me like an obscene and consequently horribly desirable trick.'[4] Death is not only the corpse we will have (who has not directly imagined it?), nor even the one we already have; it is what we *are*. Bataille seems in his way to have made the brutal and beautiful ellipsis of Louis-Ferdinand Céline his own: 'Can't even manage to think the death one is.'[5]

This 'trick', this rage, seems to have caused some of his closest friends to keep their distance. He seems to have been determined not to make the slightest concession that would have drawn him out of his isolation: he expected his friends to join him, not that he should join them. Six years later, he took up the same watchful and distrustful care he had taken in 1925 not to enter surrealism in order to reject (or accept *conditionally*), to provoke and to pronounce himself against all he seemed almost to be in agreement with, even at the price of no one understanding him any longer: 'There are, perhaps, declarations which, for want of anything better, ridiculously need an Attic chorus . . . But one does not address a chorus in order to convince or rally it, and certainly one does not submit to the judgement of fate without revolting, when it condemns the declarant to the saddest isolation.'[6]

An episode from Bataille's life could be placed here, as it is difficult to know where else it should go (no doubt between 1928 and 1932), an episode that remains itself absolutely unknown, testifying quite well to the character of total secrecy of a work that one could only mistakenly see as revelatory. At the time, Georges Bataille was violently in love with a young prostitute, Violette, whom he seems to have wanted at all costs to 'take out'. It seems he saw her so often that the young woman's employers transferred her so she could avoid her overzealous client. In fact Bataille never saw her again. He never said anything about this event (nothing at any rate that might look like autobiography) to which he undoubtedly attached great importance, in any of his books, which might cause one to doubt it happened. On the contrary, we shall find its trace in two (at least two) fictional narratives, which *a priori* are presented as fictional (we shall see that this is not the case for all of them), not without intermediary influences being superimposed, in *Madame Edwarda* and *Sainte*.[7]

III

'Someone able to see clearly'

The year he met Bataille, Boris Souvarine was one of the most fascinating, certainly one of the most highly regarded, of revolutionaries. He was thirty-six in 1931 when he created one of the most remarkable journals to emerge from the extreme left between the wars, *La Critique sociale*. It was not properly speaking a marxist journal. While it was concerned with Marx, Lenin, Trotsky and Stalin, it was in a way that never conformed to a party line. Admittedly, there was the question of the Soviet Union and what fourteen years of the communist regime had made of the revolution but, critical of Lenin as well as Trotsky, increasingly hostile with each passing day to Stalin, *La Critique sociale* even challenged Marx. Boris Souvarine, a communist until 1924 when he was expelled, an 'independent communist' thereafter, as he described himself, opened up with *La Critique sociale* what, retrospectively, can be considered the first left-wing critique of communism: 'There was a need for someone able to see clearly. Rising before the dawn, disenchanted almost as soon as it appeared, Boris Souvarine was thus the person who, before anyone else, realised what was happening.'[1] Would it not leave me open to misunderstanding, I would be tempted to say that through these years Souvarine occupied a position on the margins of the French Communist Party analogous to that of Bataille on the margins of surrealism, a position of critical withdrawal around which the excluded and dissidents rallied . . . Except for this – important – difference: if Bataille was never a surrealist, Souvarine had, if only briefly, been a communist, indeed he was among the first and most influential of them.

Souvarine was born Boris Lifschitz in Kiev on 24 October 1895. The son of an ordinary worker in a firm (the Marchak Studio) of church goldsmiths (chasubles and decorations of icons adorned with gems), he emigrated with his parents and elder brother to Paris in

1898. There, after experiencing relative poverty, Boris's father managed to establish himself as a self-employed craftsman. French rather than Russian was spoken at home. The culture and education Boris Lifschitz received were French: the lay culture and education of a modest environment. It soon led him to sympathise with socialist and anarcho-syndicalist ideas, but he was unaware of marxism, which thus had no part in them. Called up in 1913, he contributed as a soldier to *Populaire*, a socialist journal.[2] It was then that he entered into correspondence with Lenin. At the time, Lenin was only an indistinct reference point. Very few people had even heard of him. Trotsky, Martov and Lozovsky were better known. Before the Russian Revolution, Lenin was only hazily known in France as one pacifist and Tolstoyan militant among many. If Souvarine learned more about him, and more quickly than anyone else, it was due to the correspondence the two men exchanged. He was introduced into Leninism by Lenin himself before the October Revolution had taken place.

Boris Lifschitz's choice of the name of Souvarine as a pseudonym (adopted, it seems, from his first articles) calls for comment (neither he nor his friends ever explained it, at least never in a way to dispel doubt about it). It is interesting that Souvarine was initially the name of a character in Émile Zola's novel *Germinal*, seemingly inspired by the lives of several Russian nihilists. The names of Solovyev, a locksmith who shot at the Tsar in 1879, or Leon Hartmann who tried to blow up the Tsar's train on 1 December of the same year come to mind . . . We know Zola was also interested in the assassins of General Mezentsov on 4 April 1878 and Alexander II on 13 March 1881.[3] By choosing this name, Lifschitz was showing that his initial political leaning was not only anarcho-syndicalist but also very likely terrorist. The most notable things about the character Lifschitz took as a model from Zola are nothing if not ambiguous. This Souvarine has a cowardly heroism and the convictions of a visionary ready for the worst, something that Souvarine (Souvarine-Lifschitz) never was. He was not averse to political violence, nor to blind violence: the portrait Zola gives leaves no room for doubt about his hero: 'His fair girlish face, with its thin nose and little pointed teeth, had taken on a savage expression, reflecting his mystic dreams about the International and bloody visions'.[4] 'His features twisted into a horrible expression, the expression of one of those fanatical religious passions that can exterminate whole nations.'[5] Extermination is what he will bring about by sabotaging the mine where his friends work. So it remains difficult to see what strange fascination this character could exercise over Boris Lifschitz to the point that he would appropriate his name. Nothing we know about him seems able to explain it.

Nothing can do so, even though his first years as a workers' militant could be placed under the sign of 'illegal', if not violent, action.[6] If, in 1917–18, he was the discreet correspondent of Maxim Gorky's *Novoia Jizn*, he spent ten months in prison along with sixteen other members of the federal committee of the workers' union CGT and leaders of the extreme left during 1920–1 for having called for a general strike in May, a strike launched by the powerful federation of railway workers and supported by the dockers, miners, steelworkers and builders. The strike, harshly broken by Alexandre Millerand, was a failure, but Souvarine, from his cell at La Santé, was elected to the managing committee of the PCF (French Communist Party), which he had helped to create by his attitude within the Socialist Party, favourable to the holding of the Third International. When he was released, Souvarine left Paris for Moscow in May 1921: 'My heart tormented with emotion, I was going to get to know the land of the Revolution, but also the land of my birth.'[7] He stayed until January 1925 and became a member of three of the leading bodies of the Comintern: its presidium, its secretariat and its executive committee. Souvarine's influence over the leading bodies of the CPSU was considerable, and it is unlikely that any subsequent representative of the French party has ever had as much. It was significant right up to the moment when the issue of Lenin's successor was raised in 1924; he was the first person to make a stand against the accusations starting to be raised against Trotsky. True, his was a strictly revolutionary point of view: there was no doubt in his mind that to accuse Trotsky unjustly could only harm the Soviet Union in the eyes of the young militants among international workers, for whom he was still a historical figure of the Revolution. But he also defended Trotsky from a moral point of view, which he openly explained:[8]

> If I found arguments in the criticisms you [Zinoviev], Kamenev, Stalin or others have made against Trotsky's ideas, I would not for one moment hesitate to refine my point of view. I have tried to trace your arguments but I cannot. I find personal attacks, appeals (most often incorrect) to the past, more or less arbitrary interpretations of

Trotsky's conceptions. But I do not see that you have refuted the considerations and propositions of Trotsky.[9]

At the Eighth Congress of the Bolshevik Party on 28 May 1924, Souvarine (translated by Lunacharsky) defended Trotsky against the accusation of Menshevism. Again, he described the allegations against him as 'calumnies and falsehoods'. The break was inevitable.

Upon returning to Paris, Souvarine was intransigent and ratified the statements he had made in Moscow in an exemplary way. He published Trotsky's pamphlet *The New Course*, which was banned, as might have been expected. He wrote a preface for it: 'We stand against the already apparent tendency . . . to turn Leninism into a religion and make the work of its founder a gospel.' He then used the *Bulletin communiste* (the only official theoretical organ of the PCF), which he had edited since 1920, to publish letters from the man the new Soviet government was trying to discredit. He was the first person to stand up against the Stalinism that followed Lenin's death, for which he would pay with his expulsion in 1924 and the suppression of the journal he edited.

But Souvarine did not let matters rest there. Alone, using his own resources, he republished the *Bulletin* in 1925 without any further need of the marxism and Leninism of the 'fanatics' and 'devotees' of official communism. He had entered into dissidence and thereafter called himself an independent communist. The *Bulletin* appeared regularly until 1928, irregularly after that, continuing until 1933. No one escaped Souvarine's criticism. Neither Lenin, whose sincerity he did not doubt, but who he described as 'fanatical and narrow-minded'; nor Soviet Russia, which he declared to be neither bourgeois nor proletarian, but bureaucratic (we owe the expression, 'The dictatorship of the secretariat' to him); nor the intellectuals, those 'orthodox people who are satisfied with cultural formulas' and 'ersatz marxism'; nor, of course, Stalin: Souvarine was the first person to denounce him as a tyrant and to foresee that he would be responsible for 'the incompatibility between post-Leninist Bolshevism and marxism' becoming absolute.[10] Against them, the work and life of Marx in themselves constituted a protest. He would appeal to them, return to them, ask that they continue critical reflection, while recognising that they were themselves not beyond criticism either. A responsible marxism requires analysis, using the methods provided by Marx, recognising what was open to correction in Marx, and what had happened since Marx to modify its nature and conclusions.

Such was the attitude adopted by Souvarine between 1925 and 1930, the attitude of a man determined to 'accept nothing except conditionally, to avoid all confusion between a postulate and a relative deduction'.[11] Thus, in 1927, in the commemorative issue of the tenth anniversary of the October Revolution, he pushed his critique further. He denied the appointed representatives of the Revolution the right to take precedence over those for whom it had been made. He claimed that at most they formed only a 'new privileged class', a class whose interests were no longer the same as those of the proletariat: 'There is the Party and there is everyone else.'

Such a phrase, such a disavowal pronounced by the person who had most actively worked for the reconciliation of the French workers' party and the Communist Party of the Soviet Union justified *a posteriori* the excommunicators of 1924, be they 'fanatics' or 'devotees'. This excommunication has wrongly been imputed to Souvarine's Trotskyism: wrongly because, if he was one of the first members of the opposition, he was not a Trotskyist, any more than a good many others at that time were. Souvarine recalls it in one sentence: 'The inept accusation of *Trotskyism* made against whoever Stalin and the Stalinists wanted has never been a definition but an insult.' This accusation, made against Souvarine too, simplified the task of propaganda. If bloodletting there was, better it should have a single name. In fact, Souvarine never chose Trotsky against Stalin, but the truth due to Trotsky against the calumnies emanating from Stalin ('State capitalism is not socialism', he wrote to Trotsky himself in June 1929). It is not even certain that Lenin appeared to him preferable and that he believed he should submit to his action and thought. On the whole, he returned to the origins of revolutionary thought, to Marx in fact, although not without reservations, to Marx and to the analytical and critical means he developed. An intellectual must continue the thought of the social revolution starting from Marx (Souvarine, faithful even in this respect to Marx, did not call himself a 'marxist'), even if the party sycophants are roused against it.

This recollection may appear lengthy. But Souvarine is today so little known it is right to give him the place he is legitimately owed, a place due to him in this account.[12] At the time Bataille met him, his importance and prestige meant that he was one of the most influential and admired intellectuals of the extreme and far left. There is no doubt that his views were important for many people, including Breton and the surrealists, for whom he was a beacon until Breton rallied to Trotsky. Curiously, almost paradoxically, Souvarine was completely engrossed in the importance and gravity of the political stakes and had little sensitivity to aesthetic ones, and even less to ways in which politics and aesthetics could be brought together.

Pierre Pascal, Amédée Dunois, Pierre Kaan, Lucien Laurat, Aimé Patri, Jacques Mesnil, Jean-Jacques Soudeille, Max Eastman, Karl Korsch and Joachim Maurin[13] were among those who collaborated on the *Bulletin communiste* and several of them (principally Lucien Laurat) would also participate in Souvarine's new journal, *La Critique sociale*. They formed what one could call the Souvarine group. Jacques Baron, Raymond Queneau and Michel Leiris, dissidents of surrealism and three of the signatories in 1930 of the pamphlet *A Corpse*, also joined, as did Jean Piel (who would become a close and loyal friend of Bataille), Doctor Dausse (who, it will be recalled, provided Bataille with an introduction to his analyst Adrien Borel) and Jean Bernier, a former member of *Clarté* and an active intellectual of the 1920s and 1930s (it will be recalled that it was principally on his initiative that several attempts were made to bring together the surrealists with the journal *Clarté*). Georges Bataille, therefore, did not join *La Critique sociale* on his own. His friends, without forming what it would be hasty and no doubt false to describe as a 'Bataille group', supported him whenever his collaboration influenced editorial policy in a direction Souvarine could only have approved with the most serious reservations.

Another figure distinguishable among the varied grouping constituted by *La Critique sociale* was Colette Peignot.[14] Admittedly, she appeared only later, and rarely, among the contributors to the journal, under the pseudonym of Claude Araxe,[15] publishing little more than a few notes and reviews of Russian literature. But *La Critique sociale* is intimately linked with her for two reasons: first, because she would finance it thanks to funds she donated to the publisher Marcel Rivière, resulting from a share of an inheritance; second, because she was at the time the companion of Boris Souvarine, with whom she would undertake all of the editorial responsibilities (revision of texts, translations, corrections, layout, dealing with the printer, publisher and readers). It can therefore be assumed that her presence had a (perhaps determining) influence less on the political orientation of the journal (presumably Souvarine alone determined the *political* position of *La Critique sociale*) than on its being open to less immediately political horizons and on its enlargement towards 'heterodox' collaborations. We shall certainly return to discuss Colette Peignot at length. But perhaps it is not without significance to suggest at this point – however different she was then to what she would soon become – that her extreme vitality, the intensity in which she lived each moment, the lack of esteem she had for anything devout or conformist, even her instability which Souvarine complained of, led *La Critique sociale* away from what he, had he been alone, would have liked the journal to be. His lofty standpoint is not an issue. As far as he was concerned, and to say this is neither unlikely nor prejudicial to him, the aesthetic and intellectual stakes (which surrealism and Bataille shared) barely counted compared to the political stakes, about which he was better informed than anyone else. Besides, no one would have dreamed of doubting this lofty standpoint. (It was Souvarine who saw the surrealists in a delegation when they applied to join the party, and wanted his advice. Souvarine sensibly pointed out that, as someone who had been expelled, he was not well placed to give them advice. Yet, the fact that Breton approached him speaks volumes for the political authority he then held.) But, politically isolated (what leverage did *La Critique sociale* have faced with Soviet reality and the PCF? At most, it marked time), constrained to forge alliances at the very margins of his own position, which was itself marginal, Souvarine would – and this was his unexpected merit – offer a choice platform for positions that were never homogeneous and some – those of Bataille as it happens – that were all too heretical. Justice should be done to him, considering his reputation for intolerance which he had himself done much to create: he would never censor these positions. (At most, as a man who knew what it means to forbid something, he took his distance both from Bataille and from *La Critique sociale*.) Did the discreet but active presence of Colette Peignot encourage this? This can be supposed, even if he never really admitted it.

Did he, moreover, ever fully accept Bernier's and Bataille's presence on *La Critique sociale*? It must be stated that, if the journal gave rise to an anomalous political grouping, it also – and this is not so well known – gave rise to an anomalous emotional grouping. In fact Colette Peignot, Souvarine's companion, had earlier – desperately – been

Bernier's (for whom she tried to commit suicide), before becoming that – perhaps suicidally? – of Bataille (for whom she left Souvarine). Did this strange emotional agglomeration have any influence on *La Critique sociale*? It is not very likely. At least it must be recalled that the accounts of those involved (especially Souvarine), when evaluating this, owe as much to distortions due to feelings as to the facts and ideas themselves. When it comes to Bataille, these distortions would be very influential.

The Democratic Communist Circle

Without being its official publication (Souvarine insisted on keeping the two separate), *La Critique sociale* was born from the constitution of a discussion group, run by him, and open to 'comrades who have been excluded from or for whatever reasons have left the Communist Party': the Democratic Communist Circle (the Cercle communiste démocratique was the circle's second name; founded in 1926, it was called the Marx-Lenin Communist Circle until 1930). This circle brought together nearly all of the future collaborators in *La Critique sociale*, plus on occasion a few surrealists: Breton, Éluard, Aragon, Tzara, Péret, Naville, Queneau and Desnos.[1]

On the Circle's existence and activity – about which Souvarine says nothing explicit and which, following the distinction he himself drew, we should beware of purely and simply equating with *La Critique sociale* – practically nothing is known except the eyewitness account of Simone Weil who, while not a member, was nevertheless sufficiently close to it for the question of her participation to be raised several times. This account is curiously enlightening: it highlights the very divergent trends making up the Circle, the opinions confronting each of those in it and, of special interest for us, what Bataille's role was. In particular it highlights what conjectures the revolutionary mind goes through once it abandons its reference to a unifying dogma (in this way the Circle, through the high quality of its participants, formed a formidable theoretical summation of revolutionary thought of strictly marxist obedience).

The question Simone Weil asked is essential (so essential it seems incredible it came from an outsider awaiting a satisfactory reply before she joined the Circle): 'How can people belong to the same revolutionary organisation when they understand revolution in two contradictory senses?' Simone Weil speaks of two senses, not several. This is perfectly clear: there was her, and there was Georges Bataille. What, she effectively asks, do we have in common, and what can we claim to undertake together when, before anything else, 'revolution is for him the triumph of the irrational, for me of the rational; for him a catastrophe, for me a methodical action in which one should try to limit the damage; for him the liberation of instincts, in particular those considered pathological, for me a higher morality?' 'What,' she concludes, 'is there in common?'[2] Evidently Bataille had once again placed himself in a position of close dialogue and action with the members of an organisation whose analyses and aims he did not share. What Breton had more or less reproached him for was this time expressed for the Circle by Simone Weil. Bataille invokes the violent chaos of desires and instincts, but paradoxically expects those with a rational – or *moral* – vision of revolution to ratify it and adopt for themselves the explosion he proclaims. The paradox is all the greater (and all the more 'Bataillean') in that the revolution Bataille proclaims with his demands is not moral at all. In a similar way to Sade, close enough to unite their two approaches and prefigure *Contre-Attaque*, within the Circle Bataille made himself the thinker of permanent insurrection against revolutionary thought (thus Simone Weil, through the intermediary of Bataille, found herself indirectly confronted with a Sadean representation of revolt):

> Insurrection . . . is not at all a *moral* condition; however, it has got to be a Republic's permanent condition. Hence it would be no less absurd than dangerous to require that those who are to insure the perpetual *immoral* subversion of the established order themselves be *moral* beings: for the state of a moral man is one of tranquillity and peace, the state of an *immoral* man is one of perpetual unrest that pushes him to, and identifies him with, the necessary insurrection in which the republican must always keep the government of which he is a member.[3]

True to the spirit of 'open letters', true to himself, once again violently anti-idealist, Bataille willed the worst to happen: catastrophe rather than revolution, disorder rather than order, the free expression of instincts (including 'pathological' ones) rather than their prohibition, the unleashing and spread of forces rather than their rationalisation . . . What is there in common? Simone Weil is insistent: What can they do together? What real content can be given to an action that first of all professes to have such notably divergent theoretical foundations?

The situation was all the more complex in that it seemed unclear who would rally to which position, hers or Bataille's. Simone Weil seemed sure (only seemed, as she says) of the support of Boris Souvarine and Pierre Kaan, presumably along with several of Souvarine's long-time supporters (for example André Dunois). But she was less certain whether anyone would rally to the position Bataille defended: 'Confusion also results', she complained, 'from the fact that Bataille is surrounded by comrades of whom it is not known – doubtless to themselves as well – how far they adopt his point of view.' Once again, Bataille appears as he must actually have been within the composite circle: a man alone, defending a position that alarmed everyone, including those close to him.

To this uncertainty, to this dividing line, which was even clearer than Simone Weil makes it out to be (Bataille's exclusion would have been all that was needed to remove it), was added a second, which divided people along a different parameter: the matter of the Circle's organisation. Some would have liked to turn it into a new party. It seems, according to Weil, that only Souvarine might have been of this opinion (he alone, but then he it was who gave birth to the Circle). Others, even including some of his supporters, remained resolutely against the idea; this was true of Pierre Kaan. In the same way, *a fortiori*, Bataille also opposed it, along with his friends (Weil does not specify her own inclination). Disagreeing on theory and organisation, the Circle also disagreed on action: for some it should not go beyond what it was; in other words, it should remain a peaceable forum for debate, or at the very most a tribune. This was apparently not the opinion of Weil, to whom this restraint seemed rather ridiculous. For her, action required the constitution of militant forces and the preparation for battles outside the law. Can one imagine Bataille agreeing with her? No doubt he would have, as long as they did not discuss the aims of such action in detail.

Simone Weil's x-ray examination is all the more precious (in reality it is the only precise account we have on the scope and limits of Bataille's role in the Circle) in that every point she raises corresponds to confusion knowingly and deliberately maintained by him, from which it irrefutably appears that he played a considerable role in the Circle, one which, it seems, Souvarine never wished to diminish. It was a confusion he did not hesitate to push to the point of absurdity (absurdity being the point beyond which Weil herself no longer understands): if there was someone who insisted that she join the Circle, it was not Souvarine, nor Bernier (whose role is unclear, although from the start Souvarine held him in low esteem), it was not any of Souvarine's supporters, but Bataille himself, in the desire – if this can really be true – to allow those who opposed him a new and choice recruit. It was at his request that she prepared these notes; it is not known whether they were debated within the Circle. The fact remains that she did not join it, even though she contributed important articles to *La Critique sociale*. It would be an omission not to cite the diagnosis she offers in conclusion: 'The Circle is a psychological phenomenon. It is made up of mutual affection, obscure affinities, in particular of repressions and contradictions between and even within its members that have not been brought out into the open.' These contradictions, she adds, even include Souvarine himself, in whom she sees two individuals who are hard to reconcile: a man who is *dated* ('a survivor of wartime and post-war political battles') and another man, this one contemporary. This is a description which might lead one to suspect that a dividing line, this time a sort of internal line, bisected the Circle's founder, Souvarine himself.

In all likelihood the same dissensions, albeit perceptibly weaker, must have been present on the editorial board of *La Critique sociale*. Souvarine (and Colette Peignot) held the reins of *La Critique sociale*. Nothing was published unless he wanted it to be and, if on occasion he expressed some reservations about an article (as was the case for Bataille's 'The Notion of Expenditure'), he did not go so far as to censor it. At most he would signal that an article's opinions were its author's and not the editors'; *at that time*, this was as far as his judgement went. Moreover, whatever regrets he had subsequently, he took pride in having Bataille at his side; thus, writing to Pierre Kaan, he referred to Simone Weil as 'the only interesting recruit since Georges Bataille'.[4]

Although considerable, Bataille's influence was nevertheless not a determining one for *La Critique sociale*'s orientation, and was far from equal to his role on *Documents*, which effectively he controlled. He nevertheless contributed several of his most important pre-war articles to *La Critique sociale*, such as 'The Notion of Expenditure', which Thirion – despite being a surrealist – considered at the time (and did not modify this opinion later) as 'one of the major texts of this century';[5] 'The Problem of the State', which indicates his political position at this time; and 'The Psychological Structure of Fascism'.[6]

The state: heartbreak and misfortune

Of the three articles just cited, 'The Problem of the State' merits our attention first. Certainly, better than any other article written at the time (in 1933) it explains Bataille's political position. And in many ways it effectively confirms Simone Weil's irritated reproaches, namely the extent to which already he was not much of a marxist. (Had he ever been? Had he done any more than selectively borrow from Marx what he could use against idealists?)

The title of the article leaves only a few doubts: the problem is less about revolution than about the state. Not only the bourgeois state, the capitalist state, but all states. From then on, everyone despaired of revolution. What revolution could be expected, what was the point of fighting for revolution, if not to make the disappearance of the state its principal, if not its only, aim? The horror of the police states in Germany and Italy and the 'darkness and chill' cast over all revolution-ary hope by that of Stalin are, he said, the image of a humanity 'in which the cries of revolt have become politically negligible, in which these cries are no longer anything but *heartbreak* and *misfortune*'.[1] Already, as far as Bataille was concerned (and in this he did not differ from Souvarine), nothing more was to be expected of the fraudsters who had made the Russian Revolution the exact contradiction of the principles it invoked; and certainly no more could be expected of the optimists and simpletons who obstinately believed the worst had not already occurred (the worst, the betrayal of the Revolution in the Soviet Union, but also its parody in Germany and Italy). In short, nothing was to be expected of anyone who did not make hatred of the state a motive to carry the heartbreak further and deepen the misfor-tune, nothing was to be expected of anyone who did not desire 'generalised disorientation'.

We see here how an indirect response to Simone Weil takes shape.

Perhaps he counted her not among the idealists but, in all likelihood, among the optimists who persisted in not seeing that the worst had already happened. (However sharp Simone Weil's political judgement, and she was among the first to become disillusioned and independent, Bataille could not fail to consider it stupidly optimistic that she continued to believe in *the* revolution, and continued to believe in it to the point of claiming to oppose it to *his* revolt.) Revolution was no longer possible. There had already been three in the century: Russian, German and Italian. (It is doubtful whether national-socialism and fascism can, without exaggeration, be considered 'revolutions'. Actually Bataille opposed this: 'Fascism is not revolutionary'.) All three had, more violently than anyone could have suspected, reinforced the state and humiliated all those who were subject to it. A revolutionary consciousness would remain so only in spite of it, and would be torn apart by it. Why would a consciousness thus rent apart not prefer catastrophe to an impossible revolution? Therefore Simone Weil was probably right: one of them believed in (revolutionary) heaven, the other did not. Bataille was without doubt no more *disabused* than Souvarine; he had spent as much time as the latter (and in part thanks to him) in understanding the extent to which Stalin was the shame of all revolutionary morality.[2] But whereas Boris Souvarine felt this disenchantment as a man convinced that the proletariat possessed resources capable of re-establishing the revolution on the right course, Bataille, for the same reasons as incurred his banishment from the surrealist circle, essentially because he had undoubtedly never considered the Leninist form of revolution as adequate for the violent illumination he expected from the flames of riots, was anxious to take every possible advantage from such disenchantment: the 'great evening' would be the evening of revenge; the class struggle must mercilessly aim for the detriment of those who had *lost* the proletariat: 'their beautiful phrases will be drowned out by death screams in riots. That is the bloody hope which, each day, is one with the existence of the people . . .'[3]

For Bataille revolutionary violence would no longer – or only indistinctly – be *useful*; it is its own end. And this, with his brief marxist interlude over (Bataille would say that he strove in a 'touching way' to become a communist), is more in conformity with his thought, which has little concern for ends, whether human or divine. This first discussion of utility would call for further consideration in 'The Notion of Expenditure', the second of Bataille's major articles in *La Critique sociale*, and one which was original in every respect. In substance what he argued was that it is an error only to take production into account, and wrong to see society as interested only in production. There is another completely different sort of activity, equally important but neglected by economic analysis, which consists of spending, spending extravagantly and uselessly. Just as much as considering what allows society to satisfy its needs, one must be alert to the fact, as old as the world itself, that it exposes itself intentionally, almost playfully, to considerable shake-ups, violent depressions, sudden destruction and anxiety crises so intense they seem to be orgiastic . . . How to describe them in a word other than as *catastrophic*?

This is not entirely new in his writing. *The Solar Anus* and 'The Use-Value of D.A.F. de Sade', which I have already discussed, had enabled him to express a series of ideas linked to loss, excretion and shame. What is new is that Bataille now dared to give these ideas a *political* meaning. It should be remembered that he had read the anthropologist Marcel Mauss, even if he had not followed his courses, and Alfred Métraux had discussed Mauss with him at length. Mauss therefore encouraged him indirectly. Mauss was also the first person to see how unproductive loss (luxury, mourning rites, wars, cults, games, spectacles, rituals, sacrifices, arts, etc.) mattered to several so-called primitive societies. None of these activities had ends other than in themselves. In addition, all tended more towards destruction than acquisition. It is not enough therefore to claim that they constitute an 'addition' to society, a surplus by which a society will reflect itself in a splendour and a vitality attesting that *all* its needs are satisfied. 'As dreadful as it is', Bataille was not afraid to affirm, 'human poverty has never had a strong enough hold on societies to cause the concern for conservation – which gives production the appearance of an end – to dominate the concern for unproductive expenditure.'[4]

This tendency had been so underestimated that for a long time classical economy claimed that barter governed exchange in primitive society. Marcel Mauss showed that these societies were governed by exchanges of a non-economic character, which obliged individuals or groups of individuals to make *gifts*, not to barter. Mauss was able to analyse these gifts, especially within several Native American tribes, and he borrowed the word from the Chinook[5] to describe them, a word which would be one of the main ones used by Bataille: the *potlatch*.

What is a potlatch? A challenge? An ordeal? Quite simply, it is an indirect battle that is on the whole peaceful. In the course of a potlatch, the chiefs come face to face and are bound to compete in squandering by giving or destroying considerable wealth. The beneficiaries then have no other option but to accept the gift, and are required in their turn to give or destroy a greater quantity, failing which they lose status, prestige and power. What Bataille discovered in discovering Mauss was that the oblative series he had opened up from his own experience had anthropological endorsement. Entire clans and tribes destroyed themselves through extravagance, with *joy*, in order to *obligate* their enemies. This challenge consisted of ostentatiously creating a superior wealth to be destroyed, so placing an obligation on whomsoever accepted it to impoverish themselves in their turn of a still greater wealth ... In any case, a person was rich only in proportion to the power to squander, and powerful only in proportion to the squandering produced. This was a long way from any need for conservation, or concern for the *useful*, a long way from any acquisitive concern: 'wealth appears as an acquisition to the extent that power is acquired by a rich man, but it is entirely directed towards loss in the sense that this power is characterised as power to lose. It is only through loss that glory and honour are linked to wealth.'[6]

In the 1930s, there was nothing comparable. The bourgeoisie more than any other social class was based in private property. If it acquired, it was not to *enjoy* its rank in an ostentatious challenge, as the aristocracy once did, but to consolidate it. If it spent, it was in a sly, threatening and depressing way. As it accumulated, it did so in such shame and fear that it became impossible to conceal 'a sordid face, a face so rapacious and lacking in nobility, so frighteningly small, that all human life ... seems degraded'.[7] We know how much Bataille hated the bourgeoisie. Even if the revolution would be nothing but an evening of revenge on it, in the 'death screams of riots', it would seem desirable to him, whatever Simone Weil might have thought.

No doubt Bataille's strange originality is hard to gauge today. In 1933, marxist analysis prevailed even among the surrealists and those close to them. It had been a decade since Mauss's article on the gift and the potlatch had been published,[8] but no one other than Bataille had thought to use it for analysis of the production processes of the contemporary economy and class struggle.

Modifying it profoundly, Bataille was later to return to the theme of this article, which Souvarine was careful to dissociate from the responsibility of *La Critique sociale* ('In many respects, the author is in contradiction with the general orientation of our thought'), in a book, *La Part maudite*, published in 1949.[9]

'A world of appearances and of old men with their teeth falling out'

'The Notion of Expenditure', published in January 1933, was followed almost immediately by another article we must consider at length, such is its value in helping us to understand how Bataille's thought developed over the space of a few months, and the lasting political position he adopted: 'The Psychological Structure of Fascism'.

'The Notion of Expenditure' ended at the class war. 'The Psychological Structure of Fascism' begins with it. Communism is not the only solution to the class war (in fact it promises the means to effect its abolition); another political and social system of thought that is equally, if quite differently, immediate and effective does so in other ways: fascism. As if to rock the boat once again, Bataille says without frills or fuss: 'In fundamental opposition to socialism, fascism is characterised by the uniting of classes.'[1]

There can be no doubt that in 1933 the really or supposedly positive stake for political thought remained communism (few apart from *La Critique sociale* had begun to voice doubts about it); the negative stake, the one most feared on the left and the extreme left, the one against which people urgently rallied (but as we know this would take a long time to organise, and Bataille still doubted whether it would ever work), was fascism. Yet Bataille was immediately cautious: joining the cause was all very well, but in no way would this be in the name of any supposed morality or idealism. Clearly either would be powerless to think through exactly what fascism *was*, and how best to fight it *effectively*.

To analyse fascism, Bataille took up the two distinctive concepts from 'The Notion of Expenditure', the useful and the useless. But on these two concepts, simple but underused in economics, he overlaid two other complex and inclusive ones: the useful is homogeneous, the useless is heterogeneous. However, these four terms do not constitute two equations: the useful and the useless only have an economic sense (the regulation of exchange), while the homogeneous and the heterogeneous have a psycho-sociological and thus political sense. The fact remains that Bataille was the first and only thinker in France to try and elucidate fascism using a conceptual method based principally on psychoanalysis.

A homogeneous society is a productive society. It is therefore, thanks to money, *commensurable*; a cynical formula could be enough to describe it: 'Everyone . . . is worth what they produce.' In an industrial society, things are not so straightforward that this formula can be applied unproblematically. Bataille is no different from marxism in recognising that the worker – relieved by capitalism of the fruits of his labour – is not the producer; he who instigates social homogeneity controls the means of production. The dispossessed workers are thus not homogeneous with the world whose wealth they create; only the bourgeoisie is. The bourgeois state regulates the play of productive organisation spontaneously, homogenising it spontaneously; in fact it does so with great skill. If it ever has recourse to what Bataille calls 'imperative forms' (authoritarian forms), this only rarely happens, and it is justified in doing so by the appearance of new means of production, and of tensions arising from this development, through the necessity to stifle any temporary unrest from the casualties of production: heterogeneous elements.

Where marxist analysis is profoundly unsatisfactory is in its inability to comprehend how a social, religious or political superstructure is formed. And Bataille, who understood the analogical relationships between high and low, noble and ignoble phenomena, between what he defined as *simultaneously* saintly and defiled, also understood that superstructures arise from the heterogeneous and not the homogeneous. It is hard to define the heterogeneous exactly: only science might do so, but as science itself belongs to the homogeneous world, heterogeneous elements inherently evade its jurisdiction. So only the possibility of an approximation is available. Bataille proposes the one established for better or worse by Durkheim under the heading of the Sacred, to be understood of course in the ethnological sense of the term; we can hazard its inventory (the one Bataille himself gives and which does not differ noticeably from the one he had already proposed in 'The Pineal Eye'). The sacred and the heterogeneous include refuse, excrement, everything with an erotic value (for Bataille the unconscious is heterogeneous), crowds, warrior classes, violent individuals . . . In a way one could say that all social phenomena characterised by violence, madness, immoderation and delirium – phenomena that have in common the fact that they cannot be assimilated – are heterogeneous: '*Heterogeneous* reality is that of a force or shock.'[2]

At this point in his study, Bataille introduces fascism. Democratic politicians represent the flat, homogeneous world. He does not name them, but we can guess at figures like Doumer, Doumergue, Chautemps, Daladier; all democrats who in 1933–4 worked to keep a weakened if not corrupt republican government functioning. Hitler, Mussolini and all of the fascist leaders are completely different from them. They clearly spring from the heterogeneous world; even more frighteningly, they are that very world. For the first time the peaceable but spineless bourgeois world finds itself confronted by a strong, violent world ('they are above men, parties, and even laws'[3]), though we cannot yet tell if Bataille finds these facts seductive or not. For in the end, this can be seductive; or more precisely, it would be if fascism did not immediately identify itself with its transcendence (a unitary, *monarchic* transcendence, bound to a single person *against* all people), if this heterogeneity – from the very beginning – was not revealed as itself unable to integrate the totality of the heterogeneous, low, infamous, servile world to its supreme power. This 'befouled, senile, rank' world which Bataille had already often defended (and which justified Breton in rejecting him) cannot be integrated by fascism any more than by any other political system; on the contrary, and even more violently than for the homogeneous, bourgeois world, it excludes it, on the pretext of its necessary purity. There is no doubt about this in Bataille's eyes: this affirmation of purity, incomparably stronger and more vital in the fascist than in the bourgeois state, is *sadistic*. Fascism integrates only what is noble, and rejects what is not. We can recall Bataille's agiology and what he wanted to bring together within it: it is what is simultaneously defiled and saintly. Fascism is *a fortiori* not this world, a world all the less sacred the more it must be military (at most it can be religious); so little is it sacred and so blatantly is it military, that it alone, apart from the Islamic Caliphate,[4] is capable of putting into practice 'a total oppression'. The few people to come from the degraded part of society, from its servile sections, could be integrated by the armed fascist state not as people but as the flesh of a 'sickening slaughter', entirely metamorphosed into its opposite: patriotic glory (where glory is *also* to be understood in a religious sense). The fascist revolution turns the masses it seduces against themselves. Nothing remains of them except militias subject to the god-master. Far from the latter filtering power right down to the lowest, to the most servile, far from rematerialising materialism as Bataille wished, ensuring that what is low remains low, that what comes from the crowd belongs to the crowd, it seizes hold of what is low and ignominious and lifts it to the heights of what can appear as divine only by falsification. Such a procedure can only be extremely violent. Bataille says this in terms which are still modern today.[5] The fatherland becomes itself divine when, 'superseding every other conceivable consideration, [it] demands not only passion but ecstasy from its participants'.[6] Far from abolishing the state, which Bataille said was the initial problem, fascism shores it up with extravagant foundations: 'nothing human or spiritual exists nor *a fortiori* does it have any existence outside the State.'[7]

A single liberal, bourgeois society finds that two revolutions are concurrently taking shape in opposition to it that are *a priori* hostile to each other: one communist and the other fascist. Were they really concurrent? Certainly in 1933 everyone thought so; all except Bataille, who saw them as homologous. The power communism had to 'stir' the proletariat against a homogeneous world from which it was excluded, and fascism's power to 'dissociate' minor homogeneous elements (bourgeois and petit bourgeois ones) from the very world they made up (even if the number of dissociated elements grows and the force of the proletariat recedes, increasing the chances of a fascist revolution while those of a proletarian revolution decrease), made democratic countries, including France, doubly vulnerable. This double erosion could not have failed to combine forces; we know how, and in what manner, this occurred. Bataille was one of the few people and, unless I am mistaken, one of the very first who did not wish to save the bourgeois state but who did not choose between the two available revolutions either. In his eyes the dilemma consisted less of a choice between communism and fascism than of a choice between 'imperative radical forms' supporting the states and the 'liberatory subversion' of human lives (which would thwart fascism, communism *and* liberalism).

'The Psychological Structure of Fascism' concludes what was central to the article 'The Problem of the State', in which Bataille's political position – an anarchising position – of the years of *La Critique sociale* is stated in the clearest possible way; the socialist state is 'dictatorial';

the fascist state is 'totalitarian'. 'It is therefore necessary to consider things on a new level and to give the already tense struggle against fascism the general meaning of a struggle against the state.'[8] If Bataille continued to consider the revolution, it was no longer with historical reference; worse than this, it was with his back to the wall of the hateful bourgeois state, caught in the searchlights of the two most powerful revolutionary forces of the day.

In applying itself to the analysis of infrastructure, marxism did not see, or did not wish to see, how a social, religious or political superstructure was formed. Not least among the article's claims to originality was that Bataille used the very means of bourgeois thought that had arisen since Marx, those he said must be integrated, to achieve his aim: French sociology (Durkheim and Mauss), German phenomenology and Freudian interpretation. The article's title pointed to this: a superstructure can have a psychological constitution. He was the first person in France (Jacques Chatain makes the opportune comment that he had no equal, at that time, except for a 'German he doesn't know about and who doesn't know about him', Wilhelm Reich, author of *The Mass Psychology of Fascism*[9]) to introduce the effective methods of psychoanalytic analysis into the body of political analysis, methods that, even more remarkably, had been filtered through his own personal experience. These unaccustomed references indicated better than any other both the failings of marxist analysis and the gravity of the fascist threat. It was through not having integrated them at once into their bland recriminations that the idealists had been caught unprepared by the rites at fascism's disposal. Freud could help in the understanding of the *anguish* and *death* by which fascism fascinated. Francis Marmande puts it precisely:

> Behind this multifarious and unstable argument, endlessly sidetracked by its own flight from linearity, there is a novel principle which theory would long ignore: an attempt at a mass psychology which manages to integrate, into a conceptual system one did not imagine was made for the task, a consciousness of potential death and *anguish*, the motor elements of a renewed conception of revolutionary claims.[10]

This is the blinding violence of this article, a premonition that came sooner and clearer than many others, and the last of any importance that Bataille contributed to *La Critique sociale*. Souvarine did not feel himself obliged to dissociate this article from the editors' responsibility, as he had for 'The Notion of Expenditure'. Yet he would have been justified in doing so. Bataille alone continued to think that which had not been thought in his time, even against those who welcomed him as a contributor to their publications.

This 'unthought-of thought' would not have taken much to turn into a book; a 'rigorous' – at least this was how its author announced it – as well as a coherent one (in other words, methodological considerations – French sociology, German phenomenology and psychoanalysis – would have played the parts their interpretative contribution merited, which was not possible within the constraints of the article). The book even had a title: 'Le fascisme en France'.

But the book never appeared, and judging from the outlines found later,[11] there is every reason to doubt that Bataille ever progressed very far with it. This might seem a pity: who else could have presumed to write such a book, even though it would probably have been no more successful than Boris Souvarine's *Stalin*, published in 1935, a book as prophetic as it was premature? It is rather harder to find adequate reasons for the book not being finished. One, of course, is how impossible Bataille found it to see any fully developed 'literary' project through. We do not need to be reminded that, by the age of thirty-seven, he had yet to publish anything under his own name apart from *The Solar Anus* (around ten pages long). 'Le fascisme en France' was the first book we see him wanting to write; but it was not the first project he abandoned, and it was far from the last. It is even a significant feature of his character that for a long time he was only able to resort to concise, dense forms of expression and that, extraordinarily insightful as they were, he then refused to develop them further:

> However I might approach the subject, the feeling I have is an awareness of dispersion, of humiliating confusion. I write a book – and the supposition is, I'll put down ideas in order. To me, delving into particulars while working on a project lessens me. Discursive thought always implies that attention is paid to some single point at the expense of others,[12] pulling us out of ourselves, reducing us to a link in the chain that we are.[13]

Was this arrogance – 'delving into particulars . . . lessens me' – ? Or annoyance? Only insight interested him. No sooner was it stated, and become fodder for interpretation by other people, than he felt the need to turn his attention to other matters, new ones. This was also a sign of his age. For all his thirty-seven years, Bataille persisted in living with all the renewed desire for new experiences and understanding. One has to say that the answer is not only intellectual and psychological. We shall see how Bataille's life in 1934 could scarcely permit such a book being completed.

Bataille's insight is nevertheless most revealing. Does he force this feature or see to it that no one can claim not to have seen it? Fascism 'requires the unreserved submission of each person under pain of unrestrained violence'.[14] Fascist violence is that which is set in motion every day by its 'leader', even if only at the level of a threat. 'Leader' is the word commentators would use; Bataille used another, and it was revealing in other ways: the leader is the 'god-master'. He alone is sovereign. And he alone knows how, in order to be so, to obtain the abdication of all 'personal sovereignty'; he alone understands (since he refrains from being just a master and since he must also be a god) how to make the thoughts and the will of all his own, unreservedly (even if it means pretending that his thought and will is shared by all). Borrowing the Pauline image of the body of Christ from Christian metaphor, Bataille reduces everyone to the level (made fascist) of a part of the great divine patriotic body ruled by the theophanic head of the god-master. It is not enough to hold this monster, the most recent form of the sacred teratology, up to horror or ridicule, one must also understand how he dies and sustains himself. The plundering he does is in proportion to the degeneracy and insanity of the bourgeois world: 'a world of appearances and of old men with their teeth falling out'.[15]

'With a single blow, like an ox
in the abattoir'

The urgency by which Bataille, like others, was seized, an urgency which in all likelihood distracted him from continuing to write his book on fascism in France, became more immediate during the winter of 1933–4. On 8 January 1934, in a chalet in Chamonix, Alexandre Stavisky died in circumstances questionable enough for both the left-wing and right-wing press to be immediately agreed in insinuating that the police had been ordered to make him commit 'suicide'. The 'crime' certainly benefited those who wanted to keep him quiet. But it also benefited those on the extreme right who made anti-parliamentarianism the chorus of their compelling hostility to the republican state.[1] This right wing, as a whole hardly distinguishable from the clerical, nationalist and anti-communist, parliamentarian right, saw it as a perfect opportunity. On 9 January, Action française called them into the streets; or at least its gangsters, the leagues, came out on its behalf: the Jeunesses Patriotes, whose leader was Pierre Taittinger, Lieutenant-Colonel de La Roque's Croix-de-Feu, the Volontaires nationaux (these last two leagues had the benefit of approval of the army), Solidarité française and Francisme, both clearly inspired by Italian fascists. When Chautemps was forced to resign the day after Alexandre Stavisky's death, Daladier succeeded him for a short time ... until the violent riots in front of the Palais Bourbon on 6 February forced him from power as well.[2] Parliament was highly unstable at that time and this aggravated even more the prospect, widely considered imminent, of a fascist take-over of power.

Through these events, the communist left adopted a very ambiguous attitude. It was so poorly represented in the Assembly (just ten elected communists) as to feel no immediate obligation to defend the institution. Moreover, it did not completely eliminate the possibility of being able to take advantage of the crisis of the bourgeois-radical government. It went so far, if we are to believe Thirion, as to infiltrate the 6 February demonstration, adding its cries to those of the fascists: 5,000 workers thus allegedly gave it their proletarian backing.[3] The Communist Party took several days to decide unequivocally the attitude it should adopt and which side to support: that of the left and of a left united for the moment, making alliances as and where it could. The extreme left also called for a union of the two largest workers' parties, the socialists and the communists. Thus the Democratic Communist Circle drew up a tract enjoining the workers' organisations to form a single Front 'now or never', a matter so urgent as to be, in its terminology, 'a question of life or death'. Charles Ronsac has revealed that this tract was written by all its members, both the 'established' ones (Pierre Kaan, Édouard Liénert, Lucien Sablé, etc.) and the 'irregulars' (Simone Weil, Bataille, Bernier, Bénichou, etc.): 'It should be seen that, for all of us, the feeling of immediate peril was stronger than all our aversions and resentments.'[4] The surrealists were not to be outdone: on Breton's initiative, a *Call to the Struggle* was drawn up. The realignment on the left took a long time (proportionate to the importance of the events), and resulted in the unanimous decision to make the struggle against fascism take precedence over disgust for the established powers. The police who, one month earlier, had been accused of shooting to order suddenly revealed that whatever happened it would prove to be mostly republican during the 6 February riots, and in fact constituted an ally in the battle against the leagues which were trying to take advantage of the disorder into which they were all ready to throw France. The peaceful demonstration of 12 February (the police were discreet and there were no significant provocations on either side) attracted a considerable number of demonstrators and all the left-wing parties joined in together.

Bataille's position on these events is barely distinguishable from that of the far left. He did not hide his hatred for bourgeois liberalism, as his articles in *Documents* and *La Critique sociale* left not the slightest doubt. Equally, he did not hide (remember with what dark enjoyment he evoked 'general disorientation' and the 'death screams in riots') his fascination for violence degenerating into disaster. During these days of agitation, he kept, as he rarely did, a brief but detailed diary covering the days from 11 to 13 February 1934, a diary of the events themselves, admittedly, but also of his participation in them.[5] It was in fact a bit more than a diary, analysis being superimposed on the account of the events as if these notes could in one way or another usefully become part of the book he had begun to write, 'Le fascisme en France'. As his first observation, Bataille said he did not believe the necessary break between the right in government and the fascist-inspired agitation had actually taken place. The fascists could count on, if not the support, at least the indulgence of the elected republicans. There was no clear division between on one side a liberal and republican right and on the other an extreme right that was seditious and fascist inclined. The second observation was that reason dictates that the 12 February demonstration should not degenerate. By doing so, it would serve the purposes of those it intended to denounce. In other words, for the fascist-inclined leagues violence would constitute a provocation to raise the stakes. The third observation, unfortunately, responded to the two others and rendered them vain beforehand. In any case, the processes of propagation of fascism had begun and nothing allowed any hope that it could henceforth be contained . . . Bataille found the reasons for such pessimism in the foreign situation. It was abroad that fascism had started, and it was from abroad that, by an inevitable effect of contagion, one was justified in fearing that it would reach France. As André Thirion said bitterly, very few in France, the surrealists included, had realised the gravity of the fact that Hitler had come to power in Germany, and what threatening prospects were revealed by the collapse of the German workers' party, the most powerful and best organised of all workers' parties.[6] Simone Weil considered this when she said forcefully: 'it is useless and dishonours us if we close our eyes. For the second time in less than twenty years, the best organised, most powerful and most advanced proletariat of the world, that of Germany, has capitulated without resistance . . . The significance of this collapse goes far beyond German frontiers.' Georges Bataille also expressed (and one can imagine that his agreement with Simone Weil was a result of their numerous conversations during 1934), with his habitual cheerful brutality, the importance of the collapse of the powerful Austrian workers' movement: 'struck down with a single blow like an ox in the abattoir'. There could be no better evaluation or a greater insight into the risks that could result than this: '30 January 1933 is certainly one of the most sinister dates of our time.'[7] Pacifism, clearly dominant on the left (we shall see that, clear-headed as she was, Simone Weil was among the most ardent pacifists, and in this respect she was clearly distinguished from Bataille and distanced from the armed militias whose constitution in 1933 she asked the Democratic Communist Circle to support), paved the way for an archaic revolutionary contagion in which Bataille saw the crushing of the socialist uprising of Vienna as a supplementary and decisive phase. He noted in his diary, on 13 February 1934, that is the day after the demonstration of the French left in the Vincennes esplanade: 'Writ large, without the slightest doubt, in this catastrophic news is: *Nazi Austria*. On all sides, in a world in which it will soon be impossible to breathe, the fascist grip will tighten.'[8] It was fresh from his thinking about the nature of fascism (and it matters little on the whole whether or not it was completed) that Bataille spoke out, in a tone of urgency and in the most trenchant way, about the events of January and February 1934. There is no doubt that he was one of the very few to be neither foolish nor confident enough to fail to see clearly how important these events were and towards what horror they were leading.

It was in this turmoil that the colourful and completely ineffective (according to Bataille) demonstration took place in Vincennes on 12 February. Although he was not well (rheumatism had confined him to bed since the beginning of the year), Bataille took part along with Roland Tual and Michel Leiris. He met several members of what he called his 'organisation' (in all likelihood, the Democratic Communist Circle[9]). The dominant impression for Bataille – which was not shared by all his friends like Queneau, Morise, Piel, Simone Kahn – was one of failure. Admittedly, the demonstration could for a moment seem to him grandiose (at the very least it was impressive), but at no moment did it seem comparable with what it claimed to oppose. It is apparent that for him the predominant impression was that the European workers' movement was headed for an impasse. He was not far from believing that they were all witnessing its last gasp. The immediate future would prove him wrong: the combined gathering of 12 February eventually gave birth to the Popular Front. The longer term proved him right: the coming to power of Hitler and the 'Nazification' of Austria were already more important than any possible popular fronts. The defeat of the European workers' movement in fact predated its more extensive achievements. The latter did not know, and no doubt this is the principal failure Bataille saw in them, how to pose the question he considered essential: that of the state – the state in its more intensified form, which is the fascist state.

History and its ends; the end of history

He is neither the best known of philosophers – he deliberately culti-
vated his own obscurity – nor the least extraordinary. His place cannot
be compared to any other, and no one ever challenged him for it,
perhaps ultimately through not knowing *how*, or even if, he was a
philosopher at all.

Yet philosopher he was, in the most rigorous if not the most
conventional way, and it was as a philosopher that, in a little hall in
the École des hautes études, from a symbolic rostrum, he *spoke* over
the course of several years to some of his closest friends. He would do
this for six years, every Monday at half past five. His name was
Alexandre Kojève, born Kojenikov in Moscow in 1902. This man, who
was the same age as his audience (in fact younger than some of them,
since in 1933 he was thirty-one while Bataille, for example, was thirty-
six), *read*, in a perfect French that, according to his listeners, was
unlike any other (a French with a half Slavic and half Burgundian
accent), *read*, translated and gave a commentary, a commentary 'on
the hoof', improvised, without notes, allowing itself to be discovered,
even as the text discovered itself simultaneously, speaking as though it
was speaking to itself, revealing a truth that was as fortuitous as it was
unexpected, that until then most had refused to accept, Alexandre
Kojève read, translated and gave a commentary on Hegel's *Phenomenology of Spirit*. This reading ended with the outbreak of war, in 1939,
yet without being interrupted by it: chance had it that the declaration
of war coincided with the completion of a reading that gravely pronounced that history was finished.

This reading in the form of seminars was attended by Jacques Lacan
(did not the form of his own seminars, as well as their commentary
and some of their concepts too, owe much to it?), Raymond Queneau
(it is thanks to the notes he took that this oral teaching has not entirely

been lost[1]), Raymond Aron, who would retain an edgy admiration for him all his life (edgy because Kojève defined himself as a Stalinist), Roger Caillois for whom he was a master as, he said, he was for his whole generation, Maurice Merleau-Ponty, Eric Weil, sometimes André Breton . . . and, of course, Georges Bataille. Perhaps Sartre was the only person one might have expected to find there who was missing. There is no doubt that some of the most significant works of the post-war period had this origin in common.[2]

Born in 1902 into a comfortably off Moscow family, Kojenikov decided to leave the Soviet Union in 1920, not because he disapproved of the October Revolution (on the contrary, he was and continued to be a declared communist until the war) but because his class origins barred him from access to the university. Moving to Germany, he enrolled at Heidelberg University, choosing Karl Jaspers' course rather than that of Edmund Husserl, and taught himself Sanskrit, Tibetan and Chinese (Bataille was learning the latter two in France at the same time) as a result discovering Buddhism, towards which his own research into the nature of wisdom had led him before he eventually discovered pre-Socratic Greece. He also began, though without success, to read Hegel: 'I read the *Phenomenology of Spirit* four times, in full. I pursued it doggedly. I couldn't understand a word.'[3] After leaving Heidelberg, he reached Paris where he set up home in 1928 (taking French nationality and the name Kojève). In 1932–3 he attended the class on Nicolas de Cues ('Learnèd ignorance and the coinciding of contradictions') led by Alexandre Koyré, who was to become his friend, and in 1933–4 those on 'The religious philosophy of Hegel's early writings', also led by Koyré.[4] Alexandre Kojève liked neither the institution of the university, nor the publications. But, at Koyré's request, he agreed to take over his class on Hegel: 'I read the *Phenomenology of Spirit* again, and when I reached chapter four I understood that it was Napoleon. I started my class. I didn't prepare anything, I read and gave a commentary, but to me everything Hegel said seemed luminous.' What had become luminous for him was that for Hegel after Napoleon history was over:

> Hegel said so. I just explained that Hegel said so and nobody wants to admit it. . . . Nobody takes it in. . . . Hegel had simply got it wrong by a hundred and fifty years. The end of history was not Napoleon, it was Stalin, and I would have the task of announcing this. . . . Then came the war and I understood. No, Hegel was not

wrong, he had indeed given the correct date for the end of history: 1806.[5]

Georges Bataille attended the seminar assiduously. The reading he had made of Hegel so far, one partly derived from Émile Bréhier (in his *Histoire de la philosophie allemande*), Gurvitch and Nicolaï Hartmann (reading Hartmann via Gurvitch), was no doubt a hasty one (he did not read *Phänomenologie des Geistes* until 1934, under Kojève's guidance; until then he had read at most no more than *The Philosophy of History*, *Philosophy of the Mind* and the *Logic*,[6] an approach by turns marxist, through the intermediary of Benedetto Croce, or frankly hostile (he called Hegel a 'valet of German nationalism'[7]). It was thus Kojève who encouraged him towards a true discovery of Hegel: an overwhelming discovery, as overwhelming and staggering, to all intents, as that of Nietzsche had been. Bataille would say that he came away from Alexandre Kojève's Monday readings 'bursting, crushed, killed twice over: suffocated and transfixed'.

'No one more than him understood in depth the possibilities of intelligence (no doctrine is comparable to his – it is the summit of positive intelligence).'[8] There is little doubt that for the rest of his life Bataille regarded Hegel as the finally fulfilled possibility of being God, the God of an impossible positive theology. In him, knowledge would be made complete in a single whole, so nothing escaped it, completely formed, complete in its occurrence (revealed) like the occurrence (the revelation) of evident truths; Hegel seemed to him to be the evident truth, but one which was 'hard to tolerate'.[9]

Was it completely formed and complete in its occurrence? It was indeed. Such a knowledge, so absolute (Bataille would say this later, but it can be mentioned now without anticipating too much), is no different from definitive non-knowledge. Admittedly, beyond such a knowledge lies not the unknown but the unknowable: nothing within what I know will ever correspond to the knowledge *I might have*. This unanswerable issue represents the most profound rending. In old age, Hegel reached these profound depths (and no doubt he said *yes* to them without worrying any more whether it had an unknowable sense beyond his knowledge); in old age, he took on that air of an 'old bestower of blessings' for which Bataille reproached him. A bestower of blessings (remember that this is also how Bataille described Breton) is a man who has run away. No doubt as a young man, Hegel came into contact with the extreme. But if he elaborated his system it was to 'escape', because he 'thought he was going mad'. What interested Bataille from beginning to end in the reading he made of Hegel (and this reading would last his whole life) was how such a system, because it is perfect, because more than any other it exhausts mutual understanding and discursivity, reveals its own ruin, its 'setting in motion of madness', in non-knowing. Hegel's positive theology is impossible because it can only include God if he is mad; and only someone who would manage to perfect the stupefying Hegelian evidence (in making the leap Hegel never made) would know this: the leap of laughter, ecstasy and madness. Bataille would never alter this opinion, and it is strange indeed that his lasting friendship with Alexandre Kojève directed the latter in a direction that came closer every year to non-knowledge, one Kojève himself would call *silence*.[10] And, a year before his death, Bataille told Alexandre Kojève how much still remained to be said about Hegel (and no doubt these are the last words Bataille wrote about him): 'It is a question of situating at the very basis (or the end) of Hegelian thought an equivalence with madness. I could not really say exactly what this consists of – or rather what it will consist of – until I have written it. But this sort of outcome seems to me to be implied in the principle, if not of Hegelianism, then of its object.'[11]

The animal-headed journal: *Minotaure*

Strictly speaking, *Minotaure* does not concern Bataille. He was not involved in it, except distantly; it was something he did not fully participate in (he was excluded and excluded himself from it) but cannot be fully dissociated from. *Minotaure* was a journal. Ultimately, it was a surrealist journal, the most beautiful, if not the most emblematic (for the question remains as to what the 'surrealism' of *Minotaure* was: if the surrealists profoundly influenced it, it was not completely or not only surrealist[1]).

Having been forced to abandon *Documents* (in January 1931), Bataille was the first person Albert Skira – who was to be its publisher – approached to collaborate on his project. According to Skira, Bataille spoke to Pierre Reverdy, who spoke to Breton and Éluard, which was how 'my journal became surrealist'.[2] Skira's idea, shared by his associate Tériade,[3] was for a luxurious art journal (and as we shall see, several surrealists viewed this elegance as a betrayal), that would be both contemporary (cataloguing and sustaining creation) and provocative ('Contrary to all retrograde conceptions').

Two recent models still prevailed as far as provocation was concerned: *Le Surréalisme au service de la révolution* (although, for Skira and Tériade, there was no question of supporting or continuing its political violence) and *Documents*. From these two journals, they had envisaged making one, even if this meant disregarding what the two had so virulently disagreed over (but disregarding it corresponded equally well to their will to preserve only the artistic, at the expense of the 'ideological', character of the two journals). It was Bataille, then, to whom Skira first spoke. And it was in the direction of *Documents* that Tériade was also at first inclined. Their idea therefore seems to have been to bring together under the same rubric surrealists and surrealist dissidents, privileging the latter, however, at least privileging

Documents, which they saw as a safety-wall against the orthodox surrealism of *Surréalisme ASDLR*.

The choice of title (*Minotaure*) would seem to confirm without any possible equivocation this initial and, on the whole, assumed ascendancy. Whether due to Bataille and Masson, as Masson asserted (without remembering which of them, or how it happened), or to Roger Vitrac,[4] the fact is that the Minotaur was connected to what *interested* both Bataille and Masson (since 1924 both had had a liking for the myths and tragedies of Greece) and had only a distant link, if any at all, with what surrealism had up till then been interested in exploring. On the contrary, to plunge the iron a little deeper into the surrealist soul and, as if to divest Breton of the oldest and most marked of his aversions, the figure of the Minotaur is emblematically Nietzschean. By rights, labyrinthine 'thought' and 'knowledge' was Nietzschean, as was this definition (also Bataillean and anything but surrealist) Nietzsche gave of it: 'An entrance but no exit.'

André Masson retained a more polemical interpretation of the origins of *Minotaure*: for him there was no doubt that, responding to Skira's first proposition, the journal was projected as being reserved only for the 'dissidents of surrealism, to the exclusion of those who remained true to Breton',[5] and it was only due to Tériade's lack of resolve and pressure by the surrealists (and Picasso) that the balance was reversed and the dissidents were forced out.[6]

It is more likely (Skira's interests suggest it) that an agreement between the two parties was sought briefly before being deemed unrealisable. The disagreement would then have aided Breton and his friends. This likelihood is given credence by a letter from Paul Éluard to Valentine Hugo: 'I don't know about the magazine journal Schira [*sic*] has asked Breton to run for him. It seems impossible to me for us to collaborate with such repulsive elements as Bataille, who compares André to Cocteau and, praising *Voyage au bout de la nuit*, says that man lives with his own death. Mystical vomit.' A few days later, however, Éluard, notwithstanding the repulsion he felt for Bataille, seemed prepared to accept the idea of such agreement: 'If, however, he [Bataille] would take the first step towards a public reconciliation, everything might be arranged. I hope it will be.'[7]

We do not know whether Bataille did anything to facilitate such a reconciliation. Besides, it is remarkable that he never spoke in a way that reveals that he might have been involved in this project, less still that he could have had anything to do with editing it, even later when the dispute that had opposed him to Breton and surrealism had lost its intensity. The only mention he made of *Minotaure* was in a note published in *La Critique sociale* reviewing the first two issues, and it is indecisive, if not uncertain. Admittedly, if he mocks 'the fact that the word *dialectic* is to be found almost all the way through' without indicating anything but 'a confused good will', this time he did not attack Breton (but perhaps because Breton discussed Picasso in it), and even indirectly praised him for publishing Jacques Lacan ('the only article contributing a new element') and Maurice Heine (for unpublished work by Sade).[8] This was a long way from the open violence of the earlier clashes.

The fact is that *Minotaure*, without immediately becoming a journal over which the surrealists took complete control, welcomed the former dissidents only from time to time (Bataille for just one text, and only in issue 8) and otherwise excluded them altogether.[9]

Yet Bataille's shadow looms over *Minotaure*. In fact, he not only (with Masson) gave a title, and by that very fact, a theme, to a journal he did not, as it were, collaborate in, he not only imposed a motif for its painters, he even, in an artful way, put his mark on surrealism, *inspired* it.

Documents, as I said, was the abscess of surrealism that burst each month, what surrealism dared not be, or what its violence would have been had it not been caught *in extremis* by Breton's obsessive will to blend it with the best, that is the highest, reasons. The partiality *Documents* exhibited for what is *base*, for what is so for no other reason than this *baseness*, for no possible sublimation or dialectical reversal ('When the word *materialism* is used, it is time to designate the direct interpretation, *excluding all idealism*'[10]), this partiality for the night and its monsters it revealed to the point of provocation, insidiously penetrated *Minotaure* (but under such auspices, could it have been otherwise?), penetrated it to the point of fascination: 'These poets and artists ... turned towards the night, sometimes towards crime, as if in search of an exorcism, but without escaping an anguished fascination.'[11] Anguished fascination: the very thing Breton reproached Bataille with delighting in!

Even the 'method' of *Documents* (and of Bataille since 'L'Amérique disparue') took hold of *Minotaure*. This is what Jean Jamin suggested: with issue 2 (devoted to the Dakar–Djibouti expedition), 'the staff of

Documents had attained one of their goals. The works, the objects of others, whose symbolic effectiveness ethnology had established by their exegesis, contributed positively to challenging the real and the rational.'[12] Even Breton himself, giving way in his turn to this strange contagion and seized with a ventriloquism rare in his work, significantly borrowed Bataille's tone to speak . . . about evil: 'The problem of evil merits being raised only to the extent that we have not freed ourselves from the idea of the transcendence of some good which could dictate mankind's duties. Until we have, the "exalted" representation of innate evil will retain the greatest revolutionary value.'[13] As if yielding to the Greek night and its chthonian monsters, Breton after the event approved the reading of Sade that Bataille had made against him.

Recent surrealists also recognise this strange phagocyte process, even at the price of taking pride rather simplistically that in the end 'poetry triumphed': 'It was nonetheless easy to see the influence of Bataille and *Documents* in *Minotaure*, particularly in a marked bent for the horrible and also in a semblance of scientific analysis applied in a "frenzied style"' (José Pierre). Cited as other examples of this hypothesis of 'frenzy' clad in scientific garb are Roger Caillois (on the praying mantis), Maurice Heine ('A look at anthropoclassical hell' and 'Martyrs in copper-plate engravings'), Pierre Mabille ('On the enucleation of Victor Brauner') and others: 'It would seem, in short, that the example of Georges Bataille had been followed only better to do without him.'[14]

This was simplistic because the terms in which this apostle rejoices that surrealism had, in the end, triumphed over the oblique influence of Bataille and *Documents* clumsily reproduce the very ones Bataille had always opposed to Breton and, in spite of themselves, even vindicate the attacks Bataille always made against surrealism: issue 7 'above all from a glance at the pages of this number, *Documents* as a model had been thrown away, forgotten, superseded, obsolete and commonplace. *Minotaure* is poetry.'[15] 'Obsolete and commonplace' simply puts a pejorative – at least the intention was pejorative – slant on the rematerialisation of the materialism applied by *Documents* against the surrealist 'treasure islands of poetry', that in eliminating both Bataille and his shadow from it, *Minotaure* made a fresh triumph. A triumph Bataille ceaselessly tried to prevent (the strange thing, in *Minotaure*, is not that he did not absolutely prevent it, but that he prevented it for so long): 'Aesthetics and literature (literary dishonesty) depress me . . . So I'm snubbing vague, idealistic, and elevated views and seeking a humdrum reality – humiliating truths.'[16]

Breton and his friends were finally able to cast off this shadow that Bataille had from afar introduced into *Minotaure* like an insidious suspicion bearing on the very principle of surrealism. However, for a long time Breton had to accommodate himself to this strange and undesirable alliance which no exclusion could this time remedy. This required more patience than he had until then displayed, a patience all the greater in that, beautiful as this journal was, it was no less *only* beautiful. In other words, Breton most likely would have wished at that moment, precisely at that moment (from 1933 to 1939!), to have had a less luxurious, less bourgeois journal at his disposal, one that would not have restrained the 'commitment' the rise of the fascist danger called for. Proof of this could be seen in the fact (and this is not the least odd thing about this strange exchange of shadows that was *Minotaure*) that, difficult as Breton found it to get rid of the contamination of his own lands by Bataille, it was nevertheless Bataille whom he joined to respond to what *Minotaure* had rejected: commitment to anti-fascism.

'The saint of the abyss'[1]

If what Bataille alone tells us can be believed, he and Colette Peignot probably met for the first time in 1931 (even he was not sure). It was a brief encounter: from one table to another in the Brasserie Lipp where they were each dining with someone else (Bataille with his wife, Colette with Souvarine, with whom she was then living). He confesses to having been struck by her beauty, although he said later her beauty was only apparent to those with eyes to see it. He was also struck by the complete transparency he immediately sensed would be established between them.

But according to him, they saw each other again only seldom if at all before 1934 when, in January and February to be precise, while he was confined to bed (he was suffering from rheumatism), Colette apparently twice came to visit him at his home in Issy-les-Moulineaux. This is not how Souvarine remembered it; he said quite plausibly that Bataille frequently met Colette Peignot, as well as Simone Weil, at his home between 1931 and 1934, in other words during the life-span of *La Critique sociale*. This hypothesis is all the more credible in that it is hard to imagine how, since all four collaborated on the same journal, they would not have met each other repeatedly, even regularly, however distinct Colette Peignot's involvement in editing *La Critique sociale* was and however minimal (?) her participation in the Democratic Communist Circle may have been.

In May 1934 (their relationship does not seem to have developed significantly between February and May), they spent a weekend together with Boris Souvarine and Sylvia Bataille. It seems their initial affair dated from this occasion. Certainly their more frequent meetings date from it ('I think we were most often alone together'),[2] though they did not become lovers openly until 3 July 1934, on the eve of Colette's departure with Souvarine for the Austrian Tyrol.

Of course, they wrote to each other . . . until unexpectedly, with a change of plan (he was to stay in Font-Romeu with his daughter), Bataille joined her. Did he do so alone, or did his wife accompany him? Only one thing is certain: Bataille was in Innsbruck on 20 July 1934. It is not clear whether this stay was – and was only – secret, or whether Souvarine knew about it in one way or another. We cannot settle unreservedly for either of the two versions we have available, although Bataille's, which was written at the time, has much more of a ring of truth to it than Souvarine's, which was written fifty years later.[3] From Innsbruck, it would seem, Bataille followed one step behind Colette Peignot's itinerary, meeting up with her in town after town: Bolzano, Mezzocorona, Andalo . . . until 25 July, the day she abandoned Souvarine to stay with Bataille in the town of Trento. This is about all it is possible to know about this trip (and does not dispel much uncertainty), which he ended by returning to Paris alone, via Zurich on 6 August. (It was very rare for Bataille to keep a diary. He did so in 1934 from June to November and in 1935, but these notebooks are still hard to decipher.)

Little should be deduced from their first exchange of letters (thus before their reunion in Austria) other than information on the initial state of their relationship. But it is significant all the same: the letters clearly state who Colette was at that time, and what 'demands' were immediately placed upon her (we only have her letters from this correspondence, and not Bataille's).[4] She protects herself in advance from the anguish this new love is within her with an even greater anguish: 'The idea of death when one follows it to the end, to the point of putrefaction has always relieved me, and that day more than ever.'[5] As though death – death meaning right up to putrefaction – had to be understood as the first gauge of this love, a gauge that was paradoxically a deliverance . . . This is far from some pious wish. To this gauge, Colette Peignot added a coincidence, in the sense that Bataille himself gave the word, a coincidence that is, moreover, Bataillean (the eye) when she wrote to him: 'you were like the eye that followed I don't know anymore who in a "poem".'[6] Was this an act of chance, or did she know that she had caused a sheaf of significations to converge on her reader which, we now know, he was obsessed with? (In all probability she was acting unconsciously here: 'Coincidences' formed the epilogue to *Story of the Eye*, a book Souvarine, concerned for her mental health, prevented her from reading.) It is understandable, in so far as all this arose without anything prearranged or explicit having thus far happened between them, that they responded to it unreservedly: less as to what might seem to be the result of providence (this word always made Bataille laugh out loud) than as to a 'trick' of what he would soon call *fortune*.

Once these 'coincidences' emerged, Colette Peignot gave them a meaning, at least one she perceived as being at stake for her: reconciliation with herself. This calls for comment: she is unlikely not to have known Bataille's reputation, and it is unlikely Boris Souvarine or Simone Weil kept their opinions about him (he was a sexual deviant for the former, and a sick man for the latter) to themselves.[7] Did she wish to believe (like Xénie, one of the characters in *Blue of Noon*) that only those who are profoundly unhappy become debauched and 'deviant' (a self-punishing breakdown in the clinical version; or a penitent breakdown in the moral version), and thus logically that less unhappiness would mean less of a breakdown and a new love would mean a complete cure (the redemptive love version)? In any event it seems not unlikely that she might have believed in the possibility, which for her was the promise of this new love, that Bataille *too* might change, since this was what she sought for herself, given that reconciliation was what she was putting at stake. She said so unwaveringly: if she herself had been debauched before, had been a deviant, it was through despair; thus if she had to be so again, it would in no way be through predilection (although, as we have seen, such was Bataille's predilection), but in response to the despair to which she had once again been driven: for her nothing could be repugnant which was not *also, in advance*, beyond hope. It was this young woman's rare strength that she could situate a man like Bataille at the foot of such an intransigent truth: 'even if I were to say or write something that would ruin me in your eyes forever, it would have to be.'[8] No one was as 'uncompromising' and as 'pure' as her, Bataille would later write. No one had more strength, the 'fury' of the most scrupulous truth. Yet it was not impossible that she and Bataille had different things in mind, or that what made this strength uncommon became, in order to live with him, if not a weakness then at least a vulnerability. However 'uncompromising' and 'pure' she was, the fury she put into everything (for instance into wanting to be able to know what her despair – or her powerlessness – hid from her) defined the limits of this love (at the same time as it was its limitless freedom). Whatever goals she ever reached – alone or with Bataille – another, further away, higher up, would make what she reached vain and disappointing. This restless desire, this unquenchable thirst to desire what was only desirable for being out of reach, weighed heavily over her (and over them both) with the weight of the absolute. But there is nothing to suggest Bataille ever felt the desire for an impossible, absolute goal – quite the reverse. There is no doubt, above all at this time, that he was totally hostile to any goal: the impossible for him was like something ensuring that nothing had a goal. He was totally hostile to what was idealistic about such a desire for a goal that always lay just beyond what could be reached.

Colette Peignot was not such a young woman in 1934 (she was thirty-one) that she had not had several opportunities to experience the possibility of this absolute, whether it was love – with Jean Bernier whom she knew in 1926 – whether it was erotic – with Trautner, with whom she shared a debauched life in Berlin (though nothing suggests that she liked this lowest of absolutes that he made her live through; perhaps people have been too quick to see her as a woman who loved pleasure and debauchery, rather than as a woman who was not afraid of them when she wanted to find out the limits beyond which innocence *still* lay) – or whether it was political – when in the face of the deceitful, stuffy morality of her bourgeois, religious and patriotic family, she discovered with Bernier that only communism, to which she committed herself in 1926, offered an uncompromising response.

She remained a communist for a long time (for nine years, even if as a dissident towards the end). And for being a communist to make sense, she needed to be completely committed to it, not, of course, in the same way as the surrealists, whom she knew a little[9] (and considered 'fashionable'), but at personal risk. So she set off for socialism's homeland, no doubt without really knowing either what she would do there or how she could be of use to it even in a small way. She lived in Leningrad, then in Moscow, joined the writer Boris Pilniak, who became her lover, and then (one cannot help thinking of Simone Weil, who would become her friend) decided to live with impoverished peasants on a kolkhoz. She fell ill, and had to be first hospitalised and then repatriated. Bataille speaks tersely about this as 'vain and feverish agitation'; it cannot have escaped him to see what was great and at the same time laughable – vain and feverish – about wanting to be a poor person among the poor while being able to avoid their fate when the moment came, which they were unable to do. Perhaps this was their innocence in Colette Peignot's eyes. Perhaps, in becoming one of them, she felt she could redeem herself from the fault of being born a bourgeois, and win some of their innocence for herself. She returned to Paris in a sleeping compartment reserved by her brother.[10]

Once back ('disgusted, she would tempt men and make love with them even in the toilets of trains. But she never took any pleasure from it'[11]), she became involved with Boris Souvarine, with whom she lived from 1931 until 1935.

There is no reason to give Colette Peignot more than her due or to dream her life for her. All in all, little is known of her life, and moreover what we do know is thanks to Bataille, who outlined it briefly, even coldly, as if this reticence and coldness alone could explain how brightly it burned, and for how long.[12] The path of Colette Peignot's life crossed that of other men who, for other reasons – perhaps by chance, a parallel and often significant literary history passes through love – entered this story and rightfully belong to it.[13] Among them was Jean Bernier, with whom she lived a passionate and seemingly brief love, one he was no doubt too lucid to share entirely; for his sake she shot herself in the heart, which did not kill her but left her a little more anguished about death. There was also Boris Pilniak whom she knew in Moscow and saw again in Paris in 1930. The little we know of this affair suggests another failure. Finally, there was Boris Souvarine who, to judge from the hatred he showed Bataille fifty years later[14] (twenty years after his death) loved her, in his way (Bataille said like a father rather than a lover) passionately.[15]

Souvarine ill concealed that his relationship with Colette Peignot was like that of a healthy man with a patient, that he was 'entrusted with her soul', and had to protect (unbeknown to her – this was the hardest part of it, he said) a sick woman in prey to demons he felt were alien and even a matter of indifference to him: 'of this kind of thing, neither heaven nor hell strikes the slightest chord in me'. For him, was Colette's 'extreme pessimism' not pathological, as much so as her fascination with death? And was it not demented (or suicidal)[16] for her to choose Bataille, the least 'healthy' man, the furthest from what he had been for her paternally, to replace him? Should we hypothesise that she saw Bataille as a cross between Boris Souvarine (he too was a political militant, between *La Critique sociale* and Contre-Attaque) and Édouard Trautner, the doctor and writer with whom she lived a disordered but impassioned life in Berlin, who treated her cruelly, made her wear a dog collar and beat her (according to Bataille, Trautner was a scatologist too)?[17] He could just as easily, and just as little, be either of them.

But all the same she went further than Bataille in a pride and intransigence that were all her own, while offering him possibilities he accepted for a while, only to refuse them later. Bataille continued to live out his own disorders, and to live them to the point of anguish (evidently she did not participate in all of them), to the point where they became intolerable, and destroyed not the love uniting them, but the absolute under whose auspices she had naïvely seen him. And what is fascinating, and what distinguishes them from every other couple is that their love had nothing 'romantic', nothing that 'transforms' or 'reconciles', about it. Nothing that puts love above everything and gives it meaning and salvation. Nothing could be less surrealist, either: no unity (in the sense of what Breton made an imperative), nothing of the marvellous (in the sense of what constituted surrealism's love poetry), no devotion of any kind. One might even go so far as to say that happiness was ruled out of Bataille's concerns with this love (happiness was too weak a concept ever to have interested him). On the contrary, he exacerbated both their wounds, even when they came at the highest cost. In fact this love resembles a twin descent into the depths; anguish is its key.

Colette Peignot's courage lay in responding to all of this. There is no doubt that everything pointed to her meeting Georges Bataille. If she is not, as has been claimed to the point of absurdity, the matrix of *every one* of Bataille's heroines, she is the only *living* person who might be one, the only one unafraid of what Bataille was blindly setting in motion.[18] They were connected in advance in two of their aspects, those of *heaven* and *hell*, albeit unequally divided. The only difference was that everything in her led her to seek heaven, even in hell (this was her absolute: what woman would not fear going to such depths to find heaven *even there*?), while for him everything led him to make *even* heaven into a hell. There was nothing in her which was not, or should not have been, ultimately saintly; nothing in Bataille which was not, or should not have been, ultimately defiled. (Did not Bataille want the most saintly to be the most defiled and the most defiled the most saintly?) She wanted only what was ultimately innocent, even if she had to reach this innocence through what was sordid in the extreme. This difference gave rise to a voiceless, violent and for the most part unconscious battle to see either heaven or hell prevail, without either of them offering any salvation in any way for one another. (Heaven and hell should not be misunderstood here; I do not use them in the *Catholic* sense, but with reference to William Blake's poem, which fascinated Bataille profoundly.)

Bataille was unfaithful (as he always was with every woman, systematically and copiously unfaithful to the point that fidelity certainly never appeared to him necessary to love); she was jealous.[19] She was uncompromising and pure; he – perhaps intentionally – was odious. Fragile in health (physically and 'mentally'), she gave in to all of his disorders (and to his follies, as we shall see) in an almost sacrificial manner (perhaps, as in Russia, and like Simone Weil, through a part of her that remained *Christian*?). He took these to the extreme; it has been insinuated, without proof but no doubt not without justification, that he hurt her violently. She wanted to hide away, to give up drinking ('I hate getting drunk or drinking too constantly . . .'[20]); and often wanted to run away ('I hated our life, I often wanted to run away, to go off alone into the mountains (it was to save my life I understand that now)'.)[21] But, sick and fascinated as she was, she stayed.

For Bataille was fascinating: his voice, the profound and complex lucidity of his thought, his willingness to go to extremes, his dangerous play with forces normally repressed, the ferocious and malevolent *god*[22] he tried hard to be (it might have been ironically that Colette Peignot several times called him 'the God Bataille') were all fascinating. But she was fascinating too: 'Those who got close to her knew how unshakeable was her demand to rise above things, and how violent was her rebellion against the norms to which the majority subscribe.' It is not Bataille who says this but Leiris.[23] In another book, Leiris says in more emotional terms that this demand and rebellion were those of a 'saint of the abyss'.[24]

Bataille would say the same thing, less lyrically but just as powerfully: 'her face responded abruptly to the anguish I have of human beings justifying life'.[25] And justifying his works as well. Saint and bitch, angel and devil at the same time, Bataille expected the *impossible* of a woman; a bitch barking at the orgy and throwing whoever took pleasure in her into the excesses of anguish. In meeting Colette Peignot, Bataille allowed his life and his work to come together in a dangerous way: he lifted the woman who shared them up to their height, 'to the height of death', even if the price to be paid was the highest possible and if his work was turned upside-down in turn.

'I am being a bitch today – Driver – take me anywhere: "to the furnace, to the garbage dump, to the whorehouse, to the slaughter-house." I must be burnt, torn apart, covered in filth, smell like all the fucks, and repel you – and then afterwards – fall asleep on your shoulder.'[26] This impossible innocence springing from the darkest evil, revealing its nature as it exhausted it, this extreme violence inflicted on herself at the same time as on what she thought was her due, no doubt were lived out by her as if they were the most exquisite torture, the only one to be truly divine. There is a despair and fury in this; there is death as well: the death she knew as a child, to the point of exultation and disgust.

Colette Peignot was born on 8 October 1903, into a family that had only very recently become wealthy,[27] from the marriage of Georges Peignot and Suzanne Chardon, a marriage that no doubt would have been unremarkable (its education and morality were Catholic, liberal and bourgeois) if war had not broken out and snatched away from the child's world (Colette was eleven in 1914) her father (on 28 September 1915)[28] and her three uncles, André (25 September 1914), René (15 May 1915) and Lucien (after 1915). The fourth of her uncles, Robert, had died before the war, on 15 June 1913. Within four years, the Peignot women found themselves having to mourn five men: the five boys born to the marriage of Gustave Peignot and Marie Laporte. Apart from Colette's mother, no one remained alive but her aunts Jane and Julia (a third aunt had been stillborn), and her grandmother, Marie Peignot, a pious and bourgeois woman who seems to have ruled the lives of what remained of this family. A mass grave, around which circled women dressed in black, more than ever proud of – and chosen for – the sacrifice made for the homeland ... [29] Colette stubbornly thought of death again, according to Souvarine, after having tried to kill herself for Bernier's sake. This death, which no woman better or more violently than Colette tied to the most repugnant and the most desirable eroticism, was the very same that fascinated Bataille (we have seen that he did not wait until meeting her to let himself be fascinated by it), he who pleaded that it should be lived to the point of gambling with it daily, with love's dice: this death smells of the brothel, as love smells of the abattoir.

This death – a sort of promise kept by Colette Peignot (she died at the age of thirty-five in Bataille's bed) with which, on her death, he could push the game still further, avidly, amazed, his writing anguished – was a profound agreement between them, making it the only possible limit of their love (not at all a limit of *reparation*, like that of Tristan and Isolde; closer rather, if a reference point really is necessary, to that of Heathcliff and Cathy in *Wuthering Heights*, a book Bataille admired), a death for itself, with nothing left but the soil to cover it over, making it sacred in their eyes, and so that whoever dared risk it at every moment was sacred. Colette Peignot and Georges Bataille were in this sense sacred lovers: they spoke the horror of love as least as much as its beauty.

Thunderbolts and forebodings

It must not be assumed that Georges Bataille and Colette Peignot lived together immediately after the fleeting stay of August 1934. It took them a long time to find one another, longer still to become definitively linked. On returning from Italy, Bataille accompanied his wife and daughter to Tossa de Mar in Spain, staying with André Masson, who had been exiled there since the fascist machinations of February 1934 in Paris. We do not really know whether Bataille actually reached Tossa in August 1934, or whether, as indicated by his diary, he left his wife and child at Bayonne, near the Spanish border, from where they travelled on to Tossa alone.[1] The diary indicates a departure from Paris on 25 August and a return on the 28th. This would mean that, had he gone to Tossa, it would only have been for a brief stay.

In Paris, he was alone, in the exclusive sense that he was not with Colette Peignot. Souvarine had placed her in a clinic in Saint-Mandé under the care of Doctor Weil (Simone's father), according to him to lavish the unfaithful girl with the care she needed due to her state (of love?). Bataille lived no more nor less alone than he had before knowing her. Attached or not, he changed nothing about his way of life. The same disorder prevailed, and he was still as dissolute as ever, according to Leiris. From reading his diary, it would seem that he had numerous mistresses during the months from September to November 1934 alone: Simone, Janine, Denise, Florence, and especially Edith, disembodied first names about whom we know nothing more – disembodied but interesting in that they maintain the image of a free Bataille, unfaithful twice over (to his wife, from whom he would soon separate, and to his new companion), more protective of the disorder in which he lived than the propriety due to love, still in no way subscribing to the traditionally expected (even among the surrealists) obligations of fidelity and exclusivity. Georges Bataille spent these months between the Bibliothèque Nationale, where he rarely went, his political comrades (he often saw Simone Weil and others of the Democratic Communist Circle), his friends, Doctor Borel among others (who we know was also Colette Peignot's therapist), his mistresses who were as numerous as they were ephemeral, brothels (the Sphynx) and topless night-clubs (he was a regular of Le Tabarin as well as the Concert Mayol). It seems clear that whatever disorder Colette Peignot might have been ready for, she could not have claimed to be, herself, *the whole* of Bataille's disorder. Even before they were fully attached, he established a considerable distance between them which she could never completely close and which caused her suffering. She was not and never would be the whole of his world, violent as his passion for her may have been.

The year 1934 was one of transition for Bataille. At thirty-seven, he was no longer a young man. *La Critique sociale* was no longer being published and, a few months earlier, the Democratic Communist Circle had ceased to attract oppositional communists. He had all in all written just one book, *Story of the Eye*, which had been privately distributed, and that was already seven years ago; nothing else since then (except *L'Anus solaire*, which was too short and private really to count). The projected book on fascism in France not only did not appear, but there is every chance that he had barely done any work on it. The writer he regretted not yet being, faced with Breton and his friends in 1925, he had still to become nine years later. If he had married and had a child, the marriage was a failure and in 1934 he and his wife separated. The year 1934 also revealed the first signs of his illness. During January and February he had been in pain and was confined to bed. Admittedly, this was only rheumatism, but he could hardly have failed to think of his father's sickness and the possibility of a hereditary syphilis belatedly emerging (it is more likely that the rheumatism was due to overindulgence in alcohol). In April 1934, to restore himself completely, he decided to go to Italy. He found not the hoped-for sun, but rain. Rome was a nightmare. But Stresa, on the shore of Lake Maggiore, fully restored him. He rested there from the 'holiday afternoons draped over hotel beds'.

In Rome, he did not fail to go to the exhibition commemorating the fascists' assumption of power. In a letter to Queneau, he did not hide the fact that what he saw was 'striking'. Fascism displayed in this way, without its militias and blood, without its police raids and screams, quite effectively theatricalised symbols of power and death. But there was nothing, he predicted, that would be of a nature to change his opinion about it. He returned to Paris.

I have said that it could be imprudent to read Bataille as one would an autobiography. There is always at work in his writing something of the order of what fascism stages in revealing itself: a violent and abstract dramatisation. The rare times he evoked his mother, it was under the sign of the worst; we nevertheless know what patient affection he showed for her. He said nothing about Sylvia Bataille in which any happy moments are recalled. He spoke of her only allusively, later, so much later, when he associated *Le Bleu du ciel* with the crisis that separated them. It would be the same with Colette Peignot. From their first letters,[2] we can guess at the agitation, the impatience of a man in love ... And, quite to the contrary, describing his return to Paris and their encounter, he employed words that completely turn back on themselves: it could well be expected that a special place would be made for this meeting in his work (no surrealist would have failed to do so), a place where the passions aroused, in one way or another, might find expression. And he did the opposite. The word *horror* emerges in place of the word *love*:

> I came back to Paris, restored to health: it was in order to enter suddenly into horror. I encountered horror, not death. Tragedy moreover dispenses with anguish, intoxication and rapture to one to whom it is wedded, as to the being it invites. I returned to Italy and although I was chased 'like a madman' from one place to the next, I lived the life of a god (the flasks of black wine, thunderbolts, the foreboding). However, I can barely speak about it.[3]

This second stay in Italy, the stay of a god chased from one place to the next, was certainly undertaken in Colette Peignot's footsteps. But about her and about the love which impelled him: nothing! Horror took its place, horror, he said, and tragedy. Horror and tragedy have their thunderbolts and forebodings. Certainly what he himself called 'the frightful night of Trento' belonged to the thunderbolt: 'Next to me lay the second victim. The utter repugnance on her lips made them resemble the lips of a certain dead woman. From them dribbled something more dreadful than blood.'[4] In the same way, even if he said nothing about it, the assassination of Chancellor Dolfuss on 25 July 1934 in Vienna (the day after Bataille's night in Trento) belonged to *forebodings*. The first time he stayed in Austria was to bring him close to an assassination which encapsulated the full meaning of the book he had started about fascism.

Yesterday's political collaborators, today's rivals in love, Souvarine and Bataille, even in their private lives, were brought together by the trail of Nazi gunpowder over the territory of Europe. The oddest thing is that the assassination of Dolfuss, which had serious consequences, had at that moment only a displaced influence over them. (As we have seen, the importance of the failure of the Viennese workers' uprising in February 1934 had not escaped him, but of the importance of this assassination, he said nothing.) *Blue of Noon* (was it *Blue of Noon* that Bataille wanted for a time to call *Foreboding*? But this title could have been just as suitable for the book on fascism in France) would push further the impossible, the unliveable relationship between political and amorous disorders.

The sky turned upside down

The year 1934 was not just transitional but also crucial. Everything I have suggested in passing – the streets taken over first by fascist leagues and then by the massed left; the daily more serious and urgent threat of fascism which claimed Vienna after spilling blood in Paris; sickness adding its weight to this news as it reached Bataille, confined to his room; the women he found and then left one after the other (from his separation from his wife to Colette Peignot, with whom his relationship had its concealments); the brief trips abroad, to Stresa in Italy (a sort of enlightening, Nietzschean trip), a convalescent stay; to Rome where fascism had already arrived in its splendour of a revolution totally committed to the forces of power and death; then to Innsbruck (chance could hardly have arranged more or better than this) the very day Chancellor Dolfuss was assassinated in Vienna – all these things made 1934 a crucial year.

Bataille was a 'god', by turns sick, drunk, rheumatic, drifting from one hotel to the next, and going crazy, from the dark Italian wine and from this woman who was more uncompromising and pure than any other, whose track across a Europe becoming darker every day left a trail that, bedazzled and hungry as he was, he followed like a portent of impending death and the convulsion, at once repulsive and desirable, into which it would throw him. Bataille was that man of whom *Blue of Noon* was to make itself the faithful and absolutely baffling mirror, as real as it was fictitious, borrowing from real life the characteristic signs of its strictest authenticity, and from desire the effects of its least controllable slippages. *Blue of Noon*, written at the beginning of 1935, pushed this drifter to the last stronghold of his ungraspable logic. It is worth considering what Bataille himself had to say about it the day he decided to publish the book, long after writing it, in 1957: *Blue of Noon* describes a character 'who spends himself to the point of touching death by means of drinking bouts, sleepless nights and promiscuity'.[1] No doubt this is real. But perhaps it has been claimed too hastily that *Blue of Noon* is *entirely* real. This is far from being so. It is a story, and should be read as such: in other words, there is no justification for seeing anything in it beyond the reasons its author offers it to us to read. Admittedly, the story is scandalous, all the more so for not being just imaginary; cunningly set into it, woven into its fabric, emerging here and there, are a number of details about events and characters from which more alert readers have felt they could draw some conclusions.

Troppmann finds himself in London, in dives and luxury hotels, with the most beautiful young woman, one who is indecent to the point of saintliness. The story begins with her, her thighs naked, a dirty curtain in her mouth to stop her screams . . . surrounded by rats. It continues with her, under the disgusted eye of the lift attendant with the face of a grave digger, and a trembling, nauseated maid. This young woman, 'beet-red, . . . squirming on her chair like a pig under the knife', drunk, from beneath her the sound of 'slackening bowels', is called Dirty (short for Dorothea). Her indecency has a guilelessness fit to lay you low. Troppmann, made impotent by such indecent guilelessness, would gladly throw himself at her feet; Dirty, it appears, is the saint of *Blue of Noon*, its first and central character. We will not meet her again, however, until late in the story; this is her inaccessible assumption.

A second character appears, a second young woman, a sort of double negative, who is ugly, black, filthy (an 'unwashed virgin', a 'disgusting rat'), yet no less fascinating: Lazare. The name Lazare, even given to a woman, might evoke resurrection and its celebration. For Bataille, however, it evokes rather a long stay among the dead, the greenish and mucal tinge of flesh, the journey through hell. Lazare is Bataille's other world or, depending on the circumstances, the other name of the world he knew in 1934: the world of politics. We soon learn that Lazare is a communist, a dissenting communist, that she dreams of revolution with the same fervour that Christians dream of resurrection. For her the world is no longer flesh (unless it is a dulled flesh); it is nothing more than an idea . . . an idea of salvation (we know how much Bataille hated any salvation). Yet she is the one to whom Troppmann chooses to tell all, it is in her company that he goes as far as he can with his impossible confession, it is to her, who he knows will understand none of it, that he says what level of shame a sick desire, his desire, can attain. If he is impotent, it is because Dirty is too pure. And if she is too pure, it is because she is lost to debauchery. But this will never be enough. Pure or debauched, she nevertheless does not attain what alone stimulates him to erection in a woman's bed: she is not sufficiently *death*. Twice, once here to Lazare, then to another woman (Xénie), there appears the story of the indecent, obscene homage paid to his dead mother (we have seen what kind of real or imaginary story Bataille made of this on the occasion of the death of his mother in 1930).

Troppmann does not really choose between this old woman taken over by her corpse, his absent wife (since Troppmann is married; he even has two children) whose resignation overwhelms him ('Today, I am overjoyed at being an object of horror and repugnance to the one being whom I am bound to),[2] and Dirty, whom he has to admire; prostitutes would be best, they alone would be *sufficiently* death:[3] 'I realised in any case that my attraction to prostitutes was like my attraction to corpses.'[4] What his wife Edith and Dirty are not, in her own way Lazare is, and this makes her fascinating: she is death. Not the death of a woman (Lazare is scarcely a woman in Troppmann's eyes), still less that of a desirable woman; she is, through the impossible, the hypostasis of death, the annunciation to him of the death expected to spill across Europe, communist or fascist, it is the world covered in blood, that of the convulsion of war, of the sacrifice offered to its consumption. She moves through this story, from beginning to end, like its ultimate promise: like the ghost of a wider fate to whose emotional and sexual contortions one must submit with resignation.

In Paris, Troppmann goes to the Dôme, to Chez Francis, to Chez Fred Payne, to the Tabarin, to the Sphynx (remarkably, the text is full of details of identifiable places; from now on this rarely happened), all places where Bataille himself often went. A third female character appears, Xénie. Xénie has everything going for her: she is rich, seductive, and no fool; and she shows a concern and an eagerness that no man would refuse. But this concern and eagerness annoy. She is certainly not death (except in an incidental, pitiful way: threatening to swing out of the window), she is not even debauchery which she views with pity, saying: 'Everybody knows you lead an abnormal sex life. It seemed to me that more than anything else you were very unhappy.'[5] Nothing about her grabs or terrifies him. Yet Troppmann will lure her into his *joy*, into his game. It is to her that for the second time he tells the story of the *homage* paid to his dead mother; it is against her above all that he takes violent offence on the subject of Sade, accusing her and those who use him to show off (perhaps Xénie represents the surrealists in this narrative) of being frauds. What does she know, what do they know about shit?[6] Troppmann will try and make himself repellent to her as he had to Lazare, by pushing to an extreme the role of the sexually deviant sick man: 'You've come here to make my death even fouler. Now get undressed. It'll be like dying in a whorehouse.'[7]

Shortly afterwards, while convalescing, Troppmann leaves Paris for Barcelona, on the very days of the Catalan separatist insurrection of 5, 6 and 7 October 1934. In Barcelona, if luck would have it that he was there at a crucial moment, it was not to rally to the insurgents but as a tourist, taking a rest after the days of sickness in Paris. He only sees the revolution from afar: as an additional slippage. Like part of a nightmare begun elsewhere, differently, with other people. In Barcelona it is the Criolla, a shady transvestite spot, or the bars of the Ramblas that take up his time and his desire, though not without shame: 'At such a time, I realised, my life had no justification.' In Barcelona, Troppmann meets Lazare again; he will also meet Xénie and Dirty: indeed it is the same nightmare, started elsewhere and continued here. Lazare is there but of course she has come to take part in the insurrection. An idealist, she proposes storming a prison . . . [8] The Spanish workers find it more judicious to storm an arms depot. Troppmann witnesses all this with a sense of irony and despair. He waits for Xénie to join him, and she does so. But so does Dirty, who is weak and ill. She has grown thin, her skeleton is visible beneath her flesh. The riots take place without them being interested or becoming involved at all: they stay outside Barcelona, in a little fishing village, until the end of October 1934. Then they take a quick trip to Trier, Coblenz and Frankfurt, where they part; but first in a hallucinatory scene, they make love in a field overlooking a German cemetery, open to them like the void of an inverted sky, lit with a multitude of candles placed on each tomb like so many stars: 'We still had the graves below us. Dorothea opened wide, and I bared her to the loins. She in turn bared me. We fell onto the shifting ground, and I sank into her moist body. . . . The earth beneath that body lay open like a grave, her naked cleft lay open to me like a freshly dug grave. . . . We were as excited by earth as by naked flesh.'[9] In the end Dirty is death: her body is death.

And beneath her the earth, an upturned sky, a sky below, is peopled with those already dead and with those to come, with those the war promises. Dirty lies open just as the earth promises annihilation. She is no longer just a woman. Troppmann, in his bewilderment, calls her tenderly 'my skeleton'. Their embraces take place in Trier (Francis Marmande pertinently remarks in *L'indifférence des ruines* that Trier is the town in which Karl Marx was born, while *Blue of Noon* begins in London, where he died), a town whose name is paradoxical since what grips Troppmann and Dirty is the fear of – and desire for – war, its convulsion and death.[10] War and death are signalled everywhere, augured everywhere.

Having left Dirty, a petrified Troppmann, standing in the rain, witnesses an obscene concert by Nazi children 'in their sticklike stiffness', prey to a 'cataclysmic exultation', children laughing at the sun 'entranced by a longing to meet their death', who, Troppmann says, will go on to spread devastation and blood: 'inordinate laughter was making my head spin. As I found myself confronting this catastrophe, I was filled with the black irony that accompanies the moments of seizure when no one can help screaming.'[11]

Blue of Noon is hallucinating, which can be understood in several ways. It is hallucinated; the narrative is not linear (as what I have said so far may suggest); it slips endlessly from dream to reality, and from reality to the impossible, seeming to obey a multiplicity of tiny implosions, negating all sense and all becoming.[12] It is hallucinatory: nothing can be grasped. Whatever sense one thinks one can grasp at any given moment so as to stay afloat in the narrative weakens and dissolves, carried off by yet another slippage or a new switch from reality to dream, from dream to exhausted numbness, from exhaustion to convulsion, and from convulsion to stupefaction. Nothing in it is really as it seems, yet everything comes together in incessant metamorphoses.

This is why it is inappropriate to make more of this than an imaginary narrative, what it is and nothing more, offered up to the reader. It has been said that Troppmann is evidently Bataille, and even that he is so clearly, so conspicuously that *Blue of Noon* is none other than his diary for 1934. Nothing is less certain. One could not cast doubt on this any more clearly than Bataille himself did when he said, speaking of himself in the third person, 'after some months of sickness experienced a serious moral crisis . . . separating from his wife wrote

Blue of Noon which is not at all the narrative of this crisis but is if need be a reflection of it.[13] Certainly the places described are places Bataille knew well, and which appear regularly in his diary. Certainly, as we have seen, he visited Trier, Frankfurt and Coblenz on the same dates as given in the narrative, 1 and 2 November.[14] Certainly he knew Barcelona from having stayed with André Masson in Tossa de Mar, visiting it several times (it was moreover in Tossa that he completed *Blue of Noon*, on Wednesday, 29 May 1935). But as I have mentioned, we do not know if he went there in 1934. He knew London too, having stayed there in 1920 and 1927, but we do not know if he returned afterwards. This is as far as the places have parallels. Two things are certain: it is not true that he went to Vienna on 26 July 1934, just after the assassination of Chancellor Dolfuss (he was in Molveno and Innsbruck and did not visit Vienna during his stay in Austria); and it is not true that he was in Barcelona on 5, 6 and 7 October 1934, the dates of the Catalan insurrection: he was in Paris (but though he was not in Barcelona, his wife Sylvia was). These two facts come as no surprise: what appears to be the least political of books has no qualms in claiming as the background for the most violent private disarray two of the most important dates of historical disarray in the year's calendar; two moments at which if he was not in fact present, he very nearly was.

The same is true of the characters of *Blue of Noon*. It has been called a *roman à clef*, not without reason, and this has been thought reason enough to move straight to an explanation of what the keys are and what the narrative means. Thus Lazare represents Simone Weil; in *literary* terms, there is little doubt of this.[15] Every portrait sketched of her at the time, however unfavourable, evokes this possibility, the strange morbid fascination she was able to exert over Bataille reappears here in the most traumatised and (as has not been noted enough) most respectful way: 'For a moment I wondered if she weren't the most humane being I had ever seen.'[16] There is little doubt that Bataille, who knew Simone Weil in the Democratic Communist Circle, saw her frequently in 1934. And no doubt one can retrace here something of the conversations they might have had.[17] Bataille insists to an unpleasant degree on her dirtiness, of which everyone was aware, so much so that she was sent on her way by the peasants who employed her, reproaching her for never changing her clothes and not washing her hands before milking the cows. That her stance as a working-class militant (in other words, an active militant) amused others is not in doubt either; her brave rallying to the Spanish Republican cause (she reached Spain on 8 August 1936) earned her nothing more by way of active service than a badly scalded foot from a kitchen frying pan (it was in vain that she begged to do more, and go into combat; her shortsightedness encouraged her doubtless sceptical comrades to restrict her to an ideological role).[18] But there are even more precise details: it is true that in the summer of 1933 (as indicated in *Blue of Noon*), Simone Weil was in Barcelona, accompanied by Aimé Patri. It is true, unlikely as it may seem, that she was a regular at the Criolla. It is also true (according to Patri, and as Michel says in *Blue of Noon*) that she asked him to thrust pins under her fingernails as a way of training herself for torture.[19] These facts would be enough to identify Simone Weil beneath the name of Lazare beyond doubt. Bataille evidently knew about them, though we do not know if it was through Weil herself or through Aimé Patri, which would be more likely. In either case he included them in the narrative, thus giving it an additional guarantee of veracity, one which nevertheless stops there. According to Simone Pétrement's account, it is highly unlikely that Simone Weil was in Barcelona in October 1934 and played a part in the insurrection. If she had been, it would be too important for Pétrement not to have knowledge of it; but she knows nothing about it.

Twenty-five years later Bataille would give a portrait of Simone Weil in which it is certainly not difficult, approaching from the opposite direction, to identify the features of Lazare ... But the friendship which might for a while have existed between them also reappears, stripped of any fictional and traumatic trimmings:

> very few human beings have interested me to this point. Her incontestable ugliness was alarming but personally I claimed that she also had, in one sense, a genuine beauty (I think I was right). She charmed with a very sweet, very simple authority; she was certainly an admirable being, asexual, with something inauspicious about her. Always black, black clothes, hair like a crow's wing, tanned. She was undoubtedly very virtuous, but she was for certain a Don Quixote who was liked for her lucidity, her determined pessimism and for her extreme courage that was attracted to the impossible. She had very little humour, nevertheless I'm sure that internally she was crazier, more lively than she believed herself to be ... I say this without wanting to diminish her, there was in her a marvellous will for inanity.[20]

The problem posed by Dirty still remains. It has often been said that Colette Peignot can be recognised in her. This is doubtful.[21] First, it should be remembered that the character of Dirty was born with the abandoned project *W.-C.*, thus long before Bataille knew Colette Peignot. Next, Colette did not go to Barcelona with him either in 1934 (if in fact Bataille himself was there) or in May 1935. Finally, the journey to Trier, Coblenz and Frankfurt, the towns in which the final scenes of *Blue of Noon* take place, was not made with Colette Peignot but with a woman about whom we know nothing but her first name, Edith, who was then to leave for Heidelberg.[22] As we can see, the discrepancies are too numerous to sustain a literal interpretation. Michel Leiris goes even further in these reservations: according to him Colette Peignot disliked *Blue of Noon*, and this should be seen as one of the reasons it was not published sooner.

For Bataille did not publish *Blue of Noon*. By a strange after-shock, all of the effects of slippage, uncertainty and erasure related one by one in the narrative affected the narrative itself; obeying the same disarray, it never came out. In fact, Bataille does not appear to have made any effort to have it published. Friends read the manuscript, but that was all. Bataille took twenty-two years to resign himself to the publication of a book that counts among the most important of its century.[23] Was this due to the friendly pressure by those close to him, as he claimed, or, as is more likely, for more trivial financial reasons? In the meantime he reworked it, making revisions that consisted of lightening it still further, and making its character of loss and evasion more acute.

By 1935, at thirty-eight years of age, he was still no more in a position to put some order into his life. *Blue of Noon* saw off the project of 'Le fascisme en France' or, more dreadfully, it was that project's underside, its violent, dilapidated, warped version, 'the leap of rage', to be seen off in its turn by considerations that partly elude us. Certainly if it had been published the book would have caused a scandal: there could have been no more violent exposure or more sarcastic denial of that for which Bataille was known in Paris, as an ultra-left militant convinced of the urgent need to bring together every intellectual force against the rising tide of fascism. If it had been published, the book would have said just the reverse: his indifference to all this, and worse still his desire: the horror of an awakening world that marvellously (to the point of disaster) corresponded to that of a warped life – so far that no landmark now remained to stand for what is desirable and what is not, what is just and what is to be condemned. Who would have been well enough informed to understand that what Bataille was writing – so odiously and vilely – announced the way that the rise of fascism might satisfy an evil humour? Those who had only badly understood Sade (those 'cheats') could no more have understood this: *Blue of Noon* is the book of a man alone (rarely has this been so true of a book), one who has no reply to give to his life but the corpse-like taste of prostitutes, and that of Dirty overlooking the cemetery in Trier.

'Revolutionary offensive or death'

It may be difficult to understand how the same man could, within only a few months, have written *Blue of Noon*, which without exaggeration could be read as a treatise of abandonment to the worst and of political ridicule, and created Contre-Attaque, one of the final and most significant displays of the French intellectual far left before the declaration of the Second World War. The contradiction is nevertheless only apparent: in November 1935, Bataille did not think differently than he had in May,[1] and without doubt his state of mind was no less fundamentally melancholy. This is shown by the words he used in one of the Contre-Attaque leaflets: to save the world from the 'nightmare', from the 'powerlessness and carnage into which it is sinking'. Nightmare, powerlessness and carnage are three of the key words in *Blue of Noon*, and these are the words with which the narrative closes.

Contre-Attaque simply added to them, as one wagers or despairs ('nothing is possible any more except on condition of rushing headlong into the tumult'[2]), however pessimistic one could be about the possibility given to people to deflect fate: only an 'ocean of people rising up' could save the world from the horror into which Bataille was one of the few to predict that it might sink completely. Contre-Attaque was that wager. What is interesting is that to succeed he became reconciled with his everlasting enemy André Breton, for the first time undertaking to act in agreement with him.[3] This reconciliation underlines the urgency Bataille felt: 'The current political situation requires urgency.'[4]

We have the good fortune to have available the remarkable testimony on Contre-Attaque of the historian Henri Dubief, a member of the organisation and a friend of Bataille.[5] This will provide my major reference source.

The first meetings at which the organisation was worked out in draft took place at the Regency (!) café. It was in this café that Breton and

Bataille set out their agreement, although we do not know how the meeting was arranged, who facilitated it, what feelings they shared, and what allowed them to forget the insults they had exchanged five years earlier. It was September 1935.

The first, inaugural, manifesto bears the date 7 October and thirteen signatures.[6] This manifesto was inserted into the text *Position politique du surréalisme*, published at the time by Breton. This is significant: Contre-Attaque, whose instigator was certainly Bataille, according to both Dubief and Leiris was the godchild of a stictly orthodox surrealist publication. Even before it had been formed, the conditions of the next breach were established.

Like everything Bataille undertook, Contre-Attaque was an idiosyncratic group comprising the most important surrealists – it is tempting to call them the old guard, Breton, Éluard and Péret (Aragon was not of course included, having joined the Communist Party) – the Batailleans – in so far as the word then had a meaning and does not just describe the left-overs of existing organisations (it would be more accurate to say those of the former Souvariniens who followed Bataille at the time of the dissolution of the Democratic Communist Circle; in any case, they had almost all been part of it) – and finally the independents, the most important being Maurice Heine, admired by both groups but, on account of Sade, perhaps closer to Bataille than to Breton, without this proximity ever really amounting to support or even (we shall see this would have been useful) enabling him to act as their mediator. Let us take a futher look at what will really have to be called the Bataille group. It was not negligible in number, and some, like Georges Ambrosino, René Chenon, Henri Dubief, Pierre Klossowski (whom he met in 1933) and Dora Maar (his beautiful mistress at the end of 1933 and the early part of 1934, whom he had met in the Masses group, of which she was a member), would remain his friends. Others are less known: Pierre Aimery, Jacques Chavy, Jean Dautry, Pierre Dugan and Frédéric Legendre.[7]

The next meetings took place at the café de la Mairie in the place Saint-Sulpice. These were meetings of two groups divided geographically between the right bank and the left bank under the two names, emblematic as much as distinctive, of Sade and Marat. The Sade group immediately gained considerable ascendancy over the Marat group: Bataille and Breton were both part of it. The decisions taken by Contre-Attaque were made by the Sade group alone.

But what was Contre-Attaque? This definition seems to be sufficient: 'The Contre-Attaque movement has been founded with a view to contributing to an abrupt development of the revolutionary offensive.'[8] But there is nothing here to distinguish it from numerous other movements which did not claim to have any different aim. Several of the power lines were in fact similar: anti-nationalism, for example, violent anti-nationalism: if there is to be a revolution, this was on no account to be for the benefit of any nation or country at all. The first line of the first Contre-Attaque tract makes this clear without any possible ambiguity: 'Virulently hostile to any tendency, whatever form it takes, that harnesses the Revolution to the advantage of ideas of nation or country . . .' This is its very first article. From the beginning, therefore, a distance was taken from fascism and National Socialism; also from the Soviet Union, land of socialism. For Contre-Attaque, an anti-nationalist is an anti-patriot. Contre-Attaque hammered a nail into Mauras's Maginot line:

> A great many people love their country, sacrificing themselves and dying for it. A Nazi can love the Reich to the point of delirium. We are also able to love to the point of fanaticism [Jean Piel recalled that the 'fana movement' was the friendly nickname given to it] but what we love, even though we come from France, is not at all the French community, but the human community; not at all France, but the world.[9]

Another axis was anti-capitalism, yet another was anti-reformism (reformism has meaning only when power is in the hands of the workers; in fact it is preliminary to it). This was mingled with anti-democracy and anti-parliamentarianism: we are not unaware of the hatred this generation of the extreme left shared with the extreme right for the impotent and corrupt French Republic, corrupt to such a point ('the nauseating spectacle of bourgeois parliamentarianism') that Contre-Attaque did not see how it could 'be saved'. Nothing in any of this was really new, it contained nothing that might not have been shared with other intellectual groupuscules of the far left or with anarchist groups for example. If Contre-Attaque was distinctive, it was not through any of this but through what would follow. More than anyone else, Bataille was aware of the risks fascism made Europe run (Henri Dubief said forcefully that no one 'taught people so much about fascism' as Bataille[10]) and was also more certain than anyone else of where its strength lay. For fascism was the only 'revolution' which had got rid of a democracy. Equally, it furnished collective myths to disoriented people thirsting for faith. By that at least it showed an uncontestable superiority over all the workers' movements of which two of course had been incomprehensibly defeated: in Germany and in Austria (it should not be forgotten that Contre-Attaque preceded the victory of the Popular Front and that in 1935 the leagues of Colonel de La Roque were flexing their muscles more often than the workers' parties). Bataille saw in this one more reason not to believe in the capacity of the proletarian movement to emerge from the situation in which it found itself, and still less from what seemed to be promised to it by democratic and parliamentary means alone – fascism. Dubief speaks about this frankly: Bataille was convinced of 'the intrinsic perversity' of fascism, but was forced to recognise its superiority. He therefore advocated that Contre-Attaque should replace the myths created by fascism with others: 'We intend in our turn to use for our benefit the weapons created by fascism, which has been able to use humanity's fundamental aspirations for affective exaltation and fanaticism.' But this exaltation and fanaticism, in radical opposition to fascism, must be placed in the service of humanity's universal interest. It was no longer tolerable for one man to exploit for his own benefit, in one country, a movement of disorientation stirred up among the very poorest classes.[11] The revolution of the poorest, of the slaves, must benefit the poorest and the slaves. Production will then belong to them alone as the sole producers.

Contre-Attaque was remarkable for several other reasons. First, it posed problems symptomatically absent from all revolutionary ideology, which was prudish if not priggish. In this respect, Bataille drew André Breton and his friends in his wake (and in the wake of Maurice Heine and Pierre Klossowski) further than surrealism was perhaps prepared to go. The revolution would *also* be a moral revolution, which must also be understood as a revolution in morals. This is how Contre-Attaque inscribed pell-mell in its programme nothing less than the liberation of children from parental educational tutelage (both bourgeois and capitalist), the free expression of sexual urges (including those considered to be 'neurotic', a beautiful revenge for Bataille over those who had once criticised him. Maurice Heine, the reader and editor of Sade, was to draw the programme up), the free play of passions, the free man a candidate for all the pleasures due to him, and

so on. It was under the triple signs of Sade, Fourier and Nietzsche that
Bataille placed the revolution promised by Contre-Attaque: Sade for
perversity(?), Fourier for passion and Nietzsche for the abundance of
forces and consent to the world.[12] But in order to attain this programme, a violent revolution would be necessary. From the initial
manifesto, Contre-Attaque was full of appeals to violence and the
dictatorship of an armed people 'capable when the time comes of
assuming a pitiless authority'. This was the only way for the French
workers' movement to avoid the disaster that had overcome the
German and Austrian workers' movements.

The first public meeting of Contre-Attaque took place on 5 January
1936 at Grenier des Augustins in rue des Grands-Augustins, in premises
loaned by Jean-Louis Barrault. The theme of this meeting was 'Country
and Family'. Contre-Attaque did not equivocate: respect for either
made 'a human being a traitor to his fellows'. The trinity father-
country-boss is that of the old patriarchal order, that also 'today of
fascist nastiness'. Bataille, Breton, Péret and Heine were to have taken
the floor. Breton, it seems, did not, and did not even attend, according
to Georges Mouton, who with Marcel Jean was one of the unexpected
and improvised speakers of the evening.[13] The second meeting took
place some days later, on 21 January 1936. This time the advertised
speakers, Georges Bataille, André Breton and Maurice Heine, were to
address the question of the 200 families chosen for 'the justice of the
people'. Again, this time according to Charles Ronsac, Breton was not
present for this second evening, nor was any 'notable surrealist'.[14]

The first public demonstration of Contre-Attaque – moreover the
only one – took place on 17 February 1936. Forgetting for a moment
their anti-parliamentarianism, they joined the demonstration in support
of Léon Blum after he had been violently attacked by Action française.
A tract was published and distributed between the Panthéon and the
place de la Nation, under the title 'Comrades, the fascists are lynching
Léon Blum'. The tract and its watchword were brief: 'Defence is death!
Revolutionary offensive or death!'

Apparently there were no major problems until February 1936. No
major problems? This seems doubtful. The absence of the co-initiator
of Contre-Attaque at both meetings when he was supposed to have
spoken allows us to assume that dissensions had already emerged
between the two men which justified Breton failing to support an
enterprise about which they had agreed at its inception. Or had Bataille

excluded him due to the fact that Breton had made two errors which he was not willing to excuse him? Breton had failed to correct a journalist, the fascist sympathiser Georges Blond, who had, in an article in *Candide* on 18 November 1935, insidiously credited him alone with the creation of Contre-Attaque. The second was more grave, at the very least more surprising: he agreed to an interview with a journalist from *Figaro*, a newspaper regarded by the left as under the control of Colonel de La Rocque – an interview from which, to say the least, Breton did not emerge with much credit. It was surprisingly rash for Breton, who had always mistrusted journalists, unreservedly to hand himself over to one of their most dubious representatives! The first damage caused to Contre-Attaque had been done, due to clumsiness no doubt, by Breton: one day it would not fail to be exploited.

The freedom taken by Breton to appropriate the prestige of the movement – something he was in the habit of doing – and of acting from that moment as he liked, was appropriated by Bataille in his way – 'his way of being calm and obstinate, almost bovine and asinine'.[15] In March 1936 he wrote a tract with his friends Bernier and Lucie Collard (others appeared meanwhile which did not pose apparent problems) entitled 'Workers, you have been betrayed'. This was not the first tract Bataille had written without the consent of Breton and his friends (although, in a letter to Pierre Kaan, Bataille mentions that Éluard did consent). It was a ferociously anti-fascist 'call to action', and fundamental because it includes several of Bataille's political concepts, sovereignty for example (although it was a long way from the sovereignty that Bataille would later conceptualise: 'We affirm that the time has come to act as MASTERS, not for one but for ALL'), and created a precedent. But pushing provocation further, Bataille abused their trust by adding at the end of the tract the signatures of Breton and some of the surrealists, although it seems they knew nothing about it. The rupture was about to be accomplished.

It took place in April and, contrary to what might be feared, without any recriminations. Bataille had already been thinking about forming a new group, and had been careful to add a subscription form for it to the litigious tract (acting in this way, he considerably anticipated the rupture and at the very least placed himself in a position of alone being responsible for it). This was the Comité contre l'Union sacrée.

Paradoxically, and Dubief was right to say so, Breton left strengthened by this experience: it enabled him to reunite the surrealist movement, still damaged as it was by Aragon's recent departure. However, che leaves no doubt that Contre-Attaque belonged to Bataille, that the ideas promoted and the style adopted were his, and in this his political ascendancy over Breton was fully played out, forcing him, time after time to protest, to exploit alternative positions, each time trying to redeem a course another was conducting, aided this time by his friends. He was never able to take things into his own hands, as had been his habit. No doubt this explains his aggressiveness. He had imprudently placed himself in the position of being given a lesson by younger people (only Bataille, of the Batailleans, was of his generation) who were less well known than him. After all the only person in the group who could have had an ascendancy recognised by all was Maurice Heine. He was the only one who could reconcile the irreconcilable, at least to maintain the fragile equilibrium constructed entirely by Bataille and agreed by Breton. Tired and sick, Maurice Heine was unable to do so. Contre-Attaque was dissolved.

The surrealists immediately made it known in the press that the dissolution was necessary. 'Souvarinean surfascism' was the accusation they made, and this requires an explanation. Souvarine never participated in any way in Contre-Attaque (moreover, he was respected by the surrealists). Those the surrealists conveniently, and at the risk of causing confusion, described as Souvarineans were members of the old Democratic Communist Circle who left along with Bataille when it was dissolved. In substance, then, by a curious and ironic displacement (all the more ironic in that, for completely different reasons, Souvarine could not fail to entertain many grievances towards Bataille), it was the Bataillean group the surrealists described as Souvarinean. As for 'surfascism', the word must be understood as it had been created, as clumsily as possible, by Jean Dautry, who meant to convey the idea of fascism surmounted (at any rate, that is how Dubief explained or excused it). That there should be an ambiguity all the same, that no one thought there could be a way through from the anguish and vertigo, Dubief was well aware of this, even adding that ambiguity and vertigo were inevitable. Should Bataille be blamed for this? What he had until then controlled, did others – less hardened and less accustomed to the demoralisation he had put into play – control less well? It is too soon to reply. The fact is that Bataille (but Breton and the surrealists as well) countersigned a tract written by Dautry (entitled 'Sous le feu des canons français') that was, to say the least, imprudent, in which we can read without any possible ambiguity: 'We are against the scraps of paper and the slave prose of chancellors' offices . . . To them we prefer in *every case* and without being duped the antidiplomatic brutality of Hitler, less surely mortal for peace than the dribbling provocation of diplomats and politicians.'[16]

This is extraordinary, for Bataille was a long way from being able to subscribe to such a declaration himself. He wrote nothing which authorises us to suspect or allows us to think that his hatred of clerical bourgeois parliamentarianism was such that he preferred the unbridled brutality of National Socialism. Nothing at all, and yet . . .

A comment is immediately called for: not only was Bataille one of the first people to denounce fascism, but he had also started to think about it before anyone else. It was a thinking that was so elaborated (although no book had in its entirety developed from it) that it offered a model for many people and instructed (and alerted) as no other did. To what, then, should we attribute such a slip? We cannot *a priori* exclude the need to see in it a similar slip to that endured by Troppmann in *Blue of Noon*: the nightmare might certainly be so profound that in it all things would be equal. But the reality is more complex: what Bataille expected was a human uprising carrying along with it everything that constituted its limits; in a word, it would become sovereign. It should be recalled that in *La Critique sociale* he called for a generalised disorientation, and did so of his own volition. In this respect at least, if in no other, Bataille was not a man of the left, at least not as generally understood: he had hardly any belief – if any at all – in mankind. He did not believe in progress (any more than did André Masson; we shall see that this is not without significance): he therefore did not believe in history. Of the revolution he expected and attempted to make inevitable, the hostile words Simone Weil used about it should be recalled: it would resemble a catastrophe more than a peace, an irrationality rather than a rationality, a liberation of the instincts rather than their equitable ordering. If he was therefore only on the left to a slight extent, if he was even less on the right (he was one of those most violently disgusted by it), he was where no one expected him to be, exhorting the servile person to violence, to be finally raised up and impassioned all the more for being destined to failure. There was strength in acting without any real reason to hope. Bataille had it, even if he could only find himself caught in his own trap. As Dubief rightly said: he was 'fundamentally pessimistic'. Sowing

the storm, he reaped the whirlwind. Where he expected revolution, it
was war that came. But before, 'at least until Franco's uprising, this
human ocean that Bataille had consigned to the storm produced waves
of revolutionary romanticism which carried him along with his friends
and so many others.'[17]

It was the Popular Front as much as internal dissensions that got the
better of what had justified Contre-Attaque. What Bataille had retained
from the Democratic Communist Circle was definitively dispersed with
Contre-Attaque. Souvarine himself was well ahead: in 1936, he published several pamphlets about the monstrosities of the terror in the
USSR, anticipating by several years those who had worked with him.
Simone Weil was on the point of leaving for Spain, as were Fraenkel
and Péret. Masson was also in Spain, but in order to flee fascism, not
to fight it.[18] And the surrealists were trying to settle accounts with the
Communist Party, and clearly showing a deficit (several had joined it,
others would do so). 'Ferrymen' like Bernier no longer seemed to know
on what altars to sacrifice: he seemed for a while to rally to Bataille
though this did not last. What is certain is that communists or
Trotskyists now had nothing to do with the intellectual extreme left.
There was no longer anything to 'ferry'. Contre-Attaque appears to
have been the last blaze of a theoretical uprising that had begun fifteen
years earlier. It is not without interest that this should end in a fresh
and it seems definitive divorce of the two greatest intellectuals of the
period before the war.

Two facts merit consideration – although the second is of a more
anecdotal nature – if only because, in a certain way, they prolonged
Contre-Attaque. At the very least, because they let us assume that its
break-up and the dispersion of those who participated in it were not as
instantaneous as the official dissolution which took place in April 1936
might lead one to believe. The first, in January 1937, associates the
names of Bataille, Breton, Éluard and Péret (but those also, among
many others, of Naville, Hugnet, Prévert, etc.) who all signed a petition
demanding the truth about the Moscow trials of August 1936 which
resulted in the executions of Zinoviev and Kamenev among others, 'a
political trial which leaves behind it, with the corpses of sixteen
accused, a profound stupefaction'.[19]

The second fact offers the discreet interest that it was the only thing
publicly to associate the name of Colette Peignot with Georges Bataille
and Contre-Attaque (was this due to discretion or disapproval? She

signed none of the group's tracts): on 29 and 30 September 1936, supporting young women who had escaped from a reform school in Boulogne, former members of Contre-Attaque protested at a performance of a play directed by Marcelle Géniat, its principal. Several were 'beaten up', among them Georges Mouton and Henri Pastoureau,[20] others (Léo Malet, Georges Hugnet, Gaston Ferdière, Georges Bataille and Colette Peignot) were arrested and taken to the police station.

The angel and the beast, part 2

In saying that the split between Breton and Bataille was definitive, I mean that until the war nothing would significantly alter their relations. Parting company without coming to blows after Contre-Attaque, they put an end to what had opposed them and, beyond this, what from time to time might have brought them together. It is not going too far to say that they exerted a mutual fascination, but that during this period only violence emerged from it.

What is surprising is not so much their discord as their obstinacy in not completely ignoring each other. It is less surprising that Contre-Attaque did not really reconcile them than that they believed they could realise its ambitions *together*. If we cannot know what – after the hostility, insults and the heavy debit of the pamphlet *A Corpse* – brought them together (for the first time in fact), we know what divided them once again. Dubief spoke of an antipathy as 'the principal reason for Contre-Attaque's failure', but it was not so simple. No doubt the surrealist André Thirion is closer to the truth: 'Contre-Attaque [sealed] the temporary pact between the two French writers with the richest minds in the twentieth century, Bataille and Breton.'[1] This is closer because he states implicitly that only the extreme gravity of history could justify their coming together. Nothing less would have been enough to effect the reconciliation of the only two men free enough, to the left of the official left, to think through the peril posed by fascism. Certainly Breton enjoyed prestige, but it was a prestige that can be described, and not simply pejoratively, as poetic. But the man who – alone and to general censure – had thought through what filth meant, the only one not to compromise himself in some ethereal world, the only one to have said and written – obstinately and sometimes (as his critics noted) delightedly, but also furiously – about how ignominious the world is, screaming it out loud, was Bataille. And the ideas of

Contre-Attaque were his. Breton, who had less talent for thinking of the world as it really was, *a fortiori* at a time it promised to get worse still, largely left things to him. Bataille stood as a master in the arena of political analysis. Where one man answered fascism with rebukes, ones that were undoubtedly morally clear but short on analysis, the other (and here is the book he never wrote) was the only one knowledgeable enough about the subject to alert others; Breton enrolled in Bataille's school.

Breton is unlikely to have accepted this ascendancy unreservedly. It would have meant reassessing *everything* surrealism had been: its aesthetic choices (Bataille would not have passed up the opportunity to turn them to his advantage) and its choice of social revolution: in other words, making an absolute conception of liberty submit to a strict ideological discipline, and dispensing with 'that margin in which the sovereignty of desire, the savagery of thought, the exultation of poetic love, imagination and experimentation could take root and bloom'.[2] Ultimately it would have meant reassessing the aesthetic and political lucidity of the sole leadership Breton wished to continue exercising. The rivalry between the two men, since this is what it was, became simple: the role of federator of the movement *had to be* occupied by either Breton *or* Bataille. The alliance forged between several dissident surrealists and Bataille and the *Documents* group was the first expression of this problem; the pamphlet *A Corpse* was its second, violent form.[3] These were the stakes.

Does this mean Bataille coveted Breton's position? André Masson, who knew them both, seemed close to thinking so.[4] Even if this was so, it is not sufficient to explain their complex conflict. Bernard Noël is doubtless closer to the truth in proposing the hypothesis that there is 'within Breton an unrecognised Bataille: one can sense it behind *Nadja* in which the spark of poetry is revealed outside the beautiful moments it achieves, in its failure, but this Bataille then continues to pass unnoticed, even if now and again his Other is recognised'; and that 'in Bataille there is a Breton who is recognised and rejected, like a double on the point of being reconciled to itself'.[5] This hypothesis is convincing in other ways too: the Bataille of *Documents* and the one of Contre-Attaque, the Bataille soon to emerge of the College of Sociology and of *Acéphale*, knew the Breton within him, as well as Breton's power, which he found it difficult to conceal he wanted *as well*. And there is another Bataille, the one who in 1925 preferred solitude to any possible concession, the scandalous one of brothels, drinking bouts, sleepless nights and sexual encounters, the one who hated 'fine poetry' so much that he wrote books that would be unpublishable except under the counter. More than one of the challenges of their age might incline one to think of them as the two sides of the same coin, and that they were fighting over the same ground. There can scarcely be any doubt that this ground belonged to Breton (even if he was no more able than Bataille to proclaim his ownership), and Bataille coveted it only at best by way of defiance, at worst by contagion.

Contre-Attaque put an end to this 'rivalry'. With the war imminent, and the coming of age, little by little and with the disputes behind them, they would vouch for a lively esteem and even a deep admiration for each other. More than this, they understood and responded to one another from afar. After the war Breton would lead a surrealist group already at least twenty years old; Bataille would live away from Paris. Only then could what united them finally appear: less than some would have liked, and more than they could ever have admitted to themselves before the war.

From Contre-Attaque to *Acéphale*: André Masson

Introduced to one another by Michel Leiris, Georges Bataille and André Masson met in 1924, in Masson's studio in the rue Blomet, where a considerable number of people informally gathered who would rally to Breton, following Masson's lead. We have seen that, enthusiastic as this move was, it was not without reservations; for example, Masson's friends did not attach the same importance as Breton and his friends at the rue Fontaine to questions of individual behaviour and still less to those of morality. We have also seen, and André Masson insisted upon this fact, that whatever fascination Breton exercised, it never quite overcame his feeling (no doubt shared with his friends) that, fascinating as the undertaking was, it was no less in more than one aspect ludicrous: for example, the pretension *ex nihilo* to found a religion. Should we believe Masson when he spoke later of it in terms which, he said, had to be religious: several of his friends called Breton 'great pope' without him taking offence? Or that the rue Fontaine consequently should be called the Vatican and the rue Blomet, a chapel?[1] I could have said that this was not necessarily immediately the case, and only gradually did differences become quarrels. But the immediate truth was that people visited the rue Blomet who would never have set foot in the rue Fontaine or, to put it another way, whom the rue Fontaine would not have welcomed: 'rue Blomet . . . always attracted . . . potentially unusual or schismatic people . . . It was always a hearth of dissidence.'[2] Bataille was one of these unusual and schismatic people: if not the only one, then the most determined.

However, Masson was part of the first surrealism: he was even counted among its most important painters. The rupture of 1928–9 was not definitive for him, as it was for several others (moreover he was not associated with the pamphlet *A Corpse*[3]). This crisis having passed (it was, however, longer for him), he resumed relations and again collaborated with Breton – bizarrely through the mediation of Bataille. And the rare thing, according to him, was that he was able to recover what he described as being 'orthodox surrealist activity' (but, he hastened to add, orthodoxy at that time was considerably relaxed) and to be 'very close to Bataille'. Masson, more than Leiris, bridged the gap between 'the surrealists of strict allegiance' and their constant detractor.[4] His importance is therefore considerable.

It was also so much more considerable in that he was there at each of Bataille's earliest steps. It was he, we know, who anonymously illustrated *Story of the Eye* in 1928.[5] In 1931, he also illustrated *L'Anus solaire*. It was while staying with Masson in Spain, at Tossa de Mar, that Bataille completed *Blue of Noon* (if he did not write it all there). It is with him that in 1936 he published a little book called *Sacrifices* (the publication of this very short book was considerably problematic, as can be seen from the abundant correspondence the two men exchanged between Tossa and Paris. Intended for publication in 1933 by Éditions Jeanne Bucher to accompany an exhibition of drawings, sketches and water-colours by Masson at the gallery of the same name, it was published only three years later, by Éditions GLM, after for a long time being due for publication by NRF thanks to André Malraux). It was from André Masson that Bataille decided to borrow the title – 'Forebodings' – for one of his books, although we do not definitively know which one, possibly *Blue of Noon*.[6] It was also with him that in 1933 Bataille imagined – as we have seen – bringing out a journal, with the title *Minotaure*, bringing together the surrealist dissidents, a project which Breton and those loyal to him appropriated from the first issue.

But what united them does not stop there: the two men had in common a taste for Nietzsche and Dostoevsky (which distinguished them both from surrealism). They had a taste for Greece, for the tragic Greece of myths, a taste for the divinities, Dionysus, Mithras, Theseus, Orpheus and Ariadne, a taste for grave and transgressive eroticism, and a taste for Sade. We also cannot neglect the fact that the two men also had in common close family ties. By marrying Rose Maklès, the sister of Sylvia Bataille, Masson became the – attentive – uncle of Bataille's daughter, Laurence. He looked after her on several occasions, notably at Tossa, where she stayed for long periods between 1934 and 1936, stays which corresponded to the separation of her parents. However, in one thing they were very different, and on this it took them a long time to agree, if ever they did. This was political action. Masson was absent from *Documents* as well as from *La Critique sociale*, and from Contre-Attaque as well. Circumstantial reasons are not sufficient to explain this; the reasons are substantive. As far back as one goes, Masson was always hostile to any sort of marxist commitment. This was the reason for his first exclusion from surrealism: Breton affably accused him of 'social absenteeism'; and, affably or not, dismissed him. The same reasons distanced him from Bataille, as long as the latter had an allegiance to the communist revolution, be it oppositional.

When Bataille (with Breton) was committed to Contre-Attaque, he scrupulously kept his friend (who was absent from Paris, having been in Tossa since 1934) informed. Masson replied in a way and according to principles which could not have surprised Bataille but which still merit our attention. Two letters dated 6 October and 8 November 1935 must have been in response to Bataille having sent him the declaratory tract of Contre-Attaque. These two letters constitute replies that could hardly have been clearer. On 6 October he wrote: 'I think that to support marxism, *no matter how slightly*, is a mistake . . . [It is] to support a failure . . .' On 8 November Masson is even more precise (if he had not previously been): 'I am sure that everything based on marxism will be squalid because this doctrine is based upon a false idea of humanity.' The first of his reasons is the incapacity of marxism to be anything other than utilitarian and rational (in some ways Masson made himself the paradoxical advocate of Bataille's important essay 'The Notion of Expenditure'). The second is Marx's stupidity in wanting to institute a society without myths, which did not prevent Moscow from finding ridiculous substitutes for them like the 'stuffing of Lenin'.

Masson's reservations would have been those of just another anti-communist if they had not gone together with reasons to which Bataille could not have failed to be responsive: like him, profoundly Hellenist and Nietzschean, Masson took exception in advance to a society which claimed not to integrate in all their destructive strength the myths that Greece (and after it Nietzsche) had brought to their highest intensity. 'We need to emerge from it and begin by denouncing all the poverty of communism', he wrote to Bataille in the letter of 6 October, adding on 8 November, to amplify and enlarge his critique: 'I cannot get interested in any political activity which does not first of all denounce the unconsidered activity of so-called exact sciences.' The two letters, though displacing their critique, have in common that they bring attention to their reprobation of utilitarianism, functionalism and rationalism. But, in some way, they also drew up the score: Masson announced being unable to join with 'any revolutionary surge which does not accord first place to mankind, its impassioned nature, and the mysteries of life and death (not from the biological point of view in any case)'.

Can it be doubted? Masson shared the direction of Bataille's evolution; he may even have precipitated it. In fact it can be assumed that he precipitated, from afar, what Bataille would replace Contre-Attaque with: *Acéphale*. These letters were dated October and November 1935. In December, Masson and Bataille met (we do not know whether it was in Tossa or in Paris) and in April 1936 Bataille again visited Tossa de Mar. It was a decisive stay. There he drew up the first programme of *Acéphale* and the long inaugural text for the journal. In both, the shift provoked (or at the very least encouraged) by Masson was clear. Against the utopia of a possible happiness, it now strongly affirmed that such an aim was 'not only inaccessible but hateful'. The reality of values and 'the human inequality that results from it' are no less strongly affirmed. Finally, affirmed in a disordered way are existence, play, violence, power: all the notions which no less belong to one man or the other, but which it can scarcely be doubted that Masson encouraged Bataille to renew and embrace publicly. Bataille made a simple admission of this in the first issue of *Acéphale*: 'What I think and what I represent, I have not thought and represented alone.'

'Everything calls for the death which ravages us'

By April 1936 the end of Contre-Attaque was inevitable. A brief article published in *L'Œuvre*, on 5 May 1936, made it official. But Bataille did not wait for this. From April onwards, in Tossa de Mar where he was staying, he was setting out *Acéphale*'s initial programme. Contre-Attaque was not yet dead, and *Acéphale* was already born.

On 29 April 1936, 'in a cold little house in a fishing village' (as Bataille described André Masson's house), he completed the first major text of the first issue of this new journal, *Acéphale*, one which can be read as its inaugural manifesto. Its title is 'La conjuration sacrée'. A preliminary comment is required: this manifesto emerged as quite different from any other (only those of the surrealists, for entirely separate reasons and for completely different ends, might resemble it). It is untrue to say, as it often has been, that it was not political. But it was so in a way over and above what is commonly considered as such: even beyond anything Bataille had previously undertaken that could be described in this way. And if it is true that it was *also* religious (and it was – he stressed this), it is in a way that permits several levels of misunderstanding. Certainly it was religious, fiercely so even, on condition that this is understood in a Nietzschean and, without any doubt, virulently anti-Christian, sense: 'Nietzsche set aside, for good reason, the word *religion*, which alone lends itself to a confusion almost as unfortunate as the confusion between Nietzschean Dionysianism and fascism – and a word that can only be used, in the present world, in defiance.'[1] The fury in it was no less acute than in Contre-Attaque: 'Who dreams before having struggled to the end to make way for people it is impossible to watch without experiencing the need to destroy them?' Clearly he was not among these people. But since there was no possibility of destroying them, since there was no possibility even of changing them, this fury resigns itself to embarking on a quite different war, one quite different in scope, a sacred war (perhaps the same war engaged with different means). It was effectively too late: what was at stake was to be totally other or not to be at all. It was too late to hope the world would change, too late to prevent its slide into war. But there was still time to say *Yes* to it, unreservedly, time to assent to what it was, whatever it was to become. Time above all to love it, even if by doing so your world was turned upside down, even if the price was death. Any other love, any other agreement that would be accompanied by one or another reservation or condition, would be merely that of self-interest and obligation. If one did love, it had to be to the point of ecstasy; strictly speaking, to the point of losing one's head.

What was at stake in entering this war was being; and what was at stake in being was this war. Unlike everything political Bataille had hitherto written, this manifesto reconciled them. This being and this war were innocence; an innocence such that they were also a crime. A beheaded man (*Acéphale* is the man who despises the mind and reason so much that he willingly portrays himself as removed from their dual power), given over to the free play of his passion of being in the world, no longer has either God or reason; he is no longer entirely a man or entirely a God; perhaps more than anything he is both. He is surely more than anyone the *self*, a hybrid monster, a happy monster.

In Tossa de Mar, a few days before the Spanish Popular Front's victory (the second round of the legislative elections took place on 5 May) Bataille *and* Masson gave birth to this man (critics have noted his archaic nature) who has escaped from his head like a condemned man from prison. Bataille described him; Masson drew him. We have seen the influence of Masson on Bataille's writings. One feels, or at least guesses, how Bataille was involved in what Masson drew. There is little doubt, effectively, that the severed head which reappeared in the form of a skull in the exact place of the genitals was due to Bataille: both *Story of the Eye* and *Blue of Noon* had described how eroticism has no other meaning than what is given to it by death; that it has its obsessive meaning in just this way.

The first issue of *Acéphale* contained only eight pages. Pierre Klossowski contributed a text on Sade, adding to those of Bataille and to Masson's drawings. Sade, moreover, along with Nietzsche, would be among the guardian spirits of *Acéphale* (in a way they had also been those of Contre-Attaque, but accompanied by Fourier), along with Kierkegaard, Don Juan and Dionysus.

The first issue was published immediately Bataille arrived back in Paris, on 24 June 1936. On 31 July, he invited his potential future collaborators to a meeting in the basement of the café 'À la Bonne Étoile', 80 rue de Rivoli, to prepare the second issue. I say potential since we do not know exactly who attended. Only Pierre Klossowski, Roger Caillois, Jules Monnerot and Jean Wahl were named as participants in the magazine. It may thus be presumed that they participated in this preparatory meeting (Masson was absent of necessity, since he was living in Spain). Accompanying them were Jean Rollin (who contributed an article) and in all likelihood several former members of Contre-Attaque (from among those the surrealists had labelled 'Souvarineans'): Jean Dautry, Pierre Dugan, Henri Dubief and, it would appear, Colette Peignot.

All of this calls for a significant comment: *Acéphale*, above all, is part of the Bataille legend, one that was all the quicker to develop for being founded on an initial confusion and on a continuing lack of knowledge about its aims and outcomes (I do not think it will ever be possible to resolve this lack of knowledge; its secret is the key to *Acéphale*). It should therefore be stated at once that *Acéphale* is the name for two things, which I do not see as being equal or similar. It is the name of a magazine, which we know in its entirety, and here there can be no difficulties. And it is the name of a secret society, one about which we have very little information. Each participant agreed not to speak about it, and whatever occasional private revelations they have made, no one really broke this vow. Commentators have had to rely on guesswork, some of which has been unfounded, some pure speculation. *Acéphale* names two distinct projects, so distinct that not exactly the same people participated in both. What was at stake in each was perceptibly different enough for some to stop short of joining one or the other. Klossowski, Ambrosino and Waldberg made no secret of having belonged to both (this is no doubt also true of several others). We cannot even be certain that they participated closely enough for us to reduce the secret society's activities to what they disclosed about it (which in any case was largely by way of allusion); and others who chose not to be part of it probably knew more, since Bataille kept them informed: this is true for Michel Leiris, Jacques Lacan and also André

Masson, by dint of his being abroad. The simplest explanation would be that the magazine was the exoteric face of this esoteric society. This was not so: clarifying the journal *Acéphale* does not suffice to make clear the secret society Acéphale.

Not until January 1937, six months after the first issue, did the second issue of *Acéphale* appear. Such a long interval between the first two issues can be explained by the importance and number of pages in the second number (thirty-eight compared to the first number's eight), but also by the time Bataille needed to establish the Acéphale secret society.

It is worth pausing at the second issue, which was entirely devoted to Nietzsche. The intention here was not to rescue Nietzsche from obscurity; everyone knew his name, and doubtless his works too. It was a matter of reclaiming him from the hands of those who were using and abusing him: the fascists. In fact, a fascist reading of Nietzsche had appeared some years before, and this was tending to become the only one possible. From then on, there were those who celebrated the fact that Nietzsche might have been a deliberately anti-Semitic and prefascist philosopher,[2] and those who reproached him for it. Few remained who, having read and understood him sufficiently, knew it was not a case of praising or apologising for him; Bataille was among these. Alone, he attempted to turn the accusation back on this reading and to make a claim for Nietzsche's initial innocence. His courage was unusual; to more than one onlooker it could appear as a provocation. In fact, what other figure of the left, of the ultra-left even, known by all, *L'Humanité* included, for having undertaken with Breton in Contre-Attaque a revolutionary process that could be located, in Georges Sadoul's phrase, 'beyond communism', would have dared to claim that Nietzsche did not belong on the right and the only possible price of maintaining that he did was an unspeakable falsification? Better still: what figure of the left would have dared publicly to put his name to this? Yet this is what Bataille did, supported in this process of rehabilitation by Masson, Klossowski, Wahl and Caillois. And for this rehabilitation to be total and beyond criticism, he joined his voice to Nietzsche's in a telling elegy to multiracialism.

Would it have been possible to be any more, or more pertinently, political in 1937 (the year, remember, of the publication of *Bagatelles pour un massacre* by Louis-Ferdinand Céline)? We need to ask why it was so rapidly claimed that Bataille had abandoned his political positions (that he no longer spoke of politics in the way he hitherto had, that he no longer spoke of it in terms understood by everyone, makes no difference): in 1937 (as in 1938 and 1939) Bataille was and remained *political*. But who was (and still is) perturbed by this?[3] At best, it is claimed, Bataille lost interest in politics after Contre-Attaque; at worst, in so far as he continued to take an interest in it, he did so in a dubious, suspect way, in a way that might offer more than one troubling analogy with the neo-paganist mythology of Hitler's followers (we shall see how he did not escape considerably more direct and serious accusations). The texts of *Acéphale* are enough to answer these criticisms; if we can be absolutely certain of one thing about this magazine, it is that Bataille, in opposition both to a right that was predominantly (and odiously) anti-Semitic, and a left that was sometimes no less so (if less openly and without making it a political tenet), restates the honour of Nietzsche in having rid himself in advance of the racial farce. Bataille quotes him eloquently in the text: 'Don't associate with anyone implicated in the brazen humbug of racism' (this quote here assumes the tone of a decisive command) and 'But when it comes to it, what do you think I feel when the name of Zarathustra comes out of the mouth of anti-Semites!' Whatever Nietzsche's disgust, it was no less felt by Bataille; this is so clearly true that one of the few customs we know to have been observed by the Acéphale secret society consisted of refusing to shake hands with anti-Semites (in anticipation, a kind of reversed yellow star whose shame would strike out at anti-Semites!); this practice was adhered to.

Nietzsche is irrevocably distinguishable from the fascists not only in the rejection of anti-Semitism. *All* his thought *a priori* excludes the possibility of reducing it to this infamous urge:

> Fascism and Nietzscheanism are mutually exclusive, and are even violently mutually exclusive, as soon as each of them is considered in its totality: on one side life is tied down and stabilized in an endless servitude, on the other there is not only a circulation of free air, but the wind of a tempest; on one side the charm of human culture is broken in order to make room for vulgar force, on the other force and violence are tragically dedicated to this charm.[4]

This was perhaps Bataille's most important declaration at this moment. The moment should be specified, since his thought now differed perceptibly from what he had expressed in *La Critique sociale*. The reason is that in 1933–4, his critique of fascism was not very, if at all, Nietzschean. In 1937, it is *paradoxically*, by using Nietzsche that he continued this critique. Admittedly, following Nietzsche and using his example, he set force and violence in play, but not in any way to give legitimacy to servitude. Nietzsche (Bataille) and the fascists certainly share the fact that they valorise force and violence, but it is neither the same force nor the same violence. The fascists enslave while Nietzsche/ Bataille liberate. The fascists alienate in favour of the god-master, of him alone and in his sole service. Nietzsche/Bataille obey the free play of mankind's passions in the world, serving individual sovereignty, rallying to the common cause (the common cause here is Acéphale), and collective liberty (even if this meant the unleashing of servile forces called for by Contre-Attaque).

Nietzsche only responds to the fascist use of the energies he set in play at the price of a work of falsification. The exegetes are falsifiers and the texts are faked (like *Beyond Good and Evil*); the interpreters are falsifiers and the aims of his thought are diverted. Who is responsible for this monumental philosophical falsification? Bataille names them: Elisabeth Foerster-Nietzsche who, on 2 November 1933, welcomed Hitler into the Nietzsche-Archiv and brazenly offered him a sword-stick that had belonged to the philosopher (who had been dead for thirty-three years) as a gift; Richard Oehler, Nietzsche's cousin and Elisabeth's collaborator at the Nietzsche-Archiv. He was responsible for *Nietzsche and the Future of Germany*, a pious lampoon whose argument consisted of nothing less than highlighting the close relationship between the philosopher and the author of *Mein Kampf*; and Alfred Rosenberg, whose reading of Nietzsche, even if not the official one, conveys just as well the servitude to which National Socialism strove to reduce the philosopher, a servitude that other, more impassioned authors (Hauer, Bergmann and Reventlow) would accentuate.

The patient work of fascist theorists only encouraged the deployment of individual energies in order to channel them to the advantage of the *single individual* to whom they were due: Mussolini in Italy and Hitler in Germany (but perhaps Stalin was no different; we have seen what similarities Bataille found in them). Here were the replacement gods offered to the adoration of the kneeling masses: 'The comedy which – under the pretence of democracy – opposes German Caesarism and Soviet Caesarism, shows what frauds are acceptable to a mob constrained by misery, at the mercy of those who basely flatter it.'[5] This is the opposite of *Acéphale* in every way. *Acéphale* did not boast of having *politically* noted the death of God only to resign itself compliantly to his substitute sham. A man without a head is like a man who has abandoned God, who has cast him out of his body as the Evangelist cast swine out of the possessed. But with God dead, gods are no longer possible; no more master, no more king (the second of Acéphale's known customs was the commemoration in the Place de la Concorde of the beheading of Louis XVI), no more Führer to live or die for . . . Nothing left ratified by God's past life, nothing that uses it for justification. This is not the least significant nor the least political of the consequences of the death of God. Monocephalous societies are no longer possible: 'The only society full of life and force, the only free society, is the *bi- or polycephalic* society that gives the fundamental antagonisms of life a constant explosive outlet, but one limited to the richest forms. . . . the very principle of the head is the reduction to unity, the *reduction* of the world to God.' And in case this might not be clear (and not clearly political), Bataille takes care to add: 'The head, conscious authority or God, represents one of the *servile functions* that gives itself as, and takes itself to be, an end; consequently it must be the object of the most inveterate aversion.'[6]

Is there any need to recap this? The means have nothing in common but their appearance. It is not the same force, nor the same violence, that *Acéphale* and fascism wield (in the same way that the 'power' wielded by Nietzsche and fascism are not at all the same). As for the ends, they are diametrically opposed. For the fascists, this force and this violence serve a fiercely unitary society locked around a substitute for the dead God. For *Acéphale*, they serve the individual, free of any *function*, and *a fortiori* free of any servitude, devoted within the individual solely to the unleashed play of his most violent and most tragic passions, the only ones that are enlightening. The fascists serve a 'finite' monocephalous ossification; *Acéphale*, an infinite acephalous dismembering. The presence of God – or of his sham – looks inward to the closed racialism of the former; the death of God opens onto the indefinite universality of the latter.

This brief summation (I am well aware of the other developments it suggests) is still enough to show as opposites two types of thought that, through (perhaps intentional) exaggeration, some people have blended together (perhaps constituting a redress of what *Acéphale* wanted to be in the same way that *Acéphale* wished to redress the status of Nietzsche).[7]

Could *Acéphale* have incurred the displeasure of fascism and its devotees more openly than with this second issue? But this is what it did, by taking as the subject for its third number the most deleterious of gods, the one held by Alfred Rosenberg as the origin of the worst indulgences of German romanticism ('the god of the dead', as he would say), Dionysus, the one who gave birth to the profound rooting of romanticism within 'the instinctive, the unformed, the demoniacal, the sexual, the ecstatic, the chthonian – into the cult of the Mother'.[8] As the third issue of *Acéphale* appeared (in fact, a double issue, numbers 3 and 4), war was approaching: this was July 1937. The Popular Front had collapsed in June, but at no point had it been discussed in the three issues contemporaneous with it. In this sense *Acéphale* was not political, at least not as it might have been expected to be. It was as if for Bataille national history had lagged behind its actual course (but had he not reacted in the same way to the left's show of solidarity of 12 February 1934?); as if what was happening in Paris and France masked what was being played out elsewhere, in Germany, Italy and Spain,[9] a game whose scope was completely different. Bataille is quite consistent on this point. And it is not going too far to say that *Acéphale* – by other means and to other ends – was pursuing the work begun in 1933 with 'The Psychological Structure of Fascism', as well as what should have followed that article (unfinished as we have seen) with the book begun in 1934, 'Le Fascisme en France'. And if Bataille was not afraid of stating that dull (and virtuous) moral protest is something for toothless old women, he also knew that the social revolution he himself called for, and to which the Popular Front might for an instant have been believed to give rise, was not strong enough to counteract the unchecked haemorrhage of fascism across Europe.

Dionysus (numbers 3–4 of *Acéphale*) provided the opportunity to restate what was essential, and the essential, if one can put it so bluntly, is death. The community of the living is what is bound together by the anguishing promise made to one and all that they will die. Without question, Bataille considered that nothing joyful or luminous binds humanity together. He does not hide the fact of looking to the death of others to awaken the being in each one of us (we have seen that what was at stake in *Acéphale* was both war and being).

What awakens the being in humanity and shows people what they are hiding from is death rising up among them, among the living: the promise made to each of them of being annihilated in their turn. Death, through sacrifice (the analysis of sacrificial death was the magazine's business; the desire for sacrifice, as I shall explain, was the business of the Acéphale society), binds together the survivors who are held in the grip of the corpse. Death binds together the anguished community experienced together by the living in the fact of the rending of their separation. Bataille would return at length to this fascinated discovery. It is sufficient here for us to understand that in 1937, in issue 3–4 of *Acéphale*, under the sign of Dionysus, he made explicit, in a way permitting no confusion, what religious tragedy is for him: 'In the existence of a community . . . the sure grip of death has become the thing most foreign to man. No one thinks any longer that the reality of a communal life – which is to say, human existence – depends on the sharing of nocturnal terrors and on the kind of ecstatic spasms spread by death.'[10] The living only gather together 'in anguish'; the greater this is, the stronger being is in them, and the stronger their community, a tragic community (for Bataille there can be no other kind). He may have feared being misunderstood (though perhaps misunderstanding was inevitable): this tragedy has nothing to do with that which will soon spread death around the world. The death and devastation spread by National Socialist and fascist Caesarisms were conquering ones. Only the death Bataille appealed to, that he called upon himself and upon those who, along with him, formed the idea of a community, is ecstatic because only it depossesses, only it lays waste. The former bind dense communities by creating lacerations to which they feel immune or, worse still, they feel strengthens them. Bataille appeals to a death (more precisely to the *consciousness* of death) that is tragic everywhere and for all; a death that awakens being everywhere and for everyone (only the consciousness of this death sets us free). Acéphale was this community bound in such a way without a head, in other words with no God. And a community with no God (and no leader) is a community unreservedly opened to the ravages of death: 'Everything calls for the death which ravages us.' To kill God, to kill the leader, is tragic, in the mythical sense of the word. It is even a tragic *duty*.

Bataille reminds us: 'Putting the leader to death is itself tragedy. A truth that changes the appearance of human things starts here: THE EMOTIONAL ELEMENT THAT GIVES AN OBSESSIVE VALUE TO COMMUNAL LIFE IS DEATH.'[11]

Death, so overabundantly present in everything he wrote from the very first, is here as well; and, perhaps for the first time, it is truly *political*. The community of men (in no way to be confused with the state, nor in any way with the nation) would be totally different and totally differently constituted if death reassumed its due. Fascism, like democracy (even more than democracy), denies what death is; worse still, in turning it into a glamorous solution (a patriotic one, for instance), it eludes it.

Three issues of *Acéphale* were published in 1936–7, none in 1938; the final number to appear – in 1939 – scarcely resembled that of 1937. Much smaller in format, with no title, and with no theme, it would be written just by Bataille. Certainly it commemorates Nietzsche as its predecessors had done, but in a tragic way. Bataille had descended a little deeper into the horror of death being called forth every day; Colette Peignot was dead. Twenty years later he would say, soberly, that 'A death tore him apart in 1938.' The silence of *Acéphale* in 1938 bears the weight of this death that had sprung up like that invoked to hold the survivors in the grip of the horror of a communion in an intolerable identity. *Acéphale* would be placed in 1939 under the tragic sign of a long text insolently entitled 'The Practice of Joy Before Death'. Death is horror, and it is bedazzlement. No one could understand this but Bataille *alone*. He alone wrote the texts of the last issue of *Acéphale*: after a death had ravaged him, before the war ravaged all and sundry.[12]

Is it necessary to question Bataille's position in relation to fascism in 1936–7 again? Or, more precisely, to answer the insinuations made in various quarters by people once close to him, insinuations that come down to the claim that what *Acéphale* set in play, by unleashing obscure forces, barely conceals a close relation to what fascism set in play at the same moment? The texts we possess assure us of the contrary; they do not contain a single line that might justify the slightest reservation. As we have seen, *Acéphale*'s texts are nevertheless heavily political, much more so than is generally agreed. After Contre-Attaque, Bataille did not shy away from analysis of his times;

in fact he actually devoted himself to it with rare acuity, even if this analysis had no place for the Popular Front (its nature had effectively changed: the attention paid to current events was minimal; that paid to the predictability of events to come, linked to fascism, was more significant). As for Acéphale and the rituals summarily described as neo-paganist (rites about which we really know very little; and secondary questions might include asking if the only possible paganism is that of the right, or if a paganism of the left is 'unthinkable'. Did not Acéphale on the contrary try to think this through?), the texts exist which fully answer this charge, and they do so in the most decisive manner (or should we be taking no notice of the texts? Could interpretation dispense with them and pay heed to rumour?). Instead of inviting anyone to adopt energies spawning destruction and death (as fascism does), Bataille bound, or attempted to bind, strong communities once more around the *awakening* to the fatality of destruction and death; a fatality, as he sombrely informs us, that must be adopted if there is any chance for the being to spring up once more in each of us, the being for which *Acéphale* is the strange war waged against itself.

But was Bataille's truth also that of those around him? This is less certain. In this regard the Bibliothèque Nationale holds a text by Pierre Dugan,[13] apparently a member of *Acéphale* although he had nothing published in it, a text of dubious sentiments to say the least; as dubious as Dautry's word ('surfascisme') which caused the surrealists to break with Contre-Attaque. Evidently not all those around Bataille were as scrupulous in responding to the highly complex contradiction he set in play. In this text, Dugan valorises the victorious force of fascism against a 'purulent infamy of the Stalinism of divine right' that is not only sterile but 'abject'. Fascism's irrationality is force: this had got the better of communism as it had of the democracies. Dugan rashly (?) concludes:

> Any power that sets itself this task [of overcoming fascist force] will have to assimilate with ease and make explicit for its own liberating ends all the propaganda methods and even the existential forms of fascism, just as fascism assimilated and made explicit marxist methods and forms (while being opposed to marxism on an affective level). .... Just as fascism is ultimately only a surmarxism, a marxism set back on its feet, so the power that will overcome it can only be a surfascism.[14]

Thus reappears the rash – and dubious – concept of 'surfascism' that was not used at any point by Bataille himself or by anyone published in *Acéphale*. Could Bataille have agreed with what was equivocal in such a text? In notes hastily drawn up by him for future issues, he seems to have been ready to find room for Dugan's texts (whether this one, or similar ones, we do not know); and he accompanied this intention with a phrase that is strangely rash in its turn (though this is just a note found among his drafts): 'The great difference between the surrealists and my friends consists in the fact that my friends had no respect for words; they were in no respect idealists.'[15] Was the immoralist in him ready to gamble on the radical harmlessness of words? Would it have been idealistic, for once, to indicate carefully (even respectfully) the horror in question (and no one was predicting better than Bataille what this horror was), with a word not prone to the worst kind of confusion? This would be the second time Bataille let words and statements be uttered in his vicinity that, even if they were not his, carried him in the direction of something entirely different from what he was himself saying. The extreme complexity of the contradiction developed by him (a highly Nietzschean contradiction) created such slippages, and this was sometimes held against him.

This reproach – at least as far as one can imagine it – is perhaps not entirely innocent. One rarely hears about the fascination Bataille exerted over others. His intellectual influence was considerable at this time, and so was his power of fascination. Pierre Klossowski puts this unambiguously: 'Bataille was such a powerful presence that he undeniably had, from the first, an extraordinary ascendancy over me, as he had over much in the "convulsive" context that went beyond surrealism towards joining the Popular Front.'[16] This scarcely differs from the fascination evoked by Roger Caillois: 'the power Bataille could exert was not at all a political power, comparable to that of Breton over the surrealist group. Bataille's power was rather charismatic in nature, an ascendancy. This was a strange, placid, almost awkward man, but his very gravity had something fascinating about it'.[17] It is difficult to picture what kind of horror he could have used this ascendancy and fascination for; a horror to flee from. The worst was not that he could have been a closet fascist (it is clear he was not), or that his unconscious fascination with it might be contagious: this would be identifiable and could be unmasked. He would have been just one among many who, in this period, found it hard to discern whether to choose the side of the angels or the devils, and who sided first with one, then the other in a dangerous oscillation that today makes it hard to distinguish them. But the horror to which Bataille drove others had a completely different meaning: that of the death promised to them all. He does not merely say how little being each of us has, he also says that each of us only has a being equal in intensity to the experience we daily have of the death that annihilates us. To what does Bataille invite people (as we shall see, this was the meaning of the Acéphale society), other than this terror? That some should rid themselves of it by giving it other, undeserved names was perhaps inevitable. Bataille scared people, and to expose fear is to lessen it. The unspeakable was finding its nature again, and the unnameable its name.

Could such an ascendancy and such a fascination 'fascisize'? Would he ultimately have been the black god of this headless community he dreamed of, the merciless god (rising up not only just against himself but against his faithful)? Klossowski points in this direction, in seeing Bataille himself emblematised in the figure drawn by Masson, contemplating his own experience.[18] Such an accusation evokes the possibility of something which in religious terms is called a denial.

But to cut short any mistaken interpretations, one should acknowledge the fact that the other side of Acéphale, the secret society, eludes us. Conceived by Bataille in secret and to be secret, save for the two or three details confided by others on various occasions, this secret alone holds the truth: no one truly broke the code of silence. And even the details confided should be treated with caution (other than those from Bataille himself): it is not certain whether all participants *really* knew what Acéphale's project was, and whether they did not just know the limited facts Bataille agreed to supply about it (or managed to explain; as we shall see, the experience of Acéphale was ultimately perhaps his alone, and no one really understood its meaning). This is no doubt what happened with several of them: the game was in his hands alone, and he let others take part as he pleased, according to a hierarchy of players he alone controlled.

The project was that of a community, and of a religion. Essentially it was a community of men; it would seem that Colette Peignot was its only woman (after her there was Isabelle Waldberg too, later considered a surrealist sculptor; at the time she was working on a thesis on Nietzsche). We should be cautious about listing those who formed this community: Georges Ambrosino, Pierre Klossowski and Patrick

Waldberg were participants without a doubt, and strong supporters. Also probably taking part were Jacques Chavy, René Chenon, Henri Dubief, Pierre Dugan, Dussat (?), Jean Dautry (and others we do not know). Some of these are likely to have participated; others may be supposed to have (for example Jules Monnerot); finally, Roger Caillois's membership is altogether problematic. Thanks to him, and Pierre Klossowski, we know the little we do of Acéphale. Clearly, if he was not part of it, he was as close to it as possible, in other words close enough for Bataille rigorously to keep him informed about its activities, about what was being *enacted*. He says he was not a member – he even stressed this: 'I was one of the most reticent: I'm alluding here to the group about which Bataille kept me frequently informed and which I always refused to join, even whilst collaborating in the magazine of the same name that was its journal.'[19] This emphatic statement is above suspicion; yet it so happens that he did say, in private, that he had been a member, as it is also true that in public he admitted to too close a proximity to it for some doubts not to be aroused (such as those regarding Acéphale's sacrifice and Bataille's proposal to him to be the sacrificer[20]). If Caillois was a member of Acéphale, this denial might be seen as his chosen way – all the more effective for averting questions – of not betraying the vow of secrecy taken by its participants.

However we may wish to try to lift the veil of secrecy, we keep coming back to the fact that Acéphale's project was also that of a religion. Bataille admitted this twenty years later; he felt charged with the mission of founding this new religion: 'I had spent the preceding years with an insupportable preoccupation: I was resolved, if not to found a religion, at least to direct myself towards this meaning. What the history of religions had revealed to me had gradually exalted me.'[21]

Acéphale was religious, 'fiercely' so, as we have seen; and paradoxically so, as well. Bataille was a Nietzschean, and like Nietzsche he was totally hostile to Christianity. Thus it is not in any Christian sense that the meaning of this new religion should be sought. It is, rather, in the spirit of the Aztec gods, those 'fierce and malevolent' gods that impressed him so forcefully, in the spirit of the ritual sacrifices practised by a culture that more than any other was happy to be familiar with the most violent death, in the spirit too of the Chinese torture suffered by Fu Chou Li (the torture of the Hundred Pieces), in the spirit of the notion of non-productive expenditure borrowed from Mauss, in the spirit of the potlatches already evoked by Bataille ...

in short, in the spirit of everything which forces its way into mankind, awakening its being, transporting it to the state of the most intense presence in the world. Nothing but the most deranged eroticism and the blackest death can transport one into this state. If Acéphale was (or tried to be) a religion, it was in the sense in which it wished to accord death the place no one else had given it. If everyone evades it, if everyone gives it a sense of finality, or makes it a passage towards the next state of being – or the soul – Acéphale on the contrary gave it the meaning of the inevitable annihilation of being. What Bataille no doubt wished was that the horror of the death promised to each one of us should descend within everyone like a horrifying Pentecost, and that once repressed fervours and energies should rise to the measure of this horror.

Death is linked to the earth, only to the earth (and not to the heavens), to rotting, decomposition, to the buried body turning into a cadaver. The body is a root, teeming beneath the skin of the forest, or a volcano swarming with entrails. Acéphale was this *recognition*: a community of seers, eyes wide open on the stupefying work of death. We are reminded of *The Solar Anus*, the sun as a corpse at the bottom of a well, with the sky upturned. We are reminded of everything most violently anti-idealist in Bataille's writings, as a way of gaining an approximate idea of the disruptive meaning Acéphale's orgies were meant to have. Perhaps closer still to this is a dreadful text I have yet to discuss, describing the sacrifice of a female gibbon (we do not know if the scenario was real or imaginary), trussed up like a fowl and tied to a stake in a pit, head down, its anal rump opening to the sky like a flower. The participants in this sacrifice are all naked as well, all 'equally deranged by avidity for pleasure (exhausted with sensuality)'. At a signal they heap earth onto the animal, partly burying it: only the 'filthy solar protuberance' is still visible, in spasm, convulsed by anguish. Then a woman, in this story an Englishwoman,

> extends her long naked body with a charming behind over the filled-in hole: the mucous flesh of this false bald skull, slightly soiled with shit on the flower radiating from the summit is even more disturbing to see when touched by pretty white fingers. All the others stand around, holding back their cries, wiping away the sweat; their teeth bite into their lips, a slight dribble even runs from overwrought mouths: contracted by suffocation, and also by death, the beautiful boil of red flesh was set ablaze amid stinking brown flames.[22]

Let there be no mistake: I am not suggesting Acéphale practised such rites, and no such evidence exists. Yet this sense of tottering, of vacillation, has the meaning of what Acéphale wanted to be, a meaning accessible only 'at the point at which there is no longer anything but a hallucinatory void, but an odour of death which makes you gag'.[23] A sense of *alliance* as well, a sense of ecstatic nuptials; the most repellent, most binding of excessive nuptials.

Here alone is the totality of being, a totality from which Bataille forged the meaning of this new religion, as indicated by his sole surviving text that can be unmistakably attributed to the Acéphale society: 'totality requires that life reunites and so to speak is confused in the orgy with death. The object of the experience must therefore be to pass from a certain fragmented and empty state of a life freed from concern with death to that kind of brutal and suffocating ebb of everything without doubt taking place in so many death throes'.[24]

Bataille desired this irreparability. It seems he wanted a *human* sacrifice to bind Acéphale's participants (its initiates) irreparably together. Such a plan would have allowed it to reach a point of no return. A consenting victim was sought; apparently one was found.[25] A sacrificer was sought, but apparently in vain. The alliance never reached its greatest intensity, and the irreparable never took place. Bataille himself was glad of this, much later: 'This was a monstrous error, but gathering together my writings made me aware at the same time of the error and the value of this monstrous intention.'[26]

Acéphale did not always have such a grave, tragic face. Or else, because it was grave and tragic, it was no less a game and a festival: 'We have nothing in common with the avarice of Christians, we are free beings: a limitless generosity and a Greek, that is, excitable, naïvety and even movements of absurd humour . . . The sort of foolish avidity with which we approach the tragic place in which our existence develops and is played out would, without generosity, be just a new Christian avarice.' Acéphale's aim was also to turn 'human life into a festival in proportion to a game as free as this'.[27]

Two of the Acéphale society's rituals have already been mentioned: the refusal to shake hands with anti-Semites and the commemoration in the Place de la Concorde of the execution of Louis XVI. The second of these rituals, dubbed a 'hoax' by Michel Leiris,[28] was still significantly political, whatever Acéphale's allegedly apolitical status: 'The Place de la Concorde is the place where the death of God has to be announced and proclaimed because its obelisk is the calmest negation of it.'[29] Other rituals existed: culinary rituals, for example, the importance of which Bataille was well aware of, the daily lunch being ritually composed of minced horsemeat washed down with water (wine being forbidden during the day). The most important and best known nevertheless remains the one by which members travelled separately by train from Saint-Lazare station to the tiny station of Saint-Nom-la-Bretèche, strangely lost in the midst of a forest, and from there, at night, alone and in silence, proceeded to the foot of a tree struck by lightning (lightning here might have the meaning of a brutal death dealt to something that is most *rooted*). There they burned sulphur, and this is about all we know.

Thanks to Pierre Klossowski we do have an account from one of its few participants:

> About twenty of us took the train to . . . Saint-Nom-la-Bretèche. . . . We were told: 'Meditate, but secretly. Never speak a word of what you felt or thought!' Bataille never told us anything more. He never explained what this kind of ceremony represented. I can tell you that it was very beautiful . . . I only remember that particular evening as pouring with rain. There was a Greek fire at the foot of a tree struck by lightning. A whole stage set. . . . It was very beautiful. But we all had the feeling of participating in something happening within Bataille, in his head. We all felt a kind of compassion. Not compassion in the sense of pity! We were sharing . . . We were participating.[30]

Did anything else happen, that evening or any other? Was there a sacrifice, as some have variously suggested without substantiation? 'It does not matter if mortifying meditations or orgiastic rites took place in the Saint-Nom-la-Bretèche forest. Should profane curiosity grasp it, this would be enough to profane the subversive sacred nature Georges Bataille tried in vain to impart to his impossible plan: the recasting of man by changing his reality in accomplishing his own nothingness.'[31] One thing is certain: in the somewhat hierarchical society of Acéphale, each was initiated according to rank into different, graded rituals. If anyone had spoken about it (which as we have seen never happened), they would only have given a partial truth (in reality just their own truth). The only ones with everything in their grasp were Bataille and Colette Peignot; on their silence the impossible truth of Acéphale closes.

One should not forget that the lightning-struck tree in the forest of Saint-Nom-la-Bretèche, so emblematic of what Acéphale set out to be, was just a few miles from where they lived on the outskirts of Saint-Germain-en-Laye. (If this tree had symbolic value, it was above all for them.) They visited it assiduously, and doubtless 'worshipped' it. This house at 59b rue Mareil,[32] occupied by Georges and Colette at the end of 1937 and throughout 1938, and that he would thereafter share with Patrick and Isabelle Waldberg (in 1939), makes up, along with the forest of Saint-Nom, the privileged places of Acéphale's topography. There were a few others: the café L'Univers in the Place du Palais-Royal where, when he emerged from the Bibliothèque Nationale (not that he was there much: in 1939 he would arrive around midday and leave around four), Bataille would join his friends, Acéphale's 'conspirators', plus others like Jacques Lacan, who often came to these meetings[33] (if Lacan did not take part in Acéphale, Bataille can be assumed to have kept him scrupulously informed about its activities[34]); a brothel in the rue Pigalle where Bataille and Colette Peignot indulged their tastes, and another in Saint-Germain-en-Laye which they frequented more often.[35]

Colette had an essential position in all this. There is no doubting that Acéphale was first and foremost *their* community. It seems likely that the idea of such a religion came essentially from Bataille. But it seems just as likely that without Colette Peignot it would not have seen the light of day, at least not in such a form. Even though we do not know her exact role, we can justifiably conceive it as being substantial.

A final comment on this whole period: was Bataille mad, or was he playing devil's advocate? We recall that ten years earlier he was convinced he had – that we all have – an eye in the top of the skull which would allow us, once the skull was pierced, to *see* straight up, into the sun. Bataille had no doubts about this possibility, even if it appeared insane to him later. Was the project of a ritual sacrifice not equally insane? However 'luminous' the intuition of it may have been (that a community can only be tied together in the beginning by the death of one of their number), how could he have been tempted to prove it by experience? It is in all likelihood false that Bataille wished, as Caillois claimed, to make himself stronger and more important than Breton, that this master stroke (!) would help him assume a prestige greater than anything Breton could ever achieve. This supposition is not only to depreciate Bataille, it also supposes an importance for surrealism it did not have in Bataille's eyes. More illuminating is the parallel proposed, again by Caillois, between Breton and Bataille: they were both incapable of distinguishing words and things. Both, he claimed, were subject to this formidable confusion: 'Georges Bataille's attitude on this point [the ritual sacrifice] was as exasperated as Breton's definition of the simplest surrealist act: go into the street with a gun in your hand and fire at random at passers-by.'[36]

If 'madness' there was, it was Bataille's madness in never settling for knowledge: he also needed the assurance of *experience*. And this is crucial to an understanding of him. In the end he is as un-abstract and 'unliterary' as possible. He himself added that he was also as equally unphilosophical. The *theoretical* possibility of the existence of a pineal eye at the top of the skull would only have interested him moderately if all the benefits that his own experience could gain from this discovery had not also immediately appeared. The same went for Acéphale, and here too Roger Caillois's opinion is credible: the theoretical interest of shamanism seemed significant to him.[37] But it only appeared so signifi-cant to him in so far as he himself could claim to be a shaman. This is how one should doubtless understand what led him to turn himself into a 'religious' figure: it is not enough to acknowledge the interest presented by the history of religions, one must go further. One must turn oneself and one's thought into a new religion, even if such an undertaking might later appear insane or ridiculous. In 1959, in other words twenty years later, Bataille drew up some disillusioned conclusions:

> Today nothing seems further away from me than the idea of founding a religion. . . . Not only is the intention comical, not only is my current intention founded on the feeling of profound ridicule I have retained, but the foundation and effort it demands are the opposite of what I call 'religion'. All we could do is look for it. Not find it. Finding it would necessarily have a value or form of definition. But I can become religious and especially I can be religious, keeping myself above all from defining what I follow or how.[38]

It is in this way that Bataille is as unphilosophical as possible, and in this way that his biography is of capital significance for his work: he never thought about anything he did not also wish to live out, never imagined anything he did not – alone or in the company of others – also wish to experience, whatever the retractions made in hindsight.

Florid bullfight[1]

The roaring of lions, the howling of wolves, the raging of
the stormy sea, and the destructive sword, are portions of
eternity, too great for the eye of man.
(William Blake, *The Marriage of Heaven and Hell*)

To say that the irremediable did not occur is inexact. It really did
happen but not in the way that Bataille (and perhaps everyone?)
expected. If the meaning of Acéphale was that the death invoked would
come, Acéphale, darkly, triumphed. If the meaning of Acéphale was
that men and women would be definitively connected and fused
together around this death, all permeated with a terror so deep and so
alike that nothing would henceforth be able to separate them, Acéphale
was tragically a failure.

The fact is that with Acéphale, Bataille lived through two major
experiences: that of an elective – restricted and conspiratorial – community; and, at its heart, that of an amorous community. Amazing as
the 'fancy' (*lubie*: the word is Bataille's) presiding over Acéphale was,
it is intellectually exact to a point that provokes dread (the 'madness'
of Acéphale, its monstrosity, could have been to want to make the
experience of it, to *verify* it). The trepidation of a shared death (more
so than love, which alone seems to have comparable power) linked the
survivors together to the same extent as it tore them apart. Those who
remain have in common with the person they have seen dead that they
in their turn will follow; in common with the one on whom the blow
has fallen, that they have momentarily been spared. This fact of death
and this dead person grasp the community gathered around the corpse
with an anguish that, in Bataille's mind, was the whole of existence
(the aim of Acéphale was this existence and certainly not death, which
is only a paradoxical way of reaching it) and, more dreadfully, what

within existence denounces impotence. Is this what Bataille wanted to
see his friends share? Supposing this to be the case, fate, at the very
moment his challenge provoked it, decided both in his favour and
against him: in his favour in that death appeared at the rendezvous
(there was something profoundly Don Juanesque in Acéphale), in a
more terrible form than any other: it struck the woman he loved,[2] and
against him in that this death bound no one together. Admittedly, this
death was not sacrificial, not, at least, in the way Bataille understood
it. But, sacrificial or not, it did not establish around it a community of
men and women indissolubly linked by the irremediable. Other devas-
tations would follow, those of the war, which diluted this one, which
was soon no more than the sorrow of a man alone, among other men,
who were also alone. And the few exceptional friends who were present
when Colette Peignot was in her death throes, Marcel Moré, a Christian, and Michel Leiris, were not members of Acéphale. If they were
devastated, it was in the way demanded by friendship, not at all as
some sort of 'religious' way.

'The pain, dread, tears, delirium, orgy, fever and then death were the
everyday bread that Laure[3] shared with me, and this bread leaves me
with the memory of a forbidding yet immense sweetness.'[4] The community of lovers is, no less than that of men, *a* community. Perhaps it
is even the most devastating. A woman appears, rises up from the void
(from the ignorance one had of her existence) . . . This apparition
'seems to belong to the devastating world of dream'. This phrase which
a Breton could have written, Bataille immediately nuanced (unideali-
sed): 'But possession casts the face of the dream, naked and deluged
with pleasure, into the restricted real world of a bedroom.'[5] Devastating and ridiculous, the world of lovers is no less the world, the world
in its entirety. At best, it is the world more densely: more than any
other it gathers them together and brings them to the state of highest
intensity. More than politics does: 'The world of lovers is no less *true*
than that of politics. It even absorbs the totality of existence, which
politics cannot do.'[6]

The embrace of lovers closes the world over them. The existence of
each is never so close to being in communion with the other than at
the moment of this embrace, it is never so close to believing that this is
the end of all that separates one being from another . . . And it is
nowhere more profoundly, more irreparably distant: 'Two beings of

the opposite sex are lost in one another and together form a new being different from either. The precariousness of this new being is obvious: it is never something whose parts are distinct from it; there is no more than a tendency to lose consciousness in brief moments of darkness.'[7] Two bodies in a bedroom abolish the alien world in their embrace, make as though death no longer had the power to slip between them ... and death is never so intensely present as in the embrace which seemed to banish it ('and of course, the more beautiful the woman the more the tearing, her loss, or merely her being laid bare is desirable'[8]). This world is thus real, more real than any other (its paucity of the marvellous is even its proof of reality). The other vainly emerges from the most beautiful, most devastating dream, unable to realise what it seemed to promise: discontinuous they were before, discontinuous they will be afterwards. The continuity which, like all lovers, Bataille hopes for is then 'chiefly to be felt in the anguish of desire, when it is still inaccessible, still an impotent, quivering yearning. . . . [I]t seems to the lover ... only the beloved can in this world bring about what our human limitations deny, a total blending of two beings, a continuity between two disconnected creatures.'[9] What Bataille says here as a theoretician (actually he said it twenty years later and in a general way which could not be applied only to Laure) he immediately takes up again as a poet: such a love is a rage and calls for death, the death of the other rather than her loss: her death rather than the inability to maintain so great a disturbance, so violent a tremor. It is the law of such a love that the stronger the hope it brought that 'discontinuity' would be overcome,[10] the stronger is the death that comes between them as the result of the impossibility of such a promise being fulfilled. To be alone no longer, to be only one, to be part of the other and have the other as part of oneself, to melt and to mingle, this impossible miracle of love is what Bataille experienced as the highest of his desires, but he added immediately that if passion this is – and it undoubtedly is – it summons death, or murder (in reality, rather than calling for it, it already is itself death; passion is death: each person dreaming himself continuously, dreams himself unconsciously dead). Bataille would later say (disenchanted?): love is the 'full and limitless being unconfined within the trammels of separate personalities, continuity of being, glimpsed as a deliverance through the person of the beloved. There is something absurd and horribly commixed about this conception, yet beyond the absurdity, the confusion and the suffering there lies a miraculous truth.'[11] With God dead, his illusion remains, and the illusion of this love is a divine moment.

Can one, without offending, say it in this way: death is *also* a miracle? It is a dark and harsh truth. The truth, perhaps, of a crazy (or exasperated) god, no doubt a truth before which no one would not recoil. And it is a tender truth as well (there is none more tender because there is none more torn). With death ceases the expectation, the servile expectation of existence, of being one: death (if we can understand it) could be the *disenchantment* of love.

We do not know what had been 'the pain, dread, tears, delirium, orgy, fever' of which they together made their daily bread. Less still should one imagine that, however exasperating this love appears to be, it was of a 'forbidding yet immense sweetness'. When Bataille undertook writing Laure's life history, it is not least significant that he stopped at the year they met one another. Apart from a few rare confidences, what they experienced together escapes us, as if, just as for Acéphale, secrecy was the rule.

No doubt, as I have said, they were agreed that only death limited them. Moreover, how to understand their love other than as a countdown? Was Laure already condemned or not yet? Could another way of life – less harsh and less debauched – have saved her? How much longer would she have lived had she been more 'sensible'? Was that really what she wanted? There can be little doubt that in 1935 tuberculosis was so deeply within her that it was already too late (for nothing could prevent its progress). Perhaps they did not acknowledge it; perhaps she may have had the strength (we have seen and will see how strong she was) to keep it to herself, of keeping well enough so as not to change anything in their life? There is no doubt that she thought about fleeing, that at one moment or another she wanted to save her life, and she said so in such as way that it can be understood that by remaining she knew her chances of survival were slight.[12]

In 1935, Laure had three years to live, three years they lived together, though less together than has been said, yet enough for them to seem definitively linked. Less than has been said: Bataille was unfaithful, and however overwhelming this encounter was for him as well, he did not change anything in his life. They both had several trips abroad (to Spain) where they seem not to have been together: in May 1935, Bataille was at Tossa de Mar where he wrote *Blue of Noon*, but he was there alone (although he did have an affair with another

woman, Madeleine, whom we can identify without much difficulty as
Madeleine Landsberg). In her turn, Laure was in Barcelona in 1935,
but seemingly without Bataille. In May 1936, Laure was in Madrid,
although in April Bataille was at Tossa de Mar but Masson was unable
to remember whether she was with him there. In October 1936, Laure
was again in Barcelona and Catalonia; was Bataille? It seems not. The
only journey they contemplated together was to Greece in the summer
of 1937. This Dionysian journey seemed 'sacred' to Bataille or at least
that was what he said to André Masson. But they gave it up for a
perhaps even more 'sacred' journey. It was for a journey perhaps still
more 'sacred' in that they renounced it. They made their way to Sicily,
more specifically to Etna. Of this 'pilgrimage' to Etna, we know,
thanks to Bataille, rather more:

> all was as dark and as imbued with deceptive dread as the night
> Laure and I climbed Etna's slopes (climbing Etna was extremely
> important for us ... we were exhausted and, in some way, over-
> whelmed by a solitude so intensely strange and cataclysmic: there
> was a harrowing moment when we were leaning over the gaping
> wound, on the rift of the star on which we breathed ... In the middle
> of our path, as we entered an infernal region, we could clearly make
> out in the distance the crater of the volcano at the end of a long
> valley of lava; it would have been impossible to imagine anywhere in
> which the horrible instability of things could have been more evident,
> and Laure was suddenly overwhelmed with an anguish such that she
> started crazily running ahead: driven to distraction by the desolation
> into which we had entered).[13]

Laure herself spoke of it: 'I climbed Etna with Georges. It was rather
terrifying ... I cannot think about it without difficulty and I compare
everything I do at the moment to that vision. Therefore it is easy for
me to clench my teeth ... strongly enough – to break my jaw.'[14]
Should this not be compared with the unease and trepidation of the
ascent of the sacred that Acéphale claimed to lay bare? It should also
be compared with this other strange 'pilgrimage' they made in the
company of Maurice Heine (Bataille's friend of many years) to the
place where Sade wanted to be buried (at Malmaison, near Épernon,
nearer still to Saint-Hilarion): 'It was snowing that day and we got lost
as we were driving in the forest. A wild wind was blowing over Beauce.
Upon returning and having left Maurice Heine, Laure and I arranged
dinner: we were expecting Ivanov and Odoyevtsova. As we anticipated,

the dinner was just as wild as the wind. Odoyevtsova was naked and started to vomit.'[15] Laure and Bataille took the same 'journey' in March 1938, this time with Michel Leiris and his wife. But this journey was to be the last:[16] 'She walked into the daylight as if she were not being worn by death and, in bright sunshine, we reached the side of the pond indicated by Sade.'[17] On their return, she had to go straight to bed, overcome with a high temperature. She stayed in bed until the day she died, in November 1938.

Laure's death seems to have occasioned a rather curious stand-off. The two parties in attendance (Bataille and his friends on one side; the Peignot family on the other) were waiting to see, certainly with very different hopes, whether, on the edge of the abyss, Laure would be weak enough to make the sign of the cross, signifying a return, all the more harrowing for being belated, into the bosom of the Church. It is no surprise that the religious should watch over the dying to see if a rictus, a grimace or a convulsion would suggest anything resembling a repentance, anything to comfort them in their holy terror. But it is rather more surprising that Bataille's friends (primarily Leiris) were afraid she would forswear. Could they have doubted that she would be firm to the end? Or did they have doubts about themselves and their reasons for defying a God in whom they no longer believed? Marcel Moré, the friend of both parties in attendance and himself a Christian (the designated go-between), did not see the sign which would have reunited her with God. And Leiris did see a sign, a sign moreover of the cross (death throes or farce?) traced upside down: 'The wrong way up, as if a demon had inspired it, a gesture so crazy on the part of this unbeliever that I felt my unease like an onslaught from within, a sort of fluid discharge descending from the nape of my neck to the hollow of my chin . . .'[18] 'A half-sign of the cross', he said elsewhere,

> made the wrong way up – a gesture of touching one shoulder then the other and that was all – with an expression of intense joy and irony, like a little girl who would have liked to play a practical joke, to set it out but not go through with it, as though she had wished to go right to the edge in order to scare us by suggesting to us, who were her friends and nothing more nor less than atheists, the image of a possible, although clearly heterodox, conversion . . .[19]

For his part Bataille saw nothing. Was he mourning or knotting the pink or sky-blue tie he wore that day? Or was he thinking about how he would set about killing the priest who would come to set up the signs of eternity:

> A death is always dramatic, but this one occurred in the midst of circumstances that were particularly so . . . The two parties, although constantly together, never exchanged the slightest word. Several days beforehand, her mother had asked me to ask Bataille for permission to bring a priest to the house, and he had replied that as long as it was his house a priest would never cross the threshold. Her daughter having breathed her last breath, the mother said to me: 'Once she is out of the house, her body belongs to me, since they were not united in marriage.' And she insisted on a religious service. When I relayed this to Bataille, he again dispatched me with a reply: 'If anyone had the audacity to celebrate a mass, he would shoot the priest at the altar!'[20]

Bataille's violent silence in reality hid quite different terrors: obviously, he was not particularly worried about whether she would make a sign, not make it very well, or not do so at all (he clearly had no doubts about her firmness). The horrible thing was that, while dying, she had his father's face: 'a face of an empty and half crazy Oedipus. This resemblance increased during her long decline, during which the fever ate her away, perhaps in particular during her terrible outbursts of anger and bouts of hatred against me.'[21]

Then death came on 7 November 1938 at 8.15 in the morning. Bataille blamed himself for having fled in the same way as he had fled his father's death. He scattered pages of William Blake's poem *The Marriage of Heaven and Hell* into the catafalque over the dead woman's body. 'I will not say now how her death came, although the necessity to speak of it exists within me in the most "terrible" way.'[22] He never spoke of it.[23]

Sacred sociology

The period from 1937 to 1939 was one of Bataille's most active. The projects he undertook at this time hang together and relate so well that ideally they should be discussed together. Yet clarity demands the price of discursiveness (something he complained about several times), which means considering things one at a time as though they were clearly distinguishable – even if, as we shall see, they were not.

Bataille fairly soon considered adding a second, exoteric side to *Acéphale* which he had conceived in April 1936: a College of Sociology. In *Acéphale* secrecy was the rule; the rule for the College of Sociology would be openness. One should not misunderstand the meaning of the word 'college', and read anything didactic into it. Didactic concerns were and always remained alien to Bataille.[1] And one should not misunderstand the meaning of the word 'sociology': in the hands of the College's initiators, this would not be a science, 'but something of the order of a sickness, a strange infection of the social body, the senile sickness of an ascedious, exhausted, atomised society'.[2] Bataille, apparently paradoxically, would express this as follows: 'It has been formulated in the most emphatic way that the sociology we intended to explore here was not general sociology, nor was it religious sociology, but very precisely sacred sociology.'

Other than Jules Monnerot, who was soon asked to leave, the initiators of the College of Sociology formed a kind of tripartite management made up of Georges Bataille, Roger Caillois and Michel Leiris (we have seen that Caillois took part in *Acéphale* and perhaps in the secret society too, and also that Michel Leiris refrained from doing so). It is not clear whether the three men, in creating the College of Sociology, were agreed on all its tenets. We know Leiris was sceptical about Contre-Attaque and *Acéphale*; the College of Sociology would highlight rather than reduce this scepticism. As for Caillois, if he later asserted the profound affinity uniting him with Bataille ('Between Bataille and myself there was a rare meeting of minds, a sort of osmosis on the foundation of things to the extent that our respective roles were often indiscernible'),[3] what differentiated them was most probably what Denis Hollier fairly accurately describes as resulting in Caillois's case from an overwhelming desire for power, and in Bataille's from a will towards tragedy (these made Callois lean towards political and Bataille towards 'mythical' intentions). The three members of the directorate were Bataille, Caillois and Leiris. A fourth, Alexandre Kojève, was approached but wisely declined.[4] He appears to have wanted to be no more than an onlooker of this rash enterprise: 'Kojève listened to us but rejected our plan. He thought we were setting ourselves up as conjurors expecting their tricks to make him believe in magic.'[5]

A College is also a community, and it was as an elective community ('that differed in some ways from what usually brought intellectuals together') that Caillois defined the possibility open to a number of people to collaborate in common activity. But what was this activity? Two accounts aid us, by Roger Caillois and Pierre Klossowski, together with some texts, those that have survived. There seems no doubting that of the College's three initiators, Leiris's interest soon became merely distant if not distracted. Three people imagined the possibility of a College, but only two organised it, Bataille and Caillois. The truth about its fragile and tumultuous equilibrium must be sought somewhere between them.

Effectively nothing about it is certain. If the College was not a university, if its sociology was not really sociology *as such*, what could *this* College of Sociology claim to be? Caillois's reply, which cannot be doubted in the slightest (moreover, even though it is Caillois's statement alone, it was ratified by both Leiris and Bataille) was that

> The precise object of this contemplated activity can be called Sacred Sociology, insofar as that implies the study of social existence in every manifestation where there is a clear, active presence of the sacred. The intention is, thus, to establish the points of coincidence between the fundamental obsessive tendencies of individual psychology and the principal structures governing social organization and in command of its revolutions.[6]

There would seem no doubt that Bataille was in complete agreement with such a project (one can even say that everything he had been and had written until then was its principal inspiration. 'The Psychological Structure of Fascism', written in 1933, is in fact so close to such research that one could attribute its inspiration or even its origin to this article), were it not that, in addition to this first definition, which was anthropo-sociological in character, there was an ambition to steer these phenomena in an infectious and subversive direction: 'the ambition that a community formed in this way exceeds its initial plan, slipping from a will for knowledge to a will for power, to become a nucleus of a wider conspiracy – the deliberate calculation that this body find a soul.'[7]

Was this the ambition of the three initiators, or Caillois's alone? This question arises from the moment the College was created, since this ambition to turn it into something other than a *cognitive* nucleus, into an *active* nucleus (spread by infection) appears only in the text written by Caillois, and not in the one he signed jointly with Bataille and Leiris. Can we assume Bataille shared this aim, or is it not rather more likely that he saved this for Acéphale, which he alone controlled and wanted to maintain as an occult activity? This question is important. With Leiris sceptical from the start, only a two-headed directorate remained for the College. And if serious problems arose, should one not seek the reasons in a divergent understanding of its aims? Well might Caillois seek, much later and with Bataille dead, to make him the scrupulous accomplice of his goals; he made no secret, he said, of his intention to recreate 'a devastating sacred which will result in its epidemic contagion, reaching and exalting whoever had first sown its seed'. Such a statement calls for two comments: there is no doubting that Bataille wanted, even if it destroyed him, to spread the phenomena of vacillation and bewilderment. But this intention is more relevant to *Acéphale* than to the College of Sociology. The second comment is that even if what Caillois says is accurate, on this matter Bataille's opinion was fundamentally different: where, for Caillois, the issue was to subvert, for Bataille, *in the end*, it was to be subverted; where, for Caillois, the issue was to *infect*, for Bataille, following a spread of the infection, it was to be infected himself. Thus the issue was no longer so much one of making a sociology, even a sacred one, into the instrument of a catastrophe (as we have seen, Bataille did not wait until 1937 to invoke this desire) as of being oneself 'catastrophied', and experiencing the vacillation of reason. This is not just a matter of form: where Caillois may have sought to elaborate the means of his will for power (an essentially political will), Bataille would have sought to elaborate the means for a will for tragedy (a *mythical* will). There is no doubting that this distinction is more correct, and it seems likely that, perhaps unconsciously, Caillois was confusing the College and *Acéphale* (Klossowski tended to do the same) and, with Bataille's supremacy freely exercised over *Acéphale*, he may have wished to challenge this through imputing the same sort of intention to the College. For none of the texts we can ascribe to the College (none at least we know of) leads us to believe that Bataille's opinion supported this formulation by Caillois: 'We decided to unleash dangerous movements and knew that we would probably be the first victims, or that we would, at least, be carried along by the resulting current.'[8] The split between the two men, and the origin of the solitude in which Bataille found himself in the end, denounced on one side (by Leiris) and abandoned on the other (by Caillois), can no doubt be found in this difference of understanding, which was much more significant than it appeared.

The preparatory meetings of the College of Sociology took place at the start of 1937 in a dingy café in the Palais-Royal, the Grand Véfour.[9] The first lecture ('Sacred Sociology and the Relationships between "Society", "Organism" and "Being"') was held on 20 November 1937, at 9.30 in the evening in the back room of a bookshop (les Galeries du livre) at 5 rue Gay-Lussac. With two meetings a month (from autumn to the start of summer), they continued until 4 July 1939 at the same venue.[10]

What was said in the previous chapter permits us to say without undue difficulty that Bataille's contributions to the College of Sociology do not have the intellectual strength of those he was developing at the same time in *Acéphale*. Their principal interest lies in the fact that in a certain way they bring together and repeat the essential points of the themes he had introduced from 1928 (and in the article 'L'Amérique disparue', for example) up to the first three issues of *Acéphale*. If they are of less interest, it is because here Bataille was speaking publicly: without any doubt he could not speak as freely as he had in texts written for himself alone and only published after his death, or in discussions held among a few privileged individuals (his friends) or initiates (the members of Acéphale). Thus their essential interest relates to asking what Bataille allowed himself to say *in public*, to a mixed audience, on the eve of war between 1937 and 1939, and what thought he felt he could develop in front of everyone without being taken at best for a misunderstood figure, at worst for a reprobate. (We shall see that we have to wait until the last of the College's lectures, at the moment its differences had become so pronounced that he found himself alone once again, for him to display a bewildering freedom of tone, enough to stupefy the audience.)

Bataille's second lecture ('Attraction and repulsion', given in two parts on 22 January and 5 February 1938) partially answers this question: whatever brings a community together is sacred, whether its place, people, objects, beliefs or practices (we should recall that in *Acéphale* he said that death alone, and better still a sacrifice, binds a community); it is a sacredness, he said, 'of an absolutely decisive and even disconcerting specificity'. Because it is repulsive, the sacred has something of the character of corpses (one recalls how Bataille showed that the attitude of primitive peoples faced with death, shit and the gods was the same): 'Everything leads us to believe that early human beings were brought together by disgust and by common terror, by an insur- mountable horror focused precisely on what originally was the central attraction of their union.'[11] And this sacred, the nucleus of all social ties, *mediatises* all human inter-attraction, as it does with the two kinds he considered most important: sexual inter-attraction and laughter.[12] The laughter of an infant is immediate, while that of a young girl unable to stop herself laughing whenever death was mentioned was mediate.[13] Animal sexual arousal is no doubt immediate; that of a young man who could not attend a funeral without getting an erection is mediate.[14] (Evidently, unlike what we have seen so far, Bataille is not here speaking of either laughter or sexual attraction, even morbid sexual attraction, in terms that are personal to him. If, on the contrary, he had done so, he would unhesitatingly have related how he himself reacted before his mother's corpse, rather than the case of the young man aroused by funerals; here he is speaking as a sociologist, one who does not want the links between thought and experience to appear too visibly.) He deduced from this that laughter relates less to joy than to horror: 'It is always a distress; it is always something dispiriting that causes advanced laughter.' He also deduced that sexuality relates less to pleasure than to fear; and, in both cases, to repulsion. The pathological alteration of a psychological or social phenomenon reveals not so much its normality as the truth of its movement.

Of the College's three initiators, only two gave lectures in the winter of 1937 and spring of 1938: Bataille and Caillois, with Leiris (who perhaps was already expressing doubts about the enterprise) offering no more than the reading of a text. The second lecture programme (1938–9) was more eclectic: Pierre Klossowski (who discussed Sade), René M. Guastalla, Anatole Lewitzky[15] and Hans Mayer, and perhaps (according to Denis Hollier) Duthuit, Paulhan, Wahl and Landsberg,[16] and (according to Pierre Prévost) Denis de Rougement (we cannot be certain as several lectures are missing) all spoke. The diversity of speakers was matched by that of the audience. The College aroused curiosity and interest in a number of different circles, bringing together Julien Benda and Drieu La Rochelle, Denis de Rougemont and the *Esprit* circle, in all likelihood several former members of the Ordre Nouveau group founded by Arnaud Dandieu and Robert Aron (notably Jacques Chevalley), as well as several recent German émigrés, not least Walter Benjamin (that 'angel's soul', as Kojève said, 'since he really was an angelic individual'.[17] According to him, Bataille held him in the highest esteem, and it was Bataille, moreover, according to Pierre Missac, who first welcomed Benjamin to Paris), Landsberg (we know he had known Bataille for several years), Adorno and Horkheimer.[18]

Not all the lectures given by Bataille to the College of Sociology can be discussed here. But it seems the College's three initiators were agreed, before their disagreements became serious, in denouncing a major contemporaneous political event. On 29 and 30 September 1938 the accords were signed in Munich sanctioning Chancellor Adolf Hitler's blackmail attempts to make the Sudetenland, a Czech territory with a German population, part of the Reich. What is now unanimously regarded as an insult (what the French word 'munichois' means) was at the time supported by a majority of French people.[19] Flattered that Council President Daladier had congratulated them on their rectitude ('what has made success possible is the resolution shown by France. We must pay our dear and great land the homage that is its due') they believed, doubtless in good faith, that the spectre of war had retreated for good.

This was not the College's opinion, nor was it Bataille's (it was four years since he had announced that war between democracy and fascism was inescapable). Whatever distance the College adopted (distance rather than precautions: it was not the business of the College, its signatories announced, to intervene; this was a way of specifying how regrettable it was that almost universal assent to these accords forced it to do so), it said bluntly, even brutally:

Those who suffered the most crippling bewilderment end up imagining they acted heroically. The public already gives credence to the legend . . .: did not the Council's president have the cleverness to thank them for it? As it is, we have to say that these are much too petty names for feelings that only the words 'consternation', 'resignation', and fear' had fit until now. The show produced was one of immobilized and silent confusion, a sorry surrender to the event; conscious of its inferiority, it was the unmistakably frightened pose of a people who refuse to accept war as one of the possibilities of its politics when confronted by a nation that grounds its politics in war.[20]

This long declaration, as explicit as could be, in which Bataille's style can be discerned (although it is essentially Caillois's work), still bears something of the tone of Contre-Attaque: it denounced 'stupidity', 'pharisaism' and 'a certain platonic quixotism' characteristic of democracies (it is nevertheless in their name, and with the demand that they rise to the challenge of what threatens them, that these criticisms were made). Above all it denounced 'the absolute lie of current political forms and the necessity for reconstructing on this assumption a collective mode of existence that takes no geographical or social limitation into account and that allows one to behave oneself when death threatens'. Caillois's pugnacious nature was well known. Pierre Prévost offers this valuable detail about Bataille's:

I testify that Georges Bataille told me he considered it highly regrettable that in 1936, during the remilitarization of the Rhine by Hitler, the president of the Council of Ministers was not Poincaré (who was by then dead), but a left-wing politician. The old nationalist from Lorraine would not have tolerated such a breach of the Treaty of Versailles, and would have gone as far as a declaration of war – at least as far as military action.[21]

The clarity of this declaration, and its forcefulness (it was reprinted in *NRF*, *Volontés* and *Esprit* in November 1938) cut through any charge of equivocation still maintained, *in hindsight*, by some of those close to Bataille at this time (by Pierre Klossowski for example, and coming from someone who took the greatest care to absent himself from the political debate in question – from any political debate, in fact – this accusation of equivocation is no small surprise). That the apparent ambiguity of *Acéphale* might have seeped into the College is possible.[22] That the likes of Dugan or Dautry may have infiltrated it (though nothing suggests this) to spread the ill-judged concept of 'surfascism' is also a possibility (but as I have said, if the concept was ill-judged, Dautry himself was not at all). According to Klossowski, recent German exiles (Walter Benjamin first and foremost, but also Hans Meyer as we shall see) grew worried that the College was toying with explosive ideas without realistically weighing up the consequences. But to speak, as he does, about Bataille and the 'profound temptation of fascist cynicism' requires full substantiation, with written proof.[23]

This date – September 1938 – was followed by another which shed significant light on it. On Tuesday, 13 December 1938, Bataille delivered a lecture entitled 'The structure of democracies'. Unfortunately it has not survived (his lectures were often improvised).[24] The only indications we have of it are supplied by Pierre Prévost, who described Bataille that evening as having 'a face from a drama, from a tragedy even', and by Bertrand d'Astorg, who published an account in *Les Nouvelles Lettres* (no. 5). D'Astorg did not relate what Bataille said, only his conclusion: 'Bataille pessimistically pronounced a mortal crisis in which democracies would possibly perish.' A pessimism, he says, that 'must be approaching despair'. And he adds: 'There are moments, said the speaker (and I am attempting to remember the substance of his thought on this serious matter) in which man, even when he no longer knows if there are essential values involved in the struggle, must accept being on intimate terms with suffering and death, without wishing to know in advance what reality will spring from it.'[25]

Is it worth adding that between the signing of the Munich accords and this lecture came Laure's death? Or is it better to assume that these things are unrelated? In so far as Bataille was the same man as the one who wrote *Blue of Noon* in 1935 (and there is no reason to doubt he was), in so far as, for example in this book, he always mixed public and private events (political and emotional ones) in a disorder whose keys were held by him alone, the Munich accords and the death of Laure were no doubt a supplementary prefiguration, auguries – the excess value of the racial and patriotic community in proportion to the destruction of the amorous, elective community – of the war Dirty and Troppmann (the protagonists of *Blue of Noon*) call up with their admittedly frightened desires. Bataille's pessimism and despair could have this value (we shall see how the College's closing lecture would carry this unexpected combination even further than could be imagined).

*

It is true that the war put an end to the College of Sociology's activities. The new term planned for autumn 1939 naturally never took place. But it is just as true that the end of the second programme of lectures put the College through plenty of ups and downs: Caillois was absent, through illness at first (Bataille spoke on his behalf, from his notes, and one can imagine what a fragile new equilibrium this established), then through being away from Paris. And Leiris, a little more sceptical at each lecture, in the end refrained from taking part in the concluding session of the second year with Bataille, as would have been logical and as was planned. This lecture-summary was to have taken place on Tuesday, 4 July 1939; it was delivered, but by Bataille alone: 'It had been understood that there would be three of us speaking this evening, Caillois, Leiris, and myself, but I am alone. It is not without sadness that I acknowledge this.'[26] Caillois had left for Argentina a few days before, and Bataille noted: 'The few texts I have received from him are, in any case, of a sort that interrupts the harmony existing between us.'[27] What Caillois seems not to have accepted was the place Bataille gave to 'mysticism, tragedy, madness, and death'. It was owing to these very reservations expressed by Caillois and how they related to him that Bataille apparently broke off their initial agreement. Each accused the other, and what we have seen to have separated them from the start had in the meantime grown worse (though it is true that several major events had occurred in the interim).

The differences with Leiris were less acute (Leiris had been friends with Bataille for much longer), and perhaps symbolically more serious: more than a disagreement, it seemed to Bataille at least as an abandonment. Leiris explained that his reservations concerned methods. Was the College of Sociology a society of intellectuals? All three had agreed it was not. If it was a community, in what way was this true? If it was to be constituted as an Order, what would its *rules* be? And Leiris pushed these reservations further: sacred sociological phenomena are certainly numerous, and certainly determining, but they are not *all* sociological phenomena. To claim so would be to misunderstand Mauss and Durkheim, who are used too liberally. All this can be summed up in a single sentence: 'I was more and more assailed by doubts as to the rigour with which this venture has been conducted.'[28]

Left alone before the College's audience to conclude the second lecture programme, Bataille spoke as a man alone, and in a way like a man possessed. Did he feel he needed to show the co-founders of the

College a semblance of self-control? Had he forced himself until then to speak as an intellectual (or try to)? Whatever the case, with Caillois and Leiris absent, he spoke for himself, in the first person, so as 'to bring maximum disorder into habitual perspectives'.[29]

And this disorder was stupefying. One could not have imagined a more violent stripping bare. What Bataille had until then said cautiously he now exposed shamelessly, as if the absence of the College's co-founders finally left him free to go all the way and to mete out the most terrifying of lover's pleas. If one text shows what the secret of passion is, and how much Laure and he formed an impossible lacerated community, it is this, and it seems quite unbelievable he could have given it in public. The truth of *Acéphale* is given here unreservedly: 'The sacrificial tear opening the festival is a liberating tear. The individual who participates in the loss is vaguely aware that this loss engenders the community sustaining him.'[30] The same thing goes for the truth of the community of lovers:

> if the need to love and be lost is stronger in them than the concern with being found, the only outlet is in tearing, in the perversities of turbulent passion, in drama, and if it is of a complete nature – in death. . . . At this point the presence of a third person is not necessarily, as it was in the beginning of their love, the worst impediment. Beyond the common being met in their embrace, they seek infinite annihilation in a violent expenditure where the possession of a new object, a new woman or a new man, is only the pretext for an even more annihilating expenditure.[31]

And Bataille concluded this in the following way (one can picture the perplexity of an audience that thought it was attending a sociology lecture): 'In the same way that eroticism slips easily into orgy . . . the equivalent of a community must be found in the form of a universal god, in order to spread the sacrificial orgy infinitely.'[32]

Vivan le femmine, viva il buon vino, sostegno e gloria d'umanita[1]

In 1939, Georges Bataille was forty-two. Laure's death was unexpected, but not so much so that he suspended all his activities. What he lived *afterwards*, when she was dead, had nothing romantic about it ('I don't make a profession of romanticism'[2]). Amazing as it may seem, Acéphale continued. The dread sustained by this death, if it was considerable, did not cause Bataille to renounce his belief that an orgiastic god, a sacrificial god, could continue to preside over some positively tragic lives (in other words, completely open and consenting). He did not bend a knee, did not beg a vengeful god to pardon him for what that god might consider him to be guilty of (guilty, without any doubt, but before no god). The rituals of Acéphale, if they ever had a meaning – in Laure's presence – (and I could say that she gave, in the best and the worst senses, the most trenchant of possible meanings to what Acéphale claimed to be), certainly had one now she was dead. Anyone who might consider Acéphale a fancy – or a folly – would be mistaken; or would not have borne in mind how broad and violent was the rebellion Bataille set in play. This death, tragic as it was, essentially proved this rebellion right rather than refuting it. Bataille was not wrong to claim in his last lecture at the College of Sociology that the ultimate of the possible and desirable meanings of passion was its annihilation.[3] Acéphale triumphed in proportion to the horror it confronted: annihilation alone is worthy of the greatest of possible squanderings, the most vertiginous of waste. The unsteadiness Bataille appeared to experience before the audience at this lecture, the black gaiety which seems to have seized him is worthy of a man (but is it not absurd?) who cared only about knowing what an impossibility god is and what will be felt by one who persists in wanting to be his equal.

Acéphale continued. And in 1939 Patrick and Isabelle Waldberg went to live in the Saint-Germain house, which had been left empty following Laure's death, staying there until the summer. Acéphale continued to 'sacrifice' near the emblematic tree struck by lightning in the forest of Saint-Nom-la-Bretèche. To the topography now partly known by the society, Bataille added a new place: Laure's tomb, a few miles away. There was nothing that was generally respected that Bataille did not want to grasp and debase. (But it would be wrong to say 'profane'. Where a profanation might be seen, instead lies the sacred.)

Acéphale, at the point things had reached, was no longer a community; it was a challenge. And it matters rather little whether such a challenge provoked God or destiny; he summoned their remaining elements to administer the proof that they were capable of making reason stagger and reel (it *also* provoked good fortune[4]).

Madness was the stake, the stake of Bataille's investigation in 1939; the stake that was also the theme of one of the most moving issues of *Acéphale*, the last, which, unlike the previous ones, he wrote and published alone and *anonymously*.[5] It opens with a commemoration, not of a birth or of a death but symptomatically of the collapse of a mind, one of the best structured, most anti-Christian of minds, that of Friedrich Nietzsche:

> 3 January 1889
> fifty years ago
> Nietzsche succumbed to madness
> on the piazza Carlo Alberto in Turin
> He threw himself sobbing on the neck of a beaten horse
> then he collapsed
> he believed, when he awoke, that he was
> DIONYSUS
> OR
> THE CRUCIFIED

'Beyond the fulfilment and the combat, is there anything but death? Beyond words destroying one another endlessly, is there anything but a silence which drives mad by force of toil and laughter?'[6] To say *Yes* to the world, to say *Yes* unreservedly and unconditionally (this is what as *Acéphale* started, three years earlier, Bataille said was the 'totality of existence'), is to reach God; and having reached him, to kill him to become God in turn. But to be God is also, and especially, to become mad. There is one who is stronger than God: the madman. 'How did God not become sick on discovering before him his rational impotence to understand madness?'[7]

Stronger than God is the madman who says *Yes* absolutely to whatever *exists*, as happy as the greatest sensual pleasure, as unbridled as drunkenness and orgy and, at the same time, as what is most tragic. On the other hand, the God of the Christians elects and has the authority to elect; his world is not the *whole* world; his joys are those of a sick man. God is sick and so is the one who mimics his sickness by submitting. 'No outcome is sufficiently clear that it can express the happy contempt the one who "dances with the time which kills him" has for those who take refuge in waiting for eternal blessedness.'[8] No outcome is sufficiently clear that it can express the contempt (these are the words of a man who had just been torn apart by death) for any 'intellectual or moral beyond, substance, God or immutable order of salvation'.[9] Against this pallid, fawning and servile joy of people who try to find consolation by praying to God to deliver them from death, Bataille urges us to rejoice in dying, in dying absolutely, thoroughly – in reducing oneself to nothing. This is the title of the long central poem of this final issue of *Acéphale*: 'The Practice of Joy Before Death', a poem Bataille himself described as mystical. In fact it is mystical to glory in *what exists*, once *what exists* is delivered from any servile divine infirmity: mystical and divine – 'a shameless and immodest sanctity' – is the happy 'loss of self', lost not in God, but in nothingness (the idea of an unremittingly meditated nothingness is also light and liberating). The practice of joy before death is inaccessible to whoever 'would be afraid of girls and whisky' ('Now all I want is to live – intoxication, ecstasy, my existence as naked as a woman's when wracked with desire'[10]).

I cannot insist on it enough: these are Bataille's first 'mystical' pages, and they are valuable as a definition, not simply because they are among the most devastating he wrote, but also to anticipate all the misunderstandings to which the use of this word gives rise.[11]

> I reach the depth of worlds
> I am devoured by death
> I am devoured by fever
> I am absorbed in sombre space
> I am annihilated in joy before death.[12]

It might be feared that Bataille was not sufficiently precise (sufficiently anti-Christian): he made it clear that he intentionally left the expression 'the depth of worlds' as vague as possible. At the very most what is at the depth of worlds is what may be spoken of *negatively* (in imitation of the God of Denys the Areopagite): it is not God. It is so little God that it is the vision of a 'generalized catastrophe, a catastrophe that can't be stopped by anything . . . sweeping, into an abyss, both us and everything that comes from some immense terrifying depth and emerges as solid or apparently solid.'[13]

Another text immediately followed this one or, to be more exact, a project for a text, which had the same Nietzschean meaning (the same anti-Christian meaning): this is the *Manuel de l'anti-chrétien*. This ought to cut short any misinterpretations: Bataille simultaneously revealed himself as being mystical and anti-Christian. Or at the very least (for his anti-Christianity was already fifteen years old), he was careful, since he called himself a mystic (and why would this word not have a new meaning? A meaning of man without God), to reaffirm himself as violently anti-Christian, in the same way that in introducing others into the secret of Acéphale he affirmed its Nietzschean and anti-Christian religious aspect. For, if his hostility to Christianity was not new, he considered it necessary to define how the mysticism he made his own was distinct from the 'plague' Christianity is; how the object-less rage in which he revelled was distinct from this God (the obsession of mankind having become for it an object of shame and hatred); how his debauched intemperances were distinct from whining idealism.[14]

Debauched and perhaps vain. As I said, in 1939 Bataille was forty-two. More possibilities were closed to him than the future promised to open. Nothing had come of the writer he dreamed of becoming in 1925 or of the brilliant and easy life he conceived of being able to lead. In 1939 he had written only two books: *Story of the Eye*, privately published in 1928, and *Blue of Noon* which strangely remained unpublished. For two books published, how many which did not see the light of day: the study on Leon Chestov, that on 'The Pineal Eye', 'Le Fascisme en France', 'Le Manuel de l'anti-chrétien' . . . At nearly ten-year intervals he had twice occupied a dominant public position: the first was with *Documents* which, if it was one of the most innovative of all the journals that appeared at the time, fared no better than the others since it was far from equalling the success of *La Révolution surréaliste* or *Le Surréalisme au service de la révolution*; the second time with the College of Sociology, after which once more he was left alone and disillusioned.

The polemics with the surrealists benefited them more than him: those who then rallied to him did so more for the means he had available (with *Documents*) than for his thought. The year 1931 – and then 1934 – would no doubt have to be counted as the most trying of Bataille's life. *La Critique sociale* gave him the opportunity to publish some of the most important texts he wrote before the war ('The Notion of Expenditure' and 'The Psychological Structure of Fascism'). It is hardly likely that anyone outside a narrow circle had read (and understood) them. And each of the political challenges he engaged with (the Democratic Communist Circle and Contre-Attaque, which he led in a way that had to overcome André Breton's distrust) left the impression of a misunderstanding that ultimately was present virtually before the event: oscillating between a strict denunciation of the mounting dangers and a desire – according to the circumstances proclaimed more or less provocatively – for destruction and catastrophe, each time he emerged alone, denounced by his friends as much as by his obvious enemies. Finally, Acéphale – and the monstrous 'fancy' which presided over it – appears as a sort of exasperation with initially encountered dead-ends, more dangerous than any of them, more 'limited' and paradoxically risked by himself alone and for himself alone, no matter how much he claimed a desire to see a 'community' born of it. Acéphale retrospectively gave to these years immediately before the war a sombre if not totally catastrophic tint.

His close friends abandoned him in various ways, starting with Raymond Queneau in 1934.[15] Others did the same. What Bataille expected of friendship at that time was harsh and exasperating: 'I know my friendship is very demanding of those I most like. My way of dealing with people I like less is more familiar – and especially more human', he wrote to Michel Leiris in 1935.[16] We have seen how Leiris, like Masson, frequently had reservations about some of the projects Bataille put in motion, and often even refused to participate in them. The most active support from which Bataille benefited came not from his closest friends but from occasional collaborators who, when failure and dissolution came, returned to their own interests (moreover we cannot be sure they understood him in the way he expected; or, paradoxically, that they understood him as well as the most confrontational of those close to him at the time, Simone Weil, in 1934–5). Like Leiris and Masson the two other great friends of the years 1935–49, Alexandre Kojève and Georges Ambrosino (perhaps Pierre

Klossowski should also be included), only rarely supported Bataille in his undertakings (we shall see that these friendships would have an increasing influence and would predominate after the war). And in 1938 and 1940 two links, loose rather than close ones, but no doubt highly symbolic, were undone by death: Léon Chestov in 1938 and Maurice Heine in 1940. The role Léon Chestov played will be recalled. It is not a little odd that he died just when the profound pessimism into which he had initiated Bataille through readings of Dostoevsky, Nietzsche and Pascal carried him beyond his leanings towards social revolution. With Chestov's death, one of Bataille's first links with Nietzsche was broken. With that of Maurice Heine, in a very different way it is true, it was one of his links with Sade that was broken: 'There is something bleak, something so hard to accept, about the fact that Maurice Heine has today stopped living.'[17] The homage Bataille later rendered him ('one of the men who, discreetly but authentically, did the greatest credit to his time'[18]) gives us to infer that as far as he was concerned, an era had ended with Heine's death.

'And so I am abandoned, abandoned with an inexplicable brutality. I expected abandonment. I don't protest about it, I even sense its necessity, but its heedlessness and brutality shock me.'[19] If the evident failure of his private life (however dissolute, it must still have left him with the feeling of failure) is added to this shock, in 1939 he was a man alone who expected the darkest of his predictions to triumph: they alone had the measure of it. In 1937, Bataille wrote to Alexandre Kojève:

> The question you ask about me comes down to knowing whether I am negligible. I have often asked myself that question; the negative answer haunts me . . . A few facts – such as the exceptional difficulty experienced in making myself be 'recognised' (on the simple level at which others are 'recognised') – have led me to assume the hypothesis of an irrevocable insignificance, seriously though cheerfully.[20]

If he ever really experienced this feeling of insignificance it was in 1939: 'I can't abide sentences . . . Everything I've asserted, the convictions I've expressed, it's all ridiculous and dead. I'm only silence, and the universe is silence.'[21]

Of the convictions he expressed, there effectively remained virtually nothing the war would not soon sweep away; virtually nothing if not the war itself and the exhortation not to resign oneself to it that had been central to Bataille's work for several years. And, once more correcting the impression left here and there, and most often by himself, that he had abandoned himself to events in a fascinated defeat of the spirit, a phantom form of the book 'Le Fascisme en France' made an appearance in 1938. (He had not managed to write this book and it was replaced in 1935 by *Blue of Noon*, which he had not published, these projects destroying one another in a sort of gloomy chicken run played on the edge of the emptiness into which each of the elements of this finally utterly tragic game were hurled one after the other.) This was neither the least potent of its apparitions, nor the least eloquent: Bataille offered Roger Caillois, as part of his series Tyrants and Tyrannies ('Studies in extreme forms of power'), a very much augmented and simplified version of articles published in *La Critique sociale*, preceded, he made clear, by 'a long introduction (almost completely written) on the present development of fascism, its significance and consequences'.[22]

It was an attempt at an endlessly recommenced – and endlessly aborted – incantation.

IV

Good fortune

'A return to animal life, lying on the bed, a pitcher of red wine with two glasses. I don't think I've ever seen the sun go down so flamboyantly in a sky which is scarlet and gold with pink clouds that go on and on forever. Slowly, innocence, whimsicality, and a kind of decayed magnificence work me to a fever pitch.'[1]

Less than a year after Laure's death ('I only feel loathing for romanticism – I'm as hard-headed as they come'),[2] another woman came to sleep in the 'dead woman's' bed. Consent to the world, unrestrained abandonment to what it offers, gives good fortune the same capricious, 'mischievous' character as unhappiness. Love (even irreplaceable love) is never so great as to preclude another from appearing and assuming the same guise. It is a truth of nature: another body, other embraces ease the pain. Just the same, they too are the world, as marvellous as the abyss from which they save you is deep. Bataille did not live through Laure's death ascetically, but excessively. Upon the excess that was Laure, others overlaid their joy and their anguish. Only nudity has the meaning of death; nudity and intoxication. Between November 1938 and October 1939, Bataille was involved with several women (while continuing to frequent brothels and strip clubs), and then with one with whom he stayed for several years.

She was Denise Rollin-Le Gentil.[3] In 1939 she was thirty-two, married and with a young son, Jean.[4] She was beautiful, a beauty that would be described as melancholy if not taciturn. She spoke little or, for long periods, not at all. Laurence Bataille remembered her as someone both 'extremely open' and 'completely withdrawn'.[5] This confirms the portrait given by Michel Fardoulis-Lagrange: 'She was the woman who incarnated silence. She took in discussions metaphorically. People were amazed at the chords they struck in her.'[6]

Through her husband and on her own account she had links with a few surrealists before meeting Bataille: with Breton, whom it seems she knew well, and Pierre and Jacques Prévert. But she also had links with Jean Cocteau and with the painters Kissling and Derain, for whom she had modelled. Bataille met her and their relationship began on 2 October 1939: 'Except with Laure, I have never felt such comfortable purity, such a silent simplicity. However, this time it was only glitter in a void . . .'[7] The doubts Bataille seems to have had (the 'glitter in a void') were not dispelled for a month:

> 'The fragile illusion' into which I entered that day had nothing fragile or illusory about it: it was enough that I approached a glass door: what I saw, the room I thought I had to leave . . . pacing up and down, and not seeing me, beautiful as a multicoloured insect, blind like a sky . . . she entered into this room a month ago, no other woman could have been silent enough, beautiful enough, silently inviolable enough to enter it: at least without my suffering from it as much as a clear mirror would suffer from being tarnished.[8]

The relationship between Georges Bataille and Denise Rollin lasted until the end of 1943. The illuminating (even miraculous) air of *good fortune* that governed this meeting lasted little more than a few months. All those who witnessed this liaison thought they did not get on. Fardoulis-Lagrange, for example, believed that Denise Rollin never really took Bataille seriously, seeing him as an 'actor' contemplating himself in a kind of role he had assumed.[9] And he also believed, more unexpectedly, that it was Laure who fascinated her. Since it seems unlikely she knew her, this fascination would thus have been imaginary: linked to what she had been told, or to what Bataille told her? Should we picture Denise Rollin changing her mind about Bataille (the 'actor'), taking up a silently sarcastic place beside him as Laure's posthumous defender (with Laure convinced too late that the man she called the 'God Bataille' was nothing but a trickster god, a 'mischievous' god like the Aztec gods, 'lovers of cruel tricks')?

In 1939, between the death of Laure and the madness that the final issue of *Acéphale* ('La pratique de la joie devant la mort') seemed to set rashly in train, between the declaration of war and 'abandonment' by his friends, Denise Rollin incarnated good fortune: 'But such bewitched good fortune in a world that had become frightful made me tremble.'[10]

'I am myself war'

France was at war; Bataille wasn't. Disturbed when the world lingered in a peace which everything threatened to break, he inexplicably calmed down as the world threw itself into the most extreme of disturbance: his ecstasy was finally that of everyone. This was hard to understand and, if understood, even harder to agree with: war is ecstasy. If we find anything offensive in this, we have failed to understand the awful tremor Bataille sought (since 1925 and the torture of the Hundred Pieces). Only war attains horror, it alone lifts all limits, it alone is contagious like no other horror. Bataille applied himself to arousing the truth of the world and of existence, in their tragic truths, in every way available to him. This truth, of the world as of existence, is warlike[1] – orgiastic and sacrificial:

> I imagine the gift of an infinite suffering, of blood and of open bodies, in the image of an ejaculation, breaking down the one it shook and abandoning him to a fatigue imbued with disgust.
> I imagine a human movement and stimulation whose possibilities are limitless: this movement and this excitement cannot be *alleviated* except by *war*.
> I imagine the Earth projected into space, like a screaming woman with her head aflame.[2]

That is, war fascinated Bataille. Or more exactly, *the idea*, the possibility of war fascinated him. It is the unleashing of the passions, of death and of sacrifice. This suddenly furious world, suddenly seized by the most excessive of convulsions, a devastation spread everywhere across its surface makes it a torture victim multiplied by as many open, bloody massacred bodies as could be made. Because the torture of the Hundred Pieces was atrocious, it was illuminating. On an infinitely greater scale, the war was also illuminating. Its ignominy does not have a fraudulent meaning, as if shame and dissimulation were its only possible conditions. Finally it has the hateful and dazzling meaning all people and nations give it. Where yesterday they had been cowardly and avaricious, today they spend and squander everything, including their lives. For ten years (1929 to 1939), Bataille maintained his thinking on a horizon no idealist would accept: because peace is won at the price of a non-consumption of energies (of *all* energies, including those generally regarded as pathological), and because order is maintained only at the price of the exclusion of what is shameful, base and servile, war, which alone knows that human life *also* calls for excrement, is inevitable. Because it was not able to integrate the processes which appeared to threaten it (processes of dissolution, of loss, of destruction), peace paradoxically calls down upon itself the very war it wanted to appear to be guarding against. In more than one way Bataille exhorted this languid and depressed world towards shock, convulsion and disorientation. He said in every way and every tone that a society which only cares about accumulating (that fraudulent appropriative accumulation of the bourgeoisie) and is powerless to organise *ritualised* breakdowns, exposes itself to so much greater catastrophes because they have been repressed for so long. Through these years, the catastrophes had two names: revolution and war. Revolution should have meant heterogeneous energies overwhelming and violating a sinisterly homogeneous world (but a new order should not have failed to materialise from the disorder of revolution and Bataille had ceased to believe in it some years earlier). Revolution would have been a predictable, almost local, breakdown. But war (is this what fascinates?) would know no limits. Its disorder is hardly undertaken to create a new order (its ends being less clearly inscribed than in revolution). In this, it is a more violent *depression*; it is also more fascinating.

War fascinates (ambiguous as the word might be, its use should not be misunderstood: certainly, it fascinates everyone). It even 'enchants':

> I noticed only a succession of cruel splendours whose very movement requires that I die; this death is only a *dazzling* consummation of all that was, a joy in *existing* that all that comes into the world has: to the point at which my own life requires that all that exists, in all places, ceaselessly develops and annihilates itself. . . .
> I imagine myself covered in blood, broken but transfigured and in accord with the world, at once like a prey and like a jaw of TIME which kills and is killed ceaselessly.[3]

This enchants (the insupportable 'enchantment': saying *Yes* to the world to the point of horror, to the point of dread) and hallucinates: 'No one positively sees things straight on: the sun, the human eye flees it . . . the skull of God splinters . . . and no one hears.' (Extermination is God's skull splintered. Fragments of brain – of reason – crushed like insects on the walls of concentration camps. *Acéphale* wanted mankind to flee reason as one escapes from jail.)

For Bataille, extermination again posed the question of rationality and irrationality, which were not, however, clearly divided: a laborious, industrious reason – a technocratic reason – was certainly the exterminator, but it exterminated another kind of reason, universalist and abstract: 'there is an epic of reason, to which Jews made an authentic contribution; and does Jewish authenticity not mean that at Auschwitz it was reason that was really suffering in their flesh?'[4] Bataille was alone in considering the world never as it should be, but as it was. He alone (and Breton reproached him with delighting in it) knew its power of conflagration (a sort of Heraclitean power). In 1939 he had long been saying how inevitable war was and how fascinating it was (and let us not be mistaken: whether unconsciously or secretively, *everyone* was fascinated by it), so that when it appeared (it was a hierophany, a descent of the darkest sacred over the world), suddenly it no longer seemed to be his. The war could no longer be judged in political terms. The political is what justifies war, its results are political . . . But not war *itself*. Should this be stated more frankly? If it is not political, it is a wild game played by people finally restored to themselves (or to that part of themselves that civil and policed society does not allow to exist). As such, in 1939, whatever the reasons and the protagonists, it could not have failed to explode (give or take a few years). As a game inevitably explodes. This does not mean Bataille did not know how or why fascism desired the war and ensured its inevitability. On the contrary, no one had said so more clearly than he had. Nevertheless, if fascism had not existed, if there had not been that to which fascism wanted with all its strength the world to be reduced, a world devoid of common values and more violent than that the 'revolution' wished to overturn, the war would still have been unavoidable. For all that peace, with difficulty, contains appetites for violence and frenzy, all this senseless extravagance that peace had not found the means to extinguish, war, like a *festival*, a tragic festival, engulfs. (I do not underestimate the fact that it could be violently shocking to speak of war as a 'festival'. Yet it is less shocking than saying that peace is unable to exist without the aid of war.)

Bataille was perhaps alone in thinking that there was nothing natural about peace in a society (moreover, in *all* societies; no one else saw how they are all eroded in such a way that war alone, paradoxically, saves them from vanishing). Horrible as war is, it alone frees society from avarice, calculation and self-interest . . . But especially from time, work, projects and the ends by which it develops its world. Because peace falsely governs the world as if death did not exist in it. Or as if death had no political meaning. (*Sacrifice* used to make death unite the social community. It alone, instead of expelling death's power of dissolution, carried it to the highest point of intensity. What 'primitives' knew, evolved society seems to have wanted to forget.) This political meaning of death is the co-originating and founding heterogeneity of a society. Not a single aspect of its *existence* is spared its demise. No one composing it can be extracted from it. A society – every society – takes from death the transcendence which allows it to exist, but today without paying the tribute – real and symbolic – due to it.[5] When such a war takes revenge for this forgetting – hateful and ambivalent as the idea may be – it is sacred. This thinking does not deny how many innocents may pay the absurd tribute (although war dead are neither more nor less innocent than any other dead) or the destruction of the whole order it represents (a blind destruction). It considers war to be due to a need for excessive and destructive prodigality that people are no longer able to satisfy ritually, that is symbolically. The ritualisation of death links the living, through a sort of pact, to the power of individual and social conflagration and of the irruption of death among them . . . War, on the other hand, unleashes outside ritual and pact; it is the free and uncontrolled unleashing of death suddenly affecting *all* the living . . .

War having arrived, it is too late to judge it by complaining (the complaining of an old woman who does not know what god to blame for the fate which has befallen her): one either acts or allows oneself to be carried along by a horrified and silent fascination; if the war fascinates, it is because it is infernal. And 'of what is infernal, it should be possible to speak only discreetly, without depression and without bravado'.[6]

As Bataille accepted Laure's death, as he accepted 'abandonment' by his friends, as he resigned himself to silence after relinquishing his no longer relevant ideas, so he would accept the war, all war and everything a man – without taking part in it, or fleeing it – could know of it. And especially, he would *watch*. The war would be one of the most violent projections of the mystical and deranged life he had made his own: its ecstasies and terrors were the same (during this war Bataille wrote: 'I want to show that there exists an equivalence between *war*, *ritual sacrifice* and *mystical life*: it is the same play of "ecstasies" and "terrors" which joins mankind to the games of the heavens').[7] There was something of the fascinated and ultimately innocent child in the pitiless stare Bataille cast over the war (the way that as a child he had observed his father?); the games of the heavens which dispense fire and death, modern monsters and blind gods are also enchanting.[8] Having chosen a life detached from the concerns of others, and relieved of the oppressive duty of alerting them, Bataille was brought back to the solid pleasures of the cries of embraces that were drowned out by those of sirens. It was above Trier cemetery that Troppmann made love to Dirty in *Blue of Noon*. An earth entirely transformed into a charnel-house is not the worst place to experience fully the obscure links by which pleasure is entangled with anguish; death soils and defiles: it is the lacerated truth of love, as it is that of existence itself.

Bataille moved around occupied and free France (from Paris to the Massif Central, from Normandy to Yonne) too much not to have had the opportunity to verify the seductive power of the corrupting beauty of dead and tortured bodies, and to understand, from so many mouths finally open to what had always hallucinated him, the narratives of it: the proximity of horror, the summary executions, the round-ups, bodies thrown rotting into ditches and wells, the ever-present possibility of contagion, this one nothing less than real, an entire community in the grip of anguish, a 'human universe' descending 'straight to hell',[9] the prey and the maw, a beast which 'kills ceaselessly and is ceaselessly killed'.[10]

Bataille borrowed the lines he wrote about the war (his fascination was effectively discreet and without bravado) from Ernst Jünger:

The smell of bodies which are decomposing is unbearable, oppressive, sickly sweet, loathsome and penetrating like a viscous dough. It hangs so intensely over the fields, after large battles, that starving people forget to eat . . . the fields, covered with men mown down by their bullets, are spread out in front of their eyes. The corpses of their comrades lay at their sides, mingled with them, the seal of death on their eyelids. These frightful faces recall the frightful realism of old images of the Crucified . . . What is the good of covering the bits of flesh with sand and lime? What is the good of hiding them under the cloth of tents to avoid seeing black and bloated faces? Their number really was too great. The pick everywhere banged against human flesh. All the mysteries of the tomb were revealed, so atrocious that next to them the most infernal dreams seemed insignificant.[11]

Monnerot and Sartre (the latter with irony) have spoken about what this war, in which he had not been involved, could have been for Bataille: for Monnerot

he was only an isolated individual and the world was his sickness. This spectator no longer knew whether he was dreaming or was awake: on the stage of the world, it is his own story, but in a form he alone could recognise: he almost ceased to use the words of politics and sociology which previously he used frequently: but let's not be fooled, he had not for all that changed the subject [Monnerot seemed to be the only person to have remarked that, in spite of appearances, Bataille remained the same] . . . Bataille who is really a *contradictory person*, is not combatant but conflict.[12]

Where Monnerot understood that the war was not distinct from Bataille (is it necessary to recall the 'war-like' character of Bataille's name?) but was his very sickness, Sartre, *indicting* the mysticism Bataille laid claim to, pushed the anthropomorphic identification still further: 'If I suffer for *everything*, I am everything, at least by virtue of suffering. If my dying is the dying of the world, I am the dying world.'[13]

'I love ignorance touching on the future'[1]

Does this 'fascination' once more put Bataille's *political* attitude during the war in question? One might confidently claim it does not, that there was nothing *doubtful* about this attitude, other than in an imaginary sense. Yet it raises the question all the same. Or, at least, this word 'fascination' makes certain people ask it, and answer it, predictably, in a way that blatantly misrepresents it just to make it easier to condemn.

This is no surprise: these are the same critics who claimed that what Acéphale put at stake resembled in more than one way what the fascists were putting at stake at the same time. Thus the temptation was apparent, as apparent as the fact that war would be its fulfilment. With an imperceptible slippage, it would only remain to affirm that Bataille applauded the Reich's victories, or at the very least that they might, precisely, have fascinated him.

This accusation is itself 'fascinating'; it is fascinating how this half-truth could have been spread to become a certainty, if it was not already for some. What is it based on? Raymond Queneau noted in his diary: 'Bataille is very sceptical. No more "defending the democracies" at all.'[2] But did this represent any change in his views? Like all the extreme left (and, it is true, the extreme right) had he not often been anti-parliamentarian before the war? And Queneau added: 'He wants nothing to do with politics.'[3] Nothing is really convincing about this account (not that it is in any way accusatory). That of Jean Piel is hardly any more so, when he noted what Bataille said to him at their meeting two years later, on 11 December 1941:

Never has the antagonism been so great between people who have the true aspirations of people and the mass of those who live like animals, never has the tyranny been so total of animal-people over people-people who are called to live a more dangerous life, ever more hunted down, but all the more exuberant for it; only a true free-masonry of these implacable people can free and reunite the world.[4]

There is nothing here that suggests Bataille accepted the shame of the Occupation. More complex and doubtful is the analysis proposed by Klossowski. And his preliminary remarks, 'Bataille despised the fascists', do not exactly annul his conclusions. This is because the phrase is immediately followed by another that might well encapsulate what everyone unconsciously wished, justifiably or not, to reproach Bataille for: '*Pathologically* committed, like Sade, he was only interested in revolution [here it is revolution, but it might not be any different for war] through the play of passions.'[5] The adverb 'pathologically' is here given ballast by all the meaning implied in the surrounding sentences: 'That the profound temptations of fascist cynicism acted on his own talents is indisputable.'(!) Or else: 'in submitting to this fascination discernible on the horizon of German demi-culture, Bataille unconsciously took his place in a realm inclined to fascism – that ogre side of life, to put it another way, from which he could not escape'.[6] Bataille was said to be pathological (we see here how Klossowski, Bataille's *friend*, could join those Bataille saw as his enemies: Breton, Sartre and, as we shall see, Souvarine), and because he is pathological he is, of necessity, politically misled; confused or even suspect. What Klossowski thought he could ascribe to an analogy between Bataille and Sade, Fardoulis-Lagrange ascribes to Kojève's influence but with a distorted meaning: whereas Kojève announced that Stalin incarnated the end of history, during the war Bataille instead saw Hitler as doing so. This is why his conquests had such a strong impact on his mind.[7]

But the most violent and determined accusations undoubtedly came from Souvarine, though he was not in France at all during the war and his denunciation came much later (forty years after the events in question; perhaps he feared the denial of the witnesses he cited, who naturally were all anonymous). Souvarine's case, which consisted of calling on the accounts of 'all our mutual friends', without specifying who they were, is interesting all the same in that it was intentionally vague (but irrefutable, he must have thought), only relying on various unverifiable testimonies. Interestingly, his preliminary remarks are no different to those used as evidence by Klossowski; they are simply more violent. The first point is that Bataille was a 'sexual deviant'; his obsessions were 'libidinous' and his wild imaginings were 'sadomaso-chistic'. Such tendencies, the second point claimed, could only have harmful influences on 'intellectual chemistry' and 'healthy morals'. The implicit deduction is that a debauched man cannot have any integrity, and a 'pathological' man cannot be a 'republican' (the familiar refrain is that passion comes from a single person and belongs to him alone; *a fortiori*, so does the unleashing of passions). But for Souvarine, Bataille was not just sexually deviant, he was also intellectually perverse. Did he not make the mistake of admitting that he considered the only valid philosophy of the previous twenty years was German? This is only half true, since it underestimates the influence of Russian thought on him, and makes Kojève an entirely 'German' philosopher. If he read and admired German philosophy it was, according to Souvarine, because he was a follower of that 'fuliginous Nazi' Heidegger (his argument takes little account of the fact that Bataille read little of Heidegger's work, and without enthusiasm;[8] that he read much more of Hegel and Nietzsche, whom Bataille, alone as we have seen, cleared of all fascist and anti-Semitic interpretations before the war; and that he read more of Jaspers or Husserl than Heidegger . . . he was inevitably as unworthy as the man Souvarine considered the most unworthy). But Souvarine pushed this libel still further: if Bataille spoke ill of Simone Weil and borrowed her least favourable characteristics for Lazare in *Blue of Noon*,[9] it was because she was Jewish. It is with consummate treachery that he insinuates this: 'One can guess the word he dares not speak, thinking of the mother of his daughter.' (There is no need to recall that Sylvia Bataille was Jewish.) Because he is a 'deviant', Bataille is *necessarily* a fascist and anti-Semitic. Souvarine crowns this series of approximate and cobbled-together arguments with a final element that sums it all up:

> All of our mutual friends [I have already asked which ones, the accusation is too serious for them not to be called to the witness stand] who spoke to me about it after the war resorted to the word 'fascinated' to define his attitude towards Hitler, in private of course, since he would not have had the courage to take a risk.[10]

Such accusations are amply dismissed by the texts written and published by Bataille, as by the accounts of those who knew him better than Souvarine at the time, accounts that can all be cited, something Souvarine carefully avoids doing. What is more, not all of these

accounts are by Bataille's 'friends'; some were even by people hostile
to him; among them, that of Georges Duthuit is of particular interest:
'Bataille, unlike our enemies, considered that each individual must
engage in practical experiences leading simultaneously to joy and to
death for oneself, certainly not for others. In the last booklet he
published, in 1939, before entering the shadows of the invasion.'[11] This
sentence is one of the most crucial of all those likely to 'reframe' the
challenge of Acéphale, because it is one of the very few that aims to
distinguish clearly between the unleashing of passions (joy and death)
that Acéphale undertook, and the violent, directed unleashing of
passions provoked and stirred up by National Socialism and fascism
('our enemies', in Duthuit's words). It is crucial above all in that it
overturns the analogy often imputed between Acéphale and fascism,
and makes Acéphale, on the contrary, the most pronounced contradiction of fascism. Duthuit stresses this in fact: Bataille is 'unlike our
enemies'. This 'unlike' does not indicate a slight or even a pronounced
difference, but the most complete difference possible. And so that this
difference should appear to everyone (here to Breton, and at a time of
war) as the greatest possible, Duthuit articulates effectively the nature
of experience and of sovereignty: experience can only be known by
someone who cuts himself off, sovereignly, from all 'cephality' (contrary to this experience, fascism never stops investing the head with all
authority; in this way it is not at all sovereign, and sovereignty is alien
to its very constitution).

Proving that Acéphale should not be confused with fascism, however
difficult its challenge may have been (and however opaque to many),
proving that, *on the contrary*, it appeared to be in radical opposition
to it, was a task already begun in 1937 by Denis de Rougemont, thus
anticipating the misrepresentations by many years and perhaps guess-
ing their nature: 'Acéphale is the sign of radical anti-statism, in other
words of the sole antifascism worthy of the name.'[12] In a less theoretical but more political way, de Rougemont says the same thing as
Duthuit. He posits the most distinct opposition between Acéphale and
fascism (it is not a case of distinguishing them, not merely because
there can be no confusion between them, but because they are separated not by a difference of degree but by the opposition in their very
natures), an opposition all the more distinct, and effectively irreducible,
in that the experience sought by Acéphale is that of the reversal (the
inversion) of the signs of the experience of fascism. Just as fascism

'reversed' Nietzsche, Bataille 'reversed' fascism. He did so not to rediscover within fascism's radius some truth it may have changed or lost, falsifying itself as it falsified Nietzsche (but the falsification of Nietzsche had exactly the meaning that fascism wished to give itself), but to rediscover a truth of social links, in fact a sacred truth, that beyond a doubt – Bataille at least was certain – the democracies had lost as they grew weaker.

All the same, the fact remains that fascism was right about one thing (and Bataille maintained the difficult position that there is no greater danger than wishing to ignore this): the spectacle of truth onto which it had managed to haul itself is *superior* – that is, more seductive – to the homogeneous truth of bourgeois parliamentary democracies. That it used it to the ends of domination and servitude never escaped Bataille. But these ends were all the more formidable, they would even be all the more readily effective, in that the means of seduction it used to obtain them could count in advance on the tacit and, in truth, enraptured, approval of the crowds who were ready to do anything to reach, en masse, blindly, a lost sacred, even if fascism was nothing more than a simulacrum and ultimately a totally tragic falsification of it.

Bataille's desperate effort consisted in giving back to this need a sacred that was at least as great and as seductive, one which was not false (which did not have enslavement and terror as its ends). In other words, it would have been a matter, in extreme circumstances, of taking inspiration from fascism's means to reverse the attraction it obviously had, and to deprive it of the infectiousness it relied upon. This is a view Michel Leiris later explicitly endorsed:

> My feeling is that, in truth, Bataille was never a fascist. He was, if you like, fascinated by the genius for propaganda the Nazis had. His wish was that the left should show an equal genius for propaganda in the opposite direction. That's it. I don't know if the name Contre-Attaque came from him; it's possible. For that was really how Bataille saw things. It was a counter-attack. There was the fascist attack with its huge propaganda methods. And we had to manage to find equally powerful methods for the counter-attack.[13]

If, for his part, André Masson did not deny that he and Bataille hated democracies and their 'absolutely sickening spinelessness',[14] he nonetheless affirmed that even more they hated beyond all normal limits the 'horror of Nazism and of all possible forms of fascism, including Franco's', so reminding us that issues 2 and 3 of *Acéphale* were written and drawn 'in the midst of the Spanish Civil War' (in Spain itself in fact).[15]

Hans Mayer and Jean-Pierre Faye would later also say this in a way that leads to the heart of the matter (to that which relates to thought). Thus Hans Mayer says:

> Bataille alone, in my opinion, seems to have understood that a boundless *Aufklärung* was needed. How can I put it? That perhaps it was necessary to give up the frontiers of thought, for the simple reason that German reality, fascist reality, had itself given up the traditional taboos and values. Do not forget that, at the start of the Third Reich, Hitler and his men had decreed that those condemned to death should no longer be executed with the guillotine but with an axe. A return, then, to the horrible forms of the past; and at the same time, and this is the real problem that in my opinion Bataille alone understood at that time, this was not just a return to barbarism. There was also something quite different. On the one hand, execution with an axe, on the other, the perfecting of the gas chamber, using modern German technology. I think that, even before the news came from Poland and Auschwitz, Bataille had understood that it was all part of the same thing.

Mayer concludes this long analysis by saying: 'This is why Bataille sought a dialogue with [Walter] Benjamin, and perhaps also with me.'[16]

Jean-Pierre Faye's analysis was very similar, even if he spoke of phantasm (or myth) where Bataille spoke of the sacred, and of rationality where Mayer spoke of *Aufklärung*:

> Bataille was, along with Ernst Bloch, alone in trying to snatch away Nazism's great trump card, a formidable trump card: the force of phantasm, the buried and then suddenly unleashed energy of the mythical. To confine oneself to rationality is no safeguard, since rationality is a frontier, a line of protection ready to crack, and all of a sudden in pours the invasion.[17]

Nazism is not part of reason, at least not entirely, and Bataille was better prepared than others to understand this, since he had long paid 'incredibly close attention to the virulence of unreason'.[18] He alone, or with few others, could see that the reply Nazism necessitated was no longer part of 'reason', that it was no more part of it than Nazism itself was, that reason would be powerless to counter the unleashing of blind passion Nazism propagated.

Bataille dreamed of opposing the terrible, captive myth of Nazism with a myth having at least an equal power and seduction, one that would *set free*. There is certainly no doubt that Acéphale could not have that power, far from it, and that it did not set free. What is striking, however, is that Acéphale saw so clearly, even if in the end this was in vain or derisory. Acéphale was not just in vain or derisory (which it *also* was of course). Acéphale had a truth: a truth of disaster. However derisory and in vain the few rituals Bataille wished to give Acéphale were, they made up a truth in anticipation of the disaster Nazism would be: refusing to shake hands with anti-Semites, as though anticipating the extent to which this would obsessively expose 'boundless' reason (Mayer) and prophetic thought; sacrifice, as though anticipating for itself the *absolutely* tragic possibility of the Holocaust; the commemoration of the beheading of Louis XVI on the Place de la Concorde, as though reaffirming that one had to 'proclaim, shout out, the death of God' at the moment when his sham strove to turn his corpse into 'a monstrous slave enterprise' with no other end than the monocephalous reconstitution of society. Bataille was like the 'madness' of this truth anticipating the disaster, announcing the collapse: he spent the evening of the declaration of war on Germany pacing the Place de la Concorde.[19]

It remains to find a 'meaning' for this reputation ascribed to him. I shall try and give one (one that will nevertheless be less extravagant and will not contradict the facts in any way): Bataille terrified others, and such a terror needs to find words. A moralist, even a powerless one (especially a powerless one), is reassuring; as *a fortiori* is an idealist. Moralists and idealists are reassuring and comforting. But what about Bataille? Patiently, often violently, Bataille had for ten years been laying waste to the moral stakes dominating the aesthetic and political scene of the left from one end to the other (say from surrealism to the Communist Party). He accused the pacifists of being defeatists (see the 'Declaration' of the College of Sociology after the Munich accords), the patriots of being racists (see Contre-Attaque's tracts), the bourgeois of being corrupt (collaborators who had come to power), the proletariat of being cattle (bought out by the sham of the leader-gods). He predicted the abattoir for them all, whatever they might have to say while dying to protest their innocence. Not all died from the catastrophe he announced (nor did the democracies, even if it was a close thing), and the words some of them had to seek for vengeance (vengeance never comes too late against those who were right too soon) were drawn from this well of infamy: the time was right again for moralists to speak up loud and clear; all the louder in that in the meantime *everyone* had become a hero; and all the clearer in that everyone had agreed to forget the France that had so far accommodated itself to the Occupation as to become, against itself, the Reich's second weapon. If there was one lasting thing that the war should have silenced for good it was this arrogance of the moralists: their wrongs were such that even victory could not set this to rights.

The excretions of the war:
exodus, evacuation

Bataille started to write *Guilty* on 5 September 1939. At that time he was still living at Saint-Germain-en-Laye: 'The date I start . . . is no coincidence. I'm starting because of what's happening, though I don't want to go into it . . . No more evasions! I have to say things straight out.'[1] To speak without evasions does not mean to speak about the death-throes of the events then occurring, but to be oneself their death-throes. This does seem to have been the meaning of the experience *Le Coupable* describes, a mystical meaning, a meaning of being in death-throes.

Alone in September, Bataille was joined in October by Denise Rollin, with whom he shared his life, living either at the house in Saint-Germain he had taken for Laure or at Denise's flat at 3 rue de Lille in Paris. At that time he was still employed at the Bibliothèque Nationale[2] where he would remain until 1942. On 26 May 1940, twelve days after the Germans had entered Paris, Bataille accompanied Denise on part of her journey to Riom-ès-Montagnes:

> In the car taking her to the Auvergne, I accompanied her as far as the place we crossed the Loire [this text was written at Aubrais and he is no doubt referring to Fleury-les-Aubrais] where we tearfully separated. The car left and I remained standing on the road . . . if I did not feel a sense of rage, it is because I did not hold myself back. Besides, I knew nothing. Was anyone in the universe as oppressively ignorant as I was?[3]

Denise Rollin had evidently taken refuge in the region where Bataille was born, not at Riom exactly as would have been logical, but near Mauriac, at Drugeac, to be exact, in the Cantal. The day after their separation, Bataille noted: 'I feel I am so much closer to death, that is, I am unable to stir without death being the only escape that enters my head'[4] (death brought by war, the death that is war, once again Bataille called upon it to fall on him, in the sense that Acéphale called upon it, in the sense that experience would call upon it). On 30 May, he made his own way to Riom-ès-Montagnes and stayed only briefly at Drugeac, we do not know why (Riom: 'the only land to which something of my childhood remains attached'[5]), and he seems to have been in a state of despair: 'It only remains for me to die. I have my reasons and it would seem vain to give them . . . I do not at all curse life. I like it a lot, but if things turn out so badly.'[6] On the evening of 2 June, or the morning of the 3rd, Bataille was back in Paris where he would stay until the 11th of that month. This was in fact the date he started out for Drugeac again (where Denise Rollin had remained), a journey he described as an evacuation: 'It is the exodus and horror of the division between fortune and misfortune. Until now fortune has accompanied me: so much more clearly that an hour ago I would have considered leaving on foot down the road.'[7]

He again gathered a group of close friends (this was a constant: Bataille did not like to live alone) at Drugeac (or possibly at Ferluc, we cannot be sure but they are neighbouring villages): his own child Laurence – ten years old – Denise and her son Jean (one year old), André Masson and his wife Rose. If the notes he scribbled are to be believed, life there was not as he had expected: 'Misunderstandings, then hatred and accusations: life in the Ferluc house, where I hoped to discover an oasis, was becoming a sort of horror . . . myself? Why am I condemned to this ceaseless agitation all around me? As though my presence attracted problems . . . Faced with horrors, there is a sort of cruel indulgence.'[8]

The 'present disaster' of French defeat and the signing of the Armistice with the occupying troops at Rethondes on 22 June caused only an extremely muffled echo in the pages of his diary, paradoxically carried to tragic dimensions, dimensions from which only the storm would release him: 'Although it has collapsed, although the virtues which are in it [i.e. this country], like the possibility of a storm in a leaden cloud are ignored, it seems to me that they will be ardent.'[9]

In July 1940, Bataille was moving around the free zone: on the 28th, he was in Vichy, on the 31st in Clermont-Ferrand, where he slept in a school, 'the image of hard and dominant possession', his blanket bearing in red letters the name of Blaise Pascal. 'I debate ascesis and luxury with myself.'[10] On 3 August, he was in Bord and on the 4th in

Drugeac again. On the 8th he returned to Paris ('To go from Clermont to Paris is to risk being arrested at the German post: a dark horizon and leaden sky'[11]). On 28th, he started to move out of the house at Saint-Germain: 'I had to take Laure's dresses and linen out of the wardrobe. I found what she had hidden, her net and lace stockings, long black stockings or long white ones, and the stiff collars she had bought to wear with her little girl's smock.'[12] Bataille took a new flat at 259 rue Saint-Honoré (Paris VIII), where he lived for half the time, spending the rest at 3 rue de Lille, where Denise Rollin lived.

Nobodaddy[1]

I hope the heavens are ripped open . . . This I hoped for, but the skies never opened. There's a mystery in my crouching here like a beast of prey, flesh gripped by hunger. It's completely absurd: 'Is God the animal I'd like to tear apart?' As if I was *really* a beast of prey. But I'm sicker than that. My hunger holds no interest for me. Rather than eat, my desire is to be eaten. Love eats my living bones, and the only *release* is quick death. I'm waiting for an answer from the dark in which I exist. What if it turned out that instead of being ground to pieces, I was just forgotten about, like some kind of waste? There isn't an answer in all this flailing about. Just emptiness. Now say that . . . There's no *God*, though, for me to get down on my knees to.[2]

There is no God. Supplication is strangled in the throat. Yet it is no less terrible, even if there is no one to hear it. The cry is on the same scale as the void it leaves: it is immense.

It has often been said that Bataille was a mystic. It has also almost been said that the war corresponded to a kind of second conversion for him: that he had been active before the war and became contemplative once it was declared. The truth is more complex. In 1937 he defined himself to Alexandre Kojève as a 'negativity with nothing to do'. To Kojève the Hegelian, what a negativity could be was immediately understandable: for Hegel, action is the negative. But in that case, what was an action which suddenly found itself without a task? Not a contemplation, no doubt; even less a mysticism. An activity deprived of means and reasons for action suspends time, even if this is the time of war (and so the most vehement of activities), and takes it apart.

If Bataille had no doubt that this was also how Hegel might have understood what a negativity without a task might be, he nonetheless deduced the refutation of his entire system from the fact that he had not located this possibility at the end of history. Bataille did not become a contemplative man with the advent of war, but a man 'enraptured with' (removed from) time. The time of the useful, of waiting, of projects, of endings, were turned by the war (which in this way too was illuminating) into an ek-static time, an abstract time: the boundless time of a *death struggle*, between the two times of life and of death, no longer entirely one or the other (God or nothingness, death is no longer time).

Starting to write that strange book *Guilty* (if it really is a book, and not rather, as we shall see, a totally jumbled-up journal), it was from the nothingness of a death struggle that Bataille proposed to make up this story: 'I intend a description of mystical experience.'[3] And this experience had its trances. They are no different in nature from those produced by physical passion; they are just more intense. Bataille would go to look for ecstasy (the capacity *momentarily* to annihilate the enslaving empire of time), as he had found it when looking at the torture of the Hundred Pieces, and in the most disturbed emotions, preferably bloody ones (the emotions that wound, frothing at the mouth): a bird of prey tearing out the throat of a smaller bird; a blade going into the flesh of a knee . . . Is this an ecstasy? Can this come from a mystic?

> suddenly I felt myself become a sex in a state of erection, with an undeniable intensity . . . The idea that my very body and head were now no more than a monstrous penis, naked and injected with blood, seemed so absurd to me I thought I would collapse laughing . . . What is more, I could not laugh, so strong was the tension of my body. Like the tortured man,[4] I must have had my eyes contorted and my head tilted back. In this state, the cruel representation of the torture, of the ecstatic look, of bloody sides bared, gave me a harrowing convulsion.[5]

This scene was echoed a year later by another, scarcely less intense:

> I began to picture the most disturbing images I could imagine. I would enter a state which is impossible to describe and belongs to nightmare rather than orgy, but sustained by movements of virulent anger . . . I went down to the toilet and sitting on the throne hoped that a violent defecation would free me: I twisted convulsively, I wanted to cry out, but I found myself in my room once more, just as twisted, just as thirsty. It was then my naked body once again arched – as a year earlier – once again there was the contorted image of the tortured man[6] and I fell to the ground shaking with sudden convulsions.[7]

Such states, which are more intense than physical passion, are also more intense than God (one might also say they are God: as rending as his absence is, as voracious as the cry that cannot find peace; as strangled as someone who makes no plea for any justice). What Bataille discovered in giving himself up to every imaginable rending[8] – the war never supplied anything more than a few extra images to add to the timelessly incandescent states he went through – was that ecstasy is in no way diminished (is no less violently *divine*) for dispensing with God. God is not just dead, he never existed: the trances of Christian mystics are thus no less imaginary.

Bataille's insistence on calling himself a mystic was a provocation; all the more so since he made no secret of disliking the word: 'I envisage less "confessional" experience – to which one in general refers – than experience in itself, free of ties, be they vague, to any confession whatsoever. This is what justifies the abandonment of the word "mystical", to which I could not adhere without inviting confusion.'[9] But above all it had the advantage of designating God as the last possible word, the one after which silence begins. And since God is the last word, it is the one that says 'that all words will fail further on'.[10] And with the silence into which this word falls (along with all the others, since it is no different from them) begins the torture.

Any word beyond will fail, just as God himself fails. What Bataille meant to discover, within himself, was what had hitherto been hidden by God. The fact that the kind of experiences described here had been connected to what God seemed able to make them signify would hamper their role as a revelation. The mystic 'sees what he wants'. At best he can discover 'what he knew'. He cheats. He takes on a role. He poeticises. Where God 'enraptured', his absence tortures. Along with God one must get rid of the Whole, salvation, perfection, in short all of his sham, and know only, of all the things leading people to try and test out such states, those which leave them most naked, since such a state has no other authority but its own. Nothing justifies it, and nothing gives it meaning: '*Mystical states* are available to me, if that is what I want. Maintaining my distance from beliefs, deprived of hopes, nothing compels me to enter these states.'[11]

Nothing justifies it and nothing gives it meaning except the gratuitous whim to know 'the impossible of desire'. Robert Sasso puts this clearly: 'The experience in question is not that of a presence but far rather of an absence.'[12] And it is not only the absence of God that tortures, but the impossibility into which desire falls once God has gone. Nothing justifies desire any more where *once* God justified everything. What is worse is the paradox that God can no longer answer the desire one might have to emancipate oneself from one's desires. Thus he no longer answers the single desire that destroys them all: the desire for God. The desire for God is hopeless, and saintliness is impossible. Whim and passion justify evil (the disorder of desires, horrified intoxication), but who or what justifies good? Only laughter can answer the divine farce and the useless trance into which it throws you: the laughter Bataille designated with a word taken from William Blake, like a false nose placed on God's face: Nobodaddy. Alexandre Kojève agreed too with this play on words: 'All mysticism is contained in the word Nobodaddy.'[13]

The effect of a sham obtained is as sinister as one could wish. God is no more reassuring dead (as he is for the materialist) than he is full of drink, flies undone, in a brothel or on a binge, obscene and losing his grip (remember what a sham Lord Auch was for him: God in the shithouse), a cripple (blind above all; how many times had Bataille described him as blind?) or mad: 'This God who animates us under his clouds is mad. I know it. I am he.'[14] (Must we say once again how much, however Bataille twists its appearance, each in some way or other takes something from his memories of his father? This receives further confirmation, if any were needed, from the name chosen to describe him: *Nobodaddy*.) The doubt in which Bataille perpetually leaves us – does God exist or not? – might, for him, find this provisional reply: he exists. He exists *necessarily*, since man exists. This should not be misunderstood: man makes him exist. He exists in proportion to the desire people have to make him exist. And he is as far (as profound, as serious) as this desire goes, since he is the *impossible* of this desire. And this is what interests Bataille about mystics, and which makes one of him *too*, if we want to agree that he sees himself as different from those who went before him on this path, and for whom the title would not be challenged, in that he *does not attain* and does not seek *to attain*. His condition has no other aim than itself and the void onto which it opens: there is nothing that justifies it, nothing that appeases it, nothing that might be its goal. And in this way it is intense beyond equal. So intense that, more than eroticism, it is the most profound, most vertiginous expenditure. It rallies to it all available energies and takes them to their highest level of intensity for . . . for nothing: 'what mysticism cannot put into words (it fails at the moment of utterance), eroticism says; God is nothing if he is not a transcendence of God in every direction; in that of vulgar being, in that of horror and impurity; even in that of nothing at all.'[15] God is the impossible. In the church he is only the mask of the impossible. But outside church, what is left to him? The brothel. Like mysticism, debauchery strips him bare. We have seen how, leaving churches behind, Bataille threw himself into brothels, and how these replaced them:

> In place of God. . .
> there is
> only
> the impossible
> and not God.

Edwarda: the divine tatters

It was in a brothel that Bataille sought out the most tormented, the most distorted, as well as the most upsetting, of the images he was to give of God, God whose mystic it has too often been said that he was at that time, with no clear distinction as to *what* mysticism this was and *what* God. The name this image assumes is Edwarda, Madame Edwarda. It is also the title of the story Bataille made from his horrible 'whim'. She is a prostitute (not even the madame; ten years earlier, Bataille would perhaps have made her so: ordaining the free play of death), one whore among others or perhaps all possible whores. What a man finds in a brothel near the Porte Saint-Denis is the ritual – of a 'hallucinating solemnity' – thanks to which he knows which God – what impossible – condemns him: 'death itself was the festival in the same way that the nudity of the brothel calls for the butcher's knife' – the knife of the sacrificer.

And so that everything should be clear, Edwarda, a prostitute, needed to reveal herself for what she was: God.

> She was seated, she held one leg stuck up in the air, to open her crack yet wider she used fingers to draw the folds of skin apart. And so Madame Edwarda's 'old tatters' looked at me, hairy and pink, just as full of life as some loathsome squid. 'Why,' I stammered in a subdued tone, 'why are you doing that?' 'You can see for yourself,' she said, 'I'm GOD.' 'I'm going crazy – ' 'Oh, no you don't you've got to see, look!'.[1]

Naked, tied up, what Edwarda – God – forced the narrator to see are her 'tatters'. Because she is God, she has the right to demand: she tells him twice to look. Christ asked several people to look at his wounds. We find an echo of Edwarda's injunction in the *Liber visionum* of Angela of Foligno which Bataille was reading at the time he wrote both *Guilty* and *Madame Edwarda*: 'In his pity, God appeared to me several times in sleep or in waking, crucified: "Look," he said, "look at my wounds." This was repeated several times. He showed me the tortures on his head, the hairs torn from his eyebrows and beard, and said to me: "This is for you, for you, for you." ' And because Madame Edwarda is God, she is necessarily unclean, unclean and desirable. One would need not to have read *all* of Bataille to claim he might have changed; having yesterday been debauched, he could today be a mystic and – some people cannot resist saying[2] – a Christian. He was obviously the same man who as a child obeyed the same command to see what his father made him see. And he was the same man who said about God what he already suggested fifteen years earlier in *Story of the Eye*. This obscene and naked woman is God. She displays her 'tatters' and commands that they are seen for what they are: God's 'divine tatters'. She also commands him to seal his lips to it. 'Kiss! . . . I trembled; I watched her, motionless, she was smiling at me so sweetly that I trembled. Finally I got down on my knees, reeling, and placed my lips on the open wound.' Again, this echoes a vision of Angela of Foligno: 'Christ called to me and told me to put my lips on the wound on his side. I felt for the first time a great consolation mingled with a great sadness, for I had the Passion before my eyes. I reflected on it, seeking someone who really wanted to kill me. I was not asleep.' This is not far from the sick and mad father, who in his own way used to command his child to see him naked and 'tattered'. Was Lord Auch not 'God relieving himself', and how can we not find the extraordinary quality of the word 'tatter' arresting? How can the mad and beautiful whore, admitting, naked and in tatters, that she was God, not evoke his father's dead organ between flabby, dead legs? Women's tatters, in one case, but those of a woman whose name is that of a feminised man, Edward, the name, we shall soon see, of the dead man in *The Dead Man*. (*Blue of Noon* had already furnished examples of inversion of the names of characters: Lazare was a woman, Lenin became Lenova in a dream.) Men's tatters, in the other. The comparison is so much less avoidable than in the contemporary tale that is *Le Petit*, God is this time 'a gland' and this time still curiously, symptomatically, associated with the narrator's father: 'God is not a priest, but a gland: father is a gland.'[3]

There is no doubt of the capacity of this woman, the last woman, it is said, to be God, of the capacity of God to be the last woman, the most traumatised and devastating: 'She was entirely black, simply there, as distressing as an emptiness, a hole. I realised she wasn't frolicking, wasn't joking, and indeed that, beneath the garment enfolding her, she was mindless: rapt, absent. Then all the drunken exhilaration drained out of me, then I knew that She had not lied, that She was GOD.'[4] (Like him, she wore a mask and a domino: a character from a farce, from a tragic farce.)

And it is God – who is also an animal – who, disgusting as she is, leads the narrator to the invisible: the exhausting pleasure taken by Her, *before him*, with a taxi driver, in his cab, pleasure as *glorious* as it is terrified. The narrator (Bataille?) has this time pushed (and also awakened) torture as far as possible. He is not, as in *Story of the Eye* and *Blue of Noon*, the one who needs death in order to desire, this time he is himself death. Love develops without him; but in front of his eyes. And he watches over Edwarda – over God – the signs of death finally coming down – signs of pleasure inaccessible to God: 'from her stare, then, at that moment, I knew she was drifting home from the impossible. . . .' 'Love was dead in those eyes. . . . the stave slipped out, I helped her sit down, wiped her wet body. Her eyes dead, she offered no resistance.'[5] *She knew*. Bataille wrote: 'GOD, if he knew would be a pig.' Because she is a pig, Edwarda *knows*. To say of Edwarda that she is a pig is not suddenly to admit morality. It is an abject truth, but one that is also tender. Not the least extraordinary thing is that this book, while intended to be abject, should also be so tender. Edwarda is cherishable, even as a pig, or more accurately because she is a pig, she alone can open to the night of an empty sky. (Maurice Blanchot, in a very fine article written in 1957 in *NRF*, said that with all tragic writers Phaedra must meet Oenone. Edwarda is an Oenone whom the dying Phaedra will not curse for having brought her to the worst of resolutions. Edwarda *knows*, and what she knows is the knowledge of a God: what God alone could know if he knew but he does not know, and this is why he does not exist. What a prostitute knows, God does not know and this is why a prostitute alone is holy when God is a farce. If he knew, he would die. He would be unmasked. Edwarda is not only an excessive animality (as in her way Simone was in *Story of the Eye*). She is an excessive God. She is GOD revealed as DEATH. Existence is – its unveiling, its aletheia – and is only – its concealment – its slaughter: the slaughtering of the exposed body, *without God*.[6]

Madame Edwarda is the key to *L'Expérience intérieure* as *Le Petit* is the key to *Guilty*: the lubricious keys.[7] These two books can only be read, in fact, in the most upside-down way. *Guilty*, especially, is the most characteristic of Bataille's books. Intentionally disordered, with no more of a beginning than an end, uncompleted by nature, mingling, blending diary and thought, triviality and elevation, eroticism and the sacred, reality and fiction, biography and philosophy, beginning on one date and ending on another without either being justified, made of thematic annexes as if the object was to integrate a sort of residuality of the text, although other passages (too autobiographical, too real) have been taken out:[8] *Guilty* is like the short fragment of a long text begun with the first of the lines written by Bataille and completed (but is incompletion not at the heart of all Bataille ever wrote?) with the last of the lines written by him. (*Le Petit* is a sort of *Guilty* in a more naked, more brief, more shattering form.) Begun on 5 September 1939 and completed in May 1943, *Guilty*, more by what Bataille removed from it than by what he left in (the commendable concern to *make* a book out of what only poorly resembled one), gave a clear and biographically reliable image of him during the war.[9]

'I call myself the abomination of God'[1]

Bataille thus started writing *Guilty* on 5 September 1939. A few days before, he had started to read the *Liber visionum* by Angela of Foligno. This coincidence is significant. We have seen that, closely or not, intentionally or not, more than one element of this book is discernible, however changed in meaning, 'maddened', in *Madame Edwarda* (in such a way that *Madame Edwarda* is well and truly a mystical as much as an obscene book, at least if one understands its mysticism as *absolutely* obscene). We shall see that this book would also have just as significant and illuminating an influence on *Guilty* as on *Inner Experience*; it is their fascinating watermark. Angela of Foligno, saying to her confessor (Brother Arnaud), 'I am no longer disposed to writing, but to crying . . . I am blind . . . Yes! The gift of inventing an abyss so as to humiliate oneself absolutely', opens up the possibility of an abyss she fills with God only as a last resort. But several of the sentences she utters just as much leave in suspension the possibility of such a God in giving whoever reads them the possibility of claiming that the abyss is superior to this God – 'It is impossible to say anything about the abyss; no word has a sound that can give an idea of it; no thought, no intelligence can venture into it. They stay in their realms, in their inferior realms. Not one word, not one idea is like the God of the abyss' – and of claiming that higher still than words (and discursivity: 'A few Christians have broken from the language world and come to the ecstatic one'[2]) is silence: 'My words give me the feeling of nothingness. What am I saying? My words horrify me. Oh supreme obscurity! My words are curses, my words are blasphemies. Silence! Silence! Silence!' The words of Angela of Foligno could sometimes be attributed to Bataille, sometimes to Nietzsche, without anyone noticing: 'Deepening depth, hollowing out nothingness in its abyss, I long, I long, I hunger and thirst. I hunger and thirst for you to sink into the abyss, that you engulf yourselves in the depths of your nothingness and in the heights of the divine immensity.'

Such are the presuppositions of an experience that knows the night it must travel through; it matters little if the saint insists on believing that God holds sway over this night and that Bataille claims that God is himself this night (or that this night is God), the terror, the dread are the same; and above all the determination of Bataille and Angela of Foligno to have an experience stripped of its discursive, linguistic and reasonable trappings is also the same.[3] Between Angela of Foligno and Bataille come first Pascal and then Nietzsche. Pascal pushed absence further, so far that one no longer knows with him whether God or night is the depths of worlds. And Nietzsche, by a violent effort, perhaps a desperate one, tried to metamorphose this Pascalian night into a day that is heavy with the human promise that the mystics had taken from man before him. In this, Bataille goes beyond Nietzsche. It is night rather than day that attracts him: the night of John of the Cross; above all Angela of Foligno's night, so close in his eyes to that of Edwarda – both saints, and whores too: one of God, the other of men.

The community of friends

For Bataille 1941 was principally marked by the writing and publication of *Madame Edwarda*, one of the most important and well known
of his works, as well as by that of *Guilty*. A meeting this year, and the
friendship that ensued, seems to have had no less importance: this was
a meeting with Maurice Blanchot.

It is not at all surprising that these two men did not meet earlier:
they had very different pasts. It was therefore chance (fortune?) that
would put them into contact (for Bataille, another piece of good
fortune linked to the war): fortune, and more concretely, Pierre Prévost.

At the beginning of the war, Pierre Prévost was a young intellectual
who had first – in 1934 – been involved with the Ordre Nouveau
group in which, after the death of Arnaud Dandieu, he had been close
to Robert Aron, Alexandre Marc[1] and Jacques Chevalley. It was at
Chevalley's recommendation that he was introduced to Bataille in 1937
at the Bibliothèque Nationale (we have seen that Bataille had collaborated quite closely but anonymously in the composition of the chapter
'Exchanges and credits' in *La Révolution nécessaire*, a sort of manifesto
of the group in book form), and following this meeting he joined
Bataille in the most important of his public activities, the College of
Sociology. (But it should be made clear that Prévost was never close to
Bataille, to the point of knowing him well and participating in the
activities of Bataille's more secret activities, like Acéphale.) Prévost also
had other relations and friendships from which, as we shall see, Bataille
was able to take advantage: with Georges Pelorson (he worked on two
issues of the journal *Volonté* which Pelorson edited); and with Maurice
Kahane, at the time a theosophist (who would soon take the name of
Maurice Girodias). These relations meant that Prévost was quite close
to several study groups,[2] some informal, others clearly formalised: this
was the case of the main one which, under the name Jeune France,

brought together several people he knew at the time of Ordre Nouveau like Xavier de Lignac and Romain Petitot (who called himself François Bruel, after the war). Added to them were Paul Flamand (one of the future founders of Éditions du Seuil), Louis Ollivier (brother of Albert), Pierre Schaeffer and Georges Pelorson, who was to take charge of the literary part of the group and worked on the creation of a journal which would give material form to their debates. But Perlorson had other duties (in the government of Marshal Pétain, of which he seems to have been a member of the State Secretariat for Youth[3]), and wanted to hand over the editorial responsibilities to a young writer he claimed was the greatest of his generation, Maurice Blanchot.[4] Jeune France, which Vichy financed, in fact never had a journal: the apoliticism which prevailed in the group does not seem to have satisfied the curiosity of the Gestapo. Moreover, how apolitical could an association subsidised by a government linked hand and foot to an army of occupation claim to be? It was when this group, precariously consti-tuted around Pelorson and Blanchot, was dissolved that Pierre Prévost introduced the latter to Georges Bataille. Blanchot brought with him several members of Jeune France who would gather at the lectures Bataille organised at 3 rue de Lille.

There would certainly be a lot to say (of crucial importance) about the meeting of Maurice Blanchot and Georges Bataille if the silence both men maintained about their friendship did not reduce us to conjecture. It is clear that this encounter was decisive for both of them. But in what respect? Did Blanchot save Bataille, as Klossowski would have us believe, with 'so much strength'.[5] It seems clear, and several people – Camus, Sartre, Gabriel Marcel – remarked on this, that their thinking was analogous in several ways; the one mirrored the other, or they even completed each other (but could it be claimed, as Camus claimed to Sartre – who immediately repeated it – that *Inner Experi-ence* is 'the exact translation and commentary of *Thomas the Obscure*'? Which of the two books had Camus not read?)

Should things be put back in order? There is in fact reason to be suspicious of those people, the same people who claim that Bataille's work began with the war, who would have us believe that the meeting with Blanchot allowed him to start this work.[6] The facts are these: in 1941, Georges Bataille had written and published *Story of the Eye*, *The Solar Anus* and *Sacrifices*. He had written and published *Madame Edwarda* upon which Maurice Blanchot seems to have had no influence even if he was one of the first, and without any doubt one of the most perceptive, to discuss it (in 1956, when it was republished). Bataille had also written *Blue of Noon*; it is not unlikely that he gave Maurice Blanchot a copy to read as he had to his closest and most privileged friends. He had edited the journal *Documents* and given it some of its most dazzling essays, ones the surrealists could never have accepted. He had been, in so many people's opinion, the most important of the enemies recognised by Breton (who in fact considered him as representing the only possible alternative to surrealism). He had given *La Critique sociale* some of the most innovative and vital studies about the rising dangers of totalitarianism. He had co-directed with Breton (if not against him) Contre-Attaque (should we recall that Thirion saw in this the alliance of the two greatest intellectuals of the century?) and he undertook Acéphale simultaneously with the College of Sociology in which, whether admitted as such or not, he had the guiding role. This is a lot, but it is true to say that he reproached himself with being too unfocused and having written too little. The writer the Bataille of 1925 had dreamed of becoming he had certainly still not become by 1940. The fragile prestige the College of Sociology had allowed him to win back, had once more been dissipated with the war: by 1941 nothing remained of it. Nevertheless, if the encounter between the two men must be expressed in terms of influence (which certainly would make little sense) the advantage could rationally be presumed to go to Bataille. They were separated by ten years in age and by the books Bataille had published, few as they were. In fact it was only in 1941 that Maurice Blanchot published the first of his books, *Thomas l'obscur*, soon followed by *How Is Literature Possible?* and *Aminadab* (which Bataille considered very important) in 1942 and *Faux pas* in 1943.[7]

But something else separated them which partly justifies the provisional hypothesis of this ascendancy: the political positions of the two men before the war. Blanchot would rally to that of Bataille, at least henceforth his views would all lean towards Bataille's. If the two men influenced one another, politically among other things (which is undeniable), Bataille should in all likelihood be credited with Blanchot's ideological about-face (although neither ever said anything to confirm this). For Maurice Blanchot came from the Maurrasian right, even quite clearly from the extreme right. From 1936 to 1939 the same man who today is legitimately regarded as one of the great writers of the French language supported a violent Maurrasian nationalism, heaping on Léon Blum all the hatred of which anti-Semites of the time were capable. In fact, Maurice Blanchot collaborated on *Combat*, a monthly co-edited by Thierry Maulnier, from 1936 to 1938 and placed under the tutelary deities of Maurras, de Vallès and Drumont. (This has nothing at all to do with the daily *Combat* created during the war.) He also collaborated from January to October 1937 (for as long as it existed) on the fortnightly *L'Insurgé*, also edited, but this time alone, by Thierry Maulnier, a journal which featured those linked with the French extreme right immediately before the war: Georges Blond, Kléber Haedens, Jean-Pierre Maxence, Dominique Bertin, etc. Maurice Blanchot wrote two columns in *L'Insurgé*: one literary, the other political (at the time he was not merely a writer or a critic of right-wing tendencies, he was also a lead-writer of political polemic[8]).

However, it might be interesting to try to situate the meeting of Bataille and Blanchot on quite another level. Bataille in 1941 was incontestably alone and no less incontestably he retained his nostalgia for a community. Nevertheless there is little doubt that he now knew this community to be impossible. In fact it was at this moment that he began to define the possibility of any community as impossible (we shall see that he would use an analogous paradox on the subject of myth: 'Night is also a sun, and the absence of myth is also a myth'[9]). And by a second paradox (this one apparent), the person he was linked to through friendship, a feeling hardly different in his view from communitarian sentiment, would also support him in the idea of the impossibility of all community. And this absence of community, given as the sole community accessible to mankind, would ultimately open between Blanchot and Bataille the possibility of communication (since communication can only be justified by the impossibility of any community). In fact if two people ever really did establish communication, they were Bataille and Blanchot. It lasted for the rest of Bataille's life, that is for twenty years.[10]

Jean-Luc Nancy said in a decisive way that 'if the community is revealed in the death of the other [as we have seen that *Acéphale* claimed] it is because death itself is the true community of mortal beings: their impossible communion.'[11] *Thomas the Obscure* (and soon *Death Sentence*) and *Madame Edwarda* (or *The Dead Man*, as we shall see), admittedly in very different ways, are books which share this impossibility.

So no one but Blanchot could fall into agreement with Bataille on so disastrous a 'truth' and it is intellectually and biographically important to point out that this truth was that of friendship, a friendship which made the disaster *common* to them: 'I add that friendship is also the truth of disaster. You know mine.' Such is the final meaning of this community that it would be the disaster that death, which makes it a community, promises to it: 'The thought that you were ill has made me extremely uneasy and is a threat directed against something which would be common to us both'; 'It seems to me that in these distressing days, and that is their normal state, something has been given to us in common, to which we must also respond in common'; 'Something that could be called misfortune but that must also be left nameless could in a certain way be common. This is mysterious, perhaps deceptive, perhaps indescribably true.'[12] These extracts from the letters of Maurice Blanchot to Georges Bataille should be supplemented by this enigmatic dedication marked on the copy of *L'Attente, l'oubli*: 'Thinking of the goal we share'.

The impossible communion of two or more people is, paradoxically, the only thing which would be communicable to them; this is what Blanchot said twenty years after Bataille's death in – admirable – terms which are true to those of his friend:

'the basis of communication' is not necessarily the word, not even the silence which is its foundation and punctuation, but exposure to death, no longer of myself, but of the other of whom even the living and closest presence is already the eternal and insupportable absence, that which diminishes any work of mourning. And it is in this life itself that this absence of the other must be encountered, it is with it – its unwonted presence, always under the preliminary threat of a disappearance – that friendship takes shape and at each moment loses itself, an echo without return or with no other return than the incommensurable.[13]

From the community of the impossible
to the impossible community

Autumn 1941 saw the start, in Denise Rollin's flat in rue de Lille, of discussion readings organised by Bataille.[1] Two things are certain: first, they never had the importance people later tried to ascribe to them (comparable to the College of Sociology, for instance); and, second, these readings bore witness to the interest in the idea Bataille still cherished of founding a community and spreading *communication* as widely as possible among a group of people.

Whether with an eye to hierarchy or to appropriate activity, Bataille divided the circle of those attending into two groups: Queneau, Leiris and Fardoulis-Lagrange were part of the first, Pierre Prévost, Xavier de Lignac, Petitot and sometimes Louis Ollivier part of the second; it would seem that only Maurice Blanchot belonged to both. From what we know,[2] these meetings consisted of readings of passages from *Inner Experience* (being written at the time) and debates on the questions it raised (this book, published in 1943, indicates what these questions were: the possibilities and the value of an *experience*, its nature and authority, its field of action and its aims, if it had any). Bataille introduced each session (they seem to have taken place once or twice a month) by reading a fragment of the book in progress, and the debate, according to Prévost and Fardoulis-Lagrange, was essentially between Bataille and Blanchot.

Since *Inner Experience* was nearly complete, it would not be appropriate to see the plan drafted by Bataille (and read to his listeners) for a 'Socratic College' as anything other than an attempt to formalise the meetings that had already started in autumn 1941 and continued until March 1943. Moreover, this attempt, if it can be given a date with any precision, came only at a late stage: the end of 1942 or beginning of 1943.[3] This Socratic College was to have entailed several people, united by a common interest, *communicating*, in other words raising fundamental questions, those liable to lay bare the impossibility of their communion. 'To communicate means trying to reach unity, to become one from several, something successfully signified by the word communion.'[4] However much Bataille might have taken note of the impossibility of several people becoming one, the effort they made to communicate still constituted 'the negation of isolation'.[5] And this negation is – completely – inner experience; an inner experience that, to be precise, Bataille this time designated as 'negative', a designation offering the advantage of clearly removing any possible mystic presuppositions from its meaning (an advantage the title of the book published in 1943 did not offer: 'Negative Inner Experience' would have avoided several misinterpretations).

Bataille restated the outlines of this experience (which had already figured in *Inner Experience*), which according to him were borrowed from Maurice Blanchot. This experience can only:

– have its principle and end in the absence of salvation, in the renunciation of all hope [this could not have been any clearer, or less 'Christian']
– affirm by itself that it is authority (although all authority is paid for)
– be contestation of itself and non-knowledge[6]

Once again, the question of attributing ideas expressed by either Bataille or Blanchot early in their relationship is a slippery one. Was what Bataille here graciously credits to Blanchot – and it is no small thing: it is perhaps a kind of canon *law* of experience – really due to him alone? After all, in 1939, two years before meeting Blanchot, he had defined his mysticism in strikingly similar terms: 'the very love of life and fate means that it first commits itself the crime of *authority* it would *pay for*'.[7]

With these outlines laid down, Bataille also meant to distance the project of such a College from any means or ends that might have made it useful (no publications, no propaganda and no open meetings): the College would try solely 'to absorb, in its absence of opening outwards, the most clear activity' of each of its members.[8]

This meeting of men, formalised at last and placed under the ironic auspices of Socrates,[9] never took place as Bataille planned. Maurice Blanchot, who seems to have been more sceptical than Bataille about the possibility of such a project reaching any material form, does not seem to have been unduly surprised at this, seeing this meeting in retrospect 'as the final jolt of an attempt at a community that could never form itself'.[10]

The annunciation made to Marie

The year 1942 concentrated Bataille's solitude a little more and, in ways he could not have foreseen, brought him to states of extreme intensity. In fact in 1942 pulmonary tuberculosis was diagnosed. It will be recalled that this was not the first time this illness had affected him, since he had been discharged from the army in 1917 for the same reason. This time the illness was so grave that he was forced, from April, to take a long period of leave from the Bibliothèque Nationale. At first he was confined for a long time at the rue Saint-Honoré.[1] However, he continued to write *Inner Experience*, which he completed during the summer, when he was staying with Marcel Moré's mother at Boussy-le-Château.[2]

Leaving Boussy-le-Château at the end of August, Bataille reached Panilleuse (via Vernon), a village situated on the boundary of the departements of the Eure and Seine-et-Oise, where he seems to have stayed from September to November 1942.[3] A woman shared his solitude at Panilleuse, 'but we lived separately, less than a mile from one another, a beautiful girl, my mistress, and me'. (There is little doubt this was Denise Rollin. But was she with him during the summer, at Boussy-le Château?) From Panilleuse, Bataille travelled around: he went to Tilly, a small village situated only five miles from Vernon (Bataille travelled only by bicycle). He situated *The Dead Man*, the shortest and perhaps darkest of his tales, at Tilly (Bataille himself could not remember whether he had written *The Dead Man* during this stay or later):

> There is in any case the narrowest tie between *Le Mort* and my stay in Normandy as the consumptive I then was; in Normandy not far from the village called Tilly (which in *Le Mort* I call Quilly). The Tilly inn is modelled upon the actual one in Tilly; the mistress of the inn in the book is the same as the Tilly innkeeper. I invented the

other details, except for the rain, which hardly stopped falling during October or November 1942. Except also for the pitch black night when Julie knocks at the tavern door [the heroine of this tale was in fact called Julie before being changed to Marie]. Did I or did I not sleep at that inn? I don't remember, but it seems to me that I did. I further believe that in the taproom there were several farmhands wearing rubber boots, and even a player piano. Whatever, it was a sinister place, where anything could happen. And lastly I am also sure, or almost, that I slept – alone – in that place, which terrified me.

The rest is related to the intense sexual excitement which dominated me throughout that mad November. . . . I was ill, in an obscure state comingling fatigue, dread and exhilaration.[4]

Of this inn, terrifying to Bataille and symptomatic of the exasperated solitude where the war and sickness had repeatedly left him, he gave another barely less lacerated description:

I remember in Tilly my fondness for the people of the village, when the rains, mud and cold had ended, the bar viragos handling the bottles, and the noses (the snouts) of the big farm domestics (drunk, muddily shod); at night the rural songs would weep in the common throats; there was the coming and going of carousal, farting, the laughter of girls in the courtyard. I was happy to listen to their life, scribbling in my notebook, lying in bed in a dirty (and chilly) room. Not a hint of boredom, happy with the warmth of the cries, with the charm of the songs: their melancholy caught one's throat.[5]

Nevertheless, no place, no biographical facts (neither the solitude nor the delirious sexual excitement), are able effectively to prepare the reader for the horror of *The Dead Man*. The only thing that, at best, approaches it is the trepidation felt by Bataille faced with corpses, and one in particular, that of the German occupant of a shot-down airplane:

A foot of one of the Germans was exposed, the sole of his boot had been ripped off. The dead men's heads looked shapeless. Flames must have got to them, there was nothing intact apart from that foot [naked as it was, does not the foot of this corpse, when everything else is unrecognisable, have something – oppressive – of Edwarda's 'rags'?]. It was the one human thing belonging to any of the bodies, and its nakedness, become claylike, was inhuman: the heat of the blaze had transfigured it; this object was not cooked, it was charred; snug inside the soleless uppers, it was diabolical, no, not that, but unreal, denuded, indecent in the extreme.[6]

The naked brutality, the indecency, the diabolical lewdness of this foot have something of the limitless amorous and sexual brutality of the narrative (something in it of the *rat* which is a dwarf), the brutality of his conclusions reduced to their character of *impossible* necessity. Bataille made it clear: 'This foot announced the terrifying disappearance of "what is", henceforth I will no longer see "what is" except in the transparency of the foot which, better than a scream, announces its annihilation.'[7] The whole narrative of *The Dead Man* is constructed on the unavoidable necessity of such an annihilation, so much more violent for being, like this foot, silent.

The Dead Man is perhaps the most 'excremental' of Bataille's tales.[8] It is certainly one of the most devastated. A woman closes the door on one corpse (that of Edouard, whom she loved) and opens it on another (her own: she plans to die with the dawn). Between the two, there is a night (but also rain, mud and wind): a night to descend into annihilation. Like *Guilty* (like the war for Bataille) this night is prolonged like death-throes, like a decaying. As the body turns into excrement, so it turns into death. And as the flesh is a foretaste of decay, it prepares to pass away (it is as much ascetic as it is obscene). This woman, Marie, beautiful and lacerated, approaches love – or love in its orgiastic, dissolute form – as one approaches the abattoir. Between the door closed on her dead lover and the one open on her own death, there will be, as far as is permitted by the short, shocking and frenzied derangement of an obscene dying (but not only excrement equals the horror of death: the foot of the airman in the upper part of the shoe, neither charred nor burned to ashes, is inhumanly human), everything that flesh can know of 'what she is', and how mortal she is.

As we have seen, it had each time been death which determined the possibility of the narratives Bataille had so far written: Marcelle was this death (in *Story of the Eye*). It was beside her corpse and in its dazzling memory that the two adolescents embraced for the first time, and ever afterwards. In *Blue of Noon* the whores were this death, as was Troppmann's mother in the story in which he twice paid an indecent 'homage' to her corpse, and Dirty became it in her turn, wan, emaciated, clasped like a delicate skeleton above Trier cemetery. The narrator himself was this death in *Madame Edwarda*: but for him to be so it was necessary for Edwarda to be God.

On each occasion death alone, one is tempted to say, was the condition of *revelation* of the illuminating and saving character of erotic excess. In *The Dead Man*, on the other hand, and Bataille goes further here than he ever had before, this is no longer death opening onto eroticism, but eroticism and obscenity which prepare for death. The first line is 'Edouard fell back dead.' And the second: 'An emptiness opened inside her, a prolonged shudder went through her, and bore her upward like an angel.'[9] Death is the horror and turns her into an angel. Everything Marie does is divine, because she is henceforth freed from waiting; only the greatest obscenity could be equal to it.

And because this night of drawn-out dying will be without God (it could nevertheless be regarded as the night of Gethsemane itself, or as the Way of the Cross, made of as many stations as short chapters), it will have the devil as master of ceremonies. However, the Devil no more exists than does God; at best, he is a dwarf, a rat, an utterly broken rat and the bearer of all terrors: appearing in the recess of the inn door, Marie thought she recognised Edouard. Pissed on by Marie and wanked off by a farm-hand, this monster is evoked as horror itself: he 'spat seed up the front of the waistcoat. In his throes the dwarf was racked by little shudders which made him jump from head to toe.'[10]

Marie had to reply to the most horrible, not to say the most demented, invitation to be finally saintly enough to join Edouard in death. We can guess this: it was Edouard's lacerated fancy that she should contaminate herself to the equal of what he knew to be his own death; and the ghost of Edouard, looming up in the dwarf's face, is the annunciation made to Marie of the inevitability of her annihilation. The dwarf alone *knows*; although he does not guess everything and the *ends* of Marie will find him powerless.

In fact it was necessary for Marie to rise from hell and bring the dwarf – the devil – with her to die like an entranced animal under the sun. Every death, even the most filthy, especially the most filthy, the most excremental, is that of an ignoble God: of a pig whose cut throat means a divine entombment.

The most obscene of Bataille's stories is also the most austere and most saintly. Of all Bataille's heroines, Marie is the most tragically resolute. It is from death that she has come (naked, under her over-coat), and it is to death that she is going. Nothing would keep her from exploring her dying (dying is released from the servile expectation of ends): 'The time was coming to deny laws imposed by fear.'[11]

Sickening poetic sentimentality

'Yet, did not Zarathustra one day tell you that poets lie
too much?'
'But Zarathustra is also a poet.'

(Nietzsche)

Extraordinary as it may seem, Bataille's stay in Normandy corresponded
with an intense poetic activity. In one sense this is no surprise: the
challenge had become that of a mysticism whose language was rawer,
more cutting. Briefer utterances, collected, analogous in terms of the
image to what the aphorism is to the demonstration (the aphorism
condenses the argument, the poem gathers together the story); that is,
flashes of inspiration had to be substituted for the possibilities of
discourse. This is no surprise, and yet Bataille had never had recourse to
poetry (except as a teenager, none of which was published): of all the
genres he took stock of, poetry remained the one he neglected. Not only
did he neglect it, he violently opposed it. For example, he violently and
at every opportunity denounced surrealism's 'lands of treasure', lands
fit only for 'little castratos, little poets and little mystic-mongrels'.[1] Had
Bataille changed his mind on this point as well? The evidence suggests
that, on the contrary, he maintained his aggressive stance. Where once
he vilified 'lands of treasure', now during the war he vilified poetic
'delicacy' and 'nonsense'.[2] So he did not suddenly develop an attraction
for something he had hitherto heaped abuse upon. Poetry was and
remained hateful when it cherished fine words, subtle impressions,
lyrical sparks, sentimental naïvety, nonsense, image for its own sake,
rhetoric as reality, everything that might help it make the world a kinder,
fairer and more innocent place. In a word, any poetry – and perhaps
in Bataille's eyes this meant almost *all* poetry – that pleaded for an
ideal or, worse still, for the absolute, that 'disgusting, inhuman word'

(Bataille adds that the absolute is 'something you would imagine larvae longing for',[3] something he said not at the height of his arguments with surrealism in 1930, but in 1944). And if anyone could not understand or accept this, he made it clear in the most definitive way, by entitling one of his subsequent books *Haine de la poésie*.

If mysticism (at least such as Bataille adopted) nevertheless calls for poetry, it is for that which is its equal: it is not a question of contemplating, but of tearing apart:[4] 'Poetry would be the sign announcing the greatest inner ruptures.'[5] It is not a question of loving, but of hating: 'It seemed to me that true poetry was reached only by hatred.'[6] It is not a question of praise (or of escape, which comes to the same thing), but of breaking: 'Poetry had no powerful meaning except in the violence of revolt.'[7] It is not a question of 'raising up', or making ethereal, but of thickening: 'Poetry opens the void to the excess of desire.'[8] Such a poetry, as distant as possible from what 'larvae long for' (the larvae being those seized by the abject inclination towards the absolute), is troubling and enchanting: 'It causes a truth other than that of science to surge forth. This is the truth of death, of disappearance. Disappearance and death blind, they dazzle, they are never distinct. They are like poetry, which is made of death, disappearance, blinding and bedazzlement.'[9] Such a poetry consents to the possible, to every kind of possible (not only does it consent to it, it is also the experience of it), up to and including the *impossible*. Just as the *impossible* lays bare the possible (as its inevitable and annihilating surpassing), poetry must go all the way to where it is disintegrated, surpassed: 'If poetry isn't committed to the experience of going beyond poetry [poetry that did not will its own perdition would only be one more affectation, an aestheticism] it's not movement – it's a residue left over from excitement.'[10]

There is a weight of meaning in the violent way Rimbaud withdrew from this tumult, in which he turned his back on the fate his works were to have given him, in which he vanished into an essential silence and solitude: to fall silent is not enough (even death cannot silence things properly). For, however inevitable this silence and solitude may have been, they were also impossible.

This is not the truth of any specific work, not even Rimbaud's; it is the truth of every work to have no other end than to exhaust its beginning, and exhaust it *to the point of death*, without, for all that, letting death wipe it out altogether. It is its truth that the work cannot be renounced once it has been accepted (and the movement by which someone enters into this agreement is nevertheless benign. There is no solemn pronouncement, but at most an insubordination; and once the pact is sealed, no wiping the slate clean can challenge or criticise it).

The acute interest Bataille took in Rimbaud was not coincidental. If there had been no one but Rimbaud, every work would still find itself challenged. For this work was challenged by Rimbaud himself. Yet this challenge was neither great enough nor complete enough (however great or complete it may have been, it was not enough, nor could any have been). For evil is the work. It exists so that the work may exist. And this can all the less be challenged because the evil wrought is hardened and obsessive. Once there is a work (or once its dream begins; the dream of a work suffices), once this evil exists, forgetting or starting again is impossible. What Rimbaud's departure testifies, his exit or escape from the work, is at the same time the profound disgust for the work – *for all works* – and, *a fortiori*, the impossibility forgetfulness has of tolerating the evil forming it.

The reverse side of this coin is that this disgust testifies in defence of what remains of the work in the eventuality that, without really either renouncing or agreeing to it, the 'poet' resigns himself to it. It testifies for it at the same time as it is its sign. That is, if a clean slate or a forgetting might not be possible, at least a work's failure is: 'The greatness of Rimbaud is to have led poetry to the failure of poetry.'[11] Here Bataille does not just express a paradox, he makes this paradox poetry's aporia: poetry as he theorised it, and as he wrote it.

For he would stick to this paradox. There is certainly no reason to act as Rimbaud did, in such a radical way. If he was poetry's truth (by pushing back 'the possible'[12]), and it is poetry's greatness that he was its truth, he was so in a way through excess. That is, this is not a truth valid for just any work, since it could only be the truth of one – the truth of sacrifice. With this sacrifice made, a division was also made between those who might imitate him (in his renunciation) and those who might determine to take no notice of him (challenging Rimbaud's challenge; writing is all it takes): 'some of them continued to enjoy poetry or even to write, but with a bad conscience; others enclosed themselves in a chaos of inconsequential absurdities in which they took pleasure.'[13]

The paradox embraced by Rimbaud, to the point of failure – his own and that of poetry – could not be embraced by all those who came after; and those who earlier had been and still are satisfied by the easy path of *embellishment* are now joined by those who, far from being put off by the excess of this truth, toy with it as just another possibility. What depressing dishonesty! They are nothing but the simulacrum of the clean slate and the challenge. Instead of poetry correcting – as it should – the ways man has abused language throughout history, instead of it being 'the divining of ruins secretly expected',[14] instead of being 'a holocaust of words',[15] instead of climbing 'to the non-sense of poetry',[16] it subsides and exhausts itself in something precious, and ultimately just adds ignominiously to the 'literary treasury'. Not the least strength of Rimbaud's sovereignty is that it overpowers every imitation and every challenge. After him, poetry can hope for no more than to maintain itself in a paradoxically *subordinated* sovereignty.

Bataille recognised this without avoiding the aporia. Certainly, 'It is necessary that man reach the extreme limit, that his reason give way, *that God die* [but] words, their sickest games, cannot suffice.'[17] Certainly, the movement *of* poetry 'touches on madness if it is fulfilled'. But with its approach begins, inevitably, its ebb: 'The movement *towards* poetry seeks to remain within the limits of the possible. Poetry is in any event the negation of itself: it denies itself as it conserves itself and denies itself in going beyond itself.'[18]

The burden poetry inflicts on itself weighs heavily. However determined it may be to escape everything possible, it is, in subjecting itself to its means, nothing but the means of this possible: 'Poetry is outside the law. Yet, *to accept* poetry changes it into its opposite, into a mediator of an acceptance. I weaken the energy which sets me against nature, I justify the given.'[19] The law is that of discourse. Poetry had promised that words could for a moment escape this law. With it, it should have been possible to enter 'in a sort of fall where from the death of the logical world' the impossible would be born (or an infinite number of possibles going beyond the possible). It was mistaken.

By the same movement, what carries us *towards* poetry divides us from it. It offers the promise of attaining the sovereign *instant*. In reality, only the movement of this attainment is sovereign. With this movement over, the instant reached (or apparently reached) is simply *durable*, has nothing but a share (in this it is like any other) in the time it had promised to break. Poetry cannot help the fact that the cry, of which it should be only the instant, will *last*. There is no language that does not betray any cry from the instant it articulates it, from the instant it gives it the quality of the generality that is all enunciation (and between this generality and academism, Bataille said, there is not just a logic but a homologous relationship): 'In fact, such is the poverty of poetry that in using words to express what happens it tends to stifle the cry of an actual emotion under the disguise of a museum face.'[20] Instead of being something sacred which gives us the liberation that we are, poetry profanes this movement in tying it to time and to the literature it claimed to betray. Bataille would never relinquish this paradox.

He clung to it all the more willingly, however untenable it may in fact be, since he conceived it on the long familiar model of limits and transgression. The limit cannot be altered, and there are no grounds for hoping that after Rimbaud anyone might push it further back; but all the same it is legitimate to transgress it, obeying a movement of loss and sovereign release. Bataille sometimes suggests that we see this rare, hindered transgression on the predictable model of eroticism (poets 'laugh at poetry; they laugh at its exaggerated sensibilities. Lust laughs at the lover's timidity in the same way'[21]); but more often and more decisively as having a meaning 'close to that of sacrifice'.[22] In fact, only sacrifice is a tremor, a dejection, a ruin that breaks with the meanness of becoming and the 'sadness of logic'.[23] So this is how far one must go: poetry is only poetry if it is a violation, if it has the lewd character of sexuality beyond restraint; if it is a crime: the butcher's knife thrust into beautiful, noble, superior language, the sacrificial knife. Poetry represents for language (or it should) what is *base*, without ever wishing to be anything but *base*, like something that betrays language, wrecks it. It represents for language, or should, what the mole is to the eagle, the sewer to the ether, the toe to the Mind, the slaughterhouse to the church, the brothel to love.

In an exemplary way, the communication only sacrifice could attain (the communication that is the sacred: the instant in which the other ceases being an other for me, or I stop being an other for it) is undergone when, if poetry attains it, it can be desired. From this stems its nature as a method (in some ways analogous to that applied to meditation) or as an *experience* that Bataille does not hesitate to confer upon it. This experience might only be illuminating or ecstatic in the same way as the one produced by the torture of the Hundred Pieces; moreover, it works: it is a successful movement *towards* poetry.

As so often with Bataille, it is an experience of reversal. And this reversal is that of representation: in this case, that of a horse. (This is the example of reversal chosen by Bataille, one that might simply have demonstrative value, and no doubt it would have no other use if Bataille himself did not invite us to evoke the 'figure' of the horse that saw Nietzsche go mad – that made Nietzsche go mad – on the Piazza Carlo Alberto in Turin, throwing himself sobbing on its neck. It is also that of the horse rearing up in *Guernica*, forced back by the fire, and it also evokes the horse's skull that Bataille always kept among his possessions.)

The horse is subjugated; subjugated, it is distinct; distinct, and therefore transcendent; transcendent and therefore profane. The horse is profane as long as it is subjugated; it is sacred the moment it is free. Certainly there is no poetry (loving, legendary, mythic poetry and so on) that might free the horse (that might secure its escape from the servitude of the known; from standardisation, from work); that might liberate it. But this liberty cannot be of just any kind. It must lead from the known to the unknown.[24]

Like poetry in general, Bataille removes the horse from the known that is the stable, but unlike poetry in general, he does so for reasons that are nothing less than ennobling, he does so to lead it to the unknown that is the abattoir. Not so much to obey some 'mournful philosophy' – he denies this – as because, once struck down, the dead horse despite itself restores the immanence and communication its representation (and its naming) as a distinct and servile object had prevented. In the abattoir, at that moment the horse's felling will retrospectively turn into *the instant*, it is no longer 'the animal that men nurture and harness', it is 'a presence on the edge of an abyss (whose pit is absence)'. In this, it does not move us just because it dies – felled, cut up, dismembered (or else through the squeamishness of poetry); it moves us because 'it becomes the same thing as I am, a presence on the edge of absence'. For the butcher's knife – as we have seen, this is what poetry should be – the horse is certainly dead (it is henceforth *its* meat), but it is both more and less than this for the poem, for which it is merely *absent*. It is an absence in which 'Nothing is dead, nothing can be dead.'[25]

It is wanting to die and not being able to that Rimbaud's movement of frantic flight obeys. It is a movement that makes for poetry's *failure*, and that makes for what it became after him. The horse that Bataille takes as his example obeys an analogous movement towards an impossible death, carrying it towards *absence*.

The few poems Bataille wrote are located on the verge of this *absence* (there are not many of them; the first were written around 1942, but their dating is often uncertain). They have this character of anguish and lewdness demanded by the paradox they obey, a paradox he clung to so well that he himself tells us its limit: 'The worst eludes even poetry: nervous depression alone can reach it':[26]

> my madness and my fear
> have large dead eyes
> the fixity of fever
>
> what is looked at in these eyes
> is the nothingness of the universe
> my eyes are blind skies
>
> in my impenetrable night
> the impossible is crying out
> completely destroyed.[27]

Philosophy's 'easy virtue'

Today this might be considered ridiculous: in Paris, books are not only published – which can already seem ill-timed – but their readers declare war on them. An attentive war, which is vigilant and – even if this is stated ironically – moral. Unshakeable virtues keep watch so that, in those disastrous times, orthodoxy should not be infringed, and the aggressions which open new fronts, the necessity of which they appear not to doubt, remain intact.

Bataille seems to have been wrong to publish *Inner Experience* in 1943, during the war. Jules Monnerot reproached him for it in a friendly, discreet and, moreover, justified, way. Patrick Waldberg did so too, but publicly (in the journal *VVV*, published in the United States) and in a far more aggressive way. Souvarine later saw it as a heinous sign at least of its author's acceptance of the Occupation, if not of collusion with the occupier.[1] There were others in Paris itself who at the time responded negatively to the publication of *Inner Experience* for quite different reasons: if this book merited being denounced, it was not because it was published during the war, but because it was itself, in a *morbid* way, war.

The first of these attacks consisted of a short pamphlet entitled *Nom de Dieu* and signed by a certain number of second-string surrealists, mostly forgotten today (so forgotten that we do not really know what linked this second front with the majority of historic leaders who were exiled in the United States[2]). This pamphlet was aimed at the journal *Messages* almost as much as at Bataille himself (unless it was aimed at *Messages* because of Bataille's participation with it). What was the charge against him? Of wanting, it seems, to substitute himself for surrealism (even though it is difficult to see how Bataille was still capable of doing so) and, worse, of substituting himself by recourse to the old days ('the old idealist days'). Accusing Bataille of idealism, when he had made this the key word of his denunciation of surrealism, is admittedly more than a little comical. According to his accusers, 'Mr Bataille' was idealist to such a point that they considered themselves perfectly justified in adding to this insult (in Bataille's eyes, this was still the most extreme and compromising of insults) others which must have appeared just as necessary to them. Bataille found himself being called a priest, a canon, and his sheep (presumably we should understand by this his collaborators on *Messages*) were called black sheep.

The interest of this pamphlet is only anecdotal. As feeble from a literary point of view as it was confused (it is far from equalling the least imaginative of the genuinely surrealist lampoons), it testifies only to the embarrassment and spitefulness which Bataille seemed to engender among certain of his contemporaries, the most virtuously intentioned among them. If we are to believe what he wrote to Jean Bruno in a letter of 1943, he was not particularly affected by it: 'I've seen a surrealist tract which virulently implicates me after publication of my book [it is amazing that Bataille believed his book the target as this was not in fact mentioned by the signatories; their condemnation seems only to be addressed to *Messages*]; I am called a priest, a canon . . . It's amusing, but has no other interest.'[3]

The second of these attacks aimed at Bataille came from the Christian Gabriel Marcel (it is curious how, at this time, surrealists, Christians and existentialists all found reason to attack Bataille[4]). Strangely, the Christian critique – at least that of Gabriel Marcel – is not the most misguided precisely because he is a Christian who intends to denounce Bataille's enterprise as the least Christian enterprise possible (Gabriel Marcel could hardly conceive of proposing Bataille as a priest or canon). Bataille's nihilism leaves no doubt for someone who believes in God, and Marcel says this in a sentence which is inexact only in its excessiveness: 'In truth I doubt that anyone has ever gone further in the formulation of a radical nihilism';[5] for it is clear that in essence Gabriel Marcel reproaches Bataille for his disdainful refusal (but it is a challenge as well) of salvation, his dark determination not to surrender to any hope (he speaks of 'the pretension which aims at making a clean sweep of salvation, and more generally of hope itself'[6]).

Otherwise it is a matter of methods and language. Gabriel Marcel not only reproaches Bataille for his conceit in placing himself alongside Saint John of the Cross (and also many other mystics) and for turning the Christian lexicology upside down – for ends that deny it – but also for being nothing but a pitiful epigone of Nietzsche, who breathed the rarefied air of mountain tops, while Bataille, like a madman, merely surveys his dungeon. (Is there not something Jesuitical in a Christian setting himself up as a defender of Nietzsche?)

Could anyone be more hypocritical? Questionable and incoherent as his thought may have been, Nietzsche was, according to Gabriel Marcel, completely sincere: do not his madness and death bear this out? And because he was sincere, he undeniably would have been a mystic, even if his mysticism was used to serve a cause hostile to the Church. Yet, with Bataille and 'his friends' (again! Who are they? Marcel seems to be thinking of Blanchot), there is only an 'attitude taken', a simulation, a sham of the mystics, the true ones, those who have God and salvation as their authority and reason for their experience. At the very most there were one or two names Bataille might be justified in citing, given that whatever they thought, they thought without faith, in the 'most obstinate refusal which could be opposed to religious certainties': these names are Pascal and Kierkegaard.[7] We shall see how Pascal's name has not stopped squelching under Bataille's foot, no matter how careful he was only to invoke him rarely and however distant from him he may himself have felt. In 1929, André Breton had denounced the Pascal within Bataille. Gabriel Marcel did so fourteen years later. Monnerot and Sartre, especially the latter, did the same, no doubt with even more justification than they realised for doing so. As we shall see, Pascal lurks within Bataille (a debauched Pascal but no more dark or desperate) for the reason – if Bataille was conscious of this – that he *also* borrowed a style from him (clearly the Pascal of *Pensées* is the strongest detectable 'literary' influence on *Guilty* and *Inner Experience*) and that – perhaps in unconscious remembrance of Léon Chestov – Bataille's Nietzsche remains profoundly Pascalian.[8]

The third critique levelled at *Inner Experience* was by Jean-Paul Sartre.[9] Sartre describes the book, not without irony as an 'essai-martyre'.[10] Moreover, irony dominates this long article, an irony that is completely academic and patronising, even of the type – and Sartre must have guessed this – that Bataille generally mocked. It was ironic and spiteful, but this irony seems unable to get to the root of the unwonted object this book is and of the insufferable author who signed it: both irritated him. The article vacillates repeatedly between analysis and lampoon, only, in the end, to collapse entirely into provocative denigration. Bataille was not quite a man but a widower: 'There are some people one could call survivors. Early on they lost a dear being, a "father" [but did Sartre know what father?], a friend, a mistress [definitely!], and their life is no longer anything but the dismal consequence of this death. Mr Bataille survives the death of God.'[11] (Sartre does not appear to conceive how a father or a mistress could be quite different gods and powerful in different ways.) Widowed and inconsolable, Bataille is therefore sick, as Sartre does not hesitate to say: 'We know these celebrated icy and burning arguments, impotent in their harsh abstraction, which the impassioned and paranoiac use: their rigour is already a challenge and a threat, their doubtful immobility gives a foretaste of tumultuous lava. These are Mr Bataille's syllogisms. Proofs of the orator, the envious, the advocate and the madman.'[12] With this diagnosis complete, Sartre administers, forty pages on (did the sick man justify such interest?), the treatment: 'The remainder concerns psychoanalysis. Before you protest: I am not thinking here of the vulgar and suspect methods of Freud, Adler or Jung; there are other psychoanalysts.'[13]

The time when a sealed letter from the king could seal one's fate was certainly a fortunate one: someone like Sade could be got rid of quickly and lastingly. Unfortunately, there seem to be no intellectual means to get rid of a man and prevent him from doing harm, *intellectually*. For irony was not enough and Sartre seemed forced to admit it. He admitted it all the more willingly in that this book, as *crazy* as it was, had substantial precedents; so much more substantial and beautiful that it was Sartre himself who mentioned them: *Les Pensées* (Pascal), the *Confessions* (Rousseau), *Ecce Homo* (Nietzsche), *Les Pas perdus*, *L'Amour fou* (both Breton), *Traité de style* (Aragon), *L'Age d'homme* (Leiris). It was from on high that one should undertake the demolition (the examination of the 'madman'); and it would take time: no less than three articles spread over three months.

Sartre was not wrong: Bataille had two initiators: Nietzsche and Pascal (was Sartre not settling accounts as much with them as with Bataille?). Of the influence of Nietzsche, Sartre says: 'In truth, certain pages of *Inner Experience*, with their breathless disorder, their passionate symbolism, their tone of prophetic preaching, seem to have come out of *Ecce Homo* or *The Will to Power*.'[14] But it is essentially of Pascal and his 'feverish contempt and need to speak in haste' that Sartre was thinking; Pascal seemed positively to be the obligatory reference for critiques of Bataille. Formal analogies, according to Sartre, were plentiful (the strangled, knotted and allusive style of the 'brief suffocations of ecstasy or anguish'); they would sometimes even limit them to pastiche.

Nevertheless, Sartre has no particular aversion to Pascal. On the contrary, he seems to him the first historical thinker (Pascal would be in fact the first to have thought time, for he was the first to have assumed that it was quite distinct from God).

Bataille also had this quality: that of not preferring essence to existence, of not speaking of human nature, but of its condition. Then would there be anything necessarily to divide the two men? Yes; the death of God. In fact, Bataille had not for all that become an atheist (at least that is what Sartre claims), and the time liberated from God, which Sartre sees as ultimately and unreservedly historical, Bataille sees in suspension, having gained nothing from the death of God but this death itself. Bataille refrains from drawing anything useful from the bargain of such time freed from the empire of God and his promised ends. He did not like time, as we know – either historical time or political time. The substitution of ends due to mankind for the ends promised by God is not at all enticing. Bataille likes this suspended time, time entirely suspended to the moment, without calculation, without project, without end and without salvation of any sort. Bataillean time is *widowed*, just as Sartre believed it rang true to say of Bataille himself (he meant: a widower of God). In other words, he rejected all thought which would rely on its achievements and make the moment the revival of a project finding its ends in the future (Bataille borrows and radicalises Nietzsche's saying: 'I love ignorance touching on the future').

Paradoxically, Bataille is perhaps less mystical than Sartre, consoling himself so well over the annihilations of divine eschatology that he no longer expects anything from the promises of a revolutionary eschatology. Sartre identifies the Bataillean moment by means of several precedents: it is ecstatic in the style of the suffering of mystics, anguished and eternal in the style of Kierkegaard, sensual in the style of Gide and evocative of the past in the style of Proust . . . and more than anything mocking, indecently, insolently mocking (the moment for Bataille is that of 'fortune' or of 'impulse'). Was Sartre worried about this laughter? According to him, Nietzsche's light gaiety became with Bataille a bitter and administered laugh. Such a laugh, true or false, happy or sickly, has nothing refutable about it and Sartre, moreover, made no attempt to refute it. He contented himself with saying that it did not convince him. But he said so in a rather puerile, or disarmed, way, as though, line after line, he began to get bogged down in the bitter abstractions of this paranoiac: 'He tells us that he laughs, but doesn't make us laugh.'¹⁵ But if Bataille said that he had an orgasm, would Sartre *also* expect to have one? Unconsciously, he extended the metaphor from this slip: 'It is to be regretted simply that Mr Bataille's "ideas" should be so soft and unformed, when his feeling is hard.'¹⁶ Is this not what Sartre profoundly wants not to understand? This madman tears himself apart, and he laughs, finding pleasure in the worst (he delights in it, Breton would say), and he comes. It must be one thing or the other: either he really laughs, unreservedly, and he is mad; or else he comes and he's a pervert. It would appear better to put this in Nietzschean terms turned against Bataille: 'He is hallucinated with the afterlife', a Christian. The proof is that he does not laugh (except with bile) and he does not come (his thought is 'soft'). He is therefore a fraud; Sartre has a category at hand to describe him: *bad faith*. Bataille is no more able than anyone else to do without afterlives, whether the time of this world is divine or human; he is therefore a guilty Christian.¹⁷ And because he is guilty, at the very most his *experience* is a 'a good little pantheistic ecstasy'.¹⁸ So, in the end, is Bataille a Spinozist? Worse than this, the pantheism of Spinoza is white but Bataille's is black. And because to be a Christian or a pantheist is, as far as Sartre was concerned in 1943, of no use, he pulled from the trap-door of a humanism most harshly abused by the war definitive reasons for his *ad hominem* denunciation: 'the joys to which Mr Bataille invites us, if they should refer to nothing but themselves, if they should not find a role in the course of new enterprises, to contribute to form a new humanity which surpasses itself towards new goals, are worth no more than the pleasure of drinking a glass of alcohol or sunbathing on a beach.'¹⁹

Sunbathing is not something Bataille ever counted among his pleasures (was Sartre confusing him in anticipation with Camus?) and had Sartre been less prudish, perhaps he would have said that the only *waking* pleasures Bataille knew were in brothels or between the legs of the women he found there. In wanting too much to demonstrate Bataille's 'falsity', Sartre neglected, in a malevolent way, to explain the foundations of Bataillean mysticism and treated Bataille rather as he had been treated by those who did not want to read *Nausea*.[20]

However, it has been said too often that the misunderstanding between the two men was immediate and definitive. We shall see that this was not the case. It is true that Bataille was profoundly affected by Sartre's aggressive response. It is true that he thought about it for a long time and, in many ways, wanted to obtain redress for this affront. This is no surprise: it was a manifest feature of Bataille's character to be easily intimidated, especially to be respectful of prestige, and in some ways to envy it. Breton impressed him, as did Sartre and as would Camus. It is not certain that his work is in any way inferior to theirs but – whether through modesty (Bataille was and would remain profoundly modest), or through fear – not considering himself a philosopher and lacking the training for it, in trying to rival one of the most dazzling French logicians (and Bataille was only slightly a logician), all the same he hoped, in expecting to be recognised by them, to be included in a debate which would exclude him.

We have the opportunity to see this, for in 1944 Bataille and Sartre met often and, if their differences had not really lessened, Sartre was prepared to listen more attentively, and in a more friendly way, to someone who, as it seems, he still considered to be mad. The best proof of this provisional peace-making is shown in the lecture Bataille gave on 5 March 1944 at the home of Marcel Moré entitled 'A Discussion About Sin'. If this lecture did not really seem to modify the relationship between the two men, if it did not allow them suddenly to find real and definitive grounds for agreement, all the same it did dispel in Sartre's mind the confusion intentionally encouraged by Bataille in the use of some of his notions, beneath which Sartre finally recognised that Bataille was speaking about 'completely different things',[21] and that he had recourse to notions of morality and religion only in order to challenge them afterwards. To Sartre's exact logic, Bataille astutely opposed a fluctuating logic that was impassioned and contaminating ('this renders the position completely frail, completely fragile . . . I have spoken only of an untenable position'[22]) and withdraws the supports with which his interlocutor could claim to shore up his position. Irony, says Bataille in judging his own position, irony and casualness. Sartre allowed himself to be led into the trap of a seriousness in which Bataille ingenuously said he did not think his detractors would let themselves be taken:

What I believe all the same to be erroneous is the illusion I have given of needing this position to free me from sacrileges and, in this way, to find a moral life that I could not have found without sacrilege and, consequently, to remain within the Christian orbit ... I especially did not foresee that people would fail to notice something else, which is what I could call casualness. If I have done that, it is because I don't take myself seriously, it is because I am confined nowhere ... all I was insisting upon was not to be confined to any notion, to go infinitely beyond notions and, in order to be able to go beyond them in this way and prove ... this casualness to myself, I needed to confine myself or to leave behind notions which had confined other beings before me.[23]

This discussion was the first and last Sartre and Bataille had in public.[24] In the future, Bataille would respond to books published by Sartre, but Sartre never again responded to those Bataille published. This is a pity: something was at stake between them which was similar to what was at stake between Descartes and Pascal. Bataille as Sartre's Pascal? It was Sartre himself who floated the possibility. Bataille, more trivially and more brutally, would have willingly let it be said of him that he was the rotten tooth in Sartre's mouth. The dialogue would in any event have come to an abrupt end: Sartre would not be alone in neglecting Bataille. Bataille himself clearly preferred Alexandre Kojève, 'the greatest living philosopher'.[25]

'System is needed and so is excess'

The apparent simplicity of the Bataillean vocabulary should not mislead us: Bataille's thought, like Nietzsche's, only appears easy. Beneath an exterior of conventional language, Bataille devoted himself to a patient and hieratic work of distortion. As he said and repeated whenever he could, he is not a philosopher, and this denial is partly a matter of tact (it seems that he was often worried he might bore people), of timidity (he did not have the right education, as people like Sartre would be quick to remind him) and a measure of flirtatiousness (philosophers are old fogeys, the cuckolds of a history that can manage fine without them). There was tact, timidity and flirtatiousness in Bataille's sarcasm towards philosophy and philosophers; yet his position towards them, analogous – or so it seemed – to his response to poetry, would never be clear cut.

But one thing is certain: he was able to adopt more than one notion from philosophy and even from theology that would control the communication of his texts, and do so all the more in that these notions were often used in a way that deflected them from their purpose. Another thing is just as certain: there is a Bataille system; his thought is not as unsystematic as has been claimed. In fact, however carefully he may have tried to give the appearance of complete disorder, his thought was solidly constructed. (Would his thought have held together if this had not been the case? Would not Sartre have needed only a couple of pages to take it apart?) Bataille could be justifiably proud of having set up disorder and excess. But he would not have managed this if he did not also have – within him – the desire to conceive the most solid of systems.

If the whole of atheological thought does rest entirely on the notion of a system, it is also at the same time its excess. Texts such as *Madame Edwarda*, *The Dead Man* and *Le Petit* incontestably represent this

excess; *Guilty* and *Inner Experience* do so too in a certain way. Did
Bataille not knowingly expurgate them of what might justify this excess
so as to ruin their systems? But the system exists, and *On Nietzsche*,
the last of the great books of this *summa*, lays it bare, even if one
cannot deny that this is true once again only in an ambiguous way; if
the whole of *On Nietzsche* had been published there would have been
no possible ambiguity. But, as with his previous books, Bataille made
it 'lighter', leaving aside substantial aspects of the text as excretions (so
that one has to look to the notes to get a full grasp of its genealogy).
But even in a complete state, *On Nietzsche* would not suffice. Two
other texts would also have to be taken into account: 'Le rire de
Nietzsche'[1] and 'La discussion sur le péché'.[2] We shall see that they
contain a lexicon as well as a thought, in other words not just a mystic
system but a theology, albeit an *a*theology.[3]

'To place life (in other words, the possible) at the level of the
impossible': this is what Bataille defines in 'Le rire de Nietzsche' as the
task of spiritual experience. But what possible is it, and what impossible? The possible is organic life and its development; the impossible is
death and the need for destruction. This is the irreducible. So long as
we believe God to exist, no impossible is possible in any event (unless
as a transition, as a test); there is no impossible because salvation is an
escape from it. A world without the impossible is a world in which
nature is supposed to be good. If evil exists in it, it is because man
admits himself to be guilty of it. Thus one imagines chasing from the
earth's surface both evil and mankind who put it there: chasing the
impossible. In acting this way, humanity paradoxically sets itself face
to face with the impossible. Some will continue to gamble on the
future; others, just as cowardly, come back to God. . . . And some,
who know what mankind is (what they are), an easy prey for the
impossible, determine to live without trying to evade it in any way at
all.

Not to evade the impossible is to admit that, with God dead, man is
no less abandoned than an animal: with God dead, animals begin to
devour each other. It is to admit that, whatever good one might ascribe
to mankind (one might give it fresh bedding, give it fire and shelter), in
the end there remains just 'an impossible that nothing will reduce, the
same thing, in a fundamental way, for the most fortunate as for the
most wretched'.[4]

To live the impossible, not to evade any aspect of it, such is spiritual experience for Bataille. 'Spiritual' is certainly an outdated word; it tastes rancid. If he nevertheless used it himself it was at the provocative price of our agreeing to trim it down and clean it out. Experience it may be, but one with no salvation (the most odious of false perspectives: it is the evasion of the impossible, and experience is the impossible itself). Salvation is 'the perfect negation of the spiritual'. Bataille gives two negative definitions of the spiritual (Bataille's atheology borrows several of its configurations from a negative theology): 'Each impossible is that by which a possible ceases to be' and 'At the extreme limit of its power, each possible aspires to the impossible.'[5]

Nietzsche himself asked: 'Is it not necessary to sacrifice everything consoling, sanctified and curative, all hope and faith in a hidden harmony?' In other words, 'Is it not necessary to sacrifice God himself?' Experience requires us to follow the possible to its most difficult, most naked, most arid expressions (what one might *biographically* understand as an Etna of the possible). It requires us to expose ourselves unflinchingly to the annihilation of everything that had justified us in wanting to reach that extreme – God – and it requires us to say *Yes* to the impossible, to death, to evil, solitude and anguish. A happy and tragic *Yes* that alone is divine: 'The limit of man is not God, is not the possible, but the impossible, it is the absence of God.'[6]

The impossible is the summit, and to express this in the most devastating way, Bataille says in paradoxical fashion: this summit is moral. Only consent to the impossible, to evil, to death, solitude and anguish is moral.[7] He pronounced this with a kind of obstinate and controlled brutality, the obstinacy he always displayed (there is in Bataille a way of saying the most extreme things gently and of 'setting things alight' behind a resigned exterior; his turn of phrase often took on this false countenance). Where others, at their own summits, might cry out 'God! God answers what we have achieved, God is the summit' (and their eyes are full of recognition), where everybody, without asking what their justification might be, says 'Good is moral, only the good and nothing else is moral' (is this not the case, in principle – but what principle is this ultimately?), Bataille, as if nothing could stop him saying things back to front, in spite of everyone, calmly says: the summit is sensuality, the summit is evil, the summit is crime. He does not say this angrily, or even derisively – the divine, even when it is 'black', is not a joke – but almost playfully. At least he reminds all those who might have forgotten it that the truth of being is not its salvation (that pitiful bid for tomorrow that asks us to spare today) but its intensity. And only its *impossible* makes it intense, it alone makes the instant immeasurably sensual (sensual because it is perishable).[8] 'What characterises sensuality is that it is diametrically opposed to morality . . . Morality is founded on concern for the future [we know how much Bataille hated the hoarding of treasure, capitalization, calculation, projects, avarice, salvation], sensuality on indifference for the future'. (This indifference includes waste, the potlatch and communication.) 'To want to last is not glorious', but 'to keep nothing back, to burn hopelessly' is hell. On one side there is cowardice, the sane and sage judgement man makes of his existence, mindful of the ends he believes it to have and ascribes to it, on the other the 'erotic transports' that burn in us and 'carry the human quest for knowledge to the most shattering limits'.[9] If these devastated regions 'that indicate vice and crime' are not exactly the summit, at least they point out its presence and accessibility. This summit is also that of communication: 'The summit is nothing other than the most extreme laceration – of communication – that is possible without perishing.'[10]

What is more difficult is what Bataille contemplated under the rubric of communication. He found it necessary to elucidate what being and nothingness were for him (though this can only be outlined here) since – perhaps one should see this as an intellectual concession to Sartre – it was also as a 'classical' metaphysician that Bataille best explained his position on this point (and explained it at greatest length. But this is only a temporary concession: if it had recourse to the vocabulary of metaphysics, it only took summary account of it).

Bataille put this bluntly: 'I call nothingness what . . . is perceived as no longer being me, as ceasing to be me.'[11] Nothingness is that from which being has been separated, torn away, and which, in this way, pushes it back towards death; in this way nothingness penetrates being, challenging its being, threatening it with everything that might be able to take its being away. It performs an inner laceration, against whose effects being only takes possession of itself in wanting permanently to limit its annihilating effects (though *experience* consists of exposing oneself to these effects). The other may well be being, intensely so for itself, just as intensely but just as inadequately as 'I am' (Bataille calls this the *ipse*) is being for me. But it is also nothingness for me, to the precise extent that it is and remains other, unalterably, save for its desire to set in play the being it is with the nothingness I threaten it with, against this 'ontological' separation.

On the other hand (since Bataille ultimately does not set down this 'ontology'; it is in flux), nothingness is not only what is beyond the limits of being but, beyond these limits, that which reduces being to an annihilating powerlessness. Thus the question is what is the nature of this other which, between it and being (my own, since I have no being but myself), interrupts the feeling that being is threatened within itself by what it knows and permits the other to take from it? It is *communication*.

This is true in the sense that the latter is not being but nothingness: the nothingness that separates them, that the desired other imprints onto being in revealing it to be inadequate; the nothingness that my being is for the other, the one ultimately that is the other's impossible longing for the elements of their reciprocal and imaginary sufficiency (their embrace only lays bare what separates them – it does not join them together at all, but on the contrary what joins them together is this very separation): 'Insufficiency does not come to an end due to a model of sufficiency. It does not seek that which might bring it to a close, but rather seeks the excess of a lack which is made deeper the more it might be fulfilled.'[12]

Moving towards each other, throwing themselves upon each other, trading off each other to put an end to the radicalness of their separation, and with their separation growing from this trade, beings at the same time long for an impossible union and urge each other on to the endlessly repeated impossibility of their union. Beings, moving towards each other, neither forget their pretension in going towards being, nor hide from themselves the eventuality that in doing so they might be approaching nothingness:

> The question of being is in play in the dialectic I have spoken about which opposes the self and the other, and I precisely always envisage the other as an object of a desire, and that the self is subject to a desire and that this subject of a desire is *a priori* a conflict within itself in as much as it is desire for an other. Along with a fullness in being, there is also the feeling of a void, since it is this feeling of emptiness which expels it.[13]

Communication consists of this *external* setting in play.

Reaching the summit means that this setting in play must be as disturbed and lacerated as possible. Since laceration is the law of communication, the summit of communication requires this laceration to be the greatest possible. This is what, in Christian terms – and Bataille is not afraid of using them, even if they cloud an issue that for a moment had seemed clear – is called sin. Was this a deliberate provocation (and if so, it would be equivalent to saying that such a summit *is moral*)? If communication might be sin, it would also be sacred. And since this terminology is Christian and theological, Bataille does not hesitate to support his argument with an interpretation from the Scriptures: the crucifixion was certainly an evil, the greatest in fact (as indeed Christians believe). The crucifixion was a sacrifice offered to mankind to save it: a redeeming sacrifice. The paradox Bataille inserts into this standard Christian interpretation is that this execution that strikes at God's being re-establishes communication between his creatures, a communication they lacked before his sacrifice. Without it, creator and creatures alike would all be kept in a respective and separated integrity if it was not that (contrary to theological interpretation) the wound and the laceration inflicted by God in the putting to death of his son, as his envoy, in establishing men's guilt (an irredeemable guilt), had not bound them to the One towards whom they had become guilty (so that the crucifixion is not a redemption, but sin itself).

So what would be the key to the relationship with God? The key is not good, but evil . . . a radical evil, a crime. Without it, everyone would have carried on in isolation; crime re-establishes communication. Once again Bataille hesitates: is even the most heinous of crimes, that against the son of God, just a crime, or is it a deicide? With God dead, one would understand unreservedly that men might *communicate* in the endless memory of this murder, that an immanent communication could be re-established between them. Bataille concludes: 'Thus "communication" without which nothing exists for us, is guaranteed by crime. "Communication" is love, and love taints those whom it unites. . . . So clearly the "communication" of human beings is guaranteed by evil.'[14] In saying this he is saying what, in his opinion, Christians do not want to know. But its truth is different. The cross only has this power as a symbol and he only is justified in using it here because the most extreme shame, the greatest evil, has arisen within the legend – that of revelation. Far from Christ's sacrifice restoring mankind to God (in abolishing the sin separating them), it allies people with each other, finally forcing them to confront each other as totally and irrevocably torn asunder. And as torn beings, these men are divine: 'Even the torture of the cross links, be it blindly, Christian conscious- ness to the frightful character of the divine order: the divine is never tutelary except once a need to consume and destroy is satisfied, which is its first principle.'[15]

Born from evil, communication remains evil itself (this double linguistic play, sometimes using the vocabulary of shared morality – Christian morality, a morality Bataille describes as a 'morality in decline' – and sometimes referring to a hyper-morality, a morality *of the summit*, is nevertheless frequently ambiguous; I shall return to this later). Communication is an evil (to be understood here not in a moral sense but in the sense of anguish) because there is no God. And there is no God because if there were, no communication would be possible:

> 'communication' cannot proceed from one full and intact individual [and this, clearly, is what the Christian God must be] to another. It requires individuals whose separate existence in themselves is *risked*, placed at the limit of death and nothingness; the moral summit is the moment of *risk taking*, it is a being suspended in the beyond of oneself, at the limit of nothingness.[16]

And beings are clearly incomplete: it is even that share of nothing- ness in them, a nothingness no longer filled by God, that opens them up to the nothingness of others. Communication is that fragile, desper- ate thing that occurs between two or more beings who seek to surmount the nothingness that separates them, and to fill the nothing- ness that each of them can imagine in the other, their separated, rent being. This is the meaning of eroticism. A woman is desired and loved in proportion to how well she is able to appease the pain a being feels in knowing itself limited. '[Being] *by itself doesn't exist*.'[17] This incom- pleteness is evil. This is why God is obscene, absolutely obscene. It is the only absoluteness he still possesses. It is all the more present since the communication of beings witnesses his absolute absence.[18]

Philosophy in the old folk's home

Some places are familiar to Bataille, places in which it seems that feelings suddenly became more coarse and bare, places which would be something like a butcher's yard in a city. One after another, the stories (though *The Dead Man* and *Le Petit* had already done so) would take their place there as if they were awaiting a sort of rudimentary, acute spatiality to be offered to them ... Bataille's narratives have a topography which is, moreover, quite autobiographical. Bataille, as we recall, was born in a small Roman village, between the church and the door of the slaughter-houses.

With the war, and after it, Bataille's narratives essentially became rustic: sometimes a castle (or a strong edifice, preferably in a state of ruin), often an inn (the laughter and cries of free and easy nights), always a church. This is less because the church is as though the obligatory centre of the village than because it 'constitutes a sacred place in the centre of the village' on the threshold of which profane activity ceases, or upon which profane activity can encroach only furtively. It was as a sociologist that Bataille noted, before the war,[1] how churches and the dead surrounding them (the cemetery is often in the grounds of the church) both attract (devotion to the dead, prayers, solace) and repel (the anguished silence, repugnance, tears). With the war, Bataille rediscovered this topography in his own life.

Bataille left Panilleuse. Returning to Paris in December 1942, he stayed there only for a few months. By chance or irony? When he had to find new accommodation, he did so a long way from Paris, in a village that tourist pamphlets describe 'with its hard and heroic image', as a centre of spiritual resistance, a protestation of the faith, a mystical citadel:[2] Vézelay (a village with a legendary association with Mary Magdalen, which owes its fame to its recognition by Pope Leo IX in

1050 as a site of pilgramage to the relics of the sinner Mary Magdalen, the sister of Martha and Lazarus[3]).

It was half way up the impressive and beautiful headland of Vézelay that Bataille found a house:[4] at 59 rue Saint-Étienne, the principal thoroughfare, on the Place du Grand-Puits, in so far as the fork this narrow street makes here could be called a square: it then becomes two small streets both of which lead up to the basilica.

He did not live alone. Denise Rollin (and her son Jean who was then four years old) was with him: 'Arriving from Paris we entered the house, net curtains of black crêpe were drying on the trees in the sunny garden. This gloomy "omen" was heart rending (reminding me of the long black streamers of I. presaging my misfortunes[5]).'

> The first day we slept at the house, there was a lack of light in the kitchen where we dined. As night fell, the wind accompanying the storm reached an unprecedented violence, the trees in the garden were shaken like rags and twisted in the roaring of the wind. Night finally fell and the lights went out in the whole house. In the darkness I found a Christmas candle and some matches . . . After a while in the darkness, light finally returned.
>
> These slight difficulties comforted and even seduced me. The calm in the storm had the strongest meaning in my life: the torment coming from the outside calmed me down. I was afraid of nothing, it seemed to me, which might come from my deep depression.[6]

Michel Fardoulis-Lagrange, who at the time was in hiding, joined them there. Jacques Lacan and Sylvia Bataille, for whom Bataille had reserved a large house nearby in the Place de la Basilique, intended to join them as well, but this did not happen. Only Laurence, the daughter of Georges and Sylvia, who was then thirteen, joined her father and lived with him.[7]

The house was basic and falling to pieces: a dark, narrow corridor crossed its whole depth. It led first to a dining room, then to a kitchen with a stone sink. Between them, a steep staircase led to the first and only upper floor. The landing led to two bedrooms, which were directly above and the same size as the rooms on the ground floor. One looked onto the road and the other Bataille later made his office, since the view was magnificent, overlooking a narrow terraced garden (through lack of space, Vézelay was constructed by superimposition) and, beyond it, the valley. No stove (only fireplaces), no running water (a pump), no bathroom.

It is not difficult to imagine what the village was like in 1943. It could hardly be more austere ('heroic and hard'): dark streets bedecked with German flags, the basilica closed, contaminated wells (the occupiers having thrown dead bodies in them) . . . A heady presence of death (right down to the black crêpe curtains drying on the branches in the garden), so much more heady as the village was amazingly narrow and very soon (a few steps were enough) closed in on itself: ramparts, a path around them, two cemeteries, the basilica, the hospice . . .

Bataille stayed in Vézelay from March to October. Surprising as it seems (the stubbornness of *good fortune* emerging at the most unlikely moments and even in places – an isolated village – which *a priori* would seem more like those of seclusion or exile), it is here that Bataille's life again changed. A tall, beautiful young woman, aged twenty-three, accompanied by her daughter (who was three) took over the house he had reserved for Jacques Lacan and Sylvia Bataille. She was Diane Kotchoubey de Beauharnais, born in Vancouver – where she spent only the first eighteen months of her life – to a Russian father, Eugène Kotchoubey de Beauharnais, and an English mother, the daughter of a banker. She had lived in England (English being her first language; Russian was not spoken at home), then in France. The little girl who came with her to Vézelay in 1943 was born of her first marriage.[8]

The story of how Diane Kotchoubey de Beauharnais came to live in Vézelay and met Bataille is worth telling in as much as it belongs to what *idealistically* one could be tempted to call the Bataillean legend, but which belongs more exactly to what he, as a challenge to destiny (a provocation to laugh at it, to take it in its most ridiculous and least rational movements), stubbornly called *fortune*.[9] In 1943, Diane Kotchoubey had, some months earlier, been freed from an internment camp near Besançon. When advised by her doctor and her husband to rest, she replied, in a capricious way she said was typical of her at the time, that she would leave it to 'chance' to decree where she would go by sticking a pin into a map spread out in front of her. The pin fell on Vézelay, a place she did not know existed. She therefore went to live in the large house facing the basilica in April 1943 (she was able to take over from the owner the reservation made by Bataille that Lacan had not honoured). Chance also decreed that in Vézelay Diane Kotchoubey met a couple of Russians she knew who gave her a copy of *Inner Experience*, which had just been published. She certainly knew Bataille's name, but only as a neighbour. She made no link between this Bataille and the author of *Inner Experience*, which she read in one sitting and immediately admired, and, just as these seem to have been two different people for her, she did not link them with the third person she saw passing below her windows, wearing a felt hat and arm in arm with a ravishing young woman. A fourth person would act as an emissary: Denise Rollin's husband, who came to Vézelay to see their son. He it was who issued the invitation that enabled Georges Bataille and Diane Kotchoubey to meet.

Bataille was not alone then at Vézelay: divided between two sexual relationships, one ending, the other beginning (but also mingled together, the reciprocal seduction of the two young women apparently for a while established a triangular relationship), he received friends: Ambrosino, Limbour, Éluard and Nusch – who came several times, according to Fardoulis-Lagrange – and Monnerot.[10] Moreover, a few yards down the same street he had an illustrious neighbour with whom it is difficult to imagine he had previously had anything in common: Romain Rolland. Nothing, not even politics, other than the interest both had in negative theology (in Dionysius the Aeropagite among others) and Indian mysticism (Ramakrishna and Vivekananda).[11] Bataille would make two visits to the former Honorary President of the International Anti-fascist Committee.[12]

Diane Kotchoubey left Vézelay in September 1943 and returned to Paris. Bataille did the same in October,[13] accompanied by Denise Rollin, from whom he separated upon their return to the rue de Lille.[14]

Bataille needed to find a new place to live. Pierre Klossowski arranged for him to stay for the whole winter of 1943–4 in the studio of his brother, the painter Balthus, at 3 cour de Rohan (in the sixth arrondissement), a studio Jean Piel described as a 'garret room furnished with a gothic bed with a canopy and an accumulation of old rubbish'.[15] Garret was also the word Bataille used to describe this odd flat: 'a garret I lived in, happy to think I might end my days there, a place so baneful in appearance.'[16] If Bataille spoke at that time of the possibility of dying, he did not mean from his sickness, from which he seems never to have feared dying, but because he was trying to live in this garret in hiding from the threats of a jealous husband (Diane Kotchoubey's), who was determined to kill him. And Bataille was well aware that these threats had to be taken seriously. Moreover, the irreparable almost happened in the rue Pétrarque, one evening he was visiting friends. Was the aggressor, a handsome and powerfully built man, finally loath to kill such a visibly sick, pale and emaciated man after all? We know now that this was no more than a brief attack from which Bataille would emerge upset but unhurt.[17]

Yet he was not alone in Paris. He saw Sartre (in fact the two men saw one another quite often in 1944) who testified, if not friendship, then esteem and sympathy for him, a Sartre whose relations with Bataille went beyond his virulently polemical article, 'A new mystic'. They met either at the home of Leiris ('Sartre was there, who I had missed and wanted to see. . . . A preposterous discussion took place about the *Cogito*') or in the studio where he lived:

> Happiness, remembering a night of drinking and dancing, dancing by myself like a peasant, a faun, with couples all around me. Alone? Actually we were dancing face to face in a potlatch of absurdity, *the philosopher* – Sartre – and me. . . . The third character was a store-window dummy made out of a horse's skull and a flowing, striped yellow and mauve dressing gown. A grimly medieval canopied bed presiding over the fun.[18]

Or else they met at the home of Marcel Moré in the context of debates the latter organised and where Sartre and Bataille discussed – as we have seen – a theme already chosen and probed by Bataille, sin. So he saw Sartre, and Simone de Beauvoir and Camus as well. Bataille spoke briefly of the nature of his links to Sartre and Camus: 'We had in common only the roughness of our moral preoccupations and the taste for certain merry-making, innocent it is true, but irrepressible. In the realm of ideas, without being enemies, we were drawn in different directions.' He also saw old friends who were in Paris at the time, Leiris and Queneau, more recent ones like Jules Monnerot, and some unexpected ones like Father Deniélou whom he seems to have seen often during the war, and with whom he apparently had some long conversations.

He also often saw a young man called Henri-François Rey, with whom he explored an odd idea which appeared to him to vindicate the need to make some money ('That Parisian winter he lived in the greatest destitution'[19]): to write a film script, a script Bataille insisted would be commercial (without for all that contravening respectability as Bataille conceived it: it would be commercial and serious). And to this idea, singular as it was, Bataille added one which is even more so: giving Fernandel a starring role. Thus he tied his justifiable concern to make a commercial film to his appreciation for this actor while conceiving him in a role completely different from his usual ones: 'Here he was picturing Fernandel as an opium-addicted poet, living in a decaying château in the suburbs of Marseille.'[20] And so was born the script – unfortunately later lost – which Henri-François Rey describes thus:

> There was a bourgeois soap manufacturer (Marseille soap of course), respected and honoured in his city, belonging to the best society of notables, president of a charitable society, whose favourite pastime, when his children went on holiday, was to pretend to be the Marquis de Sade. I mean that he assumed his clothes and appearance and engaged in the practices described in the *120 Days of Sodom* or *Philosophy in the Bedroom* with local prostitutes. It all ends badly. The (Marseille) soap manufacturer really does murder one of the prostitutes. Of course, the incident is hushed up, but the fake Sade – a veritable bastard – kills himself so that morality can triumph.

The film was never made: the stunned reaction of the first producer they approached was enough to discourage the two apprentice scriptwriters.

The portrait Henri-François Rey gives of Bataille at that moment of his life is perhaps more interesting:

> A very handsome face, a gentle voice, a very abstract way of moving in space, at once present and absent. When he spoke about the most everyday things, the impression he gave, without being aware of it, was that he was about to impart something of the utmost importance . . . For he was the most fascinating person I have ever met, with his mysterious aspects, ambiguities and contradictions. I have never seen in real life someone whose existence ceaselessly followed a single quest, that of the absolute [a word that might have displeased Bataille], with so much secret passion, so much suffering and misfortune and with so much hope and doubt.[21]

We have some rare testimony about Bataille as he lived through the war, shadow and reality, with the spectre of death announced to everyone and to him in three ways (by war, illness and jealousy) and joy, fortunate joy, entirely motivated by the reasons he had to be up and living. This testimony comes from the participants at the lecture about sin he gave in March 1944 at the home of Marcel Moré. Arthur Adamov, who had known him for a long time, said he was struck by Bataille's tone of voice ('It seemed absolutely authentic to me'[22]),

Louis Massignon ('I was struck by Mr Bataille's tone of simplicity and direct disclosure'[23]) and Maurice de Gandillac ('we were all convinced by your tone'). Like Henri-François Rey, they all noted Bataille's character of lacerated confidence, which he revealed whether speaking to several of the most eminent representatives of the Parisian intelligentsia in the 1940s (sincere ... should we recall the last of Bataille's lectures at the College of Sociology?) or to a peasant in a café in Avallon or Vézelay (or in a brothel to a prostitute); a character of confidence and attentiveness which contained a sense of the extreme gravity of the word uttered (the contrary of a poetic effusion of the word) and the word received.

When he left the studio in the cour de Rohan in April 1944, Bataille also left Paris to move to Samois, near Fontainebleau, specifically to the rue du Coin-Musard, a few miles from the house in Bois-le-Roi where Diane Kotchoubey was living temporarily to avoid the battles of which Paris was then expected to be the epicentre (in actual fact, the Fontainebleau region was at the centre of the fighting on several occasions).

It should not be forgotten that Bataille was ill, and that his stay in Samois was that of a man handicapped by the pulmonary tuberculosis that had been diagnosed two years earlier. From Samois he went with Diane Kotchoubey once or twice a week, at first by coach but by bike after the arrival of the Americans, to Fontainebleau, to have his pneumothorax re-inflated. During this period, his illness ended: 'A little while after the liberation of Fontainbleau and Samois, I wanted to undergo re-inflation: the doctor inserted the needle seven or eight times between my ribs, but nothing happened. The pocket of air becoming inflated at each re-inflation was entirely empty. It was gone. That was how I discovered I was cured.'[24]

Bataille was often alone at Samois. He saw little of Diane Kotchoubey, who was looking after her daughter and two other children some friends had asked her to take care of. Equally, he was kept at home by the frequent bombardments and battles engaged by the Germans and the Americans. Apart from the few return journeys Bataille made between Samois and Bois-le-Roi, sometimes by bike, sometimes on foot, he was most often alone, reclusive ('My veritable seclusion – in a bedroom, ten days already – begins this morning'[25]) waiting for Diane Kotchoubey to visit him – and dejected:

I'm getting old. A few years ago I was tough, filled with bravado, with a take-charge attitude. It seems that's over with and was shallow, perhaps. Back then there wasn't that much risk in action and affirmation! ... My ability to bounce back seems gone for good! ... Illness is wasting me away; unrelenting anguish ends up making me a nervous wreck. .... Under the present conditions of my life, the slightest lapse of awareness brings on giddiness. At 5am I'm cold, my heart sinks, what is there to do but sleep.[26]

A book, a fiction this time, bears witness to this impatient wait, this weary, powerless and disheartened wait; this is *Julie*, which Bataille wrote in 1944.[27] *Julie* is a strange book and for more than one reason not among his best (the story vacillates between tragedy, analogous in some ways to *Madame Edwarda*, and insistent farce). Henri, the central character, sees expectation as the last and most extreme of all despairs which nothing will justify. Expectation and the desire which justifies it are both vain. What expectation reveals, a long and exasperated expectation, is the vanity of the hope it prolongs: 'He awaited Julie! He could no longer doubt this: expectation reveals the vanity of its object.'[28] Expectation is vain because its object is necessarily disappointing: because *any* object contained in expectation (the waiting, at this point, is desire itself) is disappointing. Once desire is satisfied, what is revealed is that the waiting had no meaning; that it was the anticipation of death: 'I expected this, Henri told himself, Julie is nothing. The object of my waiting is my death.'[29] 'Expectation has no object, but death arrives.'[30]

Curiously this is the book in which the war is most present. It is there in a certain – displaced – way, as it was in *Blue of Noon*. The waiting is that for death, or for the end of the war. There are those who escape the war and those who do not return from it. The sensual bedazzlement is all the more oppressive, more shattering, since on the liberty of mingled bodies is superimposed the servitude of trembling, hunted down bodies:

> The majority of people would be deprived of this sweet, divine and nevertheless monstrous – amorous and naked – liberty of bodies. And the expectation which for them was about to begin was not only without limits but would repeat itself with death, and with the sufferings formed from an interminable struggle in the cold and mud, in heat, dust and thirst.[31]

The catechism of fortune

The most impressive thing about Bataille's literary activity in 1944 (which attained a rare intensity, unequalled except by that of the previous two years) was his poems; for the most part they were written in Samois and, in so far as Bataille's poems can be thus described sensibly, they are love poems. Along with what is perhaps the finest of Bataille's texts from this period (*Alleluia*), they are the clearest and the most heart-rending testimony of his new love for Diane Kotchoubey, a testimony made up not just of love but of the powerlessness and fright into which the lover had thrown himself, as though he was discovering (this might be love's power of *revelation*) that only voluptuous intensity had the same marvellous character as death:

> your absence
> your distress
> sicken me
> time for me to love death
> time to bite its hands.
>
> To love is to be in death throes
> To love is to love dying
> monkeys die stinking
> . . .
> Enough I love you like someone crazed
> I laugh at myself the inky donkey
> braying at the sky's stars
> . . .
> I long to die of you
> I'd like to disappear
> in all of your sick whims.

Mysticism calls for poems; theology – and like it *a*theology – calls for a catechism. Bataille would write this catechism: his absolute insolence consisted of continuing to divert words from their pious usage and make them serve mocking and obscene designs. This catechism would be an *Alleluia*: a reply sent back to the point of jubilation to that first *Yes* Nietzsche enjoined mankind to say to existence, that *Yes* which was evidently Bataille's only true morality (this *Yes* designates the summit of morality; the *No* and the *Perhaps*, for which Nietzsche accused humanity of being as sick as its times, designate the morality of decline). This catechism is given by a man – no matter if he is debauched or a saint – to a young woman, in the guise of an initiation into the night she represents, for herself and for the one who loves her. Bataille wrote this book in 1944 for Diane Kotchoubey as a reply to the questions she asked him.[1] Bataille's answers have the unbearable explosion of the most fervent *Yes*; it is no longer enough to consent, one must also provoke the world, the void, the starry heavens, death, the impossible; provoke them to the point of loss. One must burn everything (pleasure says *Yes* but does not burn); only desire tears things apart: it must be kept in the state of the most fervent intensity for it not merely to lead to the untroubled and frivolous celebration of joy. Joy must not concern us; it is nothing but a sham of jubilation and the Alleluia. *Alleluia* is the catechism of Bataillean eroticism (nowhere else did he present it in such breadth, a breadth that is rightfully universal and cosmogonic); it is also the catechism of the Bataillean saint: her *mile et tre* commandments, what being means for a woman – and for all women; the impossible itself – only to sink 'finally into the horror of existence' (here existence is once again proposed as the self's other world, the one in which the self must dissolve itself to attain the only thing making existence worthwhile: its impossible).

Bataille only ever loved what was sullied; this was the meaning of his debauchery. Only what is sullied could frighten and intoxicate him: 'The more I'd experience fear, and the more divine was the message of shame I learned from a prostitute's body.'[2] And what is sullied is what a woman must open up to. She must be open to the hell of her 'hairy parts': '[which] have as much truth as your mouth'.[3] This truth is hell, and it is madness. It is the challenge of this hell that within each truth madness is able to perceive its opposite. Love should not raise up but make low; one must learn to go lower than any woman thought possible; one must dread, and shake with fear. Only this dread and this shaking answer the absolute of the absence of God and of the void of the sky as it weighs down on lovers: 'Sex organs copulating, like naked caterpillars, some bald, others like pink caves, the clamorous din, the dead eyes: continual spasms of mad laughter are moments within you that correspond to the sky's unfathomable cleft.'[4] Only this cleft is great enough for frenzy, for every storm and every disaster. Dianus enjoins the saint *to expose* herself unquestioningly to the exasperation and shame: 'a *you* immensely involved in obscenity'.[5] For the prize is this obscenity (in other words desire), not pleasure. To seek pleasure is cowardly; it is cowardly to want pleasure, to want relief: 'What you have to know secondly is: the only pleasure worth desiring is the desire for pleasure and not the pleasure.'[6] This is how one must have *being*, in a state of ultimate tension and exasperation: the slightest relaxation sets one back to the 'insipidity of pleasure' and 'boredom'. What two beings have in living together, the reason they choose each other at a given moment, is the setting in play of all the possibilities of either one of them: 'the sexual shipwreck'. One must sink, in fact: into nothingness ('Nothingness: the beyond of limited being'[7]). The shipwreck liberates us from every limit. In such a shipwreck, in such an orgy, no isolated being exists any more; for a while, being gives 'way to the horrible indifference of the dead'. What there is to discover in this unbearable and momentary annihilation is being's truth of the impossible, its intimate and sickening meaning of being, in complete tension towards everything that seems to promise to liberate it from its limitations, in tension proportionately to its separation from it. The truth of eroticism and of the orgy are truths of concealment: 'as a challenge to the very world that infinitely conceals its *object* from that desire'.[8] The truth of desire is certainly not salvation, but morality.[9] And Dianus warns: 'Make no mistake: the morality you hear – which is the one I'm teaching – is the most difficult. It won't let you attain either sleep or satisfaction . . . eternal death, revealed in the pleasures of the flesh, will reach the chosen few. Those elect will accompany you into a night where all that's human is destroyed.'[10] But this night is not yet the *summit* where the ultimate truth lies: 'Beyond sick ecstasies you'll still need laughter as you enter into death's shadow.'[11]

Bataille left Samois in October 1944 and returned to Paris, where he took a new flat at 16 rue de Condé (his tenth address since the start of the war). He spent winter 1944–5 there and left Paris once the war definitively ended. He would live for several years in Vézelay with Diane Kotchoubey, who had left her husband.

V

A potential for stench and irremediable fury

Anyone who wrote after 1945 had to take into account that since Auschwitz and Hiroshima had been possible, this was a world and a time that those events had metamorphosed. Is this world still a world, this time still a time? Are they not rather a chaos, a 'chaos in which everything has been brought into question',[1] where there is nothing, however disproportionate this chaos, that does not *question* thought, where there is nothing that thought – if it is possible to have anything resembling thought about this chaos – should not question? Nothing that did not indicate, for Bataille as for others, a *before* and an *after* of the thought of the world.

This was just as true for Bataille: since the 1928 article 'Vanished America', he had spoken of his fascination in the face of horror. But this horror is not simple. It is made up as much of dread as of attraction; its attraction is in proportion to its dread. From 1929 to 1939, Bataille would vacillate strangely between these two poles, sometimes abandoning himself to the experience of one, sometimes calling upon the other . . . each year conjoining them more. His position might well have still been what he expressed in *Documents* in 1930: 'The play between mankind and its own decay continues in the most dejected conditions without one ever having the courage to confront the other.'[2] In which case it would have been only the position of an anti-idealist who would have demanded that thought should leave pillowy clouds of morality and commit itself to recognising its own propensity to turn to the worst. In other words, it would have been necessary for mankind to say *everything*, to admit everything, and it is only at this price that the worst – fascism – could have been avoided. There are few doubts that this is how Bataille defined (even if he refrained from admitting it at the time) the conditions of the possibility of a 'hypermorality'. Or more exactly, there would be no doubt about it if Bataille had not in other respects allowed himself to be gripped by what is insidious in every seduction and if a moment had not come when he had to maintain his thought along the difficult skyline suspended between his violent denunciation of the fascist and Nazi terrors (and the fact is that in 1933 he was alone in denouncing them as he did) and his equally violent fascination with the catastrophe he willingly called for (but was it not upon himself that he first called down the devastation of this catastrophe?). The reproaches Simone Weil made to him when the question of her entry into the Democratic Communist Circle arose in 1933 should be recalled: what could two people whose opinions about the revolution were not only dissimilar but hostile to one another undertake together? For her, it was a triumph of the rational; for him, of the irrational. For her, a calculated and methodical action; for him, a free urge of the instincts, including those generally considered to be pathological. For her, a just and distinguished order; for him, a violent and enlightening violence. Bataille said this often: it was less revolution than riot that attracted him, that interested him, the catastrophic death cry of riots; of necessity any taking of power that followed had no meaning for him.

Until he saw that war had become inevitable (no doubt until the days of 1934), Bataille remained fascinated by the violent possibility formed by the perspective of proletarian revolution and by the irruption of servile forces into history. Then, although his denunciation did not weaken, this fascination gave way to the possibility of a violence and a catastrophe that were different but incomparably enlightening: war. Until now I have wanted to avoid ambiguity: Bataille was the first to hate this war the fascists and Nazis were preparing. He hated it because he was aware – in this he was better informed than many – of what this 'unbreathable' violent order was resolved to instigate by means of violence. Not for a moment did Bataille consider that this war would be to the advantage of the outcast and servile forces whose triumph he called for. It envisaged a closed world of 'overlords'. All the same the fact remained that the fall of the old, weary and senile world would be like a conflagration, and it occurred to him – with the world suddenly turned into a frightful game – that the mediocre political calculations which would be bound to justify this conflagration could in the end give way to the broadest and least expected designs such as to provoke cataclysm.

The war finally came and it would certainly have been somewhat mad to hope that it might be beautiful; it was atrocious.

Bataille said so in taking for himself, as for all, its full and immediate measure: 'There is generally an oppressive and sickening element in the fact of being a man which it is necessary to overcome. But this weight and this repugnance have never been so oppressive as after Auschwitz.' The war did not lessen the sickening element. It increased it in proportion to its atrocity. This weight had never been so oppressive or so repugnant, for not for a moment would it be possible to claim – only cowards could do so – that this oppressiveness and repugnance had not been shared by everyone: 'Like you and I, those responsible for Auschwitz had a human nose, mouth, voice and reason, they were able to make love, have children; like the pyramids or the Acropolis, Auschwitz is a fact and sign of mankind. Man's image is henceforth inseparable from a gas chamber.'³

The shallow, blessed morality, the morality of those who acquiesce in decline, this morality which has no other concern than to absolve, would pull itself together painlessly if it were permissible to claim that a difference in kind exists between those responsible for extermination and all of us who might be innocent of it. Two words would be enough for the war not to prevent morality from returning to guilty complacency: at most there might, *momentarily*, have existed *monsters* on one side and *people* on the other. The relentless anti-idealist and anti-transcendentalist that Bataille had always been could not resign himself to this. And even if he had to state it in desperate terms (reopening unbearable wounds: who among the victims could readily admit that there was *essentially* nothing to distinguish them from their executioners?), Bataille did not hesitate:

> we are not simply the possible victims of executioners: the executioners are like us. We should still ask ourselves: is there nothing in our nature that makes such horror impossible? And we really must reply: in fact, nothing. There are a thousand obstacles in us that oppose it . . . Nevertheless, it is not impossible. Our potential is thus not simply for pain, it also extends to passion for torturing.⁴

This is finally made clear: what Bataille was saying, however horrible it might appear, was not simply a cry of despair but responded to concern with the most solid and *disenchanted* of moralities. Nothing that forms a person is outside the *human*; and all of us are accountable for anything a person does. Auschwitz is not only the most extreme and most inconceivable potential to which humanity must henceforth know it is linked, it is also, from that moment, *our* potential. Everyone henceforth should recognise this fact. If there is one thing Auschwitz cannot allow, if there is one thing Auschwitz forbids for ever, it is that we could continue to be unaware (or want to be unaware) that within us there is an *awakening* to 'a potential for stench and irremediable fury'. Neither this stench nor this fury are distinct from us. To wish to ignore them would be to expose oneself to their sudden re-emergence in one form or another. Bataille, moreover, did not conceal his fear of them; he concealed it so much less since he knew the morality that was ready to restore to them a meaning which put them beyond the horizon of possibilities. This morality might be on its guard: but had it not already been caught unawares? Denying the possibility of war (or foolishly refusing to engage in it) does not prevent it from happening. Denying that the horror arising with it has a *human* sense would not prevent it from arising again, whatever the circumstances:

> there is in a given form of moral condemnation a fleeting means of denial. All in all, they say: this abjection would not have happened if monsters had not been there. This virulent judgement removes monsters from the possible. They are accused implicitly of being beyond the limits of the possible; instead it should be seen that their excess specifically defines this limit. And it may doubtless be that, to the extent that this language is addressed to the crowd, this infantile negation seems efficacious, but it fundamentally changes nothing.[5]

The executioners were not *monsters*. There is no justification for adding a new category of monsters to that of people responsible for the war: it is people who exterminate. It is people who took the stench and fury to new extremes. And it is they who have bequeathed these extremes to us as henceforth part of what humanity must *also* know of itself. They had a nose, a mouth and a voice. And no doubt they also knew how to love. In a word, they were men, neither more nor less than we also claim to be. The most crushing horror is this: morality would not be less abject than abjection itself if it claimed that anyone at all could be innocent. It would be no less scandalous, for it would be preparing for nothing other than the inevitable reappearance of the horror.

*

It is in analogous terms that Bataille takes note of the second of the chief horrors arising from the war. The unreproducibility of the extermination might convince in the last resort (it was so mad that insanity might do so . . . but Bataille was careful not to be convinced by such arguments); that of the Hiroshima explosion is a great deal less convincing. (Did it not henceforth belong to the natural possibilities of modern war?) It is not the least paradox that what put an end to the war of 1939–45 would also be from that time on the sign of all possible wars. Once again, Bataille denounced its inalienably *human* character. For this character contrasts with the 'fatality' that each year causes fifty million deaths. ('In fact we cannot avoid it – anyway, if we could, we would immediately realise that we should do nothing about it, that the misfortunes of preventing it would be graver than a thousand Hiroshimas.') It provides an exemplary contrast because it belongs to men to let other men live or be annihilated on a gigantic scale: 'The atomic bomb draws its meaning from its human origin: it is the possibility that human hands hold deliberately over the future.' And this concerns morality to the extent that it is not confused with lamentation; as all misfortune concerns it. Whoever is not prepared to admit his share of misfortune will use the pretext of Hiroshima to justify his lamentation: 'In truth, if we single out Hiroshima as a cause of lamentation, we do so because we dare not face the misfortune – this profound non-meaning of misfortune – which is not simply the effect of the avoidable violence of wars, but a component of human life.'[6] Hiroshima is not tragically distinct from what is humanly possible. It is just one more possible tragedy to add to the human tragedy. And that it should be *human* highlights rather than attenuates its meaning.

A new man must adapt to the world which has included among its possibilities the furies of Auschwitz and Hiroshima. Bataille had all his life looked horror in the face, and he had all his life required others to look at it with him (the feeling of dread his work achieves stems from what is sometimes intolerable about such a requirement). The appearance of these two greatest horrors was not going to make him shrink from this. There is no justification for being a man but to be the equal at least of *all* human possibilities. This is his justification and horror. On the subject of Hiroshima, impotence would be to say: 'let's deny it' (no moral protest would have been enough to prevent Hiroshima taking place). Strength consists in saying: 'let us live it'. Since we have in some way made it happen, it falls to us to assume its irreparable fault (say *Yes* to it). Bataille had enjoined us to 'live at the height of death'. He enjoined us, now the war was over – and this must be understood as the *political* formulation of a supreme morality – to 'live at the height of Hiroshima'.

Fascism's last sanctuary

Fascism is the creation of human beings, but we do not usually think that its responsibility and destructiveness contain an essential aspect of humanity.

It seems definitively accepted that with the war, Bataille finished with political commitment and any political writing. People have been able to criticise or attack him for this, some might even have taken advantage of it. It has even been claimed that his political activity ended with Contre-Attaque after 1936, thus ignoring how profoundly and essentially *political* Acéphale and the College of Sociology were, in their own way. In fact, in 1945 Bataille was far from being a man for whom politics could be a matter of indifference, and his silence between 1940 and 1944 has no other meaning than that the war was no longer politics but its frustrated, tragic consummation, and that other than fight one could do nothing but watch.

Only by not reading them could anyone be in doubt that his most important postwar books – *The Accursed Share* and *Sovereignty* – were also fundamentally political, even if this politics differed from that which Sartre defined for most people under the label of commitment (and this was also how Bataille understood it before the war, when he had sometimes been a 'committed' writer). But not only were his books political; so too were his articles, until at least 1953. Between 1944 and 1953 Bataille made as many political interventions as necessary, on every major subject according to the means available to his 'provocative' manner.[1] (If a definite date had to be given for Bataille's relative loss of interest in politics, 1953 would be the most appropriate, seventeen years later than generally agreed.)

It is in no small measure paradoxical that Bataille rejoined the political debate through the ambiguous intermediary of Nietzsche:

paradoxical because it was also with him that in a way he had resigned himself to silence five years earlier. The final issues of *Acéphale* tried to testify how Nietzsche was not and could never be a fascist. If Bataille testified to this once again in 1944, it was because the war had not had the effect he hoped: one of clarification. So long as Nietzsche was subject to suspicion, he would be too. The day Nietzsche appeared as he should, freed of the enslavement of Nazi ideology, would be the time for Bataille himself to speak up once more.

This was the meaning of the article he contributed to *Combat* on 20 October 1944; and once again Bataille could not have been any clearer. Was it not true that Germany in Nietzsche's time, at the end of the nineteenth century, already showed signs of anti-Semitic trends? And did Nietzsche not unreservedly take a stand against them? He did even more than decline to be a pan-German anti-Semite (despite his sister Elisabeth Foerster-Nietzsche's claims to the contrary): 'He spoke of the Germans with disgusted contempt. (He had high regard for Jews, a predominant taste for French ways and character.)'[2] Such foreboding on his part, causing him to take a stand against both Paul de Lagarde's idiotic pan-Germanism and Richard Wagner's 'Francophobic and anti-Semitic chauvinism', and his alarm at the cowardly marriage of his sister to the appalling Foerster (perhaps realising he had been too free for others not to take their revenge once he was dead, to cash in on his corpse),[3] absolved him in advance of the use people tried to make of him.

Not only can Nietzsche not be put into the service of National Socialism unless it deliberately misinterprets him (quoting him wrongly or partially) and warps his thought; not only does Nietzsche not have those traits in common with National Socialism which it tried to single out for propaganda purposes, but on the contrary, and in a clearly explicit way, Bataille insists, Nietzsche challenged in advance those qualities that unreservedly characterise National Socialism (pan-Germanism, racism and anti-Semitism), as if predicting and anticipating that they would intensify. Bataille announces this by stating: 'anti-Semitic pan-Germanism was for him the object of aggressive hostility. . . . In spite of the theatrical décor, the distance from Hitler to Nietzsche is that from police cells to Alpine summits.'[4]

It was thus significant that Bataille should use Nietzsche to rejoin the political debate in *Combat* (and it is not irrelevant that he chose *Combat* to do so): in other words, using the path of philosophy, the least advisable and the hardest to follow, and the most vulnerable to misinterpretation. In doing so, Bataille not only sought to clear Nietzsche's name. He seemed to be proposing that, if one is to talk politics, one must do so at a level demanded by a sovereign thought that could in no way be subjected to morality or gain.

In fact, with the same obstinacy as before the war, Bataille began two new projects. Both seem to have revolved around creating a journal. I say 'seem', for only one came to fruition; the second became 'notebooks' with only a fleeting existence, since only one appeared (a second was only half finished and did not eventually reach publication).

This notebook was called *Actualité* (itself a significant title), and was published by Éditions Calmann-Lévy in 1946. Bataille edited it alone, though it appears that Maurice Blanchot and Pierre Prévost helped initiate the project.[5]

The conditions of *Actualité*'s brief existence are less significant than the contents of the sole volume, published under the title *L'Espagne libre*. And this content was political, in the full sense of the word, in the sense in which an equal distribution of ideological, cultural and economic investigation seems to have taken place. Those contributors (Camus and Cassou) who forcefully reminded their readers of the warning that powerlessness to prevent the collapse of the least tractable of their number had given European democracies, were joined by other contributors who attempted to convey a vision of Spain that was not only ideological, but also economic and social.[6]

'For nine years now Spain has hung heavy on the hearts of my generation. For nine years they have carried it like an ill-omened wound.'[7] It was a wound all the more ill-omened in that Camus's moral conscience (and in this we shall see how close he was to Bataille) refused to be dissociated from those in France who condoned the assassination of this people and its poets (Lorca, Machado): 'Of course, that was Vichy, not us. But you cannot get away from the concept that a Nation is inter-dependent with its traitors as well as its heroes, or else it has no inter-dependence at all.'[8] The wound inflicted on Spain was inflicted on the whole of Europe since European democracy could not claim to have resolved its problem so long as the Caudillo could deny democracy in the country which was the first to shed its blood to defend it (neither would it be resolved so long as no one highlighted the fact that in 1936 several countries displayed a cowardly concern for not endangering their own democracy by coming to the aid of another). Democracy is *one*, Camus wrote: 'If it is despised in one place, it is threatened in its entirety. . . . We fought so free people might face one another without shame, so that every person might take charge of their own happiness, and judge themselves without bearing the weight of the humiliation of others.'[9]

What Jean Cassou says is similar, but less restrained. The European tragedy began in Spain; in Spain, too, it will end. Cassou's tone is one of rage: the Spanish generals' insurrection (Mola and Franco) had awakened the demons of 'French Nazis'. With the dramatic events in Spain 'that hideous gang of ministers, henchmen and society women, of writers, pimps, financiers, industrialists' first showed their faces in France. It was to Madrid that 'Pétain went, to his master Franco, to take lessons in imposture and betrayal. It was on the Spanish soldiers, the heroes of the first canto of the present epic, that our Nazified bourgeoisie and its henchmen first got their hand in before turning their attention to the French patriots'.[10]

Bataille contributed two texts to the collection he edited (and whose political direction was thus his responsibility). One was a homage to Pablo Picasso, 'the greatest living painter', and more specifically to the Picasso of *Guernica*. For Bataille it was highly significant 'that the freest of the arts had reached its summit in a political painting';

> This is not, it is true, the first time the struggle of the Spanish people for liberty has roused an artist to the highest degree of inspiration. The executed man in *Third of May*, dying with his eyes open in a great cry, is without doubt Goya's masterpiece. And this canvas in the Prado in Madrid, right in the heart of the last fascist 'sanctuary', continues to glorify 'resistance' in all times and places.[11]

For Bataille considered that if one country more than any other had earned the right to the title of Resistance, it was this one, the first that 'endured fascist aggression' and 'resisted it first in conditions of incredible destitution'. It was by considering this subjugated land and people that, paradoxically, Bataille invited his readers to take lessons in freedom: 'I doubt there exists today a population or people generally susceptible of offering to others a more authentic teaching than the country and people of free Spain.'[12] For if freedom must 'fundamentally' be understood in a political sense (and the challenge of Spanish freedom was political, in 1946 as it had been ten years earlier), so must it be understood in a sovereign sense. And the sole political designation of sovereignty, the only one that might by chance reconcile politics and sovereignty, was anarchy (and no people were more anarchist than the Spanish): 'Anarchism is, at root, the most onerous expression of an obstinate desire for the impossible.' Freedom is *the impossible*, and because the Spanish people more than any other have a sense of the impossible, they know better than any other what freedom means.[13] This people who more than any other are players, who are more familiar with death, light-hearted in their extreme seriousness and free in proportion to this lightness and seriousness, Bataille knew to be liberated in advance from any servitude, whether fascist or otherwise. The testaments to their liberty, in the face of every Franco, are the convulsed figures of Guernica and the wide-open eyes of the firing squad victim in Goya's *Third of May*.

Bataille's politics

> If one intends thought to be neither submissive, subordinated, nor subjugated, to struggle against the totalitarian order may not be enough.

There is undeniably good reason to speak of a 'political' Bataille. Not, admittedly, in the way Sartre became political as soon as the war had ended. Nor does it mean Bataille would continue to be committed in the way he often had been before the war (although he was never so committed as to support a particular party, nor even, for any length of time, any movement at all, his positions being those of an independent).[1] However, Bataille was political, in the sense in which he continued to create platforms from which he spoke (among other things about politics) and let others speak, from which ideas could be debated. If these ideas were not always 'political' in the restricted, narrow and datable sense of the term (if by this is meant that when we read these texts today we see in them a chronicle of contemporary events), they were in a way that, failing to find anything analogous to them, we should describe as 'Bataillean'.[2]

Thus the project for a new journal, *Critique* – finalised by Bataille at the end of 1945 and the start of 1946 (it was published in June 1946), simultaneously therefore with the single issue of *Actualité* – is political in the Bataillean sense of the term. Almost the same people were involved at the origin of both projects: Pierre Prévost, Maurice Blanchot and Georges Bataille. Maurice Girodias (formerly Maurice Kahane) had asked Pierre Prévost to create, with some friends, a journal for the publishing firm he directed (Éditions du Chêne). The proposition was picked up by Maurice Blanchot and passed on to Georges Bataille, who set up plans for a journal under the initial title of *Critica* reviewing French and foreign books and publications, in other words a project offering a place to debate ideas by means of a critique of their transmission and circulation. (This detail is important: *Critique* would not be a place of 'pure' ideas, or creation, but of critical commentaries on books dealing with ideas. Direct engagement was thereby *a priori* discarded.)[3] The definition Bataille himself gave to *Figaro littéraire* on 17 July 1947 (in an interview after *Critique* had been voted best journal by journalists) leaves no doubt about what he understood as the meaning of his project: 'It is necessary', he said, 'for human consciousness no longer to be compartmentalised. *Critique* seeks the relations that might exist between political economy and literature, between philosophy and politics.' And he illustrated this first and significant definition (at the moment when this interview was published, *Critique* had reached issue 13–14) by mentioning an article by Alexandre Kojève (he describes him in passing as the greatest philosopher of the time, which was both valuable and certainly true: only a few people at that time recognised it[4]): 'This article marks most clearly the intentions of *Critique*, which would like to be the crossroads of philosophy, literature, religion and political economy.' This crossroads should not be understood to mean a single confluence of ideas: the object was not to derive from an ensemble of writings, each belonging to a distinct discipline, a perceptible coherence in relation to one another but to begin to respond in advance to an intention Bataille clearly stated on this occasion:

> You see, I think there was then a need among people to live events in an ever more conscious way. I think it is the responsibility of Europe to create awareness of what is at stake between America and Russia. It is never a question for us of heightening conflicts. But if humanity wants to be able to realise the promises it bears in itself, it can do so only by taking full consciousness of the conflicts which tear it apart.

These definitions are both Bataillean ('to live events in a more conscious way'), and they are *certainly* not ('it is never a question for us of heightening conflicts'). He was making it clear that he had remained just as determined today as he was yesterday to confront realities, that he had as little desire as ever to dream. And it is a quite different man who sees humanity as full of promise – just as the most shallow of idealists would in his place – when yesterday he roared with laughter (and as he would again tomorrow) before all that could resemble any hope for the future. (Where is the love Bataille, like Nietzsche, had for ignorance about the future?)

Of course, the circumstances should be taken into account: the context of this interview, the first of his life, took account of the sense of intimidation the aftermath of the war and the beginning of the Cold War had cast over everyone, as well as of the influence the people who surrounded him had on him: his respect for Kojève, Éric Weil and Maurice Blanchot were not simply pure form. The influence of these people must have been considerable. The presence of Albert Ollivier and Raymond Aron on the editorial committee (one could also hardly imagine two men more dissimilar than Aron and Bataille) has equal significance. With *Critique* Bataille could only be responsible for a 'serious' journal by raising himself to the level of seriousness both of those around him and of what was required by the situation.

The success of *Critique* – although it was not without problems, suspending publication for a year and having three publishers in its first five years – bears witness to something new for Bataille (new or provisionally different). This was not the first journal he edited or created. There had been *Documents* and then *Acéphale*. It was not the first and certainly not the most significantly representative of his talent: *Documents* was, in a different way, more ardent; *Acéphale* incomparably crazier and more beautiful. *Critique* was a project of maturity: serious, reflective and fair. What Bataille gained in credibility in creating *Critique* (he was responsible for what was soon to become one of the most respected of journals), he no doubt lost in splendour. Even the longevity of *Critique* was out of character.[5] Until then he had been the man of brief and chaotic enterprises. The equilibrium of this new journal is not its least singular aspect: this man, who had only to a modest extent become solid and serene, would collaborate with people as dissimilar as possible from himself and would maintain afloat the unlikely possibility of their expressing themselves together.

Others did not fail to observe that the editor of *Critique* was the calm face of the author of *Madame Edwarda* and *The Dead Man*, which represent his monstrous face; that the extreme care for respectability that Bataille displayed his whole life found in this journal the means to place the stake of knowing ambivalence. No doubt this is true and false at the same time.

False, because Bataille was not simply 'worthy' in *Critique* (careful as he was to hide the fact). In the third issue he aggressively defended

Henry Miller in terms seemingly stemming from the irredentism of *Documents*: 'Miller expresses himself with an unprecedented vulgarity, but those who consider themselves guardians of morals will, they know, have to get used to it. . . . For someone one day to express themselves with the worst vulgarity could even finally appear as a necessary reparation of the betrayal of all morality represented by tact and foolishness.'[6] Again, it was under cover of a scientific outlook that he introduced statements of a provocative if not confessional character in a way that recalls the 'method' governing his very first article, 'L'Amérique disparue'[7]: 'We are unable to prevent the animality within us surviving and often overwhelming us',[8] or: 'for mankind the sexual act is animality; it is divine only when fallen and its fall is its condition – so much so that our conduct is always treacherous: either we betray during the day our truth of night, or we hypocritically aspire simply to denounce the conventions of day.'[9] False therefore because Bataille conceived and created *Critique* only to hide his unrepresentable side. He devoted considerable time to it (twenty articles in 1947, twenty-two in 1948, another twenty-two in 1949, that is, along with the issues of 1946, seventy-four articles comprising 570 pages,[10] until the provisional suspension of publication, during 1949). False, because Bataille simultaneously wrote and published *under his own name* three books (*Hatred of Poetry*, *L'Alleluiah* and *L'Abbé C.*), which are among the least respectable he wrote (in contrast, it is notable that these are the only three 'unrespectable' books he signed). False because this period, far from bearing witness to an appeasement in his thinking, a rallying to intellectual propriety, gave rise, on the contrary, to the major texts of *The Accursed Share* (three volumes) which are its absolute summit. False finally because it seems that, in good faith, seized in his turn by the necessity of a *historical* moral thought, Bataille was at that moment, like the majority of his contemporaries, living under the shock of a double threat: that of the end of the Second World War and of the beginnings of the Cold War. He wanted to understand both. He wanted to think them, but did not believe he could *think* them alone, think alone of the apparent fatefulness oppressing everything, at the closing of an atrocious war, of the fall of Europe into a new war (solitary as Bataille appears, he never thought that his thought alone would be enough).

'Something in the present world has radically changed: this world has seemingly lost plasticity. Nothing comes together any longer from the new forms coming into existence; ideas no longer solidify, nothing takes shape compared to socialist or fascist movements fermented in the play of ideas.'[11] The years 1946–7 were no longer a time of intellectual adventure, less still was it a time for bravado (the Dada and surrealist scandals were no more than a distant and disparate echo). What Bataille said here, in an attenuated tone, as an intellectual who seemed barely touched with regret, he elsewhere stated as a writer, with a force which did not resign itself, which, on the contrary, enjoins someone (here his addressee, a complicitous addressee, is René Char) not to resign himself to the 'universal confusion which now turns thought itself into an oblivion, a stupidity, a dog's barking in the church'.[12]

More effectively than any book or any text Bataille could have written to deplore it, *Critique* bears witness to this play that no longer forms ideas and this plasticity that has withdrawn from them. *Documents* and *Acéphale* occupied a distinct place among everything that was done before the war, among everything the period prior to the war allowed in the way of ideas, even at the risk of their becoming intoxicated in the game they played out. No other journal challenged that place and they only challenged it with others (surrealism, for example) the more effectively to define their differences. This was one of the many effects of the war: thought had fallen from grace. Surrealism was like a decimated shadow; communism had finally got the better of its internal oscillations; existentialism reigned but in a way Bataille was not inclined to consider to be more responsive than he considered surrealism at the height of his own age; fascism, which was in the end what the left in general and Bataille in particular looked to as a composite enemy, had not been simply defeated; for a long time it was outside all critical thought because it had long retreated from all possible thought. There remained, as André Thirion put it, only an insipid communism 'odious, wretched and of a nauseating conformism' and, no less odious, no less wretched, no less nauseating in its conformism, only a 'hypocritical undertaking of the moralisation of Paris'[13] led by what rallied in the most hypocritically petit-bourgeois way to Gaullism. The threat (of a new war) and the option (to be a communist or not) cut or tended to cut intellectual life down the middle. Nothing which was undertaken or that anyone could possibly undertake at that time was immune from its effects; such an atmosphere does not encourage collaborative work.

Critique was part of this. And it was primarily why *Critique* did not have the strength of the journals Bataille had earlier imagined, conceived and created. But it was also why, in its way, in a diminished way, betraying the widespread powerlessness, *Critique* bears witness to the age in which it was born (an age of ebb), and in this it was no less exemplary than the way in which *Documents* and *Acéphale* bore witness to theirs (an age of flow).

One cannot fail immediately to be struck by the apparent disparity of themes and texts appearing in the summary of the first issues of *Critique*. Obviously it was a long way from the contrived homogeneity of *Acéphale* to the played-out or deliberate dispersion of *Critique*.[14] Another disparity is superimposed onto this one which is neither less marked nor less striking, one particularly laden with consequences. For the first time, Bataille, imagining a journal, conceiving it, creating it, refrained from imagining, conceiving and creating anything which bore the traces – in general or in its details, from near or far – of what until then he obstinately thought and attempted under the title of *community*. On the contrary, it was marked by the most singular disparity. Included in the summary of the first four issues that appeared in June, July, August and September 1946 (in August and September one double issue, no. 3–4, came out) were the names of Jean Maquet, Jacques Lamarchand, Alexandre Koyré, Éric Weil, Jean Chauveau, Georges Ambrosino, Georges Balandier, Théodore Fraenkel, Albert Ollivier, Maurice Blanchot, Aimé Patri, Alexandre Kojève, Jean Piel and so on. Many were Bataille's *friends*, but not all. Many were prestigious (or would become so), but they did not all occupy similar 'ideological' positions. More remarkably, more significantly, the editorial committee was itself cut in two by the shadow of the threat weighing over Europe. Bataille the editor, who was admittedly neither a marxist nor pro-Soviet Union, but who was no more satisfied after the war than before it by what, willy-nilly, opposed marxism and the Soviet Union, relied on Blanchot, who had much the same views and established himself in a similarly intermediary position, on Éric Weil, a philosopher and a marxist (a Stalinist, some of his detractors in the journal even claimed), while Pierre Prévost (himself clearly anti-marxist), the chief editor of the first twelve issues, had as a close friend Albert Ollivier, a Gaullist (leader-writer for *Combat*, who was to be expelled from *Les temps modernes*).[15]

This definition of the tendencies and affinities of the journal's editorial committee was not simply formal. This division soon assumed a weighty significance. In fact it was around the question of communism that *Critique*'s first differences took shape. Bataille was concerned that Albert Ollivier, who was to review a book by Koestler, would do so, as he did in *Combat*, as an anti-communist. He reminded Prévost (in a letter) that they had agreed that the journal would not develop, as a principle, any position of this type, even though, in fact, positions of all kinds were *a priori* acceptable. Prévost insinuated that Bataille, by doing this, was being pusillanimous. In other words, his concern was not to displease the communists and in particular Aragon, whom he portrayed during the war as someone who might purify the arts at the Liberation. The reality was certainly of a quite different order (the proof that he did not rally to it would later be revealed in everything Bataille wrote about communism, but he was still less inclined to criticise it in a way that was described at the time as bourgeois, that is, to criticise according to principles implying an unreserved approval of capitalism), of an order which took into account the trap into which thought had been forced from the end of the Second World War and on the brink of the Cold War, a trap no aspect of which he wanted to underestimate and which he believed none of the recognised solutions (whether American-capitalist, Soviet-communist, national-Gaullist, etc.) could shake off. For truth to have a chance to develop, Bataille thought that none of the responses to this division could or should be denied a place in *Critique*. At this price, the challenge might have been supposed to be able to appear in a less confused way. This is what he wrote to Pierre Prévost in terms which leave no doubt as to the central, if not moderating, position he wanted to see the journal occupying: 'I cannot for my part, even if Weil accepted it, admit the Stalinist position as taboo, and anti-Stalinism as free.'[16]

Bataille's position could be judged opportunist. In fact, it is evidence of a clear intimidation, an intimidation felt at that time by everyone who did not want to rally to either of the great geo-ideological and soon to be military powers. At the same time, it was not: the problem was one of maintaining a difficult balance, on what Bataille called a 'tightrope' in another letter to Pierre Prévost giving a wry account of the misunderstandings and difficulties:

> I cannot conceal the fact that in the political sphere you have not shown all the sagacity I expected of you. This is perhaps most serious

in the sense that, on this ground, misunderstandings are most venomous and, in any case (with contributions by Raymond Aron – which, you should note, I commissioned on an issue which is not neutral – and Ollivier on the one hand and Weil and Friedmann on the other), the journal is proceeding along a tightrope.[17]

The rope was not always so tight. Whether events no longer had the same demanding character, whether both Bataille and the journal were less compliant, the fact remains that the tension apparent in the first issues was gradually dispelled. Imperceptibly, *Critique* became less political (more 'literary' and philosophical). It is likely (and no doubt inevitable) that Bataille was no longer as interested in it as he had been at the beginning. This can be seen in the fact that each year he submitted fewer texts to it, and they were texts that were, if not of a lesser importance, at least not written especially for the journal (responding to other preoccupations than those *Critique* exhibited at the beginning: Lascaux, universal history, and so on), and were distant from debates on ideas to which the journal added its voice in its early days. This can also be seen in the fact that, with some exceptions, those who published in the journal at the beginning ceased to do so. And it can finally be seen in the desire Bataille revealed (as we shall see during 1957–8) to create a new journal. If *Critique* did not force him into the 'sad compromises' which would be inevitable if it was to last, it perhaps wearied him and he soon gave it no more than a doubtless distracted attention.

Il salto mortale

Rarely do alliances outlive what justified them. With Germany destroyed, nothing remained of the Anglo-American-Soviet alliance but a fragile balance of powers and interests that – as everyone feared – threatened to fall to pieces at any moment. No sooner was the war over than, monstrously, the spectre of another took shape: Truman, the new American president (Roosevelt died in April 1945) and the new US administration appeared convinced of the Kremlin's desire for ideological hegemony (unless they wished to break with the consensus policies maintained by Roosevelt), and Stalin threw the whole weight of the Soviet bureaucracy onto those Eastern European countries the Yalta agreement had placed under his influence (perhaps he wanted to turn these agreements into a definitive partition of Europe).

On 11 May 1947, Truman agreed US economic and military aid for Greece and Turkey. This amounted, for the first time since cessation of hostilities, to putting the American and Soviet armies face to face, with the Soviet forces supporting the extreme left's rebellion in Greece. It was the first major event of what historians have called the 'Cold War', whose beginnings they generally date a year earlier in March 1946.

On 5 June 1947, in a speech given at Harvard summing up the lessons learned from American intervention in Greece and Turkey, US Secretary of State George Marshall proposed a plan for economic and political aid to Europe, intended to combat 'hunger, poverty, desperation, and chaos'. The principle behind this simultaneously generous and self-serving plan for aid was the re-establishment of the international trade that, for opposing but complementary reasons, the United States needed as urgently as Europe. The Soviet Union, after hesitating for a moment (the Marshall Plan did not in fact exclude it), finally rejected this offer, and forced Poland and Czechoslovakia to follow suit. A second European partition, this time an economic one, had just been drawn up (this Plan was like a double-sided coin, hastening the separation of the two European blocs, West and East, at least in so far as it revitalised and unified the countries of Western Europe).[1]

Bataille was perhaps never closer to a *rational* analysis of the economic, social and military situation of Europe. He wholeheartedly supported the Marshall Plan, even if he was not so naïve as to consider it to have no ideological motives, and even if he saw the extent of its political effects straight away. Not only did he support it; he would appear to have been one of the first to call for it. In the January/February 1947 issue of *Critique* (nos 8–9) he was already outlining an aid plan as if in anticipation of the one Marshall made public only on 5 June: '*Thus the normal and necessary movement of American activity would need effortlessly to result in supplying the whole world without corresponding counterpart.*'[2]

The Soviet rejection of it meant that the Plan did not supply the whole world, and the military tensions such a financial reinvigoration was meant to ease, on the contrary, grew more acute. The question of commitment to one side or another of the two blocs, put to nearly all French intellectuals, was *also* put to Georges Bataille. And it is fairly typical of the role he had at the helm of *Critique* that, if he did not reply, he nevertheless did not in any way avoid this question.

In fact a particularly strange aspect of this was that this man, who would not be a committed intellectual again, who did not sign up to any party (while several of his closest friends became members of the Communist Party), who did not vote,[3] the man who was not a marxist let alone a Stalinist – he had after all been one of the first to point out the parallels between Stalin and Hitler – should be the man who in 1947, at a moment when Stalin had no apologists (none, not even Sartre), wanted to try and *understand* what necessity, black as it might be, could be leading the Soviet Union to act as it had. Everyone was becoming involved, criticising or supporting, signing up for one side or the other. . . . But he both encouraged the Marshall Plan and suddenly 'defended' the Soviet Union. One can understand this as the political formulation of the despair Bataille felt in seeing that, if he certainly did not resign himself to liberal bourgeois government, he no longer believed that the revolution (communism) might save him from it. The bourgeoisie was hateful, this was nothing new: 'At the basis of the democratic idea (the bourgeois idea) of the individual, there is assuredly deception, avarice and a negation of man as an element of destiny (of the universal action of that which is); the modern bourgeois appears as the poorest figure of a person that humanity has assumed.'[4] But what was the standing of those who, like him, were prepared to denounce this bourgeoisie's greed, cunning and self-interest? Bataille gave a blunt reply: 'The communists offer the leap into death.' Such a leap is so radical that whoever does not take it can be equated with the bourgeoisie. Should one concede to it? 'A movement of "antitotalitarian" opinion has formed which tends to paralyse action; its strictly conservative effect is certain.'[5] This amounted, in other words, to saying: 'This collusion, whether conscious or not, has greatly contributed to the weakness and inertia of all those who wanted to escape the rigour of Stalinist communism.'[6]

Bataille refused to join the ranks of the bourgeoisie and its greedy wish to retain its privileged position. And he refused to take 'the leap into death' communism represented. So the only option left to him was to try and understand; to understand how the intractable, exhausted, coercive Soviet world was a world of slavery, a world where work was the only possibility, one that more than any other had issued a blanket rejection of the possibilities of spontaneity, spending and extravagance. This was a work imposed on everyone in so burdensome a way that there was no possibility of anyone escaping its crushing inevitability. Did Bataille consider the collectivisation of farmland justifiable, be it at the price of human lives ('it is regarded as the cruellest moment of an endeavour that was never mild')?[7] He neither judged nor justified it. Only one thing is certain: a country at peace with itself does not have the urgent necessity the Soviet Union found to meet the threat of an even greater necessity with cruel and morally unacceptable means: acts of cruelty that harass individuals seem negligible compared to the ills they are trying to avert. What does morality have to do with such fatality?

> The truth is that we rebel against an inhuman hardness. And we would rather die than establish a reign of terror; but a single man can die, and an immense population is faced with no other possibility than life. The Russian world had to make up for the backwardness of czarist society. And this was necessarily so painful, it demanded an effort so great, that the hard way – in every sense the most costly way – became its only solution.... Without a violent stimulant, Russia could not have recovered.[8]

Once again Bataille took a stand against a bland moral protest that was as ineffective then as it had been before the war. What did the Kremlin want if not world domination? It was not enough to criticise this, and even less to join the ranks of those terrified by such a viewpoint. What mattered was to understand why the Kremlin had such ambitions and how it intended to achieve them. And one had to act, immediately: if peace were possible, it could only be an armed peace: 'To suggest that this world be given a rest is fatuous in the extreme. Rest and sleep could only be, at best, a preliminary to war.'⁹

It may be noticed that Bataille was saying exactly what he had said in the years before the war. Only the blind could believe in rest and peace. Only fools and idealists could wish for demilitarisation (Bataille had never been and would never be a pacifist). The armed peace he called for had to be a 'progressive peace'. And it was the West's paradoxical fortune that the Soviet Union bearing down on it with the weight of fear and of threat would help it to avert paralysis. The least moral of revolutions (the most 'inhuman' one, according to Bataille; 'evil' itself) allowed a threat of war to hang over the West that could only force it to liberate by its own volition the masses it subjugated. Or else, with revolution, war itself would be inevitable; in other words 'secret police', 'the muzzling of thought' and 'concentration camps'.¹⁰

The curse of history

How can we not immediately see, in history itself, an evil greater than oppression.

Classical economics seems not to have wanted to take into account the fact that not all societies have always been governed by exchange. Bataille had known this since he read Mauss, and in 'The Notion of Expenditure' in 1933 he had explored significant aspects of this discovery: he exhorted *his* society and all modern societies to be aware of it. In societies unable to manage profound depressions as primitive societies could, the accumulation of wealth in isolation led to disaster. And when they obstinately failed to realise this, in a framework and according to a code chosen by this accumulation, they would expose themselves to the eruption of these depressions in an uncontrollable and catastrophic way.

So Bataille stated in 1933 that it was false to take account only of production, and false for a society to find its only interest there. He showed that there exists as well, or that there should exist, a completely different sort of activity, of great importance even though neglected by classical economics, and this activity consists of spending, spending sumptuously, spending uselessly. What counts is not only what allows a society to satisfy its needs, but also how it exposes itself, intentionally and playfully, to exemplary shocks, profound depressions, sudden destructions and crises of anguish so intense they appear orgiastic. This was without the slightest doubt the strength of the Native American societies studied by Mauss and used as an example by Bataille: they knew they were mortal to the extent that, through a whole series of manifestations, they would bring into play the simulated spectacle of their death; two manifestations especially were among the most important of those Bataille wished to retain from the primitive world: sacrifice and the potlatch.

The dazzling 1933 analysis was not without a sequel.[1] Bataille did not write this short text and then lose interest in it: the text brought to an end an initial mature cycle that had begun, in all likelihood, five years earlier. It also began a second cycle which came to an aborted end with the book 'La Limite de l'utile', written from 1939 to 1942.[2] This second ending itself opened up a third cycle of reflection from 1944 to 1949, resulting in the publication of one of Bataille's most important books, *The Accursed Share* (in February 1949). This was not all. Bataille repeatedly and under different titles[3] envisaged continuing this work through two further volumes. And in fact, he wrote a second volume, *History of Eroticism* and a third, *Sovereignty*, neither of which was published during his lifetime. Even more: until the end of his life, Bataille dreamt of profoundly modifying – to the point of rewriting – the first volume, *The Accursed Share*.[4] These details are not simply academic. They bear witness to the extreme interest and importance Bataille attached during his whole life to critical reflection about sociology and the economy, in a way so essential and so central that one can without risk of error describe this reflection as political.

Moreover, Bataille himself announced the forthcoming publication of his work under this heading:

> For some years, being obliged on occasion to answer the question 'What are you working on?' I was embarrassed to say, 'A book of political economy.' Coming from me, this venture was disconcerting, at least to those who did not know me well. (The interest that is usually conferred on my books is of a literary sort and this was doubtless to be expected: one cannot as a matter of fact class them in a pre-defined genre.)[5]

It is necessary to avoid being carelessly reductive: 'political economy' should be understood to mean, as he made clear, 'general economy', in other words an economy in which expenditure is of more significance than production, where a sacrifice, the construction of a church and the gift of jewels are of more significance than the price of wheat. So important is the question of the economy – of a general economy – that Bataille situates it as being prior to psychology and philosophy, which could not be claimed to be independent of it, nor, without idealism, could art, literature and poetry. This entails a considerable recentring: the mystical Bataille of the war cannot retrospectively be considered as mystical except within a vaster preoccupation, an absol-

utely rational one. (This is unequivocally attested by the fact that
Bataille had written 'La Limite de l'utile', the first exploration of this
'general economy', *simultaneously* with *Inner Experience*, and simultaneously with *Guilty*.) This preoccupation could surprise only those
wanting to forget his intense sociological activity from 1931 to 1939
(in other words from *La Critique sociale* to the College of Sociology)
or who wanted to believe in a conversion as radical as it was sudden.
And in fact, this preoccupation is not simply subsidiary; on the
contrary, there is justification – Bataille himself invites this view – for
presenting it, among enigmas, as enigma itself:

> Indeed I surmounted problems whose novelty and dimensions exalted
> me. Having entered into unsuspected regions, I saw that which eyes
> had never seen. . . . In this maze, I could lose myself at will, give
> myself over to rapture, but I could also at will discern the paths,
> provide a precise passage for intellectual steps. . . . The possibility of
> uniting *at a precise point* two types of knowledge which up to now
> had either been foreign to one another or only roughly brought
> together, gave this ontology its unhoped-for consistency. . . . I felt a
> sensation of triumph: perhaps this was illegitimate, premature? . . . I
> don't believe so. I rapidly felt what was happening to me to be a
> burden. What frayed my nerves was to have accomplished my
> task. . . . Everything was giving way! I awakened before a new
> enigma, one I knew at once to be unsolvable.[6]

Bataille has thereby turned to account the solitude into which he was
thrown by the war, going as far as he could into the discovery of a
fresh enigma, of the ultimate enigma. If he thought he had for a
moment triumphantly resolved them all, including the greatest one
(what exhaustion at having completed such a task!), he almost immediately perceived that this was not the case, that in any case such could
not be the case (only God could do this if God existed). And it is
because this response slipped from him that he aborted the first draft
of *The Accursed Share* ('La Limite de l'utile'). For the same reason a
second draft was possible (*The Accursed Share*, Part One: *Consumption*) and this was successful. It was not that he had a response to the
enigma (this was doubtless the error of 'La Limite de l'utile'); the
enigma was experience itself. The search for the principles of a general
economy is not distinct from the search of *Inner Experience*. It is this
experience itself. The experience of its non-meaning (non-meaning
necessarily being the meaning of this enigma, a non-meaning more

opaque and decisive, but not the final one, a final one being impossible) must make up for it.

Naïve as this may seem, to start this search it had to be told like a children's tale: 'Once upon a time'. But this naïvety is a trick: Bataille had little sense of origins because he had none of ends. In his work there is no origin about which to be nostalgic, no earthly paradise prior to some fault or other. An origin would thus be an assumption, an assumption that there was a time when the world gave itself to mankind in a pure relation of immanence. Bataille expressed this in other terms: the world was then mankind's intimate. Intimate and immediate: excess, drunkenness and passion would have been the originary mode of humanity's existence in the world, which he defined dialectically: 'The world of *intimacy* is as antithetical to the *real* world as immoderation is to moderation, madness to reason, drunkenness to lucidity.'[7] Where everyone else would interpret the arrival in the world of moderation, reason and lucidity as the peace-bearing beginnings of humanity Bataille denounces the irremediable loss of the sacred. The intimate and immanent world was sacred. The mediate and transcendent world would be profane. The world was sacred until one day the enslaving process of work was discovered (one day and then every day down to the present day). With work mankind discovered ends. For work is an operation effected with a view to an end. And all ends are a calculation speculating on the benefits of the future, all ends break with the immediacy of intimate times, all ends *separate* humanity from itself, by promising it a surplus, separating man from his kin (each one ceasing to be immediate to others) and separating humanity from the world, suddenly reduced to usage, in other words to utility. By inventing work, mankind was inventing ends as well as time. Work is effective activity.[8] For a hypothetical benefit, it enslaves in three ways: by duty, time and completion. And it enslaves his kin: if the world became useful, if man himself became useful, how much more so could be the one in his place who would fulfil the necessary tasks. When humanity enslaved its kin, it did more than alienate itself in transcendence, it also ontologically separated itself from the idea it had of its being (Bataille suggests that primitive people would have evaluated that being in the *same* image as their kin would have been for them): the loss of sacredness would then have been total.

This is one more paradox that Bataille introduced here (it was, however, apparent in his analysis of heterology): the immanent world is free, intimate, immediate and sacred; the profane and transcendent world is servile, isolated and mediated. The paradox must be extended to this conclusion: the immanent world is certainly that of communication; the transcendent world is that which, alienating man in the sequence of *useful things*, prevents the sacred contagion of communication. There is nothing here that Bataille had not already said, nothing to which he would not be absolutely true. The transcendent world introduced death (the trembling anguish of death) at the same time that it introduced time and separation. And it also introduced, with the promised ends, the absurd idea of salvation: God, in this sense, is really on the side of transcendence, and is even at its extremity. God is the hypostasis of the profanity of the world. Work has possessed and possesses this historical and irreversible effect of having to introduce into the world a relation of mankind to itself that forces it to break with intimacy, immediacy, the depth of his desires and their untrammelled expression to subject itself to the anticipated result of its useful operations.

Only one thing, just one, breaks with this loss and restores mankind to intimacy: the potlatch (which can also be read under the name of *sacrifice*). Everything man has dominated in the profane world of transcendence, he restores in a single movement, by a sumptuary operation of the potlatch, in the sacred world of immanence. And thus lost communication is re-established. People are together only when they recognise themselves as being infinitely poor (it is the paradox of the potlatch that it enriches a glory that is all the greater for the wealth that is squandered) and mortal (it is the operation of sacrifice that everyone – sacrificers, sacrificed and audience – knows they are mortal, communicating in excess as they identify the blow falling on the victim with what they will themselves one day experience). Those primitive societies that understood this knew how to break *ritually* with the servitude of the transcendent world by periodic collapse into the world of blind consumption and sacrifice. From the origin of their being, primitives know how to offer themselves to the unsettling and collapsing spectacle of its loss. There was nothing that accumulation and capitalisation could really efface: the world remained given to mankind in a relation that was fertilely hostile.[9]

This relation has vanished with industrial societies.[10] And what Bataille earlier said through ethnology, he now states as an economist under the form of a double theorem: 'On the whole a society always produces more than is necessary for its survival; it has a surplus at its disposal. It is precisely the use it makes of this surplus that determines it',[11] and 'A population that cannot somehow develop the system of energy it constitutes, that cannot increase its volume (with the help of new techniques or of wars), must wastefully expend *all* the surplus it is bound to produce.'[12] Because they do not know or do not want to know (luxurious squandering is unjust and regarded as immoral) how to expose themselves to this ritual destruction, industrial societies nourish in their hearts this share that Bataille designates as *accursed* because the only thing left to swallow it up is war: 'between the horrors of war and the renunciation of one of the activities by which a society believes it must assure its future, society chooses war'.[13] Bataille said (but could he be understood in the aftermath of the war?) that it is overabundance at least as much as privation that lies at the root of the worst. And, according to a careful reading, the worst is, from the earliest times to the present day, the result of transcendence.

The challenge of such a book – and in that it is perhaps absolutely mad – a challenge perhaps no one had issued before, is to propose the elements of a generalised and, what is more, *non-Christian* economy. What follows would merit more extended discussion (it can be given only as brief indications of the perennial value of Bataille's thought from 1930 to 1950): all political thought of the two last centuries has, without really improving on it, made the Augustinian axiology of history its own. Even the substitutive ideologies of the nineteenth century – marxism, for example – were ostensibly eschatological. All nourished the hope of a conciliation, if only in a secularised (intra-worldly and no longer spiritual) form. In other terms, all its thoughts are similarly teleological, pursuing noble ends without doubting the capacity of history to attain them. Thus Christianity and what it taught – the march of history and its parousia, its latent sacrality, its promised eschatology – underlies the mythologies supposed to deny them. Far from denying them, the same type of ends survives, more strongly than ever ('bright new tomorrows', the classless society, the abolition of the state), in the same way that the accumulation of goods survives on the paradigm of morality, morality itself survives on the paradigm of the transcendentals of scholasticism. What Bataille tried to do (he spoke of a 'Copernican revolution') was to turn all this upside down (astonishingly, this reversal echoes what Bataille as a child promised he would become: 'convinced that one day, since such lucky insolence was sustaining me, it was I who was bound to turn the world upside down – turn the world, quite ineluctably, upside down'[14]). He chose immanence over transcendence, evil over good, the useless over the useful, disorder over order, contagion over immunisation, expenditure over capitalisation, the immediate over ends, the present over the future (and the instant over time), glory over power, impulse over calculation, madness over reason, limitless prodigality over subjection to parsimony, the subject over the object, being over salvation, communication over separation. Such is the challenge of a book so mad that in the end we do not know if it is a single and simple (but inspired) meditation on power, politics, growth, the economy or metaphysics. Undoubtedly it is all of these and, even more, this ungraspable abundance brings to mind the project Bataille nurtured his whole life to write a universal history. Though only a sketch of it, *The Accursed Share* is his one book that gives the best idea of what this might have been.

Bataille seems to have been conscious of the craziness of his project, for which he apologises, at the end, with a note: 'I am that madman', he says. In fact an economist who closes such a book in this way must be 'mad':

> It is a question of arriving at the moment when consciousness will cease to be a consciousness of *something*; in other words, of becoming conscious of the decisive meaning of an instant in which increase (the acquisition of *something*) will resolve into expenditure; and this will be precisely *self-consciousness*, that is, a consciousness that henceforth had *nothing as its object*.[15]

The empire of the double

What portrait can we sketch of Bataille as he approached fifty (his age in 1947)? One that differs little from those given in turn by Leiris, Piel, Klossowski and Rey, at least if we believe that made by François Perroux, who met him in 1948: 'From the first glance, I carried Bataille's face in my heart; where I keep the portraits of exalted seekers, of extremely violent individuals who pull us from the quicksand of the everyday and set us back on our right path.'[1] Rage and exaltation had thus not so perceptibly vanished from his face for the portrait given of it by a man meeting him for the first time to associate it with beauty, a beauty which the clearly moved Perroux calls 'terrifying'.

Yet one should also reckon with an imperceptible lightening of his personality (which would keep increasing). The 'debauched man' Bataille had been (and still was), the 'madman' and fanatic he had always claimed to be, the 'exuberant' individual François Perroux saw in him had paradoxically only ever been steady and patient; there is no trace of an 'excitable' beauty in Bataille. His speech, for example, had always been slow and circumspect, mindful of the minutiae of details. At most this might have become more pronounced over the years; he had a fine voice, as everyone said: its timbre – with a slight tremble – added to so individual a diction, did much to contribute to his patent seductiveness. Everyone said so, but none better than Maurice Blanchot: only Bataille, perhaps, ever truly *spoke*. This diction was not slow because of laziness (although it did reflect periods of apathy interspersed with sudden illuminations) or affectation, as though its slowness was designed for effect. It was slow because perhaps it alone was ever *seeking* while speaking. It is rare for people to speak without knowing what they are going to say, and rare for a phrase not to be already decided upon – and along with it the idea it bears – as soon as it is begun. Bataille on the contrary exposed himself, and exposed those listening, to the risk of a speech that discovered itself. This is how it offered itself, uncertain in its ending, often hesitant, sometimes stunning, accepting its weaknesses and calling upon the help of the right image or the memory that would support it, which would almost always be impossible to predict even for him. It sometimes happened that such a sentence would be totally in suspension within the meaning it hoped to find, and would itself have no ending. A gesture would then finish it off, or more precisely would leave it in suspense.[2] As Diane Bataille would later say, Bataille was never more brilliant than when talking, late at night . . . about God, most of all, for it seems that this was his most frequent subject, the constant preoccupation of his conversations.

As Maurice Blanchot also said, perhaps only Bataille had the same ability in speaking as in writing: 'This is the first gift given us by this true speech: that to speak is fortunate and that to speak is to seek fortune, that of a relationship that is immediately unmeasurable.'[3] This speech alone is serious because all trickery is banished from it, and in its place is play, played by two people, allowing the essence of the speech to reach a point equidistant from both, in which each accepts being played himself, a game in which forgetting and erasure are the rule – in other words, death:

> Scarcely was it spoken than it was washed away, lost for ever. It forgets itself. Forgetfulness speaks in the intimacy of this speech, not only the partial and limited forgetting but the profound forgetting on which all memory is founded. Whoever speaks is already forgotten. Whoever speaks returns himself to forgetting, in an almost premeditated way, I mean by tying the moment of reflection – of meditation, as George Bataille sometimes calls it – to this necessity for forgetting. Forgetting rules the game.[4]

But this speech was not serious through a wish for gravity or by a desire to be itself transcendent. All Bataille's friends remembered it as being the same regardless of his listener. He spoke no differently whether it was to Alexandre Kojève, for example, or to a customer in a café in Vézelay or Avallon.[5] Jean Piel recalled often having been impressed 'by the attention with which he was able to talk at length with the apparently humblest or least important people. He took an interest in their problems, inquired about their interests and the business of their daily lives as if they were matters of the utmost importance'.[6] Hélène Cadou confirmed this: 'I never saw someone so attentive to what those around him were going through.'[7] Bataille moreover did not fail to give this attitude its true meaning:

> I consider it essential to keep myself *at the height of mankind* . . . If I was not myself at the level of a worker, I would feel my supposed elevation as an impotence. I feel this in cafés, streets and public places . . . I judge physically the beings who gather around me: they cannot be below or above. I differ from a worker profoundly, but the feeling of immanence I have in speaking to him (if sympathy unites us) is the sign indicating my place in this world: that of the wave among waves.[8]

This manner of speech, which made no conscious effort to be distinguished or seductive (except to women, since Bataille was aware of its power over them), or to convince – Blanchot insisted that nothing was further from Bataille's intentions than Socratic speech, one that was resolved to teach others – was heard quite differently by others: its unctuous nature stopped them short. This unctuous quality (which is undeniable), coming from a man like Bataille, for anyone who knows his writings, could only be considered feigned, hypocritical, libertine or diabolical. It was moreover not just the unctuousness of his diction but also the clerical weightiness and solemnity of his manners that evoked the prelate, the bishop or the cardinal in Bataille. He made Jean-Jacques Pauvert, who knew him well after the war (having become his publisher), think either of an eighteenth-century cardinal, Cardinal de Bernis,[9] or of Borgia, 'not Pope Alexander, who was a scoundrel, but his brother, a man of culture'.[10] The friendly nickname given him by Alexandre Kojève sealed this once and for all when he called him 'Monseigneur'.[11]

Manuel Rainord hardly stressed this 'evil priest' aspect in Bataille any more forcefully: 'A pale brow, the fire in his eyes, a shady air', an evil priest or 'an anti-priest in the highest sense', he played on his powers (we are perhaps invited to see these as diabolical), on his presence, on his pace and his silences, the fire in his eyes and his shady air, so as to create and take pleasure in discomfort; to enjoy 'in secret the spectacle of the spectators' (Rainord is describing Bataille as a lecturer here).

As we can see, the portrait 'shifts'. For some he was exalted and violent; for others slow, patient and attentive; for others still, perverse, even diabolical . . . But it is still remarkable that no one mentions his deep, convulsive laugh. When Bataille laughed, it was his whole being that laughed, without restraint. It is also remarkable that no one mentions his apparent innocence (it was both apparent and real), a disarming, confounding innocence: a childish innocence. But this could still only be an approximate portrait if I did not say that as much as he laughed – a strong, ogre's laugh, that of a child – he also cried. His capacity to allow himself to be carried away by his emotions, the fact that he did not feel he had to control them, exposed him to every surprise, to every emotional shock.[12]

If there is just one thing that permits this long and contradictory portrait of Georges Bataille around 1950 (though it would not vary after this; or more accurately, it would keep 'shifting' in the same way) to emerge, it is in fact something remarkably analogous to the doubling that, after the war, he twice staged in the most exemplary, most significant and even most autobiographical way possible.[13]

As I have repeatedly suggested, not one of Bataille's stories fails to borrow more or less heavily from his own life. There is not one of them from which, if we knew all the details, we could not recover the traces. *Madame Edwarda*, a book that everything points to being imaginary (and ultimately it is) had one of those models Bataille was most dearly attached to. The question is not so much the principle of the outpouring of life into his works, as that of its measurability. I have said just as frequently that there is no justification for seeing Bataille's stories as other than fictitious, since there is nothing to show us exactly in what ways they are or are not.

In the same way, the two books Bataille wrote between 1945 and 1950, *The Impossible*[14] and *L'Abbé C.*, maintain a strangely close yet distant relationship with the life of the author, of which the only element that cannot be doubted is this doubling that struck all those who knew Bataille. In the first story the characters are brothers; in the second they are twins. In the first, one of them, Dianus, is a debauched man; in the second, Charles is too. In the first, the second brother is a prelate (sometimes called A., sometimes Monsignor Alpha); in the second he is a curate (an 'ercu' as Bataille writes, adding inversion to the doubling) called Robert. In the first story, the two brothers have first one, then a second mistress in common: B. and E.; just as in the second story, where she is now called Éponine. For two books written less than five years apart, this is more than enough to connect them.

The two debauched men have little to differentiate them; at most Dianus in *The Impossible* is perhaps more hesitant and anguished, and is more profoundly prey to the evil he is drawn to. He seeks out every possibility for desire to find its satisfaction. He is feverish, enfeebled, always on the brink of being reduced to zero by his excessive energy. (Perhaps he is also the closest to what Bataille was during the war.) As for Charles C. in *L'Abbé C.*, he is more resolved, closer to what is irresistibly attractive about the least pardonable deviations. There is beyond a doubt *a will to evil* in Charles C. that is absent in Dianus.

The two priests on the other hand are clearly distinct (so much so that they seem to have only their vows in common): Alpha is the soul of disquiet – a Jesuit – cold, cynical (at least this is how he first appears), and he maintains with the woman he shares with his brother the wish to make their desire at least as distant from them as the distance between them. He never questions the impossibility of desire (unlike Dianus), or that desire points to its satisfaction in the void of all satiation. Since he is a Jesuit, he is a philosopher, and since he is both, he is a libertine, not a debauched man (unlike a debauched man he has the acute lucidity of a miser torn from the disorders of the flesh). Robert C. (the curate of *L'Abbé C.* who gives the book its title) is just the opposite: he is first a coward and a fraud, unctuous and ceremonious. His desires terrify him. But he burns. If he has taken the cloth it is because he believes that only God can stem their excess.

For Dianus in *The Impossible* the world can be reduced to a woman he desires (even if he shares her) and to what he believes his possession of her will resolve. He sees the world as totally reducible to that which suffers her absence. He wants, not without bad faith (he will describe himself several times as an actor), to claim she is his whole world, bringing together death, debauchery, sex, love and solitude. Not without bad faith, since when he finally possesses her he realises this is not at all true; with her there, he is the one who is no longer able to flee. What still remains for him is debauchery – with another – and death. (*The Impossible* is the least 'literary' of Bataille's stories, and the one that takes furthest the close and untenable relationship between theory and fiction, reality and its representation. It is certainly one of the most strangely bewitching: it hides behind itself, its doubling is not just singular but multiple and reversible, ending in a spiral. It is certainly, moreover, one of the hardest to recount.)

The challenge for the curate Robert C. is quite different: it is to be

God himself. The 'summit' God has not allowed him to reach will be made possible by a woman, a 'slut', Éponine. She will have no rest until the abbot stops humiliating her by ignoring her (in preferring God). Her wishes are atrocious (since they are to *lose* them) and they are divine: she wants the abbot, she wants to take sexual pleasure in him. Her cold fury, her black determination are for him a God stronger than the one he hides behind (as he hides his instincts beneath his cassock), than the one in whom he has placed his hopes. Through Éponine's unleashed 'grace', the relationship between the two brothers, the debauched Charles and the priestly Robert, will become reversed. It is Charles who made himself the initiator of the curate's debauchery, and he who did so to take pleasure in the exasperated desire of Éponine, since his temperament echoed that of Éponine, and since they were both naturally cruel and both found in this cruelty an additional frenzy and agitation. But then a reversal takes place: Charles will show himself to be more mawkish than the abbot, less bent on extremes, less apt to confront fear, less able to take on the consequences of his most extreme actions: he will recoil. Only Éponine and the abbot will go right to the edge, driven by an equal desire to lose themselves. The abbot welcomes the chaos into which his desires throw him, in which he certainly, to say the least, denies his body, but worse still also the morality that had hitherto protected him from vice. No doubt he knew it to be only a façade, but from the day he knew he could no longer maintain the lie, he chose horror: 'I suffer for my crimes, but it is in order to enjoy them more profoundly'; 'I wanted to be this waif . . . For nothing in the world did I want to hide my memory from contempt.' No atonement must be possible, and no forgiveness. One must push abjection so far that even pardon can no longer reach it. One must deny morality violently enough to cause God himself, who created it, to become bereft of hope; with no hope of salvation. It is a question of nothing less than nullifying the sacrifice of the cross. In ignominy, it is a question of becoming the equal of this God whose son died to save mankind. The abbot, whose wish was to make the whole world see how he was the living example of such a redemptive act, will offer the example of a treacherous, abject death. (I said that for Robert it was a question of being God. In betrayal, he becomes God, for 'God betrays us! With a cruelty that is all the more resolute in view of the fact that we pray to him!'[15]).

This treacherous, abject death makes the following observation vital:

this story takes place during the war. The abbot has helped the Resistance; arrested by the enemy, he 'betrays' not his fellows in arms (he shows a fidelity towards them in no way reached by the torture he has to endure), but Éponine and his brother (his double),[16] those he had loved: 'I enjoyed betraying those I love.'[17]

This sexual pleasure and this betrayal caused an affront not, as one might have expected, to the Church (at least it never showed its displeasure), but to the editors of *Les Lettres françaises* who, and this is not the least disquieting thing about it, found a third 'brother' to add to the infernal twinning of Charles and Robert, one who 'actually existed'. Without being named, Bataille effectively found himself being accused of making himself an apologist for an 'informer' and of dishonouring his publishers:

> The patriots who knew him, who know how the problems of the Resistance are dealt with in this book, who remember how Éditions de Minuit came about and what it represented during those dark years, believe it is unacceptable for such a publishing house to publish a book like this and keep its good name.[18]

In a letter of 4 July 1950 to Georges Lambrichs, Bataille fully answers the accusations of having dealt with problems of the Resistance and being an apologist for treason; and he also denies having known of the existence of an abbot who could have been the basis for Robert C.: 'It is possible that a person existed who might have characteristics in common with the one the novel presents. But the author has never heard of any such person.'[19]

'Bataille's heroines are engaged in actions comparable to those told by certain lives of saints: their difference comes from the fact that their torments are not offered to God, and find no release in ecstatic visions. . . . These are a new kind of saint, who bring a chance for salvation to people obsessed by death.'[20] There had been Simone, Dirty, Edwarda and Marie. Éponine has now become a part of the legend of Bataille's saints. She has Simone's cruelty (*Story of the Eye*), but is less juvenile, more ferocious, more 'bestial'. It is one of the very great strengths of these characters that none of them resemble each other, but each one sets out the possibility of a new story: 'Éponine and I . . . had the vague power, at once both anguished and derisive, of evil'[21] (Éponine is the first heroine to *choose* evil). She wants evil in a fresh way, and she does so without it being possible to judge her on any moral grounds (though she is the first of Bataille's heroines to posit the problem of evil). Her passion for doing evil, in other words for acceding to the most capricious of her disorders, is no less demanding, rigorous or 'vigilant' than the passion of the saints to honour God with the good of their self-denial. If Éponine wishes to satisfy her desires, her divine caprice has no equal but the will of God to subject the world to a caprice that is no lesser nor any more justifiable. And Éponine's power to open people's eyes is considerable. She it is who reveals to Robert how hypocritical he is, how false his devotion is, and how the provocations of a determined 'slut' are enough to knock down the abject fraudulence of a false piety (she alone is the elevation of the host; her arse is the chalice before which the abbot, sincere at last, can bow).

L'Abbé C. ultimately reveals that it is the devotee who is seductive, the one who believes in good, the one who is so foolish that debauching him suits the aggravated caprice of Éponine. Nothing can essentially be taken from a debauched man, but for every virtuous and chaste man there is God. Only God can inflame sick desires: 'Even in our disarray we knew that, morally, we were monsters! There was nothing inside of us to control our passions: in heaven we were as black as the devil.'[22]

From Vézelay to Carpentras

It would be an error to see Bataille as a homogeneous man. Nothing would be less true to him than a single portrait, striving to mark out perennial features of the memory to be retained of him. No one was more complex or harder to define than he was. He was not the same integral man from his youth to his death, as unchanged by life as any one else. He was not successively several men, each corresponding to one or several detectable periods. He was one and the other, and all at once (we shall see how numerous his dualities were). Circumstances simply meant that certain features prevailed at one moment or another of his life – for example, those of the activity just before the war, those of his withdrawal and personal experience of the war – to the detriment of other features, before fresh circumstances caused their equilibrium to tilt again in another direction.

The war having ended, it makes no sense to look for a different Bataille, a Bataille who had not existed before, or who had been so different that what he was becoming no longer resembled him at all.

Even if only for a moment, *Actualité* already proved it. Bataille had only changed a little, if at all: at the very least, he revealed the same concern with political questions, and had the same will to continue in group format the reflections that had interested him since he had started to write.

What *Actualité* only briefly showed, *Critique* would establish at length: for the rest of his life he edited this journal which is still in existence fifty-five years after its creation.[1] From the war until his death he therefore had a platform at his disposal from which he could speak and write in the most complete freedom and from which he could, through his collaborators, expand as far as possible the directions in which his field of reflections led. In this, he appeared unchanged. But there are several reasons why he was not. Age is one: in 1947, Bataille was fifty. Although he was still as much of an 'enragé' as he had ever been, he was so now in a different way, in a way that was also less open. The way he defended Henry Miller in 1946 admittedly still displayed ardent commitment (it was not very different from his tone in 1930 in *Documents*), but this must not blind us to the fact that such a tone was now becoming rare. From then until his death, Bataille would burn with a more internal and better-directed rage. There could be several reasons for this suddenly acquired interiority. Not the least of these reasons is that the situation had obviously changed. As soon as the war ended, the incredible profusion, the incredible richness of the theoretical debate of the inter-war period gave way to a strange peace armed with ideas permeated with intimidation (who had the war not intimidated?) and no doubt with culpability (guilty or innocent, did not all thought from before the war appear to have a disproportionate lightness when measured against it?). Only shadows remained of surrealism and communism, both of which had in their different ways and sometimes together, represented the double aesthetic and political challenge of the commitment of young intellectuals from 1924 to 1939. Surrealism had the touching weight of the marvellous into which Breton entered; communism had the crushing weight of the person who first and foremost carried it beyond its promises: Stalin. (Communism was as powerful a challenge after the war as before it, but in a different way. Soviet communism, Stalinist communism had prevailed. The opposition communists, Trotskyists, Luxemburgists, Souvariniens and so on had more or less vanished.) Admittedly one could consider Bataille's thought as essentially distinct from these two challenges (and in fact, it could also be read, though not without distortion, independently of them); these two challenges were no less those *in relation* to which he had most often defined himself from the very moment there was a question of his public existence. The challenge had been surrealism, with *Documents* and Contre-Attaque (it would remain so, as we shall see, in a way that brought Bataille closer to Breton). The challenge had been communism with *La critique sociale*, *Masses* and Contre-Attaque (Contre-Attaque tried to make a single project of this double challenge). Whether negatively or in opposition – and it is negatively and in opposition to surrealism and communism that Bataille was most often placed – it is relative to all the challenges that he determined and elaborated his own (in the form of a sort of counter-challenge).

There can be no doubt that Bataille's thought before the war was, for the most part, that of a violent and ferocious negator. However, he retained from this thinking two axes he had evidently been almost alone in making his own at the time (that is, he made them his own in a complementary and heterodox way): one was given by Marcel Mauss, the other by Friedrich Nietzsche. We now know that Mauss was not responsible for Bataille discovering his taste for loss, expenditure and what at that time he conceptualised under the name of heterology. But the reading of Mauss (and conversations with Métraux) gave him a conceptual ethno-sociological apparatus upon which he was able to draw quite considerably from the time of his essay 'The Notion of Expenditure' until the College of Sociology. If there was one thing Bataille alone thought, and if there was something he had thought about that the war has not made obsolete (compared to his analysis of fascism[2]), it was the interpretative possibilities of sociology. This was what he returned to. Nietzsche is the second of these axes. Bataille undoubtedly had two intensely Nietzschean periods. The first corresponded with his loss of faith and his consent to the world. It could be said that if Bataille was all his life faithful to a morality, and to one alone, it was one that was drawn from his reading of Nietzsche. In 1923 Bataille decided to say *Yes* to the world. From that time on he neither said nor wrote anything which did not respond to this *Yes* and make it the yardstick by which he was committed to judge both experience and thought. Bataille nevertheless lived for a time in relative disaffection – sometimes affirmed – with Nietzsche. Not until 1936, in the aftermath of Contre-Attaque and the end of all historical hope in him (*hope* allows us to imagine on his part a messianism, which had never been the case; it would be better to say all historical engagement), did he make a new allegiance to the Nietzschean injunction with *Acéphale*. And he never denied this allegiance again. He never denied it, although its form would vary. Admittedly Nietzsche took Bataille from the religious experience of his youth, Nietzsche caused him to withdraw from the desire for confinement, making him discover the agitation of the world. But it was, paradoxically, also Nietzsche who, in 1939, plunged him back into a religious experience of a quite different type, and forced him to condemn agitation.

At the beginning of *Inner Experience*, Bataille makes a passing evaluation of the man he had been. What he sharply criticised about himself to Alexandre Kojève in 1937 ('an insignificance without appeal') he said in 1941 in already alleviated terms: the activity which had been his responded to the obscure, unconscious desire 'to be everything'. If *Inner Experience* has a motivation, it is not, as might be thought, to become *everything* but no longer to be it; this is even 'the acknowledged suffering of a detoxicated man'. The solemn and far-away exigencies of morality – of Kantian morality, for example – are of little significance and value, compared to what alone is true, and is true to the extent to which it rends apart: existence only has proximate limits. And it has such short limits because it is mortal. In comparison with this same and double truth, of this disheartening truth (almost enough to lead to impotence), the assurance in which he lived was shameful: 'For I see it now, it was to sleep'. Shameful for himself and shameful for those who had shared this unjustifiable 'sleep' with him and his era: 'the old preoccupations . . . have corrupted those who possessed them and cannot surpass them.'[3]

It is clear that Bataille here gives his reasons for his withdrawal (he said himself that he appeared 'singularly distant from the living world'). It is clear that he denied his past, that he could no longer see anything but vain agitation in it, an agitation all the more mediocre in being unconsciously attached to an absurd desire to be everything, in other words to an absurd desire for *salvation*. This is no doubt unreasonable. *Blue of Noon*, for example (to take only one case), is enough to put in doubt the fact that Bataille ever considered action to be more than an energy that was always on the point of being resumed, suspended, retracted, a wild energy, a fiery energy which had difficulty in reconciling the 'solemn requirements' of morality and the ridicule he was at any moment ready to heap on them. Nevertheless, the fact is that in the years preceding the war, action had prevailed in his life, a feverish and disordered action, and that it was brought to an end (like a disavowal) by solitude, his enigmatic withdrawal from the war.

Bataille would not remain in this entrenched position of remoteness from the world, of withdrawal. The war, which he had experienced as absent or faraway, had caught hold of him. Or more exactly, what caught hold of him when the war ended was its insupportable moral question. It was put to him forcefully, divested of solemnity (besides, what solemnity could be possible: the war was too much of an unbearable moral trick for it to be claimed otherwise). Bataille no longer wanted to be everything, which in simpler terms should be understood to mean that he was no longer committed. He no longer believed in the possibility of once and for all committing oneself, conforming to the idea of a totality assumed by commitment (I discuss what he meant by commitment shortly). On the other hand, he now tried to *think* everything. If there is one aspect which predominates in this period of his life, it is the determination he showed to examine and understand the world. In a certain way he was still the same man as the one who before the war was consumed with rage and took sides (which was where the extreme violence of his commitment came from). After the war this rage only slightly diminished (at most age gradually moderated it) but it was another man who spoke and wrote, a man dominated by his intellectual (and, as we shall see, sometimes moral) concern for understanding.[4]

Certainly not everything is so clearly delimited. It seems that in 1948 Bataille wanted to participate once more alongside David Rousset and Jean-Paul Sartre in the recently created Rassemblement démocratique révolutionnaire.[5] A little later it seems he wanted to play a mediating role between Camus and Sartre and to reconcile the two men at the time of publication of *The Rebel*. The dominant impression remains, however, of a paradoxical disengagement, due more to critical and interpretative intelligence than to political abstention. Bataille appeared to have finally regarded this rage as being irremediable, and said so later in his life, tragically. No mitigating political world could exist for him. At most war and servitude could be avoided: his rage towards them could certainly have lessened.[6] It would nevertheless not have vanished.

There were other, more simply biographical, reasons for this 'disengagement': from 1945 to his death Bataille lived outside Paris, first at Vézelay and then at Carpentras, finally at Orléans. It may certainly be thought that the debates around existentialism and *Les Temps modernes* did not interest him as those around surrealism and the 'different' oppositional communist groups had in the past. One could not however fail to observe that, if such had been his desire to join his voice with those of Sartre, Camus and Merleau-Ponty and take sides (as he had always done, for example in creating a new group) his distance would doubtless have prevented him from doing so.

In fact Bataille set up home in 1945 at Vézelay, in the same house in which he had lived in 1943, but this time with Diane Kotchoubey. In a certain way, a new life started for him. It was new in several ways. Henceforth his emotional life was stable: Diane Kotchoubey would share the rest of his life, as his companion until 1951 and then until his death as his wife (a stability which did not exclude consent to 'fortune' and 'caprice'). It was also new in that for the first time, except for the three last years of the war, Bataille found himself unemployed. He had not returned to the Bibliothèque Nationale after his health forced him to leave in 1943. Without employment, he was also without resources. For a while he thought about living from his books (this had never happened until then and never would); as a letter to his publisher in which he announced an idea for a novel – 'The Clothes of a Dead Priest' – seems to indicate. He was careful to insist on the commercial aspect of the project (more commercial at least than *A Story of Rats*, he made clear), 'putting it first in order to get out of my difficulties'.[7] The creation of the collection *Actualité* and of the journal *Critique*, both in 1946, could have justified the same hope. But *Actualité* only had the lifespan of a 'pamphlet', and for a long time *Critique* lost money and its successive publishers were only able to offer its editor a meagre renumeration.[8] This is the one thing everyone who knew Bataille never forgot about him: for his whole life he was short of money. Admittedly there is no doubt he was a spendthrift (it is inconceivable that the theoretician of the economy of consumption would be a miser), and the rare times he had money at his disposal, as happened in 1930 when he received the inheritance from his mother, he 'burned' it in a few months in nightclubs and brothels. He therefore lacked money not like someone who was resigned to not having any: he would still have been short, no matter how much he received. Whether or not he was in employment, he was always similarly in need. Jean-Jacques Pauvert recalled that 'money problems occupied a quite amazing place in his life. I knew a period when his friends helped him, or they knew they had to come to his aid. He was in a state of perpetual need. Everyone knew it and everyone helped him. Everyone around him knew that Georges was on the edge of mendicity.'[9]

Without any doubt money problems were never graver for Bataille than from 1945 to 1948 at Vézelay, so much graver on 1 December 1948 when Diane Kotchoubey gave birth to a little girl, Julie. What had until then been possible certainly wasn't any longer.[10] He found himself forced to resume work as a librarian. On 17 May 1949 he was appointed the librarian for the Inguimbertine library at Carpentras, where he remained until June 1951. There is no need to comment at length about his activity as a librarian. It is likely that he never had more than a distant, if not bored, concern for it, even if some people generously saw him as not only competent (there is no doubt about this) but conscientious too. It is true that he was especially careful to improve the collection (the Carpentras library, like that of Orléans, seems at the time to have been neglected), and to care for and evaluate the stock of ancient books. In the same way, he improved the access and the content of the two museums of Carpentras of which he was in charge at the same time as the municipal library. His interest stopped there, however. On the rare occasions Bataille spoke about his new position, it was to emphasise its obligatory aspect. Responding to several correspondents on 28 May 1950, he confided with resentment: 'I've been forced to become a librarian'; 'I have had to become a librarian.' If he hoped around 1945 to be able to devote himself exclusively to his books and to editing *Critique*, he bitterly realised how inane this hope had been. Bataille was only exceptionally able to devote himself to literature alone; and only then thanks to the unhappy circumstances of war and sickness.

It is, moreover, appropriate to say that the stay in Carpentras corresponded to one of the most difficult periods of Bataille's life. Neither he nor Diane Kotchoubey was ever happy there. This must have been due to its distance from Paris and his concomitant separation from his most loyal friends. Vézelay was not so far from the capital that his friends could not come to see him: Ambrosino, Fraenkel, Kojève, Leiris often or occasionally came. Bataille himself went to Paris whenever required by publication of *Critique* and for the lectures he gave during this time.[11] At Carpentras friends were rare: René Char, Pablo Picasso (with whom Bataille attended bullfights) and Claude Lefort. The first part of his stay also corresponded with a very long depression that seems to have spared neither Georges Bataille nor Diane Kotchoubey. Bataille was clearly alluding to it in the (already mentioned) series of letters dated 28 March 1950, which at the same time marked its end: 'I am sick all the time'; 'After months of depression'; and more gravely: 'I have always had such a lot of difficulty in writing, but now this has become even worse and has become for a time a real sickness. Following the demise of *Critique*, I have lost the energy which prevented me from letting myself go completely.'[12] Added to the difficulties of adapting to the town and to the distance from their Parisian friends was also (and no doubt this is one of the most serious reasons for his depression) the suspension of the publication of *Critique*, which Bataille was convinced was definitive and he thought it was finished. In fact, *Critique* ceased to be published by Éditions Calmann-Lévy in September 1949, having reached issue 40. It reappeared only in October 1950 with Éditions de Minuit. But between these two dates there were several months in which Bataille did not know whether Minuit would take *Critique* over[13] and was unable to make any efforts himself to find another publisher (Jean Piel seems to have taken it upon himself to do so).

With *Critique* suspended, Bataille also needed to reckon with the indifference, if not the hostility, with which *L'Abbé C.* was received, a book in which, if we are to believe what he said in a letter to Georges Lambrichs, he had placed clear if modest hopes: 'I won't be able to understand it if *L'Abbé C.* does not find a welcome, I mean a minimum welcome, given the place that my recent general books have received, in spite of everything, in contemporary literature'.[14] It seems that *L'Abbé C.* did not receive the minimum of welcome and, surprisingly, this amazed Bataille. He could have calculated the provocative effect of his book and should have expected this provocation to do it a disservice (he could even, if necessary, have enjoyed it); but his character was such, provocation was so natural to him, that he was only ever provocative in an innocent way, it is tempting to say in an ingenuous way. And, innocently and ingenuously, each time the effects of his provocations amazed him (an amazement which does not seem to have been feigned). Bataille's solitude from 1949 to 1951 was that of a man forced by necessity to return to his profession with regret, in a town he did not like, far from the friends with whom he had forged a sort of community *in fact*, and, what's more, cast out into an intellectual 'emptiness' which corresponded to the suspension of *Critique*. He asked his friend Julien Cain, the director of French libraries, for a transfer and, exchanging posts with his opposite number, was able to be named as head of Orléans library in the summer of 1951.[15]

Communal demands

The question of communism is elsewhere, it is intimate in
a different way.

A few years later, in 1957, Bataille finally relented and replied to
Marguerite Duras when she pressed him by repeated questions to
admit he was a communist, not by denying it but by saying that he
was not *even* a communist.[1] 'Not even' is a jarring reply: it does not
indicate a place outside communism (a critical or oppositional communism, perhaps Trotskyism, etc.); and less still a hostility to communism (in principle, an anti-communism). What it says is that if Bataille
was not *even* a communist then he certainly should have been, that the
communal demands Duras says are answered by communism could
certainly only be his *as well*, with the sole proviso that however
sovereign it might be or wish to be, communism demands hope and
responsibility. Now Bataille refused to place any kind of hope in the
world (and said so), and even more than this rejected the suggestion
that this hope should commit him to any responsibility at all in the
world: 'I don't have the vocation of those who feel responsible for
the world. Up to a certain point, on a political level, I lay claim to the
responsibility of the insane . . . I'm not that mad myself, but I take no
responsibility in the world, in any way whatsoever.'[2] Bataille was not
only turning his back on the demands communism might have represented, he was also refusing any demands committing him to any kind
of responsibility in the future, any commitment the world might
demand for him to *share* something. Should one suspect a disenchantment born with age (and the effects of a deeper erosion: Bataille was
only a communist on rare occasions, if he ever was really one at all;
his participation in *La Critique sociale*, like that in the Democratic
Communist Circle, among others, leave no doubt about this)? Should

one also perceive in it the cumulative effect of historical disappoint-ments brought about by communism (though Bataille still refrained from criticising communism; for example, he was more willing to do so than Sartre, but less so than Camus)? One would be justified rather in reading it as a double affirmation which is only apparently paradox-ical: an affirmation of the suspicion he always showed in the face of action and commitment (a suspicion, however, which hardened when the war ended); and the much less frequent affirmation that commu-nism belongs *elsewhere*, that it is, as he enigmatically put it, *intimate*.[3]

Such an affirmation of the intimacy of communism cuts right across what is generally thought of under the general heading of commitment and under the elective heading of communism. Commitment and communism are suddenly no longer that *step taken beyond* literature and thought that all of us should make in order to respond *to* communal demands (to that hope placed in the world) and to answer *for* that demand (just as we say one answers for a responsibility). Such a demand is clearly political and it is as such that Bataille could not make it his own, it is in this regard that he calls himself 'irresponsible'; in other words, he asks to be permitted the irresponsibility accorded to the insane.

The only demand Bataille had determined to respond to, the only one he considered sovereign enough to justify his response, is in the end fairly uncommon. This is not at all true in the sense that commu-nism understands it; it is true in the sense sought by the community which, as we have seen – whether a community of friends, of lovers, or of the conspirators of Acéphale – could only be limited and uncertain.

Commitment demands action; and Bataille only took a limited interest in action: 'the supreme value attributed to it seems to me highly debatable (whatever could be said about it after the event, action is in a sense only a necessity, of the same order as a bitter remedy or the payment of a debt).'[4]

Bataille was in no way denying that one must sometimes act: no more than anyone can a writer hide himself completely from the obligatory nature that commitment and action sometimes have. But the writer has to do so as little as possible in his capacity as a writer; for the incompatibility of literature and commitment, 'which is obligatory', is 'that of contraries': 'Committed people have never written anything which was not a lie, or went beyond commitment' (perhaps this text could be referring to Sartre, without naming him).[5] Action subordinates literature. It accords it aims, *useful* aims that are frankly incompatible with its sovereignty.

This incompatibility is notorious. It is irreducible, but to try to ignore it is to diminish it. Whoever ignores it harms literature without realising it (realising it all the less in that for some, commitment can become an overriding motive for literature; in extreme cases commitment can *justify* literature). Bataille says this with a rare disdain: 'what often falsifies this play is the concern of a weak writer to be useful.'[6] The anxiety some writers have to be useful (to respond to communal demands even in their work) alters literature – it *weakens it*. Bataille is close to saying that only those writers who have this *weakness* (the weakness of wanting literature to *serve* for something: a cause, goals) try to be useful and become committed. If he stops short of saying so, he nonetheless reaffirms that in contrast literature (true literature, he implies, the one that does not falsify its play) is only sovereign when, at the moment it makes the desire for usefulness its own, when it allows itself to take on goals, literature *subordinates* itself: action 'assumes interests opposed to those of literature'.[7]

Bataille stumbles on his own words. He could just as well have said that, because it is useful, because it can only be useful, because it strives only to be effective, action assumes *benefits* where literature does not; when it is obliged, on the contrary, not to assume any, for its obligations are owed to itself and not at all to what might constrain it. What are the consequences of literature failing to be totally *disinterested*? What are the consequences of literature being subordinate to utility? An alienated literature. This led him to formulate this principle in the form of a paradox: if there can be no doubt that a writer might have more than one set of obligations to be committed (to answer the communal demands), it is still on condition that he does so 'in the least literary way he can'.[8] In other words, if a writer gives his commitment 'the authority of his name', he must not forget that 'the spirit without which this name would have had no meaning' (a justificatory meaning, permitting commitment) cannot *follow* from this. It cannot do so because 'the spirit of literature is always, whether the writer wants it or not, on the side of squandering, of the absence of defined aims, of the passion which eats away with no other end than itself, with no other end than to eat away'.[9]

Wild collapse, the absence of a definite goal and of salvation, the passion that eats you away with no other aim than the passion it is itself to eat away, are what, without defining them, Bataille enigmatically calls communism's *elsewhere*, an elsewhere that in this instance it might be helpful to imagine in the form of what revolt always was for him in the face of revolution,[10] of the tension represented by revolt and which no revolution can release, an endless tension which for this reason alone is quite *intimate* and does not commit literature to anything at all because at that moment it is solely and unreservedly sovereign.

The angel and the beast, part 3

If it appears that, as opponents, André Breton and Georges Bataille each incarnated to the highest degree what today could be considered the major challenge of the inter-war period (an intellectual, aesthetic, ideological and political challenge), that they incarnated it to a devastating extent (the violence 'linking' them attained the heights of this challenge and this period), what they were is still not reducible simply to their opposition. For if their opposition was not completely effective, it was still harmful. The challenge and the period were effective for surrealism (although not *all* surrealism relates to Breton alone) and for opposition to it (although Bataille was not all alone in this opposition, even if his was the sharpest), *exhausting* the most important possibilities of this challenge. There is no other movement, no other person who so concentratedly played it (its irruption is of an unequalled prodigality). The harm would be that this opposition also weakened its two principal protagonists. It weakened them as such. It left them with no residue, no residue of what they had each been for themselves and for one another. No residue by which they would both be more or less than the roles they *played* and than what set their opposition in play.

The question was not only that the Unrivalled One (Breton; pejoratively, the Pope) by means of a clever play of ideological strategies (but no one could have denied that it was also through a powerful authority of incitement), could rally others to the detriment of the one left out of this movement (Bataille). Certainly, of the two, Bataille was more, and more often, alone. However, the second *Manifesto*, *Documents* and *A Corpse* (defections, realignments, expulsions) had caused Breton to fear that everyone would abandon him, and made Bataille hope that what Breton was unable to be, he might henceforth be in his place. He would do so for a 'restored' surrealism, one taken to the limits and 'made monstrous'.

The question at issue was just as much completely different: in fact, it is not enough to portray Bataille as secreting himself on the margins of surrealism, in a solely predatory posture, nourishing himself here and there on what it rejected (whether of a personal or an ideological character). On the contrary, Bataille was very precisely what surrealism was not (what Breton was not). This was not by default (everything it was not, for example, because he could not be what it was), but what he was not *precisely*. The logic into which Bataille had once and for all placed himself as regards Breton, feeding on the 'carrion' of surrealism, the logic by which, as he grasped it, if he had been able to do so, would have lured him away, is a logic of catastrophic collapse (a logic of the impossible). Breton, or part of him, believed in the marvellous (or was determined to believe in it). Bataille made it clear that such a belief was cowardly (it was cowardly to believe a certain point existed . . . ; this was to flee to the references espoused by surrealism: Sade, Lautréamont, the elusive revolution . . . or it meant that surrealism had got the better of its references), and to it he had, in advance and by provocation, to the point of impotence and the impossible, opposed the monstrous. 'The play of mankind and its own decay' is monstrous, thundered Bataille (philosophising with hammer blows), and the play is cowardly 'that continues in the most dejected conditions without having the courage to confront another'. Bataille would have liked a surrealism that responded to the idea he had formed of this decay (this *lowest point* that cannot be redressed or restored by any point, that would be idealised by any rectification and restoration). He would have liked it 'to the point of shame', he would have liked it with 'spume on the lips'.

With the war over, the two men no longer had the same relationship, nor the same words. A discreet but profound understanding took the place of the violence and invective that separated them. Doubtless this was not as great as has been claimed.

Admittedly, no further polemics emerged between them (except, but very briefly and no doubt without any comparison, on the subject of Camus). Equally, nothing again pitted them against one another with the sort of violence we have seen. On the contrary, from 1946–7, the idea of a collective myth once more preoccupied them both, and this time preoccupied them together. It so happens that, with the frightful cleansing of the war over, they were in agreement. They were in agreement at least in considering themselves reciprocally the most appropriate individuals to define its nature and possibilities. As Bataille said of Breton, 'Of all those who scan the horizon or the skies to decipher the signs of what is to come, there can be few who have subjected them to a more persistent interrogation and with a greater avidity for discovery than André Breton.'[1] And Breton of Bataille: 'In everything that has to do with the development of this myth, I think that Bataille, as much for the breadth of his knowledge and views as for the remarkably untamed nature of his aspirations, is qualified to play a central role.'[2]

Bataille would not play this central role. Nor, moreover, would Breton, who no doubt knew that surrealism's ability to give rise to a new myth had elapsed. This sudden as well as delayed understanding could well have been that of men who were no longer disposed to confrontation, or worse, who knew that further clashes were pointless. Neither had changed the world, nor even turned it from its foreseeable course. But this was not the handshake of gravediggers. Surrealism profoundly said *No* to the world and called upon a surreal to redeem it. Bataille no less profoundly said *Yes* to the world to the point of its frightfulness. History completely contradicted one and, tragically, justified the other.

If there is no doubt that after the war the two men came closer, it was still at the price of specifying that Bataille came closer to Breton rather than Breton coming closer to Bataille. It was less Breton, in fact, who made the effort to understand the world Bataille set darkly in train than Bataille who made the effort to understand what surrealism dreamed about. An effort to which Bataille returned with an insistence which resembles him – with tenacity. Bataille thought through what surrealism was, or what it had wanted to be, after the event, from as close a standpoint as possible for someone who had not joined it. This means that, whatever proximity to it he acknowledged, he did not do so without numerous reservations and elaborations.

It was finally possible for Bataille to say that he was no longer *teaching* (he rarely used this word and we should therefore pay attention to its importance here) externally to surrealism, an external maintained by polemical separation, but from *within*. He was inside not in the sense that he had finally joined it, but inside it as an *enemy*, its 'old enemy from within', as he put it in a kind of sudden tenderness as much as with irredentism:

I would appear a poor choice. Whenever the occasion has arisen, I have opposed surrealism. And I would now like to affirm it from within as the demand to which I have submitted and as the dissatisfaction I exemplify. But this much is clear: surrealism is defined by the possibility that I, its old enemy *from within*, can have of defining it conclusively.[3]

What seems to have allowed Bataille to speak of himself as 'inside' surrealism (no one after all invited him in) was that he understood it better than surrealism itself (in having submitted to its demand *and* to its disappointment). Admittedly, this is neither the time nor the place to debate surrealism (which would be to ascribe it a life no longer testified to by its works), but to speak of what surrealism would have been, and what it would have continued to be, if *its thought* had supported its demands.

Not only did Bataille positively not agree with Breton on the essential points that divided them, he also, displacing or renewing the challenge, praised surrealism and admired it only in order more effectively to deplore the fact that Breton defined and maintained it so poorly at the level of the *thought* that, without knowing it, he too represented. What surrealism was, in an inflamed and spectacular way, was only true at the price of the contempt in which it held itself: unaware that it survived the fever and the spectacle only on the condition that Breton held sway over it less through authority than through thought. Bataille said this on several occasions and clearly enough to allow us to discern in it the meaning of the strange 'entryism' he would henceforth make his strategy: 'It is unfortunate that the intellectual aptitude of the surrealists could not have been up to the same level as their undeniable power to undermine.'[4] Elsewhere Bataille said that, if Breton was capable of 'profound views' and 'ventured illuminations', he 'abhorred analysis', and did not feel 'the need to raise himself to a comprehensive view'. 'If he finally settles for the quietism of the captain of a sinking ship (something which does sometimes seem worthy of admiration), it is a quietism that remains *unaware* of the leaks which would awaken him to the sentiment of death.'[5]

Such a force of reversal, to whose height an intellectual incapacity (whether this was through tiredness or a facile satisfaction) had not allowed surrealism really to elevate itself, nevertheless had a power rocked by thought: it was a matter of nothing less than tearing mankind from itself. And Bataille formulated this in a phrase which describes surrealism (or what it should be) so much better in that, when it comes to this tearing apart, it disqualifies everything else: 'there is surrealism and nothing'.[6]

Two lures distanced him from it. One consisted in believing that surrealism could be exempt from entering 'into *the night*' (the night *Documents* might have been, for example) and entering into anguish (the seepages which would awaken one to the sentiment of death). In 1945, Bataille said that surrealism could still prevail, it could prevail by force of provocation as much as, if not more than, it had between the two wars, on the condition that it divested itself of all the weaknesses towards which it was inclined and on the condition that it no longer fled what alarmed it, on the condition that 'anguish colours it to the end'.

The other lure – although connected and not distinct from the first – was that surrealism should sacrifice without realising it the principle which ruled the attraction *its works* had over it from the beginning. Instead of following this facile path, as it had, surrealism should engage 'arduously' on the side of existence: 'Here only the slightest attention could be paid to the attraction of works; not that this was trivial, but what was then laid bare – the beauty and ugliness of which no longer mattered – was the essence of things, and it was here that the enquiry into existence in the night began.'[7]

The enquiry of existence in the night: no doubt there are few definitions of surrealism less 'surrealist' than this. And certainly it would be to add inconsistency to obstinacy to bring together Bataille and Breton to the point of claiming that what the latter said could in any way satisfy the former (neither Bataille nor Breton was so made that what had once opposed them so violently could suddenly vanish, even following the miseries of the war). Anguish, existence in the night, the awakening to the sentiment of death, and in the end silence are what Bataille, intentionally misunderstanding surrealism as it existed, enjoined it to be in order to raise itself to the heights of its principles. The silence, especially, to which surrealism did not know how to consent, to which moreover it could not make itself consent; instead of 'being quiet', 'they had to devote themselves to writing these texts and tracts that tear at the heart, which call so portentously for the silence that should have been safeguarded at all costs, but that *simply could not be.*'[8]

Such an impossibility is not only logical (what silence could a surrealism be without its works, its texts and tracts, even if they clutch at the heart); it relates to the principle of surrealism (at least, the one Bataille attributed to it, which is certainly untenable. Nevertheless it is the same as the one he said poetry should obey, the same, as we shall see, that painting should tend towards). Surrealism was 'dumbness' – or should have been: 'if it spoke it would cease to be what it wanted'.[9] Carried away by the attraction of works it could not be, this silence that surrealism, giving way to display, did not know how to be (but from dumbness to display there is an abyss), meant that surrealism did not respond to what, very strangely, Bataille said was 'the first demand it admitted: to form an impersonal authority'.[10]

Strangely: the word 'impersonal' has little in common with what Breton thought and said (it shows rather more the influence of Maurice Blanchot). Nevertheless it is not simply displaced or paradoxical: in fact, if Breton's error was to have been exaggeratedly authoritarian, if this authority that was not supported by any true thought and which he used 'with insufficient care and without real discretion' damaged surrealism as a movement (making it easy prey to every possible entropy), this authority was no less indispensable. Indeed, it alone sought to respond to, yet without being able to satisfy, the principles of surrealism: 'there was in Breton a desire for common consecration to a single sovereign truth, a hatred of all forms of concession regarding this truth of which he wanted his friends to be the expression, otherwise they would cease to be his friends, something with which I still agree.'[11] There was no authority powerful or immediately 'exceptional' enough to prevent pride and individualism from prevailing against any common consecration to some sovereign truth. The community Breton dreamed about (as did Bataille subsequently) was therefore impossible, was so in itself, if it had to reconcile 'the liberty essential to surrealism and the rigour without which it fades away and any way of life replaces the sovereign course it lays claim to'.[12]

No doubt there would have been no surrealism had the names who made it so brilliant not rallied to it, and there was no longer any surrealism because, instead of the movement absorbing them to the point of making it an *impersonal authority* its principle would call for, their works had distanced them from it, because they had drawn from it a share of the affirmation which had separated them from it.

This end is not, however, definitive.

Buried as surrealism was under the weight of its works (clearly Bataille opted for the principle over the works born from it), what he called enigmatically 'the great surrealism' could begin. This was so enigmatic that there is reason to wonder what it is. A new surrealism finally divested of its tediousness, its affectation, its escalation, its preciosity, its whining? Of course! A surrealism returned to its unadorned share in the rending apart of mankind from itself, to its will to fundamental insubordination? This too. But if this is what surrealism should be, what it would have been if ostentation had not reduced it and if anguish had finally elevated it to the 'enquiry into existence in the night', what would such a surrealism, even exalted and renewed, still owe to André Breton? Would he remain its founder (in the sense in which one understands for a religion) or would he have to share this foundation retrospectively with what Bataille wanted and said it should be? Or did Bataille dream of a history recommenced, admittedly shaped by surrealism, or at least what he assumed André Breton would have wanted of it and dreamed about from its origin, and of a 'Bataillism' that might be finally accepted by Breton, if by this meaningless word (that has as little meaning as the one formed from Nietzsche's name) it is possible to represent what *Documents*, Contre-Attaque and *Acéphale* (*Acéphale* especially, which best bore witness to what Bataille sought to designate by referring to an impersonal authority) were on the margins of triumphant surrealism, and to portray them – different as they had been and as violently as they opposed one another – finally as allies.

'I situate my efforts', Bataille once said, 'as a continuation, at the side of surrealism.'[13] At the side? This is merely what we have already seen. But its continuation? As if assuming that surrealism was completed? Completed at least under the form which meant that its works and authors had carried it off (including how they had prevailed *over* surrealism). There would no longer be anything to save such a surrealism, anything beholden to it, and Breton would be wrong to persist in it. Instead, everything calls for a 'great surrealism' to begin against the other one, and only Breton and Bataille himself would be in a position finally to constitute an 'impersonal authority'.

In 1929, *Documents* rallied surrealism's disappointed and dissidents. In 1930 (with *A Corpse*) Bataille, then an enemy from the outside, undertook to harm André Breton in the most violent way. Inversely, after the war, he undertook, against the surrealists and as an enemy from within, to save Breton and the dream he ascribed to him from a principle of surrealism that time, people and works seemed to have altered and then betrayed. André Breton (as though surrealism instead of being judged by what it had been should be so by what it wanted to be, as though surrealism, however great it had been, was less than the dream he made of it) was entitled to these words that Bataille all his life only used about a few people: 'There can be no doubt that during the past twenty or thirty years no one has shown more concern than André Breton to imbue even the smallest action with a meaning that engages the fate of mankind.'[14] This homage introduces an essay on *Arcane 17* of which Breton dedicated the copy he gave to Bataille as follows: 'For Georges Bataille, one of the few people in life who it has been worthwhile for me to take the trouble of getting to know.'

It was a kind of epitaph.

Continuity discontinued

The Vézelay years, as we shall call the four years spent in the Yonne from 1945 to 1949, strangely did not correspond to a period of intense 'literary' activity. Bataille wrote a lot, certainly, but mostly for *Critique* (as already noted, nearly 600 pages from 1946 to 1949). Strictly *literary* creation showed the effects of this considerable quantity of work. He wrote 'Histoire de rats' which, added to 'Orestie', enabled him to put together a volume – a varied one as so often – under the title of *La Haine de la poésie*. He did indeed publish a very short text in the spring of 1949 called *La Scissiparité*, but it should immediately be pointed out that, apart from this text being made up partly from notes drafted during the war in Samois, it also constitutes a kind of relic of a fuller text, a 'novel' whose publication had been announced by Gallimard in September 1945 as due in 1946. This book was to have been called 'Le costume d'un curé mort', and was ultimately never written.[1] This was not Bataille's only project to be announced by his publishers but abandoned. Two others, also to be published by Gallimard, were announced in a letter of 29 December 1948 as 'Maurice Blanchot et l'existentialisme' and 'Philosophie et religion surréalistes', but neither of them went beyond the project stage.

Rather stranger was the case of the book *Théorie de la religion* which, although written and within a few pages of completion, was announced by the publishers[2] for 1949 but was not published. It seems inconceivable that Bataille might have suddenly lost interest in it, as proved by the fact that at several points he considered integrating it into larger works. This hesitation and about-turn might be evidence of Bataille's lack of resolve; and might remind us, albeit distantly, of his description of himself as a young man: 'Almost every time, if I tried to write a book, fatigue would come before the end. I slowly became a stranger to the project which I had formulated.'[3] More definably, it is evidence of his recently developed determination to build various books into larger, coherent wholes. We have seen that on several occasions he wished to follow *The Accursed Share* with one or several sequels. Though this whole project never materialised, for Bataille it would always carry the virtual overall title, *La Part maudite*. The same happened when Gallimard suggested a re-edition of the major wartime books, *Inner Experience*, *Guilty* and *On Nietzsche*. Bataille chose a generic title for them that was significant in itself: *Somme athéologique*. In a letter to Raymond Queneau of 29 March 1950, he proposed the publication of three volumes under this overall title, bringing together in the first volume *L'Expérience intérieure*, *Méthode de méditation* and 'Études d'athéologie', in the second 'Le monde nietzschéen de Hiroshima', *Sur Nietzsche* and *Mémorandum*; and in the third *Le Coupable*, *L'Alleluiah* and 'Histoire d'une société secrète'.[4] It goes without saying that none of the planned series ever came to fruition. Bataille formulated several other projects which replaced them, which all included plans to publish new works (*Le pur bonheur*, *Le système inachevé du non-savoir*) that also never appeared.[5] The case of *Théorie de la religion* is no different. He considered integrating it either into *La Part maudite* or into *Somme athéologique*, and then hoped to create a distinct ensemble for this short book bringing together texts and lectures relating to the effects of 'non-knowledge', to be called 'Mourir de rire et rire de mourir'.[6]

These details are not simply a matter of form; they perceptibly alter what was at stake. Bataille went a long time before writing 'real' books (that is, books that might interest major publishers), and once he did start writing and publishing them he was dissatisfied by what they represented. They soon appeared, to the man who was nevertheless very fond of brief and digressive forms, as only making sense when communicating between themselves, brought together in communities, 'summoned together' somehow (this was true for the essays more than for the stories).

One should also not forget that all his life – or at least from 1934 until his death[7] – Bataille wished to undertake the writing of a 'Universal history'. Both *Théorie de la religion* and before it *La Part maudite*, and others subsequently (I shall return to these in due course), clearly and distinctly suggest this possibility at the same time as they only appear at worst as its outlines, and at best as its fragments. It is possible (though there is nothing to prove it) that from 1950 until his death Bataille wrote nothing that was not a preparation for this impossible work (longed for all the more for its impossibility); if this is so, it explains why he left so many projects unfinished although he had so much set his heart on them that he devoted most of his time to them. It also explains why some of his finest books from this period were not published while others – perhaps by default – of a no doubt lesser interest were (*Lascaux, Les Larmes d'Éros* and so on). In this case Bataille, like Nietzsche, would have been accumulating material for just one book, perhaps an *ideal* one in that it would bring them all together, because it would bring from each one something that in their separate publication only gave them a partial and provisional meaning. There would seem no doubt that Bataille dreamed, by analogy with the possibility of the community of men, of a theoretical *continuum*.

It is in no small measure paradoxical that Bataille's thought, from just after the war until his death, was impressive both for its power (his thinking was at its height; nothing he had hitherto patiently set in place was not taken up again, developed and taken to an extreme of intensity) and its powerlessness. It appeared to be a kind of retrospective fact that Bataille succeeded in writing just as long as he shaped his thought within the short format of the insight, the trenchant statement, the aphorism or the image: the articles for *La Critique sociale* were not substantially different from what Bataille thought after the war, but they appeared as brief, cutting shots – he himself would probably have talked of eruptions – that were more critical and negative than constructive, and that could themselves be perceived as parts of a larger whole (a revolutionary one) and a (private) experience that gave them their meaning. This abbreviated, interrupted form was itself the thought developing itself: a ruin. From the moment Bataille decided to elaborate or systematise,[8] he found himself trapped in the impossibility of thought that was inherently present in his desire to think the impossible. Whatever goal *Sovereignty* reached, for instance, this goal itself slipped away (it could not have been otherwise: this is the very meaning of the book), and with it the book itself. If throughout his life Bataille exposed the idea that anything might have any other end other than death it was not without impunity, since death itself would one day put an end to his books before they were finished.

Bataille's thought obeyed a process of self-destruction all the more pronounced for having appeared to push back the limits of the possibility of thinking through how death itself destroys all thought. In a double and paradoxical movement, he wanted to think through the annihilation of thought just as, at the moment he thought it, annihilation would sweep over it. In acting thus, he placed himself in the position of subjugation to an excess of force and to its total deficit. He was no doubt aware of this. On 8 and 9 May 1952, during lectures given in Paris under the title 'L'enseignement de la mort',[9] he made a kind of violent and resigned confession of this:

> I am speaking, in accordance with the title of my two lectures, on the teachings of death and, in fact, in my mind it is not a question only of the supposed teachings of death, but of the teaching of the death of thought. Rightly or wrongly ... I shall pass via a sort of dialectic from the first, a simple physical death, to the second, in which the first founders. In truth, thought also founders in the first, but in the second the thought which founders is finally shipwrecked, so to speak, within thought, in other words in the thought in which the awareness of foundering subsists.[10]

Bataille not only attempted to think through annihilation, which is already to think *the impossible*, he brought upon his thought the lasting effects of this annihilation. This comes down to saying that nothingness is not just the truth that brings thought *to an end*, it is its very condition, in the grip of and fleeing in the promise of its annihilation. This is both terrifying and 'mad' at the same time. The void of death in which, along with the body, thought will collapse, was thought through by him in a thought that had itself already collapsed. This collapse (this catastrophe) is thought's way of being, its paradoxical and impossible condition of possibility. It is all the more terrifying and all the more mad in that just as he had done all his life, Bataille (unbeknown to him, admittedly) tested the effects of this collapse on himself (in any case, even if he had not wished it his thought would sooner or later have 'collapsed'; in other words, as distinct from physical death, the death of thought – Nietzsche's collapse – would have occurred within a conscious awareness of its death). From 1954 until his death eight years later, he was able to measure tangibly the fatality of such a fall: from the day he fell ill (an illness that above all affects thought and the brain) until the day the illness laid him low. It was no longer as an abstract idea that Bataille was now fascinated by death. For nearly eight years this fascination had a perceptible, measurable object: his own death inflicted on him in the gradual effects of his decline. Horror could no longer be excluded from this fascination: it was its other face. It is both horrible and fascinating to be reduced to nothing: horrible because annihilation puts an end to desire, and fascinating because it is its excess. (This might be put another way to eliminate any doubt. Bataille's thought did not diminish for one instant, did not criticise, disparage or speak ill. Less still was it that of a man powerless to answer the overabundance of existence; Bataille adored existence, and if he answered the fascination death exercised over him, it was in the same impulse by which he answered that exercised over him by life: by an impulse of excess.) And everything makes us want to know the excessive limits of this desire: only fear – that avarice – holds us back:

> The movement carrying us along would require that we break down. But the object of aggravated desire, before us, reconnects us to the life desire exceeds. How comforting it is to remain in the aggravated desire, without going to the extreme, without taking that step. How comforting to remain for a long time before the object of this desire, to maintain ourselves in life within desire instead of dying by going to the extreme and giving way to excesses of violence and desire. One has to choose: either desire will consume us, or its object will cease to burn us.[11]

Death is not the tightening jaws of a vice (though desire is): it is their reopening. Dying is filthy: 'In the end, the fall into death is dirty', and dying is wonderful: 'We are not used to taking account of it as we think or speak but death will interrupt us. I will not always be able to pursue the enslaving search for the truth. Every question will finally remain unanswered.'

And every book will remain unfinished.

Non serviam

'*Non serviam* is, they say, the motto of the devil. In this
case literature is diabolical.'
　　'How can we linger over books to which their authors
have manifestly not been *driven*?'[1]

We are not all driven to write. This compulsive quality is indeed the
distinguishing feature of a writer. Yet this quality of compulsion may
not be sufficient to define literature. This principle that Bataille
advances in the preface to *Blue of Noon* and refuses to justify (he
deigned only to include some major examples of it), decisive as it is, is
undoubtedly exaggeratedly 'psychological' (not all books exhibit an
equal or flagrant guarantee of it). And because this constraint is initially
unquantifiable, Bataille paired it up with evaluations that are admittedly better known but hardly more verifiable.

Thus, if he rejected a work or its author (which on the whole was
fairly rare), it was in the name of a *truth* he considered was due to
literature and of which he would make an at least implicit principle of
the art of the novel, which he conceived as being able to survive itself.

The truth? In this respect, Giono lies; even *Le Hussard sur le toit* is
'imbued with falsehood'. If the indecency of his declaration in *La
Gerbe* of July 1940 is confusing, it is not only because it translates a
political attitude that Bataille described as 'at least disorderly', but
because it has the 'fleeting' aspect of fleeing the man he himself was
'crossing horror with all the fearlessness of the unconscious'.[2]

More often, with a feigned good nature, Bataille mingled his violent
opinions with insinuating praise which, far from attenuating the overall
effect, intensified it. Of Julien Benda, whom he disliked, whom he liked
so little that he said that one could without being mistaken see him as
'man elevated to the contented perfection of animals', he said that

instead of his conceit (his 'arrogant platitude') condemning him, it is a virtue – and this is 'absolutely endearing', he insists rather theatrically – in that it allows one to grasp 'an essential defect of the spirit that others dissimulate or correct'.[3]

It was no different with Gide, even though he admired *Le Journal*. After having written of *Thésée* that it had a 'dazzling execution' and as if to show that this praise, instead of convincing, is meant to denigrate, he adds: but 'perhaps he went further when he wrote the very insipid *Symphonie pastorale*'.[4] Instead of the praise, a praise too ironical not to be suspect, mitigating the violent judgement (as it did with Benda), with Gide it is irony that dilutes the praise. In the end, in both cases, the effect is to leave judgement suspended.

The judgement made by Bataille on the first book by Isidore Isou, *L'Agrégation d'un nom et d'un messie*, also remains suspended. Is the author of this 'often superb' tale, a genius, he asks. Everything would lead one to believe so, and the only thing this apparent genius lacked was simply talent. In the absence of making a decision (though not every book qualifies for a decision; many fall short of it), Bataille *plays* (with Isou's literature, with literature in general, and what is more with his own) by means of a magnificent sentence that is hard to imagine belonging to the 'critical' genre the title of the journal in which these lines were written would suggest: '*L'Agrégation* is a touching, frightful, stupid, bungled, ridiculous and inspired book that is as risible and as embarrassing as a bare backside.'[5]

Arthur Adamov (*L'Aveu*) provides the pretext for a clearly more incisive, surely more recognisable, contradiction. Appearances could make one expect Bataille to be close to Adamov. He could not fail to be close to someone who, he said, 'went so far along the paths of confession', who is 'humiliated to such a degree'. As close as he had never denied being to Dostoevsky, for example: to a shame which had wanted to be *infinite*.[6] Yet one thing (and this means everything) separates them. This will to shame is infinite only in appearance; in fact it is sentimental and idealist. Bataille is drily cutting: 'It is more than an error to speak of "the ancestral grandeur of the night of the flesh": it is a laziness of the spirit. However strange this may be, there is no laying bare in this confession.' If it is not a pretence, this shame is thus false because it is arranged so that it ends in the 'hideous materiality of this world'. It has the fleeting character of religiosity. *L'Aveu* harms the truth it claims to reach (that it claims to lay bare).[7]

There are some writers who did not tremble at or flee this materiality, hideous as it was (to flee, the word is the same whether used about
Giono or Adamov, who have nothing in common, however), who on
the contrary are enchanted by it (they seem to delight in it), and
Bataille felt he was close to them, in the *truth* to which, after the war
as before the war, he intimately paid homage. Before the war, this was
the case with Louis-Ferdinand Céline whose *Voyage au bout de la nuit*
he admired for the same reasons and with the same words that he did
not admire *L'Aveu*:

> the grandeur of *Voyage au bout de la nuit* consists in the fact that it
> makes no appeal to the demented feeling of pity the Christian
> sensibility linked to consciousness of misery: today, discovering this
> misery, without excepting its worst degradations – from filth to
> death, from stinginess to crime – no longer signifies the need to
> humiliate human beings before a superior power.[8]

To humiliate oneself is possible, but for the anguish of humiliation
alone. So that nothing transcendent should come to answer for it.
There is no possibility of being low, of being *infinitely* low, except in
the face of what is low, and this is so to the lowest degree. To humiliate
oneself sexually humiliates man only before himself. If he falls, it is not
towards any superior power that could not entirely be incarnated by
the prostitutes at whose feet his disgrace is humiliated.

After the war, this was so for Samuel Beckett. Beckett responded
without hedging to the truth and the endless laying bare to which
Bataille urged literature to respond. This truth is unbearable; unbearable is the one Beckett strives to approach. Unbearable is what literature must be; Beckett's in its way is unbearable. Bataille was among
the first to notice this, seeing it in his first book *Molloy* which, he said,
'is marvellously sordid' (which prolongs the definition Breton gave of
surrealism, although it mocks it). It is even precisely in making his own
what Adamov fled (at least in *L'Aveu*) that Beckett is important: 'what
Molloy exposes is not simply reality, it is reality in its pure state: the
poorest and most infallible reality, this fundamental reality which
proposes itself to us ceaselessly, but in which a dread ceaselessly repels
us . . . Molloy was *being* finally *run aground*, the enterprise that we all
are in a state of wreck.'[9]

The wreck is not just one more trope (a mask added to a hundred
others). It would be rather the effacement of all tropes. Nothing is

more profoundly indistinct, more profoundly anonymous than the *wreck*: the words 'vagabond', 'wretched' – which Molloy also is – betray it (overburden it). It is saying too much, and too clumsily. Bataille marks violently that *what* is there is 'the depths of existence', so utterly, so profoundly the depths of being, that 'we could not give a name' to it (nor should, we could add; it is *unnameable*, he anticipates) and 'is no less dumb than death' – it reaches the same degree of *silence*.

The movement, we have seen, which carries poetry *towards* silence (which must reach it yet without being able to dissolve itself in it), literature, is also obeyed in any literature which counts (which breaks: Beckett and, as we shall see, Blanchot). It obeys it without concealing its aporia: 'It may be that *literature* would already profoundly have the same meaning as silence, but it recoils before the final step that silence would be.'[10] Like the death that is this wreck (Molloy), even this 'step beyond', would remove it from humanity, which would prevent it from being this *absence* of humanity it represents, even the 'step beyond' would withdraw it from the very possibility of literature.

> silence [is] really the last thing language could suppress, and which it nevertheless cannot take for its object without a sort of crime.
>
> Crime against language first of all . . . crime also against silence itself. I do not know how the writer could better enter into the inextricable paths of scandal, how he could better elevate himself against the weight which rules the behaviour and judgements of all people.[11]

This object of literature designated by Bataille here and in these terms is analogous to the object in the form of a definition he gave to *experience*. As experience, literature is authority itself (it obeys only itself; from this comes its character of transgression and scandal); and as experience, it expiates itself (this silence is a crime).

The greatness of Maurice Blanchot ('one of the greatest [writers] of the century', Bataille makes clear) lies in the fact that, without fleeing, he has raised this crime to the highest rank – in other words, the most guilty. Blanchot knows that in wanting to support guilt, literature is dishonest.[12] Inevitably dishonest, and exhaustive (the effort that compels towards sustaining it is 'astounding and frightful'). But such dishonesty is literature's truth: Maurice Blanchot fails in the end (for he fails; he is a failure of literature just as Rimbaud was the failure of poetry) 'only at the limit of his strength'. The same is true of literature and experience: the limit alone has the strength (the authority) of the failure which justifies them (which, in this sense, is a triumph).[13]

The words are the same as Bataille employed on the subject of two 'shameful' and 'magnificent' novels: *Roberte, ce soir* by Pierre Klossowski and *The Story of O*.[14] So much the same that, no doubt, they define if not an 'art of the novel' ('I am often asked what a *novel* could be. Most of the time, the very question, no sooner asked, seems stupid to me: could I not continue to read, perhaps even write, *novels* without knowing exactly the meaning of the word'[15]), then at least its movement. A movement of constraint (how can we linger over books to which the author has not been driven?) and of annihilation: *Roberte, ce soir*, although nothing equals it, because nothing equals it, announces not the renewal but the impasse of literature. A literature which 'aspires to the silence of a horror which alone has the strength of understanding it'.[16]

A hypermorality:
for the love of anguish alone

'Killing is not the only way to regain sovereign life, but sovereignty is always linked to a denial of the sentiments that death controls.'[1] Here is yet another about-turn: Bataille was constructing a morality; or, following Nietzsche, trying to. Significantly, it was a morality he placed under the headings of the *summit* and the *decline*. Bataille had already turned metaphysics around (like a finger); now in turn he was turning morality around: evil belongs to the summit, and good to the decline (in the sense that social convention defines and uses the concepts of good and evil). For sovereign morality (which to avoid all misinterpretations Bataille called *hypermorality*), good would be evil and evil good. Evil was the summit, but it was a good; good was a decline, and it was evil. What pre-eminent, sovereign good is this evil which is proscribed in principle by morality? The superabundance of forces, prodigality, ruin, luxury, perversity, sexual release, vice and crime, tearing apart and ecstasy, extreme anguish and death ... And what evil, in that case, is the good that forms everyone's morality, but which Bataille labels with the term decline? Is this evil the cowardly, debilitating desire to endure? The desire most in opposition to all the anguished desires called forth by death, the furthest away. If this morality of the summit only had to obey a single commandment, it would be this: 'Hold nothing back!' This is a commandment in which we find what eroticism demands in the bringing together of the excessiveness of desires so as to mobilise its means to reach the summits of the moral world: 'What characterises sensuality is that it is diametrically opposed to morality. Morality is founded on concern for the future' (and Bataille says this with marked disdain, 'the desire to endure is inglorious') 'and sensuality is founded on indifference for the future'.[2] This heroic, torn 'morality' seeks the worst extremes: it is hell, a hell that bears 'the human questioning of its extreme rendings'. These are extreme rendings that vice and crime make accessible to distress (to extreme anguish) as well as to force; to the twin desires that force and distress mobilise so as to know, in their anguished excess, their limit. For such a summit has no goal; it is not itself a goal (it neither represents nor recognises any end). At most it might be a matter of seeking the summit for its own sake, in other words desiring it for 'the love of anguish alone'.[3]

Like ecstasy, the summit cannot be reduced to anything one might make one's own, to anything one might use (or make useful). Anyone claiming to have reached the summit (even to have momentarily brought himself up to that height) would topple back down in the process, in other words go into decline. In the same way, it is not reducible to anything one might say about it: 'To conclude I will express a principle: we speak of the summit only in misrepresenting it, placing it at the level of decline.'[4] Only the *impossible* might describe it without misrepresentation; an *impossible* definable on the model of the theology of the same name – by negation: all possibilities constitute decline in advance. This is the logic of such a morality of sovereign excess, of this hypermorality which at every moment is only ever totally satisfied by the pure instant of loss, the instant of death.[5]

Moral evil

Such a reversal, because it is full of possible consequences, forces us to signal its potential ambivalence. In no way did Bataille forget the morality of history (the morality of decline) to which the time of everyone was constrained to return. A hypermorality of a single person tendered towards the summits is sovereign; morality in which the declining time of history has constrained us all to enter is relative.

The question is thus once again that of evil. It is remarkable that Bataille had for so long avoided it. It is remarkable that, setting in play the forces he did, representing death as nonchalantly as he did, assuming, at least until the war, the worst scenario as often as he did, that he did so while avoiding the problematic of an *ordinarily* (one is tempted to say, simply) moral point of view.

And this singularity did not disappear all at once; it is not certain it ever completely disappeared. There can be little doubt that his books and essays, from *Story of the Eye* to *Acéphale*, dispensed with this problem without difficulty. Admittedly, *Somme athéologique* grasped it, but in a deceptive way: in fact Bataille was more interested in 'sin' at that time, and in doing so to turn its Catholic meaning upside down and provoke everyone's morality, an inferior morality or one of decline, by challenging it with a superior morality, of one from the *summit* (he remained Nietzschean in this). And the works of the postwar period (*L'Abbé C.*, *Gilles de Rais*), if they have the appearance of a reflection of a moral character (at least they appear to announce such a possibility), it is more at the level of the relation between evil – transgression – and eroticism rather than judgement. As for the three volumes of *The Accursed Share* (we shall see later how this affects *History of Eroticism* and *Sovereignty*), they once more turned morality on itself, returning to what for Bataille prevailed until the end of the war: the morality of the instant, intensity, squandering and sacrifice . . . So this conclusion

seems beyond question: Bataille would once and for all have chosen a
sovereign and Dionysian morality, a hypermorality.

There would be no doubt if not for an intriguing passage (maybe
even a confession):

> Not being more amoral than anyone else, even having in this way
> always submitted to the attraction of evil, I nevertheless early on had
> to recognise that the attraction of the good dominated me. Of all the
> ordeals through which I have passed, none was more difficult than
> this. All around me I heard nothing but condemnation. The words
> *disgusting, swine, filth*.[1]

Unfortunately we do not know to what (and whom) Bataille is alluding
or even if he is alluding to specific people. (He may have been thinking
of the surrealists at the time of the *Second Manifesto*. Some of Bataille's
hints may lead one to think this. However, he never implied such an
aggressive or insulting confrontation on their part.)

If the moral problematisation might thus not have taken place, one
should no less take account of the fact that Bataille could, for a long
time, have been ambivalently and contradictorily attracted by both
good and evil, not without our needing, despite appearances, to ascribe
to him a preference for the former (in spite of appearances, for this
passage, written later, corrects the impression he generally gave; in
recalling a passage like this for example: 'I allowed myself to be
murkily seduced everywhere – guillotines, sewers, prostitutes –
bewitched by degradation and evil'). The difficulty involved in understanding it is due to the fact that Bataille abstained, as often as the
occasion was presented to him, from pronouncing himself *morally* on
any particular fact (the events of 1934, the rise of fascism, for
example), from judging as a moralist; which is to say judging – in the
way the surrealists among others did – from the perspective of what
had to be and what must be. (But in the end, he said, in the name of
which principles?) The moral truth of surrealism was politically obvious. And the condemnation made by Breton, in the name of his friends,
against Bataille (whose terms we have seen) was on the whole not very
acceptable, however justified, since it did not derive from the sole good
in the name of which Bataille would perhaps have tolerated being
judged: an irreducible good (without doubt the condemnation of a
Catholic would have seemed more logical to him, although even the
principles justifying it would not have been his own).

According to him idealism consists in believing, since an irreducible good does not exist, that a relative good might exist. All judgement (all non-religious judgement) emanates from a world in which evil does not have the meaning of a judgement pronounced in the name of the good. Their double relativity annuls them in the same movement: only an irreducible, absolute, good would give a no less irreducible, no less absolute, meaning to evil.

What, in this case, could be the meaning that appeared to the frightful benefit of the war, of Auschwitz, that Bataille marked out as the radicality of evil ('the decisive, undisputed and irreducible sign of *evil*')? Is the question of a sovereign Good compelled to rest on this radicality, which in fact seems absolute? It is no longer the evil which would withdraw its character of inherent infinity from the infinity of the good, but the good which owed it to the irreducibility of evil to recover a lost irreducibility. And how would Bataille's fascination henceforth be distinguished from this radical evil? The irreducibility prevented him from speaking of it in terms of degrees: of a greater or lesser evil, of an evil beyond which it would be irreducible. Evil is either entirely irreducible or it does not exist. Just as good is entire or does not exist. Neither good nor evil now governs any morality that has the sacred character it once had: 'The poverty of morality is of having turned away, out of powerlessness, from this abysmal character of the *good*.'[2]

Bataille wanted to think evil, and thought it – so we must now assume – from a moral and no longer sovereign point of view. In fact he had a project for a specific book, a 'System of morals' (note the plural), the title of which would not have failed to introduce, from the first, a major provocation and a paradox: *The sanctity of evil* (a familiar provocation and paradox for anyone who had grown used to Bataille's inverted conceptualisations, but which here, for want of clarification, could disconcert). But clarifications are rare. In fact all one has to go on are some draft lines in which we are immediately returned to the paradox of the title: 'The good is the base, evil is the summit . . . In doing good, we contribute to evil . . . "inferior" morality disapproves of sovereignty (in its eyes it is evil), but in the eyes of anyone who wants sovereignty, it is the good . . . Who is free if not he who is sovereign? Liberty thus belongs to evil.'

Some of these passages, extracted from this outline plan, far from diminishing the paradox in fact make it denser. What is the good? 'To sacrifice for evil'. The good is 'the entire awakening of the being to evil'. Which, Bataille makes clear, 'does not at all mean doing evil', etc. There is nothing here that we have not seen already, nothing which differs from what Bataille had hitherto thought under the titles of sovereign morality, of 'superior' morality or of hyper-morality.

The only truly unambiguous passage bears witness to him maintaining an anti-idealist position:

> It is not that evil would be the contrary of justice: that would suppose precisely a light to which a shadow would remain a rebel, but the light one ceases to admit as a foundation, reason ceasing to be divine, remains an awakening not to reason, nor to the absence of reason, but to this most complete reason, the reason which is its own night for itself, the reason which, as reason, judges itself not to be unreasonable, but which is just as obscure as the absence of reason.[3]

If there is one thing that appears to make this quotation certain, it is that at the moment Bataille undertook to constitute a 'System of morals' he affirms that he intends to use none of the means (God, justice, reason . . .) upon which it was hitherto founded.

Some essays also bear witness to this concern to elaborate a system, but they do so in a way that is hardly any more explicit. Moreover, the point of departure is the same; in other words, it had the same character of an implicit autobiography (the same aspect of restrained confession): 'Those who, instead of being calmed by fear (hidden under the name of various "moral feelings"), give way, and can only give way, to the solicitation of "evil" are considered "sick".'[4] Evil has this superiority over the good that it attracts and solicits, which the good is powerless to do. And this solicitation is all the more irrepressible in that the good and 'moral feelings' no longer have an element of fear sufficient to reject it. Such feelings are besides moral in name alone. The *immoralist* that Bataille was (though he never says so) is justified in treating them with contempt; a contempt which he makes no secret of having for the pages in *The Plague* in which Camus was at that time building his own moral representation; contempt for these feelings which have only the appearance of the character of morality and which it would be better, as far as Bataille was concerned, to describe negatively as the irreducible effects of fear, *of the fear of misfortune*: 'Concern about misfortune is the generator of a whole hateful morality.'[5] It is a morality that, in this text, he calls a 'morality of misfortune'; as elsewhere a 'morality which curses'.[6]

Hating, cursing, this morality that has sustained fear *subordinates*. Sovereignty is inaccessible to it because the good is no longer unfathomable, is no longer sacred (although crime, incontestably, is).

Bataille always preferred to be sovereign rather than moral. Since there is a choice, and whatever attraction good exercised over him, for *his* part he chose sovereignty, yet without neglecting the fact that a division persists that obliges us to *make up our minds*:

> In a profound way, doubt remains on the subject of morality, and yet we cannot refuse to admit the importance of a decisive step, which opposes Good to Evil and gives people the alternative of one or the other. We can go further, defining a possible 'beyond Good and Evil': we could not for a moment forget that humanity still traces out the dividing line for us. Even the will to surpass prolongs if not the desire to find the Good, at least a concern for moral truth, which is within us an unsatisfied passion *par excellence*.[7]

This concern for moral truth is 'on this side' of the Nietzschean beyond Good and Evil.

This book, which there is little doubt was one of the most determining for Bataille (evil, he said, is the stumbling-block of all philosophy), was not written. The little that is known about it (which belongs to this project or which belongs to some related texts) allows us to understand it without difficulty: what philosophy could be possible which deprived itself of the means of philosophy? Thus the title would indicate ('The sanctity of evil'; but he seems also to have called this book 'The sovereignty of evil' or 'The divinity of evil') that he would have undertaken the exploration of evil as a mystic rather than as a philosopher; in other words, in the present case, more than as a moralist.

Instead of this book, Bataille went on to write another, *Literature and Evil*.[8] What was no doubt impossible for him to say as a philosopher he would say as a writer, as a writer fascinated by other writers, all of whom, in his eyes, and each in their own way, seemed before or *with* him to have chosen the infantile and cruel innocence of evil. With him? In fact, one might question whether he shared their choice. There is nothing to confirm that 'The sanctity of evil' would have resolutely taken this line, or in a way which would not have been paradoxical from cover to cover – as indeed the introduction to *Literature and Evil* is paradoxical, to the point where it is not possible to extract an unreserved judgement from it: 'I believe that the Evil – an acute form of Evil – which [literature] expresses, has a sovereign value for us. But this concept does not exclude morality: on the contrary, it demands a hypermorality.'[9]

This preamble is not surprising; at the very most it confirms that there does not seem to be anything that would allow the opposition between morality and hypermorality (in which Bataille seemingly imprudently placed himself) to be surmounted, just as it still does not seem that he could in any sense give way when it came to sovereign morality so as to give morality (everyone's morality) the place demanded by the declining time of history. However, he tried to do so in what followed, by means of a new notion, *value*:

> So what I call *value* differs where *Good* and pleasure are concerned. Sometimes the value coincides with Good, sometimes it does not. It sometimes coincides with Evil. The value is situated *beyond Good and Evil*, but in two opposed forms, one connected with the principle of Good, the other with that of Evil. The desire for Good limits the instinct which induces us to seek a value, whereas liberty towards Evil gives access to the excessive forms of value. Yet we cannot conclude from this that authentic value is on the side of Evil. The very principle of value wants us to go 'as far as possible'.[10]

For the first time and by the approximate means of this sort of median term constituted by value, Bataille distinguishes morality of a sovereign character (the free unleashing of passions of a man intimate with the world and provoking extreme intensity) from social and political morality. He does so in the continuation of the quotation I have just given. There is the *Good*, and morality responds to it as it does in turn to morality . . . and there is *value*, which could not be absolutely the same thing as *Evil*, even if they often resemble one another. Value is intensity, in other words at all moments of existence its 'furthest possible'. And 'in this respect the association with the principle of Good establishes "the furthest point" from the social body, beyond which constituted society cannot advance, while the association with the principle of Evil establishes the "farthest point" which individuals or minorities can temporarily reach. Nobody can go any "further".'[11]

What is true for the individual is not true for everyone, that is to say for an organised society, whose concern is to last. The liberty of one (or some) to provoke an extreme and awakening intensity is sovereign even if, in order to attain it, it entails slipping towards what universal morality designates as *Evil*. But the liberty of an organised society to expose itself to a similar slippage is limited, and must be limited, for it is no longer death (self-destruction) which discharges it, but power, extermination. The first slippage grasps a supplementary degree of intensity and trepidation in the interdiction it transgresses: it knows what the law is, and the Evil it reaches has the meaning it gives to it. The second slippage, that of everyone, no longer belongs to the order of transgression but to a new and exceptional law. Auschwitz is the 'decisive, undisputed and irreducible' sign of this law that became for a whole nation that of Evil, of radical Evil. There are really two moralities, two distinct moralities: individual horror has the sense of an unleashing of passion. What it seeks is not annihilation, but *awakening* to this annihilation; collective horror has the meaning of an unleashing of *power*. Clearly, without the slightest ambiguity, Bataille links radical Evil to power and, among other forms of the most effective power, to the state. Radical Evil enters history, ravages it, only from the moment 'bestiality' is placed in service of power, of a state's power:

> one cannot say exactly that evil lies in power (otherwise there would be evil in the tiger): evil lies in the fact that passion is rendered servile, is rendered in the service of a legal power. . . . Pure passion is naturally revolt, it never seeks legal power: it does not even generally have power, but destruction, as its end, since unrestrained expenditure rapidly destroys power.[12]

Bataille had expressed his own moral position (his hypermorality) long before. But if he had expressed or obeyed it earlier (this hypermorality is in fact sovereign, and it has the sovereign character of grace: it is given and cannot in any way be acquired), he had started to think about the conditions of the possibility of a collective morality – of a social morality, of a political morality – only recently: in the aftermath of the war, more precisely in the aftermath of Auschwitz and Hiroshima. The problem was thus immediately posed to him of distinguishing *his* liberty from the liberty of all, *his* passions from those which were unleashed (and could threaten to be so again). The problem became that what he was able to maintain on a hard and sovereign skyline (the play with evil and with death) should not serve as a pretext to those less scrupulous who might make a blind use of them without in any way exposing themselves to them. And this distinction now no longer suffered from any obscurity: morality is historical, hypermorality is *a*historical. The first belongs to time (to the time of the useful, the time of work, the time of decline); the second to the instant (to the intense instant, the individual instant, the instant of death).

In becoming historical, the moral question now became that of history's excess. Not without regret did Bataille remind himself that he belonged to a generation in which ideas proliferated: Dada, surrealism, communism, fascism . . . All were ideas of history (or they belonged to history). This would allow us to suppose, if their innocence should not be brought retrospectively into question, that history was still at that moment worthy of ideas (a period would need to be naïve or archaic if it left the erroneous impression that ideas could have *made* history). The war spared nothing of such a period: the juvenile 'innocence' of ideas was only apparent. In 1950, communism was extending the reign of mankind's 'reduction to being a thing'; and this is why humanity combats it 'to the death'. Fascism had extended the scope of humanity's reduction to the state of an animal. And the confrontation, in the aftermath of the war, of the Western (from which the reduction of mankind to the status of an animal had been born) and Soviet worlds (from which the reduction of mankind to a thing had been born) 'inexorably drives mankind to suicide'.

Whether history drives it to suicide, moral anguish is in effect what sustains its exaggeration. And, in posing the question of this anguish, he entered, in a more disorderly and more tumultuous way, the issues Camus was raising at the same moment. This may surprise us: it was with Camus, from Camus, in response to Camus – to whom he sometimes felt close, sometimes violently distant (as we have seen) – that Bataille tried to come to terms with the question of a historical morality. It may surprise us (what in fact does the author of *The Plague* have in common with that of *L'Abbé C.*?), but the fact is that Camus seemed to Bataille to be the only person determined to found a revolt *in morality* while not accepting a revolutionary solution. Bataille's position in respect of communism had not changed since 1933. He hated bourgeois liberalism no less (no less than Sartre, for example); nevertheless he would certainly no longer substitute com-

munist morality for the morality of Western democracies. The effort
Camus made to clarify the possibility of the distinctive historical moral
aspects of both is close to what Bataille was attempting at the same
time.

There was no doubt, at least for Bataille, that in the end this attempt
failed. If he was close to Camus, admittedly more so than he was to
Sartre and to *Les Temps modernes*, he was still not so close as to forget
the fundamental opposition which had already justified Simone Weil's
reservations in 1934 and underpinned their disagreements. If he did not
want revolution (and in 1950, the Soviet model of revolution dominated)
it was because it is reason, while revolt is passion. The calm – calm or
resigned – revolt of Camus is as far from his position as were reasons
to hope for revolution. Revolt is passion, and because it is passion it is
sovereign. Revolt is passionate, sovereign *and* moral, and nothing could
prevent Bataille from proclaiming it as the first and last of his principles
of insubordination: 'I cannot *submit to what is*, I cannot resolve to
serve an established order, the moral question is for me one of never
placing anything above a possibility without a firm limit, to which we
could – maliciously or honestly? – give the pejorative name of caprice.
Life and the world are nothing in my eyes if not caprice.'[13]

If Camus is certainly closer to Bataille than Bataille is to Sartre,
Bataille did not, however, fail to note that something in Camus's revolt
is not sovereign, but *depressed* (and therefore does not belong to the
summit but to the decline: where one sees that instead of establishing
his position in conformity to the morality Camus defined, he judged
Camus in the name of notions belonging to his 'hypermorality'). This
is enough in his eyes to compromise Camus's position to the hilt.
Without it having been said explicitly, it may be guessed that revolt
according to Camus would be nothing but the unfortunate impotence
of the dreamt-for revolution, whereas, for him, revolt holds in suspense
the possibility of a negation of the historical world, a negation and
disorder that a revolution, whether ideal or not, will put an end to:

> The only way for me to respond was by striving to be a communist.
> But, in spite of a certain obstinacy, I have never managed to do so. I
> never succeeded in hating our bourgeois civilisation more, and never
> have I been able to free myself of a scepticism which said to me: the
> idea of a revolution is intoxicating, but what happens afterwards?
> The world will remake itself and remedy what oppresses us today to
> take some other form tomorrow.[14]

The only attitude which maintains revolt in suspense to something other than its results demands a platform above history. In the face of history, which has determined our perdition, in the face of it and within it (thought is 'entirely enclosed' in it), we should be 'strong enough – especially lucid enough – to take it upon ourselves to oppose it with a refusal, against history, in a word we could *revolt*'.[15] It is not against some or other government and some or other of its laws that we are justified in wanting revolution (for a just government, for legitimate laws), it is against all governments and against all the laws that govern reason (there are only illegitimate governments and laws) that passion prescribes revolt. It is not a particular form of history (bourgeois, communist or otherwise) which justifies us in not submitting, it is with history itself as a principle that morality (all morality) hastens us to have done: 'How can we not immediately see, in history itself, an evil greater than oppression.' Strangely, by way of Camus, Bataille gets closer *in fine* to his two positions, morality and hypermorality, and to turn the revolt against the oppressive and *baneful* time of history into the echo of its passing to a sovereign instant of non-history.

The sovereign individual

> I am at the heart of the immensity, the greatest, the exuberance. The universe could do without me. My strength, my impudence flow from this superfluous character.

Of all of Bataille's essays, *Sovereignty* is perhaps the strangest, perhaps the most 'mad'. Its object, as its title might unambiguously suggest, might be for humanity finally to be accorded free and limitless sovereignty. There is nothing really surprising about this; this object and this challenge are Nietzschean, so much so that from 'The Notion of Expenditure' to *The Accursed Share* (Volume 1, *Consumption*) Bataille had analysed their development from archaic man through to industrial society. If modern people were able to rediscover those archaic traits they still possess (from which they have one by one been alienated by their hopes), they would be sovereign: 'We can now recognise that man is himself and that he *alone* is the sovereign value of man, but this means above all that man was the real content of the sovereign values of the past. There was nothing in God or in the magnificence of the kings that was not first in man.'[1] The challenge that might consist of reappropriating humanity from what false or deferred sovereignties have usurped would thus be effectively Nietzschean. Sovereign man would be the one before the invention of God (archaic man) or after the announcement of his death (modern man): sole master of himself and with sole responsibility for himself.

This would be its theme and its challenge if reconciling humanity and God were enough; but humanity must also be freed from whatever justified the invention of God. *The Accursed Share* explained that in inventing work, humanity invented time, and by so doing also invented the most insane promises for itself. *Sovereignty* adds to this message the fact that among these promises, of all the possible promises mankind made to itself, God is the most senseless in claiming to answer them all. In inventing the anguished and comforting anticipation of time, humanity invented the anguished anticipation of death. (Death ends time, cutting expectation off from the supposed fruits of the future.) In the same movement, it needed to invent ways of consolation for death itself: how to mitigate this heartrending break. Death itself needed to have the meaning that expectation has; better still, it has to become all possible meanings of expectation, and their apotheosis. Far from death destroying the expectation, far from it making it heartrending, God gave it the transcendent meaning in which all possible and consoling expectations might find their reward; henceforth death *justified* the expectation (since death had become God).

In wishing to reconcile mankind and God, Bataille tried to reconcile it with time. Or, more precisely, instead of attempting to find the means to reconcile mankind – with God or with time – he devoted himself to a terrifying fascinated meditation on the *moment* in which all time of expectation is reduced to nothing, on the instant of death: 'May we not say of death that in it, in a sense, we discover the negative analogue of a miracle.'[2] This is an insane, shattering truth: the instant 'where expectation dissolves into NOTHING', in which we are cast outside expectation, out of the enslaving expectation of ends, is miraculous. What binds mankind to something other than itself is that very thing binding the present moment to its supposed outcome.[3] Immoderate spending, prodigious wasting of riches and sacrifice all had this ritual and social character of reconciliation with transcendence; but better than them all, individual death has this character to the highest degree, to a tragic degree. So cowardly is the future, so enslaving, and so false are its promises, that infinitely preferable is not only the instant (the dense, joyful, excessive instant) but even the tragic instant, the miraculous character of the tragic instant, that 'impossible yet existent' nature whose sovereign meaning is that of *Nothing* (if anyone can know what *Nothing* is; only the tragic instant holds the key to its meaning as impossible[4]) raised up like a *Yes* that is 'awful, yet, in spite of ourselves, marvellous',[5] in the face of all the *maybes* miserably trafficked by tomorrow. This *'impossible coming true, in the reign of the moment'*[6] demands, requires death.

*

For death destroys; it alone reduces things to *Nothing*.

It is the loss of the sacred meaning of the instant (be it happy or tragic) that has sustained the foolish illusion that what is no longer nevertheless *exists*, whatever its form, shadow, double or soul, that the being one *has*, the being one *is*, will endure. First it was claimed that the future would justify the 'happy end' of anticipation; gradually we came to be horrified by the death which reduces being to nothing, and the anticipation in which being by its nature exists, so reducing death to nothing by promising existence the overcoming of that which seemed to negate it.

Death revolts us. Everything in us condemns it. Everything in us asks only that we deny it, that we believe it to be nothing but a passage, better still an accession to fulfilled being, to *more than being*. Everything leads us to believe that death, far from destroying being, reinvests it, lifts it up to itself, and completes (satisfies) its expectation. Death is no longer just being's destiny, it is its assumption, its miracle. Expectation, however uncertain the satisfaction it was promised, leads to plenitude; it is *justified*.

'From the very beginning, as a result of an immense confusion in which the consciousness of death takes hold, men have placed the beyond at a safe and distant remove from this undefinable menace, but their effort is futile.'[7] It is not only futile, it is anguished. The sovereign individual who exists only in the instant, who is not separated from himself by promising himself reconciliatory ends, does not imagine death; or at least not the anguished interruption of death, and the anguished destruction of its expectation. Only someone subjected to expectation really dies (and has the anguished awareness of dying), for 'in the perspective in which he constantly strives to attain himself, possible death is always there, and death prevents man from attaining himself'.[8] The reconciling image of death, its religious representation, may not be enough to appease the anguish born of the time into which humanity has languished (or fallen). Nothing can in fact prevent death, even a religious one, from being 'a negation brought into operation in the world of practice: the principle of that world is submerged in death like a city in a tidal wave. It is the world of the thing, of the tool, the world of identity in time and of the operation that disposes of future time.'[9] The world built up around the function of work, and the presupposition of its benefits in a world that is threatened every day, is a world daily threatened with dissolution by death and its real or imagined effects. It is the meaning of limits, of laws and interdiction, to try and avert these effects. And the sacred meaning presented to the sovereignty of modern man is their transgression. Just as death negates them, murder transgresses them and promotes the sovereign subject into an intimate, immediate, miraculous world: 'sovereignty is essentially a refusal to accept the limits that the fear of death would have us respect in order to ensure, in a general way, the laboriously peaceful life of individuals'.[10] Of course murder is not the only thing that can give humanity back its sovereignty. But murder replies *supremely* to the fear of death that commands interdictions, by transgressing them; not only murder, but 'sovereignty is always linked to the denial of the sentiments that death controls'.[11]

Such a sovereignty is elective, naturally. It is, like grace, *given*. There is no way of acquiring it. Whoever has it cannot have it taken away. Whoever does not have it can never attain it. How could it be otherwise? A sovereignty one could acquire would be reducible to the category of useful works. Bataille is a Jansenist in this too: merit is to be awarded to labour, and sovereign grace to fortune, caprice or miracle.[12] And this character of grace, like its instantaneous nature, completely distinguishes the sovereignty of history – this was the first time Bataille put this so clearly. Was he afraid of being misunderstood? It would make absolutely no sense, but all the same he clarified it to distinguish sovereignty clearly from communism: 'Of course, sovereignty ... cannot be given as the goal of history. I even maintain the contrary: that if history has some goal, sovereignty cannot be that goal, and further, that sovereignty could not have anything to do with that goal.'[13] Sovereignty is nothing to do with goals but is also nothing to do with history itself. As in *The Accursed Share* but in a more distinct way, elements can be seen appearing in *Sovereignty* which could serve as a basis for the formulation of a 'Universal history'. It is not the least of Bataille's paradoxes that all his life he cherished the project of a global interpretation of history even while, for whoever declares himself as sovereign, it is the non-existence of history that is called forth by sovereignty.

The catechism of 'saints'

Was it because Bataille foresaw that *My Mother* would be the last of his narratives, or did he think he needed to give a model, an initiatrice to his heroines from Simone to Éponine? Whatever the case, Hélène, the last of the saints he created, would be a sort of archetype of all those who preceded her, not because she resembles them exactly, but because she collects together so many secrets about herself and her reasons to act as she does that, step by step, she has a little of those of all Bataille's other heroines.

To find a genealogy for this final story, one would need to look not in the narratives which preceded it but in one of the books of *La Somme athéologique*, *Alleluia*. As an initiator, Hélène (the *mother*) gives men an erotic catechism just as Dianus, through a woman, does for women. *Alleluia* prescribed in a catechistic canon what a woman needs to do to be a saint. *My Mother* teaches men what they need to be in order to understand the sanctity a woman can attain and what mystics they must be to join her. (But reaching sanctity is not at issue for them; there are no holy men in Bataille's books. At most it is a question of raising them to the level of an unbearable feminine sanctity.)

Pierre, the narrator, is a young man and is pious. As far as he is concerned, his mother is the most worthy of mothers, and his father is a debauchee. When his father dies, suddenly, his mother reveals what she really is: a bitch 'I do not want your love unless you know I am repulsive, and love me even as you know it.'[1] This filthy woman wants to be loved by a son who is not afraid to know her and who, knowing her, could still know her to be pure: 'I like my filth. Today I'll end up being sick, I have had too much to drink, I'd feel better if I threw up. Even if I did my worst in front of you I'd still be pure in your eyes.'[2]

It is not enough for this woman that her son knows. Her cruelty requires him to make himself the equal of such knowledge. In order to equal her it is necessary for him to set out on the discovery of what is ignominiously pure in debasing himself to the utmost state of bestiality. Thus will she initiate him. First, in leaving obscene photos within his reach, though his hands are usually joined in prayer (it should not be forgotten: this initiation enlightens a pious young man). As he pauses, trembling, Pierre is unsure whether these show his own mother and father:

> Interwoven joy and terror strangled me within. I strangled and I gasped with pleasure. The more these pictures terrified me, the more intense was my excitement at the sight of them . . . my joy was all the greater since, with regard to life, I had long since entrenched myself in an attitude of suffering, and now, in the throes of delight, I progressed even further into vileness and degradation. I sensed that I was damned, I defiled, I defiled myself before the filth in which my father – and perhaps my mother too – had wallowed. It well became the swine I was going to turn into, born of the coupling of the boar and the sow.[3]

What this woman cannot do, her friend (Réa, 'the craziest girl in the world') will do to her son – *My Mother* is not a novel about incest or, if it is, this is only incidental, only a plus. The meaning that it was appropriate to give to this indirect initiation is indicated to the future lovers: 'Are you beginning to see? my mother went on. Pleasure only starts once the worm has got into the fruit, to become delightful happiness must be tainted with poison.'[4] For it is not happiness that should be sought in debauchery, not even pleasure: it is a filthy bonding together in evil and terrors; it is necessary to go to the point of no longer being able to respond to one's desires; one should not be able to recoil before any of them, they should all be welcomed and push abjection as far as can be imagined; so far that it is no longer possible to recoil, so that death alone would be its filthy conclusion: 'Pierre, you will soon find out what unsatisfied passion is; it's the treadmill, you begin with whorehouse frolics, then it's drinking and lies, then it's going deeper and deeper, death without end.'[5] The ends of the orgy are not satiety. Eating is not debauchery, even eating excessively, except to the point of indigestion. An orgy would only really find meaning if it has no future. Only death would remain at the level of such spending; only death would have this character of an abandoned release: 'Her idea was to involve Hansi in an orgy so thoroughgoing that death alone could terminate it.'[6] Such sexual pleasure has no equal except death, which in the constantly Christian language of this book (Christian by provocation, an ambiguous and fascinated provocation) may also be called God: the only alternatives to debauchery are death and extreme piety. Is this an alternative or the end? Réa eventually becomes a Carmelite; Hélène – the mother – kills herself. Just as, exhausted and sick, Charlotte, Pierre's last mistress, dies (she wanted to die in a brothel. Bataille seems to have fluctuated between the brothel and the convent all his life). '[God?] Undeniably my ideas are of another world (or of the end of the world: sometimes I think that death is the only possible outcome of the filthy debauch, especially of the filthiest.)'[7] Pierre will say this having in his turn reached the extremity his mother wanted him to reach: the only place at which it is possible to leap into the void.

Hansi, who replaces Réa (who has gone to Cairo with Hélène, where she intended to become a white slave), will give Pierre love, sexual pleasure and happiness, none of the things his mother destined him for. She will try even to cure him of his sick inclinations: 'the happiness she cherished . . . she would never have sought it, as the depraved do, in unhappiness.'[8] The pages devoted to the relationship between Pierre and Hansi are the only pages Bataille devoted to love in which happiness is present. But Pierre, like his mother ('I hate even the word happiness'), finally condemns it. To happiness, he would prefer disaster, collapse and the leap into the void of his mother's return: 'I loved only on this shattering condition of taking as love what was only the shattering of my love, and as a desirable object what was only the satisfied desire for misfortune.'[9]

'What madmen say about God pales beside the cry this shattering truth wrests from me.'[10] *My Mother* is the cry of a voluntarily exhausted and debauched woman – tired of herself but avid in this lassitude, disgusted that she can no longer be saved (there is one thing stronger than God's pardon, as *L'Abbé C.* also said, there is what is unforgivable for God), bound to her unquenchable thirst to have done with what separated her from the woods into which she would go as a child, as an *animal*, to seek the most tremulous intimacy. This cry is the one her son emits in his turn when his mother's truth, once she is dead, has become his own: he *knew*, as Edwarda had earlier known;

as Robert C. finally knew. Bataillean narratives have a truth, an enraged truth: the truth of a void about which there is nothing to know.[11] But which, in equal measure to what one does not know about it, must violently and *in vain* be defied: '[My mother] had the right to conduct herself as she did, I could conceive of nobody of greater energy, of greater forcefulness: she was audacity itself and conscious of the abyss she was defying.'[12]

My Mother remained uncompleted.[13] However, he wrote a brief story that provided a continuation of it: *Charlotte d'Ingerville.* (Bataille wanted *Madame Edwarda*, *My Mother* and *Charlotte d'Ingerville* to form a compendium brought together under the title *Divinus Deus*. In fact only *Madame Edwarda* was published in his lifetime.) Charlotte d'Ingerville is Hélène's niece, and has her unbridled debauchery (it is, moreover, her aunt who 'initiated' her). She is called 'rotten bottom'. But unlike Hélène she is pious and meditates devoutly for hours under the Cross, not to repent but because she is herself an angel as much as a 'bitch on heat'.

Pierre, with his mother dead, appears to hesitate between her and a return to the God she forced him to abandon. In the end he will choose to be true to what she taught him: is she not herself God, in any event? This is what Charlotte reveals to him, completing Hélène's teaching: 'when I see God, it is under the form of the passion which consumed itself in the heart of your mother, and that nothing could satisfy. It is under this form that I love him and am ready to die for him'.[14] Besides, she will die and thus Pierre will experience, happy and afraid, a second descent into the underworld: 'I am terrified, but I know that she was overjoyed finally to be what she wanted to be, an abhorrence.'[15]

An abhorrence and a saint: that saint about whom Bataille wrote a short narrative (which in the *Œuvres complètes* is included as an appendix to the compendium entitled *Divinus Deus* under the title of its principal character, 'Sainte'). 'Sainte' has no right to any other name but this name for someone anonymous and absent. She is a girl (in a 'massage' house in the rue Poissonnière) and used to be religious: she loves God and likes a 'spree'. Through her silence, her absence (she is an Edwarda who has abandoned gaiety and ardour) and her over-whelming sadness, she is perhaps the most tormenting of Bataille's heroines. Her body, 'rather like those fragments of verses that twist in an interminable and inert thrill',[16] in the vacillation and rage it inspires (it seduces and frightens), this body is no longer that of a whore, if it is even that of a living woman: 'I no longer saw her, my hands were still, as though a horror within was gnawing away at me, I no longer opened up except to the night and to suffering.'[17] They drank to be sick, to vomit (yet without being able to), especially so as not to know, on awakening next day, whether they had 'tangled'. It is the last of Bataille's erotic narratives: and for the first time he takes the story so far as to want the sick embrace to sink into unconsciousness. This is nausea taken a stage further, to the ultimate nausea and unconsciousness beyond which no further stories are possible.[18]

In writing *My Mother, Charlotte d'Ingerville* and *Sainte* in Orléans in 1954–5, Bataille returned for the last time to the narrative form, something that reminds us that he wrote very little 'literature' in total. *Story of the Eye* dated from 1927 as a continuation of *W.-C.*, which had been destroyed, and it seems unlikely that it took Bataille more than a few months, at most a year, to write either of these books. *Blue of Noon* was written seven years later, in the early months of 1935. Between the two, nothing! It would be another six years before he wrote his third story, *Madame Edwarda*, immediately, it is true, followed by *The Dead Man* and *Le Petit* (in so far as these books can be considered stories). In 1945–6, *The Impossible* followed (published first as *Haine de la poésie*, but in the meantime there had been 'Julie' and 'La maison brûlée'); then he only wrote *L'Abbé C.*, in 1949 and *Divinus Deus* six years later. In thirty years, this is not very much, particularly as only *L'Abbé C.* and *My Mother* are full-length novels, while the others are marked by their brevity; not very much also because, especially because, only six of these titles were published while Bataille was alive (*Story of the Eye, Madame Edwarda, Le Petit, Blue of Noon, The Impossible* and *L'Abbé C.*) and only three, the last three, under his own name rather than clandestinely (the three others, as we have seen, were published privately under pseudonyms). There is evidently a curse at work in Bataille's stories; there is also a curse on his very literature.

The servitude of utility

On 16 January 1951, in Nantua in the Ain, eight years after they met and two years after the birth of their daughter Julie, Georges Bataille married Diane Kotchoubey. The difficulties Georges and Diane experienced all the time they were together in coping with administrative requirements made the preparations for this marriage awkward. The difficulty they both had in satisfying the formalities necessary for the civil ceremony meant that one of their close friends from their time in Vézelay, André Costa, sub-prefect of the Ain, had to come and guarantee the validity of this union to the mayor of Nantua. For all Bataille's training as a Chartist, he was throughout his life powerless to fulfil administrative requirements: not only were they alien to him, they also caused him great anguish.

Bataille gave the following indirect explanation of the significance marriage had for him – one of compromise between interdiction and transgression:

> Without the intimate understanding between two bodies that only grows with time conjunction is furtive and superficial, unorganised, practically animal and far too quick, and often the expected pleasure fails to come. A taste for constant change is certainly neurotic, and certainly can only lead to frustration after frustration. Habit, on the other hand, is able to deepen the experiences that impatience scorns ... Habit itself owes something to the higher pitch of excitement dependent on disorder and rule-breaking. We can ask whether the deep love kept alive in marriage would be possible without the contagion of illicit love, the only kind able to give love a greater force than that of law.[1]

In the summer of 1951, Georges Bataille arrived in Orléans with the woman who had become Mme Diane Bataille several months before they left Carpentras.[2] Testimony of this move to Orléans has been given by the person who would become Bataille's closest collaborator at the municipal library, Hélène Cadou, wife of the poet René-Guy Cadou who died in 1951. Their meeting, as she described it, took place under the symptomatic sign of a major 'absurdity' (we have seen how, whether talking to Kojève or someone he'd met in a café, Bataille never varied the extreme gravity of tone that, according to the circumstances, the subject matter or his listener, could appear 'absurd'):

> A little hunched, as though the weight of his head took precedence over his bearing, smoothing the air with his prelate's hands, a stranger was holding forth at the end of the room with the duty staff. He was talking about nuts and bolts, nails and screws and patiently, in minute detail, in a liturgical voice, was cataloguing, itemizing, listing like an entomologist bent on seeing the lowliest of systems conform to a universal order, however absurd this might be.

Hélène Cadou deduced from this unexpected ordering in a waiting room, with an equal seriousness that later delighted everyone: 'If he was, as he seemed to me to be, an ironmonger, it was an ironmonger of genius.'

Georges Bataille, appointed director of Orléans library, was the 'devil' come to town, at least for those who had read his work.[3] He was all the more the 'devil' in that, if he did not bring trouble, he arrived when trouble was at its height: the mayor of this bourgeois town (it is hard to imagine a town more solidly hostile to the excess of passion) had just been murdered by his wife the day after his appointment to a ministerial post.

Bataille found 'peace' in Orléans (if the word makes sense in his case). During the few years he had left before illness overtook him he felt at ease there, thanks to the proximity of Paris, frequent stays in the capital, visits from many friends, and the comfort and beauty of his surroundings (Bataille had never lived in such a big – 400 square metres[4] – or elegant flat): a former bishop's palace attached to the library itself, with a fine garden overlooking the cathedral apse. One would have needed to go to Orléans, and see the place Bataille had moved to, then and for the final ten years of his life, to judge the level of his self-effacement: the long years spent in the ground-floor study looking out onto the garden, the anonymity of a curator doing the rounds between the rows of desks in the reading room (they made him think of butchers' stalls[5]), the long and arduous (and ultimately unpublished) development of the basis of *La Part maudite* (volumes 2 and 3); and imagine that here he might have found something of the withdrawal and seclusion he had aspired to in his youth.

'Under the appearance of a Sage', as Michel Leiris put it, nothing perceptible remained of whatever used to set him aflame. Of the extreme disturbance of the years from 1925 to 1945, nothing was now apparent. He had become a man alone, imprisoned by the need to work ('I think', Hélène Cadou said, 'that in those days he knew how, or he strove, to place his taste for gratuitousness in the service of the needs that bound him. His obsession with detail took on the value of ritual. He established a game at the very heart of obligation') and, in a paradoxical way, sovereignly absent from the obligation forced upon him to combine the most violent trepidation (the descent into the 'depths of worlds') with the slavery of the real world: 'Then his outburst of laughter would open up the "depths of worlds". He came back from this strangeness with a sort of wise gentleness, and the nature of his concern was as though made up of all those black rays that had stolen him away from reality for a moment.'[6]

For Bataille, certainly, no 'peace' was possible. In Orléans several of his most weighty, difficult – and 'scandalous' – books were written. But at least the appearance, the resemblance of peace were attainable: a settled life. The Orléans years settled a tumultuous life, shot through with lightning, that had led to disaster as often as possible, that had not just thought through anguish and evil, but had allowed their attainment, to the point of suffocation; a disordered, free life devoted to 'fortune' and 'caprice', as others are to career or profit. Bataille had been a 'gambler'. He had gambled all his life, and in Orléans he was not so much someone who had forgotten what his games were (*his game*, for ultimately it was all the same game), but someone who could look back and weigh up its anguished excess. But this does not mean that the time had come for him to learn the lessons of the past. Nothing could be less like him than to sum up experience, and turn this summing up into a knowledge. Growing old and with impending illness, Bataille took up new challenges, and devoted himself to new experiences, new anguished excesses. They only differed from those he had lived until then in now being his and his alone, accessible to no one else. Bataille had 'played' with death, had provoked it more than once, had on numerous occasions instigated it, even if only to inflame eroticism further . . . Now he would live out death, live it for its own

sake and upon himself; in the same way that the slow, patient work of
the executioner of the Chinese torture victim had fascinated him (and
still did), so he would be fascinated by the slow, patient work of death
on him. There is no doubt that the texts in which the tragic and
conscious dimension of death is most present date from this period:
History of Eroticism, *Sovereignty*, and several lectures. In Orléans
Bataille did not become the philosopher that age and solitude might
finally have entitled him to be; he was the same mystic as from 1941
to 1944, the same but with the one proviso of being 'blacker' still,
blacker because he was colder. In those days he had pictured death in
fever and exultation (there was the war, and there had been Laure's
death); it was in anticipation, in the patient anticipation of the sovereign moment of self-effacement, that he would henceforth live. Death
is the beginning and the end. From his work table turned to face the
windows, he wrote as he thought through *actual* death like a coming
of spring in the garden. 'The sovereign world doubtless has an odour
of death, but this is for the subordinated individual; for the sovereign
individual, it is the practical world which has a bad smell; if he does
not sense death, he senses anguish, in which the crowd sweats anguish
faced with shadows, death subsists there in a suppressed state, but it
fills it.'[7]

The accursed body

For a long time an ambiguity has weighed upon Bataille's work. Since his work, as everyone agrees, is one of the most scandalous there is, it contributed to reducing sexual interdictions. This might lead us to assume that Bataille would have applauded the sexual liberation that emerged soon after his death (it had started even earlier). It might even be thought that he would have seen it as the fulfilment of his yearning.

This is certainly not so. Bataille's eroticism is black; it is ill-omened and accursed. This is so in a manner that time and a shift in what is acceptable could in no way remedy; essentially and irredeemably, nothing would ever cure what it is born from (as eroticism and not as sexuality), nothing could do so because it draws its dark and wounding character of bedazzlement from death. His narratives all describe the atrocious and 'holy' fever of bodies debauching themselves only because they are promised to death. They all speak of the fact that there is no reason for loving their ignominious trade – thrown against one another – but the absence of God: their separation is thus absolute (the absoluteness of the separation of bodies is all that remains of the absent absoluteness of God).

When Bataille says: 'our sexual activity finally rivets us to the distressing image of death', or, on the contrary, in the same sentence: 'and the knowledge of death deepens the abyss of eroticism',[1] he places death and eroticism in a double and reversible yet anguished relationship: death exalts eroticism and eroticism renders death desirable.

This is confirmed in that, during his lifetime, Bataille, the first person to affirm desire and eroticism as antecedent to religious, moral and social corruption, was subject to the rather absurd scorn of people thirty years younger than him. On 12 February 1957, in the course of a lecture he gave under the title 'Eroticism and the Fascination of Death',[2] those who expected the speaker to say that eroticism is free and happy were bewildered to hear him gravely assert that, on the contrary, it is, essentially and by its very nature, accursed, accursed to a terrifying degree; and that this curse makes the sexual embrace rending and desirable (to the point of decay); that eroticism is in all times contained within the narrow limits of religion and morality because it is accursed; that these limits had and will always have the meaning humanity needs to give its fear of death, and for this reason it is pointless and impossible to seek to abolish them; that whoever wants to be sovereignly – but alone – free to transgress them must seek the dark, frightful and infernal pleasure of this curse and this fear.

At the time Bataille must have felt he was at risk of not being properly understood[3] (in 1957 people began to present him, in a hasty or calculated way, as a theorist of eroticism and a reader of Sade); he wanted to avoid the beatifying interpretation of the new eroticists: 'I must first make plain the futility of the common contention that sexual taboos are nothing but prejudice, and it is high time we were rid of them.'[4] He addressed this in more detail when *Haine de la poésie* was republished in 1961 under the new title of *The Impossible*. What he said was not due to age or sickness, and he did not at all disavow the book published fifteen years earlier. It is exactly what he would have said then if he had realised that the book would disturb not only puritans but also those who reject morality (it is necessary to quote it at some length so that all misunderstanding is cleared up):

> I am no doubt also clearer about stressing the sexual disorder which marks the two first parts of this edition. However, I have no intention of praising this disorder here. On the contrary. In my view, sexual disorder is accursed. In this respect and in spite of appearances, I am opposed to the tendency which seems today to be sweeping it away. I am not among those who see the neglect of sexual interdictions as a solution. I even think that human potential depends on these interdictions: we could not imagine this potential without these interdictions . . . Moreover, I do not believe this book could exert an influence towards an unliveable sexual liberty. On the contrary: what emerges from it is unbreathable about sexual madness.[5]

What is frightful is death. The disorder is that of death. And it is death which makes the disorders of desire possible. To applaud them, to wish for them, worse, to believe a solution to them is possible, is the response of fools and idealists (again!). There is no healthy flesh, because there is no flesh which is not separated and mortal. The gulf into which the flesh falls, tearing itself upon that of another, is the same as the one into which it will fall in the end: decay is the sense of this fall of and into the flesh. This leads Bataille to speak of his disgust for nature, something of which he had until then spoken little, a disgust which in one respect could be surprising coming from someone long considered a Chthonian: 'as if decay finally summed up this world from which we emerge and into which we return, so that shame – and repugnance – is linked both to death and to birth.'⁶ Nature disgusts as a woman's animality does, it is a 'horror' that its beauty makes 'bearable and fascinating at the same time', of which its 'obscenity itself is nothing but natural animality'.⁷ This confession is among the most naked Bataille ever made. (Admittedly it did not essentially differ from those Edwarda or Marie in *The Dead Man* implicitly made: it only appears more brutal because it is freed from the emotion that accompanies it in these two stories. In a certain way, this emotion would change its meaning.) It was all the more naked in that he insisted on it, as though moved by a sudden complacency to speak of himself, of what terrified and fascinated him, of terror more than fascination;⁸ the flesh is tortured, and it is death which tortures it. But the most terrible and troubling thing is not the torture, but that it is *enjoyed*; that the flesh takes delight in what has made it accursed, its mud, its atrocious origin; and it is its atrocious end:

> There is horror in being: this horror is the repugnant animality whose presence I discover at the very point where the totality of being takes form. But the horror I experience does not repel me, the disgust I feel does not nauseate me. . . . I may, on the contrary, *thirst for it*; far from escaping, I may resolutely quench my thirst with this horror that makes me press closer, with this disgust which has become my delight. For this I have *filthy* words at my disposal, words that sharpen the feeling I have of touching on the *intolerable* secret of existence. I may say these words in order to cry out the uncovered secret, wanting to be sure I am not the only one to know it: at this moment I no longer doubt that I am embracing the totality without which I was only *outside*: I reach orgasm.⁹

There is no book by Bataille in which he states more clearly and brutally how horrible is the animality of the sexual embrace, as though, beyond this animality, was nature in its entirety, which it so happens we may have left only to be certain to fall back into it, whose filthy and desirable contagion one must experience (there is no reason to flee it; on the contrary!): 'For an embrace is not just a fall into the animal muck, but the anticipation of death, and of the putrefaction that follows it. Here eroticism is analogous to a tragedy.'[10] The moment of the 'little death' – announcing the greater one – of orgasm is that negative miracle of which Bataille spoke in *Sovereignty*: the shattering moment in which everything is momentarily reduced to nothing, anticipating a more considerable annihilation. The promise this tragic moment makes of returning to horror is the secret of existence.[11]

It is also the meaning of the first passages of *Eroticism*: 'Eroticism, it may be said, is assenting to life up to the point of death.'[12] It is necessary to say *Yes* to the embrace, to say yes to it and to seek it to the point of unpardonable vice in such a way that, equal to the greatest disturbance in its intensity, the fall into death would be the deepest, and the bitterness of love would equal that of death. The greater the erotic metamorphosis (of the worthy woman into a bitch), the more vertiginous is the fall into what the flesh hides of her, her horror and her death:

> A madness suddenly takes possession of a person. That madness is well known to us but we can easily picture the surprise of anyone who did not know about it and who by some device witnesses unseen the passionate lovemaking of some woman who had struck him as particularly distinguished. He would think she was sick, just as mad dogs are sick. Just as if some mad bitch had usurped the personality of the dignified hostess . . . Sickness is not putting it strongly enough, though; for the time being the personality is *dead*. For the time being its death gives the bitch full scope, and she takes advantage of the silence, of the *absence of the dead woman*. The bitch wallows – wallows noisily – in that silence and that absence.[13]

What lies behind misfortune

Philosophy of a constitutive sort is an ancillary activity.

Should we attribute it to what is normally associated with age and the process of slowing down? Should we attribute it to the fear that he may have suddenly felt that, in gaining a readership (and a notoriety), his work was losing its dark secret and provoking outraged or shocked reactions? The fact is that, with an insistence hitherto absent from the comments he made about his work, Bataille set about if not playing down its 'blackness' then at least giving an unexpected meaning to it, sometimes in its transitions, sometimes in its method. His work and thought were only apparently black and unbearable, it seemed, and only as the conditions of a possibility of something beyond this blackness and 'unbearableness'.

The first time Bataille took this position was to make a plea about its appearance and nothing more:

> I do not know if I love the night, maybe I do, for fragile human beauty moves me to the point of discomfort only in knowing that the night from which it comes and into which it passes is unfathomable . . . It is more moving in the platitude, when night is made dirtier, when the horror of night turns beings into a vast rubbish tip . . .
>
> I'm told about my 'unbearable' universe, as though my books displayed open wounds the way unfortunates do. It is true that I appear to have a fondness for denying, or at least neglecting or considering insignificant, the multiple resources which help us to *endure*.[1]

Everything leads to disturbance (the dirty night, the dull horror of rubbish); everything demands its provocation (to love is to love to the point of discomfort) – and we do not know if Bataille ever avoided such a necessary provocation; but this disturbance should not indicate misfortune, 'it does not indicate something black'.[2]

But such a disturbance – it has to be great; it has to be violent – is not in fact intended to frighten; it is just a form of philosophy, in any case the philosophy Bataille wrote (and he did not deny that such a philosophy is probably rare, even that, were it not for Nietzsche, such a 'passionate' philosophy would ultimately be hardly philosophical). But even in coming to its defence he affirms it: without this tangible passion, 'absolutely nothing would remain' of his thought.[3] And without further explanation or justification of how he considered this to be the sole condition of accessibility to something lying beyond its appearances, he gave his description a twist that, far from dissipating, heightened their paradoxical effects: 'I would rather say I am a happy philosopher.'[4]

How should we take this? Certainly not as the final attainment of a 'wisdom', even a Hegelian one. (Nothing could be more opposed to what his thought struggled to set in motion. Right to the end this thought affirmed its sovereign 'fever'. No despair set in so profoundly that he would have resigned himself to anything resembling a 'wisdom'.)[5] It should much rather be understood in the sense that method and transition (to what lies beyond misfortune) are, in this strange affirmation, indissociable. What Bataille's philosophy is capable of, and only at the price of creating disturbance, cannot be achieved by philosophy (though this might not be philosophy in general, since Bataille cannot but be thinking of Hegel more than Nietzsche). Or, more precisely, it cannot since it has taken away from being 'the possibility of torrent, of bedazzlement, of cry, *that it is*', since, by depriving it of its frenzy, it prevents being from being *unleashed* within itself (and only this unleashing would make it being[6]). It contains everything that philosophy no longer attains – the seduction of a pretty young woman, the exceptional nature of desire, luxury and sensuality, *fortune* (which cannot be 'profound', so philosophy ignores it) – that it no longer attains through powerlessness ('sick from a morose virtuosity'). But it is not enough that powerlessness prevents its attainment; even powerlessness is out of reach: 'In fact it can resolve nothing. And even the absence of solution cannot be reached by it.'[7]

In taking from being this possibility of the torrent, the explosion and the cry, philosophy *denies*, and in denying subjects itself to misfortune, 'at the other extreme from a perfect absence of misfortune that the universe is'.[8] Even Nietzsche, however powerful was his will to insubordination, however violent his desire to rediscover in himself the torrential and screaming being, only attains it in a mediocre way: if he was happy, it was at best in not giving his thought over to the ill fortune that overwhelmed him, it was by having not 'allowed the misfortune within him to speak'.

What philosophies could not prevent, from the moment they allowed misfortune the place they gave to it, is that in them affirmation became impossible and they *de facto* metamorphosed into a morality. Reversing the accepted sequence, Bataille affirmed that it is less misfortune that has produced morality (philosophy) than morality that has produced misfortune. So much so that for him these two words can no longer be dissociated; he said this pointedly – as we have seen – about Camus, in accusing him of it, effectively accusing Camus of being as far as possible, in the dry, harsh pages of *The Plague*, from a morality that might lead to revolt. Instead of this morality *consenting* (in consenting it would effectively be happy, it would measure up to the perfect absence of misfortune that is the universe), it *denies*. This negation that Camus claims in his turn Bataille calls a 'morality of misfortune'.[9] It is a morality of misfortune which is not only an *unhappy* morality, but is also by this very fact 'a hateful morality' (which is 'to passion what treason is to battle'[10]).

This accusation is not without consequences; these are in fact serious, and give an *affirmative* sense to what is unexpected about Bataille's *pro domo* plea:

1. My work is only black and unbearable in its appearance;
2. However great misfortune may be, however great the place I myself have given it, it is still not enough to subordinate me;
3. If I deny, it is not in order to help anyone *acquiesce*, it is not in order to lead anyone into subordination;
4. Morality has led philosophy into misfortune;
5. One only attains sovereignty on condition of 'going beyond' what is hateful about the *No* of moral philosophy;
6. My negation denies only the *No* of moral philosophy;
7. This is how my philosophy, whatever its appearances, is happy (has the universe's absence of misfortune), how it alone is *sovereign*.

However tragic it may be, Bataille dismisses all judgement of the world (in this he safeguards the meaning of the word 'tragic'; in other words, he prevents its reduction to the meaning of the word 'misfortune'), since judgement adds hatred (the hatred of the world) to fear. Taking Nietzschean assent even further, Bataille calls upon us to reach something beyond fear (in that its negation is also a passage), to reach something beyond morality (which, if it is not a revolt, can only be a decline or a misfortune), perhaps also something beyond philosophy (which no longer even attains the truth which its powerlessness to attain anything represents for it), to what he calls upon with a simplicity – a finesse – that can be disconcerting, something beyond *seriousness* (a finesse that should be understood in the sense that there is no concept that needs reducing, in other words that needs 'refining'). 'Misfortune [is] ineluctably seriousness.' As far as possible from this seriousness there exists a certain point, as different from surrealism as it is from philosophy, and just as different 'from articulated thought as, in life, the inertia of the abattoir, where nothing remains that is not cut to pieces, nothing that is not the contrary of what it is. *What happens*, then, whatever the outcome, no longer differs from *what does not happen*, which is, which was, which will be, without anything happening.'[11]

Felix culpa

The expression *Felix culpa* safeguards the artful sentiment that the love of Christ, in which the depth of the shattering of souls is revealed, *would not exist* were it not given in the intoxication of a torture.

Evil was an issue that became more insistent with each year Bataille wrote. We have seen how evil as such entered his work rather late. Or more exactly, it took what could be said to have long been a natural place within it. Was not Simone in *The Story of the Eye* already evil? Her transports, however, had a burning and joyful quality. It is not possible to judge her morally without reducing her to something quite different from what she was. Evil has as little interest for her as it appears to have had for Bataille at the time (in other words, in the 1920s, and this is so much stranger in that *Story of the Eye* is his first story and Simone the first heroine after his abandonment of his faith). Evil is equally of little interest to Troppmann (*Blue of Noon*), Edwarda and Marie (*The Dead Man*), if not to everyone in the novels: until the war, it is rather death – exclusively death – that interests Bataille's characters. *L'Abbé C.* is the first of his characters to broach and ponder the moral question of evil, and if, just like those before him, he ponders the question of death, it is in such a way that death appears as the only possible response made to the unreserved affirmation of evil.

Evoking evil, linking it to the most extreme of affirmations one can offer it, a character – the most monstrous of sexual madmen (who in a way is to reality what Sade is to literature) – loomed on Bataille's path: Gilles de Rais. Georges Bataille was already sixty, and was sick, when he embarked on a response to the most archaic of figures of sacred sovereignty and, in the general opinions of the world, the most abject.

Bataille does not judge (except in passing, responding when appropriate to his subject). Not only does he not judge, he is not afraid to add to the paradox that the existence of this monster creates for the world of moralists, a paradox that is one of the least susceptible of being understood by them: Gilles de Rais may have been a monster, but a monster who is a child: 'In effect, the question is of monstrosity. Essentially this monstrosity is childlike.'[1] 'This monster before us is like a child. We cannot deny the monstrosity of childhood. How often children would, if they could, be Gilles de Rais!'[2] Let there be no mistake: if he is prepared to see him as providing 'a rare document about sexual pathology', in no way does he interpret him by means of psychoanalysis.[3] If this must be said, it is drily, without in any way diminishing the provocation: 'I insist on this: he was a child.'

He has the sovereign humour of childhood – and this is what is fascinating – as the world of violence offered to his violent and dreadful appetite was sovereign: 'In Gilles' eyes, mankind was no more than an element of voluptuous turmoil; this element was entirely at his sovereign disposal, having no other meaning than a possibility for more violent pleasure, and he did not stop losing himself in that violence.'[4] This man was sovereign, even though it was at the price of being equally monstrous. Sovereign was the man whom 'calculation never dominated'. Sovereign was this excessive and ostentatious prodigality: 'Having to provide for needs demanded by delirium, he wasted a vast fortune without calculation.' Sovereign was this 'insane prodigality', this crazy man who 'must fascinate at any cost'.

And he fascinates whatever the crimes of which he was accused, fascinating Bataille just as the bloody sacrifices of the Aztecs in Mexico had some thirty years earlier, 'the most streaming human abattoirs'. He is so fascinated because more is involved than simply a trial; not just Gilles de Rais was on trial, but his society, that feudal world which also brought into focus the principles of Christianity: 'The crimes of Gilles de Rais are those of the world in which he committed them. The convulsive tremblings of this world are what these slit throats expose. The world had sanctioned the cruel differences that left these throats defenceless. It had permitted – or very nearly so – these tragic games: the games of an energumen, at the limit of his sovereign power.'[5] How should this accusation be understood if not, contrary to the fascination exercised by this 'funereal magnificence', as the sudden revival of a moral protest? (Speaking of the Aztecs, Bataille never tempered his fascination with any reservations.) For there can be no doubt that fascination – for Gilles de Rais but also for his time – or, at least, ambiguity dominated (unless one takes at face value words Bataille did not intend to be taken as such): fascination for wars in which this violent world is swallowed up ('a terrifying game, but a game'[6]), fascination for what the nobility, more than any other class, savoured by disdaining work ('Gilles de Rais represents in a pure state the movement which tends to abandon man's activity to enchantment, in the play of the privileged'[7]). For Bataille, the moral problem is posed in the following terms: there is a place to love *or* a place to judge. His desire is drawn towards the world his morality condemns, while he is repelled by the world that is drawn to morality. He confesses this laconically: 'Violence involves an ambiguity between seduction and terror.'[8]

Instead of blaming Gilles de Rais specifically (which is what morality would do, condemning the excess of the system, and not wanting to accept that excess is the very meaning, but the *accused* meaning, of the system), Bataille blamed feudalism, its violent coarseness and lack of culture. Gilles de Rais was condemned less for sexual excess (what were a few ragged adolescents compared to the impressive fortune of the Lord of Machecoul?), than because, twice over, he contravened the religious order by assuming the rule of an ecclesiastic and invoking the devil. These two 'excesses' that the system held against him and used to condemn him say more about the truth of the feudal system than any moral judgement. But by denouncing the feudal system, the crimes of Gilles de Rais also denounce – in a fundamental way – the Christianity that is its keystone. This provided Bataille with the opportunity to return to what he had said in *Eroticism* on the subject of happy sin (*Felix culpa*). Sin is necessary to Christianity: 'Perhaps Christianity is even fundamentally the pressing demand for crime, the demand for the horror that in a sense it needs in order to forgive.'[9] The greater the crime, the less excusable the crime to humanity, the more evident the forbearance of the Christian God. The crime therefore had to be the greatest possible in order to emphasise with the greatest brilliance how immense, how infinite is the kindness of God. Infinite is God, infinite the sin. I have said that Bataille needed God his whole life because only God made sin infinite (infinite in a way that error cannot be). Infinite is the sin from which man is born, infinite is that of the crucifixion of Christ (as he said in *On Nietzsche*), infinite is thus the relation of man to God, a relation of culpability. The key to the relation to God is not the good, but evil: an evil equal to God, infinite (all the more infinite in that to conclude this precarious and paradoxical construction, Bataille never failed to repeat that God does not exist). The most abject of criminals fascinates because he has this character of archaic and sovereign infinity.[10]

Universal history

Consideration of the life of Georges Bataille would certainly be incomplete if we did not examine what might have resulted from his 'Universal history', the project he nurtured so long and so faithfully. The first time the idea appeared (so far as we know) goes back to 1934, when he asked Raymond Queneau to help him with it. In 1960, or thirty years later, his idea of it had not changed;[1] it had just become padded out by several hundred, if not several thousand pages. No doubt from 1950 until his death Bataille wrote few pages that cannot and should not be read as the endlessly restarted outline for this project. What is, moreover, extraordinary about this is that it erases itself even as it elaborates itself, or if it does not entirely erase itself, it displaces itself, is always out of reach, deviates to such an extent that Bataille did not regard the publication of a book as essential as *Sovereignty* (or, to a lesser degree of involvement, *Theory of Religion*) as necessary. Others were significantly revised, as was the case for *Histoire de l'érotisme*, which appeared with the significantly shortened – dehistoricised – title of *L'Érotisme*.[2]

Two books from this 'History' nevertheless appeared, one in 1955, the other in 1961, *Lascaux* and *The Tears of Eros*, which both in their way testify to it in a 'localised' way (since both books are on the history of art). No one will know what this 'History' might have been. It would not be enough to put together the three books written under the generic title of *The Accursed Share*, adding to them *Theory of Religion*, *Lascaux*, *The Tears of Eros*, and finally a few lectures or articles delivered or published here and there,[3] circumstantial ones for the most part, to have even a slight idea of it. We have seen how Bataille's projects 'shifted', how they metamorphosed when they did not cancel each other out. There is no doubt that the nature of such a project was impossible for Bataille, not because he lacked the intellectual means, but because for him there was no possible end, no key, no enigma to resolve; incompletion was the rule. And even had Bataille written a complete 'Universal history', no doubt he would unfailingly have wished to start it all over again: in fact, there is no possible end for it, no possible end because there is death which is not an end but a way of making incompletion definitive.

Nevertheless a plan for such a work exists. Is it the one for this book, or for something else (which itself would have joined *all* the others to become part of *this* book)? A series of articles, including the one on 'La vallée de la Vézère', to be rewritten, were to have formed the basis of a first section that would have been completed using, also no doubt rewritten, a few of the most important pages from *Sovereignty*;[4] a second section would have been made up of themes developed on war as play and on royal religion; a third section was to cover work and slavery, Christianity and royal immoderation and finally equality (moderation); a fourth and final section was to discuss revolution and immoderation, and relations between the French, Russian and Chinese revolutions, and finally sovereignty.[5] No doubt it was not the only plan Bataille drew up (he made all kinds of plans on all subjects, including plans for his daily routine); nonetheless it is, like any other that might necessarily replace it, one of the possible plans of this impossible book.

Four years earlier (in 1955) *Lascaux ou la naissance de l'art* was published,[6] which represented a restatement rather than an elaboration of *The Accursed Share* and *Sovereignty* (no doubt because this was a de luxe publication intended for wide distribution by the publisher). It nevertheless retains something of *Sovereignty*'s accusatory tone: 'prohibitions preserve intact – if and when possible, and so far and for as long as possible – the world work organises and shelter it from the disturbances repeatedly provoked by death and sexuality: the enduring animality within us forever introduces raw life and nature into the community, which act as the mud from which we emerge.'[7] (But transgression is not at issue here.)

The article 'Le berceau de l'humanité', which remained unpublished in Bataille's lifetime, is certainly the closest to what could justifiably be regarded as an origin for this 'Universal history'. And, it comes as no surprise, this origin is death (Bataille intended nothing provocative in this paradox): 'In this way we could grasp, as a departure point, the horrible realm of death.'[8]

What the extraordinary wall paintings of Lascaux bear witness to (what Bataille did not say in the book published under this title) is the way in which primitive man was seized by the horror of death which, rather than fleeing, he managed as best he could to overcome. The representation of animals has the meaning of the death to which the hunts consign them:

> Whether they were hoping, as they portrayed these horses and bulls on the walls, to prepare, through sympathetic magic, a path of access to these elements of their subsistence is not in question [this is the traditional propitiatory and Agonistic interpretation] but in portraying those they killed, they also aimed at something other than their commonplace interest: what they wanted to resolve was the nagging question of death. Admittedly death did not cease to terrify them, but they went beyond it in identifying with it, through a *religious* sympathy with their victims.[9]

It was through representing and contemplating death that archaic man seems to have gained the greatest of his powers, the one that creates religions in all times: the one of living 'at the level of death'.[10]

This representation, this impossible taming of death, quickly took other, more elaborate forms, such as the one that consisted in giving the deceased a tomb: Bataille saw in this the first signs of hominid behaviour.[11] Other signs immediately followed: 'it is out of this awareness that eroticism appeared, distinguishing the sex life of man from that of the animal.'[12] This is how he introduces the reader to the history of eroticism (or more precisely the history of the representation of eroticism) in his final book, *The Tears of Eros*. In this way it is possible to imagine the opening sentences of this never-written 'Universal history', its anti-historical origins that would have preceded the anti-historical exhortations of *Sovereignty*.

The bit between the teeth[1]

> Essentially, the painting I am speaking about is in a
> ferment, it lives . . . it burns . . . I can no longer speak of
> it with the distance demanded by judgement and
> classification.

Art does not occupy a chance place in Bataille's work that can be
explained by circumstances alone, such as those favourable to surrealism (which brought together more effectively than is usual, painters,
writers, photographers). On the contrary, it has a key place, being
central to the way Bataille always (from the time of the article
'Vanished America') used elements that were *a priori* external in order
to intensify and sustain the core of his thinking (in obedience to what
he theorised as heterology). This could be stated, albeit exaggeratedly,
thus: Bataille immediately seized and made his own everything he
experienced. Anything his thought came across was liable to be used
to serve his own processes, processes that were a sort of 'regurgitation'.

Art would penetrate into this work just as ethnology, anthropology,
economy, physics, religion, mysticism and so on had done before, as a
kind of 'proof'. This was because the elaboration of the means of his
theorisation preceded its penetration and this theorisation was then
developed concurrently with this penetration. Art does not emerge in
this work in a way that would modify it to the slightest degree. On the
contrary, its emergence supports and justifies it (thus *Tears of Eros*
constitutes an illustrated application of the principles of a reading of
universal history by means of the *representation* of tragic eroticism).
Art did not lure Bataille into new avenues of thought, but made him
think about the same things through new elements. These were the
themes he had ceaselessly explored as a philosopher (the sacred,
sacrifice, work, eroticism, transgression, death, etc.) and played with as

a writer (the uncertain relations of fear, scandal, convention and so on).

Painting is not simply given (in which case, it would only be *visible*): equal to the convention to which everyone expects it to respond (that ostentation by which people conjure away their death in readying themselves to see it in a wider context); *without residue*. The fear Bataille sought, and that he still calls fever, is the grace by which painting suddenly escapes convention, suddenly exceeds it. Painting is not simply given: it is, on the contrary, as it escapes, as *escaping*, as it eludes (genre, motive, convention), *setting* them right or *setting* itself to rights, that it accidentally emerges.

However, for Bataille more than fear is involved in the principle of this emergence. It is not enough that it frightens, indeed terrifies, as in the example of the tortured Chinese man who is patiently and meticulously cut up, cut up a hundred times while still alive, so that this dread and this terror grab something other than our attention (even a shaken attention). He also has to have an unbearably happy appearance; what's worse, this happiness has a joy which entrances (his smile in the photographs of his torture is certainly disturbing). It is in this happiness, dreamed by him, and because it is unbearable (it is unbeknownst to reason that one wants to bear it) that the *elusive quality* occurs thanks to which painting emerges. Everything takes a spectacular turn for the worse, and yet there is something worse than all possible fear (all fear to which reason would respond), there is his sick excess, his pleasure and delectation. The elusiveness is to the genre what ecstasy is to reason: its rending logic.[2]

A work, this one a painting (*Anatomy* by Gautier d'Agoty), which Bataille reproduced in *The Tears of Eros*, brings this torture to mind (as do many others: scenes of mutilation, decapitation and emasculation, torture wheels and racks, quarterings and calcinations, etc.). It brings this torture to mind, but strangely *stylises* it. Cut up, opened, pulled to pieces, the tortured Chinese man is not just atrocious, but *also* happy (at least this is what Bataille, looking at him, wanted us to see). The woman Gautier d'Agoty painted – stripped to the bone, dissected, her back naked and cut away to her backside – is not only above suspicion, not only hallucinating, she is *also* desirable. This *excess* would then be what, though it is cast outside all convention, in advance would make a work also be more (or less) than itself, would even elude its expectation, and it could always give rise to the worst.

This excess, this eluding, this worst, would be what Bataille called 'mannerism': 'This word no longer carries any sense of disparagement in the minds of those who use it. I have recourse to the word only in the sense that it interprets a tensed violence, without which we could never free ourselves from convention ... mannerism is the quest for fever!'[3]

At the end of his life when Bataille was tired and sick he thus used a word in a way that was intended to imply neither judgement nor classification. It was a word rare or disparaged enough to be altered by neither the frequency nor the emphasis of its use, and it carried just enough of a notion (no doubt not, in his mind, a category) both to save surrealism from usury[4] and to describe less an art than an attitude of art, less a moment of it than its breaks from it, less a time and a few names than, of all times and names, intensity carried to excess – breaking. 'Today, no one restricts the word surrealism to the school that André Breton wanted to claim under this name. I prefer however to speak of mannerism; I want to indicate a fundamental unity between painters whose obsession it is to interpret fever: fever, desire, burning passion.'[5]

Bataille, one imagines, did not have the ingenuity to think that art could ever release itself from convention, in other words that it could ever do so definitively. Nothing in him allowed him to believe in a history of art, in the sense in which teleologically there would be a reason to believe in a History of history; in the sense in which a revolution (political, aesthetic or both together) would finally confer a definitive meaning on the traces that insurrections might leave in one place or another. Each age has its convention, just as each has its order, and each time art has to free itself from both to attain, if only in flashes, in lightning flashes, the 'excitement', the 'desire, 'burning passion', the yardstick by which, far from judging or classifying, Bataille deciphered and was moved by painting.

As the historian he also was (of a history from which art is not separated), Bataille did not fail to note that order is never so hard, so coercive, and its conventions never so *inflated*, as when its dominion is weakened and when they lose the means to hold, united in their hands, at their mercy, entire *inspired* crowds. Because for a long time edifica-tion was art's purpose, its enslavement (bowing down on the steps of churches and palaces). For a long time, it was only 'an integral part of a majestic *whole* set up to dazzle the masses by the powers-that-be'.[6]

The world painting thus showed was first intelligible faced with this stale, disconnected intelligibility by which, provoked by its eloquence, it wore itself out.

Because it inevitably happened that, as this power of edification weakened, as its representations elapsed, so it took a newer and suddenly subversive meaning:

> There came a day, however, when this vast didactic structure – erected and renewed time and again in the form of castles, churches, palaces and works of art calculated to awe the masses and bend them beneath the yoke of authority – lost its power to sway. It fell to pieces, its message was shown up as mere grandiloquence, and the once obedient masses turned away in search of something else.[7]

Even in speaking of painting, Bataille was speaking of history, not the history of art, but history as a whole and essentially its transitions and breaks. Art – painting – interested him above all by dint of what history places at stake in it, by dint of what history sees in it. Goya gave him the opportunity to make this plain: 'His history belongs to that of art only in a secondary way.'[8] Van Gogh allowed him to say exactly the same thing: 'It is not to the history of art that Vincent Van Gogh belongs.' He moderated this paradox by clarifying it in a critical way: 'Few intellectual enterprises have greater interest than the sociological analysis of works of art.'[9] And he adds, deploring it: 'Traditional criticism had taken little account of the social situation, of economic conditions and of class oppositions which are involved at the moment a work is developed.'

Until painting finally became 'modern', the greatest painters, those responsible for the movement of painting, have painted under constraint. They were first 'commissioned' and rewarded for painting what the powerful (the lords and the priests) wanted them to depict in order to increase their authority proportionately.[10] Yet, far from painting appearing to Bataille to be a more enslaved art than any other, it is, he says, speaking enigmatically about *Guernica* (but indirectly about Goya as well), the freest:

> It is strange that the freest of the arts reached its summit in a political painting. . . . This is not, it is true, the first time the struggle of the Spanish people for liberty has roused an artist to the highest degree of inspiration. The executed man of the *Third of May*, dying with his eyes open in a great cry, is without doubt Goya's masterpiece.

And this canvas from the Prado in Madrid, right in the heart of the last fascist 'sanctuary', continues to glorify 'resistance' in all times and places.[11]

Contrary to appearances, it is therefore untrue that painting had not been free – or did not become so; it is even the freest of all the arts. And its liberty is of such a kind that it reaches an apogee in two *political* works.

Politics: the word is elusive. It eludes both aesthetic convention and its commentary. The fear painting provokes is therefore not simply theatrical (a stage upon which only the effects of emotive affinities are perhaps produced); nor is it simply metaphysical (God did not so much withdraw from the world which owed its authority to him; rather, he was finally driven out of it). It is not so much unexpected as essential that everything combined to lead Bataille to talk about Goya (the Goya of the *Caprices*, the *Disasters of War*, the *Follies*; Goya, the painter whom he discussed most assiduously) in terms analogous to those in which he discussed the improbable ecstasy of the tortured Chinese, the happy taste for death of the Aztecs or the 'innocent' cruelty of Gilles de Rais, etc., that is, in terms of affinities and fascination (not without leaving the sense of such a comparison in suspense; Bataille twice points out that Goya is 'almost the contemporary' of Sade). Yet it would not have been enough to say what Goya put in his paintings. In particular, it would not have been enough to state the price he paid for including it: Reason liberated him (a violent liberation) from 'the order established by the hated Church'.[12]

Reason made Goya a passionate liberal, who lived alongside the people as someone 'oppressed'. Honours could have made him submissive, but instead he became isolated (deafness also isolated him). The fear he found, like that found in painting which fascinates, touches on liberty and that of a people; and the anguish to which he consented is exactly that of their *impossible*: 'It is precisely the impossible that these drawings try to depict; the wastage of poverty, infirmity, old age, madness, stupidity and massacre; the terrible figures of dream and, like a dominant obsession, life hunted down in the tortures of the Inquisition.'[13]

Just as, in order to *fascinate*, it is not enough that the tortured Chinese man was atrocious, he also had to be happy; just as it was not enough for Gautier d'Agoty's *Anatomie* to be hallucinatory, the figure also had to be desirable, so the degradation Goya drew, that he drew to the point of obsession, *fascinates* because we do not feel it as something distinct from him, because on the contrary complicity ties him to it profoundly, a complicity 'if not with the degradation of the executioner', at least 'with that of the victim'.

Goya occupies a rare place in the history of painting: he is the end, the strangling of eloquence. This end and this strangling were convulsive (from this comes the *nocturnal* aspect of his paintings). However, they retain an eloquence that Manet abandoned: they are not *indifferent* (the violence they denounce, they assume by contagion), which means they still belong to the world they strive to destroy. Of all the breaks painting had to effect, without any doubt this one is the most brutal. However, it was not completely effective. What Goya started, Manet brought to completion, a completion that Bataille evaluates like this: 'True, the picture relates an incident, no less than Goya's does, but – and this is what counts – without the least concern for the incident itself.'[14] The strange thing is that Malraux had already said this, and in a notably drier way: '*The Execution of Maximilian* is Goya's *Third of May*, less what this painting represents.'

Should we conceive that Malraux's looming shadow would incline Bataille (although no one was further from Malraux than he was) *also* to privilege this lack of concern (to make it the argument of his looking)? In fact, the concession is only apparent, in the sense that if Bataille does not deny that Manet's painting is indeed the one which should be acknowledged to have finally made painting 'modern', this is not his primary concern, it is not what most affects him. For his look is primarily drawn neither to empty eloquence nor to the pure insignificance (like the asparagus painted by Manet, for example) of which Malraux speaks so highly, but, from one to the other, the brutal and intense instant of vacillation in which painting is no longer absolutely one without absolutely attaining the other. This is a moment that Goya represents better than Manet ever could: 'Goya came as a thief in the night to burn the temple; he was the fierce negative product of academicism, whose positive side was mere death – emptiness, decline and death.' Goya is the *sick* excess of a logic: admittedly, his means 'resemble those that went to build and decorate the temple of the past, but straining his forces to the limit he undermined the temple's foundations. Out of step with his times, he did violence to everything that structure stood for.'[15]

What grips and disturbs in Goya's painting is the inability any longer to be able to *signify* an ancient, worn-out world (one no longer able to *edify*). In no longer wanting or being able to do so, it reaches the highest degree of fallen and lacerated art. Bataille seems tempted to say that the revolution Manet will come to represent ('Stains, colours, movement', as Malraux said) frustrates the revolt Goya represented. Nevertheless, there was something inevitable about the fact that Manet attenuated the sovereign moment represented by Goya (the thief in the night burning the temple), installing it in time (and which time consumes). It was in a sense inevitable that Manet soothed and settled painting from this unbearable tension of the end, turning it back towards what it was necessary for it to become, that is the equal of the world in which it is painted, and which awaited it: 'It was not the painter's anguish alone, for it had spread, though they did not realise it, to the scoffers and revilers as well, who *lay in wait* for the paintings which were so repulsive to them then, but which in time filled the yawning emptiness of their hollow souls.'[16]

However, Manet is important for the fact that he destroyed what Goya had only started to erode. He destroyed the (metaphysical) subject which was now, by the sheer effort by which the ecclesiastical and political authorities had used it, simply *eloquent*. On the subject of Manet's *Bal Masqué de l'Opéra*, Bataille speaks forcefully of a 'shipwreck of the subject': it is because the subject is freed from representation and *slips* from the solemnity and the nobility by which it was ruled in order, finally, to sink into *insignificance*, that painting suddenly became 'modern': instead of the signifying subject characteristic of 'earlier' painting, 'a majesty of everything and nothing' has been reached, which belongs 'to what *is* by reason of its *being*'.[17]

As he often did, Bataille tempered his affirmation. Admittedly, he praised the 'shipwreck of the subject' that painting realised with Manet, but this was in order to affirm immediately that Manet himself sometimes escaped this. 'Indifferent' as his paintings were to what they narrated, no matter what insignificance they attained, they did not do so to such a point that some of them could not share, with those of Goya, *the silence of death*: this is tantamount to saying that, in Bataille's eyes, there is more than a disappearance of the 'subject' from the scene of depiction. More precisely, there is something more than the subject having henceforth vanished, there is the *disappearing* subject. Just as the break in representation interests him more than its effect (this moment, we have seen, is incomparably more intense), the 'putting to death' of the subject fascinates him more than its proclaimed death. There is an 'after' of this moment which was only its decline (inevitably, it would give painting a place to rest). Goya alone, or at least Goya before anyone else, knew how to foreground the vanishing subject (appearing in this disappearance) in that same violent movement by which it disappeared, in the indescribable burst of this weakness, on the scene of its depiction:

> In that vision of a man about to die, flinging up his arms with a shriek, which we call the *Third of May*, we have the very image of death, such as man can hardly ever know it, since the event itself wipes out all consciousness of it. In this picture Goya caught the blinding, instantaneous flash of death, a thunderbolt of sight-destroying intensity, brighter than any known light. The eloquence, the rhetoric of painting has never been carried further, but here its effect is that of definitive silence, an outcry smothered before it can rise.[18]

Without doubt, Goya's work is *still* eloquent. But with an eloquence that extinguishes eloquence, that is equivalent to silence. It is a silence Manet also attained with *The Dead Toreador*, *The Funeral* and *The Suicide*, a silence the *pure* presence of *Olympia* accomplishes in an exemplary way: 'In her provocative literalness she is nothing. Her real nudity (not merely that of her body) is the silence that emanates from her, like that from a sunken ship. All we have is the "sacred horror" of her presence – a presence whose sheer simplicity is tantamount to absence.'[19] Nothing equals the representation of the horror of death but that of the *absence* that is a pure and naked presence. It is a sacred horror.

In correcting Malraux, Bataille asserted that it is not enough for a work to cease to *signify* in order to reach this silence, in order to reach *nothing*. It is equally not enough for it to meet the requirements of its modernity. Certainly this is sufficient from Malraux's point of view (as well as for a large part of historiography), a point of view that, in order not to be ingenuous, is overly 'teleological', and so sees Goya as announcing Cézanne, by means of Manet, Daumier and so on. This complies with a finalistic point of view which takes Cézanne and his intentional 'insignificance' as a *completion* towards which Goya, followed by Manet and then Daumier (etc.) had deliberately led. For Bataille, on the contrary, there were only, here and there, dysteleological conflagrations between a completed time (and this time is not only that of art, indeed it is even that of art only secondarily), a completed time in which ideality now only exerts a conventional attraction (an attraction in which the nostalgia for a delicate and eloquent world is soon played out for no longer having anything left with which to oppose the *nothing* unleashed by fear), and a dawning, arising time; conflagrations by means of which entire genres of depiction slipped and finally collapsed. Whatever laughter they provoke (but whatever fear as well), nothing can prevent these collapses. A painting is 'modern' only for the brief moment in which in it an art lets go of the time of the representation in which it exhausts itself, suspends it in silence, before replacing it by another, unknown one, that will, however, be recognised even by those who mock it.[20]

To die of laughing and to laugh of dying

The day came when death took on a real meaning in Bataille's life. From 1954 onwards he seems to have been subject to violent attacks of illness. These were not just isolated incidents, but on the contrary began to be significant enough for a consultation to be arranged by one of his oldest friends, Dr Théodore Fraenkel, involving several professors at the Lariboisière hospital. Their diagnosis was immediate: Georges Bataille was suffering from cerebral arteriosclerosis, a terminal condition (Diane Bataille was informed of the terminal nature of the illness; Georges was not, and no doubt only guessed it later, without, however, ever knowing his precise medical condition). In 1955, Bataille was fifty-eight, and he had seven years left to live.

This can be described in blunt rational terms (as Bataille himself, who always demanded that one should look death in the face, invites us to do): cerebral arteriosclerosis is not an aggressive condition in its early stages; the illness producing almost imperceptible symptoms starts insidiously, and they are all the less perceptible in that they only slightly accentuate certain character traits already present in the patient (at least, they were present in Bataille): emotional behaviour (Bataille was always emotional), egocentrism and childishness (one might, if one were being unkind, consider Bataille's child-like spirit as egocentric and childish even before he became ill), and depressive anxiety (Bataille had other words, fearful on a different scale, to indicate something considered symptomatic by medical science: *anguish in the face of the abyss*).

Then more serious effects set in: a weakening in intellectual activity, only occasional and partial, certainly, but dispiriting all the same since for a long period it still retains the distressed consciousness of progressive degeneration (did not Bataille speak, as if in premonition, of a foundering consciousness within a consciousness which knows it is foundering?), a consciousness still in command of automatic functions and the means of self-reflection.

As the years went on, Bataille suffered greatly. He underwent violent disturbances of memory and of temporal and spatial orientation (so bad that in the end he no longer knew where he lived); he also suffered brief but extreme lapses of consciousness in which he lost all self-control (and none of the treatments he was prescribed – intravenous heparin for instance – perceptibly improved his condition or reduced his suffering). Little by little, one by one, he lost his faculties. But what caused him the most suffering was no longer to have unlimited use of his intellectual capacities. (It was not true, in fact, that these faculties ever left him altogether. As we shall see, he thought through his death right to the end, and in terms that were among the most intense ever conceived. What he complained of was that his mind was suddenly subject to blackouts as virulent as they were unexpected, and which prevented him from carrying out long and detailed research.)

He told Hélène Cadou that his mind was 'undoing itself'. In a letter of 2 June 1961 he told Alexandre Kojève he was devoting himself to an examination of the deficiencies themselves (to thinking through the degeneration of the means of thought, for want of still being able truly *to think*): 'Besides, I am partly reduced to reflecting on the at least relative dilapidation in my head: I am no longer sure that I still possess the few possibilities I once had.'[1] To his friend and doctor Théodore Fraenkel, and to several other friends (Jean Piel for example), he admitted that he could only write with extreme difficulty and unbearably slowly. This was all too true: it took him nearly three years to write the eighty pages of the introduction to *Gilles de Rais*. And *The Tears of Eros* not only demonstrated a discernible reduction of his capacities (in it Bataille's writing is sometimes disjointed, and rarely stunning; one senses how a violent night has left the morning exhausted and overwhelmed); this book required an effort of will whose completion he had to postpone for months on end (it took him two and a half years to write a book he expected to finish in a few months).[2]

This illness can nevertheless be seen in quite another light, in a way that is probably no less true: Bataille had too often wished to experience for himself the death of God, and the agony of the world he had left behind, for illness not one day to lead him gently into knowing for himself, *really knowing*, the agony of a man in the world without God.

He suddenly felt the double and complicitous effect of the fall of the world (it is *the* whole world that falls with the death of a man) into the abyss opened up by the death of God. It was complicitous since Bataille did not rebel against it. He was what he had wanted to be: the pitiful and glorious truth of mortal flesh. The flesh is the same whether in orgasm (the sexual tremor) or in dying (the annihilating tremor). Illness too is made up of moments which, like those of eroticism, are alert and entreating. In his illness, Bataille was simply a little bit more in that world whose marvellous and annihilating truth he had wanted to think through and to feel. Maurice Blanchot put this perfectly: 'It has long seemed to me that the nervous problems you suffer from . . . are just your own way of living this truth authentically, of keeping yourself at the level of that impersonal misfortune that is the world's heart.'[3]

The illness set in straight away and was soon severe, but was not so bad that it entirely stopped the patient from carrying on his life. On the contrary, these years even corresponded to the only – modest – fame he ever enjoyed. The publication of *Lascaux ou la naissance de l'art* in 1955 was to be the impetus for a series of lectures he continued through a number of significant articles (like 'La vallée de la Vézère') that showed his lucidity still intact.

The question of whether a kind of 'madness' came into his life along with the illness is doubtless of secondary importance in Bataille's case. This is first because the process of 'gradual loss of sanity' threatened by the cerebral arteriosclerosis did not have time to progress to such a degree that Bataille ever *totally* lost his capacity for thought (certainly it diminished, but only for brief acute spells, as was also sometimes true for his self-control). Second, this was because 'madness', or at least its possibility as the limit of experience, was too essential a part of his thought and work for there not to be a danger of over-interpreting their encounter – their violent confrontation – with the loss of faculties which he never again managed to shake off.

Was the fascination held for him by the bloody eccentricities of the Aztecs and the impossible Chinese torture of the Hundred Pieces 'madness'? Was the conviction that humans had an eye on top of their heads that could confront the blinding sunlight without blinking 'madness'? Was the project Bataille devised for a human sacrifice so the Acéphale community could attain the sacred 'madness'? There is too much *reason* in Bataille's thought for him not to have expressed, on several occasions, this hypothesis, one he voiced as a self-reproach and a regret. However, he certainly did not so greatly reproach and regret it that he did not confirm his preference, in the last resort, for the irrational (even if such a violent irrationality was close to a loss of reason):

> Having nothing against reason and rational order, in the numerous cases in which it is clearly opportune (like anyone), I support them both. I do not know if anything in this world has ever appeared *adorable* which does not exceed the needs of utility, does not devastate and freeze the blood, even as it charms, which was not, in short, on the point of being no longer endurable.[4]

He even stressed this preference so firmly that he was not afraid, when the need arose, of the close complicity of excess, transgression, ecstasy and so on, as he thought and *played* on them, and the madness they exposed or even engendered in the self. He was neither unaware of this, nor did he hide it from himself: 'The sovereign disposition of self which touches the limit of madness' does not allow one to know for certain 'if we will not break the mechanism'.[5]

Bataille gave a frankly negative definition of this mechanism in advance, in which he not only calmly associated reason and mental health (perhaps to reduce reason to nothing but mental health), but which he also gave as that which *subordinates*: 'mental health is the gratifying functioning of a machine whose effective activity is the end, but to which it is human not to be reduced'.[6] Art – art in general, and his own in particular – are insubordinate. There is no art that does not (and should not) wish this, and which, darkly, tragically, does not triumph when it attains madness (in his words, mental pathology). Madness is the risk run by art, but not as in having something missing (not in the sense that madness would end in the failure of the work), not as in failing to reach its goal (the only goal it can have is not to have any goal), it is a risk it runs, 'by rigour and necessity', as an end in itself: 'From this comes the intimate, overwhelming, meaning of the immeasurable victory that the madness of Hölderlin, or those of Van Gogh or Nietzsche, represents.'[7]

So what was the meaning of the loss of reason Bataille underwent in fits and starts from the moment he was plunged into illness? To consider this meaning as consubstantial with his work and thought (a solar thought that was excessive or utterly sombre, that itself produced first the faltering and then the collapse of reason) would be pointless lyricism. It might be better, if only to cut short any kind of literary sentimentality, to imagine an effect of fortuitous and, what is more, highly effective verification. This 'madness' *verified* the work at the same time as it fulfilled what constantly motivated it. It was not for nothing that Bataille was endlessly haunted by Nietzsche's madness:[8] it was not that this madness had the meaning needed for any thought that takes reversal as far as it can, but because the 'immeasurable victory' represented by any madness is the price that must be paid to useful, effective reason if it is to be freed from subordination.

To think everything to a point that makes people tremble

> This harsh thirst for sensuous murder, which wrings the nerves and gives to the silent pleasure of existence a madly divine and shadowy irritation, no doubt responding alone to the first timid and anguished expectation, then, without transition, to a frenzied and always furious cutting into pieces of the possible, which is the sensuality of men and women.

In 1956, in a curious foreshortening of literary history and a supplementary effect of its dualities, Bataille, the unacknowledged author of several clandestine books, gave evidence at the trial brought against Jean-Jacques Pauvert for having published four books by D. A. F. de Sade.[1] His deposition was a model of Jesuitical equivocation, revealing a restrained fascination and 'scientific' justification (Bataille gave evidence as a *philosopher* in a quite unexpected way: when circumstances required he could always address his listener in suitable language – the need here was for Pauvert's discharge and the free circulation of the incriminated books[2]):

> We should today retain the possibility of using Sade as a means of descent into a space of abyss and horror, an abyss and horror which we should find out about and, moreover, which philosophy (the sort of philosophy I represent[3]) has a particular duty to foreground, to illuminate and disseminate.... I consider that for someone who wants to go to the depths of what man signifies, the reading of Sade is not only commendable, but essential.[4]

Bataille's position is not only clearly courageous, it is also faithful to what he always required: to elude nothing! Faithful to what Sade himself drily required: to 'say everything to a point that makes people tremble'.[5] Bataille adopted and considerably expanded this injunction, since as a philosopher he was concerned with going to the very depths of what it means to be human: there is every reason, at the point people tremble, to *think everything*. In our depths, there is no human meaning, or none that is not provisionally given to it by thought, that does not demand that we read Sade, that we read everything (without eluding anything) he wrote. To read him is, then, not only recommended; it is absolutely necessary. In this respect too Bataille was true to what he had thought (and no doubt enacted) all his life: far from betraying the free movement of sensuality, excess points to its meaning. It does so better than any celebration of its insipid (familiar) joy. On the one hand are those satisfied with pleasurable sensuality, those (and there are many of them) who are indifferent to the vertiginous aspects of passion. On the other hand are those (perhaps there are many of them too, perhaps only one) who are obsessed by the frightful overturning of the possible, who will not rest until they have attained the impossible. From the former, humanity has learned nothing except what fear had already taught it. To the latter (Sade, for example), it owes the fact that, in going beyond the possible, they lessened the impossible in some way, making it no longer definitively impossible.

Justice does not in this case fail to ascribe to their actions (the actions by which the possible has been repelled) the wrong they themselves are, that they wanted to be, and which as such it condemns (which it cannot fail, as such, to condemn; not condemning it would deprive this wrong, this passage to the impossible, of the significance it sought). Bataille said so forcefully, three years before the trial at which he was a witness:

> without the laws which condemn it, crime would perhaps be the impossible, but not considered as such. And the person hallucinated by the impossible also wants, from the object of his obsession, what would really be impossible.... Often, the criminal himself wants death as the answer to the crime, in order finally to impart the sanction, without which the crime would be *possible* instead of being *what it is*, what the criminal wanted.[6]

This is why Bataille responded 'obliquely' to the persistent questioning from the President of the Magistrates Court (who reproached him for it): Is Sade dangerous? Should it be forbidden to read him? He did so no doubt less because he feared not being understood, or being understood incorrectly as encouraging a contagion, as because the

President's questioning had little meaning except when reversed. No one will become Sade, or one of his characters, at least certainly not by *reading him*. To read him is not enough: to an unusual extent, seduction is lacking in his work. However, some people are obsessed with what obsessed Sade. They are obsessed with it because such is the logic of the play of passions that, in going beyond the possible, it wants the impossible. And this anticipated response (it dates from 1953) also concerns the law: there is in fact no reason for justice to believe itself lacking in the responses appropriate to this 'frightful reversal'. Often, the one who goes beyond the possible, in this way taking his desire to its ultimate end, expects death as the answer to his crime. Death alone – and justice is simply feeble in giving it to him – confers on his crime the character of the impossible that provoked it.

'God: a Feydeau-style situation comedy'

The year 1957 was the last to see a real literary presence on Bataille's part, but for so long his fate had been that of an unknown – one might also be inclined to say, idealistically but pointlessly, an accursed – writer that it was also the first. Three books appeared almost simultaneously from three different publishers: *La Littérature et le mal* with Gallimard; *L'Érotisme* with Minuit; and *Le Bleu du ciel* with Jean-Jacques Pauvert (the question arises of why, since he had kept this book to himself for so long – twenty-two years – when he agreed to its publication did he agree to its appearance under his own name). For the first time, his work attracted the attention of the mainstream press: the *Figaro littéraire* devoted a brief article under the title 'La littérature est du côté du mal' ['Literature is on the side of evil'] to the reception organised at the Bar du Pont-Royal by all three publishers to mark Georges Bataille's sixtieth birthday.[1]

The interview with Marguerite Duras which appeared in *France Observateur* on 12 December 1957[2] was an important one, and revealed a new – ironic – relation between Bataille and what he thought could be said and understood. This irony was all the more surprising and significant in that we know how seriously he behaved even in the most ordinary circumstances and regardless of whom he spoke to.[3] When Marguerite Duras asked if an 'external appearance' might exist to signify sovereignty, he replied that 'a cow in a meadow' seemed appropriate enough. When asked to describe God, he replied that he imagined something analogous to the idea of 'a Feydeau-style situation comedy' (he noted that God would not have to play the same pranks as Feydeau's characters to make him laugh). On a more serious note, he said something that has generally been poorly understood: 'I am not someone who lives in hope. I never understood how someone could kill themselves from lack of hope' (more important for the future than hope is understanding); and he said that God, on the contrary, if he existed, would be in a despair no human being could have the power to imagine (a despair such that he would be justified in committing suicide): 'To put yourself in God's position is such a painful position that to be God is equivalent to torture. For it supposes consenting to everything that exists; consenting to the worst.' (This is not a sarcastic comment: all his life Bataille strove to consent to *everything that exists*, including the worst, in other words *Yes*. The torture he suffered would have been the same one God suffered, if he had not died in time, if Nietzsche had not given him death before Auschwitz happened.)

A televised interview on 21 May 1958 was both the climax and the end of this first and modest fame,[4] held with Pierre Dumayet as part of the broadcast *Lectures pour tous*. In it, Bataille appeared relaxed and handsome, and scandalous (for the times) beneath an absolutely serene exterior (his way of saying the worst things with an air of innocence was all his own). He talked about literature and what was 'essentially childish' and infantile about it. It is a childishness that literature has in common with eroticism: 'It seems to me very important to perceive the infantile nature of eroticism.' Evidently Bataille was little concerned about demonstrating that eroticism was innocent in the sense morality would like to understand it. It has the cruel, black innocence of childhood. To understand it, one must reflect on what Bataille said of Gilles de Rais: 'We could not deny the monstrosity of childhood. How often would children, if they could, be a Gilles de Rais.' It is a monstrously happy childhood that Bataille was thinking of, childhood that has no limits except those imposed by law (by authority). And literature is dangerous because it is linked to childhood; because it is that element within us that is open to childhood that it is essential for us to 'confront the danger' in it, and that it is essential, through it, to 'perceive the worst'.

This was Georges Bataille's first and last television appearance. He was too tired to remember what he had found to say (though in fact he had been clear to a fault); leaving the television studio, he only recalled having talked about polygamy, and this was enough to send him into raptures. But he was nevertheless not so weary that he did not have one last great project: a new magazine. Maurice Girodias, the first publisher of *Critique*, suggested that the man who in the meantime had become the author of *Eroticism* should create an *erotic* journal. One might class the project for this magazine among Bataille's aborted projects (of which there were plenty) and say no more about it. But the idea demands some investigation, because it was Bataille's last great project – he devoted a year's work to it – and above all in it he brought together most of the themes that all his life he had made his own. These themes appeared in a list indicative of the subjects the magazine expected to cover: sexual taboos, marriage, ritual orgies, sabbaths, sacred and profane prostitution, eroticism and death; cleanliness, dirtiness, beauty, nudity and costume; psychopathology; eroticism and the 'death instinct', and so on. Everything Bataille had thought about eroticism since he had added an analytical epilogue in 1928 to *Story of the Eye* ('Coincidences'), and everything that he had set in play between 1927 and 1930 under the rubrics of the 'Pineal Eye' and the magazine *Documents* is found again here, thirty years later, with scarcely diminished force. This sentence written in 1957 introducing the project could have come from *Documents*; it has its aggressive and sombre determination: 'From the cradle to the death bed, sexuality is the basis of an unrest that the naïvety of common thought, impregnated with idealism, misunderstands.'[5] Idealism insists on misunderstanding it because it does not want to acknowledge its tragic and sacred nature: 'Eroticism opens an abyss. To want to illuminate its depths demands at the same time great resolution and calm lucidity, the consciousness of *everything* that such an intention running so counter to general somnolence might set in play: it is certainly the most horrible, and also *the most sacred*.'[6]

This journal was given the title *Genèse* (Genesis) – others considered were *L'Écharde* ('The splinter'), *Innocence*, *Sphynx* and *Transgression*. It was to come out four times a year (at one point it was to have been every two months), in French and English; an editorial board and, as we shall see, lists of contents were drawn up which give a fairly clear picture of what *Genèse* would have been and how, albeit with different contributors (perhaps greater 'authorities' – there were plenty of scientists involved), *Genèse* could have constituted a follow-up to *Documents*, for which Bataille and Leiris made no secret of harbouring fond memories.[7] This editorial team was to have been led by three men: Maurice Girodias, who was to have been its publisher as well as its financial backer (which, in the end, would not have entailed much), Georges Bataille who, as the project's inspiration, was to have been in charge,[8] and Patrick Waldberg, with whom Bataille had been linked before the war, when he participated in the Acéphale community and lived in his house in Saint-Germain-en-Laye for several months, who was to have been its editor-in-chief. Since Bataille was living in Orléans in 1957, it is thanks to the lengthy correspondence between him and Waldberg that we know some of the elements of the projected contents and the names of the expected participants: Robert Lebel ('An attempt to decipher the unconscious image in a non-figurative painting'), René Leibowitz ('Is there an erotic music?'), Man Ray (an article on the female face and some unpublished photographs), Édouard Glissant, Pascal Pia, Alfred Métraux (an article on obscenity and death), Gilbert Lély, Michel Leiris and others.[9]

It took a year to work out the plans for *Genèse*, a year in which disagreements between Maurice Girodias and Georges Bataille increased. These differences of opinion were less about the journal's orientation than about Girodias's fear that it was not interesting enough and would not gain a large enough readership. In a letter of 11 August 1958, Girodias is pleased that what he calls the 'serious' side of the journal was secure, but worries that what might potentially constitute 'its attraction for the average reader' has been 'seriously neglected' (and by average, he clarifies, he means 'mediocre'). It seems that he was soon much more explicit with Patrick Waldberg: he wanted *Genèse* to include more 'vehement images', through which it would attract a 'perverted clientele'. Waldberg, like Bataille, would not agree to this. On 6 December 1958 Maurice Girodias put an end to Bataille's last great project. *The Tears of Eros* which Bataille had begun to write at the same time in some ways took up its challenge, albeit reduced to what he *alone* (it really did seem solitude was unavoidable) could take stock of.

Regardless of the fact that it never appeared, the journal *Genèse* once again gives meaning to the lifelong interest shown by Bataille for magazines; in other words, the acute lifelong interest he showed for the community of thought that magazines make up or attempt to make up, and to which books are by their very nature powerless to lay claim. There had been *Documents*, *Acéphale* and *Critique* which he edited (the third until his death); *La Critique sociale* in which his participation was much more than just occasional, indeed to which he contributed some of his major texts of the inter-war years. There was *Minotaure* which the surrealists had taken away from him even though it was in opposition to them that, at Skira and Tériade's request, he had developed the project with André Masson. Finally there were the journals *Troisième convoi*, *Vrille*, *Verve* and *Botteghe oscure* (among others): the texts he published in them after the war are not insignificant – on the contrary, they happily accepted Bataille's 'skewed' texts, those perhaps he felt he could not publish in *Critique*.[10]

Because it never existed, although it never existed, the journal *Genèse* thus takes on a phantom position in Bataille's work. It is a phantom one just like the books he wanted to write but did not (they are innumerable; but perhaps among them all 'Le fascisme en France' bears the greatest weight), like the books he started, but did not finish (*La Limite de l'utile, Histoire de l'érotisme*), like the books he finished or nearly finished but did not publish (*Sovereignty, Theory of Religion* and so on), a position it is not enough to call a vacuum to which he himself or circumstances abandoned them; and that might be considered more appropriately as the *excreta* of the 'completed' work, anticipating its inevitable incompletion ('We are not in the habit of taking account of it, if we reflect, if we speak, but death will interrupt us'). It is a constitutive incompletion.

'One day this living world will pullulate in my dead mouth'

'It was then we could have measured the courage of this man who, tortured in his body and mind, each morning offered the most attentive face to us, the one most constantly equal to himself. . . . He nevertheless gradually became distant from us, almost excusing himself – as for a lack or some clumsiness – for this absence by which he slipped away from himself.'[1] Georges Bataille wanted to observe how one dies. He wanted to know how the body collapses, and how, in a body, awareness breaks down. He wanted to know how thought becomes stranded inside itself, 'in other words in a thought in which a consciousness of foundering survives' in a foundering thought, and – is this not the impossible? – watching itself founder. All his life Georges Bataille exalted in the thought of death (that moment which reduces every moment to itself; of all moments, that of death is the only one to be absolute). Today what exalted him – a dark and tragic exaltation – is the death of thought. The thought of death, reaching the point of the most weakened of meditations, is no more than the most intolerable (and the ultimate) thought of non-knowledge. Henceforth what is more dazzling than *not to know*, what is more dazzling than to die, is the death of thought. This is not just another paradox: the death of thought carries knowledge further. The most knowledge can 'know', its *impossibility*, is its collapse. A sudden collapse, which would coincide with a simple physical death, prevents one from knowing what death *is*. Comparable to the experience the soul has of God, thought can do what just a moment before was impossible and concealed, that is, it can experience death.[2] And for someone who, like Bataille, loved death (is this not singular? Can one *love death*; can one love life to the point of loving its limit just as much through neither weakness nor exhaustion?), to experience his own foundering is no less ecstatic: 'If the death of thought is pushed as far as the point at which it is sufficiently *dead thought* in order to be no longer either despairing or anguished, then there is no longer a difference between the death of thought and ecstasy.'[3]

Sick people are often immobilised: do they expect death to come to them when they are asleep? Bataille, in contrast, was to move around a lot in the last three years of his life. These were *sick* displacements, to be sure, whose *meaning* he needed to measure from one day to the next as so many stations in his collapse of consciousness; one day, the improvement in his condition (significantly, he judged it by the possibility being suddenly restored to him of collecting his ideas together and of writing) could convince him that it would not be fatal. Another day, its intensification could incapacitate him (the texts he was working on would then remain as they were; the worst was that correcting them made them worse); but, incapacitated or not, his condition 'enchanted' him: death is 'dirty', but for this reason it is also divine. He stayed for some time at Sables-d'Olonnes (quai Wilson), sometimes at Vézelay (to which he loved to return), but most often at Fontenay-le-Comte, with the least known and kindest of his friends from after the war, André Costa.[4] The final journey he took was to stay with Patrick Waldberg at Seillans, in the Var, in August 1960.

But this stay was not the last time he moved. There was another that, had it not been for his sickness and had it not been so serious, would have corresponded to ending the exile (the word Bataille himself used) that circumstances had imposed on him since the end of the war. On 1 February 1962 he asked Julien Cain, the Head of Libraries and also one of his friends, if he could return to work at the Bibliothèque Nationale. This request was symbolic, as much so as any of his books, of the life Bataille had been forced to lead: at sixty-five years of age, seriously ill, he was still forced to work. Nothing he had written until then had given him the means to devote himself to his writing.[5] His request being accepted, Bataille left Orléans and set himself up in the last of the flats he would inhabit, in the rue Saint-Sulpice.[6] He was to live there only for a few months. On the morning of 8 July, Georges Bataille died in the presence of a friend, Jacques Pimpanneau. In one *moment* he was, one last time, and definitively, sovereign.

In the small cemetery of Vézelay, the village in which he had lived for a long time and which he liked best of all, there would be only peasants to accompany him.[7] A simple dark gravestone is adorned with nothing but this now barely legible inscription:

GEORGES BATAILLE
1897–1962

Those substances where the eggs, germs and maggots swarm not only make our hearts sink, but also turn our stomachs. Death does not come down to the bitter annihilation of being – of all that I am, which expects to be once more, the very meanings of which, rather than to be, is to expect to be (as if we never received *being* authentically, but only the anticipation of being, which will be and is not, as if we were not the presence that we are, but the future that we will be and are not); it is also that shipwreck in the nauseous. I will rejoin abject nature and the purulence of anonymous, infinite life, which stretches forth like the night, which is death. One day this living world will pullulate in my dead mouth.[8]

And finally, incompletion

It would be pointless to speak of any last texts as final testaments in Bataille's case, since everything shows that all his writing (in the sense that death is their only limit) already has this nature of a testament. All his life Bataille wrote with his eye on death, thinking of anguish and of ecstasy; inflamed, fascinated by death. Neither illness nor the imminence of his death obliged him to consider what his life might have let him escape: at sixty-four years of age he was the same man he had been at forty.

It would also be pointless because Bataille never thought there might be anything definitive about his writing, that it might achieve anything. There was not one of his books that he did not wish in some way to change, revise or rewrite. Thus for him his illness could bring nothing that might have claimed to supply an end to his thought.[1] Death does not finish anything: it prolongs incompletion.

Only those who survived him knew that this incompletion had come to an end; that once silence had been established, the disorder in which he had left his names,[2] his papers[3] and the world would not be changed by any new disorder (nothing at all would be added or taken away from them). What he said and wrote immediately beforehand (at this moment of sudden blindness, of a 'step beyond') took on the misleading air of what should finally and definitively be known about him, lifted or pushed to that level of extreme intensity of an instant that is pure because it is annihilating: of the waking instant.

A year before his death, in March 1961, Bataille agreed to a long interview with Madeleine Chapsal for *L'Express* which gave him an opportunity to make a concise summing up of the themes of his life and work (ultimately in few writers can they be less distinguishable). And, extraordinarily, this summing up (this is an inappropriate phrase, since it suggests a finishing; it would be better to say an inventory), because of its inevitable simplification, reduced the signs under which this life and work were always placed, as if a harsh light were cast on their most trenchant incandescence.

It was no surprise that in speaking of eroticism he described it as an internal experience. Hitherto he had not only avoided saying this, he had always clearly separated them. Eroticism is an internal experience because it is 'the most powerful route to enter the instant'. It is the one thing the future cannot touch: it spends, it wastes, it inflames, but not without having to make allowances for the elation it is foolishly associated with, as well as for what it 'can bring that is extremely distressing and painful'.

In the same way that elation and anguish tear eroticism apart (what might one think of an eroticism that is not only desirable or not only repugnant but both at once?), they tear laughter apart too: 'There is in the very fact of laughing a radiance whose foundation is ultimately a collapse.' The same rift is at work, intensifying the states of hilarity and of eroticism, the same rift that brings about ecstasy (communication) and disintegration (laughter is the depth of worlds). Laughter is the depths of worlds, as Bataille had already said in 1920, but he had never said so more simply or cruelly. It is the depths of worlds because it is the most profound ambiguity: 'the human ambivalence is that we cry at death, but when we laugh we do not know we are laughing at death.' His cruelty is extreme (so extreme he seemed to hesitate for a moment. It was the *NO* of Don Juan to the 'infatuated old man'): 'Perhaps I'll be boasting, but death is what seems to me the most ridiculous thing in the world.' It was not that he might not be afraid of it (even as he spoke, death was upon him), but that only laughter delivers you from the fear of death, only laughter makes it light; laughter says *Yes* because, like eroticism, it is the most profound assent to life, to the point of death: 'But it seems to me that I first needed to devour death under its most terrible aspect, without allowing myself to be so impressed as not to laugh about it. It is really a question there of something atheist, because one cannot laugh at death in the presence of a God who is a judge.' Death is already everything. It is the profound void left by God's death. In dying in his turn, Bataille simply reached, this time definitively, the place the God had vacated: 'It is this empty place I wanted to talk about.' In dying, it was from this place he would henceforth fall silent.

One would like to quote this entire interview;[4] and quote what

Bataille said, in conclusion, about disorder ('What I am most proud about is having shuffled the cards . . . in other words having associated the practice of the most turbulent, most shocking, most scandalous laughter with the deepest religious spirit'[5]), about fever and rage. Above all about the rage that must *also* be understood as that with which Bataille settled everything he thought and undertook politically, a rage whose nature is such that nothing could claim either to appease or exhaust it, a rage against the existing state of things, against life itself: 'It is very clear that somehow, whatever type of society there is, when it comes to it, this rage will always reappear, because I do not believe one can reach a state of things that would allow us to get to the root of this rage.'[6]

The challenge was to be God: to want to think what he died of not being able to think. And now Bataille was to die in his turn. Throughout his life death exalted him just as it enraged him. As Don Juan said *NO* to the 'infatuated old man', in dying Bataille said *Yes* to death, yes to weariness, yes finally to the impotence of being God, and there is no less fury in saying yes than no, there is only, *what is more*, the feeling of a triumphant assenting to the torn apart, tragic order of the world:

> Feelings of being daring followed by a failure. But this failure was not inevitable. Not that I attribute my failure just to my growing old. There is, no doubt, something more essential. In a way I would not be up to an extreme ambition. It can be interpreted in three ways. Either I personally am not made of the right stuff, or else no one is, or else, as an old man, I might have been but no longer am – at least I would have been if I had worked on it . . . But I like death: the idea of death, which I don't see as a failure.

> There is no failure there is death
> which is not failure
> An ardent death but not
> a furious one, happy even, the opposite of failure.[7]

Afterword

Georges Bataille: It seems to me that it is important to perceive what is lacking in the world, I know that one can simply say that it is not a lack, since one can do without it, but that is not true for everyone: there are some people for whom the memory of what God represented . . . I need to be careful, for I think I might say something stupid here, in other words very oppressive things, but in the end it seems that we can perceive what Nietzsche expressed by his phrase about the death of God. For Nietzsche, what he called the death of God left a terrible emptiness, something dizzy, almost, and hard to accept. Fundamentally, it is rather like what happens the first time one becomes aware of what is signified, what is implied, by death: everything we are is revealed to be fragile and perishable, that on which we base all the calculations of our existence is fated to dissolve in a sort of flimsy mist . . . Is my statement at an end?

Madeleine Chapsal: I think so.

Georges Bataille: If it is not at an end, it would express fairly well what I wanted to say . . . [1]

Notes

Where no author of a book is specified, it is Georges Bataille. Full details of his works are given in the Bibliography on p. 581. If full details of other books are not given in the Notes, they are listed in the Bibliography.

In the beginning was death

1. *Œuvres complètes*, VI, p. 444.
2. Ibid., p. 445.
3. There can be little doubt that, given the sickness afflicting his father, this child would have been 'aborted' had he been 'conceived' fifty years later.
4. In a letter to his brother of 31 March 1961, Martial Bataille clearly stated: 'You know perfectly well that our father did not die mad and that our mother, before dying, did not lose her reason.' Was Joseph-Aristide Bataille mad or not when he died? No one knows. There are no other witnesses to his death. As for their mother, Georges Bataille never said she lost her reason before dying. What he said was that she lost it at the time her husband died.
5. In fact, Martial Bataille said nothing about it up to the time he died in 1967, and his deepest wish seems to have been for that silence to be maintained (he wrote to his brother: 'My dearest wish is to hear nothing more about it'). He must have been offended yet again by the publication in 1963 of *Le Petit* and in 1966 of *The Story of the Eye*. In 1961, in a letter addressed to his family, he did not hesitate to say that his brother was the devil.
6. Draft of a letter to Martial Bataille in 1961 (April or May).
7. *Œuvres complètes*, V, *Le Coupable*, p. 534, Notes [These notes are not included in *Guilty*, the English translation of *Le Coupable*. trans]. We can see, as brief as it may be, that this description demonstrates two things: the absence of a church (the profusion of churches in Bataille's work cannot fail to be connected to it), and the crater which will be one of the props of his disorders before he so systematically associated it with the fear and fascination of death.
8. In a college by the name of Jean Barbe, though we do not know in which town.
9. Hostile references to prisons abound in Bataille's work. This is not one of the more explicit: 'The extreme is the window: fear of the extreme enters the darkness of a prison with a hollow will of the penitentiary administration.'

10. Or before the birth of his elder son. In fact the tabetic aetiology indicates that the tabes appear between eight and fifteen years after the tumour.

11. Many inaccurate things have been said about his father. André Masson, a fellow student in 1918–19 in Paris (and an exact homonym of the painter André Masson, one of Bataille's closest friends), indicated that Bataille's father had died young and was a doctor (both of which are incorrect). This error is of interest not in itself (André Masson's good faith is not in question) but for the fact that the young Bataille needed to 'correct' his genealogy and maybe ennoble it (see André Masson, 'Notice nécrologique', *Bulletin de la bibliothèque de l'École des Chartres*, no. 122, 1964).

12. *Story of the Eye*, p. 72.

13. Ibid., p. 72.

14. Ibid. This opening may be considered brutal, and by including it I may be accused of giving way to a wish for scandal and so on. Yet, whether true or fictional (I will pose the question), these 'memories' are indispensable to the work – indispensable to the point where one might not understand the whole of its meaning if they were ignored.

15. Radio interview, 1959. In the same interview, Bataille replied to the question: 'Did you always know your father as a blind man?' with 'Yes, always!' Inclined as Bataille was to admit the conditions of his childhood, here this concerns only his father's blindness, not at all his 'madness'.

16. General paralysis is one of the neurological manifestations of syphilis in the late (or tertiary) stage of its evolution. Its symptoms, that need to be distinguished from those of paralysis in the current sense of the word, include a development towards dementia, which may or may not be accompanied by psychopathological difficulties (the dementia Martial denied), and the patient is increasingly bedridden. The tabes constitute a complication of vigorous syphilis reaching the tertiary state of its evolution. The lesions are then located at the level of the rear roots and cords of the marrow. The tabes is frequently associated with other neurological (blindness, general paralysis) or extra-neurological (syphilitic aority) manifestations.

17. Problems of the sphincter and genitals also result in disturbance of the mechanisms of the elementary reflexes: impotence is habitual and urinary problems often involve anaesthesia of urination.

18. *Story of the Eye*, p. 76. This comes from the preface published in *Le Petit* (1943), *Œuvres complètes*, III, and is published as an appendix in the English edition of *Story of the Eye*.

19. Ibid., pp. 76–7.

20. It impossible to avoid saying this *as well*; I repeat it, whether it is true or not. We shall see how a number of subsequent texts will be organised and structured around this initial obsession.

21. *Story of the Eye*, p. 72.

22. Ibid., p. 72.

23. Tabetic stabbing pains, variable in their intensity, are distinguished by their perfect localisation in time and space. A sudden, brief, flashing, sensation,

perfectly localised in one point (a pinprick more often than a dagger thrust). The same sensation is repeated at the same place with relative regularity, from a few seconds to a few minutes, constituting in this way an attack which lasts for several hours or days.

24. Ibid., pp. 72–3.

25. Bataille's statement seems to exclude his brother's presence.

26. Ibid., p. 73.

27. Ibid., p. 73.

28. Ibid., p. 23.

29. As we shall see, Marie-Antoinette Bataille lived for another fifteen years after the death of her husband. For most of these years, she lived with her sons Georges and Martial. There is no suggestion that she ever again lost her reason once these crises were over.

30. That is, *Story of the Eye*, the epilogue entitled 'Coincidences', and in the chapter of *Le Petit* entitled 'W.-C.'

31. Ibid., p. 73.

32. It is true that the mother of Marie-Antoinette Bataille, Georges's grand-mother, Anne Tournadre, was then still alive. She died on 15 April 1916. This scene could have taken place at Riom where she lived or at Rheims, where she seems to have stayed with her daughter.

33. Ibid., p. 74.

34. Ibid. This scene seems to have occurred at Riom-ès-Montagnes. At least that is what Bataille later claimed. We will see that this detail is not lacking in importance, for thus it would be prior to the departure from Rheims and in this case dates from the winter of 1914–15.

35. Ibid., p. 76. No doubt the village of R. is Riom (ès-Montagnes). 'Coincidences', as we have seen, is the epilogue of *Story of the Eye*.

36. Letter to Miss C. (emphasis added).

'Turn the world upside down, turn the world, quite ineluctably, upside down'

1. This was given as his profession when his death was registered at Rheims Town Hall.

2. *Blue of Noon*, p. 106. It is true that this text is presented as in no way autobiographical. On the contrary, it is part of a story (*Le Bleu du ciel*). Therefore to take it for real is only conjecture, though it is a plausible one.

3. *Le Coupable* in *Œuvres complètes*, V, p. 555, Notes.

4. *Œuvres complètes* II, p. 10, *Rêve*. 'There was the descent into the cellar, in relation to this childhood dream, so often and so anxiously repeated, a dream associated with a firework from 14 July – a death star. The memory of going down to the cellar with my father is without doubt the memory I most recoil from. A false memory? My father was blind, but still had to go to the cellar and from the age of two and a half or three years I was able to guide him (*Œuvres complètes*, V, p. 555).

5. *Œuvres complètes*, V, *Méthode de méditation*, p. 210. In an article in *Arts*, Marcel Bisiaux gave this strange variant in the form of a reprimand: 'What is laziest? You!' 'What is dirtiest? You!'

6. *Blue of Noon*, p. 108.

7. This was the only school in Rheims at the time. Today it is the Georges-Clemenceau School, named after the street on which it is situated. Before Bataille's time, Paul Fort had been among its pupils; after him, René Daumal, Roger Gilbert-Lecomte and Bataille's future friend Roger Caillois. For a time it was mooted that the school should be named after Caillois.

8. It is unfortunately not possible to have details about Bataille's attendance at the Rheims school since the archives were destroyed during the 1915 bombardments.

'The thunderbolt pilots all things'

1. Heraclitus.

2. He said of himself: 'was officially converted on August 14'.

3. Rheims cathedral was particularly singled out, it would seem because of the French wounded sheltering there. In a single day in September 1914, fifteen of them were killed in the shelling. It has been calculated that 245 shells hit Notre-Dame de Reims between 24 September 1914 and 5 October 1918 (Mgr Landrieux, *La cathédrale de Reims, un crime allemand*, 1919).

4. *Œuvres complètes*, III, *Le Petit*, p. 60. In another account of the same events, Bataille gives a very slightly different version, in which it was the news of his father's death which brought him and his mother back to Rheims to bury him (*Œuvres complètes*, V, *Le Coupable*, p. 505, Notes).

5. *Le Petit*, p. 60.

6. Ibid., p. 61.

7. *Œuvres complètes*, V, *Le Coupable*, p. 504, Notes.

8. *Œuvres complètes*, III, *Le Petit*, p. 61.

9. Ibid.

10. Ibid.

11. If, absurdly, Bataille's work and thought could be reduced to three or four words, the impossible would without doubt be one of them. If Bataille had not used it as the title of one of his books, it could have served for this one.

12. There is an ancient story that King Midas hunted in the forest a long time for the wise Silenus, the companion of Dionysus, without capturing him. When Silenus at last fell into his hands, the king asked what was the best and most desirable of all things for man. Fixed and immovable, the demigod said not a word, till at last, urged by the king, he gave a shrill laugh and broke out into these words: 'Oh, wretched ephemeral race, children of chance and misery, why do you compel me to tell you what it would be most expedient for you not to hear? What is best of all is utterly beyond your reach: not to be born, not to *be*, to be *nothing*.

But the second best for you is – to die soon.' (Nietzsche, *The Birth of Tragedy*, p. 42).

13. *Œuvres complètes*, V, *Le Coupable*, p. 505, Notes. The recoil would have taken the form of conversion to Catholicism.

14. *Œuvres complètes*, V, p. 447.

15. If at no point is Freudian analysis used here, it is because in this case it only appears to be of doubtful value. It is effectively of little use to say, following Freud, that 'A study of dreams, phantasies and myths has taught us that anxiety about one's eyes, the fear of going blind, is often enough a substitute for the dread of being castrated' ('The Uncanny', p. 352). Should one deduce from the fact that Bataille prays to God, in order to understand better, to give him blindness ('a rending desire that my eyes be put out! To be blind . . . so I may see!') that he unconsciously desired, rather than feared, castration . . . the better to love, to say *Yes*! What is at stake here is less Freudian logic than what its doxa might risk making of it. To those who nevertheless would venture such interpretations, it is not irrelevant to recall what Bataille himself suggested: that the castration complex, oversaturated and ultimately ineffective, should be replaced by the Promethean complex. To which one could add 'For the child, who in its terror of being cut up, seeks to provoke the bloody culmination, gives not the slightest proof of an absence of virility: an excess of strength, on the other hand, and a fit of horror hurls it blindly towards everything in the world that is most cutting, which is solar brilliance' (*Œuvres complètes*, II, p. 45).

16. *Inner Experience*, p. 153.

17. Hegel, *The Phenomenology of Spirit*.

Ave Caesar

1. The registration of the death at the town hall was made by two people unknown to the family.

2. Bataille said on several occasions how fond he was of the Auvergne landscape.

3. In all likelihood, living in Rheims, he spent his summers in Riom-ès-Montagnes. The friendship forged with Georges Delteil thus predates 1914.

4. At twenty certainly, but also at seventeen and eighteen. The whole of Bataille's period in Riom-ès-Montagnes was Catholic and even devout.

5. Georges Delteil, 'Georges Bataille à Riom-ès-Montagnes', *Critique*, nos 195–6, August/September 1963.

6. But, again, it is doubtful that philosophy was then central to his preoccupations. It is more likely that his interests lay in theology at this time.

7. At Saint-Flour, the bishopric.

8. *Œuvres complètes*, VII, *La Limite de l'utile*, p. 523.

9. Ibid., p. 524. Bataille added to these lines written twenty-five years later that he felt disgust for the 'great words' and 'great principles' he saw paraded everywhere. *Notre-Dame de Rheims*, written in 1918, shows that this is

certainly not the case; he was not above using the same words and principles himself, or nearly.

10. Of this period as a sick soldier, he said he had brought back a diary entitled *Ave Caesar*. It does not appear to have survived.

'Laid out like a corpse'

1. With, as will be seen, some recovered letters dating from the years 1919 and 1922. There must also be youthful poems by Bataille. Only one can be found among the papers of his cousin Marie-Louise: 'The old folk's brows'. It is unpublished, and no doubt better so. What could be the interest of reading poems where words like 'sabot' and 'faggot', 'bushy' and 'churlishly' are rhymed?

2. We are indebted to André Masson, Bataille's school friend, for having brought attention to the existence of this book after the author's death. It thus seems that he was the only one of his adult friends to have known about it. And it is Jean Bruno who was able to find a copy of it.

3. A sacrifice and a martyrdom. In his fine book, *La Prise de la Concorde*, Denis Hollier cites this text by Émile Mâle, *Nouvelle Étude sur la cathédrale de Reims*:

> I saw Rheims cathedral after its final damage: a phantom church in the middle of a phantom city . . . The cathedral in cinders, covered with deep impairment, baring its insides, at first appals . . . But soon a feeling emerges which causes others to be forgotten: a tender and deep veneration. The cathedral resembled a martyr who had passed through torture and whose executioners had failed to break it. It also had its Passion: its beauty will henceforth be added to its sanctity.

The school of the flesh

1. Bataille was as fascinated by this language as by what it said. André Masson says: 'Impassioned by research into language and full of scorn for the construction of classical phrases, he took pleasure in the semi-barbarous language that forms the transition from Latin to French.'

2. Odo of Cluny, *Collationnes*, book 2. Saint Odo or Odes of Cluny, 879–942, was the second reformer of the Order of Saint Benedict.

3. Anselm of Canterbury, *Le Latin mystique*, *De Contemptu Mundi*, p. 267.

'Hard brow and clear eyes'

1. Letter from Georges Bataille to Marie-Louise Bataille, 9 August 1919, Riom-ès-Montagnes.

2. Ibid.

3. Bataille only alludes to this in his letters.

4. Letter of 29 October 1919.
5. Ibid.
6. Ibid.
7. How can we not recall the obligation to *see* which his father reminded him of?
8. Letter quoted.
9. Ibid.

Tumult and withdrawal

1. It is not dated precisely but, sent from Madrid, was written between February and July 1922.
2. *Inner Experience*, p. 58.

The depths of worlds

1. Henri Bergson, *Œuvres complètes, Le Rire*, pp. 387–9.
2. Ibid., p. 395.
3. It is important not to misunderstand this 'even then'. It indicates he had an intuition of it. Later, he would freely develop some assumptions he still accepted: the assumptions of faith.
4. *Œuvres complètes*, VIII, 'Non-savoir, rire et larmes', p. 222.

La emoción

1. Bataille later jokingly implied that he *sold* his first place ranking to the eventual winner. His thesis was one of four highlighted for the Minister of Education's special attention: 'Mr Georges Bataille has also presented a good dissertation, both philosophical and historical, on a thirteenth-century story in verse. The study he has devoted to the historical sources of this poem have been particularly noted and, if the classification of the eight manuscripts from which Mr Bataille has reconstructed the poem is still in some doubt, we can confidently expect from him an excellent edition of *L'Ordre de la Chevalerie*.'
2. The journal was *Actualité*, this issue entitled *L'Espagne libre*, and his article was 'À propos de *Pour qui sonne le glas*'; I will consider it in due course.
3. Undated letter from Bataille to Marie-Louise Bataille. Three letters survive from this stay in Madrid, from February to July 1922, all undated. There is reason to believe that this stay (or at least the beginning of it) is alluded to in this passage from *Inner Experience*:

> I was far from knowing what I see clearly today, that anguish is linked to them [Bataille is speaking about 'dreamy pleasures']. I couldn't understand at the time that a trip which I had been greatly looking forward to had only brought me uneasiness, that everything had been hostile to me, beings and things, and above all men, whose empty lives in remote villages I was

obliged to see – empty to the point of diminishing him who perceives them – at the same time that I saw a self-assured and malevolent reality. (pp. 112–13).

4. *Actualité, L'Espagne libre*, Calmann-Lévy, 1946, p. 121.

5. It is highly unlikely that he ever made this journey. In 1922 he considered, without much enthusiasm, asking to be nominated for the Cairo Institute, the idea having 'come into his head to take up Coptic art, after learning some Arabic and Muslim archaeology' (letter to Miss C.).

6. Jean-Pierre Le Bouler has the following useful details to offer about Bataille's 'professional' stay: he had been advised by his former professor to work on researching French medieval manuscripts located in Spain. This seems to have added six new manuscripts to the fifteen previously catalogued. His work seems to have taken him to Seville, among other places, where he made a copy of a 'thirteenth-century mystery play', and then to Toledo where he appears, according to Le Bouler, to have become interested in redefining the periods of the construction of Toledo cathedral (along with Elie Lambert who, in 1925, became the author of *Tolède*, a book which, by coincidence, would be published by the same company (H. Laurens) as *La Cathédrale de Reims, un crime allemand* by Maurice Landrieux (Jean-Pierre Le Bouler, *Bibliothèque de l'École des Chartes*, vol. 146, January–June 1988, Librairie Droz)).

7. A monstrance is a piece of liturgical silverware, in the centre of which is set a crystal crescent containing the host presented for the adoration of the faithful. Of the same Spanish sun he would write five years later in *Story of the Eye*: 'exhausting bedazzlement', 'a torrent of the guts'; and of the sky of 'urinary liquefaction'.

8. Five years later when speaking of a Seville priest, he would formulate a phrase which in its way echoed this 'clerical grandeur': 'sacerdotal pig'.

9. In Spanish, 'deep song' (a modulated, incantatory song that is the essence of flamenco).

10. We know that during this stay in Spain, Bataille went to Miranda (south of Bilbao), to Valladolid ('The crossing of Spain from Miranda to Valladolid resembles a heroic march more than a train journey'), to Granada, where he visited the Alhambra and attended this tournament, to Toledo and Seville where the final part of *Story of the Eye* takes place.

11. 'À propos de *Pour qui sonne le glas*', p. 124.

12. Alfred Métraux, 'Rencontre avec les ethnologues', p. 677.

13. *Story of the Eye*, p. 53. The chapter this quotation comes from is titled 'Granero's Eye'.

14. 'À propos de *Pour qui sonne le glas*', p. 120.

15. Ibid., my italics.

16. The letter continues:

So I no longer want to think of her as a completely real creature. In fact I truly want to be sensible. But it would make no sense to know the very angelic person who guides humanity in such a magical way towards the knowledge of love with her pretty, incoherent face, or else cradled into the contemplation of her most multicoloured ecstasies other than through the delights of the imagination.

I have already cited, and will do so again at length in the next chapter, extracts from the letters he exchanged with this individual.

17. In *Story of the Eye.*

18. The letters from Madrid supply an important final piece of information: 'Curiously enough, I have started to write a novel, more or less in the style of Marcel Proust. I can't see how else to write.' Thus Proust seems to be the first 'contemporary' author he read; the first that mattered. Remember that at the date of his departure for Madrid (February 1922), Proust had published volumes 1 (*Du côté de chez Swann*, 1913), 2 (*A l'ombre des jeunes filles en fleur*, 1919), 3 (*Du côté de Guermantes*, 1920) and 4 (*Du côté de Guermantes II, Sodome et Gomorrhe I*, 1921) of *À la recherche du temps perdu*. Whichever of these books Bataille read, it is worth noting that they would have preceded his reading of Nietzsche, the surrealists, Dostoevsky, Gide or German philosophy. We can no doubt see it as an initial reading, and relate it to this: 'I recall having made a connection between my pleasure and those described in the first volumes of *À la recherche du temps perdu*. But I only had a partial and superficial knowledge of Marcel Proust then [*Le temps retrouvé* had not yet been published] and, young as I was, dreamt only of the naïve possibilities of triumph.'

Letters to an unknown woman

1. *On Nietzsche*, pp. 66–7.

2. Perhaps it is not unhelpful to contrast Bataille's affirmation with the testimony of Georges Delteil, his childhood friend: 'When he was twenty, in the Auvergne mountains, he led the life of a saint, imposing upon himself a discipline of work and contemplation.

3. Georges Bataille spoke several foreign languages. If he did not show a great deal of tenacity in pursuing Chinese, Russian or Tibetan, he read and wrote perfect English (in the view of his second wife Diane Bataille, whose first language was English), Spanish, German and Italian. It seems that at school he had read Greek (there is a copy of Plato annotated by him) and Latin.

4. Discretion prevents me from naming the person who received these letters. In truth it has little relevance, since she is less at issue than the person who wrote the letters which, in the long run, can give the feeling that she was only their pretext (the means of a literary process).

5. Georges Bataille, radio interview.

6. It can be regretted that, not pressing further this indecent confession, Bataille does not say what about this woman was both monstrous and beautiful. One word calls for another: sin, then inevitably confession, a rite to

which for a long time (until 1920) and assiduously (once a week), Bataille said he was compelled.

7. 'I promise you that this will not start again.'

8. Without great risk of error, it can be imagined that it was a brothel. What woman other than a prostitute could he have 'only ever seen once' and yet who could be monstrous and beautiful, and from whom he could have taken such pleasures?

9. These letters are full of phrases betraying shame and humiliation: 'Besides, you will appreciate that while I was ashamed of my attitude'; 'I am very ashamed'; 'How humiliated I am to write to you in this way: like a wretch'; 'How you humiliate me!'

10. Bataille's emphasis.

11. These letters are also those of Bataille's transition to literature. If there is still considerable naïvety of thought which, inevitably, the style betrays, here and there are sentences and phrases anticipating the tone later associated with him. 'Exuberant prodigality' (here opposed to parsimony), from this point of view, cannot be more striking, knowing the use Bataille will make of it during his whole life. Among others, I will cite the following: 'Here I am very embarrassed. I no longer know what to say, not because I do not know what I want but because words worry me as they always lie – moderately, perhaps, but don't you imagine that one could hate this moderation and throw oneself impetuously into falsehood instead of this light deception.' And: 'When they cease to be animated by a uniform movement, feelings make an absolutely dazzling play.'

12. It is following this passage that Bataille tells Miss C. about his 'personal experience' of madness: that of his father and his mother.

13. In another letter, Bataille asks his addressee to reflect: 'on the entirely contingent character of the reasons to live and also on the timid and ridiculous superstition which is the sole reason to cease living.' It was with this testimony that he told his cousin how he wanted to die when his request for the hand of Marie Delteil was rejected, the second time Bataille considered the possibility of suicide. It was also the last known occasion.

14. 'It is possible I am horribly egoistical.'

15. Michel Leiris would later say how much the young Bataille he met in 1924 was marked by this character, a character (and novel) which equally marked Léon Chestov, whom Bataille would soon meet. 'The story of the transformation of convictions! In the whole realm of literature there is no other story of such thrilling interest' (Léon Chestov).

'When you have to embark on the seas, you emigrants'

1. Nietzsche, *The Gay Science*, p. 340.
2. *On Nietzsche* p. 67.
3. Interview with Michel Leiris, 1986.
4. 'In short I was animated by a very clear religious faith, conforming to a

dogma, and ... this was very important for me, even to the point that, as completely as I could, I tried to act in accordance with my thoughts' (*Œuvres complètes*, VIII, Conférences, p. 222).

5. Interview with Michel Leiris, 1986.

6. He speaks at length and with admiration of *Paludes* to Miss C., saying in particular that he had just burnt one of his 'poems' ('written at a moment when I was very sad and disturbed'), since reading *Paludes* (specifically pp. 118–23) had suddenly made it pointless to keep it.

7. We know this from the research by Jean-Pierre Le Bouler and Joëlle Bellec-Martini who have traced the books borrowed by Bataille from the Bibliothèque Nationale from the time he started work there (published in *Œuvres complètes*, XII, pp. 553–621). Added to my study of Bataille's personal library, we can pretty well see the evolution of his reading between 1922 and 1924 and beyond.

8. *Œuvres complètes*, VIII, p. 640.

9. *Œuvres complètes*, V, *Le Coupable*, p. 505, Notes.

10. *On Nietzsche*, pp. xxi–ii.

11. It can be seen that such an interpretation of Nietzsche is paradoxically moral, and owes much to Christianity. This interpretation, moreover, would not alter.

12. *On Nietzsche*, p. 87.

13. *Œuvres complètes*, VIII, Conférences, p. 222.

14. *On Nietzsche*, p. 111.

15. Preface to *Story of the Eye*, p. 78.

16. *Œuvres complètes*, XI, p. 127.

17. Nietzsche, *The Gay Science*, p. 340; quoted by Bataille in 'Nietzsche et les fascistes', *Acéphale*, 21 January 1937.

18. Jean Piel, 'Bataille et le monde', p. 722. It goes without saying that this *Yes* was not so immediate or complete. But in fact Bataille soon made it a rule and a morality.

The joyful cynic

1. Fernande Schulmann knew neither Bataille nor Métraux at this time. Her testimony comes from what Alfred Métraux told her when she married him in 1958 (Fernande Schulmann, 'Une amitié, deux disparus', *Esprit*, November 1963, p. 322).

2. Métraux seems to have very soon left the École des Chartes to become an anthropologist.

3. Again according to Fernande Schulmann, 'Une amitié, deux disparus'.

4. *Œuvres complètes*, XII, p. 86. Although all trace of cynicism seems to have vanished from Bataille's memory of it, it seems that he is referring to the same project. Nothing has survived of it.

5. Alfred Métraux, 'Rencontre avec les ethnologues'.

6. Fernande Schulmann, 'Une amitié, deux disparus'.

'Tristi est anima mea usque ad mortem'

1. *Œuvres complètes*, VIII, p. 562.

2. Léon Chestov's philosophy was based on Nietzsche and Dostoevsky, according to Bataille, which is true for the period in which he knew him. Chestov effectively did not discover Kierkegaard, whom he quotes so often and whose thought is so close to his own, until later. But his philosophy also stems from Pascal, Martin Buber, Epictetus, Tertullian, Heraclitus, Marcion, Plotinus ... or it violently rejects others: Hegel, for example. But this, too, could be an influence for Bataille: in Chestov's eyes literature was not of lesser philosophical standing. We know the importance he always attached to Dostoevsky, but he also read and knew Tolstoy, Lermontov, Rozanov, Turgenev, Heinrich Heine, Ibsen and Chekhov.

3. Michel Leiris, 'De Bataille l'impossible à l'impossible *Documents*'.

4. Ibid.

5. Léon Chestov, *La philosophie de la tragédie: Nietzsche et Dostoïevski*.

6. Ibid., p. viii.

7. Ibid., p. 76. 'Nietzsche, in his youth, was a romantic too, a dreamer' (ibid., p. 134). 'We have followed the metamorphosis of Dostoevsky's convictions. All in all it can be pared down to an attempt at the rehabilitation of the underground man' (ibid., p. 133).

8. Christ in the Garden of Gethsemane: 'Tristi est anima mea usque ad mortem.'

9. Ibid., p. 77.

10. Ibid., p. 92.

11. 'A categorical imperative of which Kant never dreamed must ring out. The truths must penetrate our flesh like knives' (ibid., p. 198).

12. Ibid., p. iii.

13. A phrase Bataille might have written.

14. The figures of Abraham and Job would appear in Bataille's work, in *Inner Experience* for example.

15. Often, but not always. As vague as this distinction might be, let us say for the moment that it would not be Bataille's before the war, but it would be afterwards. Léon Chestov wrote: 'Pascal was reincarnated two centuries later in the person of Nietzsche' (*La Nuit de Gethsémani*, p. 51).

16. *Œuvres complètes*, VIII, *La Souveraineté*, p. 671, Notes; Chestovian and Jansenist.

17. Born in Kiev in 1866, he studied Law at Moscow University, and then moved to St Petersburg. See Nathalie Baranoff-Chestov, *Vie de Léon Chestov*.

18. Dated 24 July 1923. Chestov was in Berlin for the translation of his books.

19. 'Your plan to make a study of my works interests me greatly, of course. It proves to me that even as a foreigner I am not a foreigner for a European soul ... We shall discuss it on my return, and work together' (Letter from Léon Chestov to Georges Bataille, Berlin, 24 July 1923).

20. Chestov 'was scandalised by my excessive aversion for philosophical studies' then (*Œuvres complètes*, VIII, p. 568).

21. Bataille already had this violence, as I have said; but it was no doubt Chestov who gave it the form of thought.

22. Ibid.

23. Ibid.

24. *La Philosophie de la tragédie*, p. 37. 'The *underground voice* is a rending cry of terror let out by a man who suddenly discovers that all his life he had lied and played out a role' (Chestov). We shall see that strangely analogical tones will be found in Bataille's work: in *Guilty* for instance.

25. It is no coincidence that Chestov once more quoted Dostoevsky: 'I even affirm that the consciousness of our powerlessness to aid suffering humanity and to relieve it, joined to the certitude of its sufferings, can transform the love we have in our hearts for humanity into hatred for it' (*La Philosophie de la tragédie*, p. 110).

26. Bataille was named as joint translator. It is nevertheless doubtful whether he really collaborated on it (his knowledge of Russian never being more than elementary). There are also grounds for thinking that his role consisted in 'putting the book into French'. Whatever the case, it was the first time in Paris (and thus excluding *Notre-Dame de Rheims*) that his name appeared on a book.

27. Pierre Klossowski in Jean-Maurice Monnoyer, *Le Peintre et le démon*, p. 177. More generally the strange relationship maintained by Bataille with Eastern Europe, especially with Russia, has been little noted. I shall return to it later.

Torpid Maurras and decrepit Moscow

1. October 1924 and January 1930. Two dates in the history of surrealism, two pamphlets but with the same title, *A Corpse*. Because the second originated with Bataille and was aimed at Breton, I am taking the first, originating with Breton and aimed at Anatole France, as a point of departure.

2. 'How admirable that this literary man honoured both by torpid Maurras and decrepit Moscow (and through incredible gullibility by Paul Painlevé himself) should write, to make a packet from a completely abject instinct, the most dishonourable preface imaginable to a tale by Sade, who spent his life in prison to end up with a kick from this official ass' (Aragon, *Un Cadavre* in José Pierre, *Tracts surréalistes et déclarations collectives*, p. 25).

3. It was signed by Breton, Delteil, Drieu La Rochelle, Éluard, Soupault and Aragon.

4. *Clarté* was supported at its foundation by Maxim Gorky, Albert Einstein, Heinrich Mann, Bernard Shaw, Thomas Hardy, Léon Blum and many others.

5. Jean Bernier, 'Autobiography' in *L'Amour de Laure*, p. 9.

Magnetic field

1. Michel Leiris, 'De Bataille l'impossible à l'impossible *Documents*', p. 685.
2. Michel Leiris, interviews with the author, 1986.
3. Ibid.
4. Bataille, 'Surrealism From Day to Day' in *The Absence of Myth*, p. 36.
5. Ibid.
6. Michel Leiris, 'De Bataille l'impossible à l'impossible *Documents*'.
7. It was decided that the headquarters and journal of the movement would be set up in this brothel. Even if they never saw the light of day, one cannot consider this idea and this project as negligible. We shall see that Bataille never stopped saying *Yes*, or wanting to. Whatever subsequent refinements might have improved his thought, the evidence is that it was already entirely established by 1924. On this point it would remain unchanged until his death.
8. *The Absence of Myth*, p. 36.
9. André Masson, interviews with the author, 1986.
10. *The Absence of Myth*, p. 36. Admittedly this was written much later, but the polemics taken up soon afterwards with Breton leave little doubt about the fact that this could already have been his thought.
11. Ibid.
12. Details supplied by Michel Leiris. We do not know why Bataille attributed to him the fine 'Lettre aux médecins-chefs des Asiles de fous', more usually attributed to Robert Desnos (*La Révolution surréaliste*, no. 3, 15 April 1925). It does not seem that Fraenkel wrote anything else throughout his life, except, after the war, a sonnet-duel with Bataille (interview with Diane Bataille).
13. *The Absence of Myth*, p. 41.
14. Ibid., p. 42.
15. André Breton, *Conversations: the Autobiography of Surrealism*, p. 84.
16. *The Absence of Myth*, p. 42.
17. Ibid., p. 43.
18. This is the second individual called André Masson to appear in this account. The first, a librarian, was also the oldest of Bataille's 'Parisian' friends; he was, like him, a pupil at the École des Chartes from 1918 to 1922. He later became Inspector of the French Archives. Their friendship and common profession led them to maintain relations all their lives. The second is the painter André Masson. Born in the Oise in 1896, he spent part of his childhood in Brussels, which he only left in 1912, moving to Paris. Violently affected by the 1914–18 war (the Somme offensive, and the Chemin des Dames from which he returned seriously wounded), André Masson developed a repulsion for it which would have a major impact on his work to come. He met Bataille in 1924. They remained linked all their lives by a friendship that was among the two or three most important of those established by Bataille.

19. Michel Leiris, 'De Bataille l'impossible à l'impossible *Documents*', p. 687.

20. 'What I hate most', Breton is said to have exclaimed (André Masson, *Entretiens avec Georges Charbonnier*).

21. 'The morality of the rue Blomet was not that of the rue Fontaine (because fundamentally there is a surrealist morality), and those of us who were in an anarchist position, when we rallied to surrealism, we embraced a dogma. Except Bataille' (André Masson, interviews with the author, November 1986).

22. André Thirion, *Revolutionaries without Revolution*, p. 93.

23. Francis Marmande calls the rue du Château a 'workshop of new concepts' (*Georges Bataille politique*).

24. André Thirion, *Revolutionaries without Revolution*, p. 94.

25. 'Surrealism From Day to Day' in *The Absence of Myth*, p. 37.

26. Michel Leiris's opinion was that Bataille intentionally did not sign his translation of the *Fatrasies*, such was the extent of 'his defiance' (interviews with the author).

27. *The Absence of Myth*, p. 40.

28. Ibid.

29. Ibid., p. 41.

30. Ibid.

31. Ibid.

32. Ibid., p. 38.

33. Ibid., p. 41.

34. In October and November 1934; cf. J.-P. Le Bouler and J. Bellec Martini, *Œuvres complètes*, XII, pp. 558–9.

35. *The Absence of Myth*, p. 38.

36. Ibid., p. 39.

37. Ibid. The portrait Breton later painted of Aragon hardly differs from Bataille's: 'Most of us felt that he remained very much the "writer": even while walking with you in the street, he rarely spared you the recital of a text, finished or not. . . . just as he loved, while talking in cafés, to watch his poses in the mirrors' (André Breton, *Conversations*, p. 82).

The mortuary chasm of debauchery

1. Michel Leiris, interview with the author, 1986.

2. Jean Piel, *La Rencontre et la différence* Paris: Fayard, p. 134.

3. 'Surrealism From Day to Day', *The Absence of Myth*, p. 42.

4. *Guilty*, p. 12.

5. *The Impossible*, p. 17.

6. Ibid., p. 27 (translation slightly modified).

7. *Œuvres complètes* IV, *La Déesse de la noce*, p. 326.

8. Ibid.

9. Ibid.
10. Ibid.

The philosopher and the rake

1. *Œuvres complètes*, VIII, p. 563.

2. The sudden appearance of this destroyed text, since it was destroyed, occupies a blind spot in the works, perhaps a point from which they are founded upon a mode of disavowal, and more certainly on that of repetition.

3. In *Story of the Eye*, p. 75.

4. These details come from Francis Marmande, *L'Indifférence des ruines*.

5. Michel Leiris, 'De Bataille l'impossible à l'impossible *Documents*'.

6. The existence should also be noted of a text, published in Italy in Italian under the name Georges Bataille but without a translator's name, titled *W.-C.*, and presented by the publisher (Il sole nero) as a collection of rediscovered fragments. To all appearances these are spurious, as suggested by the details supplied by Michel Leiris on the nature of the story of *W.-C.*

'I write in order to erase my name'

1. Lord Auch.

2. *Œuvres complètes*, II, *Le Masque*, p. 409.

3. Jean-Noël Vuarnet, *Le philosophe-artiste* 10/18, 1977, p. 121–2,. As a supplementary paradox (or masked game); one of the first books that Bataille signed with his own name was called *Guilty*.

4. J.-J. Pauvert confirms that the (posthumous) edition of *Le Mort* was certainly agreed with Georges Bataille, but under a pseudonym. The same was true for the republication of *Le Petit*. Publication of *Ma Mère* was not agreed while the author was alive, but in all likelihood it would equally have appeared under a pseudonym.

5. *Œuvres complètes*, II, *Le Masque*, p. 404.

6. Only Jules Monnerot in the notes to an article published in issues 8 and 9 of the review *Confluences* (October 1945 and February 1946), establishing a bibliography of Bataille's works, attributed the paternity of *Story of the Eye* and *Madame Edwarda* to him, something he said greatly annoyed Bataille. Monnerot later explained:

> Georges Bataille was very irritated with this text. There is some interest in exploring why. Bataille, like all intellectually superior people, very easily decided the way he was or was not understood. What he did not at all like were allusions, however discreet, to his 'underground literature' (*Madame Edwarda*, *Story of the Eye*), for which he is today well known. I have no doubt that I offended both his rather ludicrous feeling of respectability (as a librarian) and also his sense not even of a secret, but of the fiction of a secret. There was something of a game in this. Bataille wanted everyone to know that he was the author of both *Inner Experience* and *Story of the Eye*,

but maintained a sort of play of duplicity. He considered he was arbitrarily simplified by this synthetic way of taking him. ('La fièvre de Georges Bataille', in *Inquisitions*, p. 216.)

Marguerite Duras did the same thing in the first issue of the review *La Ciguë*, which was devoted to Bataille in 1958, without, it seems, having incurred the same annoyance. She especially attributed to Georges Bataille the paternity of *Madame Edwarda*, although the bookshop version to which she referred was signed Pierre Angélique. *Madame Edwarda* appeared under Bataille's name only in 1973, published by J.-J. Pauvert.

The torture of a Hundred Pieces

1. Of whom I shall say more later.
2. One of these was published in Georges Dumas's *Traité de psychologie* in 1923.
3. These injections were not intended to be philanthropic, but to prolong the torture.
4. Georges Dumas (1866–1946) became head of the laboratory of the Clinique des Maladies Mentales in Paris in 1897. A doctor of medicine and of arts, he succeeded Pierre Janet as Senior Lecturer in Experimental Psychology at the Sorbonne in 1902, becoming Professor in 1912. He also published *Le Sourire et l'expression des émotions* (1906) and *Troubles mentaux et troubles nerveux de guerre* (1919).
5. *Guilty*, p. 38.
6. *Inner Experience*, p. 120.
7. *The Tears of Eros*, p. 206. Bataille also wrote 'Sade would have wished to see it in solitude, at least in relative solitude, without which the ecstatic and voluptuous effect is inconceivable' (ibid.).
8. *Inner Experience*, p. 120.
9. *My Mother*, p. 89.
10. Probably Jean Bruno, although this is not certain. In any case Bataille took up a pretty unorthodox yoga; a black, deviant one.
11. *The Tears of Eros*, p. 206.
12. Ibid.
13. Ibid.
14. Ibid., p. 207.
15. *Œuvres complètes*, I, p. 139.

The priest of Torcy

1. Or, more exactly, Dr Adrien Borel. As irony would have it, this renowned psychoanalyst played the role of the priest of Torcy in the film *Le Journal d'un curé de campagne* by Robert Bresson. [Surya is playing on the correspondence between *le curé* (priest) and *la cure* as the talking cure of psychoanalysis. *trans*.]

2. *L'Abbé C.*, p. 139.

3. Michel Leiris made no secret of the fact that a representation of Bataille as singularly dark and desperate was 'a bit strained': 'He was a man who adored life' (interview with the author, 1986).

4. These two articles were collected in an offprint, under the same title (published by J. Florange). These were Georges Bataille's first publications in Paris.

5. See Elisabeth Roudinesco, *La Bataille de Cent Ans. Histoire de la psychoanalyse en France*, Vol. 1, pp. 358–9.

6. Raymond Queneau was one. According to Leiris, Max Morise may have been another. Colette Peignot would be, as her brother, Charles, had been.

7. Elisabeth Roudinesco, *La Bataille de Cent Ans*, p. 359. Michel Leiris, who was also analysed by Borel (it was Bataille who introduced them), recalls him as a man 'full of humanity and an exemplary disinterestedness' (interview with the author, 1986).

8. This dating is his own.

9. Georges Bataille interviewed by Madeleine Chapsal in *Georges Bataille: Essential Writings*, p. 221.

10. Ibid., p. 221.

11. Later, Bataille may well have continued to see Adrien Borel, perhaps for psychoanalysis. A letter from Michel Leiris to Georges Bataille on 15 August 1934 gives us reason to think that Bataille himself may have suggested the idea. Leiris replied: 'I don't think you are wrong to see Borel: there is perhaps nothing much to expect of psychoanalysis, but one can always take it as one does an aspirin.' In 1931 he seems to have considered taking a diploma in pathological psychology. In any case, he announced in a letter to Raymond Queneau his intention to visit the demonstrations of the sick at Sainte Anne hospital.

Triunfo de la muerte

1. *Story of the Eye*, p. 9.

2. Published by Gallimard in twelve volumes between 1970 and 1988.

3. *Story of the Eye*, p. 55.

4. Ibid., p. 11.

5. Ibid., p. 43.

6. I borrow this apt word from Sarane Alexandrian (*Les Libérateurs de l'amour*), not forgetting that he found it in Bataille, who made it that of a character (Sainte) in a sequel to *Ma Mère*.

7. *Le Petit* in *Story of the Eye*, p. 75. [Part of *Le Petit* (1943) served as a preface to *Story of the Eye*. *Le Petit* itself has not been translated into English, but the preface is included in the English edition of *Story of the Eye* (trans. note).]

8. All quotations from *Story of the Eye*.

9. Michel Leiris, 'Du temps de Lord Auch', *L'Arc*, no. 44.

10. With the pseudonym Lord Auch. André Masson's drawings were not signed. *Histoire de l'œil* was not published under Bataille's name in his lifetime.

11. Published, like *Histoire de l'œil*, by René Bonnel, it too was designed by Pascal Pia with drawings by André Masson. It has been reissued several times under the title *Le Con d'Irène*.

12. A book in which he advises against or forbids all Jewish, Protestant and left-wing authors. He even finds himself having to censure uncertain and doubting Catholics like Bernanos, Max Jacob and Mauriac. In the revised edition of 1932, he sides with the rural nobility in the campaign against 'the urban cosmopolitan Jewry'.

13. Quoted by Claudine Brécourt-Villars, *Écrire d'amour. Anthologie des textes érotiques féminins (1799–1984)*.

14. *Story of the Eye*, p. 42.

15. Man Ray: 'Breton, can one be interested in two women at the same time?' Breton: 'I said that it is quite impossible.'

16. Breton: 'I could not accept the presence of a third party.'

17. Jean Piel adds that 'Breton was highly impressed by the contrast between the power and daring of this text and Bataille's appearance: shy, reserved, with little gift for conversation, a slow speaker' (interviews with the author, 1986).

The eye at work

1. Three years in all likelihood, from 1927 to 1930, but several of them cannot be dated with certainty.

2. *Œuvres complètes*, II, *Dossier de l'œil pinéal*, pp. 13–47. None of the texts included in this dossier was published during Bataille's lifetime.

3. *L'Anus solaire*: prospectus for subscribers.

4. Ibid.

5. In the clearest possible way, Bataille makes this his own, then rejects it. The final version of the text reads: 'The eye is without any doubt the symbol of the sun', after having crossed out: 'The eye is without any doubt the symbol of the sun *which is itself the symbol of the father*' (my italics).

6. Ibid.

7. 'The Pineal Eye' in *Visions of Excess: Selected Writings, 1927–1939*, p. 83.

8. Ibid., p. 83.

9. 'The Jesuve' in *Visions of Excess*, p. 74.

10. Ibid., p. 77.

11. Ibid., p. 77.

12. 'La Garandie, a village where my father lived, built without trees or church, on the slope of a crater, a simple mass of houses in a demonic landscape'. (*Œuvres complètes*, V, *Le Coupable*, p. 534, Notes.)

13. 'The Jesuve' in *Visions of Excess*, pp. 74–5. (*L'Anus solaire*, written in 1927, was published in 100 copies in 1931 under the name Georges Bataille,

illustrated with drypoints by André Masson, by Editions de la Galerie Simon, 29b rue d'Astorg, Paris. It was not republished during Bataille's lifetime.

Don't waste my time with idealism!

1. André Thirion, *Revolutionaries Without Revolution*, p. 163.
2. Among others, Soupault and Artaud did not approve. In 1930 Boiffard would comment ironically on the very sudden conversion of the surrealists to communism: twenty of them discovered 'all at once and without the slightest hesitation that they had suddenly become communists'. André Breton himself came close to sharing this ironic tone: 'I admit it looked very much like a mass conversion' (*Conversations*, p. 97). Note the religious terminology once again.
3. Louis Aragon and André Breton, *La Révolution surréaliste*, no. 7, 1926.
4. Not all: Delteil and Soupault were not invited, although former collaborators in *La Révolution surréaliste* were.
5. André Thirion, *Revolutionaries Without Revolution*, p. 186; José Pierre, *Tracts surréalistes et déclarations collectives*.
6. André Thirion, *Revolutionaries Without Revolution*, p. 166.
7. Far from bringing people together, the meeting consisted of the formal accusation of Vailland. In the end, everyone's positions remained unchanged.

The donkey's kick

1. '*Documents* which, as "Secretary-General", I would edit in agreement with Georges-Henri Rivière . . . in opposition to the titular editor, the German poet Carl Einstein' (*Le Pont de l'épée*, no. 41, 1969).
2. Jacques Baron, another surrealist, wrote: 'I have nothing in common with this foul and ludicrous journal and the Comte de Noailles' arse lickers make me puke (naturally)' (letter to Georges Bataille, 4 July 1930).
3. Letter from Pierre d'Espézel to G. Bataille, 15 April 1929. It is not possible here to present and comment on *Documents* in its entirety. I will limit myself to trying to extract Bataille's role in organising the review and the stake he had in it, referring to the republication in two volumes prefaced by Denis Hollier (*Documents*, vol. 1, 1929 and vol. 2, 1930, Paris: Jean-Michel Place, 1992).
4. Michel Leiris, 'De Bataille l'impossible à l'impossible *Documents*'.
5. Ibid.
6. This inventory rather recalls the centres of interest that excited the rue du Château and were disapproved of by the rue Fontaine.
7. Letter to Bataille, 15 April 1929.
8. All quotes from 'L'Amérique disparue' in *Œuvres complètes*, I, pp. 152–8.
9. Alfred Métraux, 'Rencontre avec les ethnologues'.
10. Ibid.
11. *Œuvres complètes*, I, 'Le cheval académique', p. 162.

12. Ibid.
13. *Œuvres complètes*, I, 'L'apocalypse de Saint-Sever', p. 167.
14. 'Le langage des fleurs', *Documents*.
15. Ibid.
16. 'Materialism' in *Visions of Excess*, p. 16.
17. 'Human life is erroneously regarded as an elevation' (*Œuvres complètes*, I, p. 200).
18. Ibid.
19. 'The Big Toe' in *Visions of Excess*, p. 23.
20. 'The Lugubrious Game' in *Visions of Excess*, p. 24.
21. Michel Leiris, 'De Bataille l'impossible à l'impossible *Documents*'.
22. Breton 'incarnated the most beautiful dreams of youth at one moment of the world' (Marcel Duchamp).
23. Belatedly, in 1955, he would partially (and exceptionally) rally to the marvellous in a passage which resonates like a deferred homage to Breton: 'It generally seems to me that the present world scorns the nostalgia people have for the marvellous. The present world tends to neglect the marvellous . . . it nevertheless seems to me that people have always lived in the expectation of the moment when they would experience this feeling' (Conference, January 1955).
24. *Œuvres complètes*, I, 'L'esprit moderne ou le jeu des transpositions', p. 273.
25. Ibid.
26. Three cases cited by him in 'Sacrificial Mutilation and the Severed Ear of Vincent Van Gogh' in *Visions of Excess*.
27. 'Base Materialism and Gnosticism' in *Visions of Excess*, p. 48.

'Excrement philosopher'

1. André Breton's description of Georges Bataille.
2. André Breton, *Manifestos of Surrealism*, p. 124.
3. *André Breton et le mouvement surréaliste*, NRF, special issue, April 1967.
4. André Breton, *Manifestos of Surrealism*, p. 165.
5. Ibid., pp. 169–70.
6. 'Au grand jour' in José Pierre, *Tracts*, p. 160. Excessive or 'misplaced' as the accusations of 'lucre' and 'notoriety' appear, they match, and even tone down, the opinions of the strictly faithful surrealists. Thus Sadoul, in his response to the call of 12 February 1929 to the meeting of the bar du Château, accused Artaud (and Vitrac) of 'filthiness of little littérateurs'. Even the peaceable André Thirion, who takes no pride in it in his fine *Revolutionaries Without Revolution*, writes more lyrically 'the corpse called Artaud and the slug that goes by the name of Vitrac drag themselves from dunghill to dunghill'. In 1952 Breton would award Artaud the justice he deserved: 'Perhaps he was at even greater odds with life than the rest of us were. . . . He

was possessed by a kind of fury that spared no human institution . . . his fury by its astonishing power of contagion, profoundly affected the surrealist procedure' (*Conversations*, p. 84).

7. All quotations taken from the *Second Manifesto of Surrealism*, pp. 123–50, except for 'social absenteeism' describing André Masson, taken from Breton, *Conversations*.

8. Philosophies was a group of young philosophers formed in 1924. It brought together Pierre Morhange, Norbert Gutterman, Georges Friedmann, Henri Lefebvre, Georges Politzer and sometimes Paul Nizan. As spiritualists and marxists (!), they more than once adopted positions close to those of the surrealists and even of Bataille: a hatred of war, patriotism, the bourgeoisie and colonialism. Politzer would join the Communist Party in 1929, the year of the *Second Manifesto*.

9. Breton, *Second Manifesto*, p. 174.

10. Ibid., p. 181.

11. Ibid., p. 183.

The castrated lion

1. Georges Ribemont-Dessaignes, 'Papologie d'André Breton' in *Un Cadavre*.

2. 'Strumpot' – gidouille: word used by Alfred Jarry to describe Père Ubu's stomach; 'strumpot' is Cyril Connolly's felicitous English equivalent [trans. note].

3. All quotations from *Un Cadavre*, in José Pierre, *Tracts*. 'The Castrated Lion' in *The Absence of Myth*, pp. 28–9.

4. André Thirion, *Revolutionaries Without Revolution*, p. 190.

5. Ibid., p. 94.

6. Boiffard, Vitrac, Desnos and Morise were included in *La Révolution surréaliste* from the first issue; Leiris from the second, Baron from the third and Queneau from the fourth.

7. Two hundred were destroyed by Bataille later, when he moved house. The crisis running through surrealism during 1929–30, and of which *A Corpse* is only one of the most marked events, ended in termination of the publication of *La Révolution surréaliste*, which was replaced in 1930 by *Le Surréalisme au service de la révolution*.

'Surrealism's secret affectations'

1. Anonymous telephone calls and the delivery of funeral wreaths.

2. These open letters were published after Bataille's death (*Œuvres complètes*, II, 'Dossier de la polémique avec André Breton'). Nothing confirms whether or not they were sent in 1930–1 rather than being kept by Bataille among his papers. In the latter case, it would be better to read them not as

elements of a sustained polemic but as recapitulating the major differences which up to that point had arisen between Bataille and Breton.

3. 'The Use Value of D.A.F. de Sade' in *Visions of Excess*, p. 92. 'One of Breton's rare inconsistencies – he who, to my knowledge, never wrote an erotic book – was to admire Sade. He should not have admired him, as I pointed out to him one day' (André Masson, interview with the author).

4. 'The Use Value of D.A.F. de Sade'.

5. It reappears, very violently, in *Blue of Noon* in 1935; but also in attenuated form much later – in 1957 – in *Eroticism*: 'Sade – or his ideas – generally horrifies even those who affect to admire him' (p. 43).

6. I am of course alluding to the term 'an obsessive' with which Breton felt he could undermine Bataille among his friends. Of Bataille's reputation at this time, Boris Souvarine and Simone Weil, among others, leave no doubt: a 'sexual deviant' according to the former, a 'sick man' for the latter.

7. This dates from 1926.

8. Bataille often used prefixes denoting privation. This by analogy could be the sense of the one in 'debauchery'.

9. Algolagnia (*algos*: pain; *lagneia*: sensual pleasure), a word coined by Schrenck-Notzing so as to 'sum up in a single word the non-contradictory notion of pain given as well as received, in its relations to amorous pleasure' (Gilbert Lély (1952) *Vie du Marquis de Sade*, Paris: Gallimard, p. 113).

10. 'The Use Value of D.A.F. de Sade', p. 92.

11. Of which I shall say more later.

12. Do the former processes relate to a 'debauched' economy and the latter to a 'libertine' one?

13. Related by André Masson.

The angel and the beast, part 1

1. 'The "Old Mole" and the Prefix Sur in the Words *Surhomme* and *Surrealist*' in *Visions of Excess*, p. 34; *Œuvres complètes*, II, p. 95.

2. Should we see this as one more Pascalian relic? Breton and later Sartre did not fail to denounce Bataille's hidden 'Pascalism'.

3. These words never emerged from the pen of Bataille. It is all the more amazing in that he had already, on several occasions, situated the abjection from which we are born in the swarming of the earth (the roots): ineradicable nature.

4. *Œuvres complètes*, II, 'Je sais trop bien', p. 87.

5. Those in which, we recall, Breton had accused him of finding pleasure.

6. This is the only reservation Bataille ever made about Nietzsche. The overwhelmed reading he began of him in 1923 would find its meaning only around 1935.

7. Bataille soon made this 'loss of the head' the emblem of a secret society, Acéphale.

8. 'The Old Mole and the Prefix Sur . . .' in *Visions of Excess*, p. 43.

'A man is what he lacks'

1. This is Marguerite Duras's word, in an interview with the author, 1986.

2. Jean Piel speaks of 'a man whose appearance was scrupulous and pathologically in conformity to the norm' ('Bataille et le monde'). All the same we should note that this account mainly relates to the period after the war.

3. *Œuvres complètes*, II, *Manuel de l'anti-chrétien*, p. 390.

4. In fact, as we shall see, he was one, briefly and just once, in Contre-Attaque.

5. André Breton in the *Second Manifesto*.

6. Jean Piel, 'Bataille et le monde', p. 134.

7. It was Bataille's job to open the shutters at the Department entrance. His repeated lateness in doing so appears to have caused a great deal of annoyance. It is certainly not hard to imagine how ill-suited his nocturnal life must have been to the demands of opening hours. It was, moreover, a feature of Bataille's character and his dramatisations that, whatever the failings he had to admit to, he could only see this reproof as an incomprehensible injustice. When he talked about it, all his friends used to laugh (knowing how dissolute his life was at that time) while he, twenty years later, choked back the tears.

8. In all likelihood this photograph dates from 1924–5. The young woman it shows next to Bataille appears to be Léon Chestov's daughter, Teresa Beresovski-Chestov, with whom he translated *L'Idée de bien chez Tolstoï et Nietzsche*, Paris: Ed. du Siecle, 1925. [This book is translated into English as 'The Good in the Teaching of Tolstoy and Nietzsche' published in *Dostoevsky, Tolstoy and Nietzsche*, translated by Bernard Martin. Ohio University Press, 1969. Chestov's name is more commonly transliterated as Lev Shestov (trans. note).]

9. There was no shortage of rumour, preferably scandalous. It is not a question of knowing whether Bataille behaved in this way or not for these rumours to be justified (as I have said, there is little doubt that *in his case* they are false), but whether he behaved like this with his wife: whether she was an accomplice or a victim.

10. Laurence Bataille, interview with the author, 1986.

11. 'Here I report two examples I consider to be significant (one of them placed me personally at stake)' (*Œuvres complètes*, II, p. 129, and *Œuvres complètes*, III, *Le Petit*, p. 60).

12. *Blue of Noon*, pp. 76–7.

13. *Œuvres complètes*, III, *Le Petit*, p. 60.

14. *Œuvres complètes*, II, p. 130.

15. Enigmatically, and in a way that lets us read no more than a furtive and perhaps involuntary echo of this scabrous scene, in 1946 Bataille lingered over this sentence by Proust: 'Sons not always having a paternal resemblance in their faces complete their mother's profanation', a sentence which he commented on thus: 'How not to see the key of these terms of tragedy in the episode in which Vinteuil's daughter, whose conduct had caused her father to

die of grief, a few days later, in full mourning, enjoyed the caresses of a homosexual lover who spat on the dead man's photograph' (*Œuvres complètes*, XI, p. 158). The article from which this sentence comes is significantly entitled 'Marcel Proust and the profaned mother'.

'An obscene and horribly desirable trick'

1. 'Notes on the Publication of *Un Cadavre*' in *The Absence of Myth*, p. 31.
2. We do not know if they were actually *read*.
3. *Œuvres complètes*, II, p. 85.
4. Ibid., Louis-Fedinand Céline, p. 87.
5. *Voyage au bout de la nuit*, a book that Bataille reviewed in *La Critique sociale* (no. 7, January 1933) in terms that could not be more laudatory:

> the greatness of *Voyage au bout de la nuit* consists in the fact that it makes *no* appeal to the sentiment of insane pity that Christian servility had linked to consciousness of poverty: to be conscious of this poverty today – without excepting from it the worst degradations (filth to death, from stinginess to crime) – no longer means the need to humiliate human beings before a superior power. (*Œuvres complètes*, I, p. 321.)

6. 'The Use-Value of D.A.F. de Sade' in *Visions of Excess*, p. 91.
7. Diane Bataille, interview with the author. In all likelihood, this encounter was during or immediately prior to 1930, Bataille having spent almost all the money inherited when his mother died in order to see and try to 'take out' this young woman.

'Someone able to see clearly'

1. Claude Roy, *Le Nouvel Observateur*, 25 November 1983.
2. Loyal to Jaurès, this journal at the time called for the renewal of the agreement between the workers' movements of the countries at war. It wanted neither vanquisher nor vanquished, neither annexations nor indemnities, nor, especially, useless massacres.
3. The murderers of Alexander II belonged to the group called the Will of the People. Sofia Perovskaya, Jeliabov and several others were hanged for it.
4. Émile Zola, *Germinal*, p. 381.
5. Ibid., p. 383. Very oddly, an oddity the evolution of the relations between Bataille and Souvarine will only reveal to the point of absurdity, there is a character in *Germinal* by the name of Bataille. It is a blind pit pony(!).
6. There were nevertheless two echoes, deferred in time to this initial, and assumed, anarchism on Souvarine's part: arriving in Moscow, he asked Lenin to visit the Boutirki prison where the anarchists were imprisoned (this infuriated Bela Kun). Later, in *La Critique sociale*, he let Georges Bataille publish openly anarchist remarks: 'Humanly there exists no scorn cutting enough to

respond to the use of this old quibble [petty-bourgeois anarchism], a ridiculous affront to all good faith, to the refusal to blind oneself.'

7. Letter from Boris Souvarine to Alexander Solzhenitsyn, March 1978.

8. What is incredible is not so much that he said this, as that he was allowed to do so. This again indicates the extent of his influence.

9. Letter from Boris Souvarine to Gregori Zinoviev, 20 March 1924.

10. *La Critique sociale*, no. 2, July 1931 p. 50. At the time of the arrest of D.B. Razianov.

11. Letter from Boris Souvarine to Solzhenitsyn, March 1978.

12. It is useful to read the foreword he wrote, a little before his death, on the republication of *La Critique sociale* (Éditions de la Différence, 1983). I will say more about the virulently polemical aspect of this text. For more on Souvarine see the special issue 'Hommage to Boris Souvarine', published on his death by the journal *Est-Ouest* (February 1985, new series, third year, no 15), and, edited by Anne Roche, *Boris Souvarine et 'La Critique sociale'* (Paris: Éditions de la Découverte, 1990). Several books of testimony and memories give him a prominent place, among others *Trois noms pour une vie* by Charles Ronsac (Paris: Laffont, 1988).

13. Amédée Dunois was a former contributor to *Le Populaire*; Pierre Kaan, a lecturer in philosophy, a former Communist Party member and contributor to *L'Humanité*; Lucien Laurat (whose real name was Otto Maschl), an Austrian economist living in Luxembourg with considerable influence over these groups; Aimé Patri, formerly of La lutte des classes (with Pierre Naville, Michel Collinet and others); Jacques Mesnil, a former socialist, the editor of *L'Humanité*, and a delegate to the Third congress of the Communist International; Jean-Jacques Soudeille, known as Souzy, the organiser with Élie Péju of the Groupe d'opposition de Lyon (future author of *La Révolte des canuts* under the name Jacques Perdu in 1934); Max Eastman, an American through whom Souvarine obtained a copy of 'Lenin's Testament'; Karl Korsch, a German, the organiser of the journal *Kommunistiche Politik*; and Joachim Maurin, Souvarine's brother-in-law and the future organiser of the POUM in Spain.

14. If *Documents* was unusual, *La Critique sociale* was no less so. Souvarine gathered around him ideologists and economists schooled in the best rudiments of political thought. Such was not the case with Bataille and his friends, far from it. Not that Bataille was less capable than any of the Souvarine supporters of writing political articles (we shall even see that he wrote the most important ones in the journal), but on account of his background he could *a priori* write only *very* different ones.

15. This pseudonym was suggested to her by Souvarine. Araxe (Arax or Araks in English) is the name of a river which rises in Turkey, skirts the Armenian–Turkish/Iranian borders, and discharges in Azerbaijan, a river so torrential that no bridge could be built across it.

The Democratic Communist Circle

1. On the Circle's constitution and role see Anne Roche, *Boris Souvarine et 'La Critique sociale'*, Éditions de la Découverte, 1990, and in particular 'D'un cercle à l'autre' by Édouard Liénert.

2. Draft of a letter to the Circle, in Simone Pétrement, *Vie de Simone Weil*, Paris: Fayard, vol. 1, p. 422. According to Charles Ronsac (*Trois noms pour une vie*, Paris: Laffont, p. 87), Simone Weil's arrival in the Circle in 1932 was closely followed by that of Queneau, Leiris and of a group made up of Paul Bénichou, Édouard Labin (alias Jean Prader) and Jean Rabaut, a group formerly close to the Trotskyists of the Communist League. The portrait Édouard Liénert gives of Simone Weil 'entering' the Circle (although as we have seen in the end she did not do so) is worth relating for the way it helps shed light on the strange relationship that linked her to Bataille: 'She was an unusual individual. Gifted with exceptional intelligence and erudition, her political judgment was very sound. . . . But she had a strange taste for vain gestures, senseless risks, even for useless sacrifices' (Anne Roche, *Boris Souvarine et 'La Critique sociale'*, p. 59).

3. D. A. F. de Sade (1965) 'Yet Another Effort, Frenchmen, If You Would Become Republicans', in *Philosophy in the Bedroom*, translated by Richard Seaver and Austryn Wainhouse, New York: Grove Press, (1965) p. 315.

4. Letter to Pierre Kaan, 20 July 1933 (?). One can date this letter, without much danger of error, to 1933 since the first appearance of Simone Weil in the pages of *La Critique sociale* dates from September 1933.

5. André Thirion, *Revolutionaries Without Revolution*, p. 478.

6. In collaboration with Raymond Queneau he submitted an important article entitled 'La Critique des fondements de la dialectique hégélienne' in which the authors, protesting against the exclusive claim to Hegel by marxists, appeal for a reading of Hegel reactivated in the light of Freud and German phenomenology. As a literary critic, Bataille also submitted important notes on publications, some positive, such as one on L.-F. Céline's *Voyage au bout de la nuit*, and others, on the surrealists for example, that were notably more polemical.

The state: heartbreak and misfortune

1. *Œuvres complètes*, I, 'Le problème de l'État', p. 332.

2. The reference Bataille makes to 'revolutionary morality' leaves no room for doubt. It is undoubtedly because he is far from it that he did not fail to remind those who stoop to it.

3. 'The Notion of Expenditure' in *Visions of Excess*, p. 128.

4. Ibid., p. 120.

5. The same could be observed among the Tlingit, the Tsimshian and the Haida, and equivalent forms were to be found in Melanesia, the Trobriand Islands, Polynesia and among the Celts where certain forms of ritual suicide

appear to affirm the pride of the chief in offering himself in sacrifice in order not to lose face.

6. 'The Notion of Expenditure' in *Visions of Excess*, p. 122.

7. Ibid., p. 125.

8. 'Essai sur le don. Forme et raison de l'échange dans les sociétés arch-aïques', *L'Année sociologique* nouvelle série, I, 1923–4. [English translation by Ian Cunnison, *The Gift: Forms and Functions of Exchange in Archaic Societies*, London: Routledge & Kegan Paul, 1954. *trans.*]

9. The ephemeral proximity of Bataille to a quite different circle from the one organised by Boris Souvarine has not often been mentioned. This was Ordre Nouveau; Bataille had close relations if not with the circle itself, at least with one of its organisers. This anti-Bolshevik, anti-capitalist, anti-parliamentarian, corporative, pro-worker (it aimed at the abolition of the proletariat) and federalist group of revolutionary thinkers had been created at the initiative of Arnaud Dandieu and Robert Aron. In the first circle, gathered around its two organisers, were found Alexandre Marc (whose real name was Lipianski), Gabriel Marcel, Jean Jardin, Claude Chevally, Daniel-Rops and Jacques Naville. The first manifesto issued by this group, Manifesto for a New Order, was published in 1930. A journal, *L'Ordre nouveau* was created in May 1933. Arnaud Dandieu edited it until his death, in August of the same year. The relations between Arnaud Dandieu and Georges Bataille are not very well known. Jean Piel specified that they met regularly for several years, for they both worked at the Bibliothèque Nationale. Bataille was not, however, a member of Ordre Nouveau, about whose activity, according to Pierre Prévost, he was 'mocking' (*Pierre Prévost rencontre Georges Bataille*, Paris: Jean-Michel Place, 1987 p. 12). The only collaboration he could recall was anonymous: Bataille had provided some comments on the chapter 'Exchanges and credits' in the book manifesto by Arnaud Dandieu and Robert Aron, *La Révolution nécessaire*. Reading the chapter this appears obvious: the majority of the themes of analysis of the 'notion of expenditure' are repeated there. It does not seem, however, that Bataille drafted this chapter. Equally, singular as this anonymous collaboration was, it does not seem to have led to anything. Bataille in any event never mentioned it.

'A world of appearances and of old men with their teeth falling out'

1. 'The Psychological Structure of Fascism' in *Visions of Excess*, p. 154. In fact one should not forget that the 'class against class' line adopted by the Sixth Congress of the Communist International in Moscow in summer 1926 did not question the principle of commitment to a classless society.

2. Ibid., p. 143.

3. Ibid.

4. Bataille points out in fact that only the Islamic Caliphate has pushed the conjunction of the religious and the military this far.

5. Jean Baudrillard and Pierre Legendre (not to mention Eugène Enriquez) later put it no differently.

6. Ibid., p. 154.

7. Benito Mussolini, 'Fascism', *Enciclopedia italiana*, quoted by Bataille in ibid., p. 155.

8. *Œuvres complètes*, II, p. 175. This should be read thus: neither liberalism nor communism is capable of successfully fighting an effective war against the advance of fascism. This is because they are not constitutionally distinct from it. Within them, and to similar degrees of violence, the same process of homogenisation is at work.

9. Jacques Chatain, *Georges Bataille*, Paris: Seghers, 1973, p. 84.

10. Francis Marmande, *Georges Bataille politique*, p. 44.

11. Published in *Œuvres complètes*, II, pp. 205–13.

12. This could also be said of any book written about Bataille, including this one: the crippling necessity to impose an order on a disorder that from the start makes it not just in vain, but false.

13. *Œuvres complètes*, VI, p. 154.

14. Ibid., p. 207.

15. Ibid., p. 206.

'With a single blow, like an ox in the abattoir'

1. A description of the leagues as *fascist* has not unanimously been agreed by historians. In fact, apart from Solidarité française and Francisme, none of them openly declared themselves as anti-capitalist in the way that foreign fascism had. Thus many of them have preferred to see in them a neo-Bonapartism, a reactive Boulangism, not to say a new anti-Dreyfusism. What matters here is that, in the eyes of the left and the extreme left, the fascination Mussolini exercised over several of the most important representatives of Action française, its anti-parliamentarianism, anti-communism and hatred of the Republic, and violence as a means of action seemed to be *fascist*. No doubt these characteristics, whether or not they were precisely fascist, justified Bataille in calling his book 'Fascism in France', making it clear that he thought a French *fascism* did exist.

2. These 6 February riots left fifteen dead and 2,000 people injured.

3. Thirion, the surrealist, asserted this from within the Communist Party, of which he was a member. Moreover, on 6 February, *L'Humanité* called for militants to demonstrate against the police and the Daladier government as well as against the fascist leagues.

4. Charles Ronsac, *Trois noms pour une vie*, Paris: Laffont, p. 103.

5. *Œuvres complètes*, II, pp. 253–63.

6. 'The French, including the surrealists, attached merely transitory importance to Hitler's victory and to the passive surrender of the German labour parties with revolutionary pretensions or reformist goals' (André Thirion, *Revolutionaries Without Revolution*, p. 335).

7. *Œuvres complètes*, II, 'En attendant la grève générale', p. 262.

8. Ibid.

9. This 'organisation' could equally well have been the Masses group, to which Bataille had belonged. Marc Richir (*Textures*, no. 6, 1970) first drew attention to this possibility, though nothing really confirms it. Marina Galleti ('Masses: un "collège" mancato? Autour de Georges Bataille dans les années trente: la politique et le sacré') uncovered the following details: the journal *Masses* was formed on the initiative of Paul Faure (later Minister of State in the Popular Front government of Léon Blum), following the dissolution of *Jeune Européen*. The political orientation of *Masses*, apparently positioned on the far left, still remains uncertain. Henri Dubief considered that the considerable influence of Jacques Soustelle over the group made *Masses* a feeler for the Communist Party. Marina Galetti, on the other hand, believes that *Masses* sought to give a fresh impetus to theoretical debates on the left thanks to diffusion of the thought of Rosa Luxemburg and the valorisation of the spontaneous movement of the masses in opposition to the inertia of bureaucratic systems. One thing seems certain: *Masses* would have been open both to marxists and non-marxists. And it was their opposition that was to be at the origin of the arrival of Bataille and his friends into the group. René Lefeuvre's appeal in favour of Victor Serge (we have seen how Souvarine and Bataille had done the same in *La Critique sociale*) would be at the root of this split. The official communists having left, *Masses* would be open to the oppositional communists: Jean Dautry, Édouard Lienert, Paul Benichou and, to a lesser extent, Simone Weil. In October 1933, *Masses* offered courses in political economy with Michel Collinet and Lucien Laurat and in sociology with Pierre Kaan, Michel Leiris and Aimé Patri. Bataille's participation would have begun in October 1933 and ended in March 1934. (Marina Galetti's article is published in English as 'Masses: a failed "collège"?' (1989) *Stanford French Review* XII (1) [trans. note]).

History and its ends; the end of history

1. Alexandre Kojève, *Introduction à la lecture de Hegel*, Paris: Gallimard, 1947. [Translated in abridged form as *Introduction to the Reading of Hegel: Lectures on the Phenomenology of Spirit* by James H. Nichols, Jr, New York: Basic Books, 1969. trans.]

2. Also present were Robert Marjolin and Father Fessard. It is all the same notable that aside from Merleau-Ponty and Eric Weil, no 'pure' philosopher attended this seminar; neither, it would seem, did Jean Hyppolite, first translator of *Phenomenology of Spirit*, nor Jean Wahl, one of Hegel's first commentators in France. For more on Alexandre Kojève, the reader is directed to Dominique Auffret's excellent biographical essay, *Alexandre Kojève, l'État, la fin de l'histoire*, Paris: Grasset, 1990.

3. Alexandre Kojève, interview in *La Quinzaine littéraire*, July 1968.

4. This class was also attended by Bataille, from November 1931. The

seminar on Nicolas de Cues took place every Friday at five o'clock. The one on Hegel was held every Wednesday at eleven (Jean-Pierre Le Bouler, written submission to the conference 'Georges Bataille et la pensée allemande'). Alexandre Koyré was also born in Russia, in 1892, leaving after the Revolution, in which he was an active participant in 1919. Moving to Paris at this date, in 1932 he founded a journal called *Recherches philosophiques*.

5. Ibid.

6. Books borrowed by Bataille from the Bibliothèque Nationale (*Œuvres complètes*, XII, p. 549).

7. One should say, however, that, for someone who was not a philosopher by education or profession, such a reading is already impressive. One should remember that in 1930 Hegel was still unknown, or practically unknown, in France. *Phenomenology of Spirit* would not be translated into French until 1939.

8. *Inner Experience*, p. 109.

9. *Guilty*, p. 105.

10. 'More and more I think the only possible attitude towards that of "Hegelians" is your own "silent" one' (letter from Kojève to Bataille, 19 July 1959); 'I have arrived at results that surprised me and which seem to be close to yours (except the terminology)' (letter from Kojève to Bataille, 5 April 1954).

11. Letter from Georges Bataille to Alexandre Kojève, 2 June 1961. The relationship between the two would be too close in the future for it to be possible to do more than outline it here: relations of friendship and of intellectual collaboration. Alexandre Kojève would participate, as we shall see, in several of Bataille's enterprises and publications: before the war in the College of Sociology, and after the war in *Critique*.

The animal-headed journal: *Minotaure*

1. Whether surrealist absolutely or only in part, *Minotaure* was the third surrealist journal. It followed *Le Surréalisme au service de la révolution* (1930–3), which had succeeded *La Révolution surréaliste* (1924–9). There is good reason to say that *Minotaure* became thoroughly surrealist only after the departure of Tériade and his replacement by an editorial group constituted of five people, Breton, Duchamp, Éluard, Heine and Mabille, with the publication of issue 10 (there were twelve issues in all).

2. '40 ans d'édition: Skira ou la perfection', *Combat*, 9 December 1967. Quoted by Valérie Holman in 'The artist in his element', in *Focus on Minotaure*).

3. Skira was the journal's administrative director and Tériade the artistic director. It does not, however, seem that their respective roles were either separated or defined in such a way.

4. As Jean Starobinski thinks ('Day Side and Night Side', translated by

A.S. and J. Shawcross, in *Focus on Minotaure*, p. 30). Roger Vitrac also contributed to *Documents*.

5. Interview between André Masson and Jeanine Warnod, 27 October, 1983, *Focus on Minotaure*, p. 83.

6. The first issue of *Minotaure* should have had a cover designed by me, but Picasso having got wind of it seized upon the idea. It was really a matter of papacy. Breton really was the Pope and the financiers were his fanatical supporters. . . . I remember writing to Tériade, who had become editor of this journal: 'You will never be more than the drover of *Minotaure*.' (interview with the author, 1986.)

7. Paul Éluard to Valentine Hugo, two letters in 1933 quoted by José Pierre, 'André Breton and/or *Minotaure*', translated by André Marling, in *Focus on Minotaure*.

8. *La Critique sociale*, no. 9, 1933; *Œuvres complètes*, I, p. 137.

9. Bataille's only contribution was entitled 'Le bleu du ciel', *Minotaure*, no. 8, June 1938. In fact, this text dates from August 1934 and is included, with few changes, in *Inner Experience* ('Antecedents to the Torment . . .', pp. 77–80). Michel Leiris was considerably more visible in *Minotaure*. Without wanting to be its editor, he organised and supervised issue 2, devoted to the Dakar–Djibouti expedition, 1931–3. For all that, Breton may have been more worried about having to share editorial direction with Tériade or Raynal, for example, who opened the journal to artists surrealism did not admit (Laurens, Lipchitz, Despaiu, Maillol, Brancusi . . .) or even with Élie Faure than with several of his old friends that his text 'Beauty will be convulsive' (no. 5, May 1934) would have more naturally rallied.

10. *Visions of Excess*, p. 15.

11. Jean Starobinsky, 'Day Side and Night Side', p. 33.

12. Jean Jamin, 'On the Human Condition of Minotaure', translated by R. F. M. Dexter, in *Focus on Minotaure*, p. 87.

13. André Breton, 'Le château étoilé', *Minotaure*, no. 8, 1936.

14. José Pierre, 'André Breton and/or *Minotaure*', pp. 95–119.

15. Ibid., p. 105.

16. *Guilty*, pp. 99–100.

'The saint of the abyss'

1. Michel Leiris.

2. *Œuvres complètes*, VI, p. 278.

3. Boris Souvarine's version is effectively different (even if it should be noted that if Souvarine specifies the facts, in relating them he never once gives Bataille's name; all he speaks of is a 'friend', an 'occasional collaborator' in *La Critique sociale*). According to him, he and Colette Peignot left Paris by car with a couple of friends (perhaps Georges and Sylvia Bataille) for the Austrian

Tyrol. And this was where Colette 'ran off' with 'the obliging friend'. This version is no doubt untrue, since Bataille's diary contradicts it, but it might perhaps indicate correctly that Sylvia Bataille was on this trip, and that he himself might have known of their presence a few miles away, in Austria.

4. Published in Laure, *The Collected Writings*.

5. Ibid., p. 134.

6. Ibid. Surely this is in fact Grandville's drawing 'Premier rêve: Crime et expiations' that Bataille had commented upon in an article in *Documents*, titled precisely 'L'œil' (*Œuvres complètes*, I, p. 188). All the same it is unlikely Colette Peignot knew this text.

7. Souvarine would speak of Bataille in these terms:

> I knew Bataille was a sexual deviant, but it was none of my business. I was well aware that this predisposition could bring with it harmful consequences for the 'intellectual chemistry' and for healthy morality, conventional or not, but there was nothing I could do. Furthermore, I had to take care of serious matters, and consequently could not concern myself with Bataille's libidinous obsessions, or with his sadomasochistic lucubrations, ill-timed rumours of which sometimes reached me. (Prologue of the re-edition of *La Critique sociale*)

8. Laure, *The Collected Writings*, p. 139.

9. She knew Crevel and Buñuel, and probably to a lesser extent Aragon and Picasso.

10. Charles Peignot, with whom, according to Bataille, she tried with his consent but without success to make love during the return journey to Paris.

11. *Œuvres complètes*, VI, p. 277. One should be aware that this kind of detail, scrupulously related by Bataille, who was careful to be truthful to a fault, aroused the indignation of those of her friends who were convinced that it misrepresented her, seeing it as a taste for scandal. Bataille, who knew that filth can also be saintly, did not think it good (or important) to hide these details, and I do likewise.

12. It should be stated just as tersely that we would know nothing of Colette Peignot (Laure) if Bataille, with Leiris, had not published the few texts she wrote (some of the finest and most violent ever written by a woman) and briefly reconstructed her life. The other accounts, from the diaries of Jean Bernier and Boris Souvarine, only appeared forty years later. These four accounts (Bataille, Leiris, Bernier and Souvarine) tell us fairly clearly who Colette Peignot was, better in any event than the legend feverishly maintained by many. Her taste for the truth, no matter how unpleasant, was too violent ever to succumb in any way to the liberties taken with her, *a fortiori* in her case.

13. Moreover, they would have belonged there just the same, even without her and, in the end, without altering much: the story of *La Critique sociale* is in effect the same whether or not Colette *afterwards* left Souvarine for Bataille; but what changes, essentially, is the account of it handed down to us by those

involved. There is no doubt that the violently hateful account Souvarine gives of Bataille would have differed in more than one respect if bitterness had not been overlaid on it.

14. I will need to come back to this hatred, since Souvarine left, almost as a testament, an account that was childishly defamatory.

15. Several of Souvarine's friends gave an account of the consequences of this brutally interrupted passion, such as Charles Ronsac who says he never saw a man 'so destroyed by regret, so distraught and miserable'. He adds the following detail: Colette Peignot announced their separation to Souvarine by telephone. Perhaps to reinforce Bataille's supposedly demonic character, Ronsac concludes this brief story with the 'illuminating' (as he insists on noting) anecdote, told him by Souvarine, 'And while she talked, I could hear the other one sniggering' (Charles Ronsac, *Trois noms pour une vie*, Paris: Laffont, p. 130).

16. It is not known when the tuberculosis from which she died was first diagnosed, but there seems no doubt that it was before 1934.

17. Édouard Trautner, a doctor and author of *Gott, Gegen-Wart und Kokaïn*. He was the second 'debauched' man Colette Peignot would have encountered; before him there was also her brother Charles Peignot, of whom Bataille himself said: 'Her name recalled to my mind her brother's Parisian orgies, which I had several times been told about' (*Œuvres complètes*, VI, p. 277).

18. To the point of absurdity: have people not gone so far as to make Simone, the heroine of *Story of the Eye*, written four years before they met and seven years before their relationship, the fictional version of Colette Peignot? Jérôme Peignot, her first biographer, claims that without her Bataille's life work 'would have remained entirely based on philosophical concepts' (Laure, *The Collected Writings*, p. 311). The matrix of Bataille's heroines (his *saints*) is found in Simone and Marcelle, characters from *Story of the Eye*, between them, and in Dirty from *W.C.*, in so far as we can judge her from what remains of the character in *Blue of Noon*. This matrix thus dates from 1926–7.

19. Bataille complained that she employed a detective to follow him. True or not, this detail conveys better than any legend the admirable truth of their love: the truth of those who know in advance both its impossibility and its base qualities.

20. Letter from Colette Peignot to Georges Bataille, published in *Cahiers Bataille*, no. 2.

21. Laure, *The Collected Writings*, p. 151.

22. The god of the Aztecs, cf. *Œuvres complètes*, I, 'L'Amérique disparue', p. 152.

23. Michel Leiris, *Fourbis*, p. 239.

24. Michel Leiris, *Frêle bruit*, p. 345.

25. *Œuvres complètes*, VI, p. 276.

26. Laure, *The Collected Writings*, p. 148.

27. In Meudon, and her full name was Colette Laure Lucienne Peignot. Laure was the given name with which she chose at the end of her life to sign her texts. It was under this name that Bataille and Leiris privately published the texts and poems she left: *Le Sacré* (1939) and *Histoire d'une petite fille* (1943). Gustave Peignot, Colette's grandfather, was responsible for the family rising from the entirely modest existence it had to that of a wealthy family. He ran a type foundry, with his studio at 68 boulevard Edgar Quinet. Two factors seem to have enabled this sudden fortune: the new law instituting freedom of the press and, at around the same time, the production of plain paper by the Imprimerie Nationale.

28. Note that this is within a month of the date (6 November) of the death of Bataille's father.

29. And an abbot more mindful of the charms of the young girl than of those of devotion.

Thunderbolts and forebodings

1. It is more likely that he went there to fetch them: the same diary indicates, without any other details, an absence from Paris from 18 to 24 October, an absence that coincides with Sylvia's return during that time.

2. Although we only know those of Colette.

3. *Inner Experience*, p. 76 [translation modified].

4. *Blue of Noon*, p. 24. The same scene appears in *Inner Experience* (p. 79): 'a second victim lay dying beside me: a liquid uglier than blood flowed from lips which disgust rendered similar to those of a dead woman.' See also *Œuvres complètes*, VI, *Sur Nietzsche*, p. 409, Notes.

The sky turned upside down

1. *Le bleu de ciel*, insert to the 1957 edition.

2. *Blue of Noon*, p. 23.

3. Cf. 'The mortuary chasm of debauchery'.

4. *Blue of Noon*, p. 38.

5. Ibid., p. 67.

6. More crudely, Troppmann asks if they have ever eaten it.

7. Ibid., p. 77.

8. Troppmann finds the idea of storming a prison seductive. We can see that he does not just accuse Lazare, but that he also makes her the intermediary of some of Bataille's most cherished ideas; these include storming a prison. The frequency with which Bataille evokes this can only make one think of a sort of posthumous provocation of his father, who had been an employee of a jail.

9. Ibid., pp. 144–5.

10. [The French word for Trier is Trèves, and 'trêve' means truce. trans.]

11. Ibid., p. 152. 'From 1935 Bataille, like Picasso with Guernica, *knew*

what was to follow. Not in an abstract, "political" way but in the private convulsion, bars, hotel rooms, the nudity of bodies. The whole world agrees, ultimately, to forbid orgasm and to demand, without saying so, the "rising tide of death".' (Philippe Sollers, *Le Monde*, 12 July 1991.)

12. Everything is in flight: 'There was now a flight in my head, everything that I thought fled me . . . even this comedy escaped me . . . I was bewildered. I had the feeling of having forgotten something – that I had known the instant before, that absolutely I would have wanted to recover', etc.

13. My italics.

14. The only difference being that 1 November 1934 was a Thursday and not a Sunday as given in *Blue of Noon*.

15. Michel Leiris and Jean Piel made no secret of this. It would seem that none of the (admittedly few) readers at the time doubted this; even Simone Pétrement, Simone Weil's biographer, does not take issue with this unpleasant hypothesis.

16. *Blue of Noon*, p. 115.

17. Simone Pétrement stresses the aspect of Simone Weil's personality that consisted of encouraging others to take her into their confidence, to the point of prying.

18. Simone Pétrement, *Vie de Simone Weil*, Paris: Fayard, 1978, vol. 2, p. 102.

19. Ibid., vol. 1, pp. 351–2.

20. *Œuvres complètes*, XI, p. 537. It is not impossible that a retrospective interest in the works Simone Weil started to write after they lost contact is present in this portrait. More than one sentence of *La Pesanteur et la grâce* (published in 1948) were likely to interest the black mystic that Bataille had meanwhile become, among them lines like: 'There is a point at which misfortune makes it impossible to continue either to tolerate it or to have done with it'; 'You have to be dead to see things stripped bare.'

21. The legend sustained by her most admiring commentator, Jérôme Peignot, suffers from this assumption. He is not alone, since Claudine Brécourt-Villars (in *Écrire d'amour*) sees her presence not only in *Blue of Noon* but also in *Story of the Eye*, published three years before Bataille met Colette Peignot for the first time and six years before their relationship started.

22. Curiously, Edith is the name of Troppmann's wife in the narrative. Nevertheless she has nothing to do with Sylvia Bataille.

23. 'The key book of our whole modernity', according to Philippe Sollers; one of the 'most atrocious' and 'most stifling' according to Francis Marmande, whose fine study of *Blue of Noon*, *L'Indifférence des ruines*, is recommended. Marguerite Duras meanwhile was struck by its writing that went 'against language': 'He invents how not to write,' she says, 'even whilst writing.'

'Revolutionary offensive or death'

1. The activities of Contre-Attaque began in November. *Blue of Noon* had been completed in May.

2. *Lettres à Roger Caillois*, p. 41.

3. 'It seems impossible to me to continue to raise narrow questions of personalities', he said in a letter to Roger Caillois of 26 September 1935 (ibid., p. 45).

4. Ibid., letter of 4 August 1935, p. 41.

5. *Textures*, no. 6, 1970.

6. There are two versions of this text. If the first, printed on white paper, carries the signatures of thirteen members, the second has those of thirty-eight. Among them were Pierre Aimery (whose real name was Imre Kelemen, a Hungarian marxist), Georges Ambrosino, Georges Bataille, Roger Blin (but he seems only to have passed briefly through Contre-Attaque), Jacques-André Boiffard, André Breton, Claude Cahun, Jacques Chavy, René Chenon, Jean Dautry, Jean Delmas, Henri Dubief, Paul Éluard, Jacques Fichbein, Arthur Harfaux, Maurice Heine, Maurice Henry, Georges Hugnet, Marcel Jean, Pierre Klossowski, Dora Maar, Léo Malet, Georges Mouton, Henri Pastoureau, Benjamin Péret, Yves Tanguy, etc. Henri Dubief estimated the membership of Contre-Attaque to have been at least fifty, at most seventy.

7. It will be noted that Michel Leiris was not part of Contre-Attaque. He found the project at best utopian, at worst 'something of a practical joke'.

8. *Œuvres complètes*, I, p. 384.

9. Ibid., p. 389. Where one will find, in a 'propagandist' way, the essence of the argument developed in 'The Problem of the State'.

10. Henri Dubief, *op. cit.* He adds that, with the help of members of the organisation, including surrealists, he deepened 'the analysis published in the three last sections of *La Critique sociale* which are still today [1970] the best studies on these questions'.

11. In fact we find here the critique advanced in the article 'The Psychological Structure of Fascism'.

12. Recall the *Yes* movement Bataille had wanted to create in opposition to Dada, eleven years earlier, in 1924.

13. 'I am able to confirm that Breton did not attend' (Georges Mouton, letter to the author).

14. Charles Ronsac, *Trois noms pour une vie*, Paris: Laffont, p. 127. But could Ronsac be mistaken? Is he really speaking of the same meeting, as he locates it in a café, whereas it had been announced, in a leaflet, as taking place at the Grenier des Augustins?

15. Henri Dubief, *op. cit.*

16. Imprudent and unfortunate as this tract was, it would be unreasonable to suspect its author, Jean Dautry, of any ambivalence or sympathy for fascist ideas. A young historian (he was born in 1910) and a pupil of Albert Mathiez, he had contributed to the organisation of *Le réveil communiste*, *L'ouvrier*

communiste and *Spartakus*, before joining Marceau Pivert's Revolutionary Left. A member of the Resistance, he was a member of the Communist Party during the war. Disappointed by Souvarine, he had, according to Charles Ronsac, joined Bataille and Contre-Attaque, in which he had only a slight hope of 'doing something, being somewhere' (*op. cit*, p. 128).

17. Henri Dubief, *op. cit.*

18. 'I went into exile to Spain after the fascist disturbances of February 1934. But that's among the ironies of life: I fled fascism to take refuge in a country about to become fascist' (André Masson, interview with the author, 1986).

19. This declaration entitled 'Appel aux hommes' ['Call to the people'] was published in *Les Humbles* the literary journal of Les Primaires (editor: Maurice Wullens), notebook no. 1, 22nd series, January 1937.

20. Georges Mouton, letter to the author.

The angel and the beast, part 2

1. André Thirion, *Revolutionaries Without Revolution*, p. 381.

2. Marco Ristić, *André Breton et le mouvement surréaliste*, NRF special issue, April 1967.

3. It is noteworthy that not one of the dissident surrealists who contributed to *A Corpse* took part in Contre-Attaque, either on Breton's side or on Bataille's.

4. 'Can one say Bataille wanted to replace Breton? I couldn't say. Overall I think so, but he never said so to me. That's what I think' (André Masson, interview with the author, 1986).

5. Bernard Noël, *Change*, no. 7, 1970.

From Contre-Attaque to *Acéphale*: André Masson

1. André Masson, interview with the author, 1986.

2. André Masson, *Entretiens avec Georges Charbonnier*.

3. 'I found it disgraceful that people wanted physically to attack Breton' (interview with the author, November 1986).

4. André Masson, *Entretiens avec Georges Charbonnier*, p. 180.

5. But he illustrated *Irène* the same year, also anonymously, with the same publisher. *Irène*, we know, has since been attributed to Aragon.

6. *Les Présages*, the title of a ballet by Léonide Massine with decor by André Masson, performed at l'Opéra de Monte-Carlo, in 1933.

'Everything calls for the death which ravages us'

1. 'Nietzschean Chronicle' in *Visions of Excess*, p. 206.

2. It would be more accurate to say pre-Nazi. The amalgamation of fascism and Nazism is not recent, and no doubt predates the war. Bataille

attempted to clear Nietzsche of the accusation of 'fascism', not of 'Nazism'. For simplicity I shall use the same word.

3. Here is one of several examples, one not at all ill-intentioned: 'From 1937 to 1946 . . . he did not publish a single political text' (Marc Richir, 'La fin de l'histoire: Notes préliminaires sur la pensée politique de Georges Bataille', *Textures*, no. 6, 1970).

4. 'Nietzsche and the Fascists' in *Visions of Excess*, pp. 185–6.

5. 'Nietzschean Chronicle' in ibid., p. 209.

6. 'Propositions' in ibid., p. 199.

7. The question of the effects of these two violences effectively remains open, regardless of their avowed ends. The question of the similarity in nature of the violence is also open; but these both go beyond the alleged relationship between *Acéphale* and fascism, at least in so far as it is possible to analyse it here.

8. Alfred Rosenberg quoted by Bataille ('Nietzsche and the Fascists', p. 189), who did not fail to note fascism's hostility towards the chthonic gods, the very ones he had recognised as his own since *The Solar Anus* and 'The Pineal Eye'.

9. Discussing at length Cervantes's play *Numance*, performed in Spain in burned-out churches (one might see this as a memory made real of *Notre-Dame de Rheims*) 'with no other scenery than the traces of fires, and no other actors than those of the red militias', Bataille once again shifts the centres of political interest. Only red militia men playing *Numance* in burned-out churches have the stature of the tragic myths that metamorphose history.

10. 'Nietzschean Chronicle', p. 208.

11. Ibid., p. 210.

12. Does it need to be said after this how Bataille played with fire? If it burned him, it was not without him wanting it to. What matters is not whether events proved him right or not, but that he should have attempted the experience of it in advance.

13. Henri Dubief describes him as a 'foreign marxist' hiding behind a pseudonym, without saying more than this. Foreign possibly, but marxist is unlikely in so far as one can trust the extract I give below. Before Acéphale he had taken part with Bataille in Contre-Attaque.

14. Bibliothèque Nationale, *Acéphale*, NAF 15952. This text is dated 17 April 1936. The text is not only rash, it also lacks rigour: to consider fascism as a marxism set on its feet is analytically speaking 'tenuous' to say the least.

15. *Œuvres complètes*, III, *Acéphale*, p. 677, Notes.

16. Jean-Maurice Monnoyer, *Le Peintre et le démon: Entretiens avec Pierre Klossowski*, p. 181.

17. Roger Caillois, interview with Gilles Lapouge, *Quinzaine littéraire*, 15–30 June 1970.

18. Monnoyer, *Le Peintre et le démon*, p. 182.

19. Roger Caillois, *L'Esprit des sectes*, preface, reprinted in his *Instincts et sociétés* and *Approches de l'imaginaire*.

20. It was Caillois himself who related this (in an interview in *Le Nouvel Observateur*, no. 521, November 1974): Bataille 'no doubt imagined I had a pitiless character'. It is hard to imagine Bataille assigning the major role of sacrificer in this extravagant ceremony to someone who was not a 'conspirator'.

21. *Œuvres complètes*, VI, p. 369. He also said: 'I then believed I was drawn towards founding a religion, at least under a paradoxical form' (ibid., p. 373).

22. *Œuvres complètes*, II, 'Le sacrifice du gibbon', p. 30. This text was written between 1927 and 1930.

23. Ibid.

24. This text is part of Henri Dubief's donation to the Bibliothèque Nationale (Acéphale, NAF 15952).

25. It has rashly been suggested that this was Colette Peignot. Absolutely nothing would support such a supposition, which says both too much and too little (and its origin needs explaining).

26. *Œuvres complètes*, VI, p. 373. This sentence should not mislead us. What he here qualifies as monstrous is not this planned sacrifice (which he never admitted to), but the plan of founding a religion.

27. Acéphale, NAF 15952, Bibliothèque Nationale.

28. Michel Leiris, interviews with the author, 1986. This insistence on Leiris's part of describing several of Bataille's projects (such as Contre-Attaque and Acéphale) as 'hoaxes' is such as to cast retrospective doubts on how 'politically' close they were from the end of *Documents* to the war. We shall see that the College of Sociology only brought them together in a superficial way.

29. *Œuvres complètes*, VI, p. 373.

30. Pierre Klossowski interviewed in Bernard-Henri Lévy, *Les Aventures de la liberté*, pp. 170–1.

31. Michel Camus, 'L'acéphalité ou la religion de la mort', preface to the reprinted edition of *Acéphale*, Paris: Jean-Michel Place, 1980.

32. It was the former home of the painter Maurice Denis.

33. Isabelle Waldberg, interview with the author, 1986.

34. The very close relationship between Bataille and Lacan between 1935 and the war has not often been remarked upon. And it has never been pointed out – not even by those involved – that Lacan followed the activities and experiences of Acéphale closely. The close intellectual and emotional relationship uniting Bataille and Lacan should one day be investigated, and it is a relationship whose effects can more than once be sensed in Lacan's works. We should also recall that in 1939 Lacan got to know Sylvia Bataille, who was to be his second wife (she had been separated from Georges Bataille since 1934).

35. Isabelle Waldberg, interview with the author. Bataille would seem not to have lost a taste for the 'cheerfully scandalous pranks' of his youth: the taste for exhibitionism, for example.

36. Roger Caillois, 'André Breton et le mouvement surréaliste', *NRF*, special issue, April 1967.

37. Shamanism was the subject of lectures given by Anatole Lewitzky to the College of Sociology on 7 and 21 March 1939.

38. *Œuvres complètes*, VI, p. 371.

Florid bullfight

1. 'The words "florid bullfight" are those [Laure] used to describe her death-throes' (Bataille).

2. To believe him capable of ritually 'sacrificing' Colette Peignot would be to make him a crazy and demented person. The pain he knew after her death shows how impossible and unthinkable it would have been for him to consider voluntarily depriving himself of her.

3. Laure, we recall, was Colette Peignot's middle name. It is the name under which she chose to sign the poems and writings discovered after her death. It is also the name by which Bataille spoke about her and of them. This is why I shall henceforth use it in preference to that of Colette Peignot.

4. *Œuvres complètes*, V, *Le Coupable*, p. 501, Notes.

5. *Œuvres complètes*, X, *L'Érotisme*.

6. Ibid.

7. 'The College of Sociology' in Denis Hollier, *The College of Sociology 1937–39*, p. 337.

8. Ibid.

9. *Eroticism*, pp. 19–20.

10. This is a word Bataille often used. It should be understood in the sense that for him existence is not finite; and in the sense that everything that it is no longer is the void.

11. Ibid., p. 21.

12. 'I hated our life, I often wanted to run away, to go off alone into the mountains (it was to save my life, I understand that now)' (letter from Laure to Georges Bataille, Laure, *The Collected Writings*, p. 151).

13. *Œuvres complètes*, V, *Le Coupable*, p. 500, Notes.

14. From a letter to Jean Grémillon dated September or October 1937.

15. *Œuvres complètes*, V, *Le Coupable*, p. 525, Notes.

16. The irony was that in Épernon, Laure saw her last film, *One Way Passage* by Tay Garnett (1932). [This film, a favourite of the surrealists, is a story of doomed lovers: he (William Powell) is a criminal being returned from China to the States to face execution, she (Kay Francis) is suffering from an incurable illness. trans.]

17. Ibid.

18. Michel Leiris, *Frêle bruit*, p. 345.

19. Michel Leiris, *Fourbis*, p. 255.

20. Marcel Moré, 'Georges Bataille and the death of Laure' in Laure, *The Collected Writings*, pp. 241–2.

21. *Œuvres complètes*, V, *Le Coupable*, p. 504, Notes. The very beautiful and violent letter written by Laure to Bataille gives an idea of this hatred and anger: 'Scatter, spoil, destroy, throw to the dogs all that you want: you will never affect me again. I will never be where you think you find me, where you think you've finally caught me in a chokehold that makes you come.' It seems that Laure accused him of infidelity, an infidelity so much more painful as she was dying:

> *Everything* you have been doing, I've known about – *everything* – for more than a year, before and after Sicily, everything that crystallised around a person who took the form of your dream, a shattering dream that knows how to shatter, a dream that relates to the most banal of daily realities that any human being is capable of living: adultery, well-organised, planned out, clever, cunning, burning because secret. (Laure, *The Collected Writings*, p. 152 [translation modified].)

22. *Œuvres complètes*, V, p. 507.

23. On the seventh November nineteen hundred and thirty eight, at eight hours fifteen minutes Colette, Laure, Lucienne Peignot, born at Meudon (Seine-et-Oise) on the eighth October nineteen hundred and three, unemployed, the daughter of Georges Louis Jean Peignot, deceased, and Suzanne Chardon, his unmarried widow, died at her home at 59b rue de Mareil. Prepared the aforesaid day at nine hours forty minutes, on the declaration of Charles Armand Gustave Peignot, forty one years of age, industrialist, Chevalier of the Legion of Honour, domiciled at 21 rue Casimir-Périer, the brother of the deceased . . . (Death certificate at Saint-Germain-en-Laye town hall.)

Sacred sociology

1. Moreover, the word 'college' was Jules Monnerot's idea, not Bataille's. A profound misunderstanding persisted between the two men about its origin. No doubt Bataille organised and developed the College's activities. No doubt its style and themes also came from him. Jules Monnerot nevertheless claimed to be its originator, saying that he 'conceived the idea, found its participants, named the project' (*Sociologie du communisme*, p. 545). Whatever their due, the differences between the two men seem to have been immediately apparent: we shall see what Bataille wanted the College to be; Monnerot on the other hand wanted it to be the basis for a real political engagement, and for the distinctions between intellectualism, art and politics to be clear within it.

2. This sentence is by Denis Hollier. On the subject of the College of Sociology, I can do no better than refer the reader to the precise and valuable book of the same name (*The College of Sociology, 1937–39*) which brings together, along with notes and comments, all of the texts of its participants.

3. Roger Caillois, interview with Gilles Lapouge, *Quinzaine littéraire*, 15–30 June 1970.

4. It should be remembered that Bataille continued to follow Kojève's seminar on Hegel's *Phenomenology of Spirit* until 1939.

5. Roger Caillois, *L'Esprit des sectes*, reprinted in his *Instincts et sociétés* and *Approches de l'Imaginaire*. Alexandre Kojève was nevertheless closer to the College than Caillois implies. Thus when informing Caillois about a meeting to settle a lecture programme, Bataille wrote to him asking 'Kojève, Wahl, [Walter] Benjamin, Leiris, Klossowski and Moré to come' (letter of 17 May 1938, Georges Bataille, *Lettres à Roger Caillois*).

6. Roger Caillois, 'For a College of Sociology', introduction, in Denis Hollier, *The College of Sociology, 1937–39*, p. 11.

7. Ibid. [translation modified].

8. Roger Caillois.

9. Ibid. This was a café near the Bibliothèque Nationale, like the Univers where the members of Acéphale met.

10. Pierre Prévost recalls the first lectures being held in a brasserie in the rue du Quatre-Septembre, the Gambrinuse.

11. Bataille, *The College of Sociology*, p. 106.

12. 'Sexual inter-attraction' is a wording that gives the term a theoretical, pseudo-scientific distance.

13. This case study is discussed by Bataille (*The College of Sociology*, pp. 107 ff.). It is taken from C. W. Valentine, 'La psychologie génétique du rire', *Journal de psychologie normale et pathologique*.

14. This case study has not been traced, but it would reappear twenty years later in Bataille's book *Literature and Evil*.

15. René M. Guastalla was a Hellenist and professor at the Lycée Lakanal, author of *Le Mythe et le livre* (Paris: Gallimard, 1940) who committed suicide in 1941. Anatole Lewitzky, born near Moscow in 1901, emigrated to France, took graduate studies at the Sorbonne as a student of Marcel Mauss and in 1933 joined the Musée de l'Homme to take charge of the Oceanic department. In 1940 he set up the museum's resistance network, the first in occupied France. Arrested in February 1941, he was executed in February 1942 at Mont-Valérien, with Boris Vildé and five other members of the Musée de l'Homme network.

16. Paul-Louis Landsberg (1901–44) was a German Jewish philosopher who emigrated to Spain in 1933, and then to France, and was sympathetic to Emmanuel Mounier's Catholicism. He died of exhaustion during his internment in Oranienburg prison, and was the author of an *Essai sur l'expérience de la mort*.

17. Klossowski, in Jean-Maurice Monnoyer, *Le Peintre et son démon*, p. 186.

18. According to Pierre Prévost, not a single surrealist ever seems to have attended the lectures (interview with the author, 1987). There is every reason on the other hand to assume that members of the Acéphale secret society attended.

19. This is suggested by one of the first IFOP surveys conducted in France.

It showed a majority in favour of these pacts of 57 per cent, with 37 per cent against and 6 per cent undecided.

20. 'Déclaration du Collège de sociologie sur la crise internationale,' Denis Hollier, *The College of Sociology*, pp. 44–5.

21. Pierre Prévost, *Pierre Prévost rencontre Georges Bataille*, pp. 23–4.

22. Nevertheless this shows that this ambiguity was only apparent. As I have said, Acéphale and the fascists laid claim neither to the same myths nor the same forces, and above all they had totally different aims.

23. I shall return to this at length with reference to the war. If there is any ambiguity about the College of Sociology, which one would strive to find (even if with the intention of taking up an impartial critical stance), it has never been better rebutted, even in its anecdotal form, than by André Masson, when he asked Paul-Louis Landsberg what, in his opinion, the Germans would do with the College if they reached Paris: 'he replied, like a shot: "They'll keep the College and shoot the collaborators." This also showed that we could not be suspected of fascism for our violent statements, even if they could come close to the "quest for glory" side of fascism. The waters between things are always clouded' (interview with Paule Thévenin, *Les Cahiers Obliques*, no. 1, January–March 1980, p. 27).

24. A few preparatory notes for this lecture were published in *The College of Sociology*, pp. 196–8.

25. Ibid., p. 195.

26. Ibid., p. 334.

27. Ibid. [translation modified].

28. Ibid., p. 354. What struck Bataille most was that his friend waited until the day before the lecture to assert his reservations and announce his abstention. Leiris, moreover, willingly agreed to make his excuses: 'I refuse to believe that such a mistake, despite the momentary trouble it may cause you, is such that can destroy our friendship' (letter to Georges Bataille, Monday, 3 July 1939, 9 p.m.)

29. Ibid., p. 336. This sudden freedom, this freeing of all reservations and all conventions, makes one think of what he did ten years earlier when running *Documents*: respectful of literary and scientific usage as long as he felt he had to be, and then suddenly (from issue 4) free in tone, insolent, provocative . . .

30. Ibid., p. 339.

31. Is this an admission of the infidelities suffered by Laure and for which she violently reproached him (Laure, *Ecrits*, p. 319)? Is it an admission of the sacrificial and annihilating nature of the meaning they had for him? It is interesting to note that this text precedes the first lines of the book *Guilty* by just a few days.

32. *The College of Sociology*, p. 340. It is important not to ignore the existence, parallel to that of the College of Sociology, of a Society of Collective Psychology with which Bataille was closely linked. In spring 1937 a symposium was held on the problem of circumcision from which was born, at the request of Drs Allendy and Borel, Bataille and Leiris, a Society of Collective

Psychology. Its aim was 'To study the role of social facts, psychological factors, in particular of an unconscious nature, to help the convergence of research thus far carried out in isolation in various disciplines.' The president of this Society was Professor Janet, and the vice-president Georges Bataille. Bataille contributed no more than an introductory talk (17 January 1938) to the debates of 1938, under the theme of 'Attitudes towards Death'. The papers took place at the rate of one a month, and were given by Julien Reinach, Denise Scheffner and Michel Leiris, Abbé Paul Jury, Haguenauer, Drs Lagache, Borel, Leuba, Schiff and Desoille, François Berge, Camille Schuwer and Georges Duthuit.

Vivan le femmine, viva il buon vino, sostegno e gloria d'umanita

1. Lorenzo da Ponte, *Don Giovanni*.
2. *Œuvres complètes*, V, *Le Coupable*, p. 522, Notes.
3. Later, he would put this differently: the community is the impossible community, the absence of community.
4. 'La Chance' 'Good Fortune' is oddly the title of a text by Bataille published in *Verve*, in November 1938, the month of Laure's death.
5. *Acéphale*, no. 5, was published in June 1939. Its title was *Folie, guerre et mort*. It contained three texts: 'La folie de Nietzsche', 'La menace de guerre' and 'La pratique de la joie devant la mort'. The format of this issue was reduced to 12cm × 17cm (rather than 20cm × 28cm for the previous issues). Patrick Waldberg's name appears on the back cover as addressee for subscriptions (the address 59b rue de Mareil, Saint-Germain-en-Laye (Seine-et-Oise); the name of Jacques Chavy appears as administrator; that of Bataille not at all.
6. *Œuvres complètes*, I, p. 546.
7. Ibid., 'L'affrontment de Dieu et du "fou"', p. 547.
8. Ibid., p. 554.
9. Ibid.
10. *Guilty*, p. 40.
11. I will have occasion to return to these misunderstandings. However, one thing is certain and can be said straightaway: Bataille has never more than today been threatened with 'recuperation' by the most varied mysticisms whether Oriental or Christian. There is perhaps no literal reading and interpretation more ill-intentioned.
12. 'The Practice of Joy Before Death' in *Visions of Excess*, p. 237.
13. *Guilty*, p. 35. A catastrophic vision is not new for Bataille. It will be recalled that Simone Weil openly accused him of this. It is also profoundly Nietzschean. Nietzsche was happy at the earthquake in Nice on 23 February 1887: 'Presaging catastrophe, himself a living catastrophe, any catastrophe pleased him' (Daniel Halévy, *Nietzsche*, p. 489).
14. The 'Manuel de l'anti-chrétien' was not completed. We know only a few sketches, notes, plans and one almost written chapter: 'For the moment

wars are the strongest stimulants of the imagination'. These sketches were gathered in *Œuvres complètes*, II, pp. 375–99.

15. *Œuvres complètes*, V, p. 514: 'Queneau was the first to abandon me.'

16. Draft of the letter of 20 January 1935 in the Bibliothèque Nationale. 'My friends avoid me. I frighten, not because of my cries, but because I cannot leave anyone in peace. I simplify: haven't I often given good pretexts?' (*Inner Experience*, p. 41).

17. *Œuvres complètes*, V, *Le Coupable*, p. 524, Notes.

18. *Literature and Evil*, p. 104. Gilbert Lély was undoubtedly wrong to take exception to the terms which Bataille chose to pay homage to Heine. If he effectively said that Heine 'squandered his fortune on his research on Sade' (ibid.), it was not to reproach him, even in a friendly way. From what we know of Bataille's thought on expenditure and squandering, it was even a compliment, one of the greatest (Gilbert Lély, *Vie du Marquis de Sade*, Paris: Jean-Jacques Pauvert, p. 709). It will frequently be the case that the intentional miscasting of Bataille's words did him a disservice when people of good faith (like Lély) or bad faith read them literally.

19. *Œuvres complètes*, V, *Le Coupable*, p. 514, Notes.

20. *The College of Sociology*, p. 90.

21. *Guilty*, p. 40.

22. Bataille proposed giving this book a new title: 'The tragic destiny' (see Georges Bataille, *Lettres à Roger Caillois*, p. 83).

Good fortune

1. *Guilty*, p. 38.

2. Ibid., p. 51.

3. Her maiden name was Denise Lefroi.

4. Jean was actually born in 1939.

5. Laurence Bataille, interviews with the author, 1986.

6. Michel Fardoulis-Lagrange, interview with the author, 1986.

7. *Œuvres complètes*, V, *Le Coupable*, Notes. Michel Fardoulis-Lagrange gives a complementary version of this meeting, to which Bataille made no allusion, and which emphasises its lovestruck nature: having caught sight of Bataille and his wife reflected in a restaurant mirror kissing, he claims Denise's husband grabbed a knife and struck it into the palm of his hand. Jean Rollin confirms this version of the incident (interview with the author).

8. Ibid., p. 515.

9. Fardoulis-Lagrange, interviews with the author, 1986

10. *Œuvres complètes*, V, *Le Coupable*, p. 516, Notes. It is doubtful whether Bataille saw her again, other than by chance. But Denise Rollin was not very far away since, to the end of her life, she maintained an apparently close relationship with Maurice Blanchot.

'I am myself war'

1. In the Heraclitean sense of the word.

2. *Œuvres complètes*, I, 'Méditation héraclitéenne', p. 557.

3. Ibid. Sentences in which one notices, in a way similar to what was said in *Acéphale*, that it was upon himself that Bataille first called for the devastation of death.

4. *Œuvres complètes*, XI, 'Note sur *Réflexions sur la question juive* de Jean-Paul Sartre', p. 228.

5. This certainly calls for a lengthy commentary, but this goes beyond the scope of this book.

6. *Œuvres complètes*, I, p. 551.

7. *Œuvres complètes*, VII, *La Limite de l'utile*, p. 251. *La Limite de l'utile* was the first version of *La Part maudite*. It was written between 1939 and 1945. Chapter VI of this uncompleted book (and unpublished while Bataille was alive) is entitled 'War'.

8. 'A little later, in the same place, a convoy of small American planes filled a clear sky. Striped black and white, they whooshed rooftops, machine-gunned roads, and a railroad. Thrilled – and catching my breath' (*On Nietzsche*, p. 119).

9. *Œuvres complètes*, I, p. 551.

10. Ibid, p. 558.

11. Ernst Jünger, *La Guerre, notre mère*. Quoted in *Œuvres complètes*, VII, *La Limite de l'utile*, pp. 251–3. Jünger's book is about the 1914–18 war. [Jünger's book appears not to be translated into English – we have translated this passage from the French translation. trans.]

12. Jules Monnerot, *Inquisitions*, 'La fièvre de Georges Bataille', p. 200.

13. Jean-Paul Sartre, speaking ironically in the first person as Bataille, in *Situations* I, 'Un nouveau mystique', p. 165.

'I love ignorance touching on the future'

1. 'Ich liebe die Unwissenheit um die Zukunft' (Nietzsche).

2. Raymond Queneau, *Journal 1939–1940*, p. 110.

3. Ibid. The meeting referred to here between Queneau and Bataille took place on 27 December 1939.

4. Jean Piel, *La Rencontre et la différence*, Paris: Fayard, 1982, p. 214.

5. Klossowski in Jean-Maurice Monnoyer, *Le Peintre et son démon*, p. 189; my italics.

6. Ibid.

7. Michel Fardoulis-Lagrange, interviews with the author, 1986. Such a suggestion calls for further detail: Fardoulis-Lagrange, who was a communist during the war and sentenced to several years in prison, nevertheless had Bataille as a defence witness in the trial. It was at Bataille's house in Vézelay

that he took refuge for several months in 1943. It is also through him that we know that Éluard (and Nusch) often visited Bataille in Vézelay in 1943.

8. 'Without ever having had, for Heidegger, anything other than an irritated attraction, I happened to read him (in fact, except exceptionally, not in German)' (*Œuvres complètes*, IV, p. 365).

9. A book Souvarine in all likelihood only read, if at all, after its publication in 1957 ('he dares claim that she was "dirty", transposing his own moral uncleanliness onto the person he alludes to. In his madness, he goes so far as to compare her to a "filthy rat". What else is this but Nazi prose?' (preface to the re-edition of *La Critique sociale*, p. 20).

10. Ibid. Souvarine's account is too violently full of hate for us not to imagine the historian at the mercy of something other than ideas. Is this a late settling of emotional accounts? Is Bataille the philosopher once again connected to the idea he allowed to be formed about him, that of a debauched individual? Ill-intentioned as Souvarine's account is, it is nevertheless not inconsequential. It was on this basis, though without naming him, that the attacks aimed at Bataille were formulated.

11. Letter from Georges Duthuit to André Breton, 18 November 1943, published in *VVV*, no. 4, February 1944, p. 42. The booklet Duthuit alludes to is *Acéphale*, no. 5, and the text is doubtless 'La pratique de la joie devant la mort'.

12. Denis de Rougemont, *Esprit*, May 1937, p. 314. This is an assertion de Rougemont exploits excessively, in alleging perfect agreement between Acéphale and personalism. Along the same lines as de Rougemont, Prévost's sentence is also worth noting: 'the whole Hitlerite movement was judged by him and by us all as a monstrous enslaving enterprise aiming to reinstate a monocephalous society' (*op. cit.*, p. 27).

13. Interview with Michel Leiris, in Bernard-Henri Lévy, *Les Aventures de la liberté*, p. 186. Since it is Souvarine's double accusation (that Bataille was 'fascinated' by Hitler, and that he was an anti-Semite) that this argument is aiming to refute, it is relevant to reprint here Leiris's two other responses in the same interview:

> In my opinion, Bataille was profoundly anti-fascist. What is certain, on the other hand, is that he was impressed by fascist methods of propaganda [we see here that 'impressed' replaces the ignominious 'fascinated' that Souvarine's account tries to use to defamatory ends]. His dream would have been to find, for the left's benefit, methods of propaganda as effective as the methods deployed by the far right. (Ibid., p. 174.)

A little later, Leiris says that Souvarine harboured a 'total hostility' for Bataille, a hostility he 'expressed in a very unjust way in the preface to the re-edition of *La Critique sociale*, in which he accuses Bataille of anti-Semitism'. 'It's an absurd accusation; pure spite' (ibid., p. 185). Jean Piel replied in 1984 to Souvarine's accusations in the article 'Quand un vieil homme trempe sa plume dans le fiel' (*Critique*, no. 444, May 1984, pp. 424–30), in which he calls upon the accounts of Waldberg, Pastoureau, Blanchot and Dubief.

14. No doubt too much is made today of the anti-parliamentarianism of the extreme left between the wars, by making it, first, analogous to the anti-parliamentarianism of the extreme right, and, second, making it the consequence of anti-democratism. This clearly underestimates the loss of confidence in parliamentary representation and the appearance of compromises by political figures (the spinelessness Masson cites) such that, for example, someone like Tardieu could place his trust in the Leagues to reclaim power in 1930.

15. 'Acéphale ou l'illusion initiatique', conversation between Paule Thévenin and André Masson, *Les Cahiers obliques*, no. 1, January–March 1980, p. 27. André Masson made no secret of the doctrinal ambiguity of an anti-democratic and non-communist anti-fascism: 'it was clear that nothing in fascism could attract us. But, if you look at all of this as a chess game, it is evident that, in renouncing democracy one gets a bit closer to the regimes that use force. . . . But in the end we've explained our position clearly enough for there to be no confusion.' There would have been ambiguity if Bataille had resolutely renounced democracy; but this was not the case. As a last resort, and with nothing to oppose the fascist peril but the democracies, bloodless and corrupt as they were, it was as a democrat that Bataille called upon them to defend themselves (cf. the College of Sociology's 'Declaration', as well as the final lectures he delivered).

16. Hans Mayer, 'Profils perdus', *France Culture* broadcasts of 12 and 19 May 1988, directed by Marc Floriot. A German born in Cologne in 1907, from 1933 Mayer was forced first into clandestine activity, then into exile after the SS raided his home. It was at his instigation and after a brief exchange of letters that he met Bataille and participated in the activities of the College of Sociology, for which he gave the lecture 'The Rituals of Political Associations in Germany of the Romantic Period' on 18 April 1939 (biographical information from *The College of Sociology*, p. 262).

17. Jean-Pierre Faye, 'Profils perdus'.

18. Ibid.

19. Related by Pierre Prévost, *op. cit.*, p. 26.

The excretions of the war: exodus, evacuation

1. *Guilty*, p. 11.

2. Where he met Maurice Heine who recorded in his diary on Tuesday, 31 October 1939:

> He [Bataille] told me: you are wrong to place yourself within a moral perspective. I place myself within the animal perspective. I am not a man among humans. I am an animal. I am ready to make the concessions of form demanded of me. I am a gnat, you can crush me, but I will not make a useless sound to signal my presence and I will not act as though I were an elephant.

We recall that Maurice Heine died on 30 May 1940.

3. *Œuvres complètes*, V, *Le Coupable*, p. 521, Notes.

4. Ibid., p. 522.

5. Ibid., p. 523.

6. Ibid., p. 527.

7. Laurence arrived with her uncle André and aunt Rose Masson. It seems they first stayed at a hotel (interviews with the author, 1986). According to Jean Rollin, Audiberti was also there. It seems that Sylvia Bataille was there too, at least for a time.

8. *Œuvres complètes*, *Le Coupable*, p. 529, Notes.

9. Ibid., p. 531.

10. We recall the terms of the letter he wrote to Mlle C. eighteen years earlier: 'What definitive reason do I have to live chastely?'

11. Ibid., p. 535.

12. Ibid., p. 536.

Nobodaddy

1. A word made from the combination of 'nobody' and 'daddy', used here and by William Blake to indicate God the father.

2. *Guilty*, p. 14.

3. Ibid., p. 19.

4. Fu Chou Li, the Chinese torture victim.

5. *Œuvres complètes*, I, *Le Coupable*, p. 518, Notes.

6. The torture of the Hundred Pieces.

7. Ibid. This double experience would be taken up again in 'La tombe de Louis XXX' (*Œuvres complètes*, IV, p. 165).

8. 'In other words, one reaches the states of ecstasy or of rapture only by *dramatising* existence in general' (*Inner Experience*, p. 10).

9. Ibid., p. 174.

10. Ibid., p. 36.

11. *On Nietzsche*, p. 44.

12. And he adds: 'This is how it is a-theological' (Robert Sasso, *Le Système du non-savoir: Une ontologie du jeu*, Paris: Éditions de Minuit (1978) p. 101). Anyone trying to establish *presence* in Bataille's experience must bear this point in mind.

13. Letter from Alexandre Kojève to Georges Bataille, 28 July 1942.

14. *Œuvres complètes*, III, *Le Petit*.

15. *Madame Edwarda*, preface, in *Eroticism*, p. 269.

Edwarda: the divine tatters

1. *Madame Edwarda*, p. 150.

2. Yet he himself gave the key. He said that the most important of the

texts of *Inner Experience*, 'The Torment' must be read after and in the light of *Madame Edwarda*, which is its 'lubricious key'.

3. The sequence which associates God with hairy and hidden parts does not stop there: this last quote is from *Le Petit*, which is a word used in brothels for the anal orifice, according to Bataille. And Bataille took a third pseudonym in these war years (*Madame Edwarda* is signed Pierre Angélique; *Le Petit*, Louis Trente), Dianus, which has to be phonetically understood as the contraction of Dieu-Anus (on the model of Lord Auch?). Bataille explained that this pseudonym seemed to him 'to reunite the savour of a bearded woman and that of a dying god, his throat flowing with blood' (*Œuvres complètes*, V, p. 437).

4. *Madame Edwarda*, p. 152.

5. Ibid., 158.

6. Of course this is not to claim to exhaust the meaning of this book. Marguerite Duras said in 1958: 'Edwarda will remain sufficiently unintelligible for centuries, for a whole theology to be based around it' (*La Ciguë*, no. 1).

7. And clandestine. Both were published under pseudonyms.

8. What he took out is included in the notes in Volume V of the *Œuvres complètes*. They contain more than enough material for Bataille to have published another book, five times as much as *Madame Edwarda* and *Le Petit*.

9. *Madame Edwarda* was published under the pseudonym of Pierre Angélique by Éditions du Solitaire (Robert Chatté) in 1941, in Paris although it is dated 1937. It was reissued by the same publisher, with illustrations by Jean Perdu (a pseudonym of Jean Fautrier) in 1945 in Paris; this edition gives the date of 1942. Still under the pseudonym of Pierre Angélique, but with the addition of a preface by Georges Bataille, it was re-issued by Jean-Jacques Pauvert in Paris in 1956. A further edition appeared under the name of Georges Bataille and illustrated with twelve plates by Hans Bellmer (Paris: Jean-Jacques Pauvert, 1966). *Le Petit* was published under the pseudonym of Louis Trente, without a publisher's name (actually Robert Chatté) in Paris in 1943 but giving the date of 1934, and then republished under the name of Georges Bataille by Jean-Jacques Pauvert, Paris, 1963.

'I call myself the abomination of God'

1. Angela of Foligno.

2. *Guilty*, p. 37.

3. Jean-Noël Vuarnet (*Extases féminines*, Arthaud) sees in Bataille's Angela of Foligno a double and cumulative *invention*: according to him this must be seen as part of the invention constituted by the translation by Ernest Hello. To this first invention must be added that of Bataille himself, which consists of reading and interpreting Angela of Foligno as one does Dionysius the Areopagite or Meister Eckhart.

The community of friends

1. Whose real name was Alexandre Lipianski.

2. It would be wrong to think that Bataille alone wanted to form study groups. In reality, they seem to have been numerous. Among them, the one formed by Marcel Moré, in which Landsberg and Koyré participated should not be overlooked.

3. After the war, Georges Pelorson also changed his name, being known as Georges Belmont and becoming a translator and publisher.

4. Pierre Prévost, interviews with the author. Maurice Blanchot was introduced as the author of several books he had burned. At the time that war was declared he had effectively published nothing.

5. Klossowski in Jean-Maurice Monnoyer, *Le Peintre et le démon*, p. 192. He said further: 'But I would attribute to this meeting with Maurice Blanchot, to their friendship that was so beneficial to him, that he had recognised in total incommunicability the condition in which a true action could then be carried out' (*Change*, no. 7, July 1970).

6. It has been seen that a similar limitation had already been attributed to Bataille: the most fervent admirers of Colette Peignot asserted that Bataille's work had not only been influenced, but made possible, by her. But there can be no doubt that in 1941 his thought was established and that, in a way that was certainly sometimes fragmentary, the books he wrote after the war were already in place. This was certainly not yet the case for Maurice Blanchot.

7. In English, *Thomas the Obscure*, translated by Robert Lamberton, New York: David Lewis, 1973; *How is Literature Possible?*, translated by Michael Syrotinski, is published in *The Blanchot Reader*, ed. Michael Holland, Oxford: Blackwell, 1995. The other books appear not to have been translated [trans.].

8. Prévost suggests that Blanchot was editor-in-chief of *L'Insurgé*. If his name does not appear as such, it is still the case that he occupied a considerable place in it. Blanchot had been a sub-editor on *Aux écoutes*; he also collaborated with the *Journal des débats*. On the political articles by Maurice Blanchot published in *Combat*, the Maurrasian mouthpiece of Jean de Fabrègues, see Jeffrey Mehlman, 'Littérature et terreur', *Tel quel*, no. 92, and *L'Infini*, no. 1. This is not the place to embark on the very problematic ideological genealogy of Maurice Blanchot. To establish it is not difficult (hardly any readers interested in this essential work are still unaware of it), but to *think* it is difficult. It will be necessary to think the whole work of Blanchot, and moreover to think *everything in it* that is essential (there is nothing in it which had been written which could not have been; there is nothing in it which could have been which does not *also* count for this work). By referring to Maurice Blanchot's collaborations before the war, I have no other aim than to account for the reasons the two men became friends and what their lives had been before they met, linking them in a way that was essential to both.

9. 'The Absence of Myth' in *The Absence of Myth*, p. 48. Catalogue of the

'Exposition internationale du surréalisme', 1947. It would be premature to see Acéphale as the experience of the impossibility of the community.

10. Without any doubt this problematic is too complex to be more than suggested here. I cannot recommend too highly the long article by Jean-Luc Nancy (certainly the most useful written on Bataille, 'La communauté désœuvrée', *Aléa*, no. 4, 1983, reprinted in an enlarged form in a book of the same title, published by Christian Bourgois in the collection 'Détroits', 1986), and Maurice Blanchot's book, *La Communauté inavouable*, whose first part, 'The Negative Community', echoes Jean-Luc Nancy's article.

11. Jean-Luc Nancy, 'La communauté désœuvrée', p. 24.

12. The letters from Maurice Blanchot to Georges Bataille have been deposited with all the recovered correspondence at the Bibliothèque Nationale in the Papiers Georges Bataille NAF. According to Diane Bataille, the vast majority of letters written by Maurice Blanchot to Georges Bataille were intentionally destroyed by Bataille before his death. Maurice Blanchot moreover did the same (perhaps in accordance with an agreement between them) to the letters he had received from Bataille as soon as he learned of his death.

13. Maurice Blanchot, *La Communauté inavouable*, p. 46.

From the community of the impossible to the impossible community

1. Pierre Prévost remembers that the first meetings took place in the rue Jean-Mermoz, and later ones in the rue de Ponthieu.

2. The accounts of Fardoulis-Lagrange and Prévost corroborate each other.

3. Spring 1943 is the date given by the *Œuvres complètes*. But Bataille clearly says: 'For some months we had been meeting now and again to talk.' This sentence would seem to date the project to early 1942, given the fact that the meetings had begun in autumn 1941.

4. *Œuvres complètes*, VI, appendix to 'Le Collège socratique', p. 279.

5. Ibid., p. 280.

6. Ibid., p. 286.

7. *Œuvres complètes*, I, Acéphale, 'La folie de Nietzsche', 1939, p. 549.

8. *Œuvres complètes*, VI, 'Le Collège socratique', p. 284.

9. Bataille made no secret of having very little in common with the Athenian philosopher. Nevertheless, he took two of his most famous maxims and made them his own: 'Know thyself' might serve to define the possibility of a negative inner experience, and 'I know only one thing: that I know nothing' that of non-knowledge approached and discovered by this experience.

10. Maurice Blanchot, *La Communauté inavouable*, p. 35.

The annunciation made to Marie

1. Laurence Bataille (who was twelve) recalls visiting her father, who had been in bed for several days, at this address (interview with the author, 1986).

2. More precisely at Boussy-Saint-Antoine near Brunoy, in Seine-et-Oise,

a village situated near Villeneuve-Saint-Georges, on the Yerres, at the borders of the forest of Sénart. Marcel Moré alludes to this stay in a letter to Georges Bataille of 19 June 1962, a few days before Bataille's death.

3. We owe to Jean Bruno the information about Bataille's exact addresses during the war. In this case, he makes it clear that Bataille stayed with a certain Mr Thoumire. Jean Bruno, Bataille's colleague at the Bibliothèque Nationale, had close and friendly personal relations with him. It seems he acted as the intermediary through whom Bataille received his salary from April 1942.

4. *The Dead Man*, p. 165.

5. *The Impossible*, p. 135 [translation modified]. These two long quotations are not superfluous, as we shall see. Their biographical interest is undeniable. We can see that there exists a topography of the Bataillean narrative, and this one, except for rare exceptions, is rural. The horror of Bataille's narratives emerges in part from landscapes like this one, from the landscape and the characters connected to it. There is reason to think that *Le Petit* also could have been written during this stay or a similar one: 'At that time I was living . . . with peasants. It rained ceaselessly for a week.'

6. *The Dead Man*, p. 166.

7. Ibid. It is difficult not to think of the article published in *Documents* on the 'big toe'. The foot, at that moment, the symbol of the oscillation from excrement to ideal, and for this reason the most human part of the body, here becomes horror alone of excrement. It no less remains – on the other hand – *what is most human*.

8. Quite clearly such an epithet involves no moral position. Bataille urges leaving to moralists the latitude to consider the ideal as noble and excrement as ignoble.

9. *The Dead Man*, p. 168.

10. Ibid., p. 184.

11. Although Bataille had sold one copy of *The Dead Man* to a bookshop in 1944, it was not be published during his lifetime. The first edition appeared with Jean-Jacques Pauvert, in 1967. Pauvert had nevertheless agreed with Bataille to publish it when he was still living, but under a pseudonym. Bataille himself designed the layout. It is not superfluous to clarify that, whether as the title of the book or the pseudonym of the signatory, Bataille prepared a preface, 'Aristide the blind man, The Dead Man': confirmation once more of the character of reminiscence in the Bataillean mystique, and of the dominion of the 'god' who died in Rheims.

Sickening poetic sentimentality

1. 'The Castrated Lion', *The Absence of Myth*, p. 29.
2. *Guilty*, p. 105, and *On Nietzsche*, p. 69.
3. *On Nietzsche*, p. 70 [translation modified].
4. *Inner Experience*.

5. Ibid., p. 169.

6. *The Impossible*, p. 10.

7. Ibid.

8. Ibid.

9. *Œuvres complètes*, III, *L'Impossible*, p. 522, Notes.

10. *Guilty*, p. 105.

11. *Œuvres complètes*, III, *L'Impossible*, p. 532, Notes.

12. *Inner Experience*, p. 148.

13. Ibid.

14. Ibid., p. 149.

15. Ibid., p. 137.

16. *The Impossible*, p. 161.

17. *Inner Experience*, p. 135.

18. *Œuvres complètes*, III, *The Impossible*, p. 532, Notes. Bataille says the same thing in *Inner Experience*: 'The one who sacrifices, the poet, having unceasingly to bring ruin into the ungraspable world of words, grows quickly tired of enriching a literary treasure.' And yet 'he is condemned to do it: if he lost the taste for the treasure, he would cease to be a poet' (*Inner Experience*, p. 149).

19. *Œuvres complètes*, XII, 'Lettre à René Char sur les incompatabilités de l'écrivain', p. 20.

20. 'From the Stone Age to Jacques Prévert', in *The Absence of Myth*, p. 147.

21. *Guilty*, p. 105. Or else, 'What one doesn't grasp: that, literature being nothing if it isn't poetry, poetry being the opposite of its name, literary language – expression of hidden desires, of obscure life – is the perversion of language even a bit more than eroticism is the perversion of sexual function' (*Inner Experience*, p. 150).

22. Equivalences abound between poetry and the sacred or sacrifice. In this way, 'sacrifice is immoral, poetry is immoral' (*Inner Experience*, p. 137).

23. *Literature and Evil*.

24. 'From the Stone Age to Jacques Prévert', p. 150.

25. This key development takes Bataille's theorisation of poetry to its conclusion, as found in the aforementioned article on Jacques Prévert. The horse had already been Bataille's justification for undertaking this development in *Inner Experience* (p. 136), without, however, raising it to the status of a method. The presence of the abattoir at the end of the development inevitably evokes the article of this title published in *Documents*, in which he draws attention to 'the staggering coincidence between mythological mysteries and the gloomy grandeur characteristic of places where blood has flowed' (*Œuvres complètes*, I, p. 200).

26. *Literature and Evil*, p. 75. The poets quoted by Bataille liable not to disappoint this demand are few: Rimbaud, of course, is one of them; so is Lautréamont, and so too in an exemplary way is William Blake, about whom he wished to write a book. There are all the same grounds for doubting

whether Jacques Prévert, in whose name he undertook this theorisation, was anything more than a pretext for it. However much his games might allow a liberation of words, it would not seem that any had the violence that might evoke the abattoir.

27. *Œuvres complètes*, IX, p. 16. Eleven poems taken from *L'Archangélique*. Not all Bataille's poems were published during his lifetime. Those collected under the title *L'Archangélique*, written between August and December 1943, were published in 1944 by Éditions Messages. They are included in the *Œuvres complètes*, III, pp. 79–91. For a more detailed study of Bataille's poetry, the reader is directed to Jacques Cels's fine book *L'Exigence poétique de Georges Bataille*, Brussels: Éditions Universitaires De Boeck, 1989.

Philosophy's 'easy virtue'

1. The year 1943 also saw the publication of *Being and Nothingness* by Sartre, *The Myth of Sisyphus* by Camus, *Epilepsy* by Leiris, *She Came to Stay* by de Beauvoir. Many others were published: Cocteau, Colette, Giraudoux, Neveu, Saint-Exupéry, Triolet, etc. In the theatre, Cocteau, Sartre (*The Flies*), Giraudoux, Claudel (*The Satin Shoe*) were performed.

2. The only notable surrealist name among the signatories of this tract is that of René Magritte, who soon after became Bataille's friend. Also to be noted is that of Maurice Blanchard (he had just published *Les Pelouses fendues d'Aphrodite* under the imprint of La main à la plume in 1942; this was the publishing house from which the pamphlet was generated) and of Christian Dotremont (in 1943 he was twenty-one; in 1947, he founded the Belgian Revolutionary Surrealist Group). We can add the names of André Stil, soon to become a communist, and Pierre Dumayet. The other signatories are the following: Noël Arnaud, Charles Bocquet, Jacques Bureau, Jean-François Chabrun, Paul Chancel, Aline Gagnaire, Jean Hoyaux, Laurence Iché, Félix Maille, Léo Malet, J.V. Manuel, Pierre Minne, Marc Patin, André Poujet, Jean Remaudière, Robert Rius, Boris Rybak, Gérard de Sède, Jean Simonpoli.

3. On the subject of this undated letter, Jean Bruno notes: 'Letter subsequent to the surrealist tract *Nom de dieu* (of 1 May 1943 and probably attacking an article by Bataille in *Messages* rather than his *Inner Experience*).'

4. This article is dated December 1943 but was published only in 1945 in a book entitled *Homo Viator* (Paris: Aubier) under the chapter title, 'Refusal of Salvation and the Exaltation of the Absurdity of Man'.

5. Ibid., p. 249.

6. Ibid., p. 258.

7. Ibid., p. 272. But was it not *also* Pascal, was it not Pascal especially, who first *thought* the absence of God or, at the very least, his absent presence?

8. It was Chestov who said Pascal had been reincarnated two centuries later in the person of Nietzsche.

9. Sartre's article 'Un nouveau mystique' was published in three parts in the October, November and December 1943 issues of *Cahiers du Sud*, nos

260, 261 and 262. It was included in *Situations I*, pp. 133–74. The page references are to the book.

10. ['Trial martyrdom'. As Bataille's book *L'Expérience intérieure* is both an 'inner experience' and an 'inner experiment', so Sartre is playing on the fact of the book being an essay in martyrdom (or a tortured essay) as well as an experiment with martyrdom. trans.]

11. Sartre, p. 142. 'Here before us, mournful and comical like an inconsolable widower who frees himself, dresses completely in black, to solitary sin in memory of the dead woman' (ibid., p. 143). In case this misleads us, the 'dead woman' is not what one might think: it is sociology. Sartre's Nervalian inflexions ('I am the shadowy one, the widower, the inconsolable one') appear to give him the power of poetic divination.

12. Ibid., p. 135.

13. Ibid., p. 174. We note that Sartre was not the first person who was solicitously anxious to send Bataille off to the couch, if only to stop him attacking virtuous intellectuality (unless it was the straitjacket rather than the couch that was meant). Breton had done so long before, then Souvarine and Simone Weil.

14. Ibid., p. 134.

15. Ibid., p. 159.

16. Ibid., p. 166.

17. Ibid., p. 166.

18. Ibid., p. 171.

19. Ibid., p. 174.

20. It was inevitable that Sartre would read *Madame Edwarda* at that time. Sartre and Bataille had too many friends in common. Even without quoting him (Bataille would not like it), he was able in the light of this book by a 'pornographer' (is this not what had been said also of the author of *Nausea*?) to draw the inevitable conclusions: except by pretending to believe in a sudden conversion, *Inner Experience* could not be by a Christian.

21. *Œuvres complètes*, VI, 'La discussion sur le péché', p. 343. This discussion was published in the journal *Dieu vivant*, no. 4, 1945.

22. 'La discussion sur le péché', p. 345.

23. Ibid., p. 349.

24. Also present and participating in this debate were: Adamov, Blanchot, Burgelin, Camus, de Gandillac, Hyppolite, Klossowski, Leiris, Lescure, Madaule, Marcel, Massignon, Merleau-Ponty, Moré, Paulhan, Prévost, de Beauvoir, the R.P. Deniélous, Dubarle and Maydieu, among others.

25. Georges Bataille, *Figaro littéraire*, 17 July 1947.

'System is needed and so is excess'

1. This was published in Brussels in 1942, in the journal *Exercise du silence*.

2. See the preceding chapter.

3. 'Everyone knows what God represents for that group of people who believe, and what place he occupies in their thought, and I think that when one suppresses the character of God, there remains all the same something in this place, an empty place. I wanted to speak about this empty place' (conversations with Madeleine Chapsal, *op. cit.*, p. 223).

4. *Œuvres complètes*, VI, p. 309. We shall see that this statement is not just metaphysical: it is *also* political. Bataille's position after the war would recall this several times.

5. Ibid., p. 310.

6. Ibid., p. 312.

7. Ibid., *Sur Nietzsche*, p. 390, Notes.

8. Ibid.

9. Ibid.

10. Ibid., p. 395.

11. Ibid., p. 445, notes for the preface to *On Nietzsche* (or 'Volonté de chance'). On the same page, Bataille gives this second definition: 'The determination of the self is the negation of what is not it. The position of the self defines the non-self as the negative, as pure nothingness.'

12. Maurice Blanchot, *La Communauté inavouable*, p. 20.

13. *Œuvres complètes*, VI, 'Discussion sur le péché', p. 340.

14. *On Nietzsche*, p. 18.

15. *L'Érotisme*, p. 200.

16. *On Nietzsche*, p. 19.

17. Ibid., p. 23.

18. *Sur Nietzsche, Volonté de chance* was published by Éditions Gallimard in 1945. That same year, Gallimard also published a collection of Nietzsche's maxims and aphorisms introduced by him with 'Memorandum': 'Morality until then led from one point to another, it was a morality of action, offering the path and the goal.'

Philosophy in the old folk's home

1. Lecture at the College of Sociology on Saturday, 5 February 1938, 'Attraction and Repulsion' in *The College of Sociology 1937–39*, pp. 113–24.

2. The same leaflet adds: 'You breathe an ascetic air, an atmosphere of combat envelops you; you can live there only in certitude and rigour.' The tone recalls that of the young Bataille writing *Notre-Dame de Rheims*.

3. Are the remains of the beautiful sinner at Vézelay or at Saint-Maximin? The devout of these two villages have long disputed this.

4. This seems to have been in January 1943, on the occasion of an initial trip.

5. The Innsbruck streamers in 1934. See the chapter 'Thunderbolts and forebodings'.

6. *Œuvres complètes*, V, *Le Coupable*, p. 558, Notes.

7. Some details concerning Jacques Lacan and Sylvia Bataille are called

for: for several years, since 1933 certainly and perhaps earlier, Lacan had been Bataille's friend and in all likelihood he was close to him in more than one of his activities (for example, in Acéphale). As for Sylvia Bataille, in 1943, it was nine years since she had separated from Georges; Jacques Lacan and Sylvia Bataille had become romantically involved in 1939, although they must have met earlier than that. From this involvement, a little girl, Judith, was born in 1940 who, unusually, would take her mother's marital name: Bataille.

Between the end of her first marriage and the meeting with Lacan, Sylvia had become a well-known actress. She worked for Renoir twice (*Le Crime de M. Lange* and *Une Partie de campagne*), for Carné (*Jenny*), for Rouleau (*Rose*), for L'Herbier (*Forfaiture*), for Feyder (*Les gens du voyage*), etc. In total, she made eighteen films between 1934 and 1940. The war did more than interrupt her career; it brought it to an end. After the Liberation, Sylvia appeared in only two films: *Les Portes de la nuit* by Carné and *Julie de Corneilhan* by Manuel in 1946 and 1949. Elisabeth Roudinesco (*Histoire de la psychanalyse en France*, Vol. 2) noted that the Maklès family and Sylvia Bataille herself had been forced by the Vichy authorities to 'renounce' their Jewish origins. At the time, Sylvia was staying at Cagnes-sur-Mer, after having stayed with Georges at Drugeac.

8. Kotchoubey is a Tartar name from the south. Eugène Kotchoubey de Beauharnais, a great Russian aristocrat, was born of the marriage of Léon Kotchoubey with Daria de Leuchtenberg, from the name of the Bavarian village established as a duchy in 1817 for Prince Eugène de Beauharnais, the stepson of Napoleon and son-in-law of the king of Bavaria. Eugène Kotchoubey de Beauharnais was first raised in Russia (in Saint Petersburg) and then, as a child, following the first Russian revolutionary riots, was sent to Germany, where he was brought up, staying with Maximilien de Bade, born in 1867, a German prince, who became Chancellor of the Empire in 1918 (he was the last Chancellor of the German Empire) and his wife Louisa, a sister of Queen Victoria. On the declaration of war of 1914, Eugène Kotchoubey de Beauharnais, a Russian living in Germany, thus an enemy, had to flee. He crossed the Atlantic and reached Vancouver where he met the woman who would be the mother of Diane Kotchoubey de Beauharnais.

9. Bataille would himself soon call fortune *caprice*.

10. There is nothing to confirm that Limbour actually visited Vézelay. Yet two letters indicate clearly his intention to do so after 1 August 1943. The visit of Monnerot was also announced by several letters between June and July 1943, the last fixing his arrival at the very end of July.

11. Romain Rolland was the author of a biography of Ramakrishna in 1929 and of Vivekananda in 1930 (*Essai sur la mystique et l'action de l'Inde vivante*), which Bataille had read and mentioned in a 1946 essay 'Expérience mystique et littérature' (*Œuvres complètes*, XI, p. 85). He also possessed in his library a book by Vivekananda, well annotated in his hand (which is somewhat rare and is only the case with his oldest books): *Raja Yoga ou conquête de la nature intérieure*, Éditions Adyen, 1930.

12. Michel Fardoulis-Lagrange, interview with the author. Romain Rolland moved to Vézelay in 1938. He died there in December 1944 at the age of seventy-eight.

13. Some 'Bataillean' anecdotes could be recounted about this stay. His daughter Laurence was apparently chased out of the church by the priest because she was the child of a bad father (the war did not excuse everything: couples splitting up, children of different parents, polygamous relationships could all shock a country priest) (interview with Laurence Bataille). On the other hand, perhaps in his capacity as a librarian (though this seems to contradict what has just been said), Bataille was the only person to have the basilica keys when it was closed for a long period. The keys of the Vézelay basilica in the hands of the author of *Story of the Eye*! Jean Rollin too recalled the bedtime stories Georges Bataille told him, stories which in fact were all part of the same narrative, told episodically: 'The Story of the Priest'. His mother later explained that if he was terrified of First Holy Communicants, it was because Bataille, in this story, claimed that a wolf was hidden under their veils (Jean Rollin, interviews with the author, 1986).

14. Leaving the flat at 3 rue de Lille, Denise Rollin offered it to Jacques Lacan. It had been Bataille who in 1942 had informed Lacan about the availability of the flat at 5 rue de Lille, where Lacan would live until his death. When Denise Rollin left the flat at no. 3, after the break with Bataille, Lacan took it for the mother of Sylvia Bataille, Laurence Bataille and Judith Bataille, the daughter of Sylvia and Jacques Lacan, to live there. It was in this flat that Lacan would receive analysands and begin his first seminar.

15. Jean Piel, *op. cit.*, p. 241. According to Pierre Prévost, Tristan Tzara shared this flat with Bataille for a while, as did Monnerot in January 1944, 'the services of the Abwher showing [him] an annoying solicitude at that time' (Jules Monnerot, *Sociologie du communisme*, p. 545).

16. *Œuvres complètes* VI, *Sur Nietzsche*, p. 397, Notes.

17. It is to be noted that Bataille nowhere mentioned this 'incident'.

18. *On Nietzsche*, p. 75. Michel Leiris recounted this anecdote in an interview: 'In the course of one of the wild parties of 1943 about which Simone de Beauvoir has spoken, I recall Sartre and Bataille performing a kind of dance together, rather in today's style, standing face to face' (*Libération*, 18 May 1980). The date indicated by Leiris is undoubtedly incorrect: the bed with the canopy in the studio of Balthus is a sure sign that it could only have been in the spring of 1944. As for the horse's head, Bataille always kept it. It was among the 'objects' to which he was most attached.

19. Henri-François Rey, *Magazine littéraire*, no. 44, January 1979, p. 58.

20. Ibid.

21. Ibid.

22. *Œuvres complètes*, VI, p. 331.

23. Ibid.

24. Ibid., *Sur Nietzsche*, p. 363, Notes. Bataille never suffered again from pulmonary tuberculosis.

25. Ibid., p. 411.
26. *On Nietzsche*, p. 84.
27. This was not published during Bataille's lifetime. It was published in *Œuvres complètes*, IV, p. 52.
28. Ibid., *Julie*, p. 63.
29. Ibid., p. 61.
30. Ibid., p. 63. In fact, Henri tries to kill himself a little before the arrival of the visitor he expects, Julie. The expectation had been exacerbated by what was only a misunderstanding. But far from this arrival solving everything (Henri is only wounded), it unbalances the frivolous, miserly behaviour of those present to the point of farce: Henri's sister, a spinster who is at the origin of the misunderstanding, their father, pusillanimous and old-fashioned, an old servant, calm and sensible.
31. Ibid., p. 113. Bataille even had recourse to an odd humour, Beckettian *avant la lettre*:

> She twisted a bottle in the ice.
> 'It will be cold in ten minutes.'
> 'It's long time,' said Henri.
> 'Yes, it is a long time.'
> 'The war will also last. We have not finished waiting.'

The catechism of fortune

1. *Alleluia, The Catechism of Dianus* included in *Guilty*.
2. Ibid., p. 159.
3. Ibid., p. 147.
4. Ibid., p. 153 [translation modified].
5. Ibid.
6. Ibid., p. 147. Bataille would retain this position, in a moral sense even:

> For having personally represented satisfaction as a death, as a negation not only of virtue but of the intimately perceptible secret of being, I am often considered the enemy of happiness. This is accurate if, by 'happiness' one understands the opposite of passion. But if 'happiness' is a response to the call of desire – and if desire, as is averred, is *caprice* itself – I would gladly say that happiness, and happiness alone, is the moral value. ('Le bonheur, le malheur et la morale d'Albert Camus', *Critique*, no. 33, February 1959).

7. *Alleluia*, p. 157.
8. Ibid., p. 148.
9. Ibid., p. 160.
10. Ibid., p. 161.
11. Ibid. *Alleluia, The Catechism of Dianus* was published in January 1947 in Bataille's name, with lithographs and illuminated capitals by Jean Fautrier, by Éditions Auguste Blaizot in Paris. It was republished in March 1947 by K. Éditeur.

A potential for stench and irremediable fury

1. *Œuvres complètes*, XI, p. 113.

2. *Œuvres complètes*, I, 'L'esprit moderne et le jeu des transpositions', p. 273.

3. *Œuvres complètes*, XI, 'Note sur *Refléxions sur la question juive* de Jean-Paul Sartre', 1947, p. 226.

4. Ibid., 'Réflexions sur le bourreau et la victime: SS et deportés', p. 266. About the book by David Rousset, *Les jours de notre mort*, 1947.

5. *Œuvres complètes*, XI, p. 226. For Bataille these articles were an opportunity to reaffirm his philosemitism (and the accusations that have been made against him make it useful to reproduce part of it):

> The fortune of humanity is perhaps linked to the power to dominate first reactions, of which anti-Semitism is the most vile. (It should be remembered here that whenever it has become acute, misfortune has regularly struck: the decadence of Spain followed the departure of the Jews, the class responsible for the Russian pogroms was destroyed and if anti-Semitism was not beforehand closed to all clear and honest sight, the German, faced with the catastrophe of which he is the author, would have had no other end than suicide.)

6. Ibid., 'À propos des récits d'habitants de Hiroshima', p. 181.

Fascism's last sanctuary

1. There is no doubt that Bataille would have had considerably more choice of means if he had bowed to the customs of morality (judging events as everyone else, marxists included, did: in an idealist way, as he thought) or of commitment (Bataille did not belong to any party, and henceforth even refused to call himself a communist, however hard his friends tried to make him do so). There is little doubt this annoyed him.

2. *Œuvres complètes*, XI, 'Nietzsche est-il fasciste?', 1944, pp. 10–11. An earlier draft of this text survives, published in *Œuvres complètes*, VI, p. 420.

3. Bataille could not have failed to have considered the significance of the fact that the freest of philosophers, who went mad and then died, was subjected to the most degrading of functions: that of a national, racial, German thinker.

4. *Œuvres complètes*, XI, 'Nietzsche est-il fasciste?', pp. 10–11.

5. The active presence of Maurice Blanchot in the editing of *Actualité* would appear confirmed by the fact that, in a letter sent in 1946 (the precise date is not given), he asks Bataille – who was titular editor of the notebooks – to send him an article. The presence of Maurice Blanchot in the notebook devoted to *L'Espagne libre* suggests the political reversal he had undergone during the war. In 1937 he had in fact been virulently against the Spanish

Republic, and just as hostile to Léon Blum's (admittedly passive) support for the Spanish Reds.

6. *Actualité*, 'L'Espagne libre', collection edited by Georges Bataille, Calmann-Lévy, 1946. The contents of the collection were as follows: Albert Camus (preface); Jean Camp ('Le passé et l'essence de l'Espagne'); Jean Cassou ('L'Espagne, lieu de notre tragédie'); chronology of events from the declaration of the Republic to the end of the Civil War; J. Quero-Morales, former Under-Secretary of State for Foreign Affairs of the Spanish Republic ('Les relations de l'Espagne républicaine et du gouvernement franquiste avec les puissances'); André Camp ('Les grands problèmes espagnols'); Robert Davée ('L'économie espagnole et les crises politiques'); Roger Grenier ('Les partis et les hommes'); Georges Bataille ('Les peintures politiques de Picasso'); Federico Garcia Lorca ('Le retable de Don Cristobal'); Albert Ollivier ('Puissance des songes'); W. H. Auden ('Espagne 1937', introduced by Max-Pol Fouchet and translated by Diane Kotchoubey); Maurice Blanchot ('L'espoir d'André Malraux'); Ernest Hemingway ('L'odeur de la mort'); Georges Bataille ('À propos de *Pour qui sonne le glas [For Whom the Bell Tolls]*').

7. Albert Camus, *Actualité*, preface.

8. Ibid.

9. Ibid.

10. Jean Cassou, 'L'Espagne, lieu de notre tragédie', ibid., p. 13.

11. *Œuvres complètes*, XI, 'Les peintures politiques de Picasso', p. 24.

12. *Œuvres complètes*, XI, 'À propos de *Pour qui sonne le glas*', p. 25.

13. As was his wont, in this article Bataille combined historical, literary (Ernest Hemingway) and private facts. I have already taken the opportunity (in the chapter 'La emoción') to quote several extracts from this article relating to Bataille's stay in Madrid in 1922.

Bataille's politics

1. I will return to the distrust that henceforth marked Bataille's attitude to commitment; see 'Communal demands'.

2. This meaning is indecisive: it could equally well signify that *nothing* is political or that everything is. The least inadequate analogy would be the one Bataille invites with what he has designated under the title of 'general economy': it thus would be appropriate to call such a politics 'general politics'.

3. Bataille said in 1947, in an interview with *Figaro littéraire*, that he had borrowed the idea for a 'journal representing the essentials of human thought as revealed by the best books' from one of the oldest French journals: the seventeenth-century *Le Journal des savants*. This reference infuriated Boris Souvarine, who pointed out – not without reason – more than one analogy between *Critique* and *La critique sociale*.

4. Those who knew this were not so numerous since by the end of the war Alexandre Kojève, who had fascinated a whole generation of intellectuals by his seminar on Hegel, had abandoned philosophy (he did it now only in his

spare time, which seems in conformity with Kojèvian irony that he became an 'amateur philosopher') to adopt a completely different but despite everything coherent trajectory: history having been completed, the possibility was open, according to him, for a philosopher to make himself a servant of the state. And Kojève became a senior civil servant of the French state. In 1945 he entered the Ministry for External Affairs as a translator, but he soon became an adviser to the Management of external economic relations of the Ministry of Finance. Several ideas which have modified the rules of international commerce are his: this is the case of 'import taxes' and the rule of 'generalised preference'. 'We rule all international economic negotiations', recalled one of his closest collaborators, Bernard Clapier, who added that Kojève's dialectic terrified foreign delegations. On the other hand he was an *éminence grise* of the French state in the negotiations of the Évian Accords.

5. 'Duration suggests only sad compromise' (*Œuvres complètes*, XI, p. 439).

6. Ibid., 'L'inculpation d'Henry Miller', p. 110.

7. 'What I say is a provocation, not a confession.' The word 'method' is to be understood in its most indecisive, that is its most paradoxical, sense. Bataille gives this sense in this passage: 'My method has as its consequence an intolerable disorder in the long run (in particular for me)' (*Œuvres complètes*, VI, p. 113).

8. *Œuvres complètes*, XI, 'La révolution sexuelle et le rapport Kinsey', p. 347.

9. 'Happiness, Eroticism and Literature', in *The Absence of Myth*, p. 187.

10. To the texts signed by him and gathered in the *Œuvres complètes* (Vols XI and XII) one should add some notes on readings signed (parodically?) Saint Melon Léon (for example in nos 3–4 on English romanticism and on Alfred Jarry), a work all the more important in being rudimentary. Bataille rewrote a number of the articles of his contributors, articles that Diane Kotchoubey typed, just as she typed those of Bataille. Besides, the distance from Paris (he lived, remember, in Vézelay) did not facilitate the relations of the director and his successive editors, Pierre Prévost, Éric Weil and Jean Piel.

11. *Œuvres complètes* XII, 'L'affaire de *L'homme révolté*', p. 230.

12. Ibid., 'Lettre à René Char sur les incompatibilités de l'écrivain', p. 17.

13. Thirion, *Revolutionaries Without Revolution*, pp. 542–3.

14. In issue 1 alone Henry Miller, Paul Éluard, Franz Kafka, Sigmund Freud, René Guénon, Hitler, Martin Heidegger, marxist dialectics and Taoist dialectics, the French economy, ondulatory mechanics, etc. were discussed.

15. Albert Ollivier and Pierre Prévost, respectively member of the editorial committee and chief editor, had, before the war, been members of the Ordre Nouveau movement founded by Arnaud Dandieu and Robert Aron, as had two contributors to the first issues, Jean Chauveau (before the war Xavier de Lignac) and Alexandre Marc (Alexandre Lipiansky). Blanchot, Weil and Ollivier were among the members of the first editorial committee of *Critique*. Also included were Pierre Josserand, an old colleague of Bataille at the

Bibliothèque Nationale (Prévost specified that he was supposed to be the reassuring element for university circles), and Jules Monnerot, who Bataille expected to cause problems (he was not in fact included among the members of the second committee; Caillois seems to have been sounded out at one point but declined). The second committee was very noticeably enlarged (thirty members, many of whom were foreigners), among them Marcel Arland, Raymond Aron, Louis de Broglie, Julien Cain, René Char, Georges Friedmann, Étienne Gilson, René Huyghe, Julian Huxley, Alan Pryce Jones, Alexandre Koyré, Lewis Mumford, Mario Praz, Louis Renou, Paul Rivet, Edmond Vermeil, Jean Wahl. Prévost and his friends had left. Among the first contributors planned were Daniel Halévy, Georges Dumézil, Jean Paulhan, Michel Fardoulis-Lagrange, Marcel Bisiaux, Jean Maquet (the three latter were young writers around the journal *Troisième convoi*); but also Max-Pol Fouchet, Henri Lefebvre and so on.

16. Quoted by Pierre Prévost *op. cit.*, p. 134. This account should certainly include the fact that Bataille found himself forced to 'contain' the change of political direction of the journal effected, knowingly or not, by the people who had come out of Ordre Nouveau and who had not lost any of the antimarxism they had developed before the war.

17. Pierre Prévost, ibid., p. 137. At the end of the 1920s Georges Friedmann had belonged to the *Philosophies* journal of Lefebvre, Guterman, Politzer, Morhange and others. It will be noted that Bataille established a division, in his mind an equitable one, between marxists (Weil and Friedmann) and nonmarxists (Aron and Ollivier).

Il salto mortale

1. Sixteen European countries came together in Paris in summer 1947. From this meeting the OECD (Organisation for Economic Cooperation and Development) was formed in April 1948. Between April 1948 and December 1951, $12 billion was given to Europe by the United States, five-sixths as aid and one-sixth as a loan.

2. *Œuvres complètes*, XI, 'A propos de récits d'habitants d'Hiroshima', p. 186; Bataille's italics. He also wrote: 'It's a choice: either the still poorly equipped parts of the world will be industrialised by Soviet plans, or America's surplus will provide for their being supplied' (*Œuvres complètes*, VII, *La Part maudite*, p. 163 [this passage has been omitted in the English translation. trans]).

3. It was less through (anarchist) principles than through forgetfulness that Bataille was incapable of remembering when elections were to take place and how to register his vote. One of the predominant traits of his character was his inability to cope with the world of duty, for example the world of administration.

4. *The Accursed Share*, p. 150. The principle, if not the tone, was the same as in the article 'Figure humaine' in *Documents*.

5. *The Accursed Share*, p. 151.

6. Ibid., p. 150.

7. Ibid., p. 160.

8. Ibid., pp. 164–5; 'one no longer imagines that cruelty can seem unavoidable' (ibid., p. 152).

9. Ibid., p. 187.

10. Ibid., p. 188.

The curse of history

1. Bataille would complain bitterly of being the only person to pursue this research: 'I feel quite alone in seeking, in the experience of the past, not the principles that were put forward but the unperceived laws that drove the world, laws the ignorance of which leaves us headed down the paths of our misfortune' (*The Accursed Share*, Vol. II, *The History of Eroticism*, p. 15).

2. Through its long analysis of the effects of death in societies and in history, *La Limite de l'utile* is closer to *Sovereignty* than to *The Accursed Share*.

3. It is difficult to mention them all. As early as 1949 and the publication of *The Accursed Share*, Vol. I: *Consumption*, there was a second volume: 'From Sexual Anguish to the Misfortune of Hiroshima'. In 1950, Bataille envisaged two other books as continuations of Volume I, 'Sexual life' and 'War and politics'. None of these projects were published. None even seems to have been started.

4. By a letter of 9 December 1961, Jérôme Lindon, editor of Éditions de Minuit, gave his agreement to Georges Bataille for the project for publication of a highly modified version of Volume I of *The Accursed Share*, *Consumption*.

5. *The Accursed Share*, p. 9.

6. *Inner Experience*, p. xxxiii.

7. *The Accursed Share*, p. 58.

8. Here we read once again Bataille's paradoxical Jansenism. Only grace interests him, because fortune alone interests him. Compared to grace, works appear to him mediocre, servile, if not obscene. Works induce a relationship to the industrious and untrustworthy world, speculating on the benefits of time. Only grace (like caprice, like fortune) is sacred.

9. On the potlatch see the chapter, 'The State: Heartbreak and Misfortune'.

10. It has not completely vanished: religions (the Catholic Church among others) bring a false and foolish response to the anguish of collapse.

11. *The Accursed Share*, p. 106.

12. Ibid., p. 108.

13. *Œuvres complètes*, XI, 'À propos des récits d'habitants d'Hiroshima', p. 181.

14. *Blue of Noon*, p. 108.

15. *The Accursed Share*, p. 190. Bataille demands nothing less than to have a consciousness of growth that is simultaneously sacrificial. To possess would

be equal to losing, to accumulate equal to destroying. *To have consciousness of* would then be precisely identical to having consciousness of nothing. No doubt this is the first attempt at a negative metaphysics of merchandise. The question has sometimes been raised of how much is owed to Georges Ambrosino in this book. One thing is certain: Georges Bataille, in a note at the bottom of the page in the introduction, thanks him in these terms: 'This book is also in large part the work of Ambrosino'. What does this mean? There is no doubt that Bataille *wrote* this book alone. But there is equally no doubt that he did not *think* it alone. What belongs to him is easily detectable: all the sociological and political parts, and without doubt a good part of the anthropological aspects, which had already appeared in texts written before he met Ambrosino. There remains what concerns the scientific aspect and most especially that to do with energy. Georges Ambrosino was a physicist and a lot more than just an adviser, he inspired and corrected the text, as can be seen from a letter of 28 November 1945 (in the Bibliothèque Nationale): 'Here are the corrections I suggest you make, without more . . .'. 'From this perspective, my suggestions have the drawback of reducing the shock value. My role is thankless, it is that of a brake. I will try to exaggerate as little as possible, trusting myself to you, moreover, to restore ardour and joy to things.' From 1945 to 1949, the date of the publication of the book, this collaboration developed to the point where perhaps the two men could have signed it together. However, in 1950 Bataille and Ambrosino were on bad terms. But their disagreement could equally well have had other and quite personal reasons.

The empire of the double

1. François Perroux, 'La part maudite et le silence', *L'Arc*, no. 44, p. 42.
2. 'He would readily finish his sentences with a gesture.' (J.-J. Pauvert); 'Sometimes he wouldn't finish his sentence but continue it with a wave of the hand and a look' (Fernande Schulmann). The portrait of Bataille given by Schulmann (though it came later, around 1955) is worth quoting in full:

> Despite his illness, his beauty was still surprising: very smooth white hair, strong even features and, above all, a way of moving with a remarkable elegance. His almost feline gestures traced a beautiful curve, full and slow. But what was most fascinating was still his muted voice, and with a smile that strangely made it complete, the same detachment and gentleness – on the very edge of absence. The voice and the smile of someone who, without ostentation or vanity, had gone beyond something, had followed a path and had brought back a complete forbearance. (Fernande Schulmann, 'Un amitié, deux disparus'. (*Esprit*, November 1963.)

3. Maurice Blanchot, 'Le jeu de la pensée'.
4. Ibid., p. 737.
5. A town near Vézelay. In Vézelay, people would affectionately call him

'poor Mr Bataille', referring to his air of overwhelmed frailty, the frailty of a man with the weight of the world on his shoulders.

6. Jean Piel, *La rencontre et la différence*. Paris: Fayard, 1982, p. 134.

7. Hélène Cadou, who was his colleague at Orléans Municipal Library between 1951 and 1961, was the wife of the poet René-Guy Cadou (interview with the author, 1986).

8. *Œuvres complètes*, III, *La Scissiparité*, p. 548. We should not misunderstand this: if Bataille felt himself the same as a worker or a peasant, it was nevertheless precisely by remaining the same and not changing any of his habits. This extreme seriousness, added to the complexity of his speech, could have comical results which on more than one occasion made everyone laugh except him. One thing was that he handed everything over to those around him, and was incapable of dealing with the real world. Another was nevertheless that on every aspect of the real world he had an explanation that, more often than not, could not be grasped by those who dealt with it perfectly well. His explanations had the gift of plunging the listener into an abyss of perplexity. His daughter recalled that, as a child, he who she had never seen lift a broom, gave her a long explanation, incomprehensible as she recalled, of how to hold a broom and then how to sweep.

9. Jean-Jacques Pauvert, interview with the author, 1986. François Joachim, Cardinal de Bernis (1715–94) was a minor poet and then, thanks to the protection of Mme de Pompadour, Minister of Foreign Affairs and ambassador to Rome: the images of a diplomat, a prelate and a libertine were represent in this single person.

10. The only brother of Don Rodrigo Borgia, Pope Alexander VI, was Don Pedro Loys Borgia. Pauvert added: 'Bataille spoke quietly, with an unctuous quality, like a prelate, and he would readily finish his sentences with a gesture: he had a cardinal's hands' (*Le Magazine littéraire*, no. 45, October 1970). Many people thought Bataille's hands reminded them of a cardinal's; they all added that they were lovely hands.

11. Among the nicknames given Bataille by his friends, it is worth quoting the ironic one given by Georges Limbour: 'Quicksilver'.

12. Only the portrait given by Pierre Klossowski seems to leave out none of the aspects of this apparently paradoxical character: he does not separate out the 'ogre aspect' from his 'exquisite sensitivity', whatever difficulty there might be in identifying them simultaneously in the same man.

13. The word 'doubling' is not entirely adequate. If it was hitherto absent from Bataille's thought, a third person would appear who has to be accounted for: the child.

14. The first title of *The Impossible* was *Haine de la poésie*. This is the title it had on its publication in 1947, but since it only exists today as *L'impossible*, *The Impossible*, I shall use this title for clarity.

15. *L'Abbé C.*, p. 140.

16. This man 'I once considered my alter ego' (*L'Abbé C.*, p. 34). The occurrences of doubling are frequent: 'The affection that bound me, that still

binds me to my brother was so strong, so thoroughly based on a feeling of identity' (ibid., p. 128). 'Robert was the image of Charles' (ibid., p. 12); 'the comical double of Charles' (ibid., p. 13, etc.).

17. Ibid., p. 157.

18. *Les Lettres françaises*, 22 June 1950; the article was titled 'La trahison en liberté. Un livre qui déshonore les éditeurs' ('Treason set free: a book that dishonours its publisher'), and was collectively signed by the magazine's editorial board. As for the triple twinning, the question could in fact be asked of the influence exerted on *L'Abbé C.* by James Hogg's *Confessions of a Justified Sinner*. Bataille wrote a highly approving and even at times eulogistic review in *Critique* in June 1949 of the French translation of this book (by Dominique Aury, entitled *Confession du pécheur justifié*). This would hardly be surprising in itself (the book is 'admirable', Bataille says, because it is 'monstrous'), were it not for the numerous analogies it offers with *L'Abbé C.* (beginning with the minor detail of the name of its principal character, Robert): the same doubling, the same devotion taken to the extremes of indefensible monstrosity, the same games of the forbidden and its transgression to the point of crime, the same solitude so hardened and dark it becomes divine. Even the narrative process (the publication of a dead man's rediscovered diary) brings them strangely together. These are no doubt coincidences, in the sense in which Bataille himself used the word at the end of *Story of the Eye*.

19. Bataille adds that it would be worthwhile for any reply Éditions de Minuit wished to make not to refer either to his name or to the title of the book. This detail is significant. *Haine de la poésie* (*The Impossible*) and *L'Abbé C.* were the first two narratives by Bataille to be published under his name. This might be explained by the fact that in 1947, the year *Haine de la poésie* was published, Bataille was not employed as a librarian, just as he was not when publication of *L'Abbé C.* was agreed (though he was once again when it came out). One should also point out that the chapter 'Éponine' had appeared on its own under this title published by Éditions de Minuit.

20. Sarane Alexandrian, 'Georges Bataille et l'amour noir', *Les Libérateurs de l'amour*. The chapter devoted to Bataille's heroines and 'saints' is one of the most acute and one of the finest written on Bataille's fictional works.

21. *L'Abbé C.*, p. 41.

22. Ibid. In one of the rare reviews to appear on the book's publication, Victor Crastre, who we saw as one of the dynamic forces behind the journal *Clarté* around 1925, wrote: 'I think that this final character – Robert – is the one who truly stands for the author's ideas.'

From Vézelay to Carpentras

1. Or more exactly, for as long as his health allowed him. For the last years, he relied on his editor-in-chief and friend Jean Piel to ensure its day-to-day direction. Piel took over the direction entirely after Bataille's death.

2. Let there be no mistake: it is likely that Bataille's analysis of fascism in

1933 remains one of the most modern. 'Obsolete' is to be understood in a historical sense. The conditions after the war were not such that this thought could appear 'current'.

3. *Inner Experience*, p. 171.

4. 'The obsession with understanding the world was what, after the first months of amical fraternity, dominated my relations with Georges Bataille. Yes, this may seem strange when we know the dominant place given, in almost all interpretations of Bataille's work, to his quasi-mystical withdrawal into the internal world' (Jean Piel, 'Bataille et le monde', p. 121).

5. It seems to have been Sartre who prevented him from doing so. It does not seem possible really to shed any light on this episode in Bataille's political life. It is all the more regrettable in being his final attempt at commitment. Thereafter there were no others. The only indication we have available comes from the contents page of an issue of the journal *Politics* (no 4, 1947) where side by side are listed the names of Albert Camus, Simone de Beauvoir, David Rousset, Jean-Paul Sartre, Maurice Merleau-Ponty and Georges Bataille (his essay entitled 'On Hiroshima'). Was Bataille a member of the RDR? He was close enough to its principal figures to be included in the contents of a journal bearing as its subtitle 'French political writing'.

6. But did Bataille ever imagine that war and servitude could vanish from the least bad of all possible political worlds? This is not only unlikely, it is comical!

7. September 1945. This book never existed, but should it be seen as the first idea for his 1949 book, *L'Abbé C.*?

8. From 1948 Bataille received a modest remuneration from Éditions de Minuit for the series he created and directed: 'L'usage des richesses', 'The use of riches'. This short-lived series began with a book by Jean Piel, *La Fortune américaine et son destin*. The second and last title would be by Bataille himself: *The Accursed Share*, Vol. I: *Consumption*. Many projects never come to fruition. This is the case for a book by Mircea Eliade, *Tantrism* and a book by Max Weber, *The Protestant Ethic and the Spirit of Capitalism*, as well as for projected books by Ambrosino, Kojève, Métraux and Perroux, all friends of Bataille, and another by Georges Dumézil. Éditions de Minuit were amazed by this strange scarcity (two books in close on three years) and complained to Bataille, asserting how detrimental this state of affairs was.

9. Jean-Jacques Pauvert, interview with the author, 1986. The generosity of Bataille's friends was not unilateral. Several recalled his generosity, for instance Roger Caillois: 'Bataille was a good and benevolent person. His lack of self-interest and his generosity were extreme (*Quinzaine littéraire*, 15 June 1970).

10. In 1948 Bataille engaged in several small editorial tasks: translations which he did not complete, one of which was of *Coming of Age in Samoa* by Margaret Mead, for Gallimard. Writing on behalf of Éditions Gallimard on 25 July 1948, expressing concern about not yet having received it, Raymond Queneau proposed that Bataille should put together the notes by Pierre Louÿs

for an erotic dictionary. Bataille also worked in 1948 as the French literary agent for the London publisher Hamish Hamilton. His role consisted of proposing French books for English translation. None of his suggestions (Philippe Hériat, Élie Halévy, *Histoire du socialisme européen*; Émile Gaboriau and Étienne Wolf, *Les changements de sexe*; among others) were in the end accepted by the publisher. His collaboration came to an end in December 1948. In 1948 Gabriel Marcel suggested, at the request of several members of the jury, that Bataille should join the jury for the Rivarol Prize, along with Gide, Schlumberger, Supervielle, Romains, Paulhan, etc. He justified his refusal by his distance from Paris.

11. Bataille seems to have placed an obligation on Pierre Prévost and then Jean Piel since, not living in Paris, he made them his intermediaries. Relations were made even more complicated by the fact that he did not have a telephone at his home in Vézelay and therefore had to fix telephone rendezvous with his successive collaborators.

12. Other letters written the same day say almost the same thing: 'I am emerging from a period of great apathy'. 'Diane and I are both in a poor state of health in Carpentras.'

13. It was Bataille who proposed to Éditions de Minuit a fusion of *Critique* and the series 'L'usage des richesses'. In fact, the series soon vanished. Only the journal remained.

14. No doubt Bataille was thinking of the book by Gérard Deledalle, *L'Existentiel, philosophes et littératures de l'existence*, an 'analytical panorama of the principal existentialist philosophies and literatures' among others, a book in which he has two pages devoted to him among the representatives of praeterexistentialist thought, along with Gabriel Marcel, Camus, Unamuno, Berdyaev, Kierkegaard, Nietzsche and Dostoevsky, who are contrasted with Heidegger, Jaspers and Sartre as the representatives of existentialist thought.

15. By ministerial decree of 23 June 1951.

Communal demands

1. Georges Bataille, interview with Marguerite Duras, *France-Observateur*, 12 December 1957. Her question about communism was: 'Can I nevertheless write that for you communism answers the communal demands?' Bataille replied 'Yes you can . . . But I repeat, I am not even a communist.'

2. Ibid.

3. *Œuvres complètes*, XI, *Critique*, 'Le mensonge politique', p. 335.

4. Ibid., p. 334.

5. *Œuvres complètes*, XII, 'Lettre à René Char sur les incompatibilités de l'écrivain', p. 23. This supposition is all the more plausible since, if Bataille rarely named Sartre, he nonetheless indirectly pursued the polemical debate that opposed and divided them on the publication of *L'Expérience intérieure*. Even the words are familiar: Sartre would say of Goetz (*Le Diable et le bon Dieu*, 1951) that he made him do what he could not do: resolve the

contradiction between the intellectual and the man of action. In 1948 Sartre published *Les Mains sales*, and in 1949 *Entretiens sur la politique*. It was in 1948 that Sartre joined David Rousset's RDR and attempted to establish a political party.

6. *Œuvres complètes*, XI, 'La littérature est-elle utile?', p. 12. Using these same terms again (with the exception of the word 'weak') Bataille soon applied them to Camus ('The author of *The Plague* is concerned to be useful').

7. *Œuvres complètes*, XII, p. 23. Elsewhere he says sovereignty is 'that which has its outcome only as the indifference to all outcomes' (ibid., p. 106).

8. Ibid.

9. Ibid., p. 25. Elsewhere Bataille put this more bluntly: 'I write authentically only on one condition: to make fun of the whole world, to trample orders underfoot' (*Œuvres complètes*, XI, p. 12).

10. 'Would revolt be revolt if it was not first of all a contempt for the possible?' (ibid., p. 246).

The angel and the beast, part 3

1. 'Poetry and the Temptation of the End of the World' in *The Absence of Myth*, p. 123.

2. André Breton, *Conversations*, p. 208.

3. 'On the Subject of Slumbers' in *The Absence of Myth*, p. 49.

4. Ibid., p. 51.

5. 'The Age of Revolt' in ibid., p. 175.

Breton has always had the habit of replacing a rigorous development of thought with an audacity and an (often subtle) displacement of the question at issue: what he says with an unrestrained power touches the sensibility or the passions. This unembarrassed lack of control has been instrumental in giving him both a wide public and a paucity of meaning and fragility of support. (ibid., p. 161.)

6. 'On the Subject of Slumbers', ibid., p. 51. Bataille had the idea for a book with the title 'Surrealist philosophy and religion'.

7. Ibid., p. 50.

8. 'Surrealism and God' in ibid., p. 184.

9. 'Surrealism' in ibid., p. 56.

10. Ibid.

11. 'Notes on the Publication of "Un Cadavre" ' in ibid., p. 31.

12. Ibid.

13. *Œuvres complètes*, V, *Méthode de méditation*, p. 193.

14. 'Surrealism and How It Differs from Existentialism' in *The Absence of Myth*, p. 57.

Continuity discontinued

1. He nevertheless wrote a preface to the new edition of Michelet's *La Sorcière* by Éditions des Quatre-Vents, included in *Literature and Evil*.

2. Éditions 'Au masque d'or', 'Miroir' collection (Angers). It was published separately in 1974 by Gallimard (Idées collection), and is in the *Œuvres complètes*, VII, p. 281.

3. *Inner Experience*, p. 57.

4. It is worth noting that apparently identical projects moved from one collection to another; thus Bataille planned to write 'De l'angoisse sexuelle au malheur d'Hiroshima' for volume 2 of *La Part maudite*, while for *Somme athéologique* he planned to write 'Le monde nietzschéen d'Hiroshima'.

5. None of these works seem even to have been begun by the author. Only a short text appended to *L'Expérience intérieure*, entitled *Post-scriptum 1953*, was added in 1954. It was not only texts but also narratives that Bataille wished to bring together in collections, for example as we shall see *Ma Mère* was to be edited into a whole called *Divinus Deus*.

6. This title is not just a play on words: one of his last declarations gives it all its (tragic) meaning: 'death is what seems to me the most laughable thing in the world'.

7. The earliest mention of this project was in 1934 in a letter to Raymond Queneau written in Rome.

8. This word can seem surprising applied to him, but there is no doubt that whatever 'whim' or digression he responded to, however multidisciplinary he was even before the word existed, he wanted to systematise.

9. Given to the Collège philosophique.

10. *Œuvres complètes*, VIII, Conférences, p. 204.

11. *L'Érotisme*, p. 106.

Non serviam

1. *Blue of Noon*, p. 153.

2. *Œuvres complètes*, XII, 'Hemingway à la lumière de Hegel', p. 254. As imbued with falsehood, Bataille said of Giono, as *The Old Man and the Sea* (which he contrasted with his work) appeared to him 'imbued with truth'.

3. *Œuvres complètes*, XI, p. 193.

4. Ibid., p. 126.

5. Ibid., 'La divinité d'Isou', p. 379. It is really the same game that Bataille plays which consists of doing as little 'critique' as possible in a journal that he nevertheless named after its function.

6. We are reminded of this sentence: 'Kierkegaard is the extremity of Christianity. Dostoevsky (in *Notes from Underground*) of its shame' (*Œuvres complètes*, V, p. 56).

7. *Œuvres complètes*, XI, pp. 162–3. This severity is amazing. First, because it is unusual in Bataille (at least since he toned down his quarrel with

surrealism). Then because, whatever shameful and hidden sentimentality one might legitimately perceive in it, this book has an undeniable audacity (and Adamov is undeniably a writer). What is more, signing a book characterised by 'sexual vice' in his own name in 1946, Adamov took more risks (exposing himself to a more brutal judgement) than Bataille had until then, for he had been careful not to recognise (by signing) *Story of the Eye* or *Madame Edwarda*, and not even to publish *Blue of Noon*. It would not be until the following year, 1947, that he would publish under his own name *Alleluia* and *Haine de la poèsie*. Besides, Mandiargues also had the feeling that Adamov, with *L'Aveu*, went further than Bataille, at least 'on the path of masochistic perversion' (*La Mort mithridatisée* reprinted in *Troisième Belvédère*, Paris: Gallimard, 1971). Yet Adamov would later show that Bataille was right to comment in this way on *L'Aveu* in a book of reminiscences, *L'Homme et l'enfant*: 'How stupid it was to invoke all that metaphysical rubbish to justify my sexual behaviour!' And Bataille would partly make amends for this excessive severity by delighting, in 1952, in the 'relative', he regretted, success of *La Parodie*.

8. *Œuvres complètes*, XI, p. 321.

9. *Œuvres complètes*, XII, 'Le silence de Molloy', p. 85.

10. Ibid. We shall see that, regarding painting, Bataille would say the same thing: with Manet painting became modern because, with *Olympia*, representation arrives at silence.

11. Ibid., 'Silence et littérature', p. 175.

12. Bataille said of William Faulkner that he was, of American novelists, 'the most significant because he had founded a world built on culpability'.

13. Ibid.

14. There is no need to judge whether Bataille was justified in elevating *The Story of O* by Pauline Réage above *Molloy*, *Death Sentence* and so on, or if he was yielding simply to the violent revelation the publication of this book involved. Yet let us note that, according to Pauvert, Bataille, along with Mandiargues, was the only person to write an actual article to welcome its publication ('Le paradoxe de l'érotisme' in *NRF*, May 1955, reprinted in *Œuvres complètes*, XI, p. 321).

15. *Œuvres complètes*, XI, 'La souveraineté de la fête et le roman américaine', p. 519.

16. *Œuvres complètes*, XII, 'Le paradoxe de l'érotisme', p. 325. The word 'renewal' brings to mind the preface to *Blue of Noon*: 'We must therefore passionately seek . . . how to orient the effort by which the *novel* renews itself, or better, perpetuates itself.' Without giving a further definition, Bataille draws up, in the same preface, a list of books (novels?) which seem to him to respond to the character of *constraint* that all books, he says, must be for their authors: *Wuthering Heights*, *The Trial*, *Remembrance of Things Past*, *Scarlet and Black*, *Eugénie de Franval* (Sade), *Death Sentence* (Blanchot), *The Idiot*, *Sarrazine* (Balzac).

A hypermorality: for the love of anguish alone

1. *Sovereignty*, p. 221. I have already discussed what the (moral) summit and what decline were for Bataille (see the chapter 'System is needed and so is excess'), with the aim of discerning in them what he conceptualised under the heading of 'communication'.
2. *Œuvres complètes*, VI, *Sur Nietzsche*, p. 390, Notes.
3. Ibid., p. 392.
4. Ibid.
5. Ibid., p. 395.

Moral evil

1. *Œuvres complètes*, VIII, *La Souveraineté*, p. 637, Notes.
2. *Œuvres complètes*, XI, 'La victoire militaire et la banqueroute de la morale qui maudit', p. 547.
3. *Œuvres complètes* VIII, p. 637.
4. *Œuvres complètes*, XI, 'Marcel Proust et la mère profanée', pp. 157–8.
5. *Œuvres complètes*, XI, 'La morale du malheur: *La peste*', p. 249.
6. Ibid., 'La victoire militaire et la banqueroute de la morale qui maudit', p. 532.
7. Ibid., 'Du rapport entre le divin et le mal', p. 198.
8. *Literature and Evil* is a series of studies devoted to writers, studies which have all been published separately in issues of *Critique*: Emily Brontë, Baudelaire, Michelet, William Blake, Sade, Proust, Kafka, Genet. It is not the most highly regarded of Bataille's books, and is not perhaps the most important. A double constraint is apparent in it: that of the subject (the authors chosen prescribe it, even if he prescribed them) and circumstances (Bataille was writing about critical studies, that is, about writers – this is the case for Baudelaire and Genet – taking a departure point from texts which themselves were critical studies, in both cases by Sartre). *Literature and Evil* still gives a very interesting glimpse of Bataille's 'critical method', a method of a writer speaking of other writers, and having a *baleful* body of work in common with them. In this he differed from Sartre, as he differed from Camus, in respect of Nietzsche, in emphasising that he speaks of Nietzsche *due to* the community he formed with Nietzsche, not as a follower.
9. *Literature and Evil*, preface.
10. Ibid., p. 55.
11. Ibid.
12. *Œuvres complètes*, XI, 'Le bonheur, le malheur et la morale d'Albert Camus', p. 410. It is in this essay that Bataille marks the agreements and disagreements by which he is linked with Camus: 'I would like to mark in this respect the point to which I feel close to Albert Camus'. 'I nevertheless see a deep opposition between the author of *The Plague* and myself. And even, a misunderstanding might follow from it that nothing could resolve.'

13. This text is from 1950 and seems to be part of a declaration to *Combat* on communism (*Œuvres complètes*, VIII, p. 643).

14. *Œuvres complètes*, XII, 'L'affaire de *L'homme révolté*', p. 232.

15. Ibid.

The sovereign individual

1. *Sovereignty*, p. 321.

2. Ibid., p. 207.

3. This is not far from Sartrean morality.

4. This Nothing is not the same as nothingness.

5. Ibid., p. 209.

6. Ibid., p. 211.

7. Ibid., p. 217.

8. Ibid., p. 218.

9. Ibid., p. 220.

10. Ibid., p. 221.

11. Ibid.

12. This is an opportunity to observe how a Bataillean idea arises and takes shape. First there is 'fortune', then 'caprice', and finally 'miracle'. Bataille had few, if any, concepts, only *notions* that were variable and uncertain; even sovereignty is not a concept.

13. Ibid., p. 281.

The catechism of 'saints'

1. *My Mother*, p. 33.

2. Ibid., p. 34.

3. Ibid., p. 41.

4. Ibid., p. 65.

5. Ibid., p. 74.

6. Ibid., p. 86.

7. Ibid., p. 89.

8. Ibid., p. 120.

9. *Œuvres complètes*, XII, *Ma mère*, p. 275. [This passage has been omitted in the English translation. trans.]

10. *My Mother*, p. 91.

11. Except in knowing that he is nothing. It was in 1952–3 that Bataille began to problematise the complex relations of knowing and non-knowing.

12. Ibid., p. 119.

13. Uncompleted and uncertain. Bataille hesitates throughout the book between a 'decent' (publishable?) version and a very raw version (fated to clandestinity?). The state in which the text has remained does not indicate a clear choice on his part.

14. *Œuvres complètes*, IV, *Charlotte d'Ingerville*, p. 285.

15. Ibid., p. 292. Sarane Alexandrian in *Les Libérateurs de l'amour* is right to point out that the saint is terrifying; faced with her, man cowers and would like to recoil.

16. *Œuvres complètes*, IV, *Sainte*, p. 308.

17. Ibid.

18. The title *Sainte* is not Bataille's. This narrative was found in his papers, like *Charlotte d'Ingerville*, not typed, and could have been a sketch for *Charlotte d'Ingerville*. It could also have been a sketch of a completely different narrative. It seems that it could date from the same period, 1954–5. It is evident that this series of narratives offers no autobiographical character. *Divinus Deus* is a fictional narrative and is perhaps even (with *L'Abbé C.*) the most fictional of all Bataille's narratives. At most it is possible to recognise in the character of Sainte the memory – diluted, mingled with others – of Violette, the young prostitute Bataille was in love with in the 1930s and who he vainly tried to 'take out'. This dialogue could evoke its possibility:

> 'Don't leave.'
> I replied gently: 'I'll leave, but with you.'
> She raised her head vindictively, and whistled contemptuously: 'You want to take me out of here!' (*Sainte*, p. 305)

The servitude of utility

1. *Eroticism*, pp. 111–12.

2. To be precise on 3 and 4 September 1951 (Hélène Cadou, interview with the author, 1986).

3. 'This was the devil arriving in Orléans. But when people saw the man himself, whose appearance was completely different, they calmed down' (Hélène Cadou, interview with the author, 1986).

4. Georges and Diane Bataille occupied the Renaissance right-hand wing of the bishop's palace (1, rue Dupanloup).

5. Ibid. The 'devil' in Bataille had his own home in Orléans library: the *Enfer*, a simple cupboard in which Bataille locked away along with the others those of his books not available for consultation.

6. Hélène Cadou. A librarian herself, Cadou stressed the overlooked professional aspects of Bataille's life: 'I discovered a man devoted to his trade, something few mention. It was fantastic to learn the trade with him. He had a totally idiosyncratic method and system of classification' (interview).

7. The totality of what Bataille wrote in this study (he no longer wrote in cafés) is considerable. One should include the ending of *History of Eroticism*; the beginnings of 'Surrealism from Day to Day' which was left unfinished (and which I have quoted several times in the chapter 'Magnetic Field'); *Theory of Religion* which remained unpublished and which he planned later to add to the text of several lectures under the title *Mourir de rire et rire de mourir*; the *Post-scriptum 1953* of the 1954 re-edition of *L'Expérience intérieure*; *Sovereignty* which he hoped to turn into volume 3 of *The Accursed Share*

(unpublished); *Lascaux* and *Manet* (which I shall come back to); *Ma Mère*, *Charlotte d'Ingerville* and *Sainte*; *L'Être indifférencié n'est rien*, poems which appeared in *Botteghe oscure*, to which he also contributed several articles; then all the articles for *Critique*, all this between 1951 and 1955 alone. Bataille had never written so much in his life. Publications, by comparison, would be rare: only *Post-scriptum 1953*, *Lascaux* and *Manet* came out. A new edition of *Histoire de l'œil* (J.-J. Pauvert) and its English translation as *A Tale of a Satisfied Desire* (Paris: Olympia Press, 1958) appeared under a pseudonym.

The accursed body

1. *The History of Eroticism*, p. 84.

2. A lecture which took place as part of the 'Cercle ouvert' organised by Jacques Nantet. This seems to have been the only lecture given by Bataille in the framework of this circle which gathered at 44 rue de Rennes. However, he was part of its honorary committee with, among others, Adamov, Barrault, Cuny, Duvignaud, Emmanuel, Guérin, Lefebvre, Leiris, Madaule, Mascolo, Morin, Claude Roy, Vilar and Wahl. Several interventions merit being quoted, such as that of Ado Kyrou: whereas the earth has been considered for centuries a valley of tears, 'I believe eroticism, along with revolt, is one of the rare means capable of leading us to immense joy'. M. Héraud spoke about the developing ideas of the speaker 'as a keystone of alienation in general and of religious alienation in particular'. Seeing in eroticism the grace by which some begin 'to break the defence which prevents them from reaching the other', he finished by saying of Bataille: 'in a very anguished tone, finally speaking like a priest'. It is necessary, on the subject of this lecture, to take account of Bataille's placid provocation. To an audience expecting him to speak about eroticism, he willingly spoke as a mystic and to an audience prepared to hear him speak about religion, he willingly spoke of eroticism, as he did in two lectures given at a women's college in Cambridge in 1949.

3. His position in fact does not fail to be ambiguous for the less enlightened readers. In 1957, he published *Eroticism, Literature and Evil* and *Blue of Noon*, all under his own name. But it should not be forgotten that all – or almost all – of his fictional work remained hidden (*Story of the Eye* and *Madame Edwarda* published pseudonymously, *The Dead Man* and *My Mother* remaining unpublished and *Le Petit* out of print). He added to the ambiguity by writing a preface, signed in his own name, to the new edition in 1956 of *Madame Edwarda* of which the author was given as Pierre Angélique.

4. Preface to *Madame Edwarda*, in *Eroticism*, p. 266.

5. *Œuvres complètes*, III, *L'Impossible*, p. 512, notes pour la préface. [Not included in English edition of *The Impossible*. trans.] Can one imagine Georges Bataille and Jacques Lacan to be profoundly in agreement on this point? It is not inconceivable that this would have been a major subject of conversation between them. It should not be forgotten in fact that they regularly met in Guitrancourt, at Lacan's home, among other places.

6. *History of Eroticism*, p. 81. Bataille would moreover make it clear that 'eroticism is never a return to nature, it is the return to the element that the *spirit* judges to be from the domain of shame' (*Œuvres complètes*, XII 'Hors des limites', p. 309).

7. Ibid., p. 149.

8. Something in this is doubtless linked to age and sickness, and this other confession gives an idea of it:

> When I made love previously, my joy was not concealed from me by the feeling that it would end – and that I would die without having grasped it. Today it happens in my happy excess that the most burning pleasure annuls itself, as in a dream: I conceive of a time when I would no longer have the means to renew it. The feeling of the exuberant richness of the festival is lacking for me, the absurd maliciousness and the laughter in which I would equal God! (*Œuvres complètes*, III, *La Scissiparité*, p. 552, Notes.)

9. *History of Eroticism*, p. 118.

10. Ibid., p. 119.

11. Bataille did not repudiate the flesh. He did not feel it was anathema. If he admits and defends the taboo that religion and morality have created, he only does so to declare himself free from it: to transgress it. In fact, Bataille remained very free, erotically, and when brothels were closed on 13 April 1946 he knew how to replace the pleasure they offered him through partouzes. He explained this jokingly to Jean Piel: 'You see, Jean, it must be understood that there is the same difference between two people making love or several making love as there is between getting into a bath or bathing in the sea' (Jean Piel, 'Bataille et le monde', p. 135). If there is no repudiation, there is, however, a fascination for the horrified representation of the flesh which, one recalls, had already fascinated him as a young man when he made Rémy de Gourmont's book, *Le Latin mystique*, his bedside reading. See the chapter 'The school of the flesh' above.

12. *Eroticism*, p. 11. Or how the affirmation Bataille had been making a morality since 1924 attains death, through contagion. By the same movement that says *Yes* to life, one must say *Yes* to death.

13. *Eroticism*, p. 106.

What lies behind misfortune

1. *Œuvres complètes*, XII, 'Lettre à René Char sur les incompatibilités de l'écrivain', p. 20.

2. Georges Bataille, radio interview.

3. Ibid.

4. The complete statement in the interview is as follows:

> Evidently, what I have to say is such that its expression is more important for me than its content. Philosophy in general is a matter of content, and for my part I make more of an appeal to feelings than to intelligence, and

from that point it is expression, through its tangible nature, that is most important. What is more, my philosophy could in no way be expressed in a form that is not tangible; absolutely nothing would remain of it. It is only from the moment I give a form that might pass as impassioned, and that might also pass for black . . . but I would rather describe myself as a happy philosopher, since I don't see myself as blacker than Nietzsche. Yet from a certain point there is a need for feelings to appeal to disturbance; one cannot move people without disturbance being in play; but, despite this, disturbance does not indicate misfortune, does not indicate something black.

5. In his excellent book *Alexandre Kojève: La philosophie, l'État, la fin de l'Histoire*, Grasset, 1990, Dominique Auffret rightly notes that far from Bataille getting closer to Kojève after the war, he constantly affirmed, in contrast to him, sometimes even to the point of irritability, his choice of Nietzschean sovereignty over Hegelian wisdom.

6. *Œuvres complètes*, XI, *Formes et couleurs*, 'L'amitié de l'homme et de la bête', p. 168.

7. Ibid., 'Initial Postulate', p. 234. Bataille also says analogously of existentialism (which he accuses of all the ills he attributes to philosophy) that it does not attain the annihilation whose attainment it seems to set itself: 'Existentialist thought is always elusive but never results in annihilation of thought in itself. Like a child in need dancing on the spot without being able to decide, this thought refuses without dying, sick with a morose virtuosity' (ibid., p. 284).

8. *Œuvres complètes*, XII, *Nouvelle NRF*, 'L'au-delà du sérieux', p. 314.

9. 'Concern with misfortune is the generator of a whole hateful morality' (*Œuvres complètes*, XI, 'La morale du malheur: *La peste*', p. 248).

10. Ibid., p. 249.

11. *Œuvres complètes*, XII, 'L'au-delà du sérieux', p. 315. There is this description of Bataille as 'philosopher' by Michel Foucault:

> perhaps, to those who strive above all to maintain the unity of the grammatical function of philosophy – at the price of coherence, of the very existence of philosophical language – one could oppose the exemplary enterprise of Bataille who has not ceased to break within himself with the relentlessness and sovereignty of the philosophising subject. In this his language and experience were his torture. ('Préface à la transgression', *Critique*, Hommage à Georges Bataille, nos 195–6, August–September 1963.)

Felix culpa

1. *The Trial of Gilles de Rais*, p. 29.

2. Ibid., p. 20.

3. On the subject of psychoanalysis, in which he was one of the most widely read in France, and was among the first non-specialists to read, this quotation is indispensable in revealing his progressive disaffection: 'my perspective is not that of psychoanalysis. It is moreover the perspective, not of

someone ignorant of psychoanalysis, but almost of someone who, from having left this perspective behind, has, so to speak, forgotten it and has become not very familiar with the representations it has introduced' (lecture: 'L'érotisme et la fascination de la mort', Cercle ouvert, 12 February 1957).

4. *The Trial of Gilles de Rais*, p. 36.

5. Ibid., p. 43.

6. Ibid.

7. Ibid.

8. Ibid., p. 38.

9. Ibid., p. 12.

10. *The Trial of Gilles de Rais* was published in 1959 by the 'Club du livre français' before being reprinted by J.-J. Pauvert in 1965. Bataille's introductory text consists of around eighty pages. The elements of this chapter are extracted from this part. It is followed by an 'Analysis of historical data', also signed by Bataille, and then by the 'Judgement of the secular court'. The texts of the two trials of Gilles de Rais were established from the minutes, and annotated by Bataille himself. The Latin minute-book of the church trial was translated by Pierre Klossowski. A bibliography closes the work.

Universal history

1. With the exception, of course, of the participation of Queneau.

2. Just as *La Limite de l'utile* was delayed by five years and then totally revised and rewritten under the title *The Accursed Share*.

3. The most interesting of these articles, 'Le berceau de l'humanité: La vallée de la Vézère', apparently written in 1959, was moreover not published.

4. The pages presented in *Œuvres complètes*, VIII, pp. 262–71, upon which I have commented.

5. The plan was published in *Œuvres complètes*, IX, p. 485; it is dated 27 July 1959.

6. The exact title is *La Peinture préhistorique: Lascaux ou la naissance de l'art*, Geneva Éditions d'art Albert Skira, 1955 (published 30 April 1955), with 68 colour illustrations by Hans Hinz and Claudio Emmer.

7. *Prehistoric Painting: Lascaux or the Birth of Art*, p. 37 [translation modified].

8. *Œuvres complètes*, IX, 'Le berceau de l'humanité: La vallée de la Vézère', p. 370.

9. Ibid., p. 373.

10. Ibid., p. 375. Is this an additional displacement? In *Sovereignty*, this power was considered as a fall from the moment that religions gave it a transcendent meaning.

11. Subsequent research has not challenged the assertion that the first tombs made for corpses must be seen as indicating the first signs of true hominid characteristics. Nevertheless there is some doubt whether this was a systematic practice: only a single piece of bone matter from a human skeleton is examined

as evidence for two million dead, the debris of fifty thousand years ago. Tombs thus would have had a privileged status.

12. *Tears of Eros*, p. 32.

The bit between the teeth

1. A phrase by Huysmans, speaking of Goya.

2. The Chinese torture called the Hundred Pieces, photographed by Louis Carpeaux, gave rise to a painted version, *Suplicio chino*, by José Gutierrez Solana (1886–1945).

3. *The Tears of Eros*, p. 157.

4. Surrealist painting 'represents the mannerism of today'.

5. Ibid., p. 160.

6. *Manet* (1983) Geneva: Skira, p. 35.

7. Ibid., p. 36.

8. Bataille insists in a decisive way that the history to which Goya belongs is that of individuality (*Œuvres complètes*, XI 'Goya', p. 309).

9. Far from all poeticising – for example surrealist poetics – this article is significantly entitled 'The Work of Goya and the Class Struggle' (*Œuvres complètes*, XI, p. 550).

10. This was the case for Goya. Called to Madrid by Mengs in 1775, he entered into the service of the king of Spain, Charles III, in order to paint the designs for the tapestries made in the Royal Workshops of Santa Barbara, tapestries destined for the apartments of the royal residences. He worked there from 1775 to 1792. Goya was the first painter of the King's Chamber.

11. This text written in 1946 was entitled 'The political paintings of Picasso'. It appears in the only issue of the Cahiers of *Actualité, L'Espagne libre*.

12. 'Goya', p. 310. As evidenced among others by this commentary by Goya about *Caprice* 23, 'The people of the curates and monks live on the festivals of the Inquisition', or of *Caprice* 13, 'Stupid monks gorging themselves as much as they can in their refectories without a care for the rest of the world; after that what else to do but make yourself comfortable!'

13. Ibid.

14. *Manet*, pp. 47–8.

15. Ibid., p. 46.

16. Ibid., p. 31.

17. Ibid., p. 69.

18. Ibid., p. 46. However beautiful and intense the light of the impressionists might have been, Bataille will reproach them for this respite. In Monet, Renoir, Pissaro and Sisley, 'There is a sort of grace present in these pacified views of a once hostile nature, brought to a human level, that of one who knows how to make peace with it, in harmony with the possible' (*Œuvres complètes*, XII, 'L'Impressionisme', p. 375). Clearer still is the reproach he made to Monet alone: 'His entire work is resonant with a passionless happi-

ness', a phrase which negatively echoes the definition Bataille gave of mannerism.

19. Ibid., p. 62.

20. The biographical and critical study *Manet* was published in 1955 by Éditions d'art Albert Skira as part of the 'Tastes of our Times' series. It is reproduced in Volume IX of the *Œuvres complètes*, and was reprinted by Éditions Flammarion in 1983 with a preface by Françoise Cachin.

To die of laughing and to laugh of dying

1. Draft of a letter to Alexandre Kojève, 2 June 1961.

2. Bataille only finished *The Tears of Eros* in May 1961 (in other words two and a half years after starting it), the last of his books, the one in which he would have liked his thought to culminate ('I'd like to make it a more extraordinary book than anything I've published before', letter to J.M. Lo Duca, 5 March 1960). Whatever his hopes for it, this was a culmination the book did not attain. In fact, his remarkable erudition could not hide the underdeveloped and, ultimately, stunted nature of this book. The extreme complexity of the work only offers a single approach towards itself, that of tragic eroticism. As a book, *The Tears of Eros* is too much a two-dimensional recapitulation to be taken for more than an assortment of images (magnificent as they may be) to which an exhausted, powerless Bataille assigned his major themes, even if it meant no longer seeing anything more than the shadows they cast. At this point the question arises of how much the book really owes to Bataille, including what it owes to weariness, illness and imminent death, and of what it does not owe to him (if not in spite of him). Two things are certain: in 1959 there were too few people interested enough in Bataille and his thought for one not to acknowledge Pauvert's role in wanting and commissioning such a book. The second is that Bataille himself was strongly in favour of it, perceiving it perhaps as a possible first instalment of the 'Universal history' he had worked on or promised to work on for several years. But the fact is that *The Tears of Eros* does not just simplify a thought of considerable complexity, it also misrepresents it. Too many approximations, too much lack of clarity, too many clumsy elements (sections that are added on or grafted in complete chunks, arguable connections, entire paragraphs repeated further on with just a few variations, and so on) spoil this book for one not to regret a hasty editing that is explained but not at all excused by the fear that Bataille might die before finishing it.

3. Maurice Blanchot, letter to Georges Bataille.

4. *Œuvres complètes*, XII, 'Lettre à René Char', *op. cit.* Bataille remained faithful to Léon Chestov in this, almost to the letter.

5. *Œuvres complètes*, XI, *Critique*, 'Marcel Proust et la mère profanée', p. 156.

6. Ibid.

7. Ibid.

8. 'He was haunted by Nietzsche's madness. He talked to me several times of his desire to become voluntarily mad' (Pierre Prévost, *op. cit.*, p. 87). To avoid reading this too literally, it is worth pointing out that this recollection relates to the period of the war.

To think everything to a point that makes people tremble

1. The four books were: *Philosophy in the Bedroom*, *La Nouvelle Justine*, *Juliette* and *The 120 Days of Sodom*. The three other witnesses called by the defence were Jean Cocteau, Jean Paulhan and André Breton. Only Paulhan and Bataille gave evidence at the trial which took place on 15 December 1956 at the Magistrates' Court in Paris. Cocteau sent a short letter to the tribunal which was read by Maurice Garçon, the defence advocate. André Breton, who was not in Paris, sent a text which was unfortunately lost and could not be read at the trial. The four texts were nevertheless collected in the book Jean-Jacques Pauvert published in 1957 under the title *L'Affaire Sade*, an accurate account of the trial brought by the Public Ministry against Éditions Jean-Jacques Pauvert, accompanied by the complete text of the plea given by Maurice Garçon. Bataille's evidence is reproduced in *Œuvres complètes*, XII, pp. 453–6.

2. Bataille's tone in *Critique* defending Henry Miller is in fact quite different: '. . . those who see themselves as the guardians of moral rules will have their work cut out, they should realise . . . that for mankind to express itself one day with the worst vulgarity might finally appear as a necessary distribution of this betrayal of all morality represented by tact and idiocy'.

3. It is remarkable that this writer who freely gave testimony on behalf of another's works (but who could equally well have borne witness for himself: *Madame Edwarda* was about to be republished) did so as a 'philosopher', he who never failed, not without exaggeration, to remind us of how little he was one. It is remarkable that he chose a court to do so: it denotes not just a very shrewd knowledge of the appropriation of languages and functions, but, in undoubtedly equal measures, a strong sense of humour.

4. *Œuvres complètes*, XII, 'L'affaire Sade', p. 455.

5. Bataille himself did not hesitate to effect the incongruous reconciliation of Sade's character with moral exigency. It is because value is passion, pure passion, thus insubordination, that, 'in spite of deceptive appearances (or intentional ambiguity), moral necessity has so much to gain in Sade's trade'. This was written ten years before the trial (*Œuvres complètes*, XI, pp. 249–50).

6. *Œuvres complètes*, XII, 'Sade 1740–1814', p. 296.

'God: a Feydeau-style situation comedy'

1. The *Figaro littéraire* article appeared on 12 October 1957. It was written by Pierre Mazara, who ended it by saying: 'Georges Bataille has signed the most fruitful of pacts with evil. Sorry! with literature.' It appears that the

instigator of this birthday reception was J.-J. Pauvert. This was the sole literary 'honour' ever awarded Bataille in his lifetime. It may be worth reminding the reader that, though he was a jury member for two literary prizes, the Prix des Critiques and the Prix de Mai, he never received one for any of his books.

2. I have already had occasion to quote extracts from this (see the chapter 'Communal demands'). This, all in all, was the third interview Bataille had with a journalist. The first happened two years previously; in 1947 he had replied in *Figaro littéraire* to the interest aroused by the prize awarded to the magazine *Critique*.

3. Bataille's sense of humour is something that has perhaps not been noted enough. Certainly laughter has little to do with humour, and even less with irony. However, one would not be far wrong in saying that he used cold sarcasm in answering questions.

4. In 1958 the journal *La Ciguë* devoted its first and only number to Georges Bataille. René Char, Marguerite Duras, Louis-René Des Forêts, Michel Leiris, Jean Fautrier, André Masson, André Malraux and Jean Wahl contributed to this homage.

5. 'La signification de l'érotisme', unpublished text reprinted with a commentary about the magazine *Genèse*, presented by Jean-Pierre Le Bouler and Dominique Rabourdin, *Revue de la Bibliothèque Nationale*, no. 17, autumn 1985.

6. Ibid. *Genèse* had headed notepaper stating: '*Genèse*, quarterly journal, sexuality in biology, psychology, psychoanalysis, ethnology, the history of morals, of religions and of ideas, in art, poetry and literature.'

7. Like *Documents*, moreover, *Genèse* was to have included several former surrealists in its ranks.

8. A letter from Maurice Girodias to Georges Bataille of 11 August 1958 indicates how much pressure there was likely to have been on his directorship: 'The directorship of the journal will be your responsibility, but I insist on our deciding jointly on anything concerning the journal's general direction, and the choice of the main articles.'

9. Unpublished letters by Artaud (supplied by Paule Thévenin), an unpublished text by Samuel Beckett (translated by Pierre Leyris), and extracts from Yves Bonnefoy's *Rimbaud par lui-même* were also planned.

10. On several occasions the possibility was raised of Bataille collaborating in the magazine *Arguments*, edited by Jean Duvignaud, Edgar Morin and Kostas Axelos. This collaboration failed to result in an article, as had been planned, but took the form of an important lecture of November 1956 on the Hungarian situation following the failure of the insurrection.

'One day this living world will pullulate in my dead mouth'

1. Hélène Cadou.

2. The thought of death is based on the representation of the death of

others; the death of thought is neither representative nor external. From it, an experience is made, that is irresistibly internal and personal.

3. *Œuvres complètes*, VIII, 'L'enseignement de la mort', p. 205.

4. Julie, the daughter of Georges and Diane Bataille, was brought up by André Costa and his wife once the condition of her father meant she had to move away from him.

5. *Le Coupable* was reissued in 1961 by Gallimard, augmented by the definitive version of *L'Alleluiah: Le coupable*, 'this work whose immoderate ambition is doubtless itself a curse'.

6. Friendship came to his aid when, to universal indifference, he was dying: on 17 March 1961 an auction was organised at Hotel Drouot, presided over by Maître Maurice Rheims, of paintings, water-colours and drawings to be sold for the benefit of Georges Bataille. Among the donors were Arp, Bazaine, Ernst, Fautrier, Giacometti, Masson, Michaux, Miró, Picasso, Vieira da Silva, Tanguy, etc. The proceeds of the sale allowed the acquisition of a new flat in Paris, 'in the very district I had always lived in, the rue Saint-Sulpice, and which will be, something I would never have believed, just as pleasant as the one I had in rue de Lille at a time when I had to go into some kind of exile' (draft of a letter to Maître Rheims).

7. Bataille died without leaving a will. He was buried according to a civil ceremony.

8. *History of Eroticism*, p. 81.

And finally, incompletion

1. 'Death and thought, so close to each other that in thinking we die, even if in dying we let go of thinking: all thought could be seen as mortal, all thought is final thought' (Maurice Blanchot, *Le Pas au-delà*, p. 7).

2. One should remember that with the death of Georges Bataille, Pierre Angélique, Louis Trente and Lord Auch died too. Bataille had refrained from 'killing them off' by revealing that they had only been his masks or doubles.

3. It is not much of an exaggeration to guess that nearly half of all his writings were unpublished at the time of his death.

4. Interview with Madeleine Chapsal, *op. cit.*, p. 223.

5. Ibid.

6. Ibid., p. 222.

7. These lines are among the last Bataille wrote. They are taken from a notebook he titled *Hors les larmes d'Éros*, 'Éléments d'un nouveau livre d'aphorismes' (*Œuvres complètes*, X, pp. 685–6).

Afterword

1. Interview with Madeleine Chapsal, *op. cit.*, p. 223.

Bibliography

Quotations from Bataille are taken from his *Œuvres complètes*, published (1971–88) by Paris: Gallimard, whose contents are:

Volume I: **Early writings, 1922–40,** *Histoire de l'œil, L'Anus solaire, Sacrifices, Articles*

Volume II: **Posthumously published writings, 1922–40**

Volume III: **Literary works,** *Madame Edwarda, Le Petit, L'Archangélique, L'Impossible, La Scissiparité, L'Abbé C., L'Etre indifférencié n'est rien, Le Bleu du ciel*

Volume IV: **Posthumously published literary works,** *Poèmes, Le Mort, Julie, La Maison brûlée, La Tombe de Louis XXX, Divinus Deus, Ébauches*

Volume V: **La Somme athéologique 1,** *L'Expérience intérieure, Méthode de méditation, Le Coupable, L'Alleluiah*

Volume VI: **La Somme athéologique 2,** *Sur Nietzsche, Mémorandum*

Volume VII: *L'Économie à la mesure de l'univers, La Part maudite, La Limite de l'utile, Théorie de la religion, Conférences 1947–48*

Volume VIII: *L'Histoire de l'érotisme, Le Surréalisme au jour le jour, Conférences 1951–53, La Souveraineté*

Volume IX: *Lascaux ou la naissance de l'art, Manet, La Littérature et le mal*

Volume X: *L'Érotisme, Le Procès de Gilles de Rais, Les Larmes d'Éros*

Volume XI: *Articles, 1944–49*

Volume XII: *Articles, 1950–61*

In addition, his letters are available in:

Georges Bataille (1987) *Lettres à Roger Caillois 4 août 1935 – février 1959,* présentées et annotées par Jean-Pierre Le Bouler, Paris: Folle Avoine.

Georges Bataille (1997) *Choix de lettres 1917–1962,* édition établie par Michel Surya, Paris: Gallimard.

In addition, the following English translations are quoted in the text:

Manet (translated by Austryn Wainhouse and James Emmons) (1955) Geneva: Skira; London: Macmillan.

Prehistoric Painting: Lascaux or the Birth of Art (translated by Austryn Wainhouse) (1955 2nd edition 1983) Geneva: Skira; London: Macmillan.

Eroticism (translated by Mary Dalwood) (1962) London: Calder & Boyars; reissued (1986) San Francisco: City Lights; (1987) London: Marion Boyars.

Literature and Evil (translated by Alastair Hamilton) (1973) London: Calder & Boyars.

The Story of the Eye (translated by Joachim Neugroschel) (1977) New York: Urizen Books; (1979) London: Marion Boyars; (1982) Harmondsworth: Penguin.

Blue of Noon (translated by Harry Matthews) (1979) London: Marion Boyars.

L'Abbé C. (translated by Philip A. Facey) (1983) London: Marion Boyars.

Visions of Excess: Selected Writings 1927–1939 (translated by Allan Stoekl) (1985) Manchester: Manchester University Press.

The Accursed Share (translated by Robert Hurley) (1988) New York: Zone Books.

Guilty (translated by Bruce Boone) (1988) Venice, California: Lapis Press.

Inner Experience (translated by Leslie Anne Boldt) (1988) Albany: State University Press.

Theory of Religion (translated by Robert Hurley) (1988) New York: Zone Books.

My Mother, Madame Edwarda, The Dead Man (translated by Austryn Wainhouse) (1989) London: Marion Boyars.

The Tears of Eros (translated by John Connor) (1989) San Francisco: City Lights.

The Impossible (translated by Robert Hurley) (1991) San Francisco: City Lights.

The Trial of Gilles de Rais (translated by Robert Robinson) (1991) Los Angeles: Amok.

On Nietzsche (translated by Bruce Boone) (1992) London: The Athlone Press.

The Absence of Myth (translated by Michael Richardson) (1994) London: Verso.

Georges Bataille: Essential Writings (edited by Michael Richardson) (1998) London: Sage Publications.

The following works are also quoted in the text:

Sarane Alexandrian (1977) *Les Libérateurs de l'amour*, Paris: Seuil.

Anon. (1987) *Focus on Minotaure*, Geneva: Skira.

Nathalie Baranoff-Chestov, *Vie de Léon Chestov*, Vol. 1 (1991) *L'Homme du souterrain (1866–1928)*; Vol. 2 (1993) *Les Dernières Années (1928–38)*, Paris: Éditions de la Différence.

Henri Bergson (1963) *Œuvres complètes, Le Rire*, Paris: PUF.

Jean Bernier (1978) *L'Amour de Laure*, texts edited by Dominique Rabourdin. Paris: Flammarion.

Maurice Blanchot (1963) 'Le jeu de la pensée', *Critique*, nos 195–6, August/September.

Maurice Blanchot (1973) *Le pas au-delà*, Gallimard.

Maurice Blanchot (1983) *La Communauté inavouable*, Paris: Minuit.

Claudine Brécourt-Villars (1985) *Écrire d'amour. Anthologie des textes érotiques féminins (1799–1984)*, Paris: Ramsay.

André Breton (1969) *Manifestos of Surrealism*, translated by Richard Seaver and Helen R. Lane, Ann Arbor: University of Michigan Press.

André Breton (1993) *Conversations: the Autobiography of Surrealism*, translated by Mark Polizzotti, New York: Marlowe & Co.

Roger Caillois (1964) *Instincts et sociétés*, Geneva: Gonthier.

Roger Caillois (1974) *Approches de l'imaginaire*, Paris: Gallimard.

Louis-Ferdinand Céline (1932) *Voyage au bout de la nuit*, Paris: Denoël.

Léon Chestov (1923) *La nuit de Gethsémani: Essai sur la philosophie de Pascal*, Paris: Grasset. (English translation (1932) 'Gethsemane Night: Pascal's Philosophy' in *In Job's Balances: On the Sources of the Eternal Truths*, translated by Camilla Coventry and C. A. MacCartney London: Dent.

Léon Chestov (1926) *La philosophie de la tragédie: Nietzsche et Dostoïevski*, Paris.

Jean-Pierre Faye *Profils perdus*. (English translation (1969) '*Dostoevsky and Nietzsche: The Philosophy of Tragedy*, translated by Spencer Roberts. Athens: Ohio University Press.)

Sigmund Freud (1985) 'The Uncanny' in *The Penguin Freud Library*, Vol. 14: *Art and Literature*, translated by James Strachley, Harmondsworth: Penguin Books.

Michel Foucault (1963) 'Préface à la transgression', *Critique*, Hommage à Georges Bataille, nos 195–6.

Denis Hollier (1974) *La Prise de la Concorde*, Paris: Gallimard.

Denis Hollier (ed.) (1988) *The Collège de Sociologie, 1937–39*, translated by Betsy Wing, Minneapolis: University of Minnesota Press.

Laure (1995) *The Collected Writings*, translated by Jeanine Herman, San Francisco: City Lights.

Michel Leiris (1963) 'De Bataille l'impossible à l'impossible *Documents*', *Critique*, nos 195–6.

Michel Leiris (1967) 'Du temps de Lord Auch', *L'Arc*, no. 44.

Michel Leiris (1955) *Fourbis*, Paris: Gallimard.

Michel Leiris (1976) *Frêle bruit*, Paris: Gallimard.

Bernard-Henri Lévy (1991) *Les Aventures de la liberté*, Paris: Grasset.

Francis Marmande (1985) *Georges Bataille politique*, Lyon: PUL.

Francis Marmande (1985) *L'Indifférence des ruines*, Paris: Éditions Parenthèses.

André Masson (1958) *Entretiens avec Georges Charbonnier*, Paris: Julliard.

Alfred Métraux (1963) 'Rencontre avec les ethnologues', *Critique*, nos 195–6.

Jules Monnerot (1949) *Sociologie du communisme*, Paris: Gallimard.

Jules Monnerot (1974) *Inquisitions*, Paris: José Corti.

Jean-Maurice Monnoyer (1985) *Le Peintre et le démon: Entretiens avec Pierre Klossowski*, Paris: Flammarion.

Friedrich Nietzsche (1968) *The Birth of Tragedy*, translated by Walter Kaufmann, New York: The Modern Library.

Friedrich Nietzsche (1974) *The Gay Science*, translated by Walter Kaufmann, New York: Random House.

Jean Piel (1963) 'Bataille et le monde', *Critique*, nos 195–6.

José Pierre (1981) *Tracts surréalistes et déclarations collectives*, 2 vols, Paris: Losfeld.

Raymond Queneau (1986) *Journal 1939–1940*, Paris: Gallimard.

Elisabeth Roudinesco (1986) *La Bataille de Cent Ans. Histoire de la psychanalyse en France*, Paris: Seuil.

Jean-Paul Sartre (1947) *Situations I, Essais critiques*, Paris: Gallimard.

André Thirion (1975) *Revolutionaries Without Revolution*, translated by Joachim Neugroschel, London: Cassell.

Émile Zola (1954) *Germinal*, translated by Leonard Tancock, Harmondsworth: Penguin.

Index

Printed and bound by CPI Group (UK) Ltd, Croydon, CR0 4YY

20/03/2025

01835117-0020